HELLENISTIC CULTURE AND SOCIETY

General Editors: Anthony W. Bulloch, Erich S. Gruen, A. A. Long,
and *Andrew F. Stewart*

Heritage and Hellenism

THE S. MARK TAPER FOUNDATION

IMPRINT IN JEWISH STUDIES

BY THIS ENDOWMENT
THE S. MARK TAPER FOUNDATION SUPPORTS
THE APPRECIATION AND UNDERSTANDING
OF THE RICHNESS AND DIVERSITY OF
JEWISH LIFE AND CULTURE

Heritage and Hellenism

The Reinvention of Jewish Tradition

Erich S. Gruen

UNIVERSITY OF CALIFORNIA PRESS

Berkeley   Los Angeles   London

The publisher gratefully acknowledges
the contribution toward the publication
of this book provided by
the S. Mark Taper Foundation

University of California Press
Berkeley and Los Angeles, California

University of California Press, Ltd.
London, England

©1998 by
The Regents of the University of California

Library of Congress Cataloging-in-Publication Data

Gruen, Erich S.
    Heritage and hellenism : the reinvention of Jewish tradition /
Erich S. Gruen.
        p.   cm. — (Hellenistic culture and society ; 30)
    Includes bibliographical references and index.
    ISBN 0-520-21052-2 (alk. paper)
    1. Judaism—History—Post-exilic period, 586 B.C.–210 A.D.
    2. Greek literature—Jewish authors—History and criticism.
    3. Judaism—Apologetic works—History and criticism.   4. Hellenism.
    I. Title. II. Series.
    BM176.G78   1998
    296'.09'014–dc21   97-38808
                                                            CIP

Printed in the United States of America
9 8 7 6 5 4 3 2 1

Manibus matris

CONTENTS

PREFACE

The intellectual odyssey of this book is readily discernible. During the past decade and more my research has concentrated upon the cultural connections between Greek and Roman societies, particularly in the era of the Hellenistic world and the Roman Republic. Two previous books explored a range of modes through which Rome appropriated Hellenism in order to reconstitute its own cultural identity. That line of investigation led naturally to a parallel question about the role of Hellenism in the reshaping of Jewish identity in this same era. The topic, a familiar one to many scholars of Jewish history, has received far less attention from those who come to it from a background in the Classics. I issued a call for "multicultural" studies of this sort in a presidential address to the American Philological Association in 1992, published in *TAPA* (1993), 1–14. It proved a useful prod to practice what I preached.

The experience has been a most salutary one. I have gained familiarity with whole areas of learning that were new to me, a range of new texts and issues, and, not least, a new and stimulating group of professional acquaintances. Some Israeli friends have twitted me for approaching the subject from the skewed perspective of a liberal, secular, diaspora Jew. I plead guilty to the characterization; others can judge how skewed is the perspective.

The book could not possibly have come into being without generous support from research grants. The National Endowment for the Humanities supplied a most welcome second award at a period when its funds were under siege from hostile lawmakers. A sabbatical leave from the University of California, Berkeley, afforded a vital stretch of time for uninterrupted research and writing. And I had the great good fortune to be named Winston Fellow in the Institute for Advanced Studies at the Hebrew University, Jerusalem, where, in the period from January to June, 1996, I was able to complete most of the book. The group brought together in Jerusalem under the rubric "The Meeting of Cultures in the Hellenistic-Roman World" and organized by Uriel Rappaport and Israel Shatzman could not have provided a more bracing—and congenial—environment. I owe much to the interchanges with its members, Dan Barag, Joseph Mélèze-Modrzejewski, Fergus Millar, Joseph Patrich, Tessa Rajak, Francis Schmidt, and Daniel Schwartz, as well as to the organizers. Others at the Institute, from different fields, added considerably to the richness of my own experience. I note in particular Richard Cohen, Elliott Horowitz, Ezra Mendelsohn, and Vivian Mann. Those six months were also markedly enhanced by the Director David Shulman, the Associate Director Laure Barthel, and their superb staff who were unfailingly courteous, helpful, cheery, and simply a pleasure to work with. The opportunity to be in Israel and to lecture in five different universities allowed me to benefit from a wealth of valuable reactions by expert audiences.

To those who read parts or the whole of the manuscript, my debts are large indeed. Constructive comments and suggestions on individual chapters came from John Barclay, Daniel Boyarin, Shaye Cohen, John Collins, Louis Feldman, Carl Holladay, Aryeh Kasher, Irad Malkin, Tessa Rajak, Uriel Rappaport, Seth Schwartz, and Israel Shatzman. I had the great advantage of seeing the unpublished manuscripts of two books by Bezalel Bar-Kochva, as well as receiving acute remarks on some of my own work by that outstanding scholar. I owe special gratitude for the sharp criticisms by my good friend Doron Mendels which resulted in some very important improvements—though not all that he might wish. Robert Doran read the entire work with keen insight and pointed me in a number of useful directions. Finally, I want to register heartfelt thanks to Daniel Schwartz, a scholar of boundless energy and a wonderful resource of knowledge. He offered much valued advice on individual chapters, then read the whole of the manuscript, and produced a twenty-two page commentary, almost all of which has had a discernible impact on the final version. The fact that he occupied an office next to mine in Jerusalem—and that we share an appreciation for Jewish humor in antiquity—immeasurably benefited my stay.

Research assistants facilitated this task in notable fashion. Miryam Segal, Hamutal Tsamir, and Peter Wyetzner rendered a significant amount of of Hebrew scholarship into intelligible English. The acute and accurate copyediting of Betsy Ditmars saved me from numerous errors. Celina Gray single-handedly accomplished the formidable task of compiling the index and the bibliography. And Mary Lamprech at the University of California Press, with characteristic skill and intelligence, efficiently ushered the manuscript through the publication process.

Berkeley, California
Spring, 1997

INTRODUCTION

The interaction of Jew and Greek in antiquity still weaves a spell, fascinating inquirers and stimulating researchers. The culture of the Hellenes traversed the Mediterranean in the last three centuries before the Common Era. In the lands of the Near East it encountered, among a motley array of nations and societies, the tenacious "people of the Book." The Jews clung fast to peculiar practices and sacred scriptures not readily assimilable to the experience of the Greeks. Both civilizations laid claim to great antiquity, their roots stretching back to legendary ancestors and divine sanction. And both carried rich traditions, with a noble heritage that gave special character to their peoples. The encounter inevitably grips the imagination.

Far-reaching consequences followed from that convergence. But the effects were disproportionate and imbalanced. In the wake of Alexander the Great's triumphant successes, Greeks and Macedonians came as conquerors and settled as ruling classes in the lands of the eastern Mediterranean. Jews endured a subordinate status politically and militarily, a minor nation amidst the powers of the Hellenistic world. For them, the experience was a familiar one. The Jews of Palestine and the Diaspora simply exchanged the suzerainty of the Persian empire for that of Alexander's successors. The Greeks, secure and content with their legacy, showed little inclination to learn the languages or embrace the cultures of peoples who had come under their authority. Nor did they engage in missionary activity designed to spread Hellenism among the natives. They took their superiority for granted. Those who dwelled in their dominions but without a share of power did not have the same luxury. Hellenic culture, as the stamp of the ascendant classes in many of the cities of the Near East, held widespread attraction and appeal. Jews were certainly not immune. Greeks may have been largely impervious to the precepts and principles of Judaism, but Jews could hardly escape the blandishments of Hellenism. The culture of the dominant party left an enduring mark upon the heirs of Moses.

The process of "Hellenization" is mysterious and obscure, not easily defined or demonstrated. No one can doubt that Jews of the Diaspora came into close contact with the institutions, language, literature, art, and traditions of Hellas in cities like Alexandria, Cyrene, Antioch, and Ephesus, even to the point of losing touch with Hebrew. The penetration of Greek culture into Palestine is more controversial. But it flourished in the cities of the coast from Gaza to Akko and in the lower Galilee at the very least, areas well within the reach of the Jews. The degree to which acculturation took place in Judaea itself and the time when it began in earnest elude any certainty. A vital point, however, undergirds the discussion in this book. " Judaism" and "Hellenism" were neither competing systems nor incompatible concepts. It would be erroneous to assume that Hellenization entailed encroachment upon Jewish traditions and erosion of Jewish beliefs. Jews did not face a choice of either assimilation or resistance to Greek culture.

A different premise serves as starting point here. We avoid the notion of a zero-sum contest in which every gain for Hellenism was a loss for Judaism or vice-versa. The prevailing culture of the Mediterranean could hardly be ignored or dismissed. But adaptation to it need not require compromise of Jewish precepts or practices. The inquiry can be formulated thus: how did Jews accommodate themselves to the larger cultural world of the Mediterranean while at the same time reasserting the character of their own heritage within it?

Ambiguity adheres to the term "Hellenism" itself. No pure strain of Greek culture, whatever that might be even in principle, confronted the Jews of Palestine or the Diaspora. Transplanted Greek communities mingled with ancient Phoenician traditions on the Levantine coast, with powerful Egyptian elements in Alexandria, with enduring Mesopotamian institutions in Babylon, and with a complex mixture of societies in Asia Minor. The Greek culture with which Jews came into contact comprised a mongrel entity—or rather entities, with a different blend in each location of the Mediterranean. The convenient term "Hellenistic" employed here signifies complex amalgamations in the Near East in which the Greek ingredient was a conspicuous presence rather than a monopoly.

"Judaism," it need hardly be said, is at least as complex and elastic a term. The institution defies uniform definition. And changes over time, as in all religions, render any effort to capture its essence at a particular moment highly problematic. "Hellenistic Judaism" must have experienced considerable diversity, quite distinct in Alexandria, Antioch, Babylon, Ephesus, and Jerusalem—also a feature common to most or all religions. Simplistic formulations once in favor are now obsolete. We can no longer contrast "Palestinian Judaism" as the unadulterated form of the ancestral faith with "Hellenistic Judaism" as the Diaspora variety that diluted antique practices with alien imports. Hellenism existed in Palestine, and the Jews of the Diaspora still held to their heritage. Each individual area struck its balance differently and experienced its own peculiar level of mixture. The distinctions, to be sure, rarely surface with any clarity in our evidence. But it is essential to emphasize that Jews were not obliged to choose between succumbing or resisting. Nor should one imagine a conscious dilemma whereby they had to decide how far to lean in one direction or other, how much "Hellenism" was acceptable before they compromised the faith, at what point on the spectrum between apostasy and piety they could comfortably locate themselves. And the idea that some form of "syncretism" took place, an amalgamation of pagan and Jewish practice or belief, misconceives the process.

An alternative conception is more instructive. Many Diaspora Jews and even some dwelling in Hellenistic cities of Palestine grew up after a generation or two as Greek speakers and integrated members of communities governed by pagan practices and institutions. They did not confront daily decisions on the degree of assimilation. They had long since become part of a Hellenic environment that they could take as a given. But their Judaism remained intact. What they required was a means of defining and expressing their singularity within that milieu, the special characteristics that made them both integral to the community and true to their heritage.

Hellenic influence exhibited itself in a range of realms. Numerous studies have traced the impact of Greek institutions, language, literature, philosophy, historiography, art, material culture, and even religion upon Judaism. The registering of such influences, however, can leave the impression of a somewhat passive receptivity or compliant adjustment on the part of Jewish thinkers to Hellenic culture. This study places the stress elsewhere. Jews engaged actively with the traditions of Hellas, adapting genres and transforming legends to articulate their own legacy in modes congenial to a Hellenistic setting. At the same time they recreated their past, retold stories in different shapes, and amplified the scriptural corpus itself through the medium of the Greek language and Greek literary forms. In a world where Hellenic culture held an ascendant position, Jews strained to develop their own cultural self-definition, one that would give them a place within the broader Mediterranean world and would also establish their distinctiveness. Those twin objectives operated conjointly.

The book endeavors to highlight Jewish creativity, ingenuity, and inventiveness. While making no claim to discovery of these features in Jewish-Hellenistic consciousness, it brings them onto center stage. Writers and thinkers developed literary strategies to redefine their people and its history in terms familiar to contemporary circumstances while simultaneously keeping faith with ancestral practices and belief. This entailed not only the manipulation of Greek forms and the adoption of Greek guises and pseudonyms, but the expansive recasting of biblical traditions to enhance the exploits of ancient heroes and embellish the legendary successes of the nation. The authors, redactors, or interpolators, often anonymous or pseudonymous, remain shadowy figures. But they reflect the creative energies and imaginative powers that characterize much of Jewish-Hellenistic literature. They also exhibit other features generally passed over by solemn scholars: a sardonic wit, mischievous sense of humor, and a pointed irony that not only poked fun at Gentiles but could expose the foibles of Jews themselves.

This work concentrates on fiction, not history—at least in the conventional sense. Its purpose is not to reconstruct the history of the Jews in the Hellenistic era but to examine the reinvention of their own past. Of course, the dichotomy itself is deceptive. Only a fine line divided legend and history in the antique traditions of Greek and Jew alike. Genre categories can too readily delude us. As an example, we customarily label II Maccabees as a work of historiography and the *Letter of Aristeas* as a fictitious narrative. Yet the first work incorporates transparent inventions and fables while the second is couched as a sober historical presentation. Where on this purported spectrum does one place the story of Alexander the Great's visit to Jerusalem, ostensibly historical fact but demonstrably fictitious creation? Or, by contrast, the recasting of the Moses tale as tragic drama in Ezekiel's *Exagoge*—plainly an imaginative version but reproducing articles of faith? The authors of these and other texts did not set out to deceive, to cloak fabrications as fact or to disguise history as entertainment. The categories converge and overlap. Readers no more confused the "tales of the Tobiads" with an archival chronicle of that family than they regarded Moses' elevation to the throne of God in the *Exagoge* as deriving from a scholarly exegesis of the Bible. Jews tapped a rich vein of legendary materials, both pagan and Jewish. Audiences for the recreations took a broad view, happily absorbing hybrid products that grafted Gentile folktales onto the Scriptures or set fables and fictions into historical contexts. The question of whether such stories were meant to be "believed" is the wrong one. Readers did not inspect these texts for clues whereby to separate reality from fantasy. Inventiveness enhanced reality rather than substituted for it. Fictive creations can in fact provide the historian with the best insights into the self-perception of Hellenistic Jews striving to articulate their own identity.

The present study does not pretend to provide a comprehensive canvas of Hellenistic Judaism, a subject of vast and unmanageable proportions. Its treatment is selective and focused rather than exhaustive, more a sampling than a survey. But it draws on a wide and diverse array of authors and texts that illuminate the mentality of Jews reexamining their tradition in lands pervaded by Greek culture. The chronological boundaries of the work are fluid rather than fixed. "Hellenistic era" has different meanings for different researchers. The conventional termini go from Alexander to Actium. But the Jewish experience underwent no sharp break in the age of Augustus, and one can justifiably stretch the period to extend to the destruction of the Temple—or even a bit beyond to encompass Josephus. Chronological fuzziness is, in any case, unavoidable. The extant works (or, more frequently, the extant fragments of works) by Hellenistic Jews rarely yield to precise dating, and the margin of possibilities can spread over two or three centuries. In general, most of the material examined here belongs to what might be termed the "Hellenistic" rather than the "Greco-Roman" phase of the Jewish experience, for the focus falls on the strategies whereby Jews endeavored to adjust to the post-Alexander world. But there are no hard and fast frontiers. Philo, for the most part, stands outside the main era under scrutiny, and Josephus beyond its limits, two authors for whom major scholarly industries already exist. Yet Philo will occasionally serve as witness for topics discussed, and Josephus, although he is not himself a subject of inspection, will frequently undergo cross-examination, for he preserves considerable material central to the inquiry. On a rough reckoning, the study pays primary attention to the span that stretches from Alexander's conquests to the early Roman Empire.

Another matter helps to delimit boundaries. We pursue here the issue of Jewish self-definition in the circumstances of a Hellenic cultural world. Hence the book addresses itself to works composed in Greek, works by Hellenized Jews who employed the language, themes, and genres of the Greeks to express the legacy of their nation and who imposed their own invented past upon Hellenic history. This by no means implies that Jews who wrote in Hebrew or Aramaic in this era lacked comparable creative skills or imaginative powers. Indeed a wealth of writings in those languages exhibit the latitude available for revamping familiar tales and fashioning new fables. One need mention only the Assumption of Moses and Jubilees in the first category, Judith and Tobit in the second. And the Dead Sea Scrolls have revealed further instances in both brackets, such as the Genesis Apocryphon and the Aramaic

I Enoch. Limitations of space and competence, however, confine attention to compositions in Greek. Here again the restriction is neither absolute nor rigid. The material includes select writings whose original language may have been Semitic but which were translated or recast into Greek, as well as some preserved now in other languages but plainly based on Greek originals. And comparisons, background, or implications require occasional reference also to texts in Hebrew or Aramaic—for which this study is heavily indebted to the good offices of friends, colleagues, and students conversant with the languages.

The selected segment may or may not be representative. Too many gaps in our knowledge prohibit confidence. Even within the limits set forth, however, a striking range and variety of components greet the researcher. The book explores works by Jewish historians, epic poets, tragic dramatists, writers of romance and novels, exegetes, philosophers, apocalyptic visionaries, and composers of fanciful fables—not to mention pseudonymous forgers and fabricators. It encompasses retelling of biblical stories, remaking of biblical figures, and accretions to the Scriptures, as well as recreations of the Greek past to incorporate the imaginary or enhanced exploits of Jews.

The approach adopted here differs from that of many modern treatments. It does not provide piecemeal analysis of writer after writer, text after text organized by genre, offering conjectures on the date and provenance of each author, the *Sitz-im-Leben* of the compositions, the circumstances that called forth the works. Scholarship has made important advances on these matters but repeatedly runs into frustration. Lack of adequate evidence leaves numerous and critical uncertainties. Chronology can only be approximate, location at best plausible, and motivation largely guesswork. And the questions themselves may be off the mark. The texts as we possess them have often gone through several versions or redactions, earlier renditions lost, subject to multiple manipulation, with authors usually anonymous or concealed under pseudonyms. To ferret out particular purposes or pinpoint dates of composition is, for the most part, an illusory exercise. And it may also be inconsequential. What matters is not so much when, where, why, or by whom an individual text was drafted but the fact that these works were read, cited, excerpted, and expanded over the course of several generations. This sets them outside the narrow confines of composition (even if those confines could be determined) and demands a broader perspective. The book treats topics that span much of the chronological spectrum, drawing on relevant texts where appropriate and calling upon them in several contexts rather than discussing them separately and singly. But all of them speak, in one way or another, to the ongoing process whereby diverse Jewish thinkers endeavored to express their people's identity in terms borrowed, manipulated, and refashioned from the Hellenic cultural corpus.

• • •

The age of the Maccabees conventionally occupies a central place in this subject. Jewish rebellion against the harsh impositions of the persecutor Antiochus IV led to a shaking off of the Hellenic yoke and the emergence of an autonomous state under the Hasmonaean dynasty. This clash supplies the locus classicus for a fundamental split between Judaism and Hellenism. Or so we are told. The idea is examined afresh here. A very different portrait emerges, suggesting that the division is artificial and that the Hasmonaean era in fact provided an atmosphere even in Palestine conducive to Jewish reconceptualization in Hellenic terms.

This work explores the reconceptualization on several fronts. The Exodus story itself, the very heart of the Jews' understanding of their past, the origin of their nation, and their relations with Gentiles, underwent notable transformation in the Hellenistic era. The Jews did not refrain from tampering even with their central myth in the light of experiences in a changed world. And that was only the beginning. Ancient Hebrew heroes appear in new guises and new circumstances. The multiple treatments of Joseph, in every variety of literary exercise, present an instructive illustration. Hellenistic Jews found no inconsistency between regarding the Scriptures as Holy Writ and rewriting them to their own taste. Some of them sought simply to explain incongruities, others to abbreviate tales, thus making them more pointed or omitting unpalatable matters. Some placed the emphasis differently and thereby improved the behavior of their ancestors, and some elevated their actions by portraying them in the form of epic poetry or tragic drama. Others took still greater liberties. They expanded the conquests of King David, invented new international associations for Solomon, blended Babylonian and Greek legends with the tale of Abraham, and turned Moses into the cultural provider for Egyptians, Ethiopians, Phoenicians, and Greeks. Nor did they stop there. Inventive writers added episodes to received texts, adapted pagan folktales and inserted amusing stories into the books of Ezra and Daniel, and even gave a wholly different tone to the book of Esther by affixing new material in strategic places. The Scriptures stimulated the creative talents of Hellenistic Jews.

Those talents gained expression outside the biblical context as well. Fictive tales set Jews at the scene of major events of Hellenistic history and gave them a dramatic part in the decisions of Hellenistic kings. In such tales Alexander the Great himself paid obeisance to their god, and successive Ptolemaic rulers welcomed them back to Egypt, sponsored the Septuagint, promoted Jews to high rank in the court, or became converted from persecutors to firm friends. The stories conveyed a harmonious setting in which Jews could live comfortably as political subordinates within the structure of Hellenistic monarchy, while also subtly advancing the idea of Jewish moral and intellectual superiority within that structure.

The emphasis on Jewish self-esteem expressed through creative fantasy recurs again and again. It appears in the claims that Greek philosophers and poets found inspiration in the Pentateuch, in the forecasts of the quintessentially pagan Sibyl who visualized Jewish triumph in the apocalypse that could sweep up compliant Greeks in its wake, and in the imaginary kinship relations between Jews and Spartans that gave a clear ascendancy to the former.

Jewish writings in Greek cover a broad expanse. They may not always reach a high level of literary quality, but their range and variety offer an invaluable perspective on the mentality of Hellenistic Jews. They contain subtleties and sub-texts often spiced with wit, humor, and irony. Their embellishments of biblical narratives and transformation of biblical heroes presuppose a readership familiar with the Scriptures, usually the Septuagint. And their elevation of the Jewish role in Hellenistic history, especially their central relationship with monarchs of the realm, leaves little doubt about the audience to which these works were addressed. Few Gentiles could be expected to read texts that straightened out the chronology of the patriarchs, had Abraham deliver the alphabet to the Phoenicians, made Plato beholden to the Pentateuch, beefed up Hebrew texts with Greek additions, or portrayed pagan kings manipulated by Jewish figures. They could have served no missionary purposes—and were surely never intended for such ends. The texts have too often been labeled as apologia or propaganda, an inadequate and seriously misleading characterization. These were not simply reactive pamphlets, the product of a defensive rear-guard action by a beleaguered minority in an alien world. They reflect the creative energies, imagination, and even whimsical caprice of their authors. Hellenistic Jews wrote for their compatriots, for their self-esteem, for their sense of identity and superiority, and for their amusement, in terms congenial to the cultural atmosphere in which they thrived. By selectively appropriating Hellenic media to recreate their past and redefine themselves, Jews made more vivid the spiritual and intellectual precedence that they accorded to their own traditions.

Hellenism and the Hasmonaeans

The revolt of Judas Maccabaeus represents for most researchers the pivotal point in the confrontation of Judaism and Hellenism. Judas' resistance to the assaults upon his people's legacy by the Hellenistic monarchy in Antioch ostensibly signaled a bitter contest between the cultures. The hitherto peaceful and piecemeal infiltration of Greek civilization in Palestine received a rude shock. The Maccabaean uprising appeared to create a deep cleavage, splitting the nation between those attracted by Hellenism and those devoted to Jewish traditions. Its repercussions reverberated through the era of the Hasmonaean dynasty, the followers and successors of Judas Maccabaeus. And it brings a central question to the fore. Did this divide sever the two cultures in Palestine, prohibiting compromise and leaving the future of Hellenistic Judaism to the Diaspora? Scrutiny of the relations between the Hasmonaeans and the Greek powers of the Near East suggests a surprising answer. They disclose an intriguing modus vivendi that could promote rather then deter Jewish adaptation to and manipulation of Hellenic ways. The behavior emblematizes in its own fashion the strategy of Hellenistic Jews that will be examined throughout this study.

The persecutions of Antiochus IV posed an awesome challenge to the Jews. Royal policy aimed at eradication of Jewish worship, traditions, and religious way of life. The defiling of the Temple and its rededication to Zeus Olympios, with the concomitant compulsion of Jews to participate in pagan sacrifices and rituals, represented a campaign to repress Judaism forcibly and to impose Hellenic institutions upon Jerusalem. The resistance of Mattathias and his sons turned back the challenge. Judas Maccabaeus' victories and Seleucid preoccupations elsewhere enabled the Jews to regain and cleanse the Temple, restore ancestral practices, and eliminate the abominations perpetrated by the Hellenistic king. The dramatic events constitute a central exhibit for the presumed clash of Judaism and Hellenism.

The sequel, however, brought apparent ambiguity and confusion. Judas' successors continued the fight; the Hasmonaean dynasty stood forth as champions of an autonomous Jewish state, with religious and political authority centered upon the Temple and in the hands of the High Priest; and its leaders rejected control by Hellenistic monarchs or absorption into a Hellenistic realm. Yet the Hasmonaeans themselves, in the course of the century that followed the Maccabaean revolt, engaged regularly in diplomatic dealings with Greek kings, adopted Greek names, donned garb and paraded emblems redolent with Hellenic significance, erected monuments, displayed stelai, and minted coinage inspired by Greek models, hired mercenaries, and even took on royal titulature. The ostensible paradox has often generated puzzlement. How could a movement that owed its origins to the rejection of Hellenism and Hellenizers within the Jewish community retain strength and appeal if its very leaders succumbed to the allure of Greek institutions? Did not the injection of Hellenic elements require compromise with Jewish faith, an encouragement to assimilation? Such questions presume a contest of Judaism against Hellenism, a struggle between traditionalists and Hellenizers, a crusade undertaken by the Maccabees but then abandoned or transformed by them.[1] Assessment of that presumption is critical for understanding the essence of the Maccabaean rebellion and the association between Jewish leadership and Hellenic culture for the next century. And it opens the way to a larger finding. The confrontation of Jew and Greek, even at its most antagonistic and even in the homeland of the faith, promoted adjustment, adaptation, indeed creative appropriation on the part of the Jews. The analysis in this chapter focuses upon political and institutional developments in

1. See, e.g., E. Bickerman, *Der Gott der Makkabäer* (Berlin, 1937) 117–39; M. Hengel, *Judaism and Hellenism* (London, 1974) I, 277–309; V. Tcherikover, *Hellenistic Civilization and the Jews* (Philadelphia, 1959) 159–265; C. Habicht, *Jhrb.Heid.Akad.* (1974) 97–110; A. Momigliano, *RivStorItal* 88 (1976) 425–43 = *Essays on Ancient and Modern Judaism* (Chicago, 1994) 10–28; Th. Fischer, *Seleukiden und Makkabäer* (Bochum, 1980) 186–88. Recent studies perceive greater complexity. U. Rappaport in M. Mor, *Jewish Assimilation, Acculturation, and Accommodation* (London, 1992) 1–13, endeavors to distinguish between a political and a cultural Hellenization, with the Hasmonaeans opposing the first but embracing the second. T. Rajak recognizes that, although contentious matters might arise over the spread of Hellenism in Palestine, Jewish traditions were not generally incompatible with Hellenic culture; in P. R. Davies and R. T. White, *A Tribute to Geza Vermes* (Sheffield, 1990) 261–80; in J. A. Crook, A. Lintott, and E. Rawson, *Cambridge Ancient History*[2] (Cambridge, 1994) 296–99; and in P. Bilde et al., *Aspects of Hellenistic Kingship* (Aarhus, 1996) 91–107. See also E. Will and Cl. Orrieux, *Ioudaismos-Hellènismos: essai sur le judaisme judéen à l'époque hellénistique* (Nancy, 1986) 120–36, 177–93.

Palestine. But it serves as prelude to the broader cultural improvisations that extended to the Diaspora and helped to define Hellenistic Judaism.

•   •   •

Did Judas Maccabaeus raise his standard against Hellenism and Hellenizers? The fact is generally taken for granted. But the texts themselves do not readily conform to the conclusion. Our evidence derives almost exclusively from I and II Maccabees, both produced probably in the later second or early first century BCE. The first, composed originally in Hebrew, is the work of a pious Palestinian Jew, steeped in the Bible and eager to demonstrate the success of the Hasmonaeans against both Gentile opponents and their Jewish collaborators, heirs to the biblical heroes of old. The second, a one volume epitome of the now lost five volumes by Jason of Cyrene, was a Greek composition from the start, indeed an elegant, occasionally florid, Greek. Its author was a Diaspora Jew, well versed in Hellenistic historiography, but one with profound theological commitments who saw the Jews' sufferings as a consequence of their own sins, their temporarily triumphant opponents as the instruments of God, and the ultimate crushing of their foes as divine vindication.[2] From such sources, one might expect a clash with Hellenism and Hellenizers, if that was its form, to be highlighted. Not so.

The term "Hellenizer" appears with frequency in modern discussions. Its usage varies confusingly and unhelpfully, sometimes signifying apostates, sometimes supporters of the Seleucids, and sometimes nothing more than opponents of the Maccabees. More significantly, however, the word appears in no ancient text relevant to the subject. Its absence should give pause to zealous over-interpreters. Further, even the term "Hellenism" or some equivalent thereof occurs only five times in all the material pertaining to the persecution and the career of Judas Maccabaeus. That puts the matter in a very different perspective.

The five allusions to "Hellenism" all turn up in II Maccabees. So also do three references to "Judaism." They comprise the first instances in which those words appear in our evidence. And nowhere does II Maccabees juxtapose them as rival or competing concepts. "Hellenism" in some form or other occurs three times in connection with actions taken by the High

---

2. This is not the place for an extended discussion of the dates and characters of these works. See the succinct treatment, with valuable bibliography, in E. Schürer, *The History of the Jewish People in the Age of Jesus Christ*, rev. ed. by G. Vermes, F. Millar, and M. Goodman (Edinburgh, 1986) III.1, 180–85, 531–37.

Priest Jason who had an affinity for certain Greek practices, installing a gymnasium and an ephebate in Jerusalem. For the author of II Maccabees, Jason, with the consent of Antiochus, led his countrymen to "the Greek way of life," and brought about a "peak of Hellenism," with the result that even the priests placed highest value upon attaining "Greek honors."[3] In a fourth passage, Antiochus IV decreed the slaughter of all Jews who declined to convert to "Hellenic ways."[4] The "Hellenic ways" receive mention again in a letter of Antiochus V which concedes that the Jews could not be brought to embrace them.[5] Whatever accuracy or meaning these phrases contain, they shed little light on the motivation of Judas Maccabaeus. Jason had fallen from power long before the beginning of the revolt. Menelaus occupied the High Priesthood when the Maccabaean movement erupted, a man for whom no trace exists of an interest in matters Hellenic. As for the royal decree, the Jews plainly resisted it, and successfully so. But the phraseology represents only a summary judgment on the mix of measures imposed by Antiochus Epiphanes upon Judaea. The Maccabaean rebellion exploded against implementation of the king's policies, not against Hellenism as such.

That the rebels may have considered themselves contending in some sense for "Judaism" is reasonable enough. II Maccabees introduces its narrative with the proud statement that the supporters of Judas Maccabaeus fought zealously on behalf of "Judaism" against Antiochus IV and his son. The author or epitomizer, however, significantly brands the enemies of the Jews as "barbarian hordes."[6] The term "Judaism" surfaces twice more in the text as the cause championed by the Maccabaean movement and one for which an adherent perished during the persecutions.[7] None of the references to Judaism singles out Hellenism or Hellenizers as the targets of Jewish wrath. Hence, even the laudatory monograph on Judas Maccabaeus, II Maccabees, the one work regularly cited as locus classicus for the battle against Hellenism, does not make the point.[8]

3. II Macc. 4.10: πρὸς τὸν Ἑλληνικὸν χαρακτῆρα; 4.13: ἀκμή τις Ἑλληνισμοῦ; 4.15: Ἑλληνικὰς δόξας. Cf. also Jos. *Ant.* 12.240–41, who confuses Jason with Menelaus: τὴν Ἑλληνικὴν πολιτείαν. As B. Bar-Kochva, *Tarbiz* 63 (1994) 464–65 (Hebrew) rightly observes, "Hellenism" here refers to *Jewish* imitation of Greek ways.

4. II Macc. 6.9: μεταβαίνειν ἐπὶ τὰ Ἑλληνικά. Cf. Tac. *Hist.* 5.8: *Antiochus ... mores Graecorum dare adnisus.* On the passage in II Maccabees, see the properly skeptical remarks of J. Goldstein, *II Maccabees* (Garden City, 1983) 278.

5. II Macc. 11.24: μὴ συνευδοκοῦντας τῇ τοῦ πατρὸς ἐπὶ τὰ Ἑλληνικὰ μεταθέσει.

6. II Macc. 2.21: ὑπὲρ τοῦ Ἰουδαϊσμοῦ ... τὰ βάρβαρα πλήθη.

7. II Macc. 8.1, 14.38.

8. Even Rajak, who questions the validity of the concept, believes that II Maccabees interprets the events as a struggle against Hellenization and against Jews who had succumbed

The campaigns of Judas Maccabaeus directed themselves in large part at enemies who had dwelled in the lands surrounding Judaea long before the advent of the Greeks. The armies of the king and his officers, to be sure, represented a chief menace. But even those armies by no means consisted exclusively of Greeks. The Seleucid general Nicanor, prior to his climactic clash with the Maccabaean forces, assembled troops of varied nationalities, a motley assemblage of peoples: παμφύλων ἔθνη.⁹ That notice is reported in II Maccabees. And it receives confirmation repeatedly and consistently throughout the text of I Maccabees which designates the foes of Judas as τὰ ἔθνη, the nations.¹⁰ More pointedly and revealingly, I Maccabees makes reference to the hostile elements as "the surrounding nations," τὰ ἔθνη τὰ κύκλῳ.¹¹ The phraseology carries significance. Greeks as such go unmentioned. The author of I Maccabees focuses attention upon the neighboring communities and peoples of Palestine and Transjordan, long-standing rivals of the Jews. Judas' campaigns therefore, on this presentation, recall the epic battles of the Bible and relive the triumphs over Canaanites, Ammonites, Edomites, and Philistines.¹² Insofar as Judas rallied his forces against the foe, he hoisted a biblical standard directed at the indigenous

to Hellenism; in Davies and White, *Tribute to Vermes*, 262. She herself employs the term "Hellenizer" too freely; *CAH*² IX, 274–75, 281–282. See also Rappaport in Mor, *Jewish Assimilation*, 2–4, and cf. S. Schwartz, *JJS* 42 (1991) 23, for whom II Maccabees presents a "Kulturkampf" between Judaism and Hellenism. The notion does not find firm support in the text. Cf. the cogent remarks of Bar-Kochva, *Tarbiz* 63 (1994) 464–65 (Hebrew). The only other passage of possible relevance has Lysias mobilize against Jerusalem with the intent of making it a "city for the Greeks"; II Macc. 11.2. Even if that report accurately reflects Lysias' designs, however, it provides no indication of a cultural crusade. On II Maccabees as a historical monograph focusing on Judas, see J. Geiger, *Zion* 49 (1984/1985) 1–8 (Hebrew); cf. *idem, SCI* 8–9 (1985–1988) 120–23.

9. II Macc. 8.9; cf. 8.16: ἐθνῶν πολυπληθίαν. Note, by contrast, II Macc. 13.2: δύναμιν Ἑλληνικήν. On the composition of the Seleucid army, see B. Bar-Kochva, *The Seleucid Army* (Cambridge, 1976) 42–53; *Judas Maccabaeus* (Cambridge, 1989) 34, 90–105. On the relationship of II Macc. 8 with I Macc. 3 here, see further Bar-Kochva, *Tarbiz* 62 (1992) 118–19, 127–28 (Hebrew).

10. I Macc. 2.68, 3.10, 3.45, 3.48, 3.52, 3.58, 4.7, 4.11, 4.14, 4.45, 4.54, 4.58, 4.60, 5.9, 5.19, 5.21, 5.43, 5.63, 6.18, 6.53, 7.23, 14.36. The phrase can be found also, with the same referent, in II Macc. 8.5, 12.13, 14.14–15.

11. I Macc. 3.25, 5.1, 5.10, 5.38, 5.57, 12.53. See also Jos. *Ant.* 12.327: τὰ πέριξ ἔθνη; 12.330: τὰ γειτονεύοντα τῶν ἐθνῶν.

12. See, e.g., Josh. 23.1; Judg. 2.14, 8.34; Sam. 12.11, 14.47. Other references in J. Goldstein, *I Maccabees* (Garden City, 1976) 293–305; Schwartz, *JJS* 42 (1991) 23–24. See further D. Arenhoevel, *Die Theokratie nach dem 1. und 2. Makkabäerbuch* (Mainz, 1967) 51–57; A. Kasher, *Jews and Hellenistic Cities in Eretz-Israel* (Tübingen, 1990) 58–59. On Judas' campaigns generally, see Kasher, *op. cit.*, 58–90, and the exhaustive study of Bar-Kochva, *Judas Maccabaeus*, 194–402.

dwellers of the region, not the Greeks themselves. That context takes shape at the very outset of I Maccabees. Its author explains the introduction even of the gymnasium, as well as other non-Jewish practices, in terms of a desire on the part of certain Jews to establish a relationship with the "surrounding nations."[13] And when Antiochus promulgated his presumed decree calling for institutional conformity throughout his realm, all of the ἔθνη adhered to the royal edict.[14] The neighboring Gentiles, in short, comprise the immediate and persistent foe, peoples not identical with the minions of the Greek king, echoing the ancient clashes of the biblical era, and providing the appropriate setting for Maccabaean heroics.[15] I Maccabees employs other terms too to characterize the opponents of the Jews: ἀλλοφύλοι or ἀλλογενεῖς, "peoples of a different race."[16] Plainly, Greeks are not singled out. The one specific usage of ἀλλοφύλοι denotes the inhabitants of Galilee, mobilized to assault the Jews.[17] The issue of Hellenism takes a decided back seat.

Of course there were enemies within. Judas had to contend with rivals in the Jewish community, collaborators, so it was claimed, with the Seleucid regime, duly branded with infamy by the author of I Maccabees. Is it appropriate, however, to label them as "Hellenizers"? The term crops up nowhere in the testimony—surely a fact of some significance. I Maccabees does characterize the Jewish targets of the Maccabees as "the impious ones," ἀσεβεῖς, a term also employed with some frequency by Josephus. It applies to those Jews who chose to cooperate with Antiochus IV, preferring their own safety to the preservation of their ancestral tradition, some perhaps serving even as garrison soldiers in the Akra to help maintain Seleucid power in Jerusalem.[18] Their wickedness consisted in consorting with the enemy, not in the embrace of Hellenic ways. That is clear enough from the fact that the

13. I Macc. 1.11: διαθώμεθα διαθήκην μετὰ τῶν ἐθνῶν τῶν κύκλῳ ἡμῶν; 1.13: τὰ δικαιώματα τῶν ἐθνῶν ; 1.14: κατὰ τὰ νόμιμα τῶν ἐθνῶν.

14. I Macc. 1.42: ἐπεδέξαντο πάντα τὰ ἔθνη.

15. That I Maccabees does not normally include Greeks among τὰ ἔθνη who oppose the Jews is indicated by I Macc. 2.48, which has the followers of Mattathias rescue the law from the hands of "the nations" and from the hands of the kings, a firm distinction between those entities: ἀντελάβοντο τοῦ νόμου ἐκ χειρὸς τῶν ἐθνῶν καὶ ἐκ χειρὸς τῶν βασιλέων. Cf. II Samuel, 22.1. Kasher, *Jews and Hellenistic Cities*, 59, 84, too readily assumes that τὰ ἔθνη refer to Hellenic cities.

16. I Macc. 3.36, 3.45, 4.26, 10.12, 11.68, 11.74. The same phrases in Jos. *Ant.* 12.336, 12.340; cf. 12.241: τῶν ἀλλοεθνῶν.

17. I Macc. 5.15. Notice the contrast here between the ἀλλοφύλοι and the coastal cities: ἐπ' αὐτοὺς ἐκ Πτολεμαίδος καὶ Τύρου καὶ Σιδῶνος καὶ πᾶσαν Γαλιλαίαν ἀλλοφύλων. Cf. the Septuagint rendering of Isaiah 8.23: Γαλιλαία τῶν ἐθνῶν.

18. I Macc. 3.8, 3.15, 6.21, 7.5, 7.9, 9.25, 9.73; Jos. *Ant.* 12.252, 12.289, 12.364, 12.399, 13.2, 13.23, 13.34, 13.40, 13.42; cf. II Macc. 8.2. Reference to renegade Jews in the Akra appears only

Seleucid choice for High Priest, Alcimus, also carried the stigma of "impiety" from the vantage point of the Maccabees. But he had certainly not forsaken Jewish traditions for the lure of Greek culture.[19] Comparable terms are slung about by our sources, tainting the enemies of Judas as "lawless men," "deserters," "sinners," even "trouble-makers"—but not "Hellenizers."[20] The nearest we have to such a suggestion is a reference in Josephus to Jews who had abandoned their native customs. Even here, however, the historian asserts that they chose instead a "common way of life," i.e. presumably common to all nations, a general allusion to Gentiles, rather than to the adoption of Hellenic ways.[21] Nothing suggests that the Maccabees hunted down Hellenizers.

Judas Maccabaeus took care over the posture he presented to the public. His cleansing of the Temple in December of 164 was consciously designed to place him in the line of ancient Israelite tradition. He made certain that the rituals of purification and rededication were performed by priests of impeccable character.[22] The event deliberately recalled the dedication of the First Temple.[23] And the commemorative festival instituted by Judas made a direct connection with Sukkot, the Feast of Tabernacles.[24] The biblical precedents for Hanukkah predominate. They form a central feature of Maccabaean rhetoric. It causes no surprise, therefore, to find the forces of Judas

---

in Josephus; see J. Sievers in F. Parente and J. Sievers, *Josephus and the History of the Greco-Roman Period* (Leiden, 1994) 198–202. But cf. I Macc. 6.21–26.

19. I Macc. 7.5, 7.9; Jos. *Ant.* 12.398–99. Josephus applies the same label to the previous High Priest Menelaus; *Ant.* 12.385. The author of II Maccabees does convict Alcimus of voluntary defilement, perhaps an implicit contrast with Judas who is elsewhere described as avoiding defilement; II Macc. 5.27, 14.3. Just what the "defilement" consisted in remains quite mysterious. But it was surely not Hellenism; cf. Goldstein, *II Maccabees*, 481–83.

20. παράνομοι or ἄνομοι: I Macc. 1.11, 2.44, 3.5–6, 9.23, 9.58, 9.69, 10.61, 11.21, 11.25; II Macc. 13.7; Jos. *Ant.* 12.286; φυγάδες: Jos. *Ant.* 12.362, 12.364, 12.391, 12.399, 13.23, 13.40; cf. I Macc. 7.24; ἁμαρτωλοί : I Macc. 2.44; cf. 2.48; ταράσσοντες: I Macc. 7.22.

21. Jos. *Ant.* 13.4: τοὺς ἀποστάντας τῆς πατρίου συνηθείας καὶ τὸν κοινὸν βίον προῃρημένους. Similarly, I Macc. 1.15: Jews shook off the holy covenant and associated themselves with τὰ ἔθνη. The statement in I Macc. 2.15 that the king's officers sought to enforce apostasy in Modein does not indicate to what end, and the policy failed anyway. Nor do we get any illumination from the letter of Palestinian Jews to Egypt forty years later, tracing the beginning of upheaval to the apostasy of Jason; II Macc. 1.7. Jews who had fallen after a particular battle were found to have possessed objects sacred to the idols of Jamnia and forbidden to observant Jews; II Macc. 12.40. But the items probably constituted plunder rather than objects of worship by Jews; cf. Goldstein, *II Maccabees*, 448–49. Or else the story was invented simply to account for the deaths.

22. I Macc. 4.42–51.

23. Cf. II Chron. 7.1–10.

24. II Macc. 1.9, 1.18, 10.6; cf. Neh. 8.18, 12.27; J. VanderKam, *JSP* 1 (1987) 31–34.

and his brothers taking aggressive action in Idumaea, Gilead, Galilee, and Philistia in 163, forceful reminders still again that the Maccabees championed Jewish heritage against its most ancient enemies.[25] The narrative of I Maccabees blames the "surrounding nations" for initiating the offensive, requiring Judas to come to the aid of beleaguered Jews dwelling in those regions. II Maccabees stresses the role played by Seleucid commanders and officers in stirring up hostilities. But their troops are foreign mercenaries, supported by indigenous enemies of the Jews, no Hellenic crusade.[26] Whatever the truth of the matter, the Maccabees set themselves (or were so placed by their chroniclers) in the tracks of ancient heroes. At Caspin they called upon the God who had enabled Joshua to take the citadel of Jericho.[27] They designated certain targets as "sons of Esau" or the land of "Philistia."[28] And they destroyed pagan temples and shrines that long predated the Greeks.[29] Hellenism and Hellenizers did not themselves constitute the targets.

The Hasidaioi or Hasidim warrant notice here. If any group could be expected to champion traditionalism against Hellenic incursions, it should have been they. The self-styled "pious" would seem to represent a principal obstacle to alien infiltration into Judaism.[30] Yet the one reasonably reliable piece of information on the Hasidaioi in the Maccabaean era has them take a moderate line and seek a peaceful resolution from Alcimus, the Seleucid appointee as High Priest, and the Seleucid general Bacchides. The effort proved calamitous, for the negotiators among the Hasidaioi were deceived and executed on the orders of Alcimus.[31] But they evidently did not look upon the representatives of Seleucid authority in Judaea, one of whom was a man of priestly stock, as unacceptable to adherents of the faith.[32] Hence even

25. I Macc. 5.3–68

26. I Macc. 5.1, 5.3, 5.9–15, 5.27, 5.37–38; II Macc. 10.14–15, 10.24, 12.2.

27. II Macc. 12.13–16.

28. I Macc. 3.24, 3.41, 5.65; cf. 4.30.

29. I Macc. 5.44, 5.68.

30. So, e.g., Tcherikover, *Hellenistic Civilization and the Jews*, 196–98, who sees them as leaders of the rebellion.

31. I Macc. 7.12–17. On this passage, see the treatment of J. Kampen, *The Hasideans and the Origins of Pharisaism: A Study in 1 and 2 Maccabees* (Atlanta, 1988) 114–35. The episode is recorded also by Jos. *Ant.* 12.395–96, without mention of Hasidaioi. Will-Orrieux, *Ioudaismos-Hellēnismos*, 179–81, question the historicity of the execution of the Hasidaioi.

32. This need not mean a split between the Hasidaioi and Judas Maccabaeus—let alone treacherous collaboration by the Hasidaioi. See the forceful remarks of J. Efron, *Studies on the Hasmonean Period* (Leiden, 1987) 22–27; cf. Bar-Kochva, *Judas Maccabaeus*, 59. Any further speculation about the Hasidaioi would be imprudent. They do receive mention in II Macc. 14.6 as backers of Judas Maccabaeus and principal sources of sedition. But that assertion is put in the mouth of Alcimus seeking the support of Demetrius I against his enemies and cannot

the most devout Jews could countenance accommodation with the ministers of Hellenic power in their land.

The cultural contest, in short, has been overplayed. And one can go further. Even the arena of warfare and diplomacy shows less than implacable enmity. Clashes between Jewish forces and Seleucid armies occupy prime place in the historical record of the Maccabaean era. But they obscure the interaction of Jew and Greek at the leadership level. The Hasmonaean age, in fact, discloses a complex pattern of reciprocal relations and mutual dependency that undermines the concept of fundamental antagonism.[33]

Negotiations between the Seleucid officialdom and the Jews took place even during the lifetime of Judas Maccabaeus. II Maccabees preserves record of four letters concerning the Jews, evidently sent in 164 and 163.[34] Two of them, composed at the Seleucid court in the reign of Antiochus IV, bear particular notice. The king himself wrote to the *gerousia* and to the "rest of the Jews," offering amnesty to those who wished to return to their homes by a specified date, granting the resumption of their dietary restrictions and other laws, and promising no mistreatment for previous actions. The letter was prompted by a visit from Menelaus who would also return with it to reassure the Jews.[35] The fact that Menelaus served as intermediary and that the addressee was the *gerousia* does not mean that Antiochus dealt here only with the "Hellenizing party."[36] The prescript includes "the rest of the Jews," and the letter, according to II Maccabees, was sent to the ἔθνος.[37] Antiochus was plainly prepared to acknowledge privileges belonging to Jews as a whole. His leading minister Lysias authored another letter, this one posted to τὸ πλῆθος of the Jews, a non-technical term clearly, perhaps

---

claim unequivocal reliability; cf. I Macc. 7.25; Kampen, *Hasideans*, 139–48. The passage in I Macc. 2.42, usually read as συναγωγὴ Ἀσιδαίων, in fact has little manuscript support. The correct reading is συναγωγὴ Ἰουδαίων, as has now been convincingly demonstrated by D. Schwartz, *SCI* 13 (1994) 7–18.

33. On relations between Seleucids and Hasmonaeans in this period, see the excellent bibliographical references assembled by Th. Fischer in A. Kasher et al., *Greece and Rome in Eretz Israel* (Jerusalem, 1990) 3–19, although the article itself does not add anything substantial.

34. II Macc. 11.16–38. Their authenticity is now generally acknowledged; see, e.g., M. Zambelli, *Miscellanea greca e romana* (Rome, 1965) 213–34; J. G. Bunge, *Untersuchungen zum zweiten Makkabäerbuch* (Bonn, 1971) 386–400; C. Habicht, *HSCP* 80 (1976) 7–12; Goldstein, *II Maccabees*, 406–407; Fischer, *Seleukiden und Makkabäer*, 64–80; Bar-Kochva, *Judas Maccabaeus*, 516–33, with extensive bibliography. The precise dates and order of the documents are not pertinent here.

35. II Macc. 11.28–33.

36. So, e.g., Tcherikover, *Hellenistic Civilization and the Jews*, 216–18; Habicht, *HSCP* 80 (1976) 10–11.

37. II Macc. 11.27: πρὸς δὲ τὸ ἔθνος ... τῇ γερουσίᾳ τῶν Ἰουδαίων καὶ τοῖς ἄλλοις Ἰουδαίοις χαίρειν.

signifying the general Jewish body, not excluding the Hasmonaeans and their sympathizers. The two Jewish emissaries who had submitted a petition to Lysias both possessed Hebrew names, and thus represented no "Hellenizing party." Lysias assured them that he would communicate certain requests to the king and would grant others on his own authority.[38] The cordial exchange between Jewish representatives and the royal minister implies the potential for mutual advantage that would supersede the overt hostility. Indeed, the entire section of the text that encompasses the correspondence is introduced by the author of II Maccabees with a negotiation between Lysias and Judas Maccabaeus. The Seleucid commander, having been defeated at Beth Zur, welcomed proposals from Judas, offered a settlement, and promised to pressure the king for an agreement.[39] II Maccabees misplaces this event, setting it after the death of Antiochus IV, and thus confounding the chronology of the letters that followed. But that gives no ground for doubting the diplomatic dealings between Seleucid authorities and the rebel leadership. Even Judas preferred a solution short of a duel to the death.

The two sides reached agreement again in early 162. Lysias had attacked Jerusalem and besieged the Temple Mount. But timing fortuitous for the Jews halted the assault. Word arrived of an insurrection at Antioch and a challenge to the throne. Seleucid troops had to be withdrawn from Jerusalem, and Antiochus V accepted terms that guaranteed to the Jews the right to practice their ancestral customs. The peace accord was concluded with the entire ἔθνος of the Jews.[40] And, if II Maccabees be believed, Antiochus marked its achievement with a gracious welcome to Judas Maccabaeus himself.[41]

The pacts proved to be impermanent, mere temporary cessations of hostility. But a basic understanding had permanence. The Seleucids no longer required abandonment of Jewish faith, let alone conformity with Hellenic practices. The appointment in 162 of Alcimus as High Priest, a scion of the Aaronite line, reinforced that conviction.[42] Seleucid nomination

---

38. II Macc. 11.16–21.

39. II Macc. 11.13–15.

40. I Macc. 6.55–61; II Macc. 13.23–24; Jos. *Ant.* 12.379–82.

41. II Macc. 13.24; Jos. *Ant.* 12.382. The author of I Maccabees does not make explicit mention of Judas, but that hardly warrants the doubts about his presence expressed, e.g., by Bunge, *Untersuchungen*, 267–68; E. Schürer, *The History of the Jewish People in the Age of Jesus Christ*, rev. ed. by G. Vermes and F. Millar (Edinburgh, 1973) I, 168–69; Goldstein, *I Maccabees*, 322–23; *II Maccabees*, 468; J. Sievers, *The Hasmoneans and their Supporters from Mattathias to the Death of John Hyrcanus I* (Atlanta, 1990) 60–61.

42. The execution of Menelaus occurred on the advice of Lysias and the orders of Antiochus V; II Macc. 13.4–8. Josephus, *Ant.* 12.383–88, gives a similar story and adds that Antiochus appointed Alcimus as his successor. Cf. II Macc. 14.3. The events are omitted in I Maccabees,

of the High Priest had probably been standard practice since the time of Antiochus III and thus consistent with acknowledging Jewish rights to live under their own laws. As we have seen, the Hasidaioi themselves were swift to recognize Alcimus' authority and to seek a peaceful resolution from him.[43] Hellenic sovereignty and Jewish traditionalism could go hand in hand.

The ensuing Seleucid intervention in Judaea came at Alcimus' own behest. The High Priest found the influence and popularity of the Maccabees to be disruptive to his own authority. The friction reflected internal Jewish rivalries, not a contest between Jew and Greek. It is noteworthy that Alcimus had to importune the new king Demetrius I with urgent appeals to dispatch a contingent of troops in 161 for the repression of his rival.[44] And more noteworthy still is the fact that the king's general Nicanor, after an initial skirmish with Maccabaean forces, offered proposals of peace. Judas consulted his soldiers and received unanimous consent to embrace the offer. In the formulation of II Maccabees, a friendly parley ensued between the leaders, the start of a personal relationship and genuine concord that permitted Judas to settle into the life of a private citizen.[45] The breakdown of the compact came only when the frustrated Alcimus renewed his appeal to the king, alleging that Nicanor undermined Seleucid policy by elevating Judas to a position of favor within the realm. Demetrius' orders to move against Judas then shattered the concord. Nicanor, in order to save his skin, had to act accordingly, thereby rupturing relations and renewing conflict.[46] The narrative attests to Alcimus' influence at court—rather than to a collision between the Jewish faithful and the champions of Hellenism.

---

whose author has Demetrius I ἔστησεν Alcimus; I Macc. 7.9. The verb may, however, mean "confirm" rather than "install," as it does in I Macc. 11.27, 11.57, 14.38; see W. Mölleken, *ZAW* 65 (1953) 205–28; Sievers, *Hasmoneans*, 61. Hence there need be no contradiction. Bar-Kochva, *Judas Maccabaeus*, 345–46, unnecessarily postulates that Alcimus did not actually serve as High Priest until the accession of Demetrius. On Alcimus' Aaronite lineage, see I Macc. 7.14; Jos. *Ant.* 12.387, 20.235.

43. I Macc. 7.13. For dependency of the High Priest upon Seleucid power, see II Macc. 3.1–3, 4.4–10, 4.23–25, 4.43–47; Jos. *Ant.* 12.237. The king's prerogative of making appointment to that office is taken for granted by II Macc. 4.8, 4.24–25.

44. I Macc. 7.25; II Macc. 14.3–10; Jos. *Ant.* 12.400–401.

45. II Macc. 14.11–25. Note the analysis of S. Schwartz, *JBL* 112 (1993) 308–309, who rightly sees Judas behaving "more like an ambitious courtier than a zealous freedom fighter." A very different version in I Macc. 7.26–30. Cf. Bar-Kochva, *Judas Maccabaeus*, 351, 354–56. The author of II Maccabees has doubtless embellished and romanticized the relationship between the two men. But the peace negotiations themselves need not be questioned.

46. II Macc. 14.28–30; cf. Jos. *Ant.* 12.405.

Judas Maccabaeus' celebrated victory over Nicanor earned great plaudits but proved short-lived. His career came to an unhappy close with defeat and death in 160. But the experiences through which he lived set a pattern that would be pursued and expanded upon in the long years of the Hasmonaean dynasty. Divisions within Judaea plagued the Maccabaean movement as much as any opposition from Antioch. Seleucid intervention took place principally in order to maintain stability and indirect control, while leaving direction in the hands of the Jewish High Priest—a long-standing policy of the Syrian monarchy since the beginning of the second century, with the aberrant exception of Antiochus IV's persecutions. This left considerable scope for negotiation and diplomacy. The future of the Hasmonaeans ironically lay not in resistance to Hellenic encroachment but in a network of reciprocal relations with Hellenic princes.

·   ·   ·

The death of Alcimus in 159 left the High Priesthood vacant. The fact is important and revealing. No one claimed or received appointment to that post for seven years thereafter.[47] That prompts an intriguing inference. It appears that both the court in Antioch and the Jewish leadership recognized the delicacy of the situation and refrained from precipitate action. With no available candidate who had the proper priestly genealogy, Demetrius I evidently stayed his hand. The king awaited a decision by the Jews, preferring a vacant post and the absence of a Seleucid nominee to offending Jewish sensibilities on so important a matter.[48] The Hasmonaeans for their part showed no eagerness to usurp an office for which they did not possess

47. Josephus, to be sure, has Judas Maccabaeus appointed to the office by the Jewish people themselves upon the demise of Alcimus; *Ant.* 12.414, 12.419, 12.434, 13.46. But the notice has no value. The Maccabaean books know nothing of it, and I Maccabees, in fact, makes it clear that Judas died before Alcimus; I Macc. 9.18, 9.23, 9.54–56. Moreover, Josephus gives the lie to his own reconstruction by asserting elsewhere that no one succeeded Alcimus and that Jerusalem lacked a High Priest for seven years; *Ant.* 20.237. The thesis of H. Stegemann, *Die Entstehung der Qumrangemeinde* (Bonn, 1971) 210–25, expanded by J. G. Bunge, *JSJ* 6 (1975) 27–28, 36–39, that the "Teacher of Righteousness," alluded to in the Qumran scrolls, held the High Priesthood after Alcimus, has been adequately refuted by H. Burgmann, *JSJ* 11 (1980) 135–76. See also Sievers, *Hasmoneans*, 76–77; P. A. Rainbow, *JJS* 48 (1997) 48.

48. Cf. Rainbow, *JJS* 48 (1997) 48–49. For Burgmann, *JSJ* 11 (1980) 141–43, the Seleucids refrained from appointing a High Priest because of three previous failures, Jason, Menelaus, and Alcimus, an unwillingness to commit themselves to the military support that such an arrangement might require, and a reluctance to provoke further hostilities by the Maccabees. An unnecesary mélange of motives.

the credentials, a usurpation which could only cost them popularity and influence among their countrymen. The empty berth at the head of the religious establishment exhibited both the knowledgeable diplomacy of the Seleucids and the precarious reputation of the Hasmonaeans among their own people.

Hasmonaean fortunes were at a low ebb after the death of Judas Maccabaeus, so we are told.[49] The assessment reflects not only recent defeats at the hands of Seleucid armies but the weakness of their position among the inhabitants of Palestine. The followers of Judas selected his brother Jonathan as their leader and general. He had considerable ground to make up.[50]

Seleucid engagement in Judaea was intermittent rather than continuous. Bacchides, commander of the forces in the area, withdrew after the death of Alcimus, and a period of peace set in for two years.[51] The outcome implies that Alcimus had been the prime instigator in what was fundamentally an internal struggle. When Bacchides returned in 157, he came upon the invitation of Jonathan's foes. The author of I Maccabees, of course, brands the collaborators as ἄνομοι, a bunch of evil-doers bent on nothing but eradication of the Hasmonaeans.[52] Whatever their motives, however, Bacchides' involvement in this instance may derive more from the need to show the Seleucid flag than to advance the interests of a particular faction. The vigorous reaction of Jonathan's forces earned some success on the battlefield and brought out Bacchides' true colors. The Seleucid general now vented his anger at the very persons who had summoned him in the first place and he announced his determination to return to his own country.[53] Bacchides accentuated his point by concluding an accord with Jonathan which not only ended hostilities and restored Jewish prisoners, but included an oath whereby, in the language of I Maccabees, the Seleucid vowed never to do harm to Jonathan for all the days of his life.[54] What Jonathan may have promised in return is unknown. The Seleucid garrison on the Akra dominating Jerusalem remained intact. Jonathan perhaps agreed not to challenge it, indeed to refrain from taking up residence in Jerusalem at all. He set up his establishment

---

49. I Macc. 9.23–27; Jos. *Ant.* 13.1–5.
50. I Macc. 9.28–31; Jos. *Ant.* 13.5–6.
51. I Macc. 9.57; Jos. *Ant.* 13.22.
52. I Macc. 9.58–60; Jos. *Ant.* 13.23.
53. I Macc. 9.69; Jos. *Ant.* 13.31.
54. I Macc. 9.69–72: ὤμοσεν αὐτῷ μὴ ἐκζητῆσαι αὐτῷ κακὸν πάσας τὰς ἡμέρας τῆς ζωῆς αὐτοῦ. Josephus tones down the biblical phraseology; *Ant.* 13.31–33: ὤμοσαν μὴ στρατεύσειν ἔτι κατ' ἀλλήλων.

instead at Michmash.[55] What matters, however, is Bacchides' vow, an action rarely stressed in the literature. In fact, it constituted a landmark. Though not binding upon the king, it bestowed a legitimacy upon Jonathan that he had not previously enjoyed. Bacchides' gesture represented reassertion of standard Seleucid policy: backing for respected Jewish leaders who could maintain stability in the area. Jonathan had attained that status in the eyes of the general. The compact between them signaled a central theme for the years to come: the mutual dependence of Seleucid and Hasmonaean.

Concord prevailed for five years thereafter, a period without recorded history in Palestine. Jonathan presumably employed it to good effect in consolidation of his authority. The modus vivendi with the Seleucids held. By abandoning the aggressive policy of his predecessor and refraining from action against Jerusalem, Jonathan had earned credit with the Seleucid regime—not as collaborator but as a pillar of stability in the region.

Dissent within the realm of the Seleucids redounded to the advantage of the Hasmonaeans. Demetrius' hold on the throne was challenged in 152 by the pretender Alexander Balas who claimed to be a son of Antiochus IV. Demetrius turned for support to Jonathan, now plainly recognized as possessing extensive influence in Judaea. The king offered still further gains of higher import. He sanctioned Jonathan's recruitment of an army, conferred upon him the formal title of "ally," and directed that the hostages in the Akra be handed over to him.[56] These were major concessions, acts of significant symbolic value. Recruitment of troops by the Hasmonaeans now had official endorsement by the throne, the status of ally meant acknowledgment of the Hasmonaeans' standing as an autonomous political entity, and the extrication of hostages from the Akra effectively invited Jonathan to reenter Jerusalem. He took swift advantage of the opportunity. Jonathan installed himself in the city and undertook a full-scale program of rebuilding structures, walls, and fortifications, thereby both to entrench his position and to leave permanent memorials to his success.[57]

There was better still to come. Alexander Balas, eager to outbid Demetrius for Jewish backing, made an even more attractive offer. He wrote to Jonathan with the salutation of "brother," accorded him the title of "friend of the king," a designation of high distinction in the Seleucid system, and, most tellingly, appointed him as High Priest of the Jews. Balas added a concrete element to his gesture by sending purple garb and a gold crown for Jonathan's

55. I Macc. 9.73; Jos. *Ant.* 13.34.

56. I Macc. 10.6; Jos. *Ant.* 13.38.

57. I Macc. 10.10–11; Jos. *Ant.* 13.41–42.

investiture.[58] The office of High Priest had stood vacant for seven years, as both Demetrius and Jonathan had exercised cautious restraint in that delicate matter. The expansion of Jonathan's influence in the interim and the exigencies of the political situation in 152, however, allowed the principals to overcome any qualms about the fact that Hasmonaeans lacked High Priestly lineage. Jonathan duly donned the vestments of office. And no opposition manifested itself.[59]

Demetrius hoped still to overtrump his rival. I Maccabees reports a lengthy missive of the king to the Jewish nation, making extravagant offers that included relief from taxation, additional territory in Samaria-Galilee, control over the Akra, release of Jewish prisoners all over the Seleucid dominions, enrollment of Jews into the royal army under the command of their own officers, a guarantee of revenues for the Temple, and handsome subsidies for all the rebuilding projects in Jerusalem.[60] The exorbitant generosity, however, only stirred suspicion in the camp of Jonathan. Demetrius' proposals lacked all credibility, and Jonathan rejected them. He already had the authority he needed from a more reliable Seleucid figure. The Jews would hold to their alliance with Alexander Balas.[61]

The episode proved beneficial for Jonathan. The Jewish leader took profit from the split in Seleucid circles to elevate his stature, attain the High

---

58. I Macc. 10.17–20: βασιλεὺς Ἀλέξανδρος τῷ ἀδελφῷ Ἰωναθαν χαίρειν ... νῦν καθεστάκαμέν σε σήμερον ἀρχιερέα τοῦ ἔθνους σου καὶ φίλον βασιλέως καλεῖσθαι, καὶ ἀπέστειλεν αὐτῷ πορφύραν καὶ στέφανον χρυσοῦν; Jos. *Ant.* 13.45. On the significance of the title "friend of the king," essentially a trusted official of the crown, see E. Bickerman, *Institutions des Séleucides* (Paris, 1938) 40–50; C. Habicht, *Vierteljahrschrift für Sozial und Wirtschaftsgeschichte* 45 (1958) 1–16; G. Herman, *Talanta*, 12–13 (1980–1981) 103–49.

59. I Macc. 10.22; Jos. *Ant.* 13.45. The effort of Bunge, *JSJ* 6 (1975) 33–43, to date the investiture to 150 does not obviate the explicit statement in I Maccabees. Sievers' claim, *Hasmoneans*, 84–85, that the appointment of Jonathan was considered irregular or controversial, has no foundation in the texts.

60. I Macc. 10.25–45; Jos. *Ant.* 13.48–57.

61. I Macc. 10.46–47. Demetrius' entire demeanor seems to be mocked by the author of I Maccabees; see, especially, 10.3–5, 10.22–24. One need not conclude, however, that the whole letter was a forgery, as was argued by H. Willrich, *Urkundenfälschung in der hellenistisch-jüdischen Literatur* (Göttingen, 1924) 37–41; see Schürer, *History of the Jewish People*, I, 178–79. It has often been noted that Demetrius addressed the letter to the ἔθνος of the Jews, rather than to Jonathan, thus leading many to the conclusion that he angled for support among the enemies of the Hasmonaeans; so, e.g., F.-M. Abel, *Les livres des Maccabées* (Paris, 1949) 185; Goldstein, *I Maccabees*, 405; Sievers, *Hasmoneans*, 93–94. That is not, however, the opinion of I Maccabee's author who plainly equates Jonathan and the "Jews" in this context; I Macc. 10.18–24. And he explicitly has Jonathan and "the people" react to the letter; I Macc. 10.46–47. Josephus certainly understood I Maccabees in this way, even adding "Jonathan" to the prescript of the letter; *Ant.* 13.47.

Priesthood, and establish Hasmonaean authority in Jerusalem. That much is clear and obvious. But the implications of Jonathan's success demand notice and emphasis. He did not grasp at the top post until nominated by a claimant to the Syrian throne, he now had royal authority for recruitment of his forces, his vestments were supplied by the monarchy, and he was formally designated as a "friend of the king." Jonathan's ready acceptance of his role needs to be understood in proper context. It was neither a sell-out of principles nor a betrayal of the Maccabaean cause. Judas had raised revolt against Antiochus IV's perverse policy but not against the Seleucid kingdom. And his campaigns directed themselves as much at indigenous foes as at the armies of the king. He had never claimed as objective the eradication of Hellenic power in Palestine, let alone of Hellenism. The arrangement between Jonathan and Alexander Balas basically reinstated the system as it had operated since the beginning of the century: the Jewish High Priest held sway in Jerusalem under the patronage of the Seleucid ruler—indeed under the supposed son of Antiochus the persecutor himself.[62]

Jonathan had bet on the right horse. Demetrius fell in battle, and Alexander Balas took the throne in Antioch. The new king also framed a marriage alliance with Ptolemy VI of Egypt, the event celebrated with grand festivities at Ptolemais (Akko) in 150. Jonathan reaped benefit from this as well. He arrived in splendor for the ceremony in Ptolemais, brought expensive gifts for the two kings and for their friends, and found favor in their eyes. Balas proceeded to make conspicuous display of his favor, robing Jonathan in purple, enrolling him among his "first friends," and naming him both general and regional governor. Those who had come to carp at him were thoroughly deflated. And Jonathan returned to Jerusalem in a position of great prestige.[63] Participation in the wedding party plainly reinforced and further elevated his public image. Jonathan's status as representative of the Jewish nation had now been openly proclaimed by two Hellenistic monarchs, and he had collected a package of titles and honors to overawe opponents at home. At the same time, however, the events set him in his proper place. Jonathan had come to Ptolemais on the summons of Alexander Balas. And the king made a show of conferring distinctions upon his nominee.[64] The grandiose

62. The one change of significance seems to be royal endorsement of the forces recruited by Jonathan—a matter of mutual benefit.

63. I Macc. 10.59–66; Jos. *Ant.* 13.83–85.

64. I Macc. 10.59: ἔγραψεν Ἀλέξανδρος ὁ βασιλεὺς Ἰωνάθη ἐλθεῖν εἰς συνάντησιν αὐτῷ; 10.65: καὶ ἐδόξασεν αὐτὸν ὁ βασιλεὺς καὶ ἔγραψεν αὐτὸν τῶν πρώτων φίλων καὶ ἔθετο αὐτὸν στρατηγὸν καὶ μεριδάρχην.

display strengthened Jonathan's hand in Judaea—but it also declared and co-opted him as a Seleucid official.

Jonathan enjoyed some heady success. After gaining important military victories against the foes of Balas, he rose higher in the Seleucid hierarchy, being registered now among the king's "kinsmen."[65] And Ptolemy himself met with Jonathan at Joppa, with proper diplomatic formalities, as if in an encounter between two heads of state.[66] But the illusion of autonomy masked the reality of dependence. When Jonathan sought to exploit his advantage by attacking the powerful citadel at Akra, he soon discovered the limits of his initiative. Alexander Balas had been murdered and a new king sat on the throne in Antioch, Demetrius II, who swiftly demanded an end to the siege and brusquely ordered Jonathan to Ptolemais.[67] The Jewish leader hurried to comply. That gesture restored the correct relationship. The new ruler had reminded Jonathan of his station, and could now afford to be gracious, even magnanimous. Demetrius accorded him all the distinctions he had possessed under the preceding monarchs, confirmed him in the High Priesthood, and counted him among the "first friends" of the king. All this occurred in public ceremony, in the presence of Jonathan's entourage that included elders and priests, and before the assembled Seleucid court in Ptolemais.[68] Demetrius had made his ascendancy plain. That having been accomplished, he could exhibit his graciousness in conferring dignities upon the man who would be his surrogate in Judaea.

Reciprocal advantage undergirded the relationship. Demetrius needed Jewish support to shore up his position against rivals and pretenders, and thus added territories in Samaria to Jonathan's realm, while affording substantial relief from taxes. At the same time, the language employed in granting the favors asserted the king's sovereignty: he offered benefactions to the Jews for their loyalty to him.[69] The pattern continues. While contenders competed for the Syrian throne, Jonathan could hope to gain concessions, but they would have to come at the hands of one Seleucid aspirant or another. So, Demetrius promised to yield up the Akra, but reneged when his fortunes improved, thus driving Jonathan into the camp of the rebel Tryphon who championed

65. I Macc. 10.89; Jos. *Ant.* 13.102.

66. I Macc. 11.6–7; Jos. *Ant.* 13.105.

67. I Macc. 11.22: ἔγραψεν Ἰωναθαν τοῦ μὴ περικαθῆσθαι καὶ τοῦ ἀπαντῆσαι αὐτὸν αὐτῷ συμμίσγειν εἰς Πτολεμαίδα τὴν ταχίστην; Jos. *Ant.* 13.123.

68. I Macc. 11.23–27; Jos. *Ant.* 13.124.

69. I Macc. 11.28–37; see 11.33: τῷ ἔθνει τῶν Ἰουδαίων φίλοις ἡμῶν καὶ συντηροῦσι τὰ πρὸς ἡμᾶς δίκαια ἐκρίναμεν ἀγαθοποιῆσαι χάριν τῆς ἐξ αὐτῶν εὐνοίας πρὸς ἡμᾶς; Jos. *Ant.* 13.125–28.

the cause of young Antiochus VI. This prompted the (by now) standard acknowledgments and guarantees: Antiochus confirmed Jonathan as High Priest, recognized his rule over the districts previously awarded, hailed him as one of the king's friends, and accorded him the privilege of wearing purple and gold.[70] The symbolic value of these gestures, however, went beyond mere formalities. The reaffirmation of distinctions both enhanced Jonathan's position and declared the crown's right to confer them at the accession of each new ruler. In a peculiar irony, the greater the Hasmonaean hold on power, the greater their dependence on Seleucid favor.

That hold was ever precarious. Jonathan made sure to advertise the backing of the throne in public pronouncements. It was essential in order to cow internal opposition in Judaea and elsewhere.[71] And when he was led into a trap and captured by the usurper Tryphon, the "neighboring nations" rose immediately to recoup losses suffered at the hands of the Jews.[72] Jonathan's fall pointed up all the more conspicuously the interdependence of Seleucid and Hasmonaean. The Maccabees prospered when their patrons succeeded, and suffered when they chose the wrong one. The "encircling peoples" of Palestine were always ready to pounce.[73]

•   •   •

In the perception of I Maccabees, a milestone in Jewish history occurred after Simon took over leadership upon the death of his brother Jonathan in 143. The nation escaped the yoke of Seleucid sovereignty, the people themselves elected Simon as High Priest, all taxes were lifted, and a whole new era would be marked by a dating scheme that began with the first year of Simon. In short, the Hasmonaeans had at last brought a genuine independence to the land of the Jews.[74] That assessment has generally been

70. I Macc. 11.57; Jos. *Ant.* 13.145–46.

71. Cf. I Macc. 10.7–8.

72. I Macc. 12.53; Jos. *Ant.* 13.196.

73. Kasher's discussion of Jonathan's years, *Jews and Hellenistic Cities*, 90–104, makes it appear that his principal quarrel was with the Greek cities of Palestine. The presentation can mislead the unwary. Jonathan's seizure of Joppa was surely motivated by his desire for a port on the Mediterranean; I Macc. 10.74–76; cf. 14.5. And the town was more Phoenician than Greek; cf. Goldstein, *I Maccabees*, 421. When he took Azotus, Jonathan conspicuously burned the temple of Dagon—no Greek shrine; I Macc. 10.83–84.

74. I Macc. 13.33–42: ἔτους ἑβδομηκοστοῦ καὶ ἑκατοστοῦ ἤρθη ὁ ζυγὸς τῶν ἐθνῶν ἀπὸ τοῦ Ισραηλ, καὶ ἤρξατο ὁ λαὸς γράφειν ἐν ταῖς συγγραφαῖς καὶ συναλλάγμασιν ἔτους πρώτου ἐπὶ Σίμωνος ἀρχιερέως μεγάλου καὶ στρατηγοῦ καὶ ἡγουμένου Ἰουδαίων; cf. 14.35. The same interpretation in Jos. *Ant.* 13.213–14; *BJ* 1.53.

endorsed in modern treatments.[75] The author's zeal for the Hasmonaean cause, however, may have overwhelmed sober judgment here. How much in fact had changed?

Conferral of the High Priesthood had long been the prerogative of the Seleucid crown. Did Simon's elevation violate that principle? I Maccabees records a bronze inscription set up to heap praise on Simon in 140 which included a statement that the "people," in view of Simon's selfless patriotism and dedication to his countrymen, made him their leader and High Priest.[76] The retrospective sanction, however, may not accurately reflect the earlier circumstances. Since the throne at Antioch was itself in dispute, with different elements enjoying Hasmonaean support at different times, any reference to Seleucid endorsement might be premature or controversial. Further, Simon's position contained its own ambiguities, for he held an authority of sorts while Jonathan was still a captive but not yet slain. I Maccabees observes that the "people" enjoined him to take the leadership in war.[77] This was plainly a temporary expedient, in Jonathan's absence, not an official inauguration. When Jonathan was executed on Tryphon's order, we hear of no assembly of Jews gathered to confer legitimacy on Simon—a remarkable omission by I Maccabees if any had, in fact, occurred.[78] It may be that Simon exercised the High Priest's responsibilities *de facto* during Jonathan's captivity and simply continued to do so without formal investiture after his death. The first acknowledgment of his office, significantly enough, comes in Demetrius II's letter to him in 142, a missive whose preamble greets him as "High Priest and friend of kings."[79] That prescript leaves open the possibility that Demetrius himself had given official authorization of the title—as he must have done for the designation "friend of kings." It is perhaps no accident that I Maccabees sets the beginning of the new calendar, signaled by "the first year of Simon the High Priest," after Demetrius' letter. Nomination to that office, in short, need not have strayed from convention.

75. E.g. Tcherikover, *Hellenistic Civilization and the Jews*, 236–40; Schürer, *History of the Jewish People*, I, 189–94; J. Goldstein in W. D. Davies and L. Finkelstein, *The Cambridge History of Judaism* (Cambridge, 1989) II, 318–19.

76. I Macc. 14.35: ὁ λαὸς ... ἔθεντο αὐτὸν ἡγούμενον αὐτῶν καὶ ἀρχιερέα.

77. I Macc. 13.7–9; Jos. *Ant.* 13.201. Sievers, *Hasmoneans*, 106, wrongly states that the people appointed him to the High Priesthood at this point as well.

78. Goldstein's thesis, *I Maccabees*, 476–77, that the author omitted this assembly out of a desire to conceal the Hasmonaeans' desertion of Antiochus VI, is strained and speculative. Far easier not to postulate an omission. Josephus, *Ant.* 13.213, does have Simon chosen by τὸ πλῆθος, but that is mere extrapolation on his part.

79. I Macc. 13.36: Σίμωνι ἀρχιερεῖ καὶ φίλῳ βασιλέων.

The breakthrough to a new era, according to I Maccabees, stemmed from Demetrius II's concessions to Simon. But close scrutiny undermines the conclusion. Demetrius, engaged in a contest for the throne with the usurper Tryphon who had murdered Antiochus VI, showed considerable generosity in order to secure Hasmonaean aid. He granted a peace treaty to Simon, proposed remission of taxes, guaranteed Hasmonaean hold over the fortresses which they had built, promised to overlook all errors and offenses committed in the past, to forgive the crown payment owed, to collect no further taxes in Jerusalem, and to encourage enrollment of Jews into the Seleucid forces.[80] These were the terms that led the author of I Maccabees to proclaim that "the yoke of the Gentile nations was lifted from Israel," thus commencing the new age of Jewish autonomy marked by Year One of Simon, High Priest, general, and leader of the Jews.[81] Yet the terms seem unsurprising, only the claim is extravagant. The promises contained in the letter do not differ substantially and, if anything, seem less sweeping than those proposed three years earlier by Demetrius to Jonathan.[82] Even if the previous offer be judged a doublet, a forgery, or an interpolation, the letter of Demetrius II should hardly have been cause for wild celebration. His position was precarious and his guarantees could easily be blown away with a shift in the political winds. The Jews had a little earlier transferred allegiance from Demetrius to Tryphon, and hence would be unlikely to pin much faith on the former's pledges.[83] Further, the letter and its context do not amount to anything like a renunciation of Seleucid sovereignty. Simon initiated the negotiations, requesting from Demetrius relief for his country which had suffered heavily from the rapacious exactions of Tryphon.[84] The request, in effect, conceded the station of the overlord, a gesture confirmed by sending a gold crown and palm branch to the king.[85] And Demetrius' reply underlined the nature of the relationship. Among other things, he magnanimously forgave all the "errors and offenses" committed by the Jews.[86] That characterization of previous Hasmonaean political behavior makes clear that the Seleucid vantage point takes precedence and the Seleucid ruler grants favor to his subordinates. It is fitting that Demetrius

---

80. I Macc. 13.36–40.

81. I Macc. 13.41–42; Jos. *Ant.* 13.213–14; see above n. 74.

82. I Macc. 11.28–37; Jos. *Ant.* 12.125–28.

83. See the appropriate skepticism of J. Dancy, *A Commentary on I Maccabees* (Oxford, 1954) 176; Sievers, *Hasmoneans*, 109–10.

84. I Macc. 13.34.

85. I Macc. 13.37; cf. Bickerman, *Institutions*, 111–12.

86. I Macc. 13.39: ἀφίεμεν δὲ ἀγνοήματα καὶ τὰ ἁμαρτήματα.

closes his letter by inviting Jewish soldiers to join the Syrian army—if they be judged suitable.[87] This is very far from an entitlement to autonomy. As for the trumpeting of the new age signaled by the first year of Simon's High Priesthood, a claim widely accepted in the modern literature, the surviving evidence supplies no support whatever. The only reference to a document dated by the years of Simon's High Priesthood comes in the inscription that honored him in 140—and that identifies the year both with regard to Simon's office and in terms of the Seleucid calendar! The text hardly signifies liberation from Seleucid hegemony.[88]

The idea of Jewish autonomy and escape from the Hellenic yoke receives decisive refutation from that very document. The Jews set up a bronze inscription in 140, affixed to a monument on Mt. Zion, detailing Simon's achievements. The decree praised him and his brothers for fighting valiantly against the enemies of his people on behalf of the Temple and the Law, for supplying his own funds to pay for the troops and finance the campaigns, for fortifying cities and strongholds, for driving out the ἔθνη, for taking over the Akra, for establishing Jewish settlements in various places and increasing the security of his nation, and for his unflagging loyalty to the interests of the Jewish people. The one item most conspicuous for its omission is any reference to liberation of the Jews from Hellenic overlordship or to the launching of Jewish autonomy. Quite the contrary. The inscription records with pride that the Syrian monarch Demetrius himself secured for Simon the office of High Priest, made him one of the king's friends, and accorded

---

87. I Macc. 13.40: εἴ τινες ἐπιτήδειοι ὑμῶν γραφῆναι εἰς τοὺς περὶ ἡμᾶς, ἐγγρα-φέσθωσαν.

88. I Macc. 14.27. Dating by years of the High Priest may have been conventional; cf. Jos. *Ant.* 14.148; Dancy, *Commentary*, 177. Goldstein, *I Maccabees*, 479–80, takes Josephus' reference here to the "ninth year" as a dating from the new era beginning in 143. But Josephus, even if inaccurate or confused, explicitly makes this "the ninth year of Hyrcanus." And Goldstein's claim that the Roman decree so dated came in 134 has no firm foundation. It rests only on a double hypthesis (not even argued by Goldstein) that the Roman praetor L. Valerius in the document was the consul of 131 and that his praetorship may have fallen in 134. The matter is much discussed; see bibliography in E. S. Gruen, *The Hellenistic World and the Coming of Rome* (Berkeley, 1984) 750, n. 13. When Alexander Jannaeus issued coins, they supplied regnal dates, with no allusion to an era stemming from Simon. Goldstein's argument, *I Maccabees*, 479–80, for an era marking Jewish liberation employs the analogy of various cities who thus signaled their emancipation from Seleucid rule. But the absence of testimony for such usage among the Jews dooms the hypothesis. Sievers, *Hasmoneans*, 110–12, rightly questions Goldstein's theory, but retains the view that the Jews adopted a new dating system beginning with Simon's years in office. Rajak, *CAH*² IX, 283–84, expresses reservations about the extent of Simon's accomplishments, but does not pursue them in detail.

him great honor.[89] Simon's accomplishments, many and admirable, did not include independence from Seleucid authority.[90]

Weakness and divisions within the Syrian realm gave the Hasmonaeans more room to maneuver. Simon's regaining of the Akra through economic blockade constituted a gain of high symbolic significance, a major step in the entrenchment of Hasmonaean power. The purging of the Akra and the joyous celebrations that accompanied it deliberately recalled Judas' purification of the Temple.[91] The acts delivered a strong message both to the Gentiles generally and to the population of Judaea that might have been hostile or reluctant to embrace Hasmonaean ascendancy. But they issued no direct challenge to the Seleucids. Their own internal difficulties progressively diminished their hold. The capture of Demetrius II by the Parthians left even wider scope for Jewish advance. Judaea enjoyed a most unusual period of peace and prosperity in the time of Simon.[92] Relations with Antioch show familiar features. Antiochus VII Sidetes, brother of Demetrius II, made a bid for the throne against Tryphon. Hasmonaean support would be serviceable, and Antiochus repeated the pattern of his predecessors with a letter bestowing a series of benefactions upon the Jews: tax remissions, acceptance of Jewish armaments, garrisons, and strongholds in various parts of the region, cancellation of debts, and the right to mint

89. I Macc. 14.38–39: ὁ βασιλεὺς Δημήτριος ἔστησεν αὐτῷ τὴν ἀρχιερωσύνην κατὰ ταῦτα καὶ ἐποίησεν αὐτὸν τῶν φίλων αὐτοῦ καὶ ἐδόξασεν αὐτὸν δόξῃ μεγάλῃ. The decree as a whole is given by I Macc. 14.27–47. Its authenticity seems assured not only by the language common to Hellenistic decrees but by the fact that the author of I Maccabees reproduces it despite inconsistencies with his own narrative. See Abel, *Les livres des Maccabées*, 254–55; Schürer, *History of the Jewish People*, I, 193–194; Goldstein, *I Maccabees*, 501–509; Sievers, *Hasmoneans*, 121–22. Goldstein, *op. cit.*, 500–501, recognizes the omission of any reference to liberation in the text, but explains it away as the influence of certain Jewish parties who believed that prophecies of Israel's future glory had not yet been fulfilled. One mention of "freedom" does occur, a statement that the decree was inscribed because the Maccabees had driven off the enemies of Israel and secured its freedom; I Macc. 14.26: ἐπολέμησε τοὺς ἐχθροὺς Ισραηλ ἀπ' αὐτῶν, καὶ ἔστησαν αὐτῷ ἐλευθερίαν. But the text is confused, the reference seems to be to the Maccabees and not just to Simon, and, in any case, it represents the interpretation of the author rather than a part of the document. On the text, see the discussions of Abel, *Les livres des Maccabées*, 255, and Sievers, *Hasmoneans*, 119. Pagan versions have the Jews obtain independence through rebellion against Demetrius, rather than as consequence of his concessions; Diod. 40.2; Justin 36.1.10, 36.3.8–9; cf. the confused account in Tac. *Hist.* 5.8. These may be indirect allusions to the capture of Akra by the Jews.

90. For a similar view, see Rajak in Bilde et al., *Aspects of Hellenistic Kingship*, 97–98.

91. I Macc. 13.49–52, 14.7, 14.36; Jos. *Ant.* 13.215–17. A good discussion by Sievers, *Hasmoneans*, 113–16.

92. I Macc. 14.4, 14.8–15. This in no way justifies the assertion of Schürer, *History of the Jewish People*, I, 193, that "the country was independent of Syrian hegemony."

coinage.[93] The Hellenistic monarch or pretender remained in a position to grant favors. Nor did Simon refuse the offers and assert autonomy. He sent soldiers, money, and resources to assist Antiochus at the siege of Dor. It was the Hellenistic king, now on the verge of victory without Jewish help, who refused the offer and repudiated his earlier promises.[94] The Jews had not cut themselves loose.

The rupture between Antiochus VII and Simon spilled over into the High Priesthood of Simon's son John Hyrcanus. And the Seleucid king had the upper hand. Antiochus besieged the Hasmonaeans for more than a year in Jerusalem, until Hyrcanus sued for terms.[95] The Hasmonaean asked that his people be granted their "ancestral constitution."[96] The phraseology is vague but conventional in Hellenistic diplomacy. Hyrcanus sought some sign of favor to mark an accord and preserve his own position, perhaps Seleucid ratification of his High Priesthood. But a show of acquiescence was required now on the Hasmonaeans' part. Antiochus demanded the surrender of weapons, tribute for the towns outside Judaea that had been seized by the Jews, and acceptance of a garrison in Jerusalem. The stipulations closely corresponded to those that he had required of Simon earlier.[97] This time they were met. The Jews agreed upon all terms except the imposition of a garrison. They could not endure the idea of another Akra. But they offered extensive compensation in the form of cash and hostages. Antiochus Sidetes now consented to lift the siege of Jerusalem—though not before he demolished the walls of the city. Negotiations concluded in a most amicable fashion. Hyrcanus became friend and ally of the Seleucid monarch and hosted his troops magnanimously in the city.[98] The implications seem clear enough. Each side cared more for recognition of its status by the

93. I Macc. 15.1–9; Jos. *Ant.* 13.213. Only the authorization for Jewish coinage is new, but there is no evidence that Simon ever availed himself of that privilege. I Macc. 15.7 includes a phrase in Antiochus' letter that Jerusalem and the Temple are to be "free." But this is not a declaration of autonomy. Cf. the remarks of Goldstein, *I Maccabees*, 514—although his proposed emendation is quite speculative.

94. I Macc. 15.26–27; Jos. *Ant.* 13.224–25; *BJ* 1.50–51.

95. Jos. *Ant.* 13.236–41; *BJ* 1.61. Under the circumstances, Hyrcanus could hardly expect a Seleucid endorsement for his High Priesthood. He seems simply to have assumed the office upon Simon's death; Jos. *Ant.* 13.230; *BJ* 1.56. But it is noteworthy that Antiochus refrained from nominating anyone else. He could anticipate an eventually compliant Hyrcanus who would be more serviceable in Judaea than opposing Jewish leaders without comparable influence.

96. Jos. *Ant.* 13.245: ἀξιῶν τὴν πάτριον αὐτοῖς πολιτείαν ἀποδοῦναι.

97. Jos. *Ant.* 13.245–46. For the demands on Simon, see I Macc. 15.25–31.

98. Jos. *Ant.* 13.247–49; cf. Diod. 34/5.1.4–5; Plut. *Mor.* 184F. Josephus' earlier version has Antiochus lift the siege after being paid 300 talents by Hyrcanus; *BJ* 1.61.

other than for fighting the war to its conclusion. Their settlement restored the relationship to its conventional form: mutual reinforcement of one another's position with Hasmonaeans controlling Judaea as surrogates for Seleucid power. The association was advertised widely in the Near East when Hyrcanus accompanied Antiochus on the first part of his campaign against Parthia in 130.[99] The public collegiality made a declaration both to the outside world and to possible dissidents within Palestine that Hyrcanus held an honored position in the Seleucid empire.

The endorsement lifted Hyrcanus' stature, as so often in the history of Seleucid-Hasmonaean relations. And, equally familiar, divisions within the Syrian ruling house gave the Jewish leader a freer hand in pursuing his own aggrandizement. The principal danger lay in selecting the wrong Seleucid pretender to support—once again a recurrent feature of this turbulent association. The patterns of preceding regimes repeated themselves revealingly in Hyrcanus' years. The successive deaths of Antiochus VII and Demetrius II threw the competition for the throne into its customary turmoil. In the contest between Demetrius' son Antiochus VIII Grypus and the pretender Alexander Zabinas, supported by the Ptolemies, Hyrcanus concluded a pact of φιλία with Alexander. The connection showed poor judgment and proved to be short-lived. Alexander fell in battle in 123 and Hyrcanus had incurred the wrath of both Antiochus VIII and his step-brother Antiochus IX Cyzicenus.[100] Fortunately for him, however, the brothers themselves fell to blows, thus giving Hyrcanus a broad field to pursue his own objectives. If Josephus be believed, these years allowed his fortunes to flourish, he enjoyed undeterred the resources of Judaea, and, as the Seleucids tore themselves apart, he could simply ignore both brothers.[101]

Hyrcanus, like his predecessors, trained his sights upon Judaea and bordering areas, not upon centers of Seleucid power. His vigorous expansionism occupied the last decade or so of the reign. Hyrcanus' forces conducted

---

99. Jos. *Ant.* 13.249. The argument of T. Rajak, *GRBS* 22 (1981) 65–81, that an intervention by Rome induced Antiochus to give up the siege, is acute but highly speculative and unnecessary. Antiochus had more to gain from collaboration with than from the crippling of the Hasmonaeans.

100. Jos. *Ant.* 13.269–70, 13.274.

101. Jos. *Ant.* 13.272–74: ὁ γὰρ πρὸς ἀλλήλους αὐτοῖς πόλεμος σχολὴν Ὑρκανῷ καρποῦσθαι τὴν Ἰουδαίαν ἐπ᾽ ἀδείας παρέσχεν ὡς ἄπειρόν τι πλῆθος χρημάτων συναγαγεῖν ... καὶ αὐτόν τε πράττοντα κακῶς καὶ τὸν ἀδελφὸν αὐτοῦ ἐν τοῖς πρὸς ἀλλήλους ἀγῶσιν ἀμφοτέρων κατεφρόνησεν. Josephus' language, indicating that Hyrcanus "revolted" from the Macedonians, is obviously imprecise and excessive. It means no more than that he ceased to provide them with any resources; 13.273: τῶν Μακεδόνων ἀπέστη καὶ οὔτε ὡς ὑπήκοος οὔτε ὡς φίλος αὐτοῖς οὐδὲν ἔτι παρεῖχεν.

campaigns in Transjordan, Idumaea, and Samaria, campaigns for which they could find biblical precedents and sanctions. This was plainly no anti-Hellenic obsession.[102] Hyrcanus encountered Seleucid forces only when he placed the city of Samaria under siege probably in 108/7. Its starving inhabitants called upon Antiochus Cyzicenus for assistance. But Antiochus' soldiers, even when reinforced by troops from Ptolemy Lathyrus, proved inadequate. Samaria fell and was eradicated. And a Seleucid commander even betrayed the city of Scythopolis to Hyrcanus—receiving rich compensation for it.[103] The aggressive thrusts built the power and spread the influence of the Hasmonaeans. Greeks were neither the initial nor the principal targets.[104]

The progressive disintegration of Seleucid authority allowed Hasmonaean ambitions to burst former confines. John Hyrcanus' successor Aristobulus, who held power for only a year, became the first of his house to take the title of king and don the royal diadem.[105] The move proclaimed that leadership of the Jews entailed both political and religious power which put it on a level with the Hellenistic states. Dependence upon or even relations with the Seleucid monarchy had now been formally relegated to the past. That

---

102. Jos. *Ant.* 13.254–58, 13.267–83; *BJ* 1.62–66. See the treatments of Schürer, *History of the Jewish People*, I, 206–10; Goldstein in Davies and Finkelstein, *Cambridge History of Judaism*, II, 324–29; Sievers, *Hasmoneans*, 141–46. On the chronology, see now D. Barag, *Israel Numismatic Journal* 12 (1992/1993) 1–12. For Schwartz, *JJS* 42 (1991) 17–20, the gains came not so much through conquest as through agreement. Kasher, *Jews and Hellenistic Cities*, 121–31, puts misleading emphasis upon Hyrcanus' campaigns as directed against "Hellenistic cities." The phrase is fair enough if by that is meant cities of mixed peoples and institutions which had taken on a mongrel character in the Hellenistic era. But that should not be confused with a notion that Hyrcanus aimed at Greeks as his victims. The case of Scythopolis is instructive. It was taken by force or betrayed to Hyrcanus. Josephus gives both versions; *Ant.* 13.280; *BJ* 1.66. In either case, the motive can hardly have been hostility between Greek and Jew. There had traditionally been warm relations between the Jews and Gentiles dwelling there; II Macc. 12.29–31. Kasher himself acknowledges that Hyrcanus' motives here were economic and strategic; *op. cit.*, 129.

103. Jos. *Ant.* 13.275–81. The version that has the Jews take Scythopolis by force is the earlier one; *BJ* 1.66.

104. Greeks and Macedonians may have occupied the city of Samaria; cf. Goldstein, *I Maccabees*, 245–46, with bibliography. But it is significant that Josephus explains the siege as retaliation for attacks on Jewish colonists and their allies. And he calls the inhabitants of the city simply "Samarians"; *Ant.* 13.275.

105. Jos. *BJ* 1.70; *Ant.* 13.301. According to Strabo 16.2.40, Alexander Jannaeus initiated this practice. But Strabo could easily have passed over the brief reign of Aristobulus. So Schürer, *History of the Jewish People*, I, 217. The numismatic evidence cannot settle the matter, for the relevant coins probably belong to the reign of Aristobulus II; cf. Y. Meshorer, *Ancient Jewish Coinage* (Dix Hills, N.Y., 1982) I, 46–47.

association, though essential to the establishment of Hasmonaean authority, represented a relic that needed to be consigned to oblivion.

The long reign of Alexander Jannaeus from 103 to 76 put the seal upon it. Jannaeus went after "Hellenistic" cities forcefully and determinedly. He attacked the coastal communities, Ptolemais, Dor, Straton's Tower, Anthedon, Gaza, and Raphia.[106] And he assaulted various cities in the Transjordan area and in the Golan: Gadara, Amathus, Dium, Gerasa, Gaulana, Seleuceia, Gamala, and Pella.[107] Jannaeus could also treat inhabitants of the cities with ruthlessness and brutality. After the surrender of Gaza, he permitted his soldiers to commit a mass slaughter and demolished the city. He destroyed Amathus. And, when the people of Pella refused to embrace the ancestral practices of the Jews, he had that city razed as well.[108]

Does this at last constitute a systematic Jewish retaliation against the Greek communities of Palestine and a blow to the culture of the Hellenes?[109] A wider perspective leads to a different conclusion. The Hasmonaeans had now broken decisively with Antioch. There was nothing more to be gained from the disintegrating dynasty whose internal divisions forecast its impending doom. It does not follow, however, that Jannaeus could operate freely outside the shadow of the Hellenistic powers. His sieges of Ptolemais and of Gaza brought rival forces from the kingdom of Egypt into play. Jannaeus was compelled to enter devious negotiations with Ptolemy Lathyrus and to solicit the support of Cleopatra, Lathyrus' mother and enemy. Only Cleopatra's forceful intervention saved Judaea from falling under Lathyrus' control—and she was barely dissuaded from occupying the land of the Jews

106. Jos. *Ant.* 13.324, 13.334, 13.357–58; *BJ* 1.87.

107. Jos. *Ant.* 13.356, 13.374, 13.382, 13.393–94, 13.397; *BJ* 1.89, 1.104–105.

108. Gaza: Jos. *Ant.* 13.362–64; Amathus: Jos. *Ant.* 13.374; Pella: Jos. *Ant.* 13.397.

109. Tcherikover, *Hellenistic Civilization and the Jews*, 242–49, recognizes that the issue was a political rather than a cultural one. But he does conceive it as a continuous struggle between the Hasmonaeans and the Greek cities, and a drive by the Hasmonaeans to Judaize the population of those cities. Kasher, *Jews and Hellenistic Cities*, 157–69, questions the extent of damage actually inflicted upon the Greeks by Jannaeus, but puzzlingly reckons that the damage was "more spiritual than physical." Schürer, *History of the Jewish People*, I, 228, goes further still in claiming that Jannaeus sought to annihilate Greek civilization. By contrast, Goldstein in Davies and Finkelstein, *Cambridge History of Judaism*, II, 337–41, finds biblical precedents and prophecies as inspiration for Jannaeus. That the destruction of cities by Jannaeus and the Hasmonaeans generally has been exaggerated by modern historians was argued on archaeological grounds by S. Applebaum in B. Levick, *The Ancient Historian and his Materials* (Westmead, 1975) 59–73; *idem, SCI* 5 (1979/1980) 168–77. Cf. I. Shatzman, *The Armies of the Hasmonaeans and Herod* (Tübingen, 1991) 72–82. But these views need modification in light of more recent excavations at Marisa, Shechem, Samaria, and Mt. Gerizim; see Bar-Kochva, *Pseudo-Hecataeus, "On the Jews": Legitimizing the Jewish Diaspora* (Berkeley, 1996) 131, 294–95.

herself. Jannaeus had to engage in supplication, and was fortunate to be accorded an alliance by the Ptolemaic queen.[110] The circumstances bear a strong resemblance to the many occasions on which Seleucid endorsement propped up Hasmonaean authority. Nor did Jannaeus' military activity confine itself to Greek cities. He campaigned in the lands of Moab and Gilead held by Arabs and he suffered defeat more than once at the hands of the Nabataeans.[111] Indeed, some of the fiercest and most determined resistance to Jannaeus came from disaffected Jews—and they suffered some of the most brutal reprisals by the Hasmonaean ruler.[112] By contrast, a substantial portion of his forces consisted of Greek mercenaries, drawn at least in part from Pisidia and Cilicia in Asia Minor.[113] It is noteworthy that Josephus nowhere suggests that Alexander Jannaeus' attacks on the various cities had as objective the Greeks who dwelled therein. In fact, the hybrid makeup of most or all of these cities renders dubious any suggestion that their "Greek" character caused offense to Jews.[114] The idea that Jannaeus conducted a systematic policy of Judaization of Greek communities goes well beyond the evidence.[115] Even in the reign most conspicuous for independence of Seleucid influence and spread of Jewish nationalist power, the Hasmonaeans

110. Jos. *Ant.* 13.324–55; note especially 13.353–55: Ἀλεξάνδρου δ' αὐτῇ μετὰ δώρων προσελθόντος καὶ θεραπείας ὁποίας ἄξιον ἦν ... ἡ Κλεοπάτρα πείθεται μηδὲν ἀδικῆσαι τὸν Ἀλέξανδρον, ἀλλὰ συμμαχίαν πρὸς αὐτὸν ἐποιήσατο. Cf. Jos. *BJ* 1.86. On Jewish-Ptolemaic relations generally in this period (for which the evidence is woefully thin), see M. Stern, *Zion* 50 (1985) 81–106 (Hebrew).

111. Jos. *Ant.* 13.374–75, 13.382, 13.394; *BJ* 1.89–90, 1.103.

112. Jos. *Ant.* 13.372–73, 13.376, 13.379–83; *BJ* 1.88–91, 1.96–98.

113. Jos. *Ant.* 13.374, 13.377–78.

114. A valuable survey of evidence on these cities in E. Schürer, *The History of the Jewish People in the Age of Jesus Christ*, rev. ed. by G. Vermes, F. Millar, and M. Black (Edinburgh, 1979) II, 85–183.

115. Only in the case of Pella does Josephus state that the Jews destroyed it because its inhabitants would not promise to adapt to traditional Jewish practices; *Ant.* 13.397: ταύτην δὲ κατέσκαψαν οὐχ ὑποσχομένων τῶν ἐνοικούντων ἐς τὰ πάτρια τῶν Ἰουδαίων ἔθη μεταβαλεῖσθαι. The city is singled out as exceptional, not representative, in Josephus' list of places under Jewish control in the time of Jannaeus. Hence, the conclusion of Schürer, *History of the Jewish People*, I, 228, that Pella's fate illustrates general policy, is unwarranted. Kasher, *Jews and Hellenistic Cities*, 156–59, plausibly argues that the encouragement to conversion was directed toward the native dwellers of Pella rather than toward the Greeks, and that Jannaeus in any case did not raze Pella to the ground; Jos. *BJ* 1.156. Kasher, however, seems to undermine some of his own findings by asserting that Jannaeus conducted an "all-out war against the Hellenistic cities," and that he pursued a "policy of Judaization in the occupied areas"; *op. cit.*, 139, 142. On Jannaeus' policy generally, see the measured and sensible remarks of Rajak, *CAH* [2] IX, 293–96; *eadem* in Davies and White, *Tribute to Vermes*, 274–77. Cf., most recently, M. Smith, *Studies in the Cult of Yahweh* (Leiden, 1996) I, 269–70, 281–82.

still operated within a Hellenistic world to which they had adapted rather than one which they had rejected.

The foregoing survey allows for some general remarks. The construct of a clash between Greek and Jew during the Hasmonaean period is a red herring, even on the political and military front. A notable fact needs to be underscored. Greek historians of the Hellenistic period rarely have an unkind word to say for the Hasmonaeans, and nowhere regard their expansionism as directed against Greek cities or Hellenic civilization.[116] That deprives the *communis opinio* of any substantial support. The Maccabaean movement arose in response to the aberrant and abhorrent policies of Antiochus Epiphanes. It soon became embroiled, however, in conflicts with other Jewish groups and directed much of its energies against Gentiles in Palestine who could be portrayed as the heirs of biblical enemies rather than against the purveyors of Hellenism. Even Judas Maccabaeus, who raised revolt and fought Seleucid armies in bloody battles, entered into diplomatic relations and framed advantageous agreements with Seleucid officials. The growth of Hasmonaean authority in Judaea and surrounding areas in subsequent decades owed much to associations cultivated by their leaders with Hellenistic princes and pretenders. Jonathan proved to be especially adept at raising the profile of his party and obtaining legitimacy through dignities conferred by Seleucid rulers and would-be rulers. Success on the battlefield had less enduring value than the marks of distinction that signaled accord and cooperation with Antioch. The much heralded "autonomy" achieved under Simon depended upon favors granted and public acknowledgment of awards by Syrian royalty. As Seleucid discord increased and their hold on the realm disintegrated, Hasmonaean power expanded notably under John Hyrcanus and Alexander Jannaeus. But the territorial aggrandizement did not constitute a crusade against the Seleucid regime or against Greeks as such. Jannaeus no longer needed to look to Antioch for legitimation but he could turn with equal effect to Alexandria. Hasmonaean success in war and politics owed more to connections than to conflict with the Hellenic world.

All of this sets the issue of Hellenism and the Hasmonaeans on an altogether different footing. The idea of a tension or an inconsistency between

---

116. The fact is documented in detail by I. Shatzman, *Zion* 57 (1992) 5–62 (Hebrew). But see the comments of B. Bar-Kochva, *Zion* 61 (1996) 41 (Hebrew). Strabo is an exception; 16.2.37, 16.2.40. Even he, however, does not claim that Hasmonaean aggression aimed at Hellenic communities. On the difficult and confusing language of Strabo here, see J.-D. Gauger, *Historia* 28 (1979) 211–24.

political resistance to Greeks and an adoption of Greek ways evaporates. And the image of a Maccabaean movement, once stoutly resistant to Hellenism, gradually giving way to compromise and assimilation under the later Hasmonaeans, no longer carries conviction. Was Hellenism as such ever an issue for the Maccabees?

The High Priest Jason installed a gymnasium and introduced the ephebate to Jerusalem ca. 174. For the author of II Maccabees, this marked a high point of Hellenism, the destruction of lawful institutions, and the entrance of illegal practices into Jewish society.[117] Did these innovations then represent the hated symbols of Hellenism, the undermining of traditional Judaism, for which Judas Maccabaeus formed a rallying point?[118]

The rhetoric of II Maccabees should not lead us astray. Its author has vastly overrated a crisis that few at the time seem to have found particularly alarming. I Maccabees offers a more sober account, but one also subject to misinterpretation. The author blames the change on παράνομοι who sought to ingratiate themselves with "the neighboring peoples" and applied to the king for permission to adopt Gentile institutions. Consequently they constructed a gymnasium in accordance with alien practices, abandoning their holy covenant and yoking themselves to the Gentiles, and even disguising their circumcision.[119] The analysis, as introduction to the policies of Antiochus IV, appears ominous. But the facts are not so frightening. A reaching out to Gentiles in the vicinity makes perfectly good sense. The installation of a gymnasium in Jerusalem certainly meant introducing Greek ways, but the idea that this entailed abandonment of the holy covenant (even though some hard-liners may have propounded it) is wild exaggeration. I Maccabees mentions only one violation of Jewish custom: the disguise of circumcision. The statement is normally taken as meaning that Jews who exercised in the gymnasium had to appear in the nude and thus sought to conceal their

117. II Macc. 4.9–13: τὰς μὲν νομίμους καταλύων πολιτείας, παρανόμους ἐθισμοὺς ἐκαίνιζεν ... ἦν δ' οὕτως ἀκμή τις Ἑλληνισμοῦ.

118. See Tcherikover, *Hellenistic Civilization and the Jews*, 163–69, who sees the change as transformation of Jerusalem into a Greek *polis*. Cf. Schürer, *History of the Jewish People*, I, 148–49; Hengel, *Judaism and Hellenism*, I, 72–75. For R. Doran in H. Attridge, J. Collins, and T. Tobin, *Of Scribes and Scrolls* (Lanham, 1990) 99–109, Jason's reform constituted a dramatic shift in the educational system.

119. I Macc. 1.11–15: παράνομοι ... λέγοντες πορευθῶμεν καὶ διαθώμεθα διαθήκην μετὰ τῶν ἐθνῶν τῶν κύκλῳ ἡμῶν ... καὶ [Antiochus] ἔδωκεν αὐτοῖς ἐξουσίαν ποιῆσαι τὰ δικαιώματα τῶν ἐθνῶν. καὶ ᾠκοδόμησαν γυμνάσιον ἐν Ἱεροσολύμοις κατὰ τὰ νόμιμα τῶν ἐθνῶν. καὶ ἐποίησαν ἑαυτοῖς ἀκροβυστίας καὶ ἀπέστησαν ἀπὸ διαθήκης ἁγίας καὶ ἐζευγίσθησαν τοῖς ἔθνεσιν. On the notion of "covenant" in I Maccabees, see Arenhoevel, *Theokratie*, 22–33.

circumcision in order to be as Greek as possible.[120] But that inference is more than questionable. II Maccabees, which provides some specifics about Jews in the gymnasium and is even more condemnatory, says nothing about nudity, let alone about the camouflage of circumcision. The worst that the author can find to say is that Jason placed the ephebes under a Greek-style hat. Had they been compelled to appear in the nude and to alter their appearance by contravening Jewish law, II Maccabees would surely have pounced upon that information. The statement in I Maccabees has to be differently understood. It may refer to the period of the persecutions when Antiochus did impose a ban on circumcision. Or else it supplies a mere metaphor for those who abandoned the Jewish way of life.[121] Neither the existence of a gymnasium nor participation in its activities required abandonment of the faith.

The conclusion is, in fact, confirmed by II Maccabees, despite the rhetorical smokescreen. As the text makes clear, Jason, High Priest of the Jews, initiated the gymnasium and the ephebate, not the Greek king.[122] The significance of that ought not to be missed. By creating the institutions as official acts of the High Priest, Jason introduced the Hellenic features with the embrace of Jewish authority. And, once the structure was in place, the priests themselves participated with eagerness in the running of the palaestra at the call of the discus.[123] II Maccabees, of course, regards this enthusiasm as coming at the expense of traditional priestly duties, an inevitable inference given its orientation.[124] The fact remains that members of Jerusalem's religious establishment found it perfectly acceptable to take part in the activities of the

120. Josephus understood it in this fashion; *Ant.* 12.241. But that is mere interpretation, not additional information.

121. The silence of II Maccabees is rightly stressed by J. Goldstein in E. P. Sanders, *Jewish and Christian Self-Definition* (Philadelphia, 1981) II, 77–78; *II Maccabees*, 229–30. For the suggestion that I Maccabees refers to the persecutions, see E. S. Gruen in P. Green, *Hellenistic History and Culture* (Berkeley, 1993) 259. The alternative idea of a metaphor is proposed by Doran in Attridge et al., *Of Scribes and Scrolls*, 106–108. It is possible that even the *petasos*, the Greek-style hat mentioned at II Macc. 4.12, is a metaphor for the Greek way of life, rather than a hat actually worn in the gymnasium. See the acute comments of H. A. Harris, *Greek Athletics and the Jews* (Cardiff, 1976) 30–31. The passages in Jubilees 3.31, 15.11–14, that strongly condemn nudity and the absence of circumcision, make no allusion to a gymnasium or to an imitation of Greek customs.

122. II Macc. 4.9–10.

123. II Macc. 4.14: ἔσπευδον μετέχειν τῆς ἐν παλαίστρῃ παρανόμου χορηγίας μετὰ τὴν τοῦ δίσκου πρόσκλησιν. The precise meaning of the text is not quite clear; see Abel, *Les livres des Maccabées*, 334; R. Doran, *Temple Propaganda: The Purpose and Character of 2 Maccabees* (Washington, 1981) 44–45; Goldstein, *II Maccabees*, 231.

124. Goldstein, *II Maccabees*, 230–31, rightly points out that priestly responsibilities were widely shared and left time for much else.

gymnasium without compromising their sacerdotal role.[125] To reckon these "Hellenic reforms" as annulling Jewish tradition is to adopt the propaganda of I and II Maccabees while ignoring the actions that they record.

Another point, rarely commented upon, needs emphasis here. No text anywhere states or even hints that Judas Maccabaeus ever sought to demolish the gymnasium. The demolition could readily have been accomplished when Judas took control of Jerusalem in 164. Indeed he could hardly have refrained from doing so if that structure stood as the very symbol of wicked Hellenism. Its razing would be a perfect counterpart to the purification and rededication of the Temple. But Judas evidently left it alone. And, as far as we know, so did his successors.[126] The gymnasium may well have continued to stand as a symbol—but it symbolized a congruence between Judaism and Hellenism.

The congruence can be perceived also through another means: the use of Greek names by Hasmonaeans and their prominent supporters. To be sure, the first generation of Maccabees exhibit only Hebrew/Aramaic names: the sons of Mattathias are John, Simon, Judas, Eleazer, Jonathan.[127] Gentile names begin in the next generation, with Hyrcanus, son of Simon, and continue consistently through the Hasmonaean years. The development has led to a deduction that the earliest members of the family were impervious to Hellenism and that subsequent generations initiated the Hellenization process.[128] The thesis, however, takes too restricted an approach and reaches questionable conclusions.

Gentile names among Jews in Palestine certainly preceded the Maccabaean period. And they do not confine themselves to any "Hellenizing party." Hyrcanus, son of Joseph the Tobiad, appears in the romantic tales of the Tobiads that refer to the late third century.[129] His supposed involvement with the court in Alexandria and service as tax collector in Ptolemaic domains perhaps explains the appellation. More pertinent, however, is Antigonus of Socho, designated in the Mishnah as disciple of the High Priest Simon the Just in the early second century and recipient of the oral tradition from him.[130] Plainly the Greek name did not signify a turning away from Jewish

---

125. Cf. the sensible remarks of Will-Orrieux, *Ioudaismos-Hellènismos*, 115–19, 125–36.

126. One might note as comparison the ξυστός, normally the covered colonnade in a gymnasium, which still existed in Jerusalem well over two centuries later; Jos. *BJ* 2.344. Sievers in Parente and Sievers, *Josephus and the History of the Greco-Roman Period*, 202–203, suggests that the gymnasium serviced soldiers stationed in the Akra.

127. I Macc. 2.2–5.

128. So T. Ilan, *JQR* 78 (1987) 15.

129. Jos. *Ant.* 12.186–236.

130. M. Aboth, 1.2–3.

tradition. A sequence of Jewish High Priests carried Hellenic names in the Maccabean period: Jason, Menelaus, and Alcimus. Of course, they, together with Menelaus' brother Lysimachus, are branded by the pro-Hasmonaean tradition as collaborators with the Syrian regime and renegades from the true cause. But all of them came from priestly families of high birth, and their names were presumably bestowed upon them by parents in the previous generation.[131] The dichotomy of Hellenizer and traditionalist certainly cannot be read in this evidence. Most telling are the names of two trusted associates of Judas Maccabaeus: Eupolemus and Jason, who represented him in negotiating a treaty with Rome.[132] And two of the men who commanded troops in Judas' army had the names of Dositheus and Sosipater.[133] As is clear, Judas had no qualms about associating himself with men whose "Hellenizing" tendencies extended to the adoption of Hellenic names. One may observe also that of the three men whom Nicanor sent to conduct what proved to be successful negotiations with Judas, two had Greek names and one a Hebrew name. They may all have been Jews.[134] And there is more. The envoys sent to develop diplomatic relations with Sparta and Rome, first by Jonathan, then by Simon, not only carried Greek names but were born of fathers with Greek names: Numenius son of Antiochus and Antipater son of Jason.[135] A firm conclusion emerges: the taking of Hellenic appellations by the second and third generations of the Hasmonaean dynasty represented no shift in attitude or ideology from the first generation.

Even the Hasmonaeans who possessed Greek names could hold Hebrew ones as well. The dual designation is attested for John Hyrcanus, his sons Judas Aristobulus and Jonathan Alexander (Alexander Jannaeus), and, in subsequent generations, Mattathias Antigonus and Jonathan Aristobulus.[136] The coinage minted by certain of these dynasts underlines their double

---

131. Josephus, to be sure, says that Jason was born Jesus and changed his own name; *Ant.* 12.238–39. But this may be guesswork on his part. With regard to Menelaus and Alcimus, he says only that they also possessed Jewish names; *Ant.* 12.239, 12.385.

132. I Macc. 8.17; II Macc. 4.11.

133. II Macc. 12.19, 12.24; cf. 12.35.

134. II Macc. 14.19.

135. I Macc. 12.16, 14.22, 14.24, 15.15; Jos. *Ant.* 13.169. These and other instances are usefully collected by Hengel, *Judaism and Hellenism*, I, 63–64; *idem* in Davies and Finkelstein, *Cambridge History of Judaism*, II, 217–18. It is hazardous to put much weight on the many Palestinian elders with Greek names recorded in the *Letter of Aristeas*, 47–50. But see the treatment of those names by N. G. Cohen, *JSJ* 15 (1984) 32–64.

136. The thesis held, e.g., by Meshorer, *Ancient Jewish Coinage*, I, 36–38, that each of the later Hasmonaeans had a double name and that each Hebrew name had a consistent Greek equivalent, has been refuted by Ilan, *JQR* 78 (1987) 8–12.

posture. Alexander Jannaeus' bronze issues display an anchor on the obverse, with the Greek inscription ΑΛΕΞΑΝΔΡΟΥ ΒΑΣΙΛΕΩΣ, while the reverse shows a lily flower with "Yehonatan the King" in Paleo-Hebrew script. Similarly, Mattathias Antigonus, Jannaeus' grandson, minted coins with Hebrew lettering on the obverse reading "Matitiah the High Priest and the [Council?] of the Jews," intertwined with double cornucopiae, whereas the reverse contains an ivy wreath and the Greek inscription ΑΝΤΙΓΟΝΟΥ ΒΑΣΙΛΕΩΣ.[137] The double message rings out clearly: the Hasmonaeans operated on the premise that Judaism and Hellenism march hand in hand. The early Maccabees no more rejected the latter than their successors rejected the former.

In this context, the readiness of Hasmonaean leaders to embrace Hellenic practices fits suitably. There is no longer a "problem." Alexander Balas, when appointing Jonathan as High Priest in 152, sent him purple garb and a gold crown. And, two years later, in state ceremony at Ptolemais, Balas formally robed Jonathan in the purple.[138] The vestments of the Jewish High priest traditionally included purple. But the gesture of Alexander Balas accompanied his designation of Jonathan as "king's friend." The garment represented Seleucid court practice. I Maccabees properly distinguishes between the purple robe which Balas supplied to Jonathan and the sacred vestments which he donned as High Priest. Acceptance of the former, indeed the personal robing by the king himself in ceremony, signaled that Jonathan took on the role of Hellenistic courtier and royal official. The position was juxtaposed directly—and with perfect consistency—to the office of High Priest.[139] I Maccabees states the fact without comment. None was needed.

The High Priesthood of Simon began with the burial of his brother Jonathan in the family tomb at Modein. But the tomb would now receive a

137. See the catalogue in Meshorer, *Ancient Jewish Coinage*, I, 118–34, 155–59, with plates 4–24, 54–55. Cf. the remarks of Rappaport in Mor, *Jewish Assimilation*, 5. The tangled arguments of Goldstein, on the basis of Jannaeus' coins, that he abandoned both royal title and diadem for a time, then resumed them, then kept the title but dropped the diadem, will not persuade many; *II Maccabees*, 73–81; and in Davies and Finkelstein, *Cambridge History of Judaism*, II, 334–36.

138. I Macc. 10.20, 10.62; Jos. *Ant.* 13.45, 13.84.

139. For the traditional garb of the High Priest, see Exod. 28.4–5. For purple as a sign of the king's friends in Seleucid practice, see Bickerman, *Institutions*, 41–44. That practice is specifically illustrated for Balas' reign by Athenaeus, 5.211b. A clear distinction between the king's gift and the sacred garments worn by Jonathan is made at I Macc. 10.20–21: ἀπέστειλεν αὐτῷ πορφύραν καὶ στέφανον χρυσοῦν ... καὶ ἐνεδύσατο Ἰωναθαν τὴν ἁγίαν στολήν. So, rightly, Goldstein, *I Maccabees*, 400–401. See further the discussion in Abel, *Les livres des Maccabées*, 183, 195. Cf. M. Reinhold, *History of Purple as a Status Symbol in Antiquity* (Brussels, 1970) 34–36.

much more striking and elaborate form. Simon raised up a lofty monument to be viewed from afar, built of polished stone from front to back. In addition he erected seven pyramids to commemorate his father, mother, four brothers, and, presumably, himself. Around the pyramids Simon set up great columns topped by trophies of armor as enduring memorials and, alongside them, sculpted ships visible to all who sailed the sea.[140] Funerary monuments designed to make a potent impression had precedents in early Israelite history.[141] But none like this. Pyramidal structures are here attested for the first time in Palestine. Simon perhaps looked to Egypt, a sign that Judaea was part of a larger multicultural scene. But models may have existed as well in the tombs of Hellenistic princes and grandees. The celebrated Mausoleum of Mausolus constructed at Halicarnassus in the mid fourth century certainly included a pyramid and an elaborate colonnade.[142] And, so it was reported, Alexander the Great planned a tomb for his father that would resemble the greatest of the pyramids.[143] In any case, columns, sculpted ships, and trophies of armor transparently imitated Hellenic archetypes, many of which Simon could have encountered in the dominions of the Seleucids.[144] Thus, the son of Mattathias and brother of Judas left an enduring memorial to the Maccabaean achievement in a form that evoked the culture of the Hellenes. I Maccabees delivers the account in straightforward reportorial fashion. In that author's view, no tension or paradox attended Simon's action.

Simon acquired his own honors in his lifetime. The *demos* of the Jews in 140, as we have seen, determined to show its gratitude for his services to the state with a formal decree inscribed on bronze tablets and fixed on stelai to be placed on Mt. Zion.[145] The resolution was passed in the presence of the people, the priests, the leaders of the nation, and the elders of the land.[146] It praised Simon and his brothers for rallying their nation and

---

140. I Macc. 13.25–30. A somewhat different description is provided by Jos. *Ant.* 13.210–12. See the comments of Abel, *Les livres des Maccabées*, 239–41; Goldstein, *I Maccabees*, 474–75.

141. Cf. II Sam. 18.18.

142. Pliny, *NH*, 36.30–31.

143. Diod. 18.4.5.

144. Goldstein, *I Maccabees*, 214–15; Sievers, *Hasmoneans*, 107–109.

145. I Macc. 14.25–27: ὁ δῆμος ... εἶπαν τίνα χάριν ἀποδώσομεν Σίμωνι καὶ τοῖς υἱοῖς αὐτοῦ; ... καὶ κατέγραψαν ἐν δέλτοις χαλκαῖς καὶ ἔθεντο ἐν στήλαις ἐν ὄρει Σιων.

146. I Macc. 14.28: ἐπὶ συναγωγῆς μεγάλης ἱερέων καὶ λαοῦ καὶ ἀρχόντων ἔθνους καὶ τῶν πρεσβυτέρων τῆς χώρας. It is possible to cite large gatherings of this sort in biblical times. See examples noted by Goldstein, *I Maccabees*, 502–503. But, as he observes, those assemblies did not debate or vote; they were simply addressed. See also Will-Orrieux, *Ioudaismos-Hellènismos*, 186–89.

resisting enemies, and noted Simon's personal subsidization of the army, his fortification of towns and settlements of Jews, his capture of the Akra, and the acknowledgment of his status by Demetrius and by the Romans. It also confirmed Simon's position as High Priest, general, and ethnarch of the Jews, and a man whose edicts were not subject to abrogation by people or priests.[147] Copies of the inscription would then be placed within the precincts of the Temple and in the treasury where they would be kept by Simon and his sons.[148] That I Maccabees does not provide a verbatim rendering of the decree has long been recognized. But it seems clear that the author had access to some documentary source whose contents are reflected in the text, even though they can hardly have corresponded precisely to the resolution as inscribed in the time of Simon.[149] There should, in any case, be no doubt that, despite variations in detail, the measure stands in a familiar pattern of Greek usage. The very fact of an honorific decree inscribed on tablets to be displayed publicly is a Hellenic institution adopted by the Jews, thereby announcing their participation in the ways of the wider world. The preamble of the resolution, with its dating formulas, recalls many Hellenic measures.[150] So does the concluding portion that provides for publication of the document and its preservation in sanctuaries and elsewhere in multiple copies.[151] The gratitude for benefits bestowed and the award of honors for the benefactor are too common in Hellenistic decrees even to require argument.[152] The Hasmonaean dynast plainly set himself in the tracks of Greek rulers and benefactors who obtained the formal gratitude of their beneficiaries through public declaration inscribed for perpetuity.

The minting of coinage would also put the Hasmonaeans in a category comparable to that of independent Greek cities and states. In negotiation with Antiochus VII, Simon allegedly gained the privilege to produce his

147. I Macc. 14.29–47.

148. I Macc. 14.48–49: καὶ τὴν γραφὴν ταύτην εἶπαν θέσθαι ἐν δέλτοις χαλκαῖς καὶ στῆσαι αὐτὰς ἐν περιβόλῳ τῶν ἁγίων ἐν τόπῳ ἐπισήμῳ, τὰ δὲ ἀντίγραφα αὐτῶν θέσθαι ἐν τῷ γαζοφυλακίῳ, ὅπως ἔχῃ Σίμων καὶ υἱοὶ αὐτοῦ.

149. See Abel, *Les livres des Maccabées*, 254–62; Schürer, *History of the Jewish People*, I, 193–94; Goldstein, *I Maccabees*, 500–509; Sievers, *Hasmoneans*, 119–22. The argument of Willrich, *Urkundenfälschung*, 69–72, that the document is a forgery, no longer has any takers.

150. I Macc. 14.27. Cf. e.g. *OGIS* 233, lines 1–10; *OGIS* 338, lines 1–2; *OGIS* 339, lines 1–2.

151. I Macc. 14.48–49; cf. e.g. *OGIS* 248, lines 53–57; *OGIS* 229, lines 107–108; *OGIS* 737, lines 20–22.

152. Of course, the honorands, if private citizens, did not normally obtain the political powers and prerogatives accorded to Simon. And if they were kings, they already had them. But this does not throw into question the clear influence of Hellenistic decrees upon this measure.

own coins. But no evidence exists to show that he ever did so. The idea of minting coins by the authority of the king might not have appealed to Simon. And Antiochus withdrew his offer shortly thereafter anyway.[153] John Hyrcanus, it appears, was the first Hasmonaean to issue coins.[154] Most of the extant ones identify the official authorities in Hebrew on the obverse: "Yehohanan the High Priest and the Council (or Assembly) of the Jews," surrounded by a wreath. The reverse exhibits double cornucopiae and a pomegranate.[155] A smaller number show a slight but possibly significant change in the inscription. It has now become "Yehohanan the High Priest, head of the Council (or Assembly) of the Jews."[156] This may imply a shift toward greater power on the part of Hyrcanus in the latter part of his tenure when he could consolidate his territorial gains in a period of peace and prosperity.[157] Alexander Jannaeus took matters a step further. As we have seen, his coins sported Greek inscriptions, at least on the obverse: his name in the genitive, "Alexander the King," around an anchor. The reverse, however, presented him as "Yehonatan the King" in Hebrew lettering, with a lily flower or a star surrounded by a diadem.[158] The blending of Hellenic and Hebrew concepts is notable. Most of the symbols employed by Hyrcanus and Jannaeus—anchor, lily, cornucopia, diadem—have Hellenistic precedents. The anchor, of course, was the preeminent symbol of the Seleucids.[159] The Hasmonaeans had no hesitation in presenting themselves as leaders who conformed to the conventions of the Hellenistic world. At the same time, they refrained altogether from placing any portraits of humans or animals on the coins, a restraint enforced by the biblical prohibitions on graven images. The fact is often noted, and generally interpreted as a limit on the degree of Hellenization permitted either by the people or by certain

---

153. I Macc. 15.6, 15.26–27. Cf. U. Rappaport, *AJS Review* 1 (1976) 172–73.

154. The matter once generated controversy which need not be rehearsed here. In the earlier view of Meshorer, *Ancient Jewish Coinage*, I, 35–47, all the coins that possess the legend "Yehohanan the High Priest" belong to Hyrcanus II in the mid 1st century BCE. Strong and persuasive arguments, however, were leveled against the theory. See Rappaport, *AJS Review* 1 (1976) 171–86; D. Barag and Sh. Qedar, *Israel Numismatic Journal* 4 (1980) 8–21; Ilan, *JQR* 78 (1987) 10–12; Sievers, *Hasmoneans*, 152–53. And recent finds at Mt. Gerizim have settled the matter. Meshorer has now conceded the point; see *Israel Numismatic Journal* 11 (1990/1991) 106–107; and in D. Amit and H. Eshel, *The Hasmonean Period* (Jerusalem, 1995) 199 (Hebrew).

155. Meshorer, *Ancient Jewish Coinage*, I, 136–50, with plates 28–45.

156. Meshorer, *Ancient Jewish Coinage*, I, 150–55, with plates 46–53.

157. Cf. Jos. *Ant.* 13.273–74.

158. Meshorer, *Ancient Jewish Coinage*, I, 118–34, with plates 4–24.

159. For discussion of the symbols, see Meshorer, *Ancient Jewish Coinage*, I, 60–68.

religious groups.[160] But why imagine that Hasmonaean dynasts would have gone further down the Hellenizing road had it not been for such constraints? An analysis of that sort simply reintroduces the dichotomy whose existence is in question. Hyrcanus and Jannaeus struck just the balance they wished: for the former a combination of Greek symbols and Hebrew inscriptions, for the latter both Hebrew and Greek inscriptions. The blending emblematized the compatibility of the cultures. No need to imagine that they sought to pacify different constituencies. The coins were all bronze issues, none of them silver, and hence would have had limited circulation among Gentiles and little value for external propaganda. Internal consumption sufficed. The coins would be seen by Jews and perhaps by recently Judaized peoples. The Hasmonaeans advertised their regime as one that absorbed the ways of the Greeks and worked within the traditions of the Jews.

None of the adaptations of Hellenic precedents interfered with Jewish customs or observances. Hyrcanus, we are told, was the first of the Jews to hire foreign mercenaries, a practice common to Hellenistic princes everywhere.[161] Our evidence for this under Alexander Jannaeus, however, shows that the troops, recruited from Pisidia and Cilicia, constituted only a minority of the forces. He had certainly not come to rely upon them exclusively, nor were they employed to replace or intimidate a national army.[162] Hyrcanus simply borrowed the Hellenic usage to advance the interests of his nation—and himself. Josephus' report of the innovation has no negative overtones.

Aristobulus enjoyed only a year in power, 104/3, but took one memorable step that culminated developments of the past two generations. According to Josephus, he assumed the title of king and donned the diadem.[163] The designation itself signaled no drastic change. Hasmonaeans had already combined supreme religious and political authority, engaged in diplomatic relations with Greek cities, Hellenistic kings, and the Roman Republic, hired mercenaries, cloaked themselves in purple vestments, received vast powers through public decree, and minted coinage. The royal title seemed only logical. And the diadem meant that Aristobulus claimed a standing equivalent to a Hellenistic monarch in terms of international dealings. Josephus reports pompously that Aristobulus was the first Jew to take the designation of king

---

160. Cf. the formulations by Rajak in Davies and White, *Tribute to Vermes*, 270, and Rappaport in Mor, *Jewish Assimilation*, 6.

161. Jos. *Ant.* 13.249; *BJ* 1.65.

162. Jos. *Ant.* 13.374, 13.377–78. Cf. A. Kasher, *JQR* 81 (1991) 344–49. Tcherikover, *Hellenistic Civilization and the Jews*, 251, puts a more cynical interpretation upon this: the ruler's desire for a loyal personal army.

163. Jos. *Ant.* 13.301; *BJ* 1.70.

since the return from Babylonian Captivity, four hundred eighty-three years and three months before, a not altogether accurate calculation. But he passes no judgment on the act, nor does he indicate that there was any inimical reaction to it among the people in the Hasmonaean domains. The omission has significance, for Josephus conveyed a hostile tradition on Aristobulus, one that condemned him for executing his mother, usurping power that was rightfully hers, and murdering his brother.[164] But in his account the title of king was evidently uncontroversial.[165]

Aristobulus' brief reign merits note on one other count that neatly exemplifies the theme of this entire discussion. The king styled himself

164. Jos. *Ant.* 13.302–17; *BJ* 1.71–84. The portrait plainly derives from Jewish opponents of Aristobulus. The pagan tradition on him was highly favorable; Jos. *Ant.* 13.318–19. Aristobulus, it appears, did not use the royal title on his coins—i.e. if the coins with "Yehudah the High Priest and the (Council?) of the Jews" on the obverse and double cornucopiae on the reverse are his issues. Aristobulus did have the Hebrew name Judah; Jos. *Ant.* 20.240. Meshorer, *Ancient Jewish Coinage*, I, 46–47, 134–36, with plates 25–27, assigns them all to Aristobulus II [67–63 BCE]. But, as Ilan, *JQR* 78 (1987) acutely points out, there is no evidence that Aristobulus II had the Hebrew name Judah or any Hebrew name at all. Further, one might note that not only the absence of the royal title but the absence of any Greek inscription on the coins would be much harder to explain after Jannaeus had used both for a generation. It makes more sense for Aristobulus I. Not that he refrained from the royal title out of constraint or reluctance. The mint officials may simply have followed the pattern of his predecessor Hyrcanus. Aristobulus only lived a year after taking office, a busy year which left little time for thinking about major changes in coin symbols or legends. It would be foolhardy to draw significant historical conclusions from this.

165. To be sure, some segments of society may have found the title objectionable—or at least resisted the idea of combining the offices of king and High Priest. The issue surfaced in 63 BCE when Pompey heard Jewish delegations including one which rejected both Hyrcanus II and Aristobulus and preferred to abandon monarchy; Jos. *Ant.* 14.41; Diod. 40.2. Hostility to Hasmonaean rule is expressed also in Psalms of Solomon 17.6, composed some time after Pompey's death; cf. 2.26–27. D. R. Schwartz, *Studies in the Jewish Background to Christianity* (Tübingen, 1992) 44–56, finds the opposition centered among the Pharisees. Cf. R. Laqueur, *HZ* 136 (1927) 243–47. Antagonism toward the Hasmonaeans existed, of course, in Qumran. One or more of them is exemplified by "the Wicked Priest" in the Pesher Habakkuk; see especially 1QpHab. 8. Cf. A. S. van der Woude, *JJS* 33 (1982) 349–59; bibliography in Schürer, *History of the Jewish People*, III.1, 435–37. Cf. also 4QNah. 1, 4; 4Q171.2; 4Q175. But the antagonism has no direct connection with the royal title. That the Temple Scroll includes a hidden attack on Hasmonaean kingship (11QT, 56–59) is questionable; see J. Maier, *The Temple Scroll* (Sheffield, 1985) 123–27; Rajak in P. Bilde et al., *Aspects of Hellenistic Kingship*, 92. The author of I Maccabees praises Romans who, among other things, shunned the crown or the purple; I Macc. 8.14. But that can hardly represent criticism of the Hasmonaeans in a work that otherwise celebrates their exploits—unless the passage itself is interpreted as an independent insertion. Goldstein's proposal, *I Maccabees*, 355–56, that the work was composed during a short period when Alexander Jannaeus purportedly renounced the kingship, is strained conjecture. Cf. Rajak, *op. cit.*, 100–101.

"philhellene."[166] In what sense and in what context we are not told, and speculation would be unprofitable.[167] Adoption of the sobriquet, in any case, declared Aristobulus' pleasure in things Greek, an attitude which apparently lost him no favor at home. More to the point, he conducted a vigorous campaign of expansion to the north, bringing the Ituraeans of Galilee or Lebanon under his authority, insisting upon their circumcision and adherence to the ways of the Jews.[168] Aristobulus within a short span of time at the helm developed the reputation of a prime benefactor to his native land and people.[169] That such a man also proudly sported the label of "philhellene"— indeed is referred to as such by Josephus in the same breath as he describes his benefactions for the Jews—speaks volumes. The historian found no inconsistency between the Hasmonaean inclinations toward Hellenism and their championing of Jewish identity.

• • •

The Maccabaean revolution sparked a process that helped to define Jewish character for generations to come. Despite internal opposition and factional friction, the Maccabees galvanized Jews against the unspeakable policies of Antiochus Epiphanes that threatened the very essence of the nation. Their successes, however limited and ambiguous, led to an increasing drive for

166. Jos. *Ant.* 13.318: χρηματίσας μὲν Φιλέλλην.

167. Kasher's suggestion, *Jews and Hellenistic Cities*, 135–36, that Aristobulus took the title in order to reassure Hellenistic cities in Galilee and Phoenicia that his policy of annexation was not aimed at them, seems unlikely. Would cities in the path of his armies be comforted by his adopted name?

168. Jos. *Ant.* 13.318: ἀναγκάσας τε τοὺς ἐνοικοῦντας, εἰ βούλονται μένειν ἐν τῇ χώρᾳ, περιτέμνεσθαι καὶ κατὰ τοὺς Ἰουδαίων νόμους ζῆν.

169. Jos. *Ant.* 13.318: πολλὰ δ' εὐεργετήσας τὴν πατρίδα. The reputation is attested to also by Strabo in Jos. *Ant.* 13.319: πολλὰ τοῖς Ἰουδαίοις χρήσιμος. S. J. D. Cohen in P. Bilde et al., *Religion and Religious Practice in the Seleucid Kingdom* (Aarhus, 1990) 211–16, wrongly takes Strabo as contradicting Josephus and speaking of a voluntary conversion to Judaism. So also A. Kasher, *Jews, Idumaeans, and Ancient Arabs* (Tübingen, 1988) 79–83; Smith, *Studies in the Cult of Yahweh*, I, 276–77. The text, in fact, states that Aristobulus won over part of the Ituraeans, attaching them with the bond of circumcision: τὸ μέρος τοῦ τῶν Ἰτουραίων ἔθνους ὠκειώσατο, δεσμῷ συνάψας τῇ τῶν αἰδοίων περιτομῇ. That is quite consistent with Josephus, and does not imply voluntary conversion. Cf. now M. Goodman, *Mission and Conversion: Proselytizing in the Religious History of the Roman Empire* (Oxford, 1994) 75–76. In the view of S. Freyne, *Galilee from Alexander the Great to Hadrian, 323 B.C.E.–135 C.E.* (Wilmington, 1980) 22–56, the inhabitants of Galilee were largely Jewish, even before the Hasmonaeans. But the evidence cited does not substantiate the claim. See further B. Bar-Kochva in A. Chastagnol et al., *Armée et fiscalité dans le monde antique* (Paris, 1977) 173–76, 191–94; and, most recently, R. A. Horsley, *Galilee: History, Politics, People* (Valley Forge, 1995) 40–45.

Jewish self-esteem and independent status among the peoples of the Near East. Hasmonaean leadership over the years gradually brought those goals within reach. They did not do so, however, by spurning the taint of Hellenism and promoting a purity of faith that pitted it against the infiltration of the Greek world. Nor did the adoption of Greek ways by the later Hasmonaeans represent a reversal of the ideals that motivated Mattathias and Judas Maccabaeus. Through all the changes and developments, an adherence to basic principles held firm. Association with Hellenistic princes and dynasts advanced Jewish interests from the start, a feature of which Judas as well as his successors took full advantage. The entrenchment of Hasmonaean authority depended in large part upon the acknowledgment, cooperation, and backing of the Seleucids—and vice-versa. The reciprocal benefits left a more enduring legacy than the intermittent antagonisms. Hasmonaean leaders practiced Hellenic ways without compromising Jewish integrity. The supposed conflict was never an issue.[170] Use of Greek names, recruitment of mercenaries, minting of coinage, and advertisement through monuments, public decrees, and display of royal finery all made the Hasmonaeans players on the international stage. They also elevated Jewish prestige and pride in their own traditions. The Jews poured out their gratitude to Simon through a Greek medium for accomplishments that advanced Jewish dignity. Hyrcanus employed Greek mercenaries to buttress a Jewish national army. The "philhellene" Aristobulus converted Gentiles to Judaism. And the coinage of the Hasmonaeans spoke in both Greek and Hebrew, but to the same constituency—the Jews for whom Hellenism expanded and reinforced their identity.

The dynasty of the Maccabees had created circumstances congenial to the application of Hellenic conventions to Jewish ends. Their achievements thereby betoken a process that stimulated the creative energies of Hellenized Jews in Palestine as well as the Diaspora. That process would promote a wholesale reshaping of the Jewish self-image.

170. There is nothing to show that the Jewish rebellion against Alexander Jannaeus (Jos. *Ant.* 13.372–83) had anything to do with his "Hellenism."

CHAPTER 2

The Use and Abuse of the Exodus Story

The Exodus was a defining moment, perhaps *the* defining moment in ancient Israelite tradition. As the legend has it, the Israelites' escape from Egypt under the leadership of Moses shook off the yoke of Egyptian oppression and gave them the impetus for articulating principles and values, surmounting an arduous journey through the wilderness, and shaping their identity as a people and a culture. The day of their release from the tyranny of Pharaonic Egypt, so the Lord declared in the Book of Exodus, would thereafter be commemorated in an annual festival, among the most sacred on the calendar, the ceremony of Passover.[1] The Exodus generated high drama, an unforgettable tale in the Bible, perhaps the single most familiar one to Jew and Gentile alike. As inspiration to subsequent generations of Jews and their admirers, its power is manifest. But what of the villains of the piece? They, or rather their presumed descendants, would not have found this story very entertaining. Indeed, we might imagine, they would have reason to feel maligned and defamed. The heartless Pharaohs, the hostile Egyptian populace, and the royal army as agent of wickedness hardly supplied models for imitation. And the tale could bring little satisfaction to the indigenous dwellers in the land of the Nile.

The spread of the story should only have aggravated matters. Jewish soldiers and Jewish settlers in Egypt occasionally appear on record in the centuries that followed the supposed time of the Exodus, most notably in the garrison at Elephantine.[2] But the principal wave of Jewish reentry into Egypt appears to have come at the end of the Persian period and in the

---

1. Exodus 12.14–20, 12.25–27.

2. See B. Porten, *Archives from Elephantine: The Life of a Jewish Military Colony* (Berkeley, 1968) 3–61. There were, of course, Jews in Egypt prior to the Elephantine garrison; cf. Jeremiah

early years of the Hellenistic age.[3] The Exodus story could have seeped into Egyptian consciousness in the course of this era, thus to stir reaction and response. Indeed, echoes of a very different variety of tale emerge in the literature produced by pagan authors in Egypt. In assorted versions, Jews appear as villains rather than victims, oppressors rather than oppressed, the perpetrators of sacrilege rather than the upholders of the faith, and ultimately the defeated rather than the triumphant. Scholars have drawn what seems to be a logical conclusion: the conflicting versions represent a form of competing historiography; pagans produced a "counter-history" to negate or reverse the effects of the Jewish legend; a polemical contest ensued, a war of propaganda between Jews and Egyptians over the nature of the biblical Exodus.[4]

Josephus, vehicle for much of the variant tradition, buttresses the interpretation. His treatise, the *Contra Apionem*, devotes itself in large part to refuting anti-Jewish tracts by Alexandrian writers and others perceived as hostile to the Jews. Diverse treatments of the Exodus constitute a substantial portion of the work, drawing Josephus' fire and prompting elaborate counteractions to undermine the negative portrayals by Manetho, Lysimachus, Apion, and Chaeremon.[5] Josephus' apologia has set the terms for modern discussion. Perhaps misleadingly so. That the Exodus narrative became transformed and manipulated seems obvious enough. But the manipulators and their motives

---

41–44; *LetArist* 13, 35; J. Mélèze-Modrzejewski, *The Jews of Egypt: From Rameses II to Emperor Hadrian* (Philadelphia, 1995) 21–26.

3. *LetArist* 12–27; Jos. *Ant.* 12.5–9, 12.17, 12.28–33. The tale itself of the deportation of 100,000 Jews by Ptolemy I and their release by Ptolemy II is questionable. Nor can one place implicit faith in the more agreeable version ascribed to Hecataeus of Abdera by Josephus, *C. Apion.* 1.186–94, that has numerous Jews follow Ptolemy I voluntarily from Palestine to settle in Egypt. See now B. Bar-Kochva, *Pseudo-Hecataeus, "On the Jews": Legitimizing the Jewish Diaspora* (Berkeley, 1996) 71–82. But the congruence of testimony does at least suggest that a significant movement of Jews to Egypt occurred at the beginning of the Hellenistic period.

4. See, e.g., the formulations of A. Funkenstein, *The Jerusalem Quarterly* 19 (1981) 59; *idem, Perceptions of Jewish History* (Berkeley, 1993) 36–40; A. Kasher, *The Jews in Hellenistic and Roman Egypt* (Tübingen, 1985) 327–34; C. Aziza, *ANRW* III.20.1 (1987) 53–63; E. Gabba in W. D. Davies and L. Finkelstein, *The Cambridge History of Judaism* (Cambridge, 1989) II, 653–55; M. Pucci ben Zeev, *JSJ* 24 (1993) 233–34; Z. Yavetz, *JJS* 44 (1993) 21; P. Schäfer in I. M. Gafni, A. Oppenheimer, and D. R. Schwartz, *The Jews in the Hellenistic-Roman World: Studies in Memory of Menahem Stern* (Jerusalem, 1996) 12, 16–17; *idem, Judeophobia: Attitudes toward the Jews in the Ancient World* (Cambridge, Mass., 1997) 17, 20–21.

5. See especially Jos. *C. Apion.* 1.223–319, 2.8–32, 2.121–22. On Josephus' apologetics and polemics, see, most recently, A. Kasher in L. H. Feldman and J. R. Levison, *Josephus' Contra Apionem: Studies in its Character and Context with a Latin Concordance to the Portion Missing in Greek* (Leiden, 1996) 143–86.

are not quite so obvious. Complexity and ambiguity adhere to the several versions, undermining trust in the stark and simplistic approach of Josephus.

Modern scholarship, taking its cue from Josephus, discerns a basic dichotomy. In general, pagan writings on the Jews are assessed along a spectrum with a clear division in the center: they were either favorably inclined, admiring of Jewish character and practices, with positive judgments on their traditions and institutions, or they were virulently anti-Semitic, hostile to Jewish customs, distorting their history and slandering their values. They might, to be sure, combine aspects of both. But analyses consistently apply the categories of "pro- or anti-Jewish." Researchers differ on where the balance lies. For some, the negative prevails: the attitude of most pagans was sharply antagonistic.[6] Others take a quite different line: pagans on the whole either looked upon Jews with favor or merely indulged in scorn and mockery, but showed no race hatred against them.[7] One can refine this division further by resorting to statistics. An eminent scholar recently reviewed the texts and tabulated the results, calculating that 18 percent of pagan assessments were favorable, 23 percent unfavorable, and 59 percent neutral.[8] Hence, a judicious selectivity can provide support for any line that one seeks to argue on this matter. But the whole approach is conceptually flawed. No numbers game will determine the issue, no reckoning of sums or statistical tables can elucidate pagan attitudes toward the Jews. Even to characterize a majority of Gentile remarks as "neutral" may misconceive the situation. It begs a critical question by assuming the existence of a war of words, a polemical setting in which all pagan appraisals of Jews can be placed. But that is the very proposition that needs reevaluation.

The story of the Exodus supplies a central exhibit. As the common reconstruction has it, that drama served as vehicle either for enhancing the Jewish image or for maliciously undermining it, depending on how the tale was told. A different perspective is offered here.

6. See, e.g., J. L. Daniel, *JBL* 98 (1979) 46: "Jews in the Hellenistic-Roman literature . . . were almost universally disliked or at least viewed with an amused contempt"; M. Goodman in E. Schürer, *The History of the Jewish People in the Age of Jesus Christ*, rev. ed. by G. Vermes, F. Millar, and M. Goodman (Cambridge, 1986) III.1, 607: "Most pagan authors who spoke about the Jews at all after c. 300 B.C. did so in a polemical sense. Hostility was almost universal after the first century B.C."

7. See, e.g., J. Isaac, *Genèse de l'antisémitisme* (Vanves, 1956) 49–126; R. Ruether, *Faith and Fratricide: The Theological Roots of Antisemitism* (Minneapolis, 1974) 23–28; M. Simon, *Verus Israel* (Oxford, 1986) 202–207.

8. L. H. Feldman in D. Berger, *History and Hate: The Dimensions of Anti-Semitism* (Philadelphia, 1986) 30; *JQR* 78 (1988) 190–91; *Jew and Gentile in the Ancient World* (Princeton, 1993) 124.

Two starkly contrasting versions of the Exodus can set the matter in a bold light. Their sharp differences make the two presentations, those of Strabo and Lysimachus, particularly useful and revealing. On the face of it, they seem to confirm definitively the notion that rival interpretations of the tale stemmed from polarized attitudes toward the Jews. Careful scrutiny might suggest otherwise.

Strabo, an indefatigable researcher, traveller, historian, and geographer from Pontus, produced most of his work, in Greek, during the age of Augustus. In the course of his monumental geographic treatise, Strabo describes the terrain, topography, and economies of Syria, Phoenicia, and Judaea. And he takes the occasion to append notes on the historical background and traditions of the region. That treatment includes a striking rendition of the Exodus events and their central figure, Moses. For Strabo, the most reliable report about the ancestors of contemporary Jews has them as Egyptians by origin. Moses indeed was an Egyptian priest who became disgruntled with the religious observances of his own people, rejecting their representations of divinity in the form of animals and even taking a side-swipe at Greeks for depicting gods in human shape.[9] In Strabo's account Moses proclaimed that God was all-encompassing, that he cannot be conceived or worshipped through images, and that he responds only to those who live temperately and through righteousness.[10] With such statements, Moses won over a substantial number of right-thinking persons who followed him out of Egypt to the site of Jerusalem. There he installed a just and pious religion where God could be properly worshipped and where Moses himself won widespread admiration.[11] Such, in brief, is the substance of Strabo's recreation of the Exodus—a very far cry from the biblical narrative. It does, however, deliver a highly flattering portrait of Moses and of those who accompanied him out of Egypt into the Promised Land. Moses did not, in this version, rescue an oppressed people. He and his followers left their native land for the best of religious motives: to pay proper homage to the supreme deity, unsullied by perverse images. Moses thus stands out as an esteemed religious leader and molder of his people, in a category with the most venerated Greek lawgivers like Lycurgus and Minos and a host of sage prophets.[12] Strabo consequently

9. Strabo 16.2.34–35. Cf. Jos. *Ant.* 14.118. What Greek art Moses might be expected to have seen remains a mystery. The idea of Moses inspecting Bronze Age figurines that turned up in Egypt requires a feat of imagination.

10. Strabo 16.2.35.

11. Strabo 16.2.36.

12. Strabo 16.2.38–39.

and for obvious reasons has been counted among those pagan writers who held the Jews and their principles in high regard.[13]

At the opposite end of the spectrum stands the Greco-Egyptian writer Lysimachus. Of the man and his time we know virtually nothing, apart from the fact that Josephus considered him as fiercely hostile to the Jews. A chronological clue lies in Josephus' remark that Apion provided the same invented figure for the number of Jews who fled Egypt as did Lysimachus. That would date Lysimachus somewhat prior to Apion, who lived in the early and middle first century CE, and possibly make him a near contemporary of Strabo.[14] It would be imprudent to claim greater precision or certainty. Lysimachus' presentation of the Exodus, in any case, puts him at very sharp odds with Strabo. According to Lysimachus, Jews in the reign of Pharaoh Bocchoris suffered from leprosy, scurvy, and other afflictions and, in seeking to alleviate their ailments, took refuge in the temples and resorted to begging for sustenance. A famine then struck the land, prompting the king to seek counsel with the oracle of Ammon. On the god's advice, Bocchoris expelled the suppliants from the holy places, drowning the victims of scurvy and leprosy and leaving the rest to perish in the desert. He then cleaned the temples, now rid of their impure and impious occupants.[15] The survivors managed to make their way through the desert, instructed by Moses to exhibit no kindness to anyone, to give wicked counsel, and to overturn all temples and altars they happened to come across. Still worse, after they reached inhabited land, the Jews treated the indigenous population with disdain, looted and burned their shrines, and built their own city of Jerusalem from which they could exercise power.[16] Not a very pretty picture.

---

13. It is not pertinent here, even if it were possible, to determine the sources of Strabo on this matter, how far he was influenced by Hecataeus, how much he paraphrased from Posidonius, and what proportion stemmed from his own researches. See the discussions by J. G. Gager, *Moses in Greco-Roman Paganism* (Nashville, 1972) 44–47; M. Stern, *Greek and Latin Authors on Jews and Judaism* (Jerusalem, 1976) I, 264–67; B. Bar-Kochva, *Anti-Semitism and Idealization of Judaism* (forthcoming), with bibliography.

14. Jos. *C. Apion.* 2.20: τὸν δὲ ἀριθμὸν τῶν ἐλασθέντων τὸν αὐτὸν Λυσιμάχῳ σχεδιάσας. Whether he is identical with "Lysimachus the Alexandrian," a writer on marvels and myths, need not be decided; see A. Gudeman, *RE* 14 (1928) 32–39; P. M. Fraser, *Ptolemaic Alexandria* (Oxford, 1972) II, 1092–93, n. 475. For Josephus' characterization of Lysimachus' animus, see *C. Apion.* 1.304, 1.319, 2.145, 2.236. Bar-Kochva, *Anti-Semitism* (forthcoming), places him at the end of the 2nd century BCE But the evidence is indirect and indecisive.

15. Jos. *C. Apion.* 1.305–307.

16. Jos. *C. Apion.* 1.310–11.

It is hardly surprising that Lysimachus conventionally ranks among the arch anti-Semites of antiquity.[17]

The two narratives, in short, move in drastically different directions. For Strabo, the Jews left Egypt on their own initiative and of their own accord, in order to promote a purer form of worship, devoid of Gentile idolatry. For Lysimachus, the Jews themselves were the impure; polluting the temples with their presence, they had to be expelled from the country, and then compounded their sacrilege with further desecration. Such presentations undergird the idea of bipolar pagan approaches to Judaism.

The matter is not so simple. A closer look at the texts of Strabo and Lysimachus breaks down the bold antithesis. How far does Strabo present an authentic pro-Jewish line and Lysimachus an anti-Semitic one? Strabo, in fact, while expressing a high opinion of Moses and ascribing noble motives to those who exited from Egypt, also finds progressive deterioration in the character and behavior of Jews in subsequent generations. Moses' initial successors held to his model of righteousness and piety, but later priests fell into superstition and aggressive behavior, promoting abhorrent dietary laws and circumcision. The rulers of Judaea engaged in plunder and seizure of land not only in their own country but in neighboring territories, even subjugating much of Syria and Phoenicia.[18] Strabo plainly found offensive the actions of the later Hasmonaeans, the transformation of priestly leadership into kingly rule, and the aggressive expansionism that marked Judaean policy from the later second century BCE to the intervention of Pompey.[19] The idea of falling away from a golden age of admirable leaders to that of unworthy successors is, of course, a commonplace in classical literature and philosophy. Nor was Strabo the first to apply that schema to

17. So, e.g., Feldman, *Jew and Gentile*, 163: "anti-Jewish bigot"; 192: "arch Jew-baiter"; 171: "arch anti-Jewish bigot"; Aziza, *ANRW* II.20.1 (1987) 56: "inspirée par des sentiments antijuifs." Aziza, *op. cit.*, 56–57, who dates Lysimachus to the mid 2nd century BCE, speculates that his animosity was provoked by the Jewish settlement at Leontopolis and that his depiction of atrocities inflicted upon the land had in mind Jewish mercenaries employed by the 2nd century Ptolemies—a tissue of unsupported conjectures.

18. Strabo 16.2.37: ἔπειτ' ἐφισταμένων ἐπὶ τὴν ἱερωσύνην τὸ μὲν πρῶτον δεισι-δαιμόνων, ἔπειτα τυραννικῶν ἀνθρώπων ... οἱ μὲν γὰρ ἀφιστάμενοι τὴν χώραν ἐκάκουν καὶ αὐτὴν καὶ τὴν γειτνιῶσαν, οἱ δὲ συμπράττοντες τοῖς ἄρχουσι καθήρ-παζον τὰ ἀλλότρια καὶ τῆς Συρίας κατεστρέφοντο καὶ τῆς Φοινίκης πολλήν. See the careful analysis of J.-D. Gauger, *Historia* 18 (1979) 211–24, although his dissection of the text accords it a greater precision than its confused character warrants.

19. Strabo 16.2.40. The formulation of Schäfer in Gafni et al., *Jews in the Hellenistic-Roman World*, 23, that "Strabo becomes a bit less pro-Jewish" misconceives the matter. Cf. also *idem*, *Judeophobia*, 25.

the history of the Jews.[20] The *topos* carries little weight as history. But it supplies a critical clue to Strabo's attitude toward Jews closer to his own day. The Greek geographer plainly did not convey his laudatory version of the Exodus in order to celebrate the qualities of contemporary Jews. To judge this account as motivated by pro-Jewish sympathies misses the point.

A comparable assessment can be made on the other side, with regard to Lysimachus. His Exodus narrative delivers a severe verdict on Jewish behavior, ostensibly reflecting retaliation by Egyptian intellectuals for the defamatory version in the Bible. Yet even Lysimachus' treatment betrays some grudging admiration. He reports that the Jews survived hardship and near death in the desert, were rallied by Moses to run the risk of pressing on, and eventually exercised power and sovereignty in Judaea.[21] Here too, therefore, the notion that this work conveys pure spleen against the Jews overstates and distorts the case. It would be wise to apply some skepticism to the thesis that these variants of the Exodus drama represent either simple denunciation of or apologia for the Jews.

Another text serves to underscore the point. Pompeius Trogus, a Romanized Gaul writing in Latin in the age of Augustus, composed a wide-ranging and massive history of Greek and Near Eastern affairs, concentrating upon the Hellenistic kingdoms, a work preserved only in a summary version by the much later compiler Justin. Trogus was, therefore, a contemporary of Strabo, and possibly of Lysimachus.[22] In the course of his discussion of Seleucid history in Syria in the later second century BCE, Trogus offers an excursus on early Jewish history.

Unlike most Greco-Roman writers, Trogus knows that the Hebrews had a history prior to Moses—or, at least, the tradition about a history. He has heard about a patriarchal period, he locates Jewish origins in Damascus, he speaks of early Jewish rulers who included Abraham and Israhel, evidently Jacob, and he transmits a highly condensed account of Joseph's experiences in Egypt.[23] More to the point, Trogus supplies a noteworthy rendition of

20. One can find a parallel interpretation in Diod. 40.3.8.

21. Jos. *C. Apion.* 1.308–11: Μωυσῆν τινα συμβουλεῦσαι αὐτοῖς παραβαλλομένους μίαν ὁδὸν τέμνειν ἄχρις ἂν ὅτου ἔλθωσιν εἰς τόπους οἰκουμένους ... ἱκανῶς δὲ ὀχληθέντας ἐλθεῖν εἰς τὴν οἰκουμένην χῶραν ... ὕστερον δ' αὐτοὺς ἐπικρατήσαντας. Elsewhere Lysimachus passed harsh judgment on Moses as lawgiver; Jos. *C. Apion.* 2.145.

22. A recent translation of Justin's epitome by J. C. Yardley includes useful introductory material by R. Develin; *Justin: Epitome of the Philippic History of Pompeius Trogus* (Atlanta, 1994) 1–10. See now also W. Heckel and J. C. Yardley, *Justin, Epitome of the Philippic History of Pompeius Trogus*, vol. I (Oxford, 1997) 1–34.

23. Justin 36.2.1–10.

the Exodus. In his view, Moses was son of Joseph, an error of course but not an especially egregious one. In the Book of Exodus, the Moses story follows almost directly upon that of Joseph—although the text does insert a sentence about much fruitful multiplying in between.[24] Trogus proceeds to describe Moses not only as having inherited Joseph's knowledge but as possessing a most handsome countenance. The Exodus story then follows in abbreviated form, a version with some familiar and some unfamiliar features. The Egyptians, in Trogus' variant, afflicted with leprosy and other skin diseases, took oracular advice and expelled Moses and others suffering from ailments, lest the pestilence spread further. Moses then assumed leadership of the exiles and took them out of Egypt—making off with a number of Egyptian sacred objects as they went. The Jews headed for Damascus, stopping at Mt. Sinai on the way, and creating the Sabbath to commemorate the end of their hunger in the Arabian desert. They began the practice of keeping themselves apart from other peoples, recalling that their expulsion had been due to Egyptian fear of contamination by plague.[25]

A detailed critique of Trogus' text would here serve little purpose.[26] But an interesting element in his digression deserves special note. The expulsion of the Jews from Egypt as consequence of leprosy and other diseases, normally considered to be a quintessentially anti-Semitic ingredient, is presented by Pompeius Trogus in a purely matter-of-fact fashion, with no polemical overtones. Indeed, the remarks follow directly upon Trogus' praise of Moses not only for his brains but even for his good looks. To be sure, he noted the Jews' theft of Egyptian objects of worship on their way out of the country. But that says no more than the Scriptures themselves, which have the Jews trick their Egyptian neighbors out of some precious articles before making their escape from the land.[27] And Trogus adds an epilogue, observing that the Jewish practice of combining kingship with high-priesthood gave them a blend of justice and religion that led to incredible power.[28]

The labels of philo-Semitic or anti-Semitic plainly have no applicability to Pompeius Trogus. The whole conceptual approach needs revision. The

---

24. Justin 36.2.11; Exodus 1.6–7.

25. Justin 36.2.12–15.

26. See the sensible discussion of Gager, *Moses*, 48–56. Cf. Schäfer in Gafni et al., *Jews in the Hellenistic-Roman World*, 24–26; *idem, Judeophobia*, 26–27.

27. Exodus 3.21–22, 11.2–3, 12.35–36.

28. Justin 36.2.16: *semperque exinde hic mos apud Iudaeos fuit, ut eosdem reges et sacerdotes haberent, quorum iustitia religione permixta incredibile quantum coaluere.* Trogus or his source evidently assumed here that the political and religious arrangements that held in the later Hasmonaean period could be traced all the way back to the generation after Moses.

categorization of pagan texts that treat the Exodus as standing on one side or another of a hostile exchange is off the mark. The episode of the Exodus held a central place in Jewish consciousness and the self-perception of Jews. But only for them. Writers of the Greco-Roman world had no comparable stake in the matter. To Gentiles who took notice of it at all, the Exodus constituted little more than a colorful sidelight or the obligatory *origo* in an ethnographic study. And one can go further. Those Hellenic intellectuals in Egypt who happened to know the tale would surely have felt no urge to refute it. Why rehabilitate the villains who represented a regime that the Greeks themselves had eventually supplanted? Egyptians, to be sure, might have had grounds for annoyance—if they were aware of the story. But how far is it likely to have spread outside the synagogues? Would Jews have propagated a narrative that highlighted their flight from Egypt at a time when they sought to establish their credentials as residents? And how urgent was it for Greeks and Egyptians to refute a Jewish legend that could safely be ignored or dismissed?[29] It is time to abandon the image of a mudslinging campaign between those sympathetic and those antipathetic to Jews. A fresh approach may be more productive.

For that purpose, we go back to the beginning, i.e., the beginning of pagan interest in the Jewish exodus from Egypt. The first extant writer to exhibit such interest is readily identifiable: Hecataeus of Abdera, a contemporary of Alexander the Great and Ptolemy I, thus active in the late fourth century BCE. Available information on his career and writings is frustratingly sparse, thereby encouraging a voluminous scholarly literature that dwarfs the ancient testimony. As pupil of the Skeptic Pyrrho, Hecataeus evidently had philosophic as well as historical interests. He traveled and lived for a time in Egypt, an intellectual who profited from the patronage of the court in the age of Ptolemy son of Lagus. Among his works, one at least was composed there, a major study of Egyptian history, culture, and traditions. From that work, in all probability, comes a lengthy extract concerning the Jews that includes a version of the Exodus.[30]

---

29. To be sure, The Wisdom of Solomon, a tract probably produced by an Egyptian Jew in the early Roman Empire, recounted the Exodus story with virulent attacks upon the oppressors of the Jews. See, especially, 10.15–21, 11.5–16, 12.23–27, 15.14–19, 17.2–21, 19.13–17. But it is most unlikely that the readership comprised many Egyptians. The treatise, composed in elegant Greek, aimed at a sophisticated and Hellenized audience. And the author in fact never identified the wicked explicitly as Egyptians. On the date and character of the work, see D. Winston, *The Wisdom of Solomon* (Garden City, 1979) 3–69.

30. See Diod. 1.46.8; Jos. *C. Apion.* 1.183. Josephus' claim that Hecataeus wrote a book entirely devoted to the Jews has generated a long and probably undying controversy. This

The fragment that survives comes at third hand. Diodorus quoted it, and his text, in turn, is preserved by Photius. How much condensation has taken place and how far the extant material has been pieced together rather than belonging together in the original remain beyond proof. Nonetheless, the transmitted text can be taken as a generally reliable indicator of the author's attitude. Hecataeus records a plague that afflicted the land of Egypt. Its severity drove the populace to interpret it as divine wrath. They concluded that ancestral religious practices were no longer being consistently observed, for there were too many foreigners in the land engaged in alien rites and rituals. Hence they called for removal of the strangers in their midst.[31] The non-Egyptians were forthwith expelled from the country, the most eminent and energetic among them landing in Greece and certain other places, under the leadership of Danaus and Cadmus. But the larger number of exiles were driven to an uninhabited land later called Judaea. Moses brought them there, a man of exemplary wisdom and courage, and responsible both for the founding of Jerusalem and for the installation of the Temple.[32] Hecataeus proceeds to ascribe to Moses a host of admirable political, religious, social, and economic institutions, including division of the people into twelve tribes, enforcement of aniconic worship, appointment of distinguished persons who would serve both as priests and heads of state, assignment of land to settlers, establishment of marriage and burial practices, and promotion of military training.[33]

The laudatory character of that presentation appears to prevail. And Hecataeus of Abdera has been reckoned by many scholars as the fountainhead for the favorable pagan tradition on the Jews. His gloss on the Exodus story and his admiration for Moses' achievement would seem to qualify as

---

is not the place to explore it, nor is it relevant to the subject at hand, for the fragments quoted by Josephus do not bear on the Exodus. A powerful argument against authenticity is delivered by Bar-Kochva, *Pseudo-Hecataeus*, 54–121. For a summary of recent scholarship on the topic, see Pucci ben Zeev, *JSJ* 24 (1993) 217–24. On Hecataeus himself, the literature is immense. See, among the more important works, F. Jacoby, *RE* 7 (1912) 2750–69; W. Jaeger, *Diokles von Karystos* (Berlin, 1938) 134–53; O. Murray, *JEA* 56 (1970) 141–71; Fraser, *Ptolemaic Alexandria*, I, 496–505; Gager, *Moses*, 26–37; B. Z. Wacholder, *Eupolemus* (Cincinnati, 1974) 85–96; F. H. Diamond in S. M. Burstein and L. A. Okin, *Panhellenica: Essays in Ancient History and Historiography in Honor of Truesdell S. Brown* (Lawrence, Kansas, 1980) 77–95; J.-D. Gauger, *JSJ* 13 (1982) 6–46; E. Will and C. Orrieux, *Ioudaismos-Hellènismos: Essai sur le judaisme judéen à l'époque hellénistique* (Nancy, 1986) 83–93; Gabba in Davies and Finkelstein, *Cambridge History of Judaism*, II, 624–30; G. E. Sterling, *Historiography and Self-Definition: Josephos, Luke-Acts, and Apologetic Historiography* (Leiden, 1992) 59–91.

31. Diod. 40.3.2–3.
32. Diod. 40.3.2–3.
33. Diod. 40.3.3–8.

the paradigmatic positive assessment by Gentiles of Jewish principles and traditions.[34] Hecataeus' acquaintance with the tale apparently indicates serious interest in the history of the Jews and the origins of their teachings. It has even been claimed that he includes in his discussion a phrase that was lifted from the Pentateuch: "a postscript to the laws at their conclusion stated that Moses declared these measures to the Jews, having heard them from God."[35]

Focus upon Hecataeus' sympathies, however, diverts attention from the larger implications of his text. Hecataeus did not write to advance a brief for the Jews. His treatment of them comes only as a digression in a broader study devoted to Egyptian culture. And his attitude toward Judaism is by no means unrelievedly appreciative. In a much discussed passage, Hecataeus describes the Jewish way of life as somewhat anti-social and hostile to others—albeit as consequence of their own experience of banishment. However one interprets the phraseology, it amounts to rather less than a ringing endorsement.[36] Further, Hecataeus' description of emigration from Egypt identifies those who went to Greece as the most eminent and most vigorous, whereas those who headed for Judaea were simply "the vast majority."[37] This too hardly adds luster to the Jewish experience. And most telling is a passage which has received surprisingly little attention. Hecataeus notes that when the High Priest announces directives from God in political assemblies or other gatherings, the Jews are so submissive that they immediately fall to the ground when he interprets those directives for them. Hecataeus' use of the word προσκυνεῖν particularly warrants notice. For Greeks, the act of

34. So, e.g., Jaeger, *Diokles*, 144–53; *JR* 18 (1938) 139–43; Will-Orrieux, *Ioudaismos-Hellènismos*, 90–93; Gabba, *Cambridge History of Judaism*, II, 624–30; Sterling, *Historiography and Self-Definition*, 78–80; Feldman, *Jew and Gentile*, 234–36.

35. Diod. 40.3.6: προσγέγραπται δὲ καὶ τοῖς νόμοις ἐπὶ τελευτῆς ὅτι Μωσῆς ἀκούσας τοῦ θεοῦ τάδε λέγει τοῖς Ἰουδαίοις. Cf. Lev. 26.46, 27.34; Num. 26.13; Deut. 29.1. The parallel is not close enough to be decisive.

36. Diod. 40.3.4: διὰ γὰρ τὴν ἰδίαν ξενηλασίαν ἀπάνθρωπόν τινα καὶ μισόξενον βίον εἰσηγήσατο (Moses). A most generous appraisal of the passage by Gabba, *Cambridge History of Judaism*, II, 629. Note also Jaeger, *Diokles*, 148–49; Diamond, *Panhellenica*, 85–86; Will-Orrieux, *Ioudaismos-Hellènismos*, 92–93. A more negative interpretation by J. N. Sevenster, *The Roots of Pagan Anti-Semitism in the Ancient World* (Leiden, 1975) 188–90; cf. V. Tcherikover, *Hellenistic Civilization and the Jews* (New York, 1959) 360–61; J. Mélèze-Modrzejewski in A. Kasher et al., *Greece and Rome in Eretz Israel* (Jerusalem, 1990) 111; Feldman, *Jew and Gentile*, 126; Schäfer in Gafni et al., *Jews in the Hellenistic-Roman World*, 11–12; idem, *Judeophobia*, 16–17. A balanced treatment by Bar-Kochva, *Pseudo-Hecataeus*, 39–40, with extensive bibliography.

37. Diod. 40.3.2: οἱ μὲν ἐπιφανέστατοι καὶ δραστικώτατοι ... ὁ δὲ πολὺς λεώς.

προσκύνησις before a man was a mark of barbaric servility.[38] None of this implies animosity on Hecataeus' part, let alone anti-Semitism.[39] To label Hecataeus in terms of his attitude towards the Jews is simply beside the point.

A more marked characteristic stands out in Hecataeus' account: the sheer volume of misinformation therein. The segment on the Jews contains numerous errors, inaccuracies, and misconceptions. To list only the most egregious ones: that the Jews occupied an uninhabited land; that Moses founded Jerusalem and erected the Temple; that he conceived God as a globe-encircling heaven which ruled the universe; that the Jews were never governed by kings; that the High Priest was chosen for his superiority in virtue and wisdom.[40] And, most central for our purposes, vast discrepancies exist between the biblical narrative of the Exodus and the version conveyed by Hecataeus. They have remarkably little in common.

Wherein lies the basis for Hecataeus' adaptation? As has long been recognized, the form and structure of the presentation owe much to standard Greek folktales about colonization, the founding of settlements abroad, and the establishment of institutions to govern the lives of the settlers. Moses therefore fits the pattern of the οἰκιστής or κτίστης. Hecataeus, in fact, employs the language characteristically applied to the leading out of a colony and the foundation of cities.[41] The schema makes it easy to see why Hecataeus would assume that the man who brought the Israelites out of Egypt would also have been responsible for founding Jerusalem and the Temple. The

38. Diod. 40.3.6: τοῦτον δὲ κατὰ τὰς ἐκκλησίας καὶ τὰς ἄλλας συνόδους φησὶν ἐκφέρειν τὰ παραγγελλόμενα, καὶ πρὸς τοῦτο τὸ μέρος οὕτως εὐπιθεῖς γίνεσθαι τοὺς Ἰουδαίους ὥστε παραχρῆμα πίπτοντας ἐπὶ τὴν γῆν προσκυνεῖν τὸν τούτοις ἑρμηνεύοντα ἀρχιερέα. Controversy over attempted introduction of the Persian practice of proskynesis plagued the expedition of Alexander the Great, a contemporary of Hecataeus; see, especially, Arrian 4.10.5–4.12.5; Curt. Ruf. 8.5.5–24, 8.7.13; Plut. *Alex.* 54–55, 74.1–2.

39. The concluding lines of the excerpt report that many of the Jews' ancestral practices were upset through their mingling with other nations in the time of the Persian and then the Macedonian overlordship; Diod. 40.3.8. But this is almost certainly Diodorus, not Hecataeus, speaking. The latter, writing in the late 4th century, would be in no position to assess the effects of Macedonian rule.

40. Diod. 40.3.3–5. The efforts of Bar-Kochva, *Pseudo-Hecataeus*, 25–33, to explain away all these inaccuracies as mere errors in dating and sequence of institutions and events is unconvincing.

41. Diod. 40.3.3: ἡγεῖτο δὲ τῆς ἀποικίας ὁ προσαγορευόμενος Μωσῆς ... ἄλλας τε πόλεις ἔκτισε καὶ τὴν νῦν οὖσαν ἐπιφανεστάτην, ὀνομαζομένην Ἱεροσόλυμα. Diodorus himself, in introducing the Hecataean fragment, refers to the establishment of the nation from its beginnings as κτίσις ; 40.3.1. Cf. the discussion of Bar-Kochva, *Pseudo-Hecataeus*, 30–33.

interpretatio Graeca pervades the presentation. Moses' measures on allocation of land and inalienability of the lots, the training of youth for military service, even the exhortation to Jews to keep themselves apart and their practices distinct from other peoples strongly recall the image of the Spartan system. Other elements, such as the equation of an encircling heaven with the deity, an elitist priesthood with special privileges that governed the land, and a broad-gauged set of laws that regulated public and religious practices, all suggest the influence of Greek philosophy and political theory.[42] The juxtaposition of Jewish migration and the legendary voyages of Danaus and Cadmus to Greece thus underscores the Hellenic character of the narrative. Jewish traditions have at best a marginal role.

The Greek shape of the narrative, however, does not account for everything. Hecataeus relied heavily upon Egyptian informants for the work as a whole, a study of the history, traditions, and culture of the land which stressed above all its place as fountainhead for civilizations all over the Mediterranean and the Near East.[43] An Egyptian substratum certainly underlies the digression on the Jews. In fact, it incorporates two separate strands, both rooted in national pride. On the one hand, the notion of foreign rites and customs diminishing respect for Egypt's religious traditions, bringing a plague from the gods, and requiring removal of aliens reflects common Egyptian attitudes: the land needs to be purged of foreign pollution in order to appease divine wrath.[44] On the other, dispatch of Cadmus and Danaus to Greece and Moses to Judaea also reinforced the idea that those cultures owed their ultimate derivation to Egypt. The impetus for the story therefore came from Hecataeus' Egyptian informants, not from the Book of Exodus.

But there is more to be said. Hecataeus was not innocent of contact with Jews. Neither the Hellenic echoes nor the Egyptian conceptualization can explain the data on the Jews, however garbled and confused, which Hecataeus transmitted. These include the Jewish sojourn in Egypt, Moses as leader and lawgiver, the division of the people into twelve tribes, the

---

42. The Hellenic influence in Hecataeus' formulation has been widely and variously noticed. See Jaeger, *Diokles*, 144–53; *idem, JR* 18 (1938) 40–43; Murray, *JEA* 56 (1970) 158; M. Hengel, *Judaism and Hellenism* (London, 1974) 255–56; Gager, *Moses*, 31–34; E. Bickerman, *The Jews in the Greek Age* (Cambridge, Mass., 1988) 16–18; Gabba, *Cambridge History of Judaism*, II, 627–29; Bar-Kochva, *Pseudo-Hecataeus*, 29–39. Numerous parallels between Greek and Israelite foundation stories have been discerned by M. Weinfeld, *The Promise of the Land* (Berkeley, 1993) 1–51—but none directly applicable to the Hecataeus narrative.

43. See Sterling, *Historiography and Self-Definition*, 64–75.

44. Cf. Jaeger, *Diokles*, 144; J. Yoyotte, *RHR* 103 (1963) 140; D. B. Redford, *Pharaonic King-Lists, Annals, and Day Books* (Mississauga, Ontario, 1986) 276–81; Will-Orrieux, *Ioudaismos-Hellènismos*, 83.

prohibition on images of the deity, the central role of the High Priest, and perhaps even a paraphrase from the Scriptures. All of these items must have been obtained through oral communication with Egyptian Jews. The deduction is incontrovertible, and generally acknowledged.[45] But it creates a dilemma. If Hecataeus drew much of his data from knowledgeable Jews, why are there such sharp discrepancies between Jewish traditions, practices, and belief on the one hand and their representation by Hecataeus on the other—not to mention the contrast between his account and that in the Book of Exodus? It will not do to ascribe to Jewish informants only those details in Hecataeus' text that are accurate, while assigning the rest to malicious Egyptians, Hellenic formulas, or Hecataeus' own errors. That is too easy. And it should now be abundantly clear that the question of whether the Greek historian was favorable or unfavorable to the Jews is quite irrelevant and devoid of meaning.

A very different proposition needs to be considered. The Diaspora Jews themselves may have had a hand in molding even the non-traditional parts of the story, thereby to have a better fit with the cultural milieu in which they found themselves. It would be a gross error to assume that Jewish intellectuals adhered rigidly to the Exodus tale as it appears in the Bible and that departures from it represent manipulation by Gentiles. Variants on the story may in fact owe more to Jewish ingenuity than we customarily allow.[46]

45. See, e.g., Jaeger, *Diokles*, 146; Jacoby, *FGH*, III A, 264, 50–51; Gager, *Moses*, 37. Wacholder, *Eupolemus*, 91–92, even speculates that Hecataeus visited Jews in Palestine. For Diamond, *Panhellenica*, 81, 87, all of Hecataeus' information came from a "reliable Jewish source." But she does not specify how or in what form. That the Greek historian had any direct knowledge of the Bible is highly unlikely. The Septuagint did not yet exist. Aristobulus, to be sure, claims that earlier translations of the Hebrew had circulated; Eusebius *PE* 13.12.1. But Aristobulus had a special axe to grind: the postulate of earlier translations was required to support his thesis that Jewish writings influenced Greek thinkers like Pythagoras and Plato. The allusions to prior Greek renditions of the Bible in the *Letter of Aristeas*, 314–16, are mere fables.

46. D. Mendels, *ZAW* 95 (1983) 96–110, offers the inventive and intriguing suggestion that Hecataeus' material came from Jewish priestly circles in the late 4th century who represent the ideology of the Persian period as reflected in the books of Ezra and Nehemiah. Mendels finds a number of provocative parallels. But the argument too often rests on strained conjectures. It is not easy to believe, for instance, that Jewish priests in the Persian period promulgated the idea of Moses as founder of Jerusalem and the Temple in order to diminish the stature of the Davidic kingdom. Nor can one readily concur with the idea that a downplaying of David's line translated itself into a denial that the Jews ever had a king. Still less probable is the notion that Moses' supposed measures on military training and land distribution reflect the actual policies of Nehemiah with a mere overlay of *interpretatio Graeca*. Mendels properly recognizes that Jews played a part in revamping the tradition that appears in the Bible. But he fails to explain how priestly opinions in Judaea would have reached Hecataeus in Egypt.

The portrayal of Moses' leadership as based on φρόνησις and ἀνδρεία, the selection of the governing class for their outstanding merit and ability, and the Exodus as issuing in the establishment of a religious and political center as well as a Temple could well be adaptation of the scriptural narrative by Hellenized Jews themselves. The concepts would strike familiar chords to those of the Diaspora brought up in an atmosphere pervaded by Greek culture. It is time to question the idea that pagans were primarily responsible for reshaping or misshaping the biblical Exodus for polemical purposes. On the contrary. Few of them would have had the occasion, interest, or motivation to do so.[47] The Jews played a large part in the refashioning of their own past.[48]

The hypothesis can be pursued through a different avenue. The Egyptian priest Manetho (first half of the third century) sketches a portrait of the Exodus that diverges widely from that of Hecataeus. The Jews possess a rather positive image in Hecataeus' narrative, although, as we have seen, that does not explain the author's objective. Manetho, by contrast, supplies an account that earned him the label of the first of the pagan anti-Semites, source of the Egyptian counter-history of the Exodus. It will pay dividends to examine how the legend fares in the hands of Manetho—or, more properly, what form it takes in a text which has been ascribed, on disputed authority, to Manetho.

A welter of textual, biographical, source-critical, and historical problems confront any researcher who treads on this slippery terrain. We focus mercifully upon those elements of Manetho's work that bear on the Exodus and its variants. Little enough is known of his life, and not all of that fully reliable. A Hellenized Egyptian intellectual, he attained priestly rank in the reign of Ptolemy I Soter or Ptolemy II Philadelphus, probably at Heliopolis, and took part in establishing or developing the cult of Sarapis in Alexandria. Most important, he authored influential works in Greek, notably his *Aigyptiaka*, addressed to Philadelphus, a political and religious history of his native land from its beginnings down to the eve of the Hellenistic period.[49]

47. On Greek attitudes to foreigners' accounts of their own origins generally, see E. J. Bickerman, *CP* 47 (1952) 68–73.

48. D. R. Schwartz, in a forthcoming article, maintains that the entire fragment actually derives from a Jewish "Pseudo-Hecataeus" of the late Hasmonaean period. This is not the place to review his incisive and attractive but ultimately unpersuasive arguments. If he is right, of course, this would only strengthen the case made here.

49. A reliable summary of what is known or conjectured about Manetho's life and career in W. G. Waddell's Loeb edition, *Manetho* (Cambridge, Mass., 1940) vii–xxvii. See also R. Laqueur, *RE* 14 (1928) 1060–1101; Fraser, *Ptolemaic Alexandria*, I, 505–10; Sterling, *Historiography*

Two long extracts in Josephus purportedly derive from that work and appear to relate versions that connect to the Exodus of Hebrews from Egypt. Both are mired in controversies that cannot here be settled. Nor is it necessary to settle them in order to discern the texts' value in illuminating perceptions of the Exodus story.

The first extract, from Josephus, can in fact be disposed of briefly. Manetho recounts an assault on Egypt by invaders of obscure origin from the east who conquered the land without a blow. They overcame the rulers of the country, burned cities ruthlessly, destroyed temples, oppressed the natives, installed garrisons, and exacted tribute. Their king Salitis established a capital at Avaris, fortifying it to protect the frontier. The invaders ruled through six generations of kings, their race known as Hyksos, which connotes some form of shepherds, and their aim was to stamp out the Egyptian stock. The "shepherds" held sway for more than five centuries, until the Egyptians rose up to overthrow their oppressors, drive them to confinement in Avaris, and eventually arrange their departure from Egypt through a negotiated treaty. The shepherds then migrated *en masse*, 240,000 strong, and crossed the desert to Syria, where they built the city of Jerusalem in Judaea.[50]

Whether this narrative has anything whatever to do with the biblical Exodus is questionable. In essence, Manetho simply retails the Hyksos' invasion and occupation of Egypt, a central feature of his nation's history. Josephus, not Manetho, makes the connection with the Jews. And Josephus has a special axe to grind. He proposes to dispel Greek doubts about the antiquity of the Jews by pointing to Egyptian and Phoenician writings that attest to his people in the remote past. Manetho serves as prime exhibit for Josephus' partisan purposes.[51] Manetho himself, it bears repeating, makes no explicit identification of Hyksos with Jews in the quoted fragment. That is left to Josephus. The reference to Jerusalem does, to be sure, evoke an association with Jews.[52] But even if it belongs in Manetho's original text (a disputed proposition), this hardly affects the principal issue. His story of Hyksos departing for Judaea under a negotiated truce carries not the faintest resemblance to the Book of Exodus. For our purposes, it can safely be set aside.[53]

---

and *Self-Definition*, 117–35. Recent scholarship is usefully summarized by Pucci ben Zeev, *JSJ* 24 (1993) 224–34. See also the interesting thesis by Mendels, *Studia Hellenistica* 30 (1990) 91–110.

50. Jos. *C. Apion.* 1.75–90.

51. Jos. *C. Apion.* 1.69–74, 1.103–104, 1.228.

52. Jos. *C. Apion.* 1.90, 1.94, cf. 1.228.

53. Josephus could plausibly seize upon the term "shepherds" for his objectives, since the Hebrews in the time of Joseph's migration to Egypt were shepherds; cf. Genesis 46.34, 47.3.

Manetho's second excerpt has greater relevance and higher significance. The narrative is drawn, according to Josephus, not from priestly records but from invented stories and rumors.[54] The Jewish historian introduces this segment by asserting that Manetho maliciously amalgamated Jews with the mob of Egyptian lepers and those with other afflictions who were banished from Egypt. He then proceeds to reproduce a substantial text ascribed to Manetho. The text has the Egyptian Pharaoh Amenophis, of uncertain date and place in the sequence of kings, manifest a desire to witness the gods themselves directly. That feat would be possible, a wise counselor advised him, only if he purged Egypt of all lepers and other polluted persons. The king thereupon gathered the afflicted people, 80,000 of them, set them to work in the stone quarries where they would not contaminate the rest of the population, then later allowed them to occupy the abandoned city of Avaris, sacred to the pernicious god Typhon, enemy of Osiris. The impure then appointed as their leader a certain Osarsiph, one of the priests of Heliopolis, who bound his people by oath and promulgated legislation forbidding them to worship Egyptian gods and indeed enjoining them to sacrifice and feast upon all animals sacred to the Egyptians. The aggressive enactments issued in even greater aggressive action. Osarsiph prepared his followers for rebellion and war, summoning to their aid the shepherd people, 20,000 strong, former occupants of Avaris and now dwelling in Jerusalem. Together the rebels and the shepherds forced Amenophis onto the defensive. The king, fearful because of a prophet's prediction, declined battle and withdrew his army, his family, as many sacred animals as he could collect, and a multitude of Egyptians across the border to Ethiopia where they dwelled in exile for thirteen years. In the meanwhile, the polluted Egyptians and their allies from Jerusalem went on a rampage, plundering the land, burning cities and villages, robbing temples, defacing images of the gods,

---

And it is possible that the name of the Hyksos' first ruler, Salitis, reflects the title of *shalit* that Joseph took as governor of Egypt; Genesis 42.6. But the absence of any mention of Jews by Manetho in this passage remains the central fact. It takes a real stretch to find contact with the Exodus tale. A valuable review of earlier scholarship appears in L. Troiani, *SCO* 24 (1975) 98–100, n. 3. Some of the more recent literature is cited by Pucci ben Zeev, *JSJ* 24 (1993) 225–26. The case for a connection between Manetho's Hyksos and the Hebrews is made, among others, by Tcherikover, *Hellenistic Civilization and the Jews*, 362–63; Stern, *Greek and Latin Authors*, I, 62–63; Sevenster, *Roots of Pagan Anti-Semitism*, 186–88; Kasher, *Jews in Hellenistic and Roman Egypt*, 328–30; Pucci ben Zeev, *op. cit.*, 225–30; Bar-Kochva, *Anti-Semitism*. The skeptics include: Laqueur, *RE* 14 (1928) 1066–70; A. Momigliano, *RivFilol* 9 (1931) 497–502; Jacoby, *FGH*, IIIC, 609, 84; Troiani, *op. cit.*, 103–10; Gabba, *Cambridge History of Judaism*, II, 631–32; Aziza, *ANRW* II.20.1 (1987) 49–50.

54. Jos. *C. Apion.* 1.229: τὰ μυθευόμενα καὶ λεγόμενα ; cf. 1.105.

persecuting priests and prophets, and using the sanctuaries themselves to roast the sacred animals of the Egyptians. Osarsiph, the Heliopolitan priest who had taken his name from Osiris and who authored a constitution and laws, chose to adopt the new appellation of Moses. And Manetho concludes the tale with a postscript, adding that at a later time Amenophis with his now grown son returned from Ethiopia with large forces, defeated the shepherds and their polluted comrades, driving them out of Egypt to the borders of Syria.[55]

Such is the gist of Manetho's—or perhaps Pseudo-Manetho's—presentation. How should one interpret or characterize it? For many scholars, it represents an exemplar of Egyptian anti-Semitism, a hostile twist on the Exodus tale, a reversal of that story, an upside-down Exodus in which the Jews serve as the powers of evil and the Egyptians as the innocent and victimized, Moses the tyrant who tramples upon tradition and terrorizes the land of Egypt until he and his villainous compatriots are driven out by the resurgent and ultimately triumphant Egyptians. Manetho's text thus delivered a stinging reply to the Book of Exodus and generated the counter-tradition that flowed into tracts like those of Lysimachus, Chaeremon, and Apion.[56] That thesis, widely adopted and influential, is less than compelling. A reconsideration is warranted.

Authorship of the second fragment itself has stimulated controversy, a long-standing dispute. Is it genuine Manetho or Pseudo-Manetho?[57] The debate can happily be avoided. Decision on the question does not affect the main issue. Does the extract, in fact, constitute an inverted Exodus, an anti-Semitic response to the biblical tale? A closer look raises doubts. The Jews as such do not appear in the narrative. The polluted persons are Egyptians, placed in the quarries to segregate them from other Egyptians; indeed some

55. Jos. C. Apion. 1.230–51.

56. So, e.g., Tcherikover, Hellenistic Civilization and the Jews, 361–64; Stern, Greek and Latin Authors, 64; Sevenster, Roots of Pagan Anti-Semitism, 186–88; Kasher in B. Oded et al., Studies in the History of the Jewish People and the Land of Israel (Haifa, 1974) III, 69–84 (Hebrew); Jews in Hellenistic and Roman Egypt, 327–32; Funkenstein, The Jerusalem Quarterly 19 (1981) 59; idem, Perceptions of Jewish History, 36–40; Aziza, ANRW II.20.1 (1987) 54–55; Mendels, JSP 2 (1988) 16; Studia Hellenistica, 30 (1990) 108–109; Pucci ben Zeev, JSJ 24 (1993) 233; Bar-Kochva, Anti-Semitism. A somewhat peculiar twist on this theory occurs in A. Catastini, Henoch 17 (1995) 279–300, who has Manetho respond to the Exodus story but then sees the Joseph tale in Genesis as a counter-retort in the polemic.

57. Doubts about authenticity have been expressed, e.g., by E. Meyer, Aegyptische Chronologie (Berlin, 1904) 71; Laqueur, RE 14 (1928) 1070–80; Momigliano, RivFilol 9 (1931) 490–95; Gabba, Cambridge History of Judaism, II, 632–33; Bickerman, Jews in the Greek Age, 224–25.

of the lepers were Egyptian priests.[58] Manetho's reference to the Σολυμῖται need mean no more than the inhabitants of Jerusalem; the text refrains from indicting Jews as a nation.[59] Explicit association of the Jews with lepers and the impure is attributed to Manetho by Josephus but does not surface in the quoted text.[60] Manetho indeed explicitly distinguishes the polluted persons who are Egyptians from the Jerusalemites who come to their aid.[61] The equation of Osarsiph with Moses might seem decisive for Manetho's attitude. But the equation itself is a jarring intrusion in the narrative, a glaring anomaly that surely did not belong in the original. Manetho had already introduced Osarsiph earlier in the story as priest of Heliopolis and lawgiver. The second introduction with a change of name is mere repetition, unnecessary, and out of place.[62]

The very concept of anti-Semitism as applied to Manetho grossly oversimplifies the matter. Even Josephus, who goes to great lengths to refute Manetho's narrative, pointing out its inconsistencies, chronological blunders, and self-contradictions, stops short of branding him with anti-Jewish prejudice. He takes Manetho to task for that part of his narrative that abandoned written records and relied on fictitious stories and rumors, thus inducing him to confuse the Israelites with Egyptian lepers and the generally polluted. Manetho did not miss truth by much, according to Josephus, when he relied on the ancient chronicles, but when he turned his attention to inauthentic legends, he either framed implausible tales or trusted those

58. Jos. *C. Apion.* 1.233–35: τῶν ἄλλων Αἰγυπτίων εἶεν κεχωρισμένοι. εἶναι δέ τινας ἐν αὐτοῖς καὶ τῶν λογίων ἱερέων φησὶ λέπρᾳ συνεχομένους.

59. Jos. *C. Apion.* 1.248: οἱ δὲ Σολυμῖται κατελθόντες σὺν τοῖς μιαροῖς τῶν Αἰγυπτίων; cf. 1.241: ποιμένας εἰς πόλιν τὴν καλουμένην Ἱεροσόλυμα.

60. Jos. *C. Apion.* 1.228–29: ἀναμῖξαι βουλόμενος ἡμῖν πλῆθος Αἰγυπτίων λεπρῶν καὶ ἐπὶ ἄλλοις ἀρρωστήμασιν.

61. Jos. *C. Apion.* 1.233–34, 1.241.

62. Jos. *C. Apion.* 1.238–40: ἡγεμόνα αὐτῶν λεγόμενόν τινα τῶν Ἡλιοπολιτῶν ἱερέων Ὀσάρσιφον ἐστήσαντο ... τοιαῦτα δὲ νομοθετήσας; 1.250: λέγεται δὲ ὅτι ⟨ὁ⟩ τὴν πολιτείαν καὶ τοὺς νόμους αὐτοῖς καταβαλόμενος ἱερεὺς τὸ γένος Ἡλιοπολίτης ὄνομα Ὀσαρσίφ ... μετετέθη τοὔνομα καὶ προσηγορεύθη Μωυσῆς. Cf. Gager, *Moses*, 117; Schäfer in Gafni et al., *Jews in the Hellenistic-Roman World*, 15; *idem*, *Judeophobia*, 20; A. J. Droge in Feldman and Levison, *Josephus' Contra Apionem*, 134–36; *contra*: Troiani, *SCO* 24 (1975) 126. The insertion of ⟨ὁ⟩ in the above text might make the idea of an interpolation a little less likely. But that insertion is itself more than questionable. The fact that Osarsiph has to be identified again not only as lawgiver but as Heliopolitan priest points almost inescapably to interpolation. Whether "Osarsiph" is actually a form of "Joseph" need not here be investigated. See Gager, *op. cit.*, 115, n. 5; Troiani, *op. cit.*, 113–18; Catastini, *Henoch* 17 (1995) 287–88.

motivated by bias.[63] This does not amount to animus against the Jews, even in Josephus' eyes.[64] Nor is it likely that a work addressed to Ptolemy II would set out an assault on Jews. The reign of that king has come down, at least in Jewish tradition, as one most generous and favorable to the Chosen People.[65]

The point can be driven home even more sharply. Does Manetho's yarn constitute a retort to the biblical Exodus at all? In fact it shares little or nothing with the Scriptures. Only a committed prejudgment could read Manetho as a counterblast to the Jewish tradition. Departure of the "shepherds" from Egypt in the first fragment came under a negotiated treaty, not as flight or escape. And the second excerpt has the Jerusalemites return to Egypt rather than seek release from it. Their eventual expulsion, together with the leprous and diseased Egyptians, appears as an afterthought and epilogue to the story, not the heart of it. As a twist or parody of the Hebrew Exodus it would fall flat.

One may go further still. An Egyptian rejoinder to the biblical version presumes circulation of the latter in Gentile circles. Yet the Septuagint, even if trust be placed in the legend conveyed by the *Letter of Aristeas*, dates no earlier than the time of Ptolemy II himself. Its effect upon Egyptian intellectuals literate in Greek, if ever it had any, could hardly have been so swift and powerful as to require a refutation by Manetho. One can, of course, postulate earlier versions or oral propagation of portions of the Pentateuch—perhaps even noisy celebrations of the Passover. But such conjectures border on circular reasoning and do not advance matters. The Jews of Egypt had no motivation for disseminating the tale in Gentile circles—nor indeed for emphasizing their escape from a land in which they now resided. The version as we have it in Josephus' second extract either belongs to a later time, foisted upon Manetho in order to give it greater authority, or, if it is authentic Manetho, has no relation to the Book of Exodus.

In fact, Manetho's narrative fits within an established Egyptian tradition. A potent strain in Egyptian literature fastens blame for evils suffered by the populace upon the impure and the diseased, carriers of pollution. The gathering of the impure in a city devoted to the rival god Typhon or Seth, enemy of Osiris, reinforces the contrast between the good and the wicked.

63. Jos. *C. Apion.* 1.228–29, 1.287: Μανέθως ἕως μὲν ἠκολούθει ταῖς ἀρχαίαις ἀναγραφαῖς, οὐ πολὺ τῆς ἀληθείας διημάρτανεν, ἐπὶ δὲ τοὺς ἀδεσπότους μύθους τραπόμενος ἢ συνέθηκεν αὐτοὺς ἀπιθάνως ἤ τισι τῶν πρὸς ἀπέχθειαν εἰρηκότων ἐπίστευσεν.

64. Contrast Josephus' more explicit blast against Lysimachus; *C. Apion.* 1.304: συντεθεικὼς κατὰ πολλὴν ἀπέχθειαν. Noted also by Troiani, *SCO* 24 (1975) 111.

65. *Letter of Aristeas*, passim; Jos. *Ant.* 12.11–118.

The ravaging of land, pillaging of temples, and sacrilegious sacrificing of the animal deities represent the malevolent enemy in characteristic fashion. The subsequent expulsion of the foreigner gives final victory and vindication to the native forces. Similar sentiments received expression in Middle Kingdom Egypt, and the echoes resonate in Hellenistic texts like the Demotic Chronicle, the Potter's Oracle, and the Prophecy of the Lamb. The traditions had special relevance in the late Egyptian period when inhabitants of the country had suffered a comparable form of religious oppression at the hands of the Persians. Nationalist overtones ring out clearly.[66] The Manethonian tale does not derive from the Exodus or some garbled form of it. In its essentials, it has nothing whatever to do with Jews.

How then did Jews enter this tangle of stories? Why should Osarsiph, otherwise a renegade Heliopolitan priest, become identified with Moses? Why should the polluted prisoners at Avaris have received assistance from persons dwelling in Jerusalem? Even those scholars who take the line that direct or indirect allusions to Jews in the narrative are accretions or interpolations, tacked on at a later time, nevertheless agree that the additions stem from anti-Semitic Egyptians or Greeks eager to set Jews in the guise of the conventional polluter, oppressor, and purveyor of impiety.[67] But what would prompt Greco-Egyptian writers to cast Jews in this particular mold? Why would they care?

Jewish mercenaries in the army of the Persians have been reckoned as the culprits. But the suggestion that they provoked a hostile misrepresentation has little plausibility. It would not easily explain the longevity of the portrait.[68] The Elephantine garrison, to be sure, could be a source of trouble. Friction

---

66. The Egyptian background to Manetho's story and others similar to it is well brought out by Yoyotte, *RHR* 163 (1963) 133–43, and Redford, *Pharaonic King-Lists*, 276–83. But Yoyotte retains the notion that Jews were cast into this villainous role. So also, most recently, H. Heinen, *Trierer Theologische Zeitschrift* 101 (1992) 143–145; J.-W. van Henten and R. Abusch in Feldman and Levison, *Josephus' Contra Apionem*, 271–309; Schäfer, *Judeophobia*, 57–58, 163–69. For discussions of these texts and others, see C. C. McCown, *HTR* 18 (1925) 357–411; S. K. Eddy, *The King is Dead* (Lincoln, 1961) 257–94; J. G. Griffiths in D. Hellholm, *Apocalypticism in the Mediterraean World and the Near East* (Tübingen, 1983) 273–93, with useful bibliography; D. Frankfurter, *Elijah in Upper Egypt* (Minneapolis, 1993) 174–83. On Seth as god of foreigners and emblematic of the enemies of Egypt, at least since Assyrian times, see H. te Velde, *Seth, God of Confusion* (Leiden, 1967) 109–51. On Persian oppression in Egypt, exaggerated by Greek sources but by no means negligible and punctuated by Egyptian uprisings, see E. Bresciani in I. Gershevitch, *The Cambridge History of Iran* (Cambridge, 1985) II, 502–12, 522–27.

67. So, e.g., Laqueur, *RE* 14 (1928) 1071–74; Gager, *Moses*, 116–18; Gabba, *Cambridge History of Judaism*, II, 633.

68. The suggestion is that of Yoyotte, *RHR* 163 (1963) 142–43.

arose between the Egyptian priests of the ram-god Khnum and the Jews of Elephantine, resulting in the destruction of the Jewish temple in 410 BCE.[69] Did the celebration of the Passover and an emphasis on the Exodus generate this reaction? So it might be surmised.[70] But Passover had certainly been celebrated for some time before the end of the fifth century.[71] And no other evidence exists for strife of this sort during the two or more centuries of the Jewish community at Elephantine. The conflict in 410 may indeed have been connected with an Egyptian revolt against Persian authority.[72]

A different argument traces the negative characterization to friction between Jews and Greeks over citizenship privileges in Alexandria.[73] Even if the friction is real, however, it hardly accounts for a fable that equates Jews with invaders who devastated the land, terrorized the populace, and assaulted the venerated gods of Egypt. If a quarrel over citizen rights produced so elaborate a scenario, it was surely overkill. Indeed, the Alexandrian Greeks are most unlikely perpetrators of the portrait. They would have had little incentive to champion the legacy of a native people whom they did not even permit to share their own privileges and prerogatives.[74]

The idea that Egyptians themselves felt resentment over the hostile representation of their ancestors contained in the Book of Exodus might seem to make more sense. But not upon scrutiny. How many of them ever had occasion to read the Book of Exodus? No intelligible version circulated in the time of Manetho. And it helps little to resort to a later "Pseudo-Manetho." The Septuagint did not have any discernible impact outside the Jewish communities—let alone among the indigenous inhabitants of Egypt.[75] Moreover, as noted above, Jews had no obvious reason for spreading to Gentile communities a legend that glorified their evacuation of Egypt—a land in which they now sought to establish roots. The idea that the story

69. A. Crowley, *Aramaic Papyri of the Fifth Century* BC (Oxford, 1923) 21, 27, 30–33, 37–38.

70. Cf. Porten, *Archives from Elephantine*, 279–93; *idem* in W. D. Davies and L. Finkelstein, *The Cambridge History of Judaism* (Cambridge, 1984) I, 388–90; Mélèze-Modrzejewski, *The Jews of Egypt*, 37–43; Schäfer, *Judeophobia*, 121–35. Rightly questioned by E. G. Kraeling, *The Brooklyn Museum Aramaic Papyri* (New Haven, 1953) 92–96.

71. See Porten, *Archives from Elephantine*, 128–33.

72. See Crowley, *Aramaic Papyri*, 27. The reconstructions of Porten, *Archives from Elephantine*, 279–81, and Schäfer, *Judeophobia*, 123–27, are highly speculative. A different interpretation by Kraeling, *Brooklyn Museum Aramaic Papyri*, 102–107.

73. Cf. Bickerman, *Jews in the Greek Age*, 224–25.

74. Cf. Jos. *C. Apion.* 2.29–32.

75. See Tcherikover, *Eos* 48 (1956) 169–93; cf. A. D. Nock, *Conversion: The Old and the New in Religion from Alexander the Great to Augustine of Hippo* (Oxford, 1933) 79; A. Momigliano, *Alien Wisdom: The Limits of Hellenization* (Cambridge, 1975) 91.

in the Scriptures roused patriotic passions or ethnic retaliation lacks any sound basis.

An alternative possibility demands a hearing: that introduction of the Jews into Manetho's narrative, as into Hecataeus', came from Jewish sources themselves. A paradoxical idea on the face of it, even altogether implausible one might assume. Would Jews really represent themselves in so ruthlessly negative a fashion? Presumably not. But further probing alters the picture. We need to bear in mind that the story went through at least two or three versions before it reached its present form. We see Manetho's text only as it came to Josephus and through the latter's eyes. That point must be stressed. From the Jewish historian's perspective, Manetho's work was the first of several Egyptian tracts that set out to slander the Jews, distorting the truth both about the Israelites' entrance into Egypt and their evacuation of it.[76] In fact, however, Josephus' specific criticisms of Manetho's version confine themselves to pointing out internal inconsistencies, implausibilities, and absurdities. None of them has anything to do with entrance into or exit from Egypt.[77]

Still more significant are Josephus' subsequent remarks. He proceeds to excogitate the motives of those authors whom he seeks to refute: jealousy and hatred of his ancestors because they had ruled Egypt and because they then prospered after return to their own land.[78] These are striking remarks rarely noted or commented upon. Josephus in short accepts the tradition that Jews had taken control of the country of Egypt! That tradition, set in a negative light by the text of Manetho which Josephus sought to ridicule, also has a fundamentally positive side which the Jewish historian found quite acceptable.[79]

To put the matter more pointedly. One can envision an earlier layer slanted to the benefit of the Jews. The coalition of shepherds and rebels overthrew Egyptian rule, drove the Pharaoh and his minions across the border, and held ascendancy for an extended period in that land, a significant

76. Jos. *C. Apion.* 1.223: τῶν δ' εἰς ἡμᾶς βλασφημιῶν ἤρξαντο μὲν Αἰγύπτιοι. βουλόμενοι δ' ἐκείνοις τινὲς χαρίζεσθαι παρατρέπειν ἐπεχείρησαν τὴν ἀλήθειαν. οὔτε τὴν εἰς Αἴγυπτον ἄφιξιν ὡς ἐγένετο τῶν ἡμετέρων προγόνων ὁμολογοῦντες, οὔτε τὴν ἔξοδον ἀληθεύοντες.

77. Jos. *C. Apion.* 1.254–78.

78. Jos. *C. Apion.* 1.224: αἰτίας δὲ πολλὰς ἔλαβον τοῦ μισεῖν καὶ φθονεῖν, τὸ μὲν ἐξ ἀρχῆς ὅτι κατὰ τὴν χώραν αὐτῶν ἐδυνάστευσαν ἡμῶν οἱ πρόγονοι κἀκεῖθεν ἀπαλλαγέντες ἐπὶ τὴν οἰκείαν πάλιν εὐδαιμόνησαν.

79. Cf. Jos. *C. Apion.* 1.252: δέδωκε γὰρ οὗτος [Manetho] ἡμῖν καὶ ὡμολόγηκεν ἐξ ἀρχῆς τὸ μὴ εἶναι τὸ γένος Αἰγυπτίους, ἀλλ' αὐτοὺς ἔξωθεν ἐπελθόντας κρατῆσαι τῆς Αἰγύπτου καὶ πάλιν ἐξ αὐτῆς ἀπελθεῖν.

military success in which the Jerusalemites could take pride. The most likely fashioners of such a tale are surely Jews themselves. The story, it is true, has the victors plunder and ravage the land, actions painted in lurid colors by Manetho or Pseudo-Manetho. But that would not preclude a Jewish origin for the narrative. The destructive deeds inflicted humiliation upon the Egyptians, a demonstration of the conquerors' power. Jewish writers would find satisfaction in recounting or embellishing those elements of the tale. According to the Book of Exodus itself, after all, God authorized the Hebrews to despoil the Egyptians before departing from the land—which they proceeded to do.[80] Desecration of the temples and slaughter of the animals worshipped by Egyptians would also announce the triumph of the Chosen People and their faith. Taking action against rival cults and abhorrent practices had a long tradition among Jews, a sign of supremacy, not a source of shame. One need cite only the imperatives of Deuteronomy, enjoining the Israelites to drive out their foes, destroy them utterly, smash their altars and sacred objects, and burn their idols.[81] Such commands were duly fulfilled by Joshua who left a trail of total destruction wherever he went.[82] And the later prophecies of Isaiah included the forecast that the land of Judah would bring terror to the Egyptians themselves.[83] On this reconstruction, therefore, the identification of Osarsiph with Moses and the introduction of Jerusalemites into the story, far from injecting anti-Semitic elements, represent Jewish expropriation of an Egyptian tradition, thus to establish the claims of Jews to a place of eminence in the history of Egypt.[84]

The rendition, as we have it, must be a composite. At least two quite independent strands are here interwoven: first, a tale of lepers and contaminated persons herded and confined to the city of Seth; and, second, a narrative of Jerusalemites who invaded, conquered, and pillaged the land of Egypt. Who

---

80. Exodus 3.22, 12.36. Only much later did apologetic Jewish writers like Philo and Josephus feel the need to justify or deny the plundering; Philo *Moses* 1.140–42; Jos. *Ant.* 2.314. Cf. I. Lévi, *REJ* 63 (1912) 211–13.

81. Deut. 7.1–5, 7.25, 12.1–3.

82. E.g. Joshua 8.24–29, 10.28–40, 11.10–22.

83. Isaiah 19.16–17.

84. A similar view was proffered long ago by Momigliano, *RivFilol* 9 (1931) 485–503, and largely ignored in subsequent literature. Momigliano, however, indulges in excessive speculation when seeking to identify separate strands deriving from Egyptians, Jewish interpolators, anti-Semites, and philo-Semitic refutations. Just which particulars can be assigned to Jewish writers remains unknowable, especially as the surviving versions have come through so many hands. Presumably, however, Jews did not designedly associate themselves with lepers, the diseased, or the adherents of Seth. It is noteworthy, as we have seen, that even Manetho clearly disassociates the lepers from the people of Jerusalem; Jos. *C. Apion.* 1.233–34, 1.241.

put them together, and when, remains beyond our grasp. But the second strand could easily derive from a Jewish construct.

A form of the story seems to have found its way even among the traditions of Jewish origins reported by Tacitus. One of the tales ascribed by the Roman historian to unidentified sources has the Jews as Assyrian refugees whose paltry land-holdings induced them to leave their country. They migrated to Egypt where they achieved dominance in part of that land.[85]

The idea of an assault by Israelites upon Egypt can, in fact, be found in a Jewish-Hellenistic source. A fragment of Artapanus, little known or commented upon, provides some startling information. The author, a Hellenized Jew from Egypt, writing probably in the second century BCE, was quite uninhibited in his recreation of biblical tales—and he was by no means alone.[86] In Artapanus' version, the voice from the burning bush instructed Moses to lead an army against Egypt. Moses took heart from this command and determined to assemble a force and make war on the Egyptians.[87] The fragment breaks off shortly thereafter and the outcome is unreported.[88] But it provides direct testimony for a Jewish tradition on mobilization against Egypt.

Hellenistic testimony exists also for the razing of alien temples and altars by Jews. The smashing of pagan shrines, indeed pre-Greek shrines, by the Maccabees is amply attested.[89] Further, a preserved text refers to similar actions in the Persian period evidently in Palestine, and the author explicitly expresses admiration.[90] There can be little doubt that a Jew composed that tale, wrongly ascribed by Josephus to Hecataeus.[91] And, whatever its historicity, it demonstrates a favorable Jewish tradition on

---

85. Tac. *Hist.* 5.2.3: *sunt qui tradant Assyrios convenas, indigum agrorum populum, parte Aegypti potitos.*

86. On Artapanus, his date, and provenance, see J. Freudenthal, *Alexander Polyhistor* (Breslau, 1875) 143–75; C. Holladay, *Theios Aner in Hellenistic Judaism* (Missoula, 1977) 199–232; Sterling, *Historiography and Self-Definition*, 167–86.

87. Eusebius *PE* 9.27.21–22: φωνὴν δ' αὐτῷ θείαν εἰπεῖν στρατεύειν ἐπ' Αἴγυπτον ... τὸν δὲ θαρρήσαντα δύναμιν πολεμίαν ἐπάγειν διαγνῶναι τοῖς Αἰγυπτίοις. Cf. also Jos. *Ant.* 2.268: καὶ θαρροῦντα ἐκέλευεν εἰς τὴν Αἴγυπτον ἀπιέναι στρατηγὸν καὶ ἡγεμόνα τῆς Ἑβραίων πληθύος ἐσόμενον.

88. Artapanus has Moses go directly to meet Aaron after the burning bush episode. And the scene then shifts abruptly to the summoning of Moses by Pharaoh; Eusebius *PE* 9.27.22. A break in the text is rightly noted by N. Walter, *Jüdische Schriften aus hellenistisch-römischer Zeit*, I.2 (Gütersloh, 1976) 133, n. 22a.

89. See, e.g., I Macc. 5.44, 5.68, 10.83–84; II Macc. 12.26.

90. Jos. *C. Apion.* 1.193: ἔτι γε μὴν τῶν εἰς τὴν χώραν, φησί, πρὸς αὐτοὺς ἀφικνουμένων νεὼς καὶ βωμοὺς κατασκευασάντων ἅπαντα ταῦτα κατέσκαπτον ... ὅτι δίκαιον ἐπὶ τούτοις αὐτούς ἐστι θαυμάζειν.

91. See, most recently, Bar-Kochva, *Pseudo-Hecataeus*, 97–101, with bibliography.

the destruction of foreign shrines, an action still worthy of praise in the Hellenistic era.[92] One might recall also that the literature of the Jews in that era did not shrink from recording and applauding what we might regard as Jewish atrocities. In the Book of Esther, Mordecai received permission from the Persian king for his countrymen to slaughter all the people hostile to them in his domains, including women and children, and to plunder their property. The Jews proceeded to cities in various satrapies of the empire and massacred 75,000 people—although they did refrain from the plunder. The event prompted inauguration of a commemorative celebration.[93] In a closely parallel case, III Maccabees portrays triumphant Jews in the time of Ptolemy IV petitioning and obtaining from the king the right to execute all the apostates from within their own ranks. They murdered more than 300 wayward Jews in a single day, exulting in the punishment and establishing the day as an annual festival.[94] As is clear, Jewish writers of the Hellenistic age quite comfortably recorded (or invented) sanguinary attacks on their foes, destruction of shrines and holy places, and brutal assertion of their own religious supremacy.

These examples help to set the various versions of the Exodus legend in proper perspective. The violent and aggressive features of the tale indeed occupied its central segment. So integral had they become that they demanded incorporation in the Egyptian version of Manetho or Pseudo-Manetho. The Egyptian author, in fact, had to supply an addendum that brought Amenophis and his supporters back into power after Egypt had long been at the mercy of its conquerors.

Of course, once those elements entered the tradition, they could be reshaped and twisted to different purposes. As we have seen, in the hands of Lysimachus, the lepers and other diseased folk were themselves Jews, the very persons who polluted the country and had to be expelled from it. That hostile version circulated already by the mid first century BCE, for it appears in a tale reported by Diodorus Siculus.[95] Even in Lysimachus' text,

92. Note also the Jewish destruction of a pagan altar at Jamnia in 39 CE; Philo *Leg. ad Gaium* 200–202.

93. Esther 8.9–12, 9.1–19. Not that Hellenistic Jews abstained from plunder when they had the opportunity. Even the author of II Maccabees revels in the fact that Judas Maccabaeus' forces ravaged the whole country and put barbarian hordes to flight; II Macc. 2.21: τὴν ὅλην χώραν ... λεηλατεῖν καὶ τὰ βάρβαρα πλήθη διώκειν. And he does not hesitate to record other Jewish savaging of the Gentiles; cf. II Macc. 8.6, 12.16, 12.26–28.

94. III Macc. 7.10–15.

95. Diod. 34/5.1.1–2. Cf. Schäfer in Gafni et al., *Jews in the Hellenistic-Roman World*, 19–21; *idem, Judeophobia*, 22–23. The source for Diodorus' tale is much disputed. See discussion and bibliography in Bar-Kochva, *Anti-Semitism*.

however, the strength of their conviction and the potent leadership of Moses allowed the Israelites not only to survive but to plunder the lands which they traversed. That central aspect adhered to the tradition. And it did not originate with anti-Semites.

If this be so, one might ask, why are there so few traces of the tale in Jewish writings themselves? A fair question. But where would we expect to find them? Extant Jewish-Hellenistic writings on this subject, it must be emphasized, are very fragmentary prior to the Roman period. And by that time the story of Israelite occupation of Egypt had been reinterpreted by antagonistic authors as a slanderous drama of evil and diseased villains who conducted sacrilegious rapine. Philo and Josephus denied by implication that Jews could have committed such acts. They suppressed the Deutero-nomic prescriptions and even claimed that Mosaic law prohibited blasphemy of other gods or plundering of alien temples.[96] To that end they could claim scriptural authority—or rather that of the Septuagint. Exodus 22.28 simply forbids the reviling of God. The Septuagint version of that text, however, renders Elohim as the plural θεούς, perhaps as a gesture toward Gentiles, perhaps as defense against Gentile criticism.[97] Philo and Josephus, in adapt-ing the passage, certainly had the latter motive. Other Jewish writers took a more militant line, magnifying the misdeeds of Egyptians and emphasizing the vengeance of the Lord.[98] One need not be surprised that few signs of the earlier story survive.

Subsequent instances of the hostile version can be treated with brevity. The Greco-Egyptian writer Apion had a clear grievance with the Jews. A grammarian, Homeric scholar, and author of a five-volume work on Egyptian history, Apion obtained citizen privileges in Alexandria and served as representative of the city on an embassy to the emperor Caligula. There he firmly opposed the claims of Jewish envoys who complained of their mistreatment at the hands of Alexandrians. Apion included some harsh comments about Jewish history and traditional customs in his *Aigyptiaka*, thus providing a stimulus for Josephus' lengthy counter-treatise, the *Contra Apionem*.[99] Apion himself, oddly enough, receives relatively little attention

96. Philo *Moses* 2.205; *Spec. Leg.* 1.53; Jos. *C. Apion.* 2.237; *Ant.* 4.207.

97. Cf. G. Hata in L. H. Feldman and G. Hata, *Josephus, Judaism, and Christianity* (Detroit, 1987) 192–93; P. W. van der Horst, *Studia Philonica Annual* 5 (1993) 1–4.

98. Wisdom 10.15, 19–20; 11.6–16; 12.23–27; 15.14–19; 16.1–9; 17.1–21; 18.5–25; 19.13–21; Sib. Or. 3.29–45, 314–18, 348–49, 596–600, 611–23.

99. On Apion, see Gager, *Moses*, 122–24; Stern, *Greek and Latin Authors*, I, 389–90; M. Goodman in Schürer, *History of the Jewish People*, III.1, 604–607; Aziza, *ANRW* II.20.1 (1987) 61–63. The hostile comments on Jews to which Josephus responds all derive from

in Josephus' tract, with few quotations and even less on his re-creation of the Exodus. What survives, however, indicates that his version has affinities with those already discussed. Apion cites the elders of Egypt for the report that Moses was a Heliopolitan who evidently took great liberties with ancestral practices, building outdoor synagogues, erecting columns instead of obelisks, and installing the image of a boat to serve as a sundial.[100] The significance of all this is unclear, but the identification of Moses as a Heliopolitan connects with Manetho's version. More significantly, Apion has Moses lead the lepers, the blind, and the lame out of the country.[101] That statement parallels the presentation of Lysimachus. The Jews themselves were the lepers and the handicapped who successfully departed from the land. The tale, Egyptian in origin but modified and transformed by Jews, had been refashioned again by Egyptian intellectuals to suit their own ends. Apion, it appears, had access to more than just Egyptian traditions. He knew of Moses on Mt. Sinai and a sojourn of forty days before he descended with the laws.[102] The Septuagint, of course, was now available, but there is nothing to suggest that Apion read it. Pompeius Trogus, doubtless among others, had already placed Moses on Mt. Sinai. Apion could get his information elsewhere than in the Scriptures. But he clearly wove the tales into his narrative. And, whatever his animus, Jewish sources indirectly provided many of the ingredients for his reconstruction.[103]

A contemporary of Apion, the Hellenized Egyptian priest and Stoic intellectual Chaeremon, offers a variant on the story in Manetho but one intermingled with still additional Jewish elements. Chaeremon, who wrote on Egyptian history and mythology, combined the training of a Greek

---

the Αἰγυπτιακά. Clement of Alexandria claimed that Apion wrote an entire work κατὰ Ἰουδαίων; *Strom.* 1.21.101.3–4. But that may be no more than an erroneous inference from Josephus.

100. Jos. *C. Apion.* 2.10–11.

101. Jos. *C. Apion.* 2.15: φησι τὸν Μωσῆν ἐξαγαγεῖν τοὺς λεπρῶντας καὶ τυφλοὺς καὶ τὰς βάσεις.

102. Jos. *C. Apion.* 2.25; cf. Exodus 24.15–18.

103. For Trogus on Moses and Mt. Sinai, see Justin 36.2.14. A curious tale repeated by three later and obscure writers, Nicharchus, Ptolemy Chennus, and Helladius, all preserved by Photius, maintains that Moses was called "Alpha" by the Jews because he had many leprous spots, *alphoi*, on his body; texts in Stern, *Greek and Latin Authors*, I, 533; II, 149, 491. The report is generally connected with the negative Alexandrian tradition that associates Jews with lepers as part of the Exodus story; Gager, *Moses*, 129–33; Feldman, *Jew and Gentile*, 240–41; but see Aziza, *ANRW* II.20.1 (1987) 63–65. That would not, however, explain why Moses received the name from the Jews. One might recall the famous passage in Exodus 4.6 regarding Moses' leprous hand. Cf. also the story of Miriam, Aaron's wife, as leper; Num. 12. The tale of Moses as "Alpha" may indeed have come through a Jewish rather than an anti-Jewish route.

philosopher with a deep engagement in native religious traditions. Later report has it that he was a teacher of Nero and, if he is the Chaeremon who appeared on an embassy to Claudius, he may well have shared Apion's animosity toward Alexandrian Jews.[104] Josephus, in any case, brackets him with Manetho, Lysimachus, and Apion as Egyptian writers whose representations of the Jews he is determined to controvert. Chaeremon's version, however, or at least those fragments of it that Josephus had access to and chose to transmit, discloses more confusion than hostility. He has king Amenophis provoked by the goddess Isis in his sleep and then advised by a sacred scribe to purge the land of its contaminated populace. Amenophis thereupon gathered and banished 250,000 infected persons who were led by two scribes named Moses and Joseph, each of whom also had an Egyptian name—perhaps implying a change of appellation, as with the purported Osarsiph-Moses. The exiles left for Pelusium, where they joined 380,000 would-be immigrants whose entrance had been blocked by Amenophis. Their combined forces allowed them to invade the land, drive Amenophis into Ethiopia, and evidently hold the country for many years until Amenophis' son, born in exile, reached maturity, chased the Jews to Syria, and restored his father.[105] The narrative has obvious similarities with that of Manetho's second extract, but also marked differences. There is little convergence with Lysimachus' account, and still less with what is known of Apion's. In Chaeremon's fragment, it is not even clear with whom the Jews are to be identified: the exiles, the blocked migrants, or some combination thereof? Josephus exploits the confusion to discredit the account.[106] But Chaeremon's presentation doubtless had a fuller tapestry than the fragment reveals—and perhaps than Josephus himself saw. The divergences in any case indicate that even in the early Empire the tradition was splintered and subject to repeated variations.[107] The Egyptian substratum, however,

104. On Chaeremon and the meager sources related to his career, see H. R. Schwyzer, *Chairemon* (Leipzig, 1932) 9–16; Gager, *Moses*, 120–22; Stern, *Greek and Latin Authors*, I, 417–18; Goodman in Schürer, *History of the Jewish People*, III.1, 601–604, with bibliography; P. W. van der Horst, *Chaeremon: Egyptian Priest and Stoic Philosopher* (Leiden, 1984) ix–xiv, 2–7; Aziza, *ANRW* II.20.1 (1987) 60–61.

105. Jos. *C. Apion.* 1.288–92.

106. Jos. *C. Apion.* 1.293–303.

107. Chaeremon's version seems alluded to in a 3rd century CE papyrus that speaks of the anger of Isis, an attack on Jews (?), and the expulsion of the "lawless" from Egypt; *CPJ*, III, no. 520; see the commentary *ad loc.*; also Stern, *Zion* 28 (1963) 223–27 (Hebrew); *Greek and Latin Authors*, I, 420, n. 289. A recent discussion, with bibliography by D. Frankfurter, *JJS* 43 (1992) 208–12. G. Bohak, *JSJ* 26 (1995) 32–41, speculatively associates the papyrus with an Egyptian reaction to Onias' 2nd century BCE temple in Heliopolis.

remains evident. And the Jewish accretions, represented here by both Moses and Joseph, as well as by Jews enjoying conquest and dominance, still held central place.

The foregoing analysis sets other pagan versions of the Exodus in a new light. It is no longer surprising that an author like Pompeius Trogus could report that Jews were evicted from Egypt as lepers and diseased persons, who purloined sacred objects as they left, while at the same time characterizing their leader Moses as a man of consummate wisdom and great beauty. Indeed the form of the story even as it came down to Tacitus, usually regarded as the chief of pagan anti-Semites, shared these mixed elements. He supplies a tale on which, he claims, most authorities agree. A plague had struck Egypt, ravaging the bodies of its inhabitants and inducing the Pharaoh Bocchoris, on recommendation of the Oracle of Ammon, to purge his kingdom by banishing the Jews, reckoned as hateful to the gods. The exiles, abandoned in the desert, nearly gave way to despair but were rallied by Moses who exhorted them to courage and self-reliance and led them to safety, culminating in their seizure of new lands, expulsion of the conquered, and establishment of a city and temple.[108] The ingredients here can be found, each with a different mix, in one or more of the Egyptian writers already discussed. Eviction of the foreigner to relieve Egypt of divine wrath reflects the indigenous legend, overlaid by Jewish supplements that celebrate an admired leader and his triumphant people. Tacitus does not stumble into inconsistency or incoherence. He transmits a tradition that had itself been repeatedly manipulated, modified, and refashioned.

•   •   •

A summation would be salutary. The distorting lens of Josephus has slanted our vision for too long. The Jewish historian relished the task of combatting Greco-Egyptian writers like Manetho, Lysimachus, Apion, and Chaeremon whose works he saw as malicious and mendacious. That angle of sight helps to account for most subsequent interpretations of the texts as anti-Semitic perversions of the Exodus tale. But Josephus shows little sensitivity to the complexities imbedded in the narratives he attacks. And he fails to see the combination of Egyptian legend and Jewish infiltration that lift those narratives outside the category of simplistic anti-Semitism.

The Book of Exodus held profound meaning for Jewish identity and memory. But those Jews scattered in the Diaspora and particularly those

108. Tac. *Hist.* 5.3.1–2.

dwelling in Egypt had strong incentive to reshape the tale. To them the reasons for escape from Egypt were less important than the justification for their return. The self-esteem of Hellenistic Jews in Egypt could be bolstered by an enhancement of their ancestors' history in that land. Their new cultural milieu presented Jews with a genre of Egyptian legends that depicted the foreigner as an alien presence who polluted the land, trampled upon native religion and traditions, and was eventually expelled. Such narratives, taking diverse forms as framed by writers like Hecataeus and Manetho, did not originate as responses to the Book of Exodus, nor were they initially directed against Jews. Instead, Jewish writers and thinkers themselves grafted their people's presence onto those stories, found analogues to Moses, set up their forefathers as conquerors, and took credit for the overthrow of false Egyptian idols. The Jews could reckon themselves as former rulers of the land—an edifying and comforting past. Such a twist on the Egyptian legends gave them a proud presence on the Nile in its remote antiquity.

Pagans did not invert the biblical story to construct a counter-history and advance the anti-Semitic cause.[109] Few would have had any familiarity with the biblical story—even after the composition of the Septuagint.[110] And oral transmission would have provided very different variants. Egyptian lore about contests with the foreign oppressor or the polluted alien is quite independent of the Scriptures. To put it boldly, the extant narratives do not derive from Egyptian distortion of the Jewish legend, but exactly the reverse. Jewish inventiveness expropriated Egyptian myth in order to insert into it their own heroes, their religious superiority, and even their military triumphs.

Later Alexandrian writers like Lysimachus, Apion, and Chaeremon did have anti-Jewish axes to grind. But they found themselves saddled with stories that made Moses an effective leader and the Jews successful warriors, undetachable elements that adhered to their own versions.[111] Josephus, in

109. Droge in Feldman and Levison, *Josephus' Contra Apionem*, 136–37, who had access to an earlier version of this chapter, agrees that the hostile pagan stories did not take an "anti-Exodus" form. But he oddly sees them as attacking Hecataeus' representation of the Jews.

110. Tcherikover, *Eos* 48 (1956) 169–93, argues forcefully for the absence of Gentile interest in or acquaintance with Jewish-Hellenistic literature. That would certainly seem to be the case with regard to the Septuagint, which has left little mark on the pagan scene. But Tcherikover somewhat overstates the case in general, relying largely on an *argumentum e silentio*; see the criticisms of Feldman, *JQR* 78 (1988) 230–41. Variants fashioned by Jewish intellectuals on familiar Egyptian folktales could readily have circulated among Hellenized Egyptians.

111. A similar idea, that traditions favorable to the Jews could be retained even in hostile accounts, is expressed (with regard to different matters) by Feldman, *JQR* 78 (1988) 249; *idem* in Feldman and Levison, *Josephus' Contra Apionem*, 269.

contending with them, saw only their animus and strained to undermine their credibility. He missed the traces of Jewish intrusion that held fast through all the variations. Hence he overlooked what may have been a pivotal step in the shaping of the tradition. The Jews freely adapted the Exodus legend and infiltrated native fables in order to elevate their own part in the history of their adopted land.

CHAPTER 3

The Hellenistic Images of Joseph

The figure of Joseph held great appeal for Jews and Gentiles of every era. His story in the Book of Genesis echoes through the ages, retold, enhanced, or distorted, down to the great novels of Thomas Mann and even the musical theater of Andrew Lloyd Webber. Joseph's character and achievements exercised unbroken fascination. Few could resist the tale of the righteous man, victimized, sold, enslaved, deported, and imprisoned, whose innate skills and adherence to principle enabled him to rise to power in an alien land, forgive and rescue his own tormentors, and wield widespread political and economic authority in the interests of communal welfare. Joseph's image not only as hero to his people but as potentate in Egypt carried special attraction to Egyptian Jews of the Hellenistic era. But that is only part of the story. Darker and less admirable characteristics of the patriarch recur in the tradition, stemming from Genesis itself. And Hellenistic Jews did not shy away from them, indeed developed and manipulated them. The varied versions of Joseph's tale make for an intriguing mix. Their propagation and elaboration offer an illuminating perspective upon Diaspora Jewry.

The Genesis narrative of Joseph portrays a complex and manifold personality, no mere one-dimensional man of virtue. The young Joseph, ambushed by his brothers, was hardly an innocent waif. His boastful recounting of dreams that forecast ascendancy not only angered his brothers but troubled his father.[1] When he went in search of his brothers on what seems little more than a spying mission, he flaunted the multicolored coat—thus leading

---

1. Gen. 37.5–11. This is not to mention the disputed text in Gen. 37.2b, which has Joseph deliver an evil slander against his brothers. On this, see E. Hilgert, *Biblical Research* 30 (1985) 5–6, with bibliography.

directly to his humiliation.[2] Joseph, of course, nobly resisted the blandishments of Potiphar's wife in Egypt, preserving his virtue and principles at the cost of imprisonment. He also, however, made a point of displaying his administrative skills, first in Potiphar's household, then in management of prison personnel.[3] His reputation as interpreter of dreams brought him to Pharaoh's attention, but the administrative talents put him in a position to run the country. With the consent of Pharaoh, Joseph obtained extensive power to govern the land and reorganize the agricultural system, and he took without hesitation the symbols of authority that elevated him to a rank second only to that of the king himself.[4] The rediscovery of and reconciliation with his brothers forms a moving story, underscoring the magnanimity of the now grand vizier who tearfully embraced those who had once sold him into servitude. But one should not omit to note that he calculatingly put them through some severe anxieties and emotional trials before revealing himself.[5] Joseph's magnanimity had its limits. He made certain also to exhibit his mastery. And not only his own. Joseph's stern and exacting management of grain allocation during the famine years brought all Egyptian land under the king's control and transformed the entire Egyptian peasantry into vassals of the crown.[6] The new ordinance obliging every farmer to reserve one fifth of his produce for the king became a permanent part of the Egyptian system.[7] Genesis thus supplies an intricate tale, a multifaceted personality, and rich material to be exploited by Hellenistic Jews.[8]

.   .   .

Joseph receives almost no notice in the remainder of the scriptural canon. Abraham, Isaac, and Jacob stand forth as the patriarchal ancestors of the Chosen People; the honor roll does not include Joseph. The ambiguous personality and occasionally dubious behavior of the Genesis figure perhaps suggested a less than altogether edifying model. Only the psalmist of Psalm

---

2. Gen. 37.3, 37.12–24.

3. Gen. 39.1–23.

4. Gen. 41.39–44.

5. Gen. 42–45.

6. Gen. 47.13–26. The Septuagint version minces no words: 47.21: καὶ τὸν λαὸν κατεδουλώσατο αὐτῷ εἰς παῖδας.

7. Gen. 47.26.

8. S. Niditsch, *Underdogs and Tricksters* (San Francisco, 1987) 70–125, offers an illuminating comparative study of folkloric patterns in the Jacob and Joseph narratives in Genesis. Cf. also the analysis of A. Meinhold, *ZAW*, 87 (1975) 306–24, who sees the story as a "Diasporanovelle."

105 makes reference to the tale in Genesis. And the verses there allude not to Joseph's character or uprightness but to his career as a sign of the Lord's favor, his liberation from the shackles of slavery, and his appointment by Pharaoh as ruler of all royal possessions and as importer of wisdom to the royal household.[9] The portrait is plainly positive, but not especially to the credit of Joseph. A brief mention occurs also in First Chronicles, though only to the rights of the first-born, forfeited by Reuben and thus accorded to Joseph.[10]

Intertestamental texts, composed in Hebrew and deriving from Palestine, gave a little more attention to Joseph. Ben Sira counts him among the ancestral heroes, a man in a class of his own, but he offers no specifics, apart from the transference of his bones from Egypt to the land of his fathers. That notice alludes to the Pentateuchal tale and implies the inclusion of Joseph among the patriarchs.[11] Joseph receives brief mention in I Maccabees, a Greek text of course but one deriving from a Hebrew original. The author gives Mattathias' dying exhortation to his sons listing Jewish ancestors whose adherence to the faith had earned them high renown. Among them he cites Joseph who under stressful circumstances persevered in keeping a commandment—an obvious allusion to resisting the temptations of adultery.[12]

A far more substantial summary of Joseph's career occurs in Jubilees, a work composed in Hebrew probably in the second century BCE and devoted to retelling the stories contained in Genesis and Exodus.[13] The author of Jubilees supplies a sanitized version. Not a hint of character flaws invades the portrait of the hero. Joseph's brothers turn upon him and sell him to the Ishmaelites for no apparent reason except their own innate wickedness. The narrator omits mention of dreams, boasts, favoritism by Jacob, embroidered coat, or even fraternal jealousy.[14] Joseph's adventures in Egypt show him

9. Psalm 105.16–22.

10. I Chron. 5.1–2.

11. Ben Sira 49.15; cf. Gen. 50.25–26; Exod. 13.19; Josh. 24.32. On the bones of Joseph and the subsequent tradition, see J. L. Kugel, *In Potiphar's House* (New York, 1990) 128–55.

12. I Macc. 2.53.

13. On the date, provenance, and objectives of Jubilees, see A. M. Denis, *Introduction aux pseudépigraphes grecs d'Ancien Testament* (Leiden, 1970) 150–62; J. VanderKam, *Textual and Historical Studies in the Book of Jubilees* (Missoula, 1977) 1–6, 207–85; O. S. Wintermuth in J. H. Charlesworth, *The Old Testament Pseudepigrapha* (Garden City, 1985) II, 35–50; E. Schürer, *A History of the Jewish People in the Age of Jesus Christ*, rev. ed. by G. Vermes, F. Millar, and M. Goodman (Edinburgh, 1986) III.1, 308–18. A skeptical and salutary assessment by R. Doran, *JSJ*, 20 (1989) 1–11.

14. Jub. 34.10–11, 34.18–19.

only in the most glowing light. He rejected the advances of Potiphar's wife by proclaiming adherence to ancestral precepts taught him by Jacob and stemming from Abraham, a solemn prohibition on adultery.[15] His accuracy in interpreting dreams gained him freedom and power. Pharaoh elevated him to a position nearly equivalent to his own, investing him with all the public symbols of authority and asserting that only occupancy of the throne indicated any differentiation between them.[16] Jubilees embellishes liberally on Genesis by depicting Joseph's administration of Egypt as one of undeviating righteousness and integrity, devoid of all arrogance or pomposity, earning him the love of all those with whom he came into contact.[17] The discomfort that he put his brothers through upon seeing them again in Egypt, which receives no clear explanation in Genesis, is rationalized in generous fashion by the author of Jubilees: Joseph simply wished to see whether there was internal harmony among the brothers.[18] This, of course, they amply demonstrated, leading to disclosure and tearful reunion. Jubilees never questions the rather drastic means employed to test the brothers' concord. Nor does the text breathe a hint of dissension among the populace in the wake of Joseph's sweeping economic changes. His powers were wide, tantamount to absolute sovereignty.[19] Jubilees picks up a key line in Genesis: Joseph was like a father to the Pharaoh.[20] And a small but noteworthy omission occurs with regard to Joseph's economic policy. He bought up all the land of Egypt, apart from priestly holdings, for the crown. The peasantry would, of course, continue to work it but would henceforth yield up one fifth of their produce to the state. In Genesis, the farmers welcomed the arrangement as rescue from famine, but described their situation as bondage to the king, a state of subjugation. Jubilees, however, presents the new system as a sheer act of generosity—no reference to indentured servitude.[21] Joseph thus combines the application of ascendant power with ethical principles of the highest order.[22]

Those same features reappear in much condensed form in the *Biblical Antiquities* of Pseudo-Philo. That text, preserved now only in Latin manuscripts,

---

15. Jub. 39.5–8.
16. Jub. 40.6–7.
17. Jub. 40.8–9.
18. Jub. 42.25, 43.14.
19. Jub. 43.19–20, 43.24, 46.3.
20. Jub. 43.19. See Gen. 45.8.
21. Jub. 45.8–12. Cf. Gen. 47.20–25.
22. Cf. the analysis by M. Niehoff, *The Figure of Joseph in Post-Biblical Literature* (Leiden, 1992) 41–46.

is generally agreed to derive from a Hebrew original, via the intermediacy of a Greek translation, and to have been written some time in the first or second century CE.[23] The author, whose extant work retells biblical stories that span from Adam to David, devotes only a few lines to Joseph. But they correspond closely in tone and substance to the much lengthier treatment in Jubilees. Joseph is hated by his brothers, without apparent reason, delivered by them to Egypt, brought into the king's service through his repute as interpreter of dreams, then put into the highest official post in the land, where his measures relieved the famine. When his brothers arrived, Joseph sought no vengeance and exhibited only magnanimity.[24] His resistance to the wiles of Potiphar's wife is omitted here but indirectly alluded to later when the author contrasts Joseph's character favorably with that of Samson.[25] The ambiguous personage who appears in Genesis, gifted and competent, faithful and sensitive, but also devious, arrogant, and domineering, is flattened out in the post-biblical texts from Palestine, transformed into a one-dimensional paragon of virtue.

A duplicate image shines forth in the Testament of Joseph, one of the texts included in the *Testaments of the Twelve Patriarchs*, the supposed final words of the sons of Jacob. Each is presented as a hortatory message by the dying patriarch, delivering ethical lessons to sons gathered about him at the end. Unfortunately, provenance, date, and original language of the work remain under considerable dispute, with little sign of consensus. Scholars debate the degree to which Christian interpolations have altered what were originally Jewish writings, or, conversely, the degree to which what are fundamentally Christian writings draw on Jewish sources. Dating is similarly controversial. Parts may go back to the pre-Maccabaean period, but the final Christian form can be no earlier than the late second century CE. Nor is there much agreement on how far, if at all, the Greek texts depend upon Semitic originals. Hence any secure categorization of the document would be illusory.[26] For our

23. See D. J. Harrington, *HTR*, 63 (1970) 503–14; *idem* in Charlesworth, *Old Testament Pseudepigrapha*, II, 297–302; C. Perrot and P.-M. Bogaert, *Pseudo-Philon: Les Antiquités Bibliques* (Paris, 1976) II, 66–74; Schürer, *History of the Jewish People*, III.1, 325–31; F. J. Murphy, *Pseudo-Philo: Rewriting the Bible* (New York, 1993) 3–7; H. Jacobson, *A Commentary on Pseudo-Philo's Liber Antiquitatum Biblicarum* (Leiden, 1996) I, 199–210, 215–24.

24. Ps.Philo 8.9–10. Cf. Jacobson, *Commentary*, 395.

25. Ps.Philo 43.5.

26. Voluminous literature exists on the subject. Among the more valuable, see R. H. Charles, *The Testaments of the Twelve Patriarchs* (London, 1908) xv–xviii, xlii–lxv; J. Becker, *Untersuchungen zur Entstehungsgeschichte der Testamente der zwölf Patriarchen* (Leiden, 1970) 371–496; M. de Jonge, *The Testaments of the Twelve Patriarchs* (Leiden, 1953) 31–36, 77–110, 117–28. As guides to the controversy see especially Denis, *Introduction*, 49–59; H. D. Slingerland, *The Testaments of the Twelve Patriarchs: A Critical History of Research* (Missoula, 1977) 1–115; J. J. Collins in M. E.

purposes it suffices that the character of Joseph possesses the same spotless virtue that one finds in the intertestamental Hebrew texts from Palestine and gives some reason to place the Testament of Joseph in that intellectual setting.

The text, like most of the other Testaments, focuses upon an episode in the dying patriarch's life which he employs to drive home a moral lesson to his attentive sons. In the case of Joseph, two events or aspects of his life form the basis for his sermonizing. An introductory segment recounts the circumstances that brought him to Egypt, asserting that his brothers hated him, were deflected by the Lord from killing him, and then sold him into slavery—once again without any provocation or apparent reason, as in Jubilees and in Pseudo-Philo.[27] Then the first episode takes over the narrative: Joseph's steadfast refusal to compromise his virtue through a sexual liaison with Potiphar's wife. The tale, of course, stems from the Bible. But, whereas Genesis treats the matter in a few verses, the Testament of Joseph elaborates upon it with great flourish. The shameless hussy importunes Joseph again and again, alternately threatening him with a variety of punishments and promising him desirable rewards, feigning motherly affection, offering to abandon her native religion and embrace Joseph's god, suggesting the murder of her husband and a new marriage so as to avoid adultery, mixing Joseph's food with drugs, whether poison or aphrodisiacs, warning that a refusal of intercourse would drive her to suicide, and making herself as alluring as possible in order to entice him to bed. The virtuous patriarch, however, withstands every temptation through faith in the Lord's precepts, bolstered by fasting, prayer, and dogged self-restraint. Such is the lesson of unyielding chastity that the patriarch passes on to his heirs.[28] Joseph then proceeds to a second lesson, diverging still further from any basis in Scripture. Here he emphasizes the importance of fraternal loyalty and devotion. Despite the treachery of his brothers, Joseph did more than

---

Stone, *Jewish Writings of the Second Temple Period* (Philadelphia, 1984) 331–44; *idem* in R. A. Kraft and G. W. E. Nickelsburg, *Early Judaism and its Modern Interpreters* (Atlanta, 1986) 268–76; H. C. Kee in Charlesworth, *Old Testament Pseudepigrapha*, II, 775–81; D. Mendels, *The Land of Israel as a Political Concept in Hasmonean Literature* (Tübingen, 1987) 89–105; M. Delcor in W. D. Davies and L. Finkelstein, *The Cambridge History of Judaism* (Cambridge, 1989) II, 436–43. On the Testament of Joseph in particular, see G. W. E. Nickelsburg, *Studies on the Testament of Joseph* (Missoula, 1975) 1–12.

27. T. Jos. 1.3–4.

28. T. Jos. 2–10. M. Braun, *History and Romance in Graeco-Oriental Literature* (Oxford, 1938) 44–94, offers a valuable discussion of the narrative in light of motifs found in a wide range of classical literature, especially the Phaedra legend. See also the analysis of H. W. Hollander, *Joseph as an Ethical Model in the Testaments of the Twelve Patriarchs* (Leiden, 1981) 33–42. On the importance of the story for subsequent exegetes, see Kugel, *In Potiphar's House*, 28–124.

forgive them. He avoided any imputation of blame, repeatedly insisting under interrogation that he was a slave of the Ishmaelites, not a free man victimized by his brothers, sticking to his story in the face of torture and imprisonment. The patriarch would thus leave to his sons as legacy the model of unblemished ethical purity.[29] The portrayal, however, omits any reference to Joseph's achievements as chief minister to the crown, as economic czar and governor of the land who set the whole Egyptian system on a new footing. Instead, he emerges as a high-minded but rather priggish prude.

• • •

Hellenistic Jews writing in Greek, mostly in the Diaspora, developed the image of Joseph beyond the one-dimensional ideal of virtuous self-control. Joseph, to be sure, could still stand as ethical model. That aspect, powerfully delineated in the post-biblical tradition, remained prominent. It occurs in the hortatory philosophical tract The Wisdom of Solomon, which seeks to suffuse philosophic wisdom with divine inspiration. The author, among other things, credits Wisdom with rescuing numerous righteous men through the ages, according them glory and reward. One of those men was sold into slavery but saved from sin, bolstered by Wisdom even when in chains. The reference plainly points to Joseph, with emphasis once more upon his unflagging piety.[30] The philosophical orientation of IV Maccabees which retells the martyr stories of the Seleucid persecutions with a blend of Jewish faith and Stoic ethics, naturally finds Joseph to be an appropriate *exemplum*. The author recalls Joseph as a prime instance of reason prevailing over passion: Joseph nobly suppressed his sexual urgings and held unremittingly to the commandment that prohibits adultery.[31] Of course, Joseph's time long preceded delivery of the commandments at Mt. Sinai, a chronological detail that did not worry the composer of IV Maccabees or other Hellenistic writers who made the same point. Divine inspiration gave Joseph insight into

29. T. Jos. 11–18. Cf. W. Harrelson in Nickelsburg, *Studies on the Testament of Joseph*, 29–35; Hollander, *Joseph as an Ethical Model*, 42–48. On references to Joseph in the other Testaments, see Hollander, *op. cit.*, 50–92. For the Testament of Joseph as a Jewish romance, see L. M. Wills, *The Jewish Novel in the Ancient World* (Ithaca, 1995) 163–70.

30. Wisdom 10.13–14. On this work, see D. Winston, *The Wisdom of Solomon* (Garden City, 1979) 3–69, a fine analysis although too confident about a dating in the reign of Caligula. Cf. also Schürer, *History of the Jewish People*, III.1, 568–79, with bibliography.

31. IV Macc. 2.1–6. The work has received much discussion; see the treatment and bibliography in Schürer, *History of the Jewish People*, III.1, 588–93; H. Anderson in Charlesworth, *Old Testament Pseudepigrapha*, II, 531–43.

the morality of abstinence. That lesson echoes in I Maccabees, Wisdom of Solomon, and IV Maccabees in remarkably similar tones. Joseph stands out as emblem of self-restraint, rational control of sexual drive, and dedication to the Law.

Another aspect of the Joseph story, however, got equal billing among Hellenistic Jews: Joseph's swift rise to power and his exercise of dominion in Egypt—a more concrete and pragmatic source of pride. The business-like chronicler Demetrius concerned himself with a range of historical problems, particularly questions of dating, that arise in certain books of the Bible. The fragments of that historian show no interest in the character, personality, or moral dilemmas of biblical personages. Demetrius strives to straighten out chronological discrepancies and solve historical puzzles, thereby to reinforce the credibility of the Scriptures. Hence the historian ignores Joseph as ethical icon withstanding the allure of Frau Potiphar or beneficently forgiving his brothers' transgressions. Demetrius focuses upon reconstructing the chronology of Joseph's career and offering reasons for the unequal distribution of gifts to his brothers. He does not, however, omit to record Joseph's ascendant position in Egypt. According to Demetrius, the Hebrew forebear ruled the land for seven years.[32] This feature, no small matter for Jews in the Greco-Roman period, finds its way also into those texts whose principal concern is with ethical values and moral character. Mattathias' death-bed comments in I Maccabees refer not only to Joseph's obedience to the commandment against adultery but to his reward: he became lord of Egypt.[33] The Wisdom of Solomon reports that divine Wisdom both saved Joseph from the torments of imprisonment and delivered to him the scepter of royal rule that gave him mastery over those who had been his tormentors.[34] And the Jewish epic poet Philo also sets a scepter in Joseph's hand, placing him directly on the throne of the Pharaohs.[35] Joseph's political power in Egypt stirred the pride of Hellenistic Jews.

32. Demetrius *apud* Euseb. *PE* 9.21.12: Ἰωσὴφ ... ἄρξαι Αἰγύπτου ἔτη ἑπτά. On Demetrius, see the cogent remarks of E. Bickerman in J. Neusner, *Christianity, Judaism, and Other Greco-Roman Cults* (Leiden, 1975) III, 72–84. A convenient text, with translation, commentary, and bibliography in C. R. Holladay, *Fragments from Hellenistic Jewish Authors, Vol. I: The Historians* (Chico, 1983) 51–91.

33. I Macc. 2.53: Ἰωσὴφ ἐν καιρῷ στενοχωρίας αὐτοῦ ἐφύλαξεν ἐντολὴν καὶ ἐγένετο κύριος Αἰγύπτου.

34. Wisdom 10.13–14: ἤνεγκεν αὐτῷ σκῆπτρα Βασιλείας καὶ ἐξουσίαν τυραννούντων αὐτοῦ.

35. Philo *apud* Euseb. *PE* 9.24.1: σκηπτοῦχος ἐν Αἰγύπτοιο θρόνοισι. See the text of Philo's fragments, with extensive commentary and references, in Holladay, *Fragments from Hellenistic Jewish Authors, Vol. II: Poets* (Atlanta, 1989) 205–99.

The figure of Joseph, therefore, had appeal to later Jewish sensibilities on two principal fronts: as consummate exemplar of rectitude whose piety embraced biblical precepts and encompassed Greek philosophy, and as preeminent statesman whose special gifts and wide authority brought rational order and system to his adopted land. Both of these conceptions are underscored in the full-scale biographical treatise accorded to Joseph by Philo of Alexandria.

Philo's *De Josepho* aimed above all to outline a model for the ideal statesman. He designed the work as a βίος τοῦ πολιτικοῦ. The treatise itself alternates between a close rendering of the Joseph narrative in Genesis and commentary by Philo, often in the form of his characteristically allegorical interpretations. Philo plainly took as his mission the idealization of Joseph, thus to present him as the epitome of statesmanly qualities.[36] The dubious or questionable features that appear in Genesis are smoothed over or rationalized.

Philo's biography, like much of the Hellenistic literature that precedes it, strains to exalt the character of Joseph. So, for instance, the treatise ascribes Jacob's special feelings for Joseph to his early perception of a noble disposition that set the youth apart from others.[37] The hostility of the brothers, therefore, stems from sheer jealousy, not any arrogance or presumptuousness on Joseph's part.[38] Philo does have Joseph report his dreams, thus infuriating his brothers and even alarming his father, but explains this as mere innocent naiveté.[39] When Jacob sends him to seek out his brothers, Philo gives the most favorable interpretation: Joseph was to give them greeting and inquire after their well-being and that of the flocks.[40] Philo clearly massages the Genesis story to leave no trace of character deficiency in Joseph.

The theme of Joseph's noble spirit recurs repeatedly in Philo's narrative and interpretation. The youth's καλοκαγαθία and εὐγένεια earned him the complete confidence of Potiphar and a free hand in management of

---

36. Cf. A. Priessnig, *Monatsschrift für Geschichte und Wissenschaft des Judentums* 73 (1929) 148–50. On Philo's notion of kingship and use of the Joseph story to advance that notion, see R. Barraclough, *ANRW* II.21.1 (1984) 491–506; Niehoff, *Figure of Joseph*, 54–83. The provocative analysis of E. R. Goodenough, *The Politics of Philo Judaeus: Practice and Theory* (New Haven, 1938) 42–63, sees Philo's treatment of Joseph as a code message, subtly reminding the new rulers of Egypt of how the land should properly be governed.

37. Philo *Jos.* 4: ἐνορῶν οὖν ὁ πατὴρ αὐτῷ φρόνημα εὐγενὲς καὶ μεῖζον ἢ κατ' ἰδιώτην.

38. Philo *Jos.* 5.

39. Philo *Jos.* 6–9: χρώμενος οὖν ἀκάκοις τοῖς ἤθεσι ... ὁ δὲ οὐδὲν ὑπιδόμενος. Cf. Niehoff, *Figure of Joseph*, 65–66.

40. Philo *Jos.* 11.

the entire household—a preview of his skills in administering the polity itself.[41] Philo does not dwell on the attempted seduction by Potiphar's wife, a tale rather marginal for his political theme. Unlike some of the other treatments of that episode, however, he has Joseph reject her advances not because of religious prohibition but because of social and moral obligations to his benefactor, Potiphar. Joseph punctuates the point by contrasting the practices of the Hebrews with the laxity of other peoples.[42] Philo, in short, stresses the superiority of Jewish conventions as well as the moral self-restraint of Joseph—with the appropriate implications for statesmanship.[43] Joseph's καλοκαγαθία also won him the admiration of fellow prisoners and set him in a position of authority even in jail.[44] His qualities immediately declared themselves upon first encounter with the king, leading to his swift elevation to eminence.[45]

Philo further offers a most generous interpretation of Joseph's behavior toward his brothers after their arrival in Egypt. The initial concealment of his identity receives an interesting twist in Philo's hands: it merits praise by contrast with what he *might* have done, namely, exact vengeance through the application of his awesome power. Instead, he curbed his inclinations and elected to hide his relationship to the suppliants.[46] That puts a most liberal construction on Joseph's behavior, but supplies no reason for his deception. The reason surfaces later when Philo accounts for the stratagem that had Benjamin arrested and that terrified the remaining brothers. As in Jubilees, it was merely a test to discover whether there was dissension among the children of Jacob's two wives. When they displayed authentic family solidarity, all could be revealed—and forgiven.[47] Even if the means might be dubious, the motives were noble. Indeed Joseph had protected his brothers' repute throughout, never once disclosing their misdeeds to others, even when he was sorely tried, and he showed his sensitivity at the close of the episode with a private reconciliation, lest any outsider might reproach them.[48]

Joseph proceeded to administer the economy of Egypt with brilliance and effectiveness, while turning down every opportunity for self-aggrandizement

41. Philo *Jos.* 37–39.
42. Philo *Jos.* 42–48.
43. Cf. Philo *Jos.* 54–57.
44. Philo *Jos.* 85–87.
45. Philo *Jos.* 105–106, 117–19.
46. Philo *Jos.* 166.
47. Philo *Jos.* 232–36.
48. Philo *Jos.* 237, 247–48; cf. T. Jos. 11–18.

and self-enrichment.[49] Philo goes so far as to suggest that Joseph not only stabilized the public revenues of Egypt but raised the level of civilization for a people otherwise decidedly inferior in their manner of life.[50] And he ends the treatise with a flourish, assigning to Joseph a host of virtues, including intelligence, eloquence, a balanced disposition, great political and administrative skills, and even good looks.[51]

The lavish praise for Joseph's superior traits of character goes hand in hand with emphasis upon political power. That aspect looms large—and inseparable from moral excellence. Philo places considerable weight upon Joseph's talent in running affairs and his lofty position at the center of governance. He interprets the Hebrew name "Joseph" as equivalent to "addition of a lord" (or perhaps "addition to the Lord") in Greek, thus presaging his hero's career.[52] The coat of many colors also forecasts the statesman's future: it represents the flexibility and variety of means whereby the true leader must deal with a range of contingencies.[53] As already noted, Joseph ran Potiphar's household and then took charge of the very prison in which he was incarcerated. Philo properly notes that when Pharaoh put Joseph in authority at court, the young man, showered with the emblems of power, was technically second in command. He was a διάδοχος.[54] Yet the treatise subtly suggests an ambiguity of roles, even a reversal of positions. When Joseph first encountered the Pharaoh, he was unimpressed by his elevated status and spoke to him more as king to a subject than vice-versa.[55] Even when describing Joseph's appointment as the number two man in the realm, Philo notes that Pharaoh retained only the title of ruler, while Joseph exercised dominion in fact.[56] The Alexandrian underscores the role reversal alluded to in Genesis. Joseph remarks to his brothers that not only does he hold the post of highest honor with Pharaoh but that the latter, though

49. Philo *Jos.* 257–60.
50. Philo *Jos.* 203–204: τὸν ἄλλον χρόνον ... τῆς χώρας ἀμαθέστερον τὰ περὶ δίαιταν ἀγούσης, ὁ ἀνὴρ οὗτος τοῖς κοινοῖς ἐπιστὰς οὐ μόνον τοῖς μεγάλοις πράγμασιν ἥρμοσεν εὐταξίαν ... ἀλλὰ καὶ τοῖς εὐτελεστέροις εἶναι δοκοῦσιν.
51. Philo *Jos.* 268–70.
52. Philo *Jos.* 28: παρὰ μὲν Ἑβραίοις Ἰωσὴφ καλεῖται, παρὰ δ' Ἕλλησι κυρίου πρόσθεσις. See the discussion of V. Nikiprowetzky, *REJ* 127 (1968) 387–92.
53. Philo *Jos.* 32–34.
54. Philo *Jos.* 119–20, 148–50, 166.
55. Philo *Jos.* 107: ὁ δὲ ταξίωμα τοῦ λέγοντος οὐδὲν καταπλαγεὶς ὥσπερ ὑπηκόῳ βασιλεύς, ἀλλ' οὐχ ὑπήκοος βασιλεῖ ... διελέγετο.
56. Philo *Jos.* 119: τὸ μὲν ὄνομα τῆς ἀρχῆς ὑπολειπόμενος αὐτῷ, τῆς δ' ἐν ἔργοις ἡγεμονίας ἐκστὰς ἐκείνῳ.

the older man, reveres him as a father.[57] The Joseph of Philo's *De Josepho* represents more than the abstract image of the ideal statesman. His exercise of power in Egypt rescued the land and its people, turned Pharaoh himself into a subordinate, and made preservation of the Egyptian legacy dependent upon a forefather of the Jews.

The golden image, however, becomes tarnished elsewhere. The Joseph tale in Genesis opened itself to diverse interpretations. And Joseph's image in the Hellenistic period could be turned to various ends. Philo himself, who manipulated the figure of the patriarch to advance his own conception of model statesmanship, also refashioned it to express undesirable characteristics and detrimental qualities. In his tract *On Dreams*, Philo takes a stunningly different line on Joseph. The youthful dreamer's report on his nocturnal visions was far from naive and inoffensive. It exhibited boastfulness and presumptuousness. Philo, in fact, surprises the reader by setting the conventional interpretation on its head. He justifies the brothers' righteous indignation against Joseph as appropriate resistance to premature over-reaching.[58] A still more ambitious dream earned him the sharp rebuke of Jacob.[59] The coat of many colors, which Philo interpreted in the *De Josepho* as signifying laudable political flexibility, gets a more sinister exegesis in the *De Somnis*: it symbolizes craftiness, deceit, and insincerity.[60] Joseph becomes emblematic of the shifting temperament that pursues diverse aims with no stability of purpose.[61] Pride and pomposity take over. The dignities and honors bestowed upon him as Pharaoh's right hand man constitute not rightful elevation to power but hybristic ambition aimed at eradicating equality.[62] Joseph's elation at the trappings of high office discloses his empty vanity.[63] Grandiose self-importance induced him to exalt himself over people, cities, laws, and ancestral practices.[64] The name "Joseph," rendered by Philo as "addition of a lord" in the *De Josepho* and thus forecasting his proper station, becomes in *De Somnis* the addition of meaningless, corrupting, and alien features to one's

---

57. Philo *Jos.* 242: τιμὴν δὲ ἔχω τὴν πρώτην παρὰ τῷ βασιλεῖ καὶ μὲ νέον ὄντα πρεσβύτερος ὢν ὡς πατέρα τιμᾷ. Cf. Jub. 43.19. Note also Pharaoh's respectful awe towards Jacob, his treating the Israelite patriarch as if he were his own father; Philo *Jos.* 257.

58. Philo *Somn.* 2.93–100.

59. Philo *Somn.* 2.110–13.

60. Philo *Somn.* 1.219–20.

61. Philo *Somn.* 2.10–11.

62. Philo *Somn.* 2.15–16: ἐμφαίνεται καὶ τὸ τῆς κενῆς δόξης, ἐφ' ἣν ὡς ἐφ' ἅρμα διὰ τὸ κοῦφον ἀναβαίνει, φυσώμενος καὶ μετέωρον αἰωρῶν ἑαυτὸν ἐπὶ καθειρέσει ἰσότητος.

63. Philo *Somn.* 2.42–46.

64. Philo *Somn.* 2.78–79.

natural character, unnecessary material goods and wealth to innate quality.[65] Or, in another formulation elsewhere, the name "Joseph" is tantamount to the mentality of the politician who seeks to juggle human and divine values, shifting back and forth between true and apparent virtue.[66] The assessment of the biblical figure's character here takes on a much more cynical cast.

The inconsistencies and tensions in this dual portrait create a baffling paradox.[67] How to account for Philo's glowing tribute to Joseph in his biographical treatise and his censorious disapproval elsewhere? On one theory, Philo employs the Joseph figure as a smokescreen to advance political ideas growing out of his immediate experience in an Alexandria governed by incompetent and malevolent Roman prefects. The *De Josepho*, therefore, constitutes a form of mirror for princes in which Joseph represents the ideal governor whom Roman officials should emulate, whereas the Joseph of *De Somnis* serves as whipping boy for Philo's criticisms, a surrogate for the Roman regime in Alexandria. The inconsistency, on this view, is deliberate and calculated, a twisting of the Joseph character for political ends, depending upon intended audience: the *De Josepho* for Gentile readers, the *De Somnis* for Jews.[68] Alternatively, one might postulate a change of mind or change of direction by Philo, who composed these works at different times and under different circumstances. The *De Josepho* thus presents a general philosophy of proper governance, whereas the *De Somnis* was composed as reaction to the turmoil and anti-Semitism provoked or aggravated by the Roman prefect Avillius Flaccus—or possibly even by Philo's nephew, the apostate Jew Ti. Julius Alexander.[69] In a quite different vein, it can be argued that

65. Philo *Somn.* 2.47, 2.63; *Mut.* 89–90; *Migr.* 203–204.

66. Philo *Migr.* 158–63: μεθόριον ἀνθρωπίνων τε καὶ θείων ἀρετῶν τιθέντες, ἵν' ἑκατέρων ἐφάπτωνται, καὶ τῶν ἀληθείᾳ καὶ τῶν δοκήσει.

67. A summary of scholarship on Philo's inconsistencies generally in R. Hamerton-Kelly, *Studia Philonica* 1 (1972) 3–26.

68. So Goodenough, *Politics of Philo Judaeus*, 21–63. See also J. Laporte, *De Josepho* (*Les Oeuvres de Philon d'Alexandrie*, 21) (Paris, 1964) 13–18; A. M. Goldberg, *Bibel u. Kirche* 21 (1966) 13–14; S. Sandmel, *Philo of Alexandria: An Introduction* (New York, 1979) 103.

69. See Barraclough, *ANRW* II.21.2 (1984) 491–506, who devotes most of his discussion to arguing with Goodenough, only to accept his basic premise that Philo had two different political objectives in mind when composing the two works; see especially 501–502. In general Barraclough stresses the influence of Greek philosophy and Hellenistic theory of kingship, rather than particular efforts to criticize Roman rule. But he offers little help in accounting for the inconsistencies in the Joseph presentations. That Philo's negative depiction of Joseph represents Ti. Julius Alexander is a thesis independently arrived at by D. R. Schwartz, *The Studia Philonica Annual* 1 (1989) 63–73, and R. Kraft in B. Pearson, *The Future of Early Christianity* (Minneapolis, 1991) 131–41. But chronological difficulties compromise that idea, requiring either a quite elderly Philo composing allegorical treatises after Ti. Julius Alexander's

Philo's divergent treatments depend upon the method adopted in a particular treatise. Philo designed the *De Josepho* as a relatively straightforward and faithful recreation of the Genesis story, drawing out the lessons for ideal rulership through allegorical commentary. Elsewhere, however, as in the *De Somnis*, an individual figure is himself allegorized, Joseph becoming emblematic of κενὴ δόξα, vacuous glory, and a vehicle for Philo to attack a human character flaw.[70] It is even possible to soften the inconsistencies between the two texts and find a certain amount of common ground between the ostensibly conflicting portraits. The *De Somnis* indeed holds out hope for Joseph's reformation and his brothers' reconciliation with him (not vice-versa), symbolized by Joseph's wish to have his bones buried in the homeland.[71] Or, on another theory, Philo's allegorical methods contrast the symbolic meanings of Israel and Egypt, manipulating the Joseph figure accordingly.[72]

The diverse explanations need not here be weighed and assessed. Whatever one's view of Philo's intentions and objectives, striking discrepancies remain in the images of Joseph transmitted in his works. And that has important implications. The predominantly positive picture of the abstemious, though rather sanctimonious, patriarch, the self-restrained, wise, and upright ruler, that appears in Hellenistic texts like Jubilees, Pseudo-Philo, the *Testaments of the Twelve Patriarchs*, The Wisdom of Solomon, I Maccabees, IV Maccabees, and Philo's *De Josepho*, did not altogether repress the more dubious characteristics of the manipulator, the artful schemer, and the man enamored of worldly goods and power. The latter was certainly no invention of Philo's. He observes that ascription of the name "Joseph" to the disposition of the politician who moves between real and merely ostensible virtue

---

prefecture of Egypt in 66 CE or the postulate of reaction to him in some lesser capacity earlier on. Neither hypothesis is compelling.

70. See Hilgert, *Biblical Research* 30 (1985) 7–13, drawing on the analysis of Philo's exegetical methods by B. Mack, *Studia Philonica* 3 (1974/1975) 71–112. This explanation would not, however, easily account for divergent attitudes within the same treatise, as, e.g., *Migr.* 17–22, 158.

71. Philo *Somn.* 2.105–109; cf. *Migr.* 16–22. See the analysis of J. Bassler, *JSJ* 16 (1985) 240–55. Alternatively, one can discern in *De Josepho* 34–36 intimations that the maneuverability of the statesman, emblematized by the coat of many colors, can border on the fickleness of the demagogue, beholden to the whims of the populace—a notion comparable to *Somn.* 2.10–11. Ambiguous rather than purely positive implications can be read also in *De Josepho*, 28–31; cf. Nikiprowetzky, *REJ* 127 (1968) 387–92. Niehoff's discussion of Philo's views, *Figure of Joseph*, 54–83, takes no note of any text beyond the *De Josepho*.

72. J. Cazeaux in J. F. Kenney, *The School of Moses: Studies in Philo and Hellenistic Religion* (Atlanta, 1995) 41–81.

was a conventional one.[73] Similarly, attraction to material goods and the comforts of the body, according to Philo, customarily receive the designation of "Joseph" as well.[74] All of this suggests that for Hellenistic Jews Joseph was more persona than personage, an acknowledged literary artifice available and versatile. No monolithic figure determined the discourse. The ambiguities of Joseph's personality and achievements made him readily malleable to serve a variety of purposes. For Philo the moralizing ends took precedence. In the hands of other writers, more imaginative constructs could emerge.

•   •   •

Artapanus offers a useful case in point. A Hellenized Jew in Egypt, he composed a work on the Jews which seems to have combined a refashioning of biblical stories, historical reconstruction, and inventive fiction. The genre of the work, if any, can hardly now be ascertained. Only a few fragments survive, quoted by Alexander Polyhistor and preserved by Eusebius. The Egyptian context of the fragments gives Artapanus' provenance and Polyhistor provides a date prior to the early first century BCE. Moderns frequently label his work as "competitive" or "apologetic" history, a response to writers hostile to the Jews, a defense of the biblical past against critics like Manetho.[75] That may not be the most profitable approach. Discussion has dwelled almost entirely upon the lengthiest extant fragment, that on Moses. Apologetic tendencies even there take a back seat to creative retelling. In the extract on Joseph, they can barely be detected, and, in any case, need not be hypothesized. Artapanus freely adapted and molded the Genesis story to his own taste.

The fragment is compact and highly condensed. But it discloses clearly enough the scope available for Hellenistic writers to reshape biblical traditions. Artapanus interestingly reconceives the narrative of Joseph's transfer from Palestine to Egypt. The young man's brothers conspired against him

73. Philo *Migr.* 158–59: τούτου τοῦ δόγματος ὁ πολιτευόμενός ἐστι τρόπος, ὃν Ἰωσὴφ ὀνομάζειν ἔθος.

74. Philo *Migr.* 203: τοῦ καὶ τὸ σῶμα καὶ τὰ ἐκτὸς ἀσπαζομένου, ὃν ἔθος καλεῖν Ἰωσήφ. Rightly noted by Hilgert, *Biblical Research* 30 (1985) 10–11.

75. See, e.g., J. Freudenthal, *Alexander Polyhistor* (Breslau, 1874/1875) 143–74, 215–18; P. M. Fraser, *Ptolemaic Alexandria* (Oxford, 1972) 704–706; N. Walter, *Jüdische Schriften aus hellenistischer und römischer Zeit* (Gütersloh, 1976) I.2, 121–26; Holladay, *Theios Aner in Hellenistic Judaism* (Missoula, 1977) 199–232; *idem, Fragments*, I, 189–93; J. J. Collins, *Between Athens and Jerusalem* (New York, 1983) 32–38; *idem* in Charlesworth, *Old Testament Pseudepigrapha*, II, 889–95; Schürer, *History of the Jewish People*, III.1, 521–24; E. Gabba in Davies and Finkelstein, *Cambridge History of Judaism*, II, 639–40. On Artapanus as Hellenized Jew, see below, p. 150.

because he surpassed them in knowledge and intelligence. But, instead of falling into their trap, Joseph foresaw the plot and persuaded some neighboring Arabs to convey him to Egypt.[76] Joseph landed in Egypt, therefore, through his own shrewdness, escaping the machinations of his brothers, not victimized by them. For Artapanus, he engineered the sequence of events, an account sharply divergent from the Genesis tale. Upon arrival in Egypt, Joseph became acquainted with the king and was installed as his chief economic minister, in charge of the entire land.[77] Not a word about Joseph as dream interpreter—let alone about a stint in prison as target of Mrs. Potiphar's spleen. Joseph evidently impressed Pharaoh with his talent and intellect upon first encounter and received his lofty post immediately, no sorcery or divine intervention needed. And the new minister proceeded to restructure Egyptian agriculture, placing land tenure for the first time on an equitable footing. He put an end to exploitation of the weak by the powerful, allocating possessions in designated lots, with clearly delineated boundaries, bringing neglected land back into cultivation, and setting aside property for the priests.[78] This account, truncated and terse though it be, is a far cry from the biblical narrative. The Book of Genesis describes Joseph's agricultural changes as extending royal authority and ownership and making the peasantry of Egypt dependent upon the crown.[79] Artapanus evidently felt free to ignore the testimony of the Scriptures. Further, he omitted the whole rationale for Joseph's policy as given in Genesis, the need to shore up resources in the years of plenty in order to preserve them for the coming famine. For Artapanus, Joseph received his post simply to reorganize the country's economic system.[80] The subsequent arrival of Jacob and the brothers appears unmotivated by any crisis, merely a reunion with Joseph and a resettlement.[81] More striking still, Artapanus makes Joseph the discoverer

76. Euseb. *PE* 9.23.1: συνέσει δὲ καὶ φρονήσει παρὰ τοὺς ἄλλους διενεγκόντα ὑπὸ τῶν ἀδελφῶν ἐπιβουλευθῆναι. προιδόμενον δὲ τὴν ἐπισύστασιν δεηθῆναι τῶν ἀστυγειτόνων Ἀράβων εἰς τὴν Αἴγυπτον αὐτὸν διακομίσαι.

77. Euseb. *PE* 9.23.2: ἐλθόντα δὲ αὐτὸν εἰς τὴν Αἴγυπτον καὶ συσταθέντα τῷ βασιλεῖ διοικητὴν τῆς ὅλης γενέσθαι χώρας.

78. Euseb. *PE* 9.23.2: τοῦτον πρῶτον τήν τε γῆν διελεῖν καὶ ὅροις διασημήνασθαι καὶ πολλὴν χερσευομένην γεωργήσιμον ἀποτελέσαι καί τινας τῶν ἀρουρῶν τοῖς ἱερεῦσιν ἀποκληρῶσαι.

79. Gen. 47.13–26.

80. The last sentence of the fragment as reported by Eusebius does make allusion to the storage of grain surplus during seven years of plenty; *PE* 9.23.4. But the passage is out of place, unconnected, and inconsistent with what went before, an afterthought at best and perhaps wrongly inserted and attributed to Artapanus; cf. Walter, *Jüdische Schriften*, III.2, 287.

81. Euseb. *PE* 9.23.3.

of measurements, a lasting contribution for which he was much beloved by the Egyptians.[82]

Artapanus' reconstruction plainly used the biblical tale as no more than a springboard. He cast his Joseph in a very different mold. In the preserved fragments divine aid plays no part, moral lessons are absent, and the hero's inner character is irrelevant. Joseph appears as a clever calculator who impressed the Pharaoh, a farsighted economic reformer, and even a pragmatic inventor. Artapanus' version skirts any ethical concerns. His Joseph merits neither praise for self-control nor blame for ambition and material desires. The trappings of power, for good or ill, make no appearance in the text. Joseph gained authority through his wits and employed it to reorder the institutional structure of Egypt. That nation owes its success, in short, to the brains of an Israelite.

• • •

A remarkable text highlights still further the malleability of the Joseph figure and the multiple forms which it could take. The romantic story, *Joseph and Aseneth*, moves in a realm quite different from those discussed above, that of novelistic fantasy. Genesis provides barely a pretext for this invention. The Scriptures report only that Pharaoh gave to Joseph as his wife Aseneth, daughter of Potiphar the priest of On, and that she subsequently bore him two children.[83] All else is embellishment. And *Joseph and Aseneth* embellishes in style.

A summary of the yarn would be apposite. Joseph, gathering grain in the course of his duties as Pharaoh's agricultural minister at the outset of seven plenteous years, reached the territory of Heliopolis. There he encountered the eminent Pentephres, priest of Heliopolis, a royal official of the highest station, adviser to Pharaoh, and a man close to the throne. Pentephres had a beautiful eighteen-year-old daughter, Aseneth, likened by the author of the tale to the most celebrated women of the patriarchal age, Sarah, Rebecca, and Rachel. Aseneth, however, like Puccini's Turandot, scorned all men and rudely rejected suitors from noble houses in Egypt and royal families elsewhere. Pharaoh's son himself pressed hard for her hand but was overruled by his father who preferred a match with another ruling house. The report of Aseneth's celebrated beauty depended upon rumor rather than witnesses, for

---

82. Euseb. *PE* 9.23.3: τοῦτον δὲ καὶ μέτρα εὑρεῖν καὶ μεγάλως αὐτὸν ὑπὸ τῶν Αἰγυπτίων διὰ ταῦτα ἀγαπηθῆναι.

83. Gen. 41.45, 41.50–52, 46.20.

she shut herself up in a lofty tower, not to be seen—let alone touched—by any man.[84] Pentephres, upon learning of Joseph's imminent arrival, immediately proposed that Aseneth be betrothed to this righteous, pious, and powerful man. But Aseneth recoiled in anger: she would have nothing to do with one who was a stranger in the land, a shepherd's son from Canaan, sold as a slave and imprisoned as an adulterer. The arrogant Aseneth would accept marriage only with the son of Pharaoh.[85] Once the young maiden spied Joseph from her bedroom window, however, everything turned topsy-turvy. Aseneth was smitten and, her haughty aloofness immediately abandoned, she was overcome with self-reproach that she had despised as a shepherd's son one who turned out to be a dazzling divinity.[86] Joseph himself had his doubts when he caught a glimpse of Aseneth: he feared that she was yet another predatory female determined to bed him, like Potiphar's wife and a host of others who could not keep their hands off him. But Pentephres reassured his noble guest: Aseneth was a man-hating, committed virgin, and no threat to Joseph's chastity. Pentephres then brought the two people together, even suggesting that they exchange a kiss as brother and sister, only to have Joseph recoil this time from the eager Aseneth. The purist devotee of a sole god would have no congress of any kind with an idolatress. Joseph took some pity on the crestfallen Aseneth, offering up a prayer to the Lord to have her mend her ways and acknowledge the true god, for only such a drastic conversion could justify any relationship.[87] Aseneth grasped at the hope and turned her religious life around at a stroke. Much weeping and wailing ensued as she repented of former heresies, removed all false idols from her home, and fell to fasting and mourning, self-flagellation and humiliation, uttering desperate prayers to her newly found god, seeking forgiveness for past sins and rescue from the fury of spurned divinities.[88]

The maiden's prayers were answered. An angel of the Lord materialized, resplendently garbed, bathed in light, with sparks shooting forth from hands and feet. He braced the young woman's courage, offered her absolution for prior offenses, proclaimed her acceptance by God, and bade her put off sackcloth and dress herself in bridal attire to prepare for a wedding with Joseph. The happy encounter climaxed with a ritual meal, featuring a magical honeycomb and bees. The angel then flew off in a fiery chariot,

---

84. *Jos. As.* 1–2.
85. *Jos. As.* 3–4.
86. *Jos. As.* 5–6.
87. *Jos. As.* 7–8.
88. *Jos. As.* 9–13.

pulled by lightning-like steeds.[89] Aseneth's new dress restored her to the fullness of her beauty. And when Joseph returned for a second visit, she declared her renunciation of false idols and embrace of the true god. Joseph's kisses now came freely, infusing his betrothed with the spirit of life, wisdom, and truth. Pentephres offered to host the wedding festivities, but Joseph declined, preferring to have Pharaoh himself preside over the ceremonies. The king therefore gave the bride away, placed crowns on the heads of the couple, and sponsored a spectacular banquet that lasted for seven days. The marriage was consummated, and Aseneth subsequently produced two sons as Joseph's legacy.[90]

The happy ending, however, had not yet come. A second part of the tale, quite different from the love story that preceded, now takes the narrative in a new direction. The seven years of plenty had come and gone, famine set in, and Joseph's family migrated from Palestine. Internal friction began to show itself both in the Hebrew patriarch's household and in that of Pharaoh. Joseph's brothers Simeon and Levi, the sons of Leah, immediately took joy in the company of Aseneth, while other brothers, the offspring of Leah's and Rachel's servants, felt only envy and hostility. Further, Pharaoh's son, still nursing fierce resentment at the loss of Aseneth, determined to take her by foul means. He hoped to win over Joseph's brothers for a plot to murder Joseph and carry off Aseneth. Simeon and Levi refused firmly, the former dissuaded from assaulting Pharaoh's son only by Levi's pacifist stand. But the villain of the piece did have success with other brothers, notably Dan and Gad who proved willing to share in the nefarious enterprise. They would lead Egyptian armed men in an ambush of Aseneth and her entourage, to be followed by massacre of Joseph and his sons, while the heir to the throne prepared to murder his own father.[91] The schemes, of course, were foiled. The Egyptians cut down Aseneth's companions, forcing her to flee, with Pharaoh's sons and fifty men at her heels. Fortunately, however, Benjamin, now a strapping lad of eighteen, stood with Aseneth in her chariot. Leaping from the vehicle, he launched fifty stones, each of which felled an Egyptian, including Pharaoh's offspring. The sons of Leah wiped out the remaining foes. And when the other brothers made a final effort to slay Benjamin and Aseneth, their swords miraculously fell to the ground and dissolved into ashes.[92] The sons of Leah, headed by Simeon, sought vengeance upon their

89. *Jos. As.* 14–17.
90. *Jos. As.* 18–21.
91. *Jos. As.* 22–25.
92. *Jos. As.* 26–27.

evil half-brothers, threatening a new blood bath. But Aseneth intervened to urge forgiveness and concord. The peace-loving Levi then stayed Benjamin's hand when he attempted to finish off Pharaoh's helpless son. Their enemies were thus spared—those who survived. Pharaoh prostrated himself before Levi in gratitude. His heir, however, perished anyway from the effects of the wound, thus bringing about the death of the grief-stricken Pharaoh himself shortly thereafter. But not before the ailing ruler turned his kingdom over to Joseph, bestowing upon him the diadem that signaled royal authority. Joseph then reigned as monarch of Egypt for forty-eight years, before yielding the diadem in turn to Pharaoh's youngest son whom Joseph had treated as his own child through all those years.[93]

So ends the narrative, an edifying and uplifting one. In fact, it consists of two narratives, a love story followed by an adventure tale, the two only loosely connected with one another. Its strikingly unusual character has called forth an extensive scholarly literature. Controversy swirls around the language, date, provenance, genre, message, and audience of the text.[94] Mercifully, most of the discussions have only a marginal bearing on our subject and the issues can be treated with brevity. A broad consensus now holds that the original language of the piece was Greek rather than Hebrew. The influence of Septuagintal vocabulary is readily documentable, as is the presence of Greek philosophical ideas. By contrast, no trace survives of a Semitic original, and later rabbinical versions of the Aseneth tale seem quite unaware of this one.[95] The work very probably emanated from Jewish circles. Christian interpolations, if any, are few and conjectural. The text as a whole betrays little knowledge of Christian ideas and advances no Christian doctrines.[96] Attribution to any particular Jewish sect, whether Pharisees, Essenes, Therapeutae, or others is highly speculative and largely pointless.[97]

93. *Jos. As.* 28–29.

94. See now the thorough and analytic review of the scholarship by R. D. Chesnutt, *From Death to Life: Conversion in Joseph and Aseneth* (Sheffield, 1995) 20–93.

95. See, especially, C. Burchard, *Untersuchungen zur Joseph und Aseneth* (Tübingen, 1965) 91–99; M. Philonenko, *Joseph et Aséneth* (Leiden, 1968) 27–32, 53–57; G. Delling, *JSJ* 9 (1978) 29–56; Chesnutt, *From Death to Life*, 69–71.

96. See the arguments of V. Aptowitzer, *HUCA* 1 (1924) 260–86; M. Delcor, *BullLittEccl* 63 (1962) 5–22; Burchard, *Untersuchungen*, 99–107; Philonenko, *Joseph et Aséneth*, 99–102; Chesnutt, *From Death to Life*, 71–76. The effort of T. Holtz, *NTS* 14 (1967–1968) 482–97, to revive the Christian hypothesis has won few converts. Additional bibliography in Collins, *Between Athens and Jerusalem*, 239, n. 72. The whole matter will undergo a thorough reassessment, however, in a forthcoming book by Ross Kraemer.

97. The sensible remarks of Burchard, *Untersuchungen*, 107–12, merit reading on this score, with references to earlier views. See further D. Sänger, *Antikes Judentum und die Mysterien*

Composition by a Jewish writer or writers, presupposing awareness of the Septuagint, with a narrative setting in Egypt, suggests but by no means proves an Egyptian provenance.[98]

Efforts to pinpoint the date of composition founder for lack of any clear historical references. In a work of imaginative fiction, the search for such allusions may itself be illusory. The scenario of Egypt in the patriarchal period hardly lends itself to precise parallels with Ptolemaic or Roman society, and it would be misguided to manufacture them. The author's familiarity with Septuagintal language would place the text no earlier than the late third century BCE. A *terminus ante quem* remains beyond our grasp. Even the standard assumption that it must precede Hadrianic times on the ground that no conversion narrative would have been produced thereafter depends on the notion that this *is* a conversion narrative—an unestablished premise. The attitudes reflected therein with regard to relations between Jews and Gentiles, tense but resolvable, may tip the balance slightly toward a Ptolemaic rather than a Roman setting. Comparable attitudes are discernible in works like the *Letter of Aristeas*, III Maccabees, and the writings of Artapanus. Beyond that it would be unsafe to go.[99]

The genre of *Joseph and Aseneth* has, of course, evoked discussion and commentary. Obvious affinities exist between the work and Greek romances like those of Chariton, Heliodorus, Achilles Tatius, or Xenophon of Ephesus, affinities rightly stressed by most moderns. Yet the erotic features are subordinated in the first part of the narrative and altogether absent in the second. Indeed the love story and the adventure tale in *Joseph and Aseneth*

(Tübingen, 1980) 22–58; Chesnutt, *From Death to Life*, 185–216. Cf. Collins, *Between Athens and Jerusalem*, 218. Further literature noted by Chesnutt, *JSP* 2 (1988) 45, nn. 7–11.

98. Most opt for Egyptian origins: e.g. Burchard, *Untersuchungen*, 142–43; Philonenko, *Joseph et Aséneth*, 102–108; Chesnutt, *From Death to Life*, 76–80. Some skepticism expressed by S. West, *CQ* 68 (1974) 79, without alternatives offered. The proposition is also questioned by A. Standhartinger, *Das Frauenbild im Judentum der hellenistischen Zeit: Ein Beitrag anhand von "Joseph und Aseneth"* (Leiden, 1995) 14–16. Philonenko, *op. cit.*, 61–79, strains to make the case that Aseneth's portrait is modeled on that of the Egyptian goddess Neith; accepted by M. Goodman in Schürer, *History of the Jewish People*, III.1, 548, but adequately refuted by D. Sänger, *JSJ* 10 (1979) 13–20.

99. Among efforts to locate a more precise time, all speculative and inconclusive, see Aptowitzer, *HUCA* 1 (1924) 286–306; Delcor, *BullLittEccl* 63 (1962) 26–27; Burchard, *Untersuchungen*, 143–51; Philonenko, *Joseph et Aséneth*, 108–109; Sänger, *ZNW* 76 (1985) 90–104; G. Bohak, *Joseph and Aseneth and the Jewish Temple in Heliopolis* (Atlanta, 1996) 84–87. More cautious and sagacious remarks by West, *CQ* 68 (1974) 79–81; cf. Collins, *Between Athens and Jerusalem*, 89–91; Burchard in Charlesworth, *Old Testament Pseudepigrapha*, II, 187–88; Chesnutt, *From Death to Life*, 80–85; Standhartinger, *Das Frauenbild*, 16–20. A much later date in the Christian era will be defended in Kraemer's forthcoming work.

bear relatively little relation to one another. Other parallels can be found in Jewish fiction of contemporary or near contemporary eras, like Judith, Esther, and Tobit. Here again the pattern is not perfect. Romantic elements play an insignificant role in those narratives, and differences loom larger than similarities. The conversion in *Joseph and Aseneth* prompts a comparison with mystical tales and sacred epiphanies, as in Apuleius' *Metamorphoses*. But that places too much weight upon a particular aspect of the work and does not account for the bulk of it. Additional speculation would pay few dividends. Placement of *Joseph and Aseneth* in a particular genre, even if that were an appropriate process, cannot illuminate the intent and significance of the tale.[100]

The work is not readily classifiable, nor is its objective readily definable. The "conversion" aspect has perhaps received undue emphasis. Most commentators ascribe a missionary purpose to *Joseph and Aseneth*, with Aseneth's adoption of Joseph's religion and his god seen as the core of the narrative, the tract aimed at demonstrating the value of embracing Judaism.[101] The text as a whole, however, gives small comfort to that idea. Joseph certainly conducts no active campaign to convert Aseneth, nor is he present when the conversion takes place. The heroine's adoption of Judaism did not inspire professions of the new faith by any other character in the tale, not even those like Pentephres and Pharaoh who show conspicuous favor to the religion. One might observe, in fact, that no mention of "Jew" or "Gentile" occurs in the text. Aseneth's transformation essentially meant abandonment of idolatry. The very concept of active Jewish proselytism in this period is debatable. *Joseph and Aseneth*, in any case, would hardly stimulate it. The work,

---

100. On *Joseph and Aseneth* as a Hellenistic romance, see Philonenko, *Joseph et Aséneth*, 43–47; West, *CQ* 68 (1974) 71–77; Burchard in W. C. van Unnik, *La littérature juive entre Tenach et Mischna* (Leiden, 1974) 84–96. For parallels with Jewish fiction, see Burchard, *Untersuchugen*, 106–107. The influence of the mystical tradition is emphasized by Kee, *NTS* 29 (1983) 394–413. That aspect is given fuller but more skeptical treatment by Sänger, *Antikes Judentum*, 88–190, evidently unknown to Kee. See also Chesnutt, *From Death to Life*, 217–53. A variation on earlier ideas was advanced by R. I. Pervo, *SBL Seminar Papers* (1976) 171–81, who set *Joseph and Aseneth* in a Jewish sapiential tradition, but oddly applied that characteristic to works like Daniel, Judith, Esther, and Tobit which hardly qualify as wisdom literature. Wills, *Jewish Novel*, 170–84, sees two layers of composition, a national hero romance overlaid by a symbolic conversion story. Ingenuity will allow the detection of whatever one wishes to emphasize in the text. Even echoes of the Homeric *Iliad* have been discovered in the second part of the narrative; Philonenko, *Joseph et Aséneth*, 41–43. The recent and stimulating but highly speculative thesis of Bohak, *Joseph and Aseneth, passim*, sees the work as a fictional history designed to justify Onias' temple in Heliopolis.

101. See, e.g., Aptowitzer, *HUCA* 1 (1924) 299–306; Philonenko, *Joseph et Aséneth*, 53–61; Collins, *From Athens to Jerusalem*, 217–18; Nickelsburg in Stone, *Jewish Writings*, 67–70.

presupposing familiarity with the tales of the patriarchs in the Septuagint, can have found few knowledgeable Gentile readers. And an author engaged in missionary efforts would not likely feature a story in which the impulse to conversion came from the convert's passion for her intended lover![102]

The imaginative tale of Joseph and Aseneth offers insight into a matter of broader consequence than chronology, provenance, literary genre, or even proselytism: the relation between Jew and Gentile in the Diaspora. Scholars often interpret the text as pitting the two cultures against one another. Joseph's insistence upon the purity of the faith and the pollution of idolatry, Aseneth's abject debasement and thorough break with her past to achieve absolution, the rigorous separation of Jews and Egyptians, and the favor of God supporting the faithful against their idolatrous opponents all seem to suggest a stark dichotomy between the forces of good and evil.[103] But the breakdown is not so simple and the polarity not so sharp. Friction exists after all *within* each of the two communities. Joseph's brothers engage in potentially murderous activities against one another, and Pharaoh's son plots the assassination of the king. The fact that the wedding of Joseph and Aseneth takes place under the auspices of Pharaoh, who had not himself become a convert, holds central symbolic significance. The enemies of the faithful had been forgiven, harmony and reconciliation followed, and the Gentile ruler of Egypt presided over the union of Hebrew patriarch and

---

102. See the climax of Aseneth's prayer for acceptance by the Lord—so that she might be a maidservant and slave for Joseph; *Jos. As.* 13.11–12. Doubts about the missionary character of the tale have been expressed by West, *CQ* 68 (1974) 78; Sänger, *Antikes Judentum,* 209–15; *idem,* *JSJ* 10 (1979) 33–36; *idem,* *ZNW* 76 (1985) 94–95; Burchard in Charlesworth, *Old Testament Pseudepigrapha,* II, 194–95; Chesnutt, *JSP* 2 (1988) 37–40; Bohak, *Joseph and Aseneth,* 88–90. Sänger's idea that it aimed to promote mixed marriages, however, has little to recommend it. So, rightly, Delcor in Davies and Finkelstein, *Cambridge History of Judaism,* II, 503. Chesnutt's extensive study, *From Death to Life,* 153–84, 254–65, questions proselytism as a motive but still sees conversion as the central motif of the work, its objective to enhance the status of Gentile converts in Jewish eyes. See also J. M. G. Barclay, *Jews in the Mediterranean Diaspora* (Edinburgh, 1996) 204–16, who reckons Aseneth's conversion as the principal theme but regards it as a vehicle to underscore the sharp differentiation between Jews and Gentiles. On the question of Jewish proselytism generally, see S. McKnight, *A Light among the Gentiles* (Minneapolis, 1991) *passim*; E. Will and C. Orrieux, *"Prosélytisme Juif"? Histoire d'une erreur* (Paris, 1992) 81–137; M. Goodman, *Mission and Conversion* (Oxford, 1994) 60–90, with references to earlier literature; P. Schäfer, *Judeophobia: Attitudes toward Jews in the Ancient World* (Cambridge, Mass., 1997) 106–18. A different view in L. H. Feldman, *Jew and Gentile in the Ancient World* (Princeton, 1993) 288–341; P. Borgen, *Early Christianity and Hellenistic Judaism* (Edinburgh, 1996) 45–69.

103. Philonenko, *Joseph et Aséneth,* 48–52; Collins, *Between Athens and Jerusalem,* 212–13; Sänger, *ZNW* 76 (1985) 96–100; Chesnutt, *JSP* 2 (1988) 22–30; *From Death to Life,* 97–108; Barclay, *Jews in the Mediterranean Diaspora,* 204–16.

the daughter of an Egyptian priest. The fable plainly promotes concord between the communities. Equally important, it asserts the superiority of Jewish traditions and morality—even against some Jews themselves.

Aseneth holds central place in the narrative, and scholarly focus has properly concentrated upon her.[104] The figure of Joseph, however, occupies our attention. His treatment in a work of imaginative fancy, a form quite different from the other literary contexts in which he appears, adds a valuable dimension to the image of the patriarch in the Hellenistic era.

Joseph as the embodiment of piety and purity comes through loud and clear. But that aspect of character is by no means an unmixed blessing. Joseph's fussiness bespeaks a cramped disposition, and his public display of abstinence borders on the offensive. Upon entrance into Pentephres' house, he immediately planted himself upon his host's "throne" (evidently Pentephres' official seat as royal representative).[105] He took his meal in private, for he would not eat with Egyptians, an abomination in his view.[106] Having caught a glimpse of Aseneth at her window, Joseph leaped to the conclusion that she was yet another in the long line of females who lusted after his body. And he did not hesitate to recount to Pentephres his stoical resistance to the flocks of beauties, the wives and daughters of Egyptian aristocrats and royal appointees, and indeed women of all classes, who were desperate to sleep with so handsome a creature. Joseph, of course, so he announced, was impervious to their charms and scorned the costly gifts with which they sought to win his affection.[107] This was not behavior designed to endear him to his hosts—who, however, were too dazzled by his position to care. Joseph consented to receive Aseneth only when told that she was a virgin who hated all men, for this suggested that he was safe from molestation. The text adds, quite notably, that he too was a παρθένος.[108] But when Aseneth eagerly approached him, ready to offer a kiss, Joseph shoved

104. See now the extensive treatment by Standhartinger, *Das Frauenbild, passim*. R. Kraemer, *Her Share of the Blessings* (New York, 1992) 110–13, argues for female authorship of the work. But see Standhartinger, *op. cit.*, 225–37.

105. *Jos. As.* 7.1: καὶ εἰσῆλθεν Ἰωσὴφ εἰς τὴν οἰκίαν Πεντεφρῆ καὶ ἐκάθισεν ἐπὶ θρόνου.

106. *Jos. As.* 7.1: παρέθηκεν αὐτῷ τράπεζαν κατ' ἰδίαν, διότι οὐ συνήσθε μετὰ τῶν Αἰγυπτίων, ὅτι βδέλυγμα ἦν αὐτῷ τοῦτο.

107. *Jos. As.* 7.2–5: ἠνόχλουν γὰρ αὐτῷ πᾶσαι αἱ γυναῖκες καὶ αἱ θυγατέρες τῶν μεγιστάνων καὶ τῶν σατραπῶν πάσης γῆς Αἰγύπτου τοῦ κοιμηθῆναι μετ' αὐτοῦ. καὶ πολλαὶ γυναῖκες καὶ θυγατέρες τῶν Αἰγυπτίων ... κακῶς ἔπασχον ἐπὶ τῷ κάλλει αὐτοῦ· καὶ ... ἀπέστειλον πρὸς αὐτὸν μετὰ χρυσίου καὶ ἀργυρίου καὶ δώρων πολυτίμων. καὶ ἀντέπεμπεν αὐτὰ ὁ Ἰωσὴφ μετὰ ἀπειλῆς καὶ ὕβρεως.

108. *Jos. As.* 7.8–8.1. so also 4.9.

her away disdainfully: no true worshipper of God could touch the lips of an alien woman polluted by contact with dead and dumb idols.[109] Joseph thus kept his principles intact and his body undefiled. But, like the Joseph figure in the *Testaments of the Twelve Patriarchs*, he boasts rather unsparingly, even unpleasantly, of his chastity and ritual purity. Only more so. This time it is not just Potiphar's wife but a host of lascivious ladies whom he had to fight off. Nor does he hesitate to humiliate Aseneth in front of her father, thus driving her to self-abuse and mental torture before he would acknowledge her rejection of idolatry. The hero of this saga evidently did not prize graciousness or even civility.[110]

Instead, Joseph exudes power and authority—more strikingly here than in Genesis or any of the other Hellenistic elaborations. The author of *Joseph and Aseneth* introduces Pentephres as chief of all satraps and grandees in the realm.[111] Yet, when he learns of Joseph's imminent visit, he is beside himself with excitement and goes to every length in preparing his household to receive so eminent a guest—one to whom he refers as "powerful man of God."[112] Pentephres breathlessly describes Joseph to his daughter as ruler of all the land of Egypt and Pharaoh's appointee as all-powerful governor.[113] Joseph then enters the gates of his host's estate in a royal chariot, resplendent in purple robes and a gold crown with precious stones. Pentephres and his entire family hastened to perform *proskynesis*. The text could not make plainer the fact that, no matter how lofty was the position of Pentephres in the court and in the realm, he was far below the station of Joseph the Jew.[114] In fact, Joseph possesses an aura that sets him apart from any mortal potentate. He was not only the "powerful man of God." His crown radiated with twelve golden rays, emblematic of a sun god. Aseneth makes a direct identification: Joseph was the sun from heaven, arriving in a chariot and shining its beams upon the earth.[115] Still more significant, the text refers to Joseph repeatedly as "son of God." This does not designate a title, nor should it be seen as Christian interpolation. But it lifts Joseph well out of

---

109. *Jos. As.* 8.4–5.

110. To be sure, Joseph does take pity upon the crestfallen and abject Aseneth, offering her a blessing and prayer for her repentance, that she may be brought into the fold; *Jos. As.* 8.8–11. But the young woman still had some lengthy ordeals to endure before she could cross that threshhold. On comparative material in T. Jos. and *Jos. As.*, see E. W. Smith in Nickelsburg, *Studies on the Testament of Joseph*, 133–35.

111. *Jos. As.* 1.4.

112. *Jos. As.* 3.1–6: Ἰωσὴφ ὁ δυνατὸς τοῦ θεοῦ.

113. *Jos. As.* 4.8; cf. 20.7.

114. *Jos. As.* 5.4–10.

115. *Jos. As.* 6.2; cf. 5.6.

the ordinary and sets him in the glow of the divine.[116] Aseneth's prayer to the Lord describes Joseph as beautiful, wise, and powerful. That last adjective has major import.[117] Phrases of this sort always issue from other persons' mouths. But Joseph's demeanor and behavior would certainly not have discouraged them. Indeed he underscored his stature by dismissing Pentephres' offer to provide a wedding banquet. Joseph would have none other than Pharaoh himself perform that task. The king consequently not only presided over the occasion but placed golden crowns upon the couple's heads.[118] Joseph disappears in the second part of the narrative, the adventure story. But he turns up again at its conclusion, to have the dying Pharaoh present him with the diadem, symbolic of royal authority. And the text has Joseph reign as king of Egypt for forty-eight years, before relinquishing the diadem to Pharaoh's youngest son. This goes well beyond the biblical tale and probably beyond any subsequent Hellenistic version of it.[119] The absence of Joseph in the second part of the tale has significance. When his enemies are forgiven, it is Aseneth and Levi who extend the clemency. Joseph would not have done so. In *Joseph and Aseneth*, he remains mighty and unbending from start to finish.[120]

The superiority of the Hebrews, their character, faith, and traditions, constitutes a central theme of the work. Joseph's contemptuous refusal to have a meal with Egyptians deliberately reverses the biblical passage that has the Egyptians shun any table occupied by Hebrews.[121] Aseneth's smashing of idols and her abject submission to the Lord accentuate the inferiority of her native religion. It is noteworthy that the author forecasts Aseneth's transformation early in the text, when he describes her beauty as unlike that of any of the Egyptians but akin to that of Sarah, Rebecca, and

---

116. *Jos. As.* 6.3, 6.5, 13.13, 18.11, 21.4, 23.10. See the discussion of Burchard, *Untersuchungen*, 115–17; *idem* in Charlesworth, *Old Testament Pseudepigrapha*, II, 191–92.

117. *Jos. As.* 13.11: κάλλος ... σοφὸς καὶ δυνατός; 18.1–2, 21.21.

118. *Jos. As.* 20.6–21.5.

119. *Jos. As.* 29.10–11: κατέλιπε τὸ διάδημα αὐτοῦ τῷ Ἰωσήφ. καὶ ἐβασίλευσεν Ἰωσήφ ἐν Αἰγύπτῳ ἔτη τεσσαράκοντα ὀκτώ. There may be an indirect allusion to this in the Testament of Levi which refers to Joseph as enshrined among kings; T. Levi, 13.9. A direct mention of Joseph as king comes in the fragmentary papyrus now labeled as "History of Joseph," but this occurs in the context of Joseph's renewed encounter with his brothers and the gathering of grain—while Pharaoh was still alive and on the throne. Cf. Genesis 44.18. See the text in A. M. Denis, *Fragmenta Pseudepigraphorum Graeca* (Leiden, 1970) 235–36, recto, 16–19, verso, 25–28. And the work is probably much later than the Hellenistic and early Roman periods; cf. G. T. Zervos in Charlesworth, *Old Testament Pseudepigrapha*, II, 468–69.

120. The sole exception is *Jos. As.* 8.8–11. See above, n. 110.

121. Gen. 43.32; *Jos. As.* 7.1.

Rachel.[122] Pharaoh makes obeisance to Joseph's god when he conducts the wedding ceremony.[123] The second segment of the narrative points up the Hebrews' physical as well as spiritual superiority. Pharaoh's son acknowledges that they are powerful men, beyond all others on the face of the earth.[124] Benjamin's superhuman strength enables him to fell fifty Egyptians.[125] And, in a climactic scene that emblematizes the Hebrews' military and moral supremacy, Pharaoh left his throne to prostrate himself before Levi, who had spared his defeated son.[126] The harmonious resolution stands at the core of the tale. But it comes only through affirmation of Jewish ascendancy.

Joseph and Aseneth supplies revealing testimony on the manipulation of the Joseph image in Hellenistic times. The romantic tale diverges in most respects from the other vehicles that conveyed that image. And certainly it bears little relation to or concern for the biblical narrative. Yet the personality of Joseph that appears in Genesis interestingly reappears in this fictitious fantasy, modified but unmistakable. Joseph emerges again as the favorite of God, trusting in divine beneficence, the loyal upholder of the faith, the fierce proponent of piety and rectitude, and the wielder of extensive authority in Egypt. But the author of the romance also heightens and intensifies those characteristics, subtly (or perhaps not so subtly) transforming them into haughtiness, prudery, self-righteousness, authoritarianism, and contemptuousness.

How would Jews react to the pomposity and arrogance discernible in the character of Joseph? None can say with confidence. Much of the audience may have read the novel simply as the tale of a pious patriarch. But others will have detected a more nuanced treatment of the flawed hero. In this writer's hands, Joseph could effectively carry the sense of Jewish superiority in a multi-ethnic society—but also some of the disagreeableness that can accompany that superiority. The ambiguous personality of Joseph gave itself readily to refashioning. This work, it may be suggested, both celebrates Jewish pride and cautions against its excess.

•   •   •

The complex and multiform features of the Joseph character recur in an indirect way through still another and altogether different vehicle. Josephus

---

122. *Jos. As.* 1.6–8.
123. *Jos. As.* 21.4.
124. *Jos. As.* 23.3; cf. 24.7.
125. *Jos. As.* 27.1–5.
126. *Jos. As.* 29.5–7.

transmits an elaborate family saga of intrigue, escapade, and adventure in the historical context of Jewish experience under the Ptolemies and Seleucids. On the face of it, the biblical Joseph is nowhere in evidence. The account follows the family of the Tobiads over two generations, spanning the third and second centuries BCE, enmeshed in the turmoils and rivalries of the Hellenistic age, ostensibly a serious historical narrative. Yet echoes of Genesis resonate in the background, and Joseph resurfaces in altered form.

The tale of the Tobiads, as presented by Josephus, warrants brief rehearsal. The account commences at the outset of the second century BCE, following conclusion of the Fifth Syrian War. Josephus reports a treaty between Antiochus III and Ptolemy V that ceded to the latter control of Coele-Syria, Judaea, Samaria, and Phoenicia. This put the revenues of the area in Ptolemaic hands and set the stage for tensions that embroiled the Jews. Onias, High Priest in Jerusalem, motivated by niggardliness and avarice, refused to pay the annual tribute that his predecessors had rendered to their Hellenic overlords, thus stirring the fury of Ptolemy. The king's envoy arrived with threats of land confiscation, spreading anxiety among the Jews but leaving Onias unmoved.[127] A young man then came to the rescue, a certain Joseph, son of Tobias and nephew of Onias on his mother's side, a man of gravity and prescience, with a reputation for uprightness. Joseph rebuked Onias for placing his people in jeopardy and failing in his roles as High Priest and chief official of the state. The youth offered to go as envoy to Ptolemy himself and, after having secured permission, skillfully prepared the way by ingratiating himself with Ptolemy's representative who was still in Jerusalem.[128]

The advance preparation did the trick. By the time Joseph reached Egypt, Ptolemy's envoy had already smoothed the path by reporting on the obstinacy of Onias and the excellence of the young man who would come as spokesman for the Jews. Ptolemy greeted Joseph with graciousness and favor, even invited him into his chariot. Joseph's wit and aplomb charmed the king still more, earning him a stay in the palace and a place at the royal table. The timing proved to be propitious. It was the occasion for the gathering of leaders and chief officials from various cities in Syria and Phoenicia, each bidding for the tax-farming rights in his region. Joseph, who had been ridiculed by these men on the journey to Egypt, now seized the opportunity to retaliate. He denounced their low bids as the product of collusion and promised to deliver twice the amount. When he then capped

127. Jos. *Ant.* 12.154–59.
128. Jos. *Ant.* 12.160–66.

his offer with another witticism, suggesting the king and queen themselves as guarantors of his proposition, Joseph had Ptolemy in the palm of his hand. The king assigned him all tax-farming rights without demanding surety, thus deflating his arrogant competitors and sending them back empty-handed.[129] Joseph proceeded to borrow 500 talents from friends of the king and 2000 troops from the royal army to help in the collection of revenues in Palestine and Syria. Nor did he tolerate any resistance. With Ptolemy's authority behind him, Joseph terrorized reluctant or recalcitrant cities, gathered the requisite taxes for the king, and amassed a fortune for himself.[130]

Joseph the Tobiad enjoyed his position and his prosperity for twenty-two years. In the course of it, one wife produced seven sons and another gave him an eighth. A romantic anecdote accounts for the second marriage. Joseph's brother, through a subterfuge, placed his own daughter in Joseph's bed during a visit in Alexandria, lest Joseph's infatuation for an Egyptian dancing girl lead him to unlawful intercourse with an alien. So Joseph, despite himself, kept faith with ancestral traditions, married his niece, and received Hyrcanus, an eighth son, as reward.[131] Hyrcanus, while still a teenager, outstripped his half-brothers in innate courage and intelligence, thus winning special favor from his father and exciting the envy of his siblings.[132]

Hyrcanus soon had occasion to reproduce the exploits of his father. King Ptolemy announced the birth of a son and planned great festivities to mark the event. Old age prevented Joseph from making the trip to Egypt, and none of his older sons proved willing to go, urging him instead to send Hyrcanus, in the expectation that he would not return. The youth was happy to oblige. He requested only a modest sum for the trip and no money at all for a gift to the king. Instead, he sought a letter from Joseph to his financial agent in Alexandria who could supply the needed cash for a handsome gift, an idea that appealed to his father. Hyrcanus departed to carry out his plan, while his brothers communicated with friends of the king who would do away with him.[133] The young man, of course, had hatched a scheme to outwit his rivals. He delivered Joseph's letter to the financial agent Arion and then requested the sum of 1000 talents. The flabbergasted agent, assuming that Hyrcanus wanted the cash for extravagant personal expenditures, refused to relinquish it, and was immediately put in irons on Hyrcanus' orders. Word of this

129. Jos. *Ant.* 12.167–79.
130. Jos. *Ant.* 12.180–85.
131. Jos. *Ant.* 12.186–89.
132. Jos. *Ant.* 12.190–95.
133. Jos. *Ant.* 12.196–202.

reached Ptolemy who demanded an explanation and got a pointed witticism about the need for discipline at every level of society, even Ptolemy's own. The king was as charmed by Hyrcanus as he had been by Joseph. The young man used his 1000 talents to purchase one hundred boys and one hundred girls as presents for the court. Hyrcanus thereby outshined and humbled all the eminent guests who had scorned him through both the acuity of his wit and the lavishness of his gifts. He even had enough cash left over to buy off the would-be assassins whom his brothers had recruited[134]

The story would not, however, have a happy ending. Hyrcanus' cleverness endeared him all the more to Ptolemy but further alienated his family. Ptolemy showered him with honors and wrote glowing letters of recommendation back home. The brothers nevertheless redoubled their efforts and even Joseph had become disenchanted. A fraternal war ensued. Hyrcanus' forces slew many of his enemies, including two brothers. But he could gain no entry to Jerusalem and was compelled to withdraw for safety across the Jordan where he turned to military and financial oppression of the natives.[135] Hyrcanus entrenched himself by constructing an elaborate fortress, replete with a moat, caves carved out of rock, and artistic embellishments. He held forth there for seven years until the accession of Antiochus IV in Syria and the death of his patron Ptolemy V of Egypt. Hyrcanus, acknowledging the irresistible power of Antiochus, elected to take his own life.[136]

Arguments over the historical value of this narrative persist, the chief focus of scholarly attention. Josephus' real or alleged blunders are regularly impugned. Confused chronology seems to bedevil the account from start to finish. Neither the twenty-two years of Joseph's tax supervision nor the seven years of Hyrcanus' installation across the Jordan fit easily into the circumstances reported by Josephus. And the scenario of Ptolemaic fiscal control in Palestine and Coele-Syria would appear to demand a period prior to Josephus' starting point. Other inconsistencies and difficulties require no rehearsal here.[137]

134. Jos. *Ant.* 12.203–18.

135. Jos. *Ant.* 12.219–22, 12.228–29.

136. Jos. *Ant.* 12.230–36.

137. Many of the problems were pointed out long ago by J. Wellhausen, *Israelitische und jüdische Geschichte*[8] (Berlin, 1921) 229–32, and H. Willrich, *Juden und Griechen vor der makkabäischen Erhebung* (Göttingen, 1895) 91–107, who denied historicity to the bulk of the narrative. Cf. the more complex and more moderate position of A. Büchler, *Die Tobiaden und die Oniaden* (Vienna, 1899) 43–106. A recent restatement on certain points was made by C. Orrieux, *Kentron* 2 (1986) 8–11; *Kentron* 4–5 (1988) 133–41. In a forthcoming article, D. R. Schwartz gives some strong arguments for accepting Josephus' placement of Joseph and Hyrcanus in the early 2nd century—but he has to embrace the notion that Coele-Syria was simultaneously controlled by

To be sure, a historical substratum exists. The tales of the Tobiads did not spring up out of whole cloth. Independent testimony, literary, papyrological, and archaeological, confirms the eminence of that family in late biblical and Hellenistic times. The Tobiads, in fact, go back to the period of the Babylonian Exile. A Tobiah receives mention among Judaean leaders who will return to crown the High Priest in the new Temple. Another Tobiah plays a prominent role among principal houses in the time of Nehemiah. And the name "Tobiah" appears on rock-cut inscriptions at the Transjordanian site of Araq el Emir in Aramaic lettering, now dated to the fourth century BCE.[138] The fortress itself, excavated at Araq el Emir, corresponds closely to Josephus' description of the elaborate structure built by Hyrcanus, although it plainly predates Hyrcanus by perhaps a century.[139] The prestige of the clan gains further confirmation from the Zenon papyri of the mid third century. They record a Toubias, clearly a notable personage in the Transjordan, in contact with the Ptolemaic ruler, his *oikonomos* Apollonios, and Apollonios' agent Zenon. The papyri attest to his wealth in the form of gifts and supplies and his authority as head of a military cleruchy situated on his own estates.[140] The site itself is termed "the Birta of the Ammonitis," which may well coincide with the powerful "Baris" or fortress that Josephus ascribes to Hyrcanus. And the "Saurabitt" that appears in another papyrus, evidently a Greek transcription of the Hebrew "Zur" or stronghold, can be linked to "Tyros," the name that Hyrcanus applied to his structure. Thus the edifice and possessions that Josephus assigns to Hyrcanus had actually been in the family for several

---

the Seleucids and taxed by the Ptolemies. For an incisive and influential reconstruction of the events, see A. Momigliano, *AttiTorino* 67 (1931/1932) 165–200, who, however, is too schematic in seeing the divisions among the Jews as reflection of pro-Ptolemaic or pro-Seleucid leanings. Similarly, V. Tcherikover, *Hellenistic Civilization and the Jews* (New York, 1959) 126–42; cf. M. Stern, *Tarbiz* 32 (1962) 35–47 (Hebrew); M. Hengel, *Judaism and Hellenism* (London, 1974) I, 267–77. J. Goldstein in Neusner, *Christianity, Judaism, and Other Greco-Roman Cults*, III, 85–123, offers some provocative insights, but surprisingly pronounces the stories of Joseph and Hyrcanus as almost entirely true. A much more skeptical treatment by D. Gera in A. Kasher, U. Rappaport, and G. Fuks, *Greece and Rome in Eretz Israel* (Jerusalem, 1990) 21–38.

138. Zech. 6.9–15; Neh. 2.10, 2.19, 6.1, 6.11–19, 7.61–62, 13.4–8; Ezra 2.59–60. See the discussion of B. Mazar, *IEJ* 7 (1957) 141–45, 229–38. For the dating of the inscriptions, see J. Naveh, *Proceedings of the Israel Academy of Sciences and Humanities* 5 (1971–1976) 62–64; Gera in Kasher et al., *Greece and Rome in Eretz Israel*, 25, with bibliography.

139. See Gera in Kasher et al., *Greece and Rome in Eretz Israel*, 24–26, with references to the literature.

140. The texts are printed in *CPJ*, I, nn. 1–2, 4–5; see discussion by Tcherikover, *op. cit.*, 115–16; idem, *Hellenistic Civilization and the Jews*, 64–66.

generations.[141] It was known also in the third century as the "land of Tobiah," a name that clung to it still in the period of the Maccabaean rebellion a century later.[142] Finally, the wealth and standing of Hyrcanus obtain verification from an important passage in II Maccabees: the man of high distinction, here identified as "son of Tobiah," had a substantial sum of money deposited in the treasury of the Temple itself.[143] That the house of the Tobiads had a long and influential history in Palestine and Transjordan from post-exilic times through the Maccabaean era cannot be gainsaid.

The significance of Josephus' narrative, however, lies elsewhere. Whatever relation it bears to historical reality, the account has obvious folktale elements and the appealing qualities of imaginative fiction.[144] More pertinently, it reverberates with allusions to Genesis. The recollections are indirect, transmuted, and modified. The biblical Joseph does not correspond in a one-to-one relationship with a particular character in the tales of the Tobiads. But the scriptural similarities are hardly random coincidences.

A number of biblical resonances can be detected. Both Joseph the Tobiad and Hyrcanus ingratiate themselves as young men to the ruler of Egypt and swiftly obtain positions of high authority, leading to substantial wealth, as did Joseph in Genesis. The division between brothers borne by different mothers recalls the house of Jacob, as does the eclipse of older brothers by the younger, and the favor of the father bestowed upon the latter. Even select details offer parallels, such as Joseph's mounting the king's chariot, and the last minute substitution of a bed partner who becomes a wife.[145] But we need to pass beyond the parallels. What traits and qualities of the Joseph figure draw attention in this narrative? And what are their implications for the Hellenistic conception of that figure?

141. *CPJ*, I, n. 1, line 13: ἐν Βίρται τῆς Ἀμμανίτιδος ; n. 2a, Col. I, line 6; Jos. *Ant.* 12.230, 12.233. See Mazar, *IEJ* 7 (1957) 140; Tcherikover, *CPJ* I, 116.

142. *CPJ* I, n. 2d, Col. IX, line 16: ἐν τῆι Τουβίου ; I Macc. 5.13: ἐν τοῖς Τουβίου; II Macc. 12.17: τοὺς λεγομένους Τουβιανοὺς; cf. II Macc. 12.35. See Mazar, *IEJ* 7 (1957) 139; Hengel, *Judaism and Hellenism*, I, 276; J. Goldstein, *I Maccabees* (Garden City, 1976) 298–99; *idem, II Maccabees* (Garden City, 1983) 439–40; Gera in Kasher et al., *Greece and Rome in Eretz Israel*, 27–30.

143. II Macc. 3.10–11: τινὰ δὲ καὶ Ὑρκανοῦ τοῦ Τωβίου σφόδρα ἀνδρὸς ἐν ὑπεροχῇ κειμένου.

144. See S. Niditch, *JJS* 32 (1981) 47–55; Wills, *Jewish Novel*, 187–93.

145. For the ascending into a royal chariot, see Gen. 41.43; Jos. *Ant.* 12.172. The story of the substitute bed-partner alludes to the switch of Leah for Rachel on Jacob's wedding night; Gen. 29.21–23; Jos. *Ant.* 12.186–89. Parallels with the biblical text were pointed to by Willrich, *Juden und Griechen*, 94–95; Niditsch, *JJS* 32 (1981) 50–51. Gera in Kasher et al., *Greece and Rome in Eretz Israel*, 31–33, adds a number of others, some of them rather unduly stretching the point.

The tales of the Tobiads do not aim at moral uplift. As in the case of Artapanus' fanciful reconstruction, the virtuous and virginal Joseph is absent. No indication points to the episode of Potiphar's wife, nor to forgiveness and magnanimous reconciliation. Perhaps more surprisingly, the saga omits reference to administrative restructuring and economic reform. The characters in this narrative evoke other features of the biblical patriarch. Joseph the Tobiad is introduced as a young man with a reputation for righteousness, an evident echo of the Genesis Joseph.[146] But that trait nowhere emerges in the story. Instead, emphasis rests upon the shrewd and calculating youth who first undermined Onias' authority, usurped his place as leader of the Jews, won the endorsement of Ptolemy's agent with extravagant gifts and entertainment, gained the king's favor through charm and wit, and outmaneuvered all the tax-bidders with clever ploys.[147] This portrait resembles the biblical Joseph who impressed Pharaoh with acuity and talents superior to those of the royal councilors. And it approximates still more closely the Joseph of Artapanus who stole a march on his brothers and earned the king's favor immediately upon arrival at court, apparently through sheer intellect.[148] The Tobiad proceeds to implement his power ruthlessly, running roughshod over opponents and squeezing revenues from the cities to fill the royal coffers and line his own pockets. The description has its roots in Genesis, where Joseph shows little clemency to despairing peasants and exploits their plight to entrench crown control over all land in Egypt.[149] Josephus' stress on the amassing of personal wealth in order to solidify personal power also has analogies with Philo's image of Joseph as exemplifying greed for material goods.[150] The concluding remarks on Joseph the Tobiad after his death make reference to his lifting of the Jews from poverty and idleness to far more splendid styles of life—a description which applies more suitably to the patriarch than to the Tobiad.[151]

---

146. Jos. *Ant.* 12.160: δικαιοσύνης δόξαν ἔχων.

147. It is possible even that Joseph had wrested the προστασία τοῦ λαοῦ away from Onias before going to Egypt; cf. Jos. *Ant.* 12.161, 12.167; see Momigliano, *AttiTorino* 67 (1931/1932) 182–84; Tcherikover, *Hellenistic Civilization and the Jews*, 132–33. But the phrase may not be a technical one; see 12.167: ... τὸ πλῆθος; εἶναι γὰρ αὐτοῦ προστάτην.

148. Artapanus *apud* Euseb. *PE* 9.23.2.

149. Gen. 47.13–26; Jos. *Ant.* 12.180–84.

150. Philo *Somn.* 2.47, 2.63; *Mut.* 89–90; *Migr.* 203–204; Jos. *Ant.* 12.185.

151. Jos. *Ant.* 12.224: τὸν τῶν Ἰουδαίων λαὸν ἐκ πτωχείας καὶ πραγμάτων ἀσθενῶν εἰς λαμπροτέρας ἀφορμὰς τοῦ βίου καταστήσας. Cf. Hengel, *Judaism and Hellenism*, I, 270. The passage also recalls a similar comment by Philo on the biblical Joseph; *Jos.* 204. See above, n. 50.

Hyrcanus carries even stronger reminiscences of the biblical and post-biblical Joseph. He outwits and outdoes his brothers, thereby rousing their ire, rather than innocently suffering at their hands, a close analogy to the dark picture drawn in Philo's *De Somnis*.[152] Hyrcanus' clever escape from his brothers' assassination plot resembles a comparable tale of Joseph in Artapanus' work.[153] The young man's wheedling of Ptolemy, his surpassing of rivals, the remorseless treatment of the financial steward, and severe repression of his subjects all duplicate in different forms his father's behavior, additional reminders of the less scrupulous side of Joseph the patriarch.[154] Open warfare between the brothers, as occurred after Hyrcanus' return to Palestine, has no analogue in Genesis but neatly parallels the battles recounted in the second part of *Joseph and Aseneth*.[155]

A point of importance needs to be insisted upon. The Tobiad stories deliver no negative verdict upon their principal characters. The saga underscores cleverness and wit, conscious manipulation of competitors and patrons, and fierce oppression of subjects. But the presentation endorses its heroes. Success counts, and the traits that bring it win admiration. When the Tobiad tales evoke the image of Joseph the patriarch, they highlight those dimensions of his character that appealed as much to Hellenistic Jews as did moral righteousness and religious piety.[156]

•   •   •

152. Philo *Somn.* 2.93–100; Jos. *Ant.* 12.190–95.

153. Artapanus *apud* Euseb. *PE* 9.23.1; Jos. *Ant.* 12.202, 12.218.

154. Jos. *Ant.* 12.203–20.

155. *Jos, As.* 26–27; Jos. *Ant.* 12.221–22, 12.228–29.

156. Speculation on the author or authors of the tales would not be profitable. Willrich's idea, *Juden und Griechen*, 99–102, that Josephus used a Samaritan source no longer finds favor, rightly so. Tcherikover, *Hellenistic Civilization and the Jews*, 140–42, assigns it to an Alexandrian Jew who drew on the family history of the Tobiads. In the view of Stern, *Tarbiz* 32 (1962) 36–40 (Hebrew), the story derives from Jewish circles in late 2nd or early 1st century Alexandria, largely as an encomium of Hyrcanus. For Hengel, *Judaism and Hellenism*, I, 269–70, the author was an advocate of Hellenism for the Jews and propagator of the contemporary values represented by the Tobiads, namely close collaboration with the Gentiles. These suggestions seem to miss the central features of the tale. Goldstein in Neusner, *Christianity, Judaism, and Other Greco-Roman Cults*, 104–16, sees it as a propaganda work by Onias IV—which makes it difficult to account for the narrative's attitude toward Onias II. Gera's idea, in Kasher et al., *Greece and Rome in Eretz Israel*, 35–38, that the author wrote to bolster the spirits of Jews in Ptolemaic Egypt, is more plausible, but misplaces the emphasis by shifting it away from the personalities of the heroes, and, like Goldstein, misconceives the tales as "propaganda." For an analogous adaptation of the Joseph theme to help mold the portrait of Agrippa I, see the pertinent remarks of D. R. Schwartz, *Agrippa I: The Last King of Judaea* (Tübingen, 1990) 33–34.

The figure of Joseph lent itself to a variety of shapes. Genesis itself supplied a disjointed combination: a person of high moral principles, mingled with pride and prudery, resourceful but calculating and manipulative, a political and economic reformer who also advanced the centralization of royal authority, a wielder of power but one largely impervious to the sufferings of its victims. Hellenistic writers exploited the biblical material at will, taking and rewriting what they liked, omitting or freely adapting what they found unpalatable. What strikes the reader most sharply, however, is how much they found *palatable*.

The Hellenistic texts certainly or probably composed in Hebrew generally take a benign position. Jubilees lavishes praise upon Joseph for his moral integrity, his unselfish and effective administration, his forgiving temperament, and his application of power for the advantage of the community. Failings are repressed or explained away. A similarly spotless character appears in the comments of Ben Sira, I Maccabees, and Pseudo-Philo. And the Testament of Joseph gives him full treatment as unbending devotee of personal chastity and fraternal loyalty, whatever the temptation. The one-sided presentation, however, stripped Joseph of balance and complexity, leaving him a pompous purist.

Hellenized Jews took a more broad-minded line and expanded the dimensions of the character. Joseph as epitome of ethical dedication still endured, cited as exemplary in works like IV Maccabees and The Wisdom of Solomon. But philosophical and historical texts also found other features to admire, particularly the vast authority that Joseph had acquired in an alien land. Demetrius and Wisdom underline that element, an appropriate means to bolster Jewish pride in the Diaspora. Joseph as a figure of eminence and dominance could be pushed further still, in imaginative ways that left the Bible far behind. So Artapanus credits Joseph not only with reordering the economic system of Egypt but with introducing its inhabitants to the knowledge of measures. In Artapanus' hands moral and religious issues recede, acuity of intellect and breadth of vision take precedence.

The malleability of the Joseph figure comes on exhibit in pronounced fashion through the works of Philo. The philosopher's biography of Joseph combines the patriarch's qualities of moral excellence with his instincts for leadership to paint a portrait of the ideal statesman. The biblical account supplied adequate material with which to fashion a pattern for imitation. But a different perspective might also discern more troubling traits. Leadership could slip into manipulativeness, self-assurance into arrogance, high station into lust for wealth and material benefits. Philo—and not he alone—employed Joseph simply as emblem, whether of political wisdom and morality or lack thereof. Philo's inconsistencies dissolve, for Joseph was representation, not reality. The richness and the riddles of the Genesis narrative gave Hellenistic Jews ample scope for imagination.

Joseph had become a stimulus for inventive minds and a model for manifold constructs. Faithfulness to the Bible story did not hold high priority. A few lines in Genesis sufficed to inspire an elaborate tale of romance and adventure. *Joseph and Aseneth* owes little to the biblical narrative, but much to post-biblical and Hellenistic fiction. Nonetheless, the multilayered character of Joseph, stemming from Genesis and a range of subsequent texts, pokes through even in creative fantasy. Joseph breathes rectitude and piety, displays a dazzling presence, wields intimidating authority, but also conducts himself with pomposity and offensive sanctimoniousness. The latter traits do not convey a primarily negative message or moral. Joseph remains a hero to the end, a devout champion of Hebrew ethical and religious superiority, elevated to royal rank with absolute sovereignty over Egyptians. Self-esteem, even when spilling over into arrogance, and a commitment to Jewish ascendancy, even when expressed through swagger and condescension, exhibit, indeed intensify, the pride of Hellenistic Jews. The figure of Joseph catered perfectly to those purposes.

The varied forms of the image could be exploited also without direct reference to Joseph. The tales of the Tobiads involve historical personages rather than legendary ones, and deal with recent history rather than a fabled past. Yet embellishment and elaboration permeate the story, replete with echoes of Joseph's escapades. In this incarnation, the characteristics that come to the fore emphasize cunning and clever schemes to outsmart competitors, accumulate wealth, and crush opponents. And here again the narrative intends no critical judgment. It condones the actions and applauds the results.

Hellenistic Jews found multiple means to express their relationship to surrounding society. A strong strain in Judaic culture pushed beyond accommodation and adjustment to stress Jewish advantage and superiority. The pliable portrait of Joseph suitably ministered to those objectives. He appeared in various genres and in various guises, recreated by historians, philosophers, exegetes, propagandists, and writers of creative fiction.[157]

157. It would seem superfluous to append comments on Josephus' treatment of Joseph, an idiosyncratic and partially autobiographical one. It has already received extensive examination; see, especially, H. Sp;rödowsky, *Die Hellenisierung der Geschichte von Joseph in Ägypten bei Flavius Josephus* (Greifswald, 1937) *passim*; Niehoff, *Figure of Joseph*, 84–110; L. H. Feldman,

Joseph could represent moral righteousness, commitment to religious principle, surpassing sagacity, fierce pride, haughty condescension, consummate shrewdness in the accumulation of wealth and power, crafty outmaneuvering of rivals, and unrelenting suppression of subordinates—or any combination thereof. Jewish intellectuals had a free hand in reshaping, excerpting, expanding, or even ignoring the Genesis narrative. The ostensibly cavalier attitude toward Scripture, however, did not constitute irreverence or creeping secularism. The adaptation of Jewish legend and the appropriation of Hellenic forms marched in tandem to reassert the admirable values and superior attainments of the Jews. The images of Joseph, in all their disparate manifestations, had that mission in common.

RevBibl 99 (1992) 379–417, 504–28. On Josephus and the Potiphar story, with classical parallels, see the exhaustive analysis by M. Braun, *Griechischer Roman und hellenistische Geschichtsschreibung* (Frankfurt, 1934) 23–117.

CHAPTER 4

Scriptural Stories in New Guise

For Hellenistic Jews writing in Greek, the Scriptures provided stimulus for ingenuity and creativity. The concept of a fixed and unalterable tradition had not yet taken hold. No scriptural "canon" existed. Composition and interpretation proceeded concurrently, and the idea of established texts was still in process of formation. The fluidity of the tradition may frustrate modern scholars. But it gave impetus to writers eager to reshape and revivify narratives long familiar but conveniently adaptable.

One discerns a developed sense of the canon as we know it only in the mid and later first century CE. Philo may allude to it in speaking of "laws, oracular sayings through prophets, hymns, and other writings by which knowledge and piety are expanded and perfected." For Philo, these amount to "holy scriptures."[1] The tripartite division occurs in Luke, where Jesus finds premonitions of his mission in the "Law of Moses, the prophets, and the psalms."[2] And Josephus provides the fullest expression by counting five books of Moses, thirteen of prophets, and four of hymns to God and rules by which to live.[3] Something like a canon had taken shape by the later first century CE.[4]

Two centuries earlier a more flexible and malleable situation prevailed. The Jews, to be sure, had a notion of authoritative writings, a tradition derived from forefathers guided by divine inspiration. The grandson of Ben Sira, providing a Greek version of his grandfather's treatise in the late second century BCE, reported that he had devoted himself to a study of the

1. Philo De Vita Cont. 25, 28: τοῖς ἱεροῖς γράμμασι.
2. Luke 24.44.
3. Jos. C. Apion. 1.37–41.
4. Cf. E. Tov in A. van der Woude, *The World of the Bible* (Grand Rapids, 1986) 156–90.

"Law, the prophets, and other books of our ancestors."[5] More elaborately, II Maccabees cites the books of kings and prophets, the works of David, and the royal letters on sacred dedications assembled by Nehemiah in founding a library.[6] But fluidity was the hallmark of the process. The Qumran texts suffice to show that variants aplenty existed and a stable canon had not yet materialized.[7]

The nearest thing to an established sacred text in the Hellenistic period was the Pentateuch. Tradition reports that learned elders rendered the Law of Moses into Greek in third century Alexandria. The *Letter of Aristeas*, our earliest testimony to that tradition, includes a notable statement: the translation was pronounced exact and unalterable, the precise wording to be preserved in perpetuity, with a curse laid upon any who would alter an iota of it.[8] That pronouncement bears little relation to reality. No such ban discouraged the retelling of Pentateuchal tales in revised, expanded, elaborated, or altogether transformed versions—in Semitic as well as Greek renditions. But the statement of "Aristeas" contains a deeper truth. The authors of these divergent treatments had no intention of challenging or replacing biblical narratives. Their creations existed as accompaniments, commentaries, alternative visions, or provocative reinterpretations, inviting readers to make comparisons or engage in reassessments of the tradition.[9]

The phenomenon is a remarkable one. Why this frenzy for reworking the Scriptures in a variety of genres, modes, languages, times, and places? No

---

5. Ben Sira Praef. 3.

6. II Macc. 2.13.

7. See G. Ulrich in G. Ulrich and J. VanderKam, *The Community of the Renewed Covenant* (Notre Dame, 1994) 77–93. The issue of "canonization" is complex and disputed, mercifully beyond the scope of this investigation. The neat process once conceived as a three stage development, with the Torah canonized ca. 400 BCE, the Prophets ca. 200 BCE, and the Ketubim ca. 90 CE, has now been largely discredited; see J. P. Lewis, *JBR* 32 (1964) 125–32; A. C. Sundberg, *The Old Testament of the Early Church* (Cambridge, Mass., 1964) 113–28; E. E. Ellis, *The Old Testament in Early Christianity* (Tübingen, 1991) 37–40. On the general question of canonization a huge literature exists. See the very useful discussion of J. A. Sanders, with bibliography, in D. N. Freedman, *Anchor Bible Dictionary* (New York, 1992) I, 837–52. One might note particularly J. Blenkinsopp, *Prophecy and Canon* (Notre Dame, 1977); J. A. Sanders, *From Sacred Story to Sacred Text* (Philadelphia, 1987); Ellis, *op. cit.*

8. *LetArist* 310–11.

9. S. J. D. Cohen, *From the Maccabees to the Mishna* (Philadelphia, 1987) 192–95, interestingly suggests that canonization itself prompted creative interpretation among Hellenistic Jews, secure in the knowledge that the sacred original remained intact. It does not follow, however, as Cohen hypothesizes, that Second Temple Jews considered themselves inferior to their forebears and dwelling in a "silver age."

full or final answer to this fascinating puzzle can be produced. Nor will any single answer suffice. This chapter represents only a beginning. The question must stand at the center of any inquiry into the Jewish drive for refashioning self-identity in a Hellenic universe. Interpretation and explanation of biblical material occupied a large number of Jewish intellectuals. We concentrate here on a sampling of diverse texts composed in Greek some time in the last three centuries before the Common Era. Multiple motives emerge.

· · ·

A substantial portion of the relevant writers' work exists only in fragments. And for most of these we rely upon an obscure, tantalizingly elusive, but indispensable scholar, Alexander Polyhistor. Of his life we know next to nothing. But a crucial chronological fact is basic. Polyhistor, a Greek from western Asia Minor, was brought to Rome as a slave in the wake of Sulla's eastern victories and taught there in the mid first century BCE. This supplies a serviceable *terminus ante quem* for the authors whom he cites. Polyhistor was a polymath, with twenty-five titles to his name, works on geography, history, philosophy, religion, and literature. Their quality and accuracy can be questioned. He was fond of reporting fabulous stories and, at least occasionally, conveyed erroneous information—such as the notice that Moses was a woman. Nor is there anything in the extant remains of his work to suggest that he contributed original ideas of his own. But no matter. Polyhistor's value lies in his preservation of others' writings, especially, for our purposes, in his book "On the Jews," the surviving parts of which come to us largely through the Church Father Eusebius. What remains indicates that Polyhistor excerpted, abbreviated, and made some alterations in the texts he records, but, for the most part, transmitted them faithfully.[10] And that is what counts. The extracts from Jewish-Hellenistic authors quoted by Polyhistor are precious items of cultural history.

One writer demands notice at the outset. The fragments of Demetrius, few and meager though they be, afford an entrance into the subject. To scholarly frustration, the date, place, and even character of his work remain uncertain, subject to considerable debate. Moderns have dubbed him "Demetrius the Chronographer," a somewhat unfair designation. His

10. The best treatments, with references, by J. Freudenthal, *Alexander Polyhistor* (Breslau, 1875) 16–35, and B. Z. Wacholder, *Eupolemus: A Study of Judaeo-Greek Literature* (Cincinnati, 1974) 44–52.

interest in chronological matters is clear enough. But the fragments evince broader concerns.[11]

Demetrius composed an account, historical in form, that treated material in Genesis and Exodus. Three fragments at least, perhaps as many as five, culled by Eusebius from Alexander Polyhistor, attest to it. A sixth quotation is ascribed by Clement of Alexandria to Demetrius' work *On the Kings in Judaea* and concerns subjects deriving from II Kings. Whether the fragments belong to one work or more matters little for our purposes.[12] More significant are certain puzzles and problems that captured Demetrius' attention and for which he offers solutions. So, for instance, he addresses the question of how Jacob managed to father twelve children in just seven years. The schedule is tight, but Demetrius works out a time-table that fits all twelve offspring, produced by four different mothers.[13] Demetrius reports the episode of Jacob's wrestling with an angel, thus to explain why Jews refrain from eating the sinew of animals' thighs: it was in the upper thigh or hip that the angel had struck Jacob, causing him to limp. The explanation closely follows the account in Genesis. But Demetrius' retelling, in the extant fragment, focuses on that issue alone, leaving out the drama of the confrontation as it appears in the Bible.[14] Similarly, he accounts for Joseph's failure to summon his father to Egypt by the fact that shepherds were held in low esteem by the Egyptians, for which he cites Joseph's own admonition to his brothers to claim that they tended cattle. The explanation is inadequate, omitting

11. The label seems first to have been affixed by Freudenthal in what is still the most fundamental and thorough study of Demetrius; *Alexander Polyhistor*, 35–82. It is used also by, e.g., Y. Gutman, *The Beginnings of Jewish-Hellenistic Literature*, 2 vols. (Jerusalem, 1958, 1963) I, 132 (Hebrew); Wacholder, *Eupolemus*, 280; and J. Hanson in J. H. Charlesworth, *Old Testament Pseudepigrapha* (Garden City, 1985) II, 843. The fragments can usefully be consulted in C. R. Holladay, *Fragments from Hellenistic Jewish Authors: Volume I: Historians* (Chico, 1983) 51–91, with Holladay's valuable introduction and notes. More recently, see the discussion by G. E. Sterling, *Historiography and Self-Definition: Josephos, Luke-Acts, and Apologetic Historiography* (Leiden, 1992) 153–67, with excellent bibliography.

12. A book on kings in Judaea would be unlikely to encompass stories about Abraham, Jacob, and Moses that appear in the other fragments—a problem not resolved by the fact that Philo refers to Moses as a king; *Mos.* 2.292. Better to assume more than one work. Freudenthal, *Alexander Polyhistor*, 36, assigns five fragments in Eusebius' *Praeparatio Evangelica* to Demetrius, although the Church historian mentions him explicitly in only three of them. R. Doran, *ANRW* II.20.1 (1987) 249–50, separates out the two anonymous ones (Euseb. *PE* 9.19.4, 9.29.16). Their style and character, however, closely approximate the others, and the second appears in the same context with another quotation of Demetrius. Cf. Sterling, *Historiography and Self-Definition*, 155.

13. Euseb. *PE* 9.21.3–5. See Freudenthal, *Alexander Polyhistor*, 54–56.

14. Euseb. *PE* 9.21.7; cf. Genesis 32.22–31.

much that is in Genesis and thus leaving the point unpersuasive.[15] But no matter. Demetrius brought up the issue only to offer a solution to a puzzle that had been posed. He does the same with regard to Joseph's feeding to Benjamin five times what he offered his other brothers and bestowing four times the amount of clothing upon him. The behavior prompts a question about Joseph's favoritism, so claims Demetrius.[16] And he supplies an answer: Leah had seven sons, Rachel but two; hence Benjamin's five portions plus Joseph's two evened the balance. The disproportion appears in Genesis, but the explanation is Demetrius'.[17] When the historian moves on to Moses, he brings up and confronts another problem: how is it that Moses could marry Zipporah, both of whom could trace descent from Abraham, if Moses was six generations distant from the patriarch and Zipporah was seven? Demetrius' reconstruction of the generational gap answers the question: Isaac was already married when Abraham married Keturah and had a second son, thus of the same generation as Isaac's son from whom Zipporah descended. The solution evidently developed from a piecing together of biblical testimonies and some shrewd calculations.[18] Finally, Demetrius tackles another puzzle in the Moses story. How did the Israelites, who left Egypt unarmed, manage to secure weapons in the desert, so someone asked.[19] An easy answer: they appropriated the arms of Egyptians who drowned in the sea. The conclusion plainly depends upon historical hypothesis, not any textual testimony.[20]

What ends were served by such exegesis? Arguments from Demetrius' location and time do not get us far, since neither is known with any certainty. Citations of his work by Alexander Polyhistor place Demetrius prior to the

---

15. Euseb. *PE* 9.21.13; cf. Genesis 46.28–34. See Freudenthal, *Alexander Polyhistor*, 45; Holladay, *Fragments*, I, 84.

16. Euseb. *PE* 9.21.14: διαπορεῖσθαι δὲ διὰ τί. A different interpretation by Doran, *ANRW* II.20.1 (1987) 249–50.17.

17. Euseb. *PE* 9.21.14–15; Genesis 43.34, 45.22. On textual problems with regard to the numbers, see Freudenthal, *Alexander Polyhistor*, 53–54; Holladay, *Fragments*, I, 84–86.

18. Euseb. *PE* 9.29.1–3; cf. Freudenthal, *Alexander Polyhistor*, 42–44; P. M. Fraser, *Ptolemaic Alexandria* (Oxford, 1972) I, 692; Wacholder, *Eupolemus*, 100–101. It may well be that by tracing Zipporah's lineage to Abraham, Demetrius was responding to concerns that Moses had married a woman outside his people; so Gutman, *Beginnings*, I, 137 (Hebrew); J. J. Collins, *Between Athens and Jerusalem* (New York, 1983) 28; Doran, *ANRW* II.20.1 (1987) 250; Sterling, *Historiography and Self-Definition*, 160.

19. Euseb. *PE* 9.29.16: ἐπιζητεῖν δέ τινα πῶς οἱ Ἰσραηλῖται ὅπλα ἔσχον ἄνοπλοι ἐξελθόντες.

20. Euseb. *PE* 9.29.16; cf. Exodus 13.18, and the discussion in Holiaday, *Fragments*, I, 89–90. It should be noted that the fragment, though very probably from Demetrius, is not explicitly ascribed to him.

early first century BCE. A date in the reign of Ptolemy IV Philopator in the late third century has won near unanimous opinion, on the grounds that Demetrius employs that reign as chronological marker in one of his fragments: 573 years from the fall of Samaria to the time of Ptolemy IV.[21] A note of caution might be injected. Demetrius does not actually denote Philopator's reign as "in my time" or anything comparable. And the fragments show a fondness for employing various chronological markers to calculate intervals between events.[22] Strictly speaking, the late third century provides only a *terminus post quem*. As for place, the same passage has sufficed to situate Demetrius in Ptolemaic Egypt, more particularly in Alexandria.[23] One might note, however, that a Ptolemaic reign, as well as a Seleucid one, is also employed as a chronological indicator by the historian Eupolemus—whom almost all moderns place in Judaea.[24] Further, if Demetrius' *floruit* in fact came in the later third century, he could well have employed a Ptolemaic date while dwelling in Palestine, at that time under the sway of the Ptolemies. Other items have also been brought into the reckoning, notably the fact that Demetrius had intimate familiarity with the Septuagint.[25] Indeed, further conclusions conventionally follow with regard to the existence and influence of the Septuagint prior to the late third century.[26] The circularity in all this is patent—and the progress illusory. Better to infer Demetrius' objectives from the fragments themselves.

21. Clement *Strom.* 1.21.141.2. Freudenthal, *Alexander Polyhistor*, 57–62, sought to push the date back to Ptolemy III to suit the correct chronology of Samaria's fall. But see the cogent criticisms of E. Bickerman in J. Neusner, *Christianity, Judaism, and Other Greco-Roman Cults* (Leiden, 1975) III, 80–84. The late 3rd century is accepted by almost all commentators; e.g. A. M. Denis, *Introduction aux pseudépigraphes grecs d'ancien testament* (Leiden, 1970) 250; Fraser, *Ptolemaic Alexandria*, I, 693; Wacholder, *Eupolemus*, 99, 280; N. Walter, *Jüdische Schriften aus hellenistisch-römischer Zeit* (Gütersloh, 1975) II.2, 282; Collins, *Between Athens and Jerusalem*, 27; Holladay, *Fragments*, I, 51; E. Schürer, *The History of the Jewish People*, rev. ed. by G. Vermes, F. Millar, and M. Goodman (Edinburgh, 1986) III.1, 515; Walter in W. D. Davies and L. Finkelstein, *The Cambridge History of Judaism* (Cambridge, 1989) II, 387; Sterling, *Historiography and Self-Definition*, 153.

22. Cf. Euseb. *PE* 9.21.18.

23. See the works cited in n. 11. Reservations expressed by Wacholder, *Eupolemus*, 280, 292, and Schürer, *History of the Jewish People*, II.1, 516.

24. Clement *Strom.* 1.21.141.4. See, e.g., Wacholder, *Eupolemus*, 8–13; Sterling, *Historiography and Self-Definition*, 207–209, with bibliography.

25. The fact was decisively demonstrated by Freudenthal, *Alexander Polyhistor*, 40–44, 48–51, 206–207.

26. So, e.g. Schürer, *History of the Jewish People*, III.1, 515; Hanson in Charlesworth, *Old Testament Pseudepigrapha*, II, 844–45.

Demetrius' agenda surely had Jewish ends in view. That he was himself a Jew can hardly be questioned. Gentiles with an interest in the minutiae of biblical chronology or a concern about the disproportionate share meted out by Joseph to Benjamin would be rare birds indeed.[27] Did Demetrius then engage in apologetic historiography, driven by a desire to defend Jewish practices like abstention from animal thigh sinew or to erase embarrassment over Joseph's nine-year neglect of his father?[28] It has even been proposed that Demetrius wrote in response to Manetho's hostile rendition of the Jewish experience in Egypt.[29] And Demetrius' obsession with chronological precision for the most remote periods of Israelite history has suggested to some the motive of demonstrating the hoary antiquity of the Jews, thus to claim a priority over other cultures.[30]

The proposals fall well short of persuasion. Apologetic purposes of any sort seem distant indeed from the sober, dry, and colorless narrative of Demetrius. Few readers would gain a vivid or memorable impression of Israelite heroes from a brief reference to Jacob's wrestling match recorded simply to account for a Jewish dietary restriction, or a bald reference to Joseph as dream-interpreter and ruler of Egypt, or the tale of Dinah's rape and the vengeance imposed on Shechem mentioned in passing only to provide the ages of the principals.[31] No hint of polemic exists in Demetrius' austere renditions, no embellishments of character, no syncretistic transformation of biblical personages into figures of universal significance. And if Demetrius had been bent upon establishing Israelite chronological precedence over the nations of the world, one would expect some comparative time reckonings. His calculations, however, are strictly internal. The exercise has a starkly

27. Josephus does list Demetrius together with the "elder Philo" and Eupolemus as Greek writers on Jewish antiquity; *C. Apion.* 1.218. But this is a manifest confusion with Demetrius of Phaleron, as Josephus himself calls the writer. Eusebius has it right in *HE*, 6.13.7.

28. So P. Dalbert, *Die Theologie der hellenistisch-jüdischen Missions-Literatur unter Ausschluss von Philo und Josephus* (Hamburg, 1954) 27–32; cf. Denis, *Introduction*, 251; P. W. van der Horst, *Essays on the Jewish World of Early Christianity* (Göttingen, 1990) 197.

29. S. K. Eddy, *The King is Dead* (Lincoln, 1961) 195; Freudenthal, *Alexander Polyhistor*, 81; Fraser, *Ptolemaic Alexandria*, I, 694.

30. Gutman, *Beginnings*, I, 136 (Hebrew); M. Hengel, *Judaism and Hellenism* (London, 1974) I, 69; Sterling, *Historiography and Self-Definition*, 163–66; cf. Bickerman in Neusner, *Christianity, Judaism, and Other Greco-Roman Cults*, 76–78.

31. The wrestling match: Euseb. *PE* 9.21.7; rape of Dinah and revenge: Euseb. *PE* 9.21.9; Joseph as ruler: Euseb. *PE* 9.21.12. The straightforward and unadorned character of Demetrius' presentation is equally well exemplified in his abbreviated and matter-of-fact recounting of the Abraham-Isaac sacrifice story—if that fragment in fact belongs to Demetrius; Euseb. *PE* 9.19.4. Attribution of the anonymous fragment to Demetrius is questioned by Doran, *ANRW* II.20.1 (1987) 249, and Sterling, *Historiography and Self-Definition*, 155.

academic quality. No wonder that some moderns regard Demetrius as engaging in exegesis for its own sake: the Jewish historian had imbibed the exacting principles of Alexandrian scholarship and put the techniques of Greek learning to the service of Jewish hermeneutics.[32] There may indeed be something in this. Demetrius wrote in Greek for a cultivated reading audience. Exposure to Hellenic modes and forms of scholarship could have served as stimulus and inspiration. Yet the extant fragments breathe hardly a hint of texts or traditions outside the Septuagint. Demetrius' narrative appears to be a rigorously internal one. Nor would he require Alexandrian techniques to engage in exegetical enterprise. The Scriptures themselves attest to it, and the Book of Jubilees provides a rewriting of Genesis and Exodus that owes little or nothing to Alexandrianism.[33] Jewish rather than Hellenic foundations undergird the history of Demetrius.

It does not follow that Demetrius provided exegesis for its own sake. His readership plainly consisted of Jews. Few Gentiles would have had the remotest interest in biblical genealogies or reconciling chronological discrepancies to account for the marriage of Moses and Zipporah. Why then rewrite a narrative for Jews already familiar with it? In fact, Demetrius, as even the scanty fragments show, avoided a mere reproduction of Scripture. He abbreviated, streamlined, and modified the text—to the detriment of its vividness and drama. Demetrius had other ends in view. For Jews who read and spoke Greek, especially those attracted by Hellenic rationalism and critical inquiry, the Bible presented some troubling problems: inconsistencies, chronological disparities, and historical perplexities. Demetrius took up the tangles, reduced narrative to bare bones, assembled chronological data, straightened out genealogies, and supplied explanations for peculiar deeds and events. His work or works, therefore, offered reassurance on the reliability of the Scriptures.[34] Demetrius engaged in ratiocination, not apologia. Nor did he offer an alternative to the biblical narrative. The authority of that narrative was taken for granted by the historian for whom it was the sole source of

32. See Freudenthal, *Alexander Polyhistor*, 65–77; M. Hengel, *FondHardt* 18 (1972) 236; Fraser, *Ptolemaic Alexandria*, I, 692–94; Walter, *Jüdische Schriften*, III.2, 281; Collins, *Between Athens and Jerusalem*, 29–30; H. W. Attridge in M. E. Stone, *Jewish Writings of the Second Temple Period* (Phildelphia, 1984) 162; Hanson in Charlesworth, *Old Testament Pseudepigrapha*, 845; Sterling, *Historiography and Self-Definition*, 160–62.

33. Cf. the general remarks on overlapping of biblical and interpretative tradition by G. Vermes, *Scripture and Tradition in Judaism* (Leiden, 1961) 127, and the cogent discussion of Demetrius by Wacholder, *Eupolemus*, 98–104, 280–82—although his conjecture that Demetrius actually influenced the Septuagintal tradition is unlikely. See also the valuable treatment by Gutman, *Beginnings*, I, 137–39 (Hebrew).

34. Cf. Collins, *Between Athens and Jerusalem*, 28; van der Horst, *Essays*, 197.

his reconstruction. He appealed to a sophisticated Jewish readership that posed tough questions as well as seeking edification. Demetrius' rewriting came at the cost of aesthetic quality and dramatic power, but it reinforced confidence in the tradition.

.   .   .

A single fragment survives of the Hellenistic Jew Aristeas—and nothing at all of his origin, life, or location. But the fragment alone excites interest, suggesting another reconstruction firmly based on the Bible but shaped to a particular purpose. The quotation again stems from Alexander Polyhistor as conveyed by Eusebius, a third-hand transmission that naturally generates nervousness about accuracy. Polyhistor cites Aristeas' work simply as "On the Jews," which may be a title but more likely a general description. Its scope and extent are beyond recovery—or conjecture. The sole fragment represents a severe condensation of the Book of Job. Aristeas has Job, formerly Jobab, as son of Esau and Bassara, thus setting him in the patriarchal age, a man of righteousness and of great wealth. God put him to the test, to probe his fidelity. Job swiftly lost all, his livestock and camels taken, his sheep and shepherds burned, and his children killed when their house collapsed. Job's whole body was then afflicted by sores. Friends hurried to offer comfort, but Job assured them that he remained firm in his piety even in dire straits. God was amazed at his great spirit, freed him from illness, and made him master of many holdings.[35] Such is the text.

How best to understand Aristeas' purpose? The author is convention-ally designated by moderns as "Aristeas the Exegete," a useful label, though without ancient authority. Certainly he did not reproduce the Book of Job but offered a highly concentrated summary which applied to it his own em-phasis and consequently an implied interpretation. Like Demetrius, Aristeas worked with the Septuagint, a fact plainly demonstrable from wording and content.[36] Nothing suggests any departure from the Septuagintal text or use of extraneous material. But Aristeas may well have put together certain items from various parts in order to reach his formulations. So, for instance, the claim that Job previously had the name Jobab identifies him with the Jobab

---

35. Euseb. *PE* 9.25.1–4. See the text in Holladay, *Fragments*, I, 268–70, with translation. The text can be consulted also in A.-M. Denis, *Fragmenta Pseudepigraphorum Quae Supersunt Graeca* (Leiden, 1970) 195–96, and translations in Walter, *Jüdische Schriften*, III.2, 295–96, and R. Doran in Charlesworth, *Old Testament Pseudepigrapha*, II, 859.

36. Freudenthal, *Alexander Polyhistor*, 136–41; Walter, *Jüdische Schriften*, III.2, 293; Collins, *Between Athens and Jerusalem*, 30.

of Genesis 36.33, a descendant of Esau. The conjecture has little claim on authority. Job was no son of Esau and Bassara, as Aristeas claims. Even the Greek additions to the Book of Job which amalgamate him with Jobab have him as great-grandson of Esau. And "Bassara" is no woman at all but confusion with a place name. Perhaps Aristeas misread the Septuagintal text or Alexander Polyhistor made a mistake in transmission. But the conflation of Job and Jobab, thus linking Job to the descendants of Abraham and the kings of Edom in the pre-Mosaic era could be Aristeas' own.[37] That would suggest some ingenuity and imagination.

More significant is the thrust of Aristeas' précis as a whole. He includes none of Job's anguish, his bitter laments and protest, his cursing of the day of his birth, the breaking of his spirit, and the fundamental questioning of divine justice. In Aristeas' summary, there is only steadfastness, no wavering, and no doubt. Job endures his afflictions, secure in his faith. It is God who is amazed at Job's great courage and then rewards him with bounteous goods.[38]

Aristeas has shifted the direction of the tale in striking fashion. Not that he challenges or alters the Scriptures. Readers of the Septuagint would find no contradiction or inconsistency. But the stress placed by Aristeas' succinct summary amounts to a wholesale reinterpretation. The ferocious agonizing over human righteousness and divine power has vanished, leaving only constancy in faith and earned rewards. Whatever the implications for Aristeas' theology, the composition of this particular synopsis demonstrates that Jewish thinkers could offer their own powerful and remarkable exegesis simply through studied selectivity.[39] Readership and reception remain a matter of guesswork. Aristeas may have been a Palestinian or an Alexandrian

---

37. Freudenthal, *Alexander Polyhistor*, 139–41, argued that the additions to the Septuagintal Book of Job, 42.17.b–e, derive from Aristeas, rather than the other way round, a not implausible conclusion; so also Walter, *Jüdische Schriften*, III.2, 293–94; cf. Denis, *Introduction*, 258. Others propose that both depended on a "Syrian book" alluded to in the Greek epilogue to Job; 42.17.b; Collins, *Between Athens and Jerusalem*, 30; Doran, *ANRW* II.20.1 (1987) 251–52; Schürer, *History of the Jewish People*, III.1, 525. But the reference to the "Syrian book" may apply only to what came before, not to the text of the appendix; so Walter, *op. cit.*, 294.

38. Euseb. *PE* 9.25.4: τὸν δὲ θεὸν ἀγασθέντα τὴν εὐψυχίαν αὐτοῦ τῆς τε νόσου αὐτὸν ἀπολῦσαι καὶ πολλῶν κύριον ὑπάρξεων ποιῆσαι.

39. Doran offers a fine analysis in *ANRW* II.20.1 (1987) 253–54; cf. *idem* in Charlesworth, *Old Testament Pseudepigrapha*, II, 855–56. But his thesis that Aristeas sought to evoke martyr tales with his allusion to wonder and admiration at steadfastness in suffering may misplace the emphasis. Aristeas points not to the amazement of persecutors but to the amazement of God, a very different and far more striking matter. The terms employed by Aristeas, ἄγασθαι and εὐψυχία, are found almost nowhere in the Septuagint; cf. Dalbert, *Die Theologie*, 69.

Jew, writing some time after the availability of the Septuagint and before Alexander Polyhistor. Little more can be said with any confidence.[40] But the lone fragment, skimpy though it be, implies an audience of Hellenized Jews open to recast versions of Scripture, with no diminution of their faith.[41] In fact, Aristeas' résumé of Job resolves biblical doubts into new certainties. Job's trust in the Lord's rectitude exceeds even the Lord's confidence in his servant. God stands in awe of the piety of man. Here is edification indeed. Aristeas' rendition directed itself to readers who were both deeply devout and receptive to alternative treatments of the Holy Book.

•   •   •

A more divergent treatment occurs in a very different medium. Alexander Polyhistor preserved record of an epic poet named Theodotus whose extant verses, composed in Homeric hexameters, treated the tale of Dinah's rape at the hands of Shechem and the consequent destruction of the Shechemite city by Dinah's brothers Levi and Simeon, the sons of Jacob.[42] The poet had obviously imbibed Hellenic culture and enjoyed thorough familiarity with Homeric language and epic technique. But he took as his text, at least in the surviving lines, an episode recorded in Genesis 34. A summary of that text as it appears in the Bible, and then of Theodotus' variant, will be instructive.

The biblical account has Jacob return to Canaan, after his lengthy absence in the land of Laban, and reach the city of Shechem. There his

---

40. See the inconclusive discussions of Dalbert, *Die Theologie*, 68; Denis, *Introduction*, 259; Walter, *Jüdische Schriften*, III.2, 293–94; Collins, *Between Athens and Jerusalem*, 30–31; Holladay, *Fragments*, I, 261–62; Schürer, *History of the Jewish People*, II.1, 525–26.

41. A comparable conclusion arises from inspection of the Testament of Job, a much longer and complete Hellenistic text, which also underscores Job's endurance and breathes not a hint of wavering or objection. See the edition of S. P. Brock, *Pseudepigrapha Veteris Testamenti Graece* 2 (Leiden, 1967). Valuable discussions by B. Schaller, *Jüdische Schriften aus hellenistisch-römischer Zeit* (Gütersloh, 1979) III.3, 303–74; *idem, Biblica* 61 (1980) 377–406.

42. The text is contained in Euseb. *PE* 9.22.1–11. It can be conveniently consulted in Denis, *Fragmenta*, 204–207, H. Lloyd-Jones and P. Parsons, *Supplementum Hellenisticum* (Berlin, 1983) 360–65, and Holladay, *Fragments from Hellenistic Jewish Authors* (Atlanta, 1989) II, 106–27, with translation. Theodotus' date and provenance remain uncertain. He preceded Alexander Polyhistor and he wrote for a Hellenized Jewish community which could have been in Palestine or in the Diaspora. No firmer finding is likely. The efforts of R. J. Bull, *HTR* 60 (1967) 221–27, to use the excavations at Shechem to date Theodotus to the mid 2nd century are inconclusive; see Collins, *HTR* 73 (1980) 100–102. Theodotus' poetic description need not reflect eyewitness testimony to the city walls. For a survey of modern opinions on date and origins, see Holladay, *op. cit.*, 68–72, with notes.

daughter Dinah wandered into the city, only to be seized and raped by the like-named Shechem, son of its ruler Hamor. The event set matters rapidly in motion. Shechem may have been initially overcome by lust, but he soon aimed to make an honest man of himself. He obtained the intercession of his father who would speak to Jacob about arranging a wedding. Hamor indeed went well beyond that initial request. He generously proposed a host of marriage alliances between Jacob's people and his own, and made his land and possessions available to the newcomers. The sons of Jacob, however, outraged at the defilement of Dinah, plotted deception and revenge. They consented to the uniting of the peoples but only on condition that the Shechemites circumcise themselves, for intermarriage with the uncircumcised would be intolerable. Hamor and Shechem readily agreed, took the lead themselves, their example was swiftly followed, and within a short time all the males in Shechem were circumcised. That provided the opportunity for Dinah's brothers Levi and Simeon. While the Shechemites still suffered the effects of their recent surgery, the two sons of Jacob swooped upon them, murdered every male, and looted everything in the city, including women and children. The underhanded scheme and the ruthless butchering of a compliant people sat ill with Jacob. He rebuked Levi and Simeon for making him vulnerable to the hostility of his neighbors generally. And he never forgave them. On his death bed, Jacob cursed Levi and Simeon for their resort to the sword and their reckless yielding to animus and anger.[43] The tale hardly casts the Israelite actions in the best possible light.

Theodotus' version adheres to the basic narrative but turns it in a quite different direction. Both his elaborations and his omissions set the events in contrasting colors. Theodotus opens with a laudatory description of the city of Shechem, whose name he traces to its founder Sicimius, a son of Hermes.[44] He proceeds to report that it was subsequently occupied by Hebrews in the time of Hamor and Shechem, a very stubborn pair.[45] Theodotus then offers an excursus for background: Jacob's sojourn with Laban after the quarrel with Esau, his marriages, and the birth of his children, including the beautiful, shapely, and noble Dinah.[46] Hamor welcomed Jacob and his family into Shechem and provided them with land. But his son Shechem immediately became enamored of Dinah, carried her off, and raped her.

43. Genesis 33.18–34.31, 49.5–7.
44. Euseb. *PE* 9.22.1.
45. Euseb. *PE* 9.22.2.
46. Euseb. *PE* 9.22.3.

Only later did he seek her hand in marriage, coming with his father to make the request of Jacob. The Hebrew patriarch responded that marriage in his clan could take place only with the circumcised, a divine commandment stemming from the time of Abraham and inviolable. Jacob required that all Shechemite males undergo the change before he would sanction Dinah's marriage. Hamor raised no objection and agreed to persuade his people.[47] He was in the course of doing so when Simeon inspired his brother Levi to action, citing an oracle that promised God's gift of ten nations to the descendants of Abraham. The Lord provided them with the idea in order to punish the impiety of those in Shechem. He struck at the Shechemites who were inhospitable to all, reckless of rights and laws, enmeshed in their own deadly deeds.[48] Simeon and Levi consequently entered the city, killing those whom they encountered, and then murdering Hamor and Shechem— the latter two deaths described in graphic, Homeric fashion by Theodotus. When the other sons of Jacob learned of the events, they joined their brothers, plundered the city, and brought back Dinah, together with their captives, to the house of Jacob.[49]

Theodotus kept his eye on the Genesis narrative throughout. Nothing in his account stands in flagrant contradiction with it. But he felt free to embroider or suppress matters, thus giving a distinctive slant and allowing for an alternative meaning. The epic poet blended Greek elements with the Hebrew legend. Theodotus identified Shechem's founder with the son of Hermes, a feature that linked the city's story to *ktisis* tales and Greek mythology.[50] And he has the divine impetus for the attack on Shechem delivered through an oracular forecast in Hellenic fashion.[51] The pagan trimmings were plainly congenial to the auditors of Theodotus' epic rendition of the Scriptures.

47. Euseb. *PE* 9.22.4–7.

48. Euseb. *PE* 9.22.8–9. On this passage, see R. Pummer and M. Roussel, *JSJ* 13 (1982) 177–82.

49. Euseb. *PE* 9.22.10–11.

50. Euseb. *PE* 9.22.1: τὰ δὲ Σίκιμά φησι Θεόδοτος ἐν τῷ περὶ Ἰουδαίων ἀπὸ Σικιμίου τοῦ Ἑρμοῦ λαβεῖν τὴν ὀνομασίαν. A. Ludwich, *De Theodoti carmine graeco-iudaico* (Königsberg, 1899) 5, long ago emended Σικιμίου τοῦ Ἑρμοῦ to Συχὲμ υἱοῦ τοῦ Ἐμμὼρ, thus eliminating the syncretism. And the supposed error has been ascribed to Polyhistor; Collins, *HTR* 73 (1980) 102; *idem, Between Athens and Jerusalem*, 48. But there is no mansucript warrant for an emendation, and such a mistake is highly implausible. It would make the ruler of the city at the time of Jacob identical with the father of its founder. So, rightly, Schürer, *History of the Jewish People*, III.1, 562; cf. N. Walter, *Jüdische Schriften aus hellenistisch-römischer Zeit* IV.3 (Gütersloh, 1983) 164; F. Fallon in Charlesworth, *Old Testament Pseudepigrapha*, II, 790. See the long note by Holladay, *Fragments*, II, 131–35.

51. Euseb. *PE* 9.22.8: λόγιον προφερόμενον τὸν θεὸν.

More important divergences, however, lay elsewhere. The biblical tale casts a cloud on Israelite actions. Shechem's ravishing of Dinah, to be sure, was hardly exemplary conduct, nor is it condoned in Genesis. But the young man hastened to turn his infatuation into a permanent relationship, his father was magnanimous in welcoming Jacob's people into his lands and property, and Shechemite males unhesitatingly subjected themselves to circumcision—a stunning display of neighborliness. Yet it earned them only massacre, pillage, and captivity, the result of deception and a sneak attack by Jacob's sons, behavior condemned even by their father. Theodotus puts a different twist on the tale. God implants the thought of revenge in the minds of Simeon and Levi. And the Shechemites got what was coming to them, for they were a godless and discreditable people, maimed by God to set them up for the slaughter by Jacob's sons. Theodotus leaves out any calculated ruse on the part of the Hebrews. Nor does he suggest that the Shechemites had circumcised themselves and were still recuperating when attacked—although Hamor did encourage them to do so. And the poet also omits any reproach or dissent from Jacob. The retaliation for Dinah's disgrace goes unquestioned.

What significance do these changes bear? Scholars have long debated Theodotus' roots: was he Samaritan or Jew? On the first hypothesis, he transformed the Genesis story of Jacob and his sons into an epic centered upon Shechem, which he terms a "holy city" and whose future is encapsulated by the forecast that God will give the "ten nations" (i.e. presumably the ten tribes of the northern kingdom) to the descendants of Abraham.[52] If advancement of Samaritan interests were the purpose, however, this epic would not seem to do the job. The city perished by divine command, its citizens godless, inhospitable, and no respecters of law and justice. Hence, some have interpreted Theodotus as conveying anti-Samaritan propaganda, perhaps indeed an apologist for John Hyrcanus who captured Shechem, destroyed the Samaritan temple, and enforced circumcision upon the Idumaeans.[53]

52. Shechem as the holy city: Euseb. *PE* 9.22.1: ἱερὸν ἄστυ; the ten nations: Euseb. 9.22.8: τὸν θεὸν ἀνελεῖν φάμενον τοῖς Ἀβραὰμ ἀπογόνοις δέκα ἔθνη δώσειν. Arguments for Theodotus as a Samaritan stem from Freudenthal, *Alexander Polyhistor*, 99–101, adopted by, among others, Denis, *Introduction*, 272–73; Fraser, *Ptolemaic Alexandria*, II, 986; Hengel, *FondHardt* 18 (1972) 242–43; Wacholder, *Eupolemus*, 283–85; Bull, *HTR* 60 (1967) 223–24. A fuller bibliography for this view in R. Pummer, *HTR* 75 (1982) 177, n. 2.

53. The case is made most forcefully by Collins, *HTR* 73 (1980) 91–104. And see now M. Mor in I. M. Gafni, A. Oppenheimer, and D. R. Schwartz, *The Jews in the Hellenistic-Roman World: Studies in Memory of Menahem Stern* (Jerusalem, 1996) 345–59 (Hebrew). The idea of Theodotus as Samaritan was questioned long ago by Ludwich, *De Theodoti carmine*, 5, 7. See also H. G. Kippenberg, *Garizim und Synagoge* (Berlin, 1971) 83–84; Walter, *Jüdische Schriften,*

On still another theory, one can view the text not as anti-Samaritan but as anti-Shechemite. This allows Theodotus to be a Samaritan who strives to distinguish contemporary Samaritans from the wicked denizens of Shechem who perished in biblical times—hence a Samaritan apologist responding to anti-Samaritan propaganda.[54]

The whole discussion, however, has proceeded on too narrowly political a front. Theodotus' revisions of Genesis do not so much excoriate the Samaritans as exculpate the Hebrew forefathers. The changes are subtle rather than radical. Theodotus does not seem driven to demonize the Shechemites. In the poem Hamor receives Jacob in welcoming fashion and provides him with land—thus going one better than the biblical version which has Jacob purchase the lot.[55] Hamor further graciously meets Jacob's conditions and undertakes to persuade his people to circumcise themselves. Theodotus holds close to the scriptural text here.[56] He avoids contradiction or challenge, let alone any suggestion of undermining the authority of the Bible. The selective omission had greater effect. No hint of duplicity on the Israelites' part, no actual circumcision by the Shechemites, no attacks while they were ailing, and no censure by Jacob of his sons. It misses the point to ascribe this to pro- or anti-Samaritan indoctrination or to advocacy of Hasmonaean expansionism. Epic poetry was not the most likely vehicle for political propaganda. Theodotus' verse rendition smoothed out some rough spots in the Genesis narrative. Jewish readers could take pleasure in an account that spared opprobrium for the patriarchs.

Contemporary rewritings of the episode in Hebrew moved further along these lines, more direct and less subtle than Theodotus. Jubilees magnifies

---

IV.3, 157–59; *idem, ANRW* II.20.1 (1987) 110–11; G. W. E. Nickelsburg in Stone, *Jewish Writings*, 121–25; Schürer, *History of the Jewish People*, III.1, 561–62; Holladay, *Fragments*, II, 58–68. Further references in Pummer, *HTR* 75 (1982) 177, n. 3. Fallon in Charlesworth, *Old Testament Pseudepigrapha*, II, 785–86, prefers to leave the matter open. The fact that Polyhistor gives the title of the work as περὶ Ἰουδαίων (Euseb. *PE* 9.22.1) suggests a broader subject than just the story of Shechem—though that title may be a generic designation; cf. Holladay, *op. cit.*, 53–58. The label of "holy city" for Shechem need be no more than an epic convention; Ludwich, *op. cit.*, 6. As for the "ten nations," this seems to refer to God's earlier covenant with Abraham, promising subjugation of ten peoples in Palestine—and would thus justify Jewish conquest of Samaria rather than support Samaritan claims on the heritage of Abraham; Genesis 15.18–21; cf. Fallon, *op. cit.*, 793; Holladay, *op. cit.*, 187–88.

54. Such is the ingenious reconstruction of D. Mendels, *The Land of Israel as Political Concept in Hasmonean Literature* (Tübingen, 1987) 110–16; cf. Holladay, *Fragments*, II, 90. A similar view in van der Horst, *Essays*, 194–96.

55. Genesis 33.18–20; Euseb. *PE* 9.22.4: τὸν δὲ ὑποδέξασθαι αὐτὸν καὶ μέρος τι τῆς χώρας δοῦναι.

56. Genesis 34.18–23; Euseb. *PE* 9.22.5, 9.22.8.

the violence of the Shechemite deed. Dinah was just twelve, abducted and raped, not seduced on a sight-seeing trip. Jacob's anger matched that of his sons and they put every man in Shechem to the sword, a judgment issued by the Lord to uphold the honor of Israelite women.[57] The same interpretation underlies the allusion to this event in Judith. The heroine's prayer to God before entering the camp of Holofernes recalls the slaughter in Shechem: the Lord had delivered its inhabitants to destruction in answer to Israelite pleas and as vengeance for the pollution of a virgin.[58] A more complex variant surfaces in the Testament of Levi. In his reference to the event, Levi acknowledges the circumcision of the Shechemites and Jacob's disapproval of his sons' actions. But he denies any deception and amplifies the iniquity of the enemy: they not only defiled Dinah, but had hoped to do the same to Sarah and Rebecca. Their annihilation represents the wrath of God and their dwelling was forever to be regarded as "the city of fools."[59] Later references to the story reinforce the sense that Israelite retaliation against the perpetrators of evil was fully justified and sanctioned by the Lord.[60]

Theodotus' poem was less blunt and more nuanced. Epic conventions allowed for bloody death scenes but need not blacken villains. Theodotus told a tale that nowhere contravened the Scriptures, that left Shechemite behavior ambiguous, but that cleared the Hebrew leaders of duplicity, passed over their internal friction, and set the outcome as execution of divine will.[61]

Epic poetry evidently had an audience among Hellenistic Jews. At least one other Jew composed in that genre. A certain Philo, a few of whose

57. Jubilees 30.1–6; cf. 30.18: Most recent discussion, from a different vantage point, by C. Werman, *HTR* 90 (1997) 3–10.

58. Judith 9.1–4. The rape of Dinah and the massacre of Shechemites in retaliation are mentioned in characteristically sober fashion by Demetrius; Euseb. *PE* 9.21.9.

59. TLevi, 5–7; see, especially, 5.3–4, 6.8. Jacob's anger is noted also in IV Macc. 2.19. J. Kugel, *HTR* 85 (1992) 1–34, provides an insightful and stimulating interpretation of the Testament of Levi on the Dinah story, but places perhaps too much emphasis upon its variants as simply exegetical in character.

60. *Jos. As.* 23.13; Philo *De Mig.* 224; *De Mut.* 193–95, 199–200; Jos. *Ant.* 1.337–41; Ps. Philo 8.7. See the remarks of Collins, *HTR* 73 (1980) 96–99; Pummer, *HTR* 75 (1982) 178–84; Walter, *Jüdische Schriften,* IV.3, 160–61. Most recently, A. Standhartinger in L. Bormann et al., *Religious Propaganda and Missionary Competition in the New Testament* (Leiden, 1994) 89–116, offers a valuable survey of the texts, focusing on the treatment of Dinah. So also *eadem, Das Frauenbild in Judentum der hellenistischen Zeit: Ein Beitrag anhand von "Joseph und Aseneth"* (Leiden, 1995) 155–69.

61. See the intelligent discussion of Pummer, *HTR* 75 (1982) 177–88, who rightly questions the anti-Samaritan interpretation of Theodotus. But he does not provide convincing reasons for his view that the poet's principal aim was to combat mixed marriages. The insistence on circumcision, after all, was not Theodotus' invention, but an integral part of the Genesis story.

verses have reached us through the double filter of Alexander Polyhistor and Eusebius, produced a poem of substantial size with the title "On Jerusalem."[62] What survives may constitute no more than a tiny fraction of the whole. The few extant lines treat only Abraham, Joseph, and the waters of Jerusalem. And even they receive expression in tortured language, enveloped in studied obscurity, the vocabulary riddled with *hapax legomena* and a variety of arcane allusions as if to compete with or outdo the opacity of a Lycophron. That should suffice to discourage protracted speculation about the poem or its author.[63] But a number of the preserved verses suggest that Philo, like Theodotus, may have endeavored to enhance the luster of the patriarchs.

Philo's inflated language, however pompous and pretentious, could serve that purpose. The context of Abraham's would-be sacrifice of Isaac proved suitable. Philo hails Abraham in words either invented or refashioned as "widely-famed," "resplendent," and "abounding in lofty counsels." The expressions intimate but by no means echo or duplicate known epic conventions. Philo has a verbiage all his own. But he applies to the patriarch some striking terms to arrest the attention even of highly cultivated Jews conversant

---

62. Text in Denis, *Fragmenta*, 203–204; Lloyd-Jones and Parsons, *Supplementum Hellenisticum*, 328–31; Holladay, *Fragments*, II, 235–45. A segment on Joseph appeared, according to Polyhistor, in the fourteenth book of the poem; Euseb. *PE* 9.24.1. This would imply a work of remarkable length. Freudenthal, *Alexander Polyhistor*, 100, proposed to emend the "fourteen" to "four," a solution preferred by many; e.g., Denis, *Introduction*, 271; Schürer, *History of the Jewish People*, III.1, 559. But it is neither compelling nor necessary; cf. Walter, *Jüdische Schriften*, IV.3, 140–41. Further bibliography in Holladay, *op. cit.*, 266–67. The poem was, in any case, an extensive one. A single reference survives to one other Jewish presumed practitioner of epic poetry: a certain Sosates described as the "Jewish Homer in Alexandria"; C. Frick, *Chronica Minora* (Leipzig, 1892) 278. But nothing more is known of him; see S. J. D. Cohen, *HTR* 74 (1981) 391–96.

63. Of course, it has not done so. The fact that the epic has Jerusalem as its subject no more makes Philo a Jerusalemite than the affinities with Alexandrian poetry make him an Alexandrian. Nor does his reference to the "pool of the High Priest" (Euseb. *PE* 9.37.3) necessarily point to the structure built by Simon II and mentioned in the Greek translation of Ben Sira 50.3, in the late 2nd century, thus narrowing down Philo's date; see the discussion with bibliography by Holladay, *Fragments*, II, 208–10, 273–78. There is no good reason to associate Philo the epic poet with a certain Philo the historian, registered by Josephus, Clement, and Eusebius—a writer who is himself otherwise unknown and hence of no help; Jos. *C. Apion.* 1.218; Clement *Strom.* 1.141.3; Euseb. *PE* 9.42; cf. Holladay, *op. cit.*, 213–17, who gives full references to the scholarship. The most valuable treatments of Philo may be found in Y. Gutman, *Scripta Hierosolymitana* 1 (1954) 36–63; *idem, Beginnings*, I, 221–44 (Hebrew); Walter, *Jüdische Schriften*, IV.3, 139–46; and the exhaustive notes of Holladay, *op. cit.*, 205–27, 246–99.

with Hellenic literature. Abraham's preeminence acquired especially exalted features.[64]

Joseph enjoys comparable elevation in another fragment. When introducing a segment on Joseph, Philo speaks of "a great leader of the whole, the most high, who founded the happiest dwelling place for them, even from before, from the time of Abraham, Isaac, and Jacob, whence stemmed Joseph."[65] The great leader and most high is generally taken as God. But Philo's penchant for overblown vocabulary and tortured syntax also allows for Joseph as the intended subject. The poetic rendition would thus give the forefather who opened Egypt to the Hebrews an especially august status.[66] Even if those epithets were meant for God, however, Joseph's image is glowing enough. Philo depicts him not only as prophetic interpreter of dreams but as holder of the scepter on the thrones of Egypt, a man who discloses the secrets of fate in the stream of time.[67] His extravagant language was more than mere bombast. Like his fellow Jewish epic poet Theodotus, Philo employed the genre to expand upon Scripture. In his verses the Hebrew patriarchs take on a pronounced eminence described in arresting terms that would resonate with a sophisticated and Hellenized audience.

•   •   •

64. The translations can only be somewhat conjectural; Euseb. *PE* 9.20.1: Ἀβραὰμ κλυτοηχὲς ὑπερτέρῳ ἅμματι δεσμῶν, / παμφαές, πλήμμυρε μεγαυχήτοισι λογισμοῖς. See Walter, *Jüdische Schriften*, IV.3, 148; H. Attridge in Charlesworth, *Old Testament Pseudepigrapha*, II, 785; Holladay, *Fragments*, II, 234–35, 249–52. Gutman, *Scripta Hierosolymitana* 1 (1954) 39–53, offers an imaginative interpretation, linking Philo's verses to Orphic themes and philosophic concepts traceable from Plato to Philo of Alexandria. Cf. *idem, Beginnings*, I, 225–36 (Hebrew). But see the criticisms of Collins, *Between Athens and Jerusalem*, 44–46.

65. Euseb. *PE* 9.24.1: τοῖσιν ἕδος μακαριστὸν ὅλης μέγας ἔκτισεν ἄκτωρ / ὕφιστος καὶ πρόσθεν ἀφ'Ἀβραάμοιο καὶ Ἰσακ / Ἰακὼβ εὐτέκνοιό θ' ὅθεν Ἰωσήφ.

66. For Joseph as subject, see Gutman, *Scripta Hierosolymitana* 1 (1954) 58–59; Dalbert, *Die Theologie*, 34. Most recent scholars opt for God; e.g., Walter, *Jüdische Schriften*, IV.3, 150; Lloyd-Jones and Parsons, *Supplementum Hellenisticum*, 331; Attridge in Charlesworth, *Old Testament Pseudepigrapha*, II, 783–84; Holladay, *Fragments*, II, 267–69, with additional bibliography.

67. Euseb. *PE* 9.24.1: ὃς ὀνείρων / θεσπιστὴς σκηπτοῦχος ἐν Αἰγύπτοιο θρόνοισι / δινεύσας λαθραῖα χρόνου πλημμυρίδι μοίρης. For the rendition of the last phrase as a chiasmus, see Walter, *Jüdische Schriften*, IV.3, 150. Lloyd-Jones and Parsons, *Supplementum Hellenisticum*, 330–31, emend σκηπτοῦχος to σκηπτούχῳ, thus making Pharaoh the holder of the scepter; adopted by Attridge in Charlesworth, *Old Testament Pseudepigrapha*, II, 784. But emendation is unjustified here. Joseph is more than once spoken of as ruler of Egypt in Jewish-Hellenistic literature—including one other reference to his holding of the scepter; Wisdom 10.13–14; see also Demetrius *apud* Euseb. *PE* 9.21.12; I Macc. 2.53.

The reframing of biblical material occurs in still another genre. The Jewish writer Ezekiel tried his hand at tragic drama—not without some success. Working within the tradition of classical tragedy, influenced particularly by the plays of Aeschylus and Euripides, Ezekiel chose Jewish themes for his subjects. How many dramas he wrote and what variety of themes he employed escape detection. But a substantial portion of one play survives, the *Exagoge*, based on the story of Moses leading the Israelites out of Egypt. The choice itself of that tale suggests an appeal to pride in national history and tradition produced in a quintessentially Hellenic mode.[68]

Ezekiel hewed closely to the narrative line contained in the Book of Exodus. He cast it in different form, of course, employing the conventions of the Greek theater, with monologues and dialogues, keeping the battle scenes and the gore off stage, even bringing on the trusty messenger's speech to summarize events that transpired between dramatic episodes. But his tale diverges little from the biblical version. It was not Ezekiel's purpose to raise any doubts about the authority or adequacy of the Scriptures. The Septuagint served as his text and he conveyed its narrative faithfully. This makes all the more intriguing those few instances when he does add new material to the mix. They supply important clues to the tragedian's intent.

Moses fled the wrath of Pharaoh and settled in Midian. So says the Book of Exodus. The account goes on to narrate Moses' assistance to the seven daughters of the priest in Midian, one of whom, Zipporah, he received in marriage.[69] In an altogether different context and much later, the Book of

---

68. The fragments are due to Alexander Polyhistor, as transmitted by Clement and especially by Eusebius. That Ezekiel wrote several tragedies on Jewish themes is noted by Clement *Strom.* 1.23.155.1: ὁ Ἐζεχίηλος ὁ τῶν Ἰουδαικῶν τραγῳδιῶν ποιητής. One may conveniently consult the fragments in the fine study by H. Jacobson, *The Exagoge of Ezekiel* (Cambridge, 1983) 50–67, and Holladay, *Fragments*, II, 344–405. On the influence of Euripides, see K. Kuiper, *REJ* 46 (1903) 52–73, *passim*, 161–62; J. Wiencke, *Ezekielis Iudaei poetae Alexandrini fabulae quae inscribitur Ἐξαγωγή fragmenta* (Münster, 1931); Gutman, *Beginnings*, II, 33–35 (Hebrew). The Aeschylean elements are stressed by Jacobson, *op. cit.* 23–28. As so often, the date and provenance of the work can be determined only within broad limits. Ezekiel employed the Septuagint version of the Pentateuch, as his language makes clear, and he must precede Alexander Polyhistor. Efforts to date him more precisely than some time between the later 3rd and early 1st century rest on no solid foundation. Nor does the subject matter of the *Exagoge* fix the place of composition in Alexandria or elsewhere in Egypt. Among discussions of these issues, see Gutman, *Beginnings*, II, 66–68 (Hebrew); R. G. Robertson in Charlesworth, *Old Testament Pseudepigrapha*, II, 803–804; Jacobson, *op. cit.*, 5–17; Schürer, *History of the Jewish People*, III.1, 564–65; Holladay, *op. cit.*, 308–13, with references to earlier literature. The argument of N. L. Collins, *JSJ* 22 (1991) 201–11, that Ezekiel wrote in Egypt, on the grounds that his calendar day seems to have opened at dawn, is speculative.

69. Exodus 2.15–22.

Numbers reports that Aaron and Miriam criticized Moses for having wed a Kushite wife—which the Septuagint renders as an Ethiopian woman.[70] The tension between these accounts did not escape notice by Hellenistic writers. The historian Demetrius, characteristically enough, set about to explain the situation to his readers and to reassure them that Moses had not taken a barbarian bride. Midian, he asserts, acquired its name from one of Abraham's children. And Zipporah, far from an alien presence, could trace her lineage from Abraham as well. The patriarch in fact had sent his sons to the east to establish a settlement—hence the explanation for Aaron and Miriam labeling Zipporah as an Ethiopian.[71] This constitutes typical rationalization by the assiduous Demetrius.

Ezekiel takes a different approach. He introduces a scene nowhere paralleled in the Scriptures. Moses engages in dialogue with Zipporah, asking her about the seven maidens. Her reply identifies them, including herself, as daughters of the priest who was also sovereign and general of the land, a ruler and judge of the city; and the land itself is called Libya, inhabited by tribes of various nations, black-skinned Ethiopian men.[72] Ezekiel is evidently untroubled by inter-ethnic marriage, even when it involves a preeminent Hebrew hero. After all, the Bible itself acknowledges the fact: Moses was an alien in the land of his wife.[73] The *Exagoge* indeed underscores the bi-national union in the subsequent dialogue. Zipporah declares to a certain Chum that her father gave her as bride to this *xenos*.[74] The father himself, even after the wedding, it seems, addresses Moses as *xenos*.[75] Unlike Demetrius, Ezekiel felt no urge to explain away or disclaim Zipporah's nationality. Nor did he take recourse in the tradition that Moses had two wives, thus distinguishing Zipporah from an Ethiopian bride—if indeed he knew of that tradition at all.[76] For Ezekiel, amalgamation of Zipporah and the Ethiopian woman was

70. Numbers 12.1: γυνὴ Αἰθιόπισσα.

71. Demetrius *apud* Euseb. *PE* 9.29.1–3; cf. Genesis 25.2. See above, p. 114.

72. Euseb. *PE* 9.28.4b: Λιβύη μὲν ἡ γῆ πᾶσα κλῄζεται, ξένε, / οἰκοῦσι δ' αὐτὴν φῦλα παντοίων γενῶν, / Αἰθίοπες ἄνδρες μέλανες.

73. Exodus 2.21–22.

74. Euseb. *PE* 9.28.4c: ξένῳ πατήρ με τῷδ' ἔδωκεν εὐνέτιν. On the character of Chum, evidently an invention by Ezekiel, see Jacobson, *Hebrew University Studies in Literature* 9 (1981) 139–46.

75. Euseb. *PE* 9.29.6.

76. It appears in Jos. *Ant.* 2.252–53, 2.258–63. On this and other legends associating Moses with Ethiopia, see T. Rajak, *JJS* 29 (1978) 111–22. Whether Ezekiel's version has any connection with the tale in Cleodemus Malchus that linked the descendants of Abraham with the conquest of Libya remains entirely speculative; Jos. *Ant.* 1.239–41; Euseb. *PE* 9.20.2–4. See the valuable discussions of Jacobson, *Exagoge*, 85–87, and Holladay, *Fragments*, II, 430–33.

unproblematic, requiring no rationalization. Indeed it added a dimension to Moses' stature—and to that of his descendants. By interpreting Midian as Libya, Ezekiel associated Moses with a vast and storied land, home of diverse peoples. And, in his account, Moses married not only into a priestly family but one that held supreme secular, military, and religious authority in Libya, a designation that could stand for all Africa.[77] Ezekiel's embellishments, fully consistent with but expanding upon the Scriptures, attached international and multicultural elements to the ancestor of the Jews.

The dramatist added a still more remarkable scene that has no biblical prototype. Moses, in dialogue with his father-in-law, reports a puzzling dream, in which he had a vision of a great throne high upon a summit extending to the cleft of heaven. There a noble man sat with diadem and a great scepter, summoned Moses to him, handed him the scepter and diadem, and departed from the throne. From that spot Moses had a view of the whole earth, both below it and above the sky, and a multitude of stars fell on their knees, whose numbers he counted as they passed like an array of troops. Moses' father-in-law provides a most heartening interpretation of the dream. It is a sign from God that Moses will lift up a great throne, will issue judgments, and will serve as guide to mortals. The vision of the whole world, things both below and beyond God's firmament, signifies that Moses will perceive what is, what has been, and what will be.[78] This striking passage corresponds to nothing in the Book of Exodus. Indeed no other tale anywhere in literature ascribes a dream vision to Moses. Further, the very idea of a dream by a Hebrew figure rendered intelligible by a non-Hebrew figure is unparalleled. Ezekiel plainly aimed to capture his readers' attention here.

The various elements of the episode do not lack precedent. For refined readers, the cultural contexts out of which it sprang would have suggested themselves. Moderns have tirelessly sought out the sources of Ezekiel's inspiration. Greek tragedy, of course, supplies dream visions in sufficient quantity. One need mention only Atossa's dream in Aeschylus' *Persae*, Clytaemestra in Sophocles' *Electra*, or the Hecuba of Euripides. They also appear in abundance in the pages of Herodotus. And a Latin drama, produced perhaps within Ezekiel's lifetime, contained a dream which was then interpreted by

---

77. Euseb. *PE* 9.28.4b: ἄρχων δ' ἐστὶ γῆς / εἷς καὶ τύραννος καὶ στρατηλάτης μόνος / ἄρχει δὲ πόλεως τῆσδε καὶ κρίνει βροτοὺς / ἱερεύς. For Libya as Africa, see Herodotus, 4.42.

78. Euseb. *PE* 9.29.6.

another party.[79] None of these instances, however, records a vision remotely comparable to that of Moses in the *Exagoge*. The learned and the devout could have found closer approximations in the Bible itself. Dream stories enliven the narrative at several points, as in the dreams of Jacob, Joseph, and Daniel.[80] Visions of God were vouchsafed to some fortunate figures, like Jacob, Isaiah, Ezekiel, Daniel, and, of course, Moses himself.[81] Of more direct relevance, a few gained a direct glimpse of a throne in Heaven. Isaiah saw the Lord on a lofty and splendid one accompanied by seraphs.[82] The prophet Ezekiel enjoyed the view of a jeweled throne graced by the radiant figure of the Lord.[83] And Daniel's vision included the Almighty taking his seat on a fiery throne.[84] A dream of Joseph presents perhaps the closest parallel to a feature of Moses' vision in *Exagoge*: Joseph claimed to see sun, moon, and stars bow down before him, a passage that may be echoed in Ezekiel's lines that have stars on their knees before Moses.[85]

Nowhere, however, does God relinquish his seat to anyone else. Those who receive the visions are awestruck by their majesty. The idea of succeeding the Lord on his throne and exercising surveillance over the world would have been quite unimaginable to them. The nearest hint might be discerned in Psalm 110, wherein God offers to David a place at his right hand, a promise that David's scepter will extend from Zion, and the forecast that his enemies will form a footstool at his feet.[86] That remains a far cry from replacing the Lord on his throne. Moses himself, of course, had a special relationship with God in the Pentateuch, including not only visions but private consultations. And Ezekiel's portrait of Moses as a seer in the *Exagoge* could well have had as its stimulus Moses' recital of the Lord's deeds in past, present, and future.[87] But no combination of episodes or accumulation of passages adds up to anything like the scene painted by Ezekiel. Closer comparisons come with post-biblical texts, notably with 1 Enoch, the Testament of Levi, and

79. Aesch. *Pers.* 181–214; Soph. *Elektra*, 417–30; Eur. *Hecuba*, 68–97. The texts are noted by Gutman, *Beginnings*, II, 41 (Hebrew); E. Starobinski-Safran, *MH* 31 (1974) 220. Jacobson, *Exagoge*, 96–97, acutely points to precedents in Herodotus; e.g. 1.107–108, 1.209, 3.30, 7.12, 7.19. One person's dream interpreted by another occurs in a play by Accius, referred to by Cic. *De Div.* 1.44–45; see P. van der Horst, *JJS* 34 (1983) 24.

80. Genesis 28.10–15, 37.5–11; Dan. 7.

81. Genesis 28.10–15; Exodus 24.9–10; Isaiah 6.1–4; Ezekiel 1.25–28; Dan. 7.9–10.

82. Isaiah 6.1–2.

83. Ezekiel 1.25–28.

84. Dan. 7.9–10.

85. Genesis 37.9; Euseb. *PE* 9.29.5: καί μοί τι πλῆθος ἀστέρων πρὸς γούνατα / ἔπιπτ'.

86. Psalm 110.1–2.

87. Deut. 32–33. Moses' prescient forecasts occur also in *The Assumption of Moses*, 2–8.

3 Enoch. The first work includes the Lord on a glorious throne ringed by fire and an invitation to Enoch to join him. Later, God places "the Elect One" upon the throne of glory where he sits in judgment on all the holy ones above and the mighty below. In the Testament of Levi, its purported author enters the heavens, observes God on his magnificent throne, and is addressed by him. 3 Enoch gives the nearest parallel: God provides a throne for Enoch, comparable to his own, sets a majestic robe and a royal crown upon him, and appoints him as vice-regent, ruler over all the realms both on high and on earth.[88] Yet even here there are no precise correspondences, no transfer of a throne, and no reason to believe that the testimony of 3 Enoch, compiled long after the era of Ezekiel, sheds light on the context of *Exagoge*.[89]

The creativity of Ezekiel should receive its due. In the Book of Numbers, God announces that, while he reveals himself to others in visions and dreams, he speaks to Moses directly, face to face, without enigmatic messages.[90] Ezekiel chose to ignore or sidestep that statement. It seemed a small price to pay. The playwright had a powerful scene in mind: the forecast of Moses' future through a dramatic dream that gave him access to divinity. Ezekiel employed forms and material drawn both from Greek literature and from Jewish traditions, but he shaped them to convey an original conception. The dramatist not only intensifies the grandeur of Moses, he reconceives Moses' relationship with God. No earlier tradition had Moses see and hear the Lord in a dream—let alone occupy the seat that God had vacated. The modern quest for sources and precedents undervalues the novelty of this treatment.

Moses encounters a "noble man" with scepter and diadem on the great throne that extends to Heaven. The image here plainly presents God as sovereign power, ruler of the universe.[91] The celestial realm appears as

88. 1 Enoch 14.18–25; see Jacobson, *Illinois Classical Studies* 6 (1981) 274–75; 1 Enoch 55.4, 61.8, 62.1–16; cf. Holladay, *SBL Seminar Papers* (1976) 450; TLevi, 2.5–7, 5.1–2; 3 Enoch 10.1–6, 12.1–4; cf. van der Horst, *JJS* 34 (1983) 24–25.

89. Jacobson, *Exagoge*, 89–97, provides valuable parallels for the several parts of the scene, but leaves little room for Ezekiel's originality. So also Nickelsburg in Stone, *Jewish Writings*, 126–28.

90. Numbers 12.6–8.

91. Euseb. *PE* 9.29.5: θρόνον / μέγαν τιν' εἶναι μέχρις οὐρανοῦ πτυχός, / ἐν τῷ καθῆσθαι φῶτα γενναῖόν τινα / διάδημ' ἔχοντα καὶ μέγα σκῆπτρον. Use of the Homeric φώς here does not mean that Ezekiel represents God in human form, as Jacobson, *Illinois Classical Studies* 6 (1981) 278–79, interprets it. Nor should one take it as an allusion to Pharaoh, soon to be replaced by Moses, the view of Starobinksi-Safran, *MH* 31 (1974) 222; Collins, *Between Athens and Jerusalem*, 208–209; Holladay, *Fragments*, II, 442. Gutman, *Beginnings*, II, 43 (Hebrew) suggests Enoch. There can be little doubt that the occupant of a heavenly throne is God. The emphasis, however, is upon God's sweeping authority as emblematic of royal power; cf. W. A. Meeks, *The Prophet King* (Leiden, 1967) 147–49.

analogous to royal governance on earth. God beckons to Moses to approach the throne, then bids him sit upon it, hands over the scepter and diadem, and departs.[92] The meaning can hardly be that God has relinquished universal dominion. Rather, Ezekiel calls attention to the analogy. Moses' ascension to the throne and acquisition of royal emblems signals his appointment as the Lord's surrogate in governing the affairs of men.[93] That meaning is reinforced when Moses' father-in-law interprets the dream. He explains that Moses will cause a great throne to rise, will exercise jurisdiction, and will be a leader of mortals. The explanation evidently foresees Moses as executor of God's will on earth, with absolute authority on a royal model.[94] As the dream proceeds, Moses gains a view of the whole earth all around, both

92. Euseb. *PE* 9.29.5: δεξιᾷ δέ μοι / ἔνευσε, κἀγὼ πρόσθεν ἐστάθην θρόνου. / σκῆπτρον δέ μοι παρέδωκε καὶ εἰς θρόνου μέγαν / εἶπεν καθῆσθαι. βασιλικὸν δ' ἔδωκέ μοι / διάδημα καὶ αὐτὸς ἐκ θρόνων χωρίζεται.

93. On the association of Moses with kingly powers in other later texts, see W. A. Meeks in J. Neusner, *Religions in Antiquity: Essays in Memory of E. R. Goodenough* (Leiden, 1968) 354–71. The argument of van der Horst, *JJS* 34 (1983) 24–27, and *Mnemosyne* 37 (1984) 364–65, that the scene implies a deification of Moses, is unpersuasive. The parallels with 3 Enoch do not suffice, since God and Enoch both sat on thrones. The additional material adduced by van der Horst concerns shared thrones and thus cannot account for the dream in *Exagoge*. Any notion of deification is, in any case, dispelled by God's later reminder to Moses that he is mortal; Euseb. *PE* 9.29.8: θνητὸν γεγῶτα. Jacobson, *Illinois Classical Studies* 6 (1981) 272–78, by contrast, takes rather too sober a view of Ezekiel. For him, the dream scene, by making Moses' ascension an illusory one, represents a deliberate reaction against those versions that saw it as a real event; Ezekiel thus demystifies Moses and the entire episode by turning it into a dream. That analysis will not carry the day. None of the texts cited by Jacobson as Moses' heavenly ascension precedes Ezekiel, thus weakening the idea that he was polemicizing against the tradition they represented. Further, the "ascension" is normally associated with the climbing of Sinai and receipt of the Law. But the dream of Moses in *Exagoge* has no ostensible connection with that event. And, most significant, the convention of the prophetic dream in both Greek and Jewish literature serves to present real events of the future in symbolic guise—not to suggest that the events themselves are an illusion. See the criticisms of Jacobson, on other grounds, by van der Horst, *Mnemosyne* 37 (1984) 365–67; *idem, Essays*, 190–92. D. Mendels, *The Rise and Fall of Jewish Nationalism* (New York, 1992) 71–72, offers a brief and thoughtful analysis of the episode as representing Moses in the form of a universal king, but ties it perhaps too closely to the Ptolemaic monarchy.

94. Euseb. *PE* 9.29.6: ἐξαναστήσεις θρόνον / καὶ αὐτὸς βραβεύσεις καὶ καθηγήσῃ βροτῶν. The verb ἐξαναστήσεις has sometimes been rendered as "overturn," thus alluding to the overthrow of Pharaonic rule; so, e.g., Dalbert, *Die Theologie*, 58; Starobinski-Safran, *MH* 31 (1974) 222; additional bibliography in Jacobson, *Exagoge*, 201, n. 25. But Pharaoh's rule was not, in fact, overturned, nor did Moses replace him. The whole idea is fully at variance both with tradition and with Ezekiel. Cf. Jacobson, *op. cit.*, 93; Holladay, *Fragments*, II, 447–48. There is no sound reason to see the functions of a prophet implied in the words βραβεύσεις and καθηγήσῃ; so, rightly, Jacobson, *Illinois Classical Studies* 6 (1981) 287–88, as against Holladay, *SBL Seminar Papers* (1976) 448–49; cf. *idem, Fragments*, II, 443–44.

beneath and beyond the sky, while a multitude of stars fall on their knees before him.[95] The remarkable passage has naturally provided support for the thesis that Moses has taken on the features of divinity and that the astral symbolism implies rule over the whole cosmos.[96] The thesis, however, runs into a major obstacle. Explication of the dream by Moses' father-in-law refutes it decisively. He takes Moses' vision of all things above and below Heaven as signifying ability to see into past, present, and future.[97] The vast dominion that Moses beholds from his lofty vantage point extends in time rather than space. The symbolism connotes the prophetic powers that he could now exercise.

Ezekiel has thereby combined familiar conventions with striking novelty to create a complex picture. He nowhere disputes or denies the biblical account. But the admixture of the dream episode both magnifies the Moses figure and renders it more accessible to the dramatist's contemporary society. Moses as prophet has scriptural roots in his final forecasts before death at the conclusion of Deuteronomy. But Ezekiel raises it to a new level, dramatized by the vast sweep of Moses' vista when set upon God's throne. He expressed the powers of the Hebrew prophets in terms that applied to Greek seers. And he draped Moses in the emblems of royal power that would resonate with those who lived in the era of the great monarchies. The author reinvents the position of Moses on the model of Hellenistic kingship, while at the same time making Moses the model and precursor of Hellenistic kingship itself. God places Moses upon his own throne, a symbolic assignment of universal authority, to sit in judgment and be a guide for all mortals. The lines have telling significance: they betoken the application of the Law as a pattern for all nations. The Israelite hero thus becomes a beacon for mankind, a

95. Euseb. *PE* 9.29.5: ἐγὼ δ' ἐσεῖδον γῆν ἅπασαν ἔγκυκλον / καὶ ἔνερθε γαίας καὶ ἐξύπερθεν οὐρανοῦ. / καί μοί τι πλῆθος ἀστέρων πρὸς γούνατα / ἔπιπτ'.

96. So E. R. Goodenough, *By Light, Light: The Mystic Gospel of Hellenistic Judaism* (New Haven, 1935) 288–91; Denis, *Introduction*, 274; van der Horst, *JJS* 34 (1983) 24–25; cf. Collins, *Between Athens and Jerusalem*, 208–11. Jacobson, *Illinois Classical Studies* 6 (1981) 273–74, rejects the whole approach, with some justice. But his minimalist interpretation is excessive. Jacobson's claim that beholding the cosmos is not equivalent to being master of it ignores the fact that the stars fell on their knees to Moses. This is more than just a "view from a mountain top." See the dissent of van der Horst, *Mnemosyne* 37 (1984) 368.

97. Euseb. *PE* 9.29.6: ὄψει τά τ' ὄντα τά τε προτοῦ τά θ' ὕστερον. Holladay, *SBL Seminar Papers* (1976) 447–52, takes this as foundation for his idea that Ezekiel portrays Moses as a mantic figure along Hellenic lines, a counterpart to Apollo, the divine representative and surrogate of Zeus. The inference has little basis in the texts. See the criticisms of Collins, *Between Athens and Jerusalem*, 208; Jacobson, *Illinois Classical Studies* 6 (1981) 287–89; van der Horst, *JJS* 34 (1983) 28–29.

representative of the divinity on earth, described in phraseology that struck responsive chords among Ezekiel's Hellenic or Hellenized compatriots.

One other extant scene of the play has no counterpart or precedent in the Bible. The Israelites at Elim in the desert encounter a magnificent and multicolored bird of stunning proportions and appearance, evidently the legendary Phoenix.[98] The brevity of the fragment precludes confident conjecture or extended discussion. But the scene plainly involved the merging of a Jewish tale with Hellenic myth in creative fashion.[99] The tragic poet held scriptural authority in awe. But that did not prevent him from occasionally improving upon it. His most inventive scenes gave heightened force to Jewish traditions by commingling them with features arising from Greek culture and society. For a readership of Hellenistic Jews, tragic drama with such themes would be a source of both comfort and pride.[100]

•   •   •

Jewish-Hellenistic writings in Greek came in assorted forms, genres, and styles. The retelling of biblical stories for those who dwelled in Greek-speaking communities proved to be an especially lively enterprise. But it was more than mere self-indulgence or entertainment. The writers treated here addressed themselves to devout Jews who knew their Scriptures, at least in Greek translation. None evoked any distrust in the authority of the text. Their renditions, however, with judicious selectivity, omission, or augmentation, could enhance the significance of the tradition for Jews conversant with Hellenic culture. The historian Demetrius addressed troubling questions arising out of the Bible—chronological disparities, problematical behavior, historical puzzles. His solutions and rationalizations, however strained or awkward, sought to make the stories hold up. Demetrius aimed to silence the skeptic and hearten the faithful. As Demetrius reduced dynamic narrative

98. Euseb. *PE* 9.29.16b.

99. For discussion, see Gutman, *Beginnings*, II, 60–65 (Hebrew); R. van den Broek, *The Myth of the Phoenix According to Classical and Early Christian Traditions* (Leiden, 1971) 121–22, 393–96. Jacobson, *Exagoge*, 157–64, offers the attractive idea that Ezekiel saw the regeneration of the Phoenix as analogous to the redemption of the Israelites in Egypt, but he also goes well beyond this in questionable speculation. See also the notes of Holladay, *Fragments*, II, 518–26, with bibliography.

100. There is nothing to suggest that the work aimed to impress pagans with Jewish values, as is maintained by Dalbert, *Die Theologie*, 55; so also van der Horst, *Essays*, 193. In the most recent treatment, J. M. C. Barclay, *Jews in the Mediterranean Diaspora* (Edinburgh, 1996) 135–37, also assumes that Ezekiel's audience would be primarily Greeks and his purpose apologetic. None of them makes a case for the audience.

to skeletal analysis, so Aristeas "the exegete" condensed the tale of Job to a compact synopsis, but one that could also play to the pious. His version erased Job's doubts, excised his challenges and bitterness, and presented a new portrait of unwavering devotion in the face of adversity. Aristeas, by stripping the text of ambiguity, made it simpler and more palatable, but nowhere undermined it. More subtle changes in the received tradition came in Theodotus' epic rendition of Dinah's rape and the sack of Shechem. His verses did not directly tamper with the tale in Genesis, but diminished the heinousness of Hebrew behavior, softened friction among the patriarchs, and set the events under a divine plan—a more satisfying, if not more satisfactory, version. The poem of Philo performed a comparable function. His overblown phraseology may seem jarring now, but it doubtless swelled the pride of Jewish readers who welcomed the exaltation of the patriarchs in the elevated tones of Greek epic. No less edifying was the representation of the Exodus story as tragic drama. Ezekiel scrupulously followed the biblical account, but added key scenes that gave it new character and meaning. Moses developed international connections. And God's elevation of him to glory signified a royal dominion familiar to Hellenistic readers and a universal message that the Jews could claim as their own. The interpreters of Scripture honored the tradition while making it speak to their contemporaries.

CHAPTER 5

Embellishments and Inventions

The Scriptures inspired reverence but also stimulated creative energies. Hellenistic Jews found in them a prod for imagination and inventiveness. The activity went well beyond hermeneutics. As we have seen, writers recast or freely adapted biblical tales in a variety of genres—history, epic, tragedy, romance—that appealed to the hellenized circles of their brethren. Many of them hewed closely to the received text and regarded themselves as faithful reproducers of it—even while adding, condensing, enhancing, or interpreting. But such compositions by no means exhaust the Jewish penchant for originality. More striking and more remarkable is the frequency with which intellectuals simply rewrote scriptural narratives, inventing facts or attaching fanciful tales. The Bible here served less as a text for exegesis than as a springboard for creativity.

The literary vitality exhibited in these writings has, of course, attracted scholarly attention. But much of the scholarship has concerned itself with recovering the *Sitz-im-Leben* of the authors, often to analyze their works as covert allusion to contemporary circumstances, whether for purposes of advocacy or of apologia. Such analysis has its merits but also its limits. It misses an important feature: the irony and wit, indeed the playfulness that marked several of these productions, the mockery that not only targeted Greeks but occasionally even deflated Jews. That dimension of Jewish inventiveness has been undervalued. By lampooning "the other" and sporadically spoofing themselves, Hellenistic Jews helped to sharpen their own self-image. The former reinforced a sense of superiority, the latter added a reminder of vulnerability.

•   •   •

To begin with a relatively sober example. The Jewish historical writer Eupolemus composed a work *On the Kings in Judaea.*[1] Its scope goes beyond the implications of the title, for even the scanty fragments include comments on Moses.[2] The principal focus, however, evidently rested upon the era of the monarchy, extending at least to the inception of the Exile. Certain passages on David and Solomon arouse attention at the outset.

Eupolemus records a surprising string of military successes for King David. In his compressed account, David subdued Syrians dwelling along the Euphrates and the area of Commagene, Assyrians in Galadene, and Phoenicians; he further campaigned against Idumaeans, Ammonites, Moabites, Ituraeans, Nabataeans, and Nabdaeans. He then took up arms once more against Souron the king of Tyre and Phoenicia, made the people tributary to the Jews, and framed a pact of friendship with Vaphres the king of Egypt.[3] Problems arise with virtually every name in the text—not to mention a glaring omission: the extant fragment passes over David's renowned conquest of the Philistines in silence. Eupolemus departs drastically from the biblical narrative. The king's exploits in II Samuel include only a small portion of these victories. The Hellenistic historian extends David's territorial advance well beyond the scriptural testimony, while evidently omitting the subjugation of Philistia, he depicts a struggle with Phoenicia that has no basis in the Bible, and he records an alliance with Egypt that is otherwise unknown and a king from an altogether different era.[4] How does one account for discrepancies of such magnitude?

1. Such is the title accorded by Clement of Alexandria, *Strom.* 1.23.153.4: περὶ τῶν ἐν τῇ Ἰουδαίᾳ βασιλέων. Whether he also produced other works entitled *On the Jews of Assyria* and *On the Prophecy of Elijah*, as indicated by Eusebius, *PE* 9.17.2, 9.30.1, is more dubious; see the important comments of J. Freudenthal, *Alexander Polyhistor* (Breslau, 1875) 82–92, 207–209. Among more recent treatments, see especially B. Z. Wacholder, *Eupolemus: A Study of Judaeo-Greek Literature* (Cincinnati,1974) 21–26; M. Goodman in E. Schürer, *The History of the Jewish People in the Age of Jesus Christ*, rev. ed. by G. Vermes, F. Millar, and M. Goodman (Cambridge, 1986) III.1, 517–18; C. Holladay, *Fragments from Hellenistic Jewish Authors: Volume I: The Historians* (Chico, 1983) I, 93. Further bibliography in G. E. Sterling, *Historiography and Self-Definition: Josephos, Luke-Acts, and Apologetic Historiography* (Leiden, 1992) 212.

2. Clement *Strom.* 1.23.153.4; Euseb. *PE* 9.25.4–9.26.1.

3. Euseb. *PE* 9.30.3–4.

4. The narratives of David's victories and annexations appear in II Sam. 5.17–25, 8.1–14, 10.6–19; I Chron. 14.8–17, 18.1–13, 19.10–19. Souron the king of Tyre, represented as a victim of David, is obviously equivalent to the biblical Hiram with whom David enjoyed a positive and productive association; II Sam. 5.11. The Egyptian Vaphres has a place in the pharaonic royal genealogy, but long after any putative date for David; Manetho, fr. 68. And a Davidic treaty with Egypt has no biblical counterpart. The absence of the Philistines is especially striking. To

The modern explanation is simple and consistent: Eupolemus reflects contemporary political circumstances. An ally and beneficiary of Judas Maccabaeus, he supplied Davidic precedents for Maccabaean expansionism and he justified Judas' anti-Seleucid policy by listing Syrians among David's conquests and blackening Phoenicians as surrogates for the subjects of Antiochus IV. Such is the prevailing theory.[5] The reconstruction, however, rests on shaky foundations, a chain of hypotheses every link of which is weak. The premise demands identification between Eupolemus the historian and Eupolemus, son of John from the priestly family of Akkos, who served as ambassador for Judas Maccabaeus on the mission to conclude a treaty with Rome in 161.[6] Reasons for the amalgamation are indirect and circumstantial rather than definitive. The historian employed as chronological marker the fifth year of Demetrius' reign and the twelfth year of Ptolemy. The kings who best fit that combination are the Seleucid Demetrius I whose fifth year fell in 157 and Ptolemy VIII whose twelfth year can be placed in 158, thus squarely in the *floruit* of Eupolemus the envoy.[7] The name Eupolemus is, in any case, highly unusual even among pagans, and unknown otherwise among Jews. Further, the extant fragments place heavy emphasis upon the Temple, an appropriate theme for a member of a priestly family and an adherent of Judas, restorer of the Temple. Those considerations have sufficed to assimilate the envoy and the historian, in the nearly unanimous view of modern researchers.[8]

---

be sure, we depend on extracts chosen by later compilers. But the relevant fragment supplies a long and detailed list of conquests. That Philistines, of all people, are missing can hardly be inadvertant.

5. The case is argued most fully by Wacholder, *Eupolemus*, 131–39; similar conclusions reached by M. Hengel, *Judaism and Hellenism* (London, 1974) I, 93–94; J. J. Collins, *Between Athens and Jerusalem* (New York, 1983) 40–41; Holladay, *Fragments*, I, 104; H. W. Attridge in M. E. Stone, *Jewish Writings of the Second Temple Period* (Philadelphia, 1984) 164; Goodman in Schürer, *A History of the Jewish People*, III.1, 518; Sterling, *Historiography and Self-Definition*, 216–17, 220–21.

6. I Macc. 8.17. On the priestly lineage, see I Chron. 24.10; Ezra 2.61; Nehemiah 3.4, 3.21, 7.63.

7. Clement *Strom.* 1.21.141.4.

8. So, e.g., Freudenthal, *Alexander Polyhistor*, 123–27; Y. Gutman, *The Beginnings of Jewish-Hellenistic Literature*, 2 vols. (Jerusalem, 1958, 1963) II, 76–78 (Hebrew); J. Giblet, *EphTheolLov* (1963) 551–52; A.-M. Denis, *Introduction aux pseudépigraphes grecs d'ancien testament* (Leiden, 1970) 252–55; Hengel, *Judaism and Hellenism*, I, 92, II, 63, with bibliography; Wacholder, *Eupolemus*, 4–9; Holladay, *Fragments*, I, 93; Attridge in Stone, *Jewish Writings*, 162–63; Goodman in Schürer, *History of the Jewish People*, III.1, 518; D. Mendels, *The Land of Israel as a Political Concept in Hasmonean Literature* (Tübingen, 1987) 29–31; N. Walter, *Jüdische Schriften aus hellenistisch-römischer Zeit* (Gütersloh, 1976) I.2, 93–98; Collins, *Between Athens and Jerusalem*, 41; F. Fallon in J. H. Charlesworth, *The Old Testament Pseudepigrapha* (Garden City, 1985) I, 863; R. Doran, *ANRW* II.20.1 (1987) 264; Sterling, *Historiography and Self-Definition*, 207–209. Doubts expressed long

The confidence is misplaced. Rarity of the name Eupolemus may simply be due to the paucity of our information. To deliver a laudatory description of Solomon's Temple hardly required the credentials of priestly lineage—and certainly demanded no attachment to the Maccabaean cause. The subject would readily appeal to any devout Jew engaged in reproducing biblical history.[9] Eupolemus, to be sure, calculated the span of time that elapsed from Adam to a date in the reigns of Demetrius and Ptolemy, thus in the era of the Maccabees. It does not follow, however, that this date must be in the lifetime of the historian or that he designated thereby the point at which he completed his work. The fragment, snatched from context, allows for no confident conclusions on that score.[10] One may go further. Even if the identity of historian and envoy be accepted, the extant fragments show little sign of Maccabaean propaganda. The Davidic conquests retailed by Eupolemus go well beyond the biblical narrative. But subjugation of Assyrians, extension into Commagene, clashes with Nabataeans, campaigns against Phoenicia, and an alliance with Egypt bear hardly the slightest resemblance to the activities of Judas Maccabaeus. To regard the Phoenicians as disguised stand-ins for the Seleucids or Egypt as a potential Hasmonaean helpmate against them is far-fetched conjecture. Still more implausible is the idea that Eupolemus included Nabataeans, Ituraeans, and peoples of Commagene on the grounds that they planned secession from the Seleucid realm. As

---

ago by H. Willrich, *Juden und Griechen vor der makkabäischen Erhebung* (Göttingen, 1895) 157, have been ignored or dismissed.

9. That Eupolemus was a Jew seems clear enough. Josephus, it is true, counts him among pagan writers, together with Demetrius of Phalerum and "the elder Philo"; *C. Apion.*, 1.218. But the passage is confused and unreliable, Demetrius of Phalerum perhaps a mistake for the Jewish historian Demetrius, and the "elder Philo" otherwise unknown. Eusebius unhesitatingly identifies Eupolemus as a Jew; *HE*, 6.13.7, as does Jerome, *Vir. Ill.* 38, and, evidently, Clement of Alexandria; cf. Euseb. *HE*, 6.13.7. The extant fragments, in any case, could hardly have been written by anyone but a Jew. See Freudenthal, *Alexander Polyhistor*, 105–30; Wacholder, *Eupolemus*, 1–3; Holladay, *Fragments*, I, 98–99.

10. Clement *Strom.* 1.21.141.4. Clement continues the quotation or paraphrase with a time reckoning of one hundred twenty years from the point in Demetrius' and Ptolemy's reigns to a Roman consular date, evidently the year of Cn. Domitius and Asinius, i.e. 40 BCE; Clement *Strom.* 1.21.141.5. Uncertainty bedevils any inferences drawn from this information. If the last passage represents a quotation from Eupolemus, he must be placed at least a century after the Maccabaean era. Of course, Clement may have taken it from his source Alexander Polyhistor—assuming that Polyhistor lived that long—or from some other work that cited Eupolemus. But even the date of 40 BCE depends upon emendation of Clement's text. And a gap of one hundred twenty years is, in any case, imprecise. The problems thus multiply and the doubts increase. For discussion, see Freudenthal, *Alexander Polyhistor*, 214–15; Wacholder, *Eupolemus*, 40–44; Holladay, *Fragments*, I, 155–56. Any conclusions resting on these data remain insecure.

advocacy for the Maccabees such allusions would be hopelessly obscure and ineffectual. A blueprint for future Hasmonaean expansionism along these lines would require remarkable prescience on the part of a historian writing in the 160s or 150s. The whole construct of a political agenda for Eupolemus is ramshackle. Of course, the historian might lapse into anachronism, inserting the Nabataeans, unknown in the days of David, adding the pharaoh Vaphres, who happened to be a name familiar to him, and omitting the Philistines who had no resonance for contemporary readers. But none of this amounts to anything like a partisan brief for the Maccabees. The striking fact remains that Eupolemus broke well beyond the bounds of biblical narrative. The mighty conquests of David extended to the Taurus range in the north, the Euphrates in the east, and the Gulf of Aqaba in the south. This may not be a Utopian vision for a Hasmonaean future but it is certainly a dramatic rewriting of the Israelite past.[11]

Departure from the Scriptures is marked also in Eupolemus' treatment of Solomon. The installation of the Temple constitutes the centerpiece of his narrative.[12] The historian, however, adds some novel features that transcend the biblical account and carry significance for Hellenistic Jews. Most notably, Eupolemus records a double exchange of correspondence: Solomon writes to and receives communications from both Vaphres the king of Egypt and Souron the ruler of Tyre. The letters derive largely from the imagination of the historian—and are all the more important for that.

The exchange between Solomon and Vaphres is sheer invention. The Bible lacks any reference to Solomonic diplomacy with Egypt. Eupolemus builds upon and advances his own earlier fabrication of an alliance between Vaphres and David. Now Solomon writes to the Egyptian monarch to announce his accession to the throne, to affirm his support by the "greatest God," and to implement the commands of David that a temple be built to the God who created heaven and earth and that Vaphres supply men

11. The case for a Utopian vision is argued by Wacholder, *Eupolemus*, 137–39, and Mendels, *Land of Israel*, 35–36. See also P. W. van der Horst, *Essays on the Jewish World of Early Christianity* (Göttingen, 1990) 205–206. In fact, Eupolemus could find biblical texts to supply some authority, however thin, for the exaggerated exploits he ascribed to David. So, for instance, the Chronicler brings David to the Euphrates (I Chron. 18.3) a border long ago foretold; Gen. 15.18; Deut. 1.7, 11.24; Josh. 1.3–4; cf. II Sam. 8.3; I Chron. 5.9. And a conquest of Arabia could be deduced from I Kings 10.15; II Chron. 9.14. But no Hasmonaean echoes can explain the geography.

12. On Eupolemus' attitude toward the Temple, see Gutman, *Beginnings*, II, 90–93 (Hebrew), and the insightful comments of Mendels, *The Rise and Fall of Jewish Nationalism* (New York, 1992) 143–47, who usefully cites parallels from the Temple Scroll and the *Letter of Aristeas*.

to assist in completion of that task.[13] The pharaoh responds with proper respect. He addresses Solomon as "great king," reports his joy at Solomon's accession for which he arranged a celebratory occasion, and expresses readiness to send workers from various parts of his realm to aid in construction of the Temple.[14] For any reader conversant with the Bible, this striking addition would immediately arrest attention. The mutual messages are polite and cordial, plainly drawing upon the Hellenistic conventions of royal correspondence.[15] But Solomon's ascendancy is clear and unequivocal. The Jewish monarch greets Vaphres as "paternal friend" but is addressed in response as "great king."[16] Solomon issues his request as a command handed down by David.[17] Vaphres is duly deferential, rejoicing in Solomon's elevation, organizing a festival in his honor, and sending laborers for the Temple without hesitation. Which does not mean that the pharaoh is abject or servile. That would strain all plausibility, discredit the narrative, and hardly enhance the stature of Solomon. Vaphres, in fact, enjoins the Jewish ruler to provide for the needs of his men, to make other arrangements for their well-being, and to see that they return home once their task is accomplished.[18] Eupolemus takes care to affirm the independence and pride of the Egyptian monarch. But the whole exchange underscores Solomon's authority.

What meaning does this invention convey? Some have seen in the appearance of Leontopolis among the places listed by Vaphres an allusion to Onias IV's temple in that vicinity: Eupolemus thus polemicizes against the Zadokite priesthood, which abandoned Jerusalem for a new shrine in Egypt, by having Leontopolis compliantly contribute to the building of Solomon's

13. Euseb. *PE* 9.31.1

14. Euseb. *PE* 9.32.1.

15. See C. B. Welles, *Royal Correspondence in the Hellenistic Period: A Study in Greek Epigraphy* (New Haven, 1934) xxxvii–l. For comparative purposes, see, e.g., Welles, *op. cit.*, 58, 65, 71. Eupolemus' use of the Hellenistic epistolary style has long been recognized; see Fruedenthal, *Alexander Polyhistor*, 109–12; Gutman, *Beginnings*, II, 86 (Hebrew); Wacholder, *Eupolemus*, 158–59; Holladay, *Fragments*, I, 143.

16. Euseb. *PE* 9.31.1: φίλῳ πατρικῷ χαίρειν; Euseb. *PE* 9.32.1: βασιλεῖ μεγάλῳ χαίρειν. There is no need to see the "paternal friend" as a *terminus technicus* implying royal adviser or court official, as do Holladay, *Fragments*, I, 145, and Mendels, *Land of Israel*, 135; cf. Euseb. *PE* 9.34.4. Vaphres, though plainly inferior in authority to Solomon, is portrayed as an independent ruler, not a member of Solomon's entourage.

17. Euseb. *PE* 9.31.1: καθότι ἐπιτέτακται.

18. Euseb. *PE* 9.32.1: φρόντισον δὲ καὶ τὰ δέοντα αὐτοῖς καὶ τὰ ἄλλα ὅπως εὐτακτῇ, καὶ ἵνα ἀποκατασταθῶσιν εἰς τὴν ἰδίαν, ὡς ἂν ἀπὸ τῆς χρείας γενόμενοι.

Temple.[19] So subtle an allusion, however, would surely have escaped the notice of all but the most intimate of Eupolemus' inner circle. And it would hardly account for the correspondence as a whole. Nor should one imagine that the historian advanced Judas Maccabaeus' cause by suggesting that the support of Egypt might back Hasmonaean interests. To a pagan readership such an implication could only be laughable or offensive. And no knowledgeable Jew could take seriously the proposition that the Ptolemies would subordinate themselves to a Judaean faction. Eupolemus' vision pierced beyond partisan politics and current events. The exaltation of Solomon through an ascendant relationship to pharaonic Egypt had wider significance. Vaphres not only acknowledges Solomon's superiority but even pays homage to the Israelite God.[20] Eupolemus may not have expected his readership to take the account literally. But it gave to Hellenistic Jews the sense of a proud heritage, of a nation whose impressive history both reflected divine favor and earned the approbation of the great powers. The historian unhesitatingly "improved upon" the biblical account, depicting the ancient kingdom at the time in which its sacred shrine was created as exercising widespread authority and achieving an international renown acknowledged even by the ruler of Egypt. For the Jews of Palestine or the Diaspora dwelling under the shadow of the Hellenistic powers, a pride in their past buoyed the spirit and uplifted perceptions of national identity.

The exchange of letters between Solomon and "Souron" reinforced those ends. Here Eupolemus did not need to create out of whole cloth. Biblical tradition already recorded correspondence that passed between Solomon and Hiram the prince of Tyre on whom Eupolemus' "Souron" is obviously based. Reports in I Kings and II Chronicles have Solomon write to Hiram with requests for building materials from the cedars of Lebanon, and for laborers and skilled craftsmen who can work with Solomon's own men to construct the Temple for the greater glory of God. Hiram responds in friendly and collegial fashion, providing an expert artist and a host of experienced

19. The thesis is proffered by Wacholder, *Eupolemus*, 164; cf. 249; and, with further elaboration, by Mendels, *Land of Israel*, 42–43; *idem*, *Rise and Fall*, 43–44. Those scholars have also interpreted Eupolemus' anachronistic insertion of Eli's presence at Solomon's coronation (Euseb. *PE* 9.30.8) as a slap at the Zadokites and, particularly, their descendant Onias IV; Wacholder, *op. cit.*, 151–54; Mendels, *Land of Israel*, 40–41; cf. Holladay, *Fragments*, 142; F. Fallon in Charlesworth, *Old Testament Pseudepigrapha*, II, 867. Gutman, *Beginnings*, II, 88 (Hebrew), rightly sees a more positive meaning in the reference to Leontopolis.

20. Euseb. *PE* 9.32.1: παρὰ χρηστοῦ ἀνδρὸς καὶ δεδοκιμασμένου ὑπὸ τηλικούτου θεοῦ.

workers who would cut the timbers, float the logs, and assist in erecting the sacred edifice.[21] Eupolemus, however, rewrote the exchange and thus reshaped the relationship in subtle and important ways. The Bible depicts Solomon and Hiram as rulers of approximately equal stature, collaborating as partners linked in alliance. Hiram readily complies with the Jewish king's wishes but receives handsome subsidies in return.[22] In the version of Eupolemus, the relationship did not arise out of a treaty contracted by allies on an equal footing but derived from David's conquest of Hiram/Souron who was reduced by compulsion to tributary status.[23] Souron's realm has a wider extent in Eupolemus' presentation. The Bible describes him simply as ruler of Tyre; in the Hellenistic historian's account, he has become king of Tyre, Sidon, and Phoenicia, his own increased stature adding still further to that of his suzerain.[24] The correspondence follows closely along the lines of that invented for Solomon and Vaphres. Souron greets the new Jewish monarch as "great king," expresses delight at his accession, praises the God who created heaven and earth, and grants the wishes of Solomon.[25] Here again, however, Souron is no cringing subject. The Tyrian prince concludes his letter by endorsing the suggestion that Solomon provide for his workmen by directing regional governors to supply their needs.[26] Souron's pride in the resources and manpower of his realm, like that of Vaphres, only enhances the esteem of the Jewish king to whom both are subordinate.

Solomon's territorial holdings, in the presentation of Eupolemus, are notable not so much for their extent as for their firm consolidation under the king's rule. In offering to furnish the needs of Souron's workmen, Solomon announces his mandates to Galilee, Samaria, Moab, Ammon, Gilead, Judaea, and Arabia for appropriate supplies.[27] That list involves both anachronism and manipulation. Ammon and Moab, independent principalities in the time of Solomon, are placed on a par with Judaea,

21. I Kings 5.1–17; II Chron. 2.1–18. Differences exist between these two accounts—alterations made by the Chronicler to improve the earlier version. But these need not concern us here.

22. I Kings 5.9–12; II Chron. 2.15

23. Euseb. *PE* 9.30.4: οὓς καὶ ἀναγκάσαι φόρους Ἰουδαίοις ὑποτελεῖν.

24. Euseb. *PE* 9.33.1. So, rightly, Holladay, *Fragments*, I, 144.

25. For Solomon's letter, the first part of which is a duplicate of that to Vaphres, see Euseb. *PE* 9.33.1. Souron's reply follows in Euseb. *PE* 9.34.1–3. His praise for the Jewish God does have biblical precedent; I Kings 5.7; II Chron. 2.12.

26. Euseb. *PE* 9.34.3: περὶ δὲ τῶν δεόντων καὶ ἀποστελλομένων σοὶ παίδων καλῶς ποιήσεις ἐπιστείλας τοῖς κατὰ τόπον ἐπάρχοις, ὅπως χορηγῆται τὰ δέοντα. Cf. I Kings 5.9; II Chron. 2.15.

27. Euseb. *PE* 9.33.1.

Galilee, and Gilead, the centers of the Jewish realm. Neither Samaria nor "Arabia" (possibly meant as the land of the Nabataeans) existed as definable entities in the Solomonic era. The historian emphasizes here that Solomon not only had wide international connections with rulers who paid him respect but also exercised tight command over his own expanded heartland.[28] The coincidence of political power and religious piety that marked the erection of the first Temple constituted a principal theme for Eupolemus. It symbolized the great legacy to which Hellenistic Jews could lay claim.[29]

The fragment of Eupolemus on Solomon concludes in remarkable fashion. After the successful building of the Temple, the king magnanimously restored the Egyptian and Phoenician craftsmen and laborers to their native lands with enormous severance pay, despatched lavish gifts to Vaphres, and to Souron he sent a golden column, set up at Tyre in the temple of Zeus.[30] Here once more Eupolemus supplies details for which no scriptural authority exists, employing the occasion to embellish the wealth, power, and generosity of Solomon. The final item, however, deserves special notice. Would the devout Solomon, having just completed the most monumental act of piety, actually send a pillar of gold to stand in a pagan temple? Scholars uncomfortable with the idea have sought to explain away the passage: perhaps Solomon simply sent the gold as a gift, which Souron then transformed into a sacred offering to Zeus; or possibly a later author tacked on this sentence to Eupolemus' text.[31]

Grasping at such solutions, however, may misdirect inquiry. Various versions of this tale, in fact, circulated among Hellenistic writers. In one

---

28. See Wacholder, *Eupolemus*, 164–65; Holladay, *Fragments*, 145. The analysis of Mendels, *Land of Israel*, 37, has Eupolemus shrink Solomon's realm from that of David, reconceiving Eretz Israel as the land dependent upon the Temple. But Eupolemus suggests no shrinkage of foreign dependencies. His stress falls upon the king's control and command of his kingdom proper.

29. The historian makes certain to underscore the continuity of that legacy down to his own day. In recording the fall of Jerusalem to Nebuchadnezzar and the removal to Babylon of all the treasures of the Temple, he adds that Jeremiah managed to retain and thus preserve for posterity the ark and the tablets; Euseb. *PE* 9.39.5. That last detail has no biblical counterpart, and is plainly a Hellenistic invention. Cf. Jeremiah 39.14, 40.1. An elaboration of the tale appears in II Macc. 2.1–8. Wacholder's discussion, *Eupolemus*, 237–42, of the relation between those texts reaches no decisive conclusion. Eupolemus, in any event, made clear that the pillage of the Temple did not affect the central symbols of Israelite tradition, preserved intact through the ages. Eupolemus' originality with regard to the Temple is properly appreciated, on other grounds, by Mendels, *Rise and Fall*, 144–45.

30. Euseb. *PE* 9. 34.18: τῷ δὲ Σούρωνι εἰς Τύρον πέμψαι τὸν χρυσοῦν κίονα, τὸν ἐν Τύρῳ ἀνακείμενον ἐν τῷ ἱερῷ τοῦ Διός.

31. See Wacholder, *Eupolemus*, 217.

formulation the king of Tyre employed Solomon's gold to erect a statue of his daughter, using the pillar to cover it. Others have him decorate the temple of Zeus with gold offerings or dedicate a golden column to Zeus—or even give his daughter in marriage to Solomon in the aftermath of the fall of Troy![32] But Eupolemus alone, so far as our evidence goes, makes Solomon supply the rich object that would adorn the temple of Zeus in Tyre. No need for tortured explanations here. The Bible itself records Solomon's penchant for foreign wives and for foreign gods. Among the deities whom he honored was Astarte, the goddess of the Sidonians.[33] Eupolemus simply pursued the point a step further: Solomon enabled the Phoenician king to honor Zeus with a handsome offering. The implications of this notice deserve emphasis. Eupolemus saw no inconsistency in presenting Solomon both as dedicated devotee of the Lord and as patron of foreign princes who honored alien cults. This is not "syncretism," as it is sometimes characterized.[34] Rather it highlights Jewish superiority in the spiritual and material spheres. Solomon requisitioned the manpower of other kingdoms to erect his magnificent structure to the supreme deity. And he could in turn take responsibility for subsidizing the worship of his compliant neighbors. That theme, here adumbrated by Eupolemus, recurs with some frequency and in more dramatic form elsewhere in Jewish-Hellenistic literature. It supplies a leitmotif for Jewish pride in ancestral achievements that extended to the enhancement or even generation of foreign cultures.

·　·　·

The theme resurfaces in another long fragment attributed to Eupolemus by Alexander Polyhistor. The author rewrote portions of Genesis, wove in Babylonian and Greek legends, and exalted Abraham as a world-historical figure.[35] Whether the work in fact came from Eupolemus' pen or was

32. The statue of the daughter is recorded by a certain Theophilus; Euseb. *PE* 9.34.19. Variants on Hiram/Souron's building program, including adornment of the temple of Zeus, appear in the largely unknown historians Dios and Menander; Jos. *C. Apion.*, 1.112–20. The story of a marriage alliance between Solomon and Hiram's daughter is ascribed to Laetus, a Greek translator of Phoenician works; Tatian, *Ad Graec.* 37 = Stern, *Greek and Latin Authors*, I, 129. On these traditions, see the valuable comments of Wacholder, *Eupolemus*, 217–23; Mendels, *Land of Israel*, 131–43. But one need not accept the proposition that Eupolemus engaged in polemics with purveyors of Phoenician traditions.

33. I Kings 11.1–6.

34. Cf. Hengel, *Judaism and Hellenism*, I, 94.

35. Euseb. *PE* 9.17.1–9.

misascribed by Polyhistor need not here be examined in detail. A nearly unanimous scholarly consensus opts for the latter, reckoning the author not as a Jew but as a Samaritan writing in the early second century BCE. Hence he now appears regularly in the scholarship as "the anonymous Samaritan" or, more frequently, "Pseudo-Eupolemus."[36] In fact, the basis for that construct has less solidity than is usually assumed. The hypothesis of Pseudo-Eupolemus' Samaritan origins depends upon a passage in which Abraham is received hospitably at the temple Argarizim (Mt. Gerizim, near Shechem), a term interpreted as "mountain of the Most High," and presented with gifts by Melchizedek, ruler and priest of God.[37] None of this proves that the author must be a Samaritan. The passage derives directly from Genesis wherein Abraham was hosted by Melchizedek, king of Salem and priest of God Most High. The fact that he added "the temple Argarizim" hardly proves Samaritan bias.[38] "Salem" or "Shalom," usually taken to refer to Jerusalem, can be rendered as "Salem, city of the Shechemites" by the Septuagint.[39] And the rift between Jews and Samaritans may not yet have arisen in the time of "Pseudo-Eupolemus."[40] The fragment is compatible with Eupolemus' exaltation of Solomon's Temple. Identification of the two

---

36. The case was argued first by Freudenthal, *Alexander Polyhistor*, 82–103, whose influential treatment has persuaded almost all subsequent scholars. Among the more important discussions, see Gutman, *Beginnings*, II, 95–96 (Hebrew); Wacholder, *HUCA* 34 (1963) 83–113; Walter, *Klio* 43–45 (1965) 282–90; idem, *Jüdische Schriften*, I.2, 137–40; Hengel, *Judaism and Hellenism*, I, 88–92; A.-M. Denis, *JSJ* 8 (1977) 42–49; Goodman in Schürer, *History of the Jewish People*, III.1, 528–30; Mendels, *Land of Israel*, 116–19; A. J. Droge, *Homer or Moses?* (Tübingen, 1989) 19–20; and Sterling, *Historiography and Self-Definition*, 187–206, with excellent bibliography. There has hardly been a whisper of dissent.

37. Euseb. *PE* 9.17.5–6: ξενισθῆναί τε αὐτὸν ὑπὸ πόλεως ἱερὸν Ἀργαριζίν, ὃ εἶναι μεθερμηνευόμενον ὄρος ὑψίστου· παρὰ δὲ τοῦ Μελχισεδὲκ ἱερέως ὄντος τοῦ θεοῦ καὶ βασιλεύοντος λαβεῖν δῶρα.

38. Genesis 14.18.

39. See the Septuagint version of Genesis 33.18. The evidence of later Jewish debates suggests that "Salem" carried a geographical ambiguity and need not always designate Jerusalem; cf. Wacholder, *HUCA* 34 (1963) 107.

40. Chronological uncertainties allow for no confident assertions here. A date for Pseudo-Eupolemus in the first half of the 2nd century BCE is plausible enough; see the discussions cited in n. 36. But nothing pinpoints the break between Jews and Samaritans. Some scholars even put it beyond the Hellenistic era into the Roman period; R. Pummer, *Église et Théologie* 10 (1979) 147–78; idem, *Biblische Zeitschrift* 26 (1982) 224–42; idem, *HTR* 75 (1982) 177–88; A. D. Crown, *JQR* 82 (1991) 17–50; S. Schwartz, *Jewish History* 7 (1993) 9–25. Most recently, H. Eschel provides a full bibliography and argues for the beginning of a rift in the 2nd century BCE; *The Samaritans in the Persian and Hellenistic Periods: The Origins of Samaritanism* (Diss. Hebrew University, 1994), in Hebrew with English summary.

authors remains a possibility.[41] Whatever conclusion one draws on that matter, however, the import of the fragment is unaffected. And on that we must focus attention.

Abraham is the central figure in this snippet. The author's representation of him departs drastically from the Bible. Abraham, described in Hellenic fashion as a man of εὐγένεια and σοφία, gets credit for the discovery of astrology and Chaldaean science, while maintaining the piety that won him God's favor.[42] He then taught these skills to the Phoenicians, explaining to them the movements of sun and moon and a host of other matters.[43] In a subsequent journey, Abraham dwelled with the Egyptian priests in Heliopolis, supplying them with a wealth of knowledge about astrology and a range of additional subjects. He associated himself here with the Babylonians, declaring that he and they were jointly responsible for their discovery, but giving ultimate credit to the fabled Enoch rather than to the Egyptians.[44]

The narrative of Genesis serves as little more than a launching pad here.[45] Pseudo-Eupolemus' elaborations embellish the tale and connect it with divergent traditions. He incorporates and expropriates Babylonian

---

41. R. Doran, *ANRW* II.20.1 (1987) 270–74, alone among recent scholars, has attempted to make a case for this identification; see also, *idem* in Charlesworth, *Old Testament Pseudepigrapha*, II, 873–78. The argument is too hastily dismissed by Mendels, *Land of Israel*, 116–17. Sterling's counter-arguments, *Historiography and Self-Definition*, 187–90, do not shake Doran's position. The fact that the author refers to Canaan as Phoenicia and that the Samaritans claimed to be Sidonians carries no weight in determining the ethnicity of Pseudo-Eupolemus. The question of the author's nationality and the question of identity or distinction between the two authors are separate matters. "Pseudo-Eupolemus" might conceivably be a Jew but nevertheless different from Eupolemus. But no compelling evidence undermines Polyhistor's identification of them.

42. Euseb. *PE* 9.17.3: εὐγενείᾳ καὶ σοφίᾳ πάντας ὑπερβεβηκότα, ὃν δὴ καὶ τὴν ἀστρολογίαν καὶ Χαλδαικὴν εὑρεῖν ἐπί τε τὴν εὐσέβειαν ὁρμήσαντα εὐαρεστῆσαι τῷ θεῷ.

43. Euseb. *PE* 9.17.4.

44. Euseb. *PE* 9.17.8. This statement hardly makes Pseudo-Eupolemus "anti-Egyptian"— any more than having Abraham visit Phoenicia before he goes to Egypt makes him "pro-Phoenician." Yet such phrases recur repeatedly in the modern literature; e.g. Freudenthal, *Alexander Polyhistor*, 95–98; Wacholder, *HUCA* 34 (1963) 96, 108, 112; *idem, Eupolemos*, 287; Walter, *Jüdische Schriften*, I.2, 138; Denis, *JSJ* 8 (1977) 46; Goodman in Schürer, *History of the Jewish People*, III.1, 529; Droge *Homer or Moses?* 20; Sterling, *Historiography and Self-Definition*, 204–205. The association of Abraham with astrology is widespread in Second Temple and rabbinic literature; see Hengel, *Judaism and Hellenism* II, 62. And also among pagan authors; J. S. Siker, *JSJ* 18 (1987) 194–97.

45. Genesis does, of course, have the Lord promise Abraham that he will be the father of many nations; Genesis 12.1–3, 17.1–6.

legends and Greek mythology. Some of it enters into the author's revised tale of the tower of Babel, here reckoned as the construct of giants.[46] And, more impressively, Pseudo-Eupolemus linked biblical genealogy with a Babylonian stemma, identifying the Babylonian Belus with the Greek Kronos, he amalgamated the Hebrew Kush with the Greek Asbolus, ancestor of Ethiopians and indirectly of Egyptians, and, since the Greeks made Atlas the father of astrology, he assimilated Atlas to Enoch as well.[47]

Wherein lay the significance of all this? The hypothesis that Pseudo-Eupolemus sought to authenticate the biblical story by finding confirmation in independent traditions seems unlikely.[48] The text shows no signs of defensiveness or argument, and it transforms rather than verifies the scriptural account. Nor should one infer that the cross-cultural identifications aimed to discredit pagan traditions or to undermine polytheistic interpretations.[49] Pseudo-Eupolemus amalgamated diverse strands and encompassed Greek and Near Eastern mythology, thus to recast his tale, not to refute others. Whether he had direct access to the Babylonian historian Berossus or to the antique legends in Hesiod's *Theogony* is irrelevant. Pseudo-Eupolemus traces the knowledge of his people to Enoch through his son Methuselah. This has less to do with the Bible than with Jewish elaborations of Enoch in the Hellenistic period as originator of the astronomical sciences and indeed of human knowledge generally.[50] Pseudo-Eupolemus partook in and contributed to the amplification of these characters and of their stories. He associated Abraham with the heritage of Enoch and had him transmit the

46. Euseb. *PE* 9.17.2–3. To be sure, Genesis describes Nimrod the descendant of Noah as a mighty warrior, rendered by the Septuagint as γίγας; Genesis 10.8. But if this lurks behind Pseudo-Eupolemus' version, he has certainly gone well beyond it. The weaving together of traditions is explored in the learned discussion of Gutman, *Beginnings*, II, 97–99 (Hebrew), who sees the novelty of the author in connecting Greek legends of the giants to Babylon—though he unnecessarily applies the label of "Euhemerism."

47. Euseb. *PE* 9.17.9. Conjectures about the author's sources are numerous but unverifiable. See the discussions of Freudenthal, *Alexander Polyhistor*, 90–98; Gutman, *Beginnngs*, II, 100–101 (Hebrew); Wacholder, *HUCA* 34 (1963) 89–99; Walter, *Klio* 43–45 (1965) 288–90; Hengel, *Judaism and Hellenism*, I, 89; Doran in Charlesworth, *Old Testament Pseudepigrapha*, II, 877–78; Sterling, *Historiography and Self-Definition*, 195–204.

48. The idea is proffered by Hengel, *Judaism and Hellenism*, I, 88; so also Sterling, *Historiography and Self-Definition*, 204.

49. So Wacholder, *Eupolemus*, 93–99.

50. Euseb. *PE* 9.17.9. The Genesis account of Enoch is evocative but quite brief; 5.18–24. All else is Hellenistic invention. On the Enochic traditions in relation to Pseudo-Eupolemus, see Wacholder, *HUCA* 34 (1963) 96–99; *idem, Eupolemus*, 74–76. A vast literature exists on the treatment of Enoch in the Hellenistic era; see the discussion and bibliography in Schürer, *History of the Jewish People*, III.1, 250–68.

fruits of his knowledge to Phoenicia and Egypt. This, so it is often said, makes Abraham a universal rather than a national figure.[51] In fact, he is both. Pseudo-Eupolemus put the biblical figure on center stage—even while straying distantly from the Bible itself. Abraham brings culture and learning to the great nations of the Near East and, through them, to Hellas. The patriarch stems from Ur of the Chaldees and shares credit for wisdom with the Babylonians. But he is simultaneously progenitor of the Israelites and mentor of other peoples of the Mediterranean. This creative rewriting of the ancient past absorbs a range of traditions but subordinates them to the achievement of the Hebrew patriarch. For a Jewish readership it could only reinforce a sense of cultural superiority.[52]

Abraham as both ancestor of Jews and purveyor of culture to other peoples reappears unmistakably in a fragment of Artapanus. The latter is no more than a name to us—and a peculiar one at that. "Artapanus" has a Persian flavor, thus prompting much scholarly speculation. The author is unquestionably a Hellenized Jew, writing some time before Alexander Polyhistor who quotes him, and very probably from Egypt since the extant fragments all deal with that land. Familiarity with the Septuagint and a firmly Jewish perspective make his sympathies clear. No more need be said on those subjects.[53] Artapanus focuses on Egypt. The brief fragment on Abraham parallels the tradition in Pseudo-Eupolemus that Abraham brought the science of astrology to Egypt, and in this instance he is actually

---

51. So Hengel, *Judaism and Hellenism*, I, 91–92; Mendels, *Land of Israel*, 116–17; Sterling, *Historiography and Self-Definition*, 204.

52. Mendels' assertion, *Land of Israel*, 119, that "from the Jewish point of view this was an abuse of their history" is difficult to comprehend. A better appreciation by Gutman, *Beginnings*, II, 108 (Hebrew). Alexander Polyhistor quotes one other short but closely related fragment which he ascribes to an anonymous author; Euseb. *PE* 9.18.2. The passage has Abraham trace his ancestry to the giants who dwelled in Babylonia, gain familiarity with astrology, and teach the subject first to Phoenicians, then to Egyptians. There are discrepancies between this fragment and the previous one, leading some scholars to posit separate authors; e.g., Gutman, *Beginnings*, II, 107–108 (Hebrew); Walter, *Jüdische Schriften*, I.2, 137–38, n. 4; Doran in Charlesworth, *Old Testament Pseudepigrapha*, II, 873–74; cf. Wacholder, *Eupolemus*, 287, n. 12; Sterling, *Historiography and Self-Definition*, 192–93. But the conclusion is unnecessary. The second reproduces the principal themes of the first and seems to be no more than a garbled summary.

53. Freudenthal's treatment, *Alexander Polyhistor*, 143–74, decisively refuted earlier speculations about Artapanus as a pagan writer, although he engaged in some dubious speculations of his own regarding the author's writings and intentions. Date and provenance have been discussed extensively but without resolution. For a summary of opinions and bibliography, see Holladay, *Theios Aner in Hellenistic Judaism* (Missoula, 1977) 199–204; Sterling, *Historiography and Self-Definition*, 167–69. Further on Artapanus, see above, pp. 87–89.

mentor of the Egyptian pharaoh.[54] The Hebrew Bible, of course, has none of this. Nor does it provide any authority for Artapanus' statements that Abraham dwelled in Egypt for twenty years and that, when he departed, he left many of his followers behind.[55] The rewriting plainly aims to strengthen the association of Abraham with Egypt, and to establish a continuity between the patriarch's endowment and the development of Egyptian culture. This goes beyond a mere competitive scramble to claim for the Jews a priority over Babylonians, Egyptians, Greeks, and others who maintained that their ancestors originated the science of interpreting the stars.[56] Artapanus sets Abraham and his people in the midst of antique civilizations, pivotal contributors to the origins of culture and learning. Equally significant, he is quite explicit that Abraham is not—or not simply—a universalist figure of vague ethnic connections. His work carried the title "On the Jews." He asserts that the original designation of that people was "Hermiouth," a term nowhere else attested and presumably another concoction by Artapanus, and he maintains that the name "Hebrews" actually derives from Abraham himself. The author appears to manipulate phraseology that might link the Hebrews to Hellenic figures (Hermes?).[57] But, more to the point, he specifies Abraham as ancestor of the Jews who played a critical part in the generation and transmission of Near Eastern learning. Artapanus' aim was not so much to have Abraham eclipse Egyptians or Greeks as to locate the Hebrew patriarch at the center of ancient Mediterranean cultures—with obvious reverberations for Hellenistic Jews in Palestine and the Diaspora.

The malleable Abraham could extend his influence elsewhere as well. An obscure Hellenistic writer Cleodemus Malchus produced a still more ingenious twist on the Genesis tale. He extracted a portion on Abraham's descendants and grafted it upon a Hellenic legend concerning Heracles, thereby dramatically expanding the patriarch's cultural and imperial legacy. Cleodemus takes as starting point the bald biblical resumé of Abraham's

---

54. Euseb. *PE* 9.18.1: ἐλθεῖν εἰς Αἴγυπτον πρὸς τὸν ... Φαρεθώθην καὶ τὴν ἀστρο-λογίαν αὐτὸν διδάξαι. The name itself seems invented, either a variant on "pharaoh" or some ingenious combination of Egyptian terms; see Walter, *Jüdische Schriften*, I.2, 127; Holladay, *Fragments*, I, 226–27, n. 6.

55. Euseb. *PE* 9.18.1. This is clearly inconsistent with Genesis 12.20–13.1.

56. So Sterling, *Historiography and Self-Definition*, 177–78.

57. On the term "Hermiouth," whose meaning remains obscure, see Freudenthal, *Alexander Polyhistor*, 153; Walter, *Jüdische Schriften*, I.2, 127. The connection with Hermes is plausible, in view of the association with Moses later in Artapanus' text. A different interpretation by G. Mussies in M. Voss et al., *Studies in Egyptian Religion* (Leiden, 1982) 112. On the title of the work, see Euseb. *PE* 9.23.1: περὶ Ἰουδαίων; Clement *Strom.* 1.23.154.2: περὶ Ἰουδαίων. A variant in Euseb. *PE* 9.18.1: ἐν τοῖς Ἰουδαικοῖς—which need not be a formal title.

children, grandchildren, and further issue through his wife Keturah. He then places his own stamp upon the tale by expropriating a legend of Heracles. The Greek story had it that Heracles engaged in battle with the Libyan giant Antaeus, overcame him, and brought civilization to barbarous Africa. A subsequent tradition added that Heracles wed the wife of Antaeus, from whom the lineage descended through Sophax and Diodorus to the rulers of North Africa.[58] Cleodemus seized upon the legend, inserted Abraham and his progeny, and gave the latter a role in the conquest of Libya. Moreover, he assigned to them the ancestry of great nations, far transcending anything that could be inferred from Genesis. In Cleodemus' rendition, two of Abraham's sons by Keturah, Apher and Aphran, fought side by side with Heracles in subduing Antaeus. Heracles then married Aphran's daughter who gave birth to Diodorus, and he in turn fathered Sophon from whom the barbarian Sophanes received their designation. The destiny of Apher and Aphran was more glorious still. The city of Aphra was named after the one, the whole continent of Africa after the other. And a third brother, Assouri, became the namesake of Assyria. Such is Cleodemus' imaginative reconstruction.[59]

The author himself escapes identification. A variety of modern suppositions have labeled him as either Jew, Samaritan, Syrian, Phoenician, Carthaginian, or some combination thereof.[60] No definitive solution is forthcoming, nor is one necessary. The scholarly debate rests on the assumption that if we could determine Cleodemus' nationality, we could discern the motives for the invention. But nothing shows that Cleodemus, whoever he might be, initiated the fable anyway; we know only that Polyhistor found it in that source. The story could have originated earlier, elsewhere, and under any number of possible circumstances. What matters is not the origin of the legend but its meaning and implications.

The link between Abraham and Heracles can only be an *interpretatio Judaica*, not *Graeca*. The line begins with the Hebrew patriarch, his son has the honor of a continent named after him, and Heracles' victory becomes

58. On the various versions of the Greek tale, see Diod. 1.17.21, 1.17.24, 4.17.4; Plutarch, *Sertorius*, 9. Cf. Walter, *Jüdische Schriften*, I.2, 116; Doran in Charlesworth, *Old Testament Pseudepigrapha*, II, 884–85. The best analysis, exploring both classical and Jewish texts on north Africa, is that of Gutman, *Beginnings*, II, 137–43 (Hebrew).

59. The text is preserved in Jos. *Ant.* 1.239–41 and Euseb. *PE* 9.20.2–4, with some variations in the names. It derives from Alexander Polyhistor. The biblical genealogy occurs in Genesis 25.1–6.

60. Among the more important treatments, see Freudenthal, *Alexander Polyhistor*, 130–36; Gutman, *Beginnings*, II, 136–37 (Hebrew); Walter, *Jüdische Schriften*, I.2, 115–18; Holladay, *Fragments*, I, 245–59; Doran in Charlesworth, *Old Testament Pseudepigrapha*, II, 883–87; Goodman in Schürer, *History of the Jewish People*, III.1, 526–29.

by inference the outcome of Jewish intervention. What had been a Greek legend of Heracles bringing the blessings of civilization to barbarous Libya became transformed into one in which the progeny of Abraham shared in that distinction and gained permanent renown by bestowing their names upon subsequent national entities. The tale of Cleodemus makes no pretense at exegesis or allegorization of Genesis. It employs the biblical genealogy simply as vehicle for absorbing a Hellenic myth and extending further the long shadow of Abraham. The biblical patriarch's reach now encompassed Africa and Assyria. This involved no diminution of Heracles or denigration of Hellenism. They found their place within the larger embrace of Jewish history. It would not be amiss to detect here a touch of playfulness, even mischievousness. The Jewish author swept Heracles into the Hebrew heritage and made his heirs, founders of a dynasty, the descendants of Abraham. As emblematic figure of the Hebraic past, Abraham could be purveyor of culture to Phoenicia and Egypt, forefather of Assyria and Africa, or ultimately responsible for the lineage of Hellas' greatest hero.

•   •   •

Abraham was not alone in possessing such awesome qualities. The figure of Moses also held great attraction for Jewish-Hellenistic writers who ascribed to him comparably multifaceted prowess. A fragment of Eupolemus names him as "the first wise man," probably an allusion to the Greek sages and thus according precedence to the Hebrew leader.[61] The historian proceeds to report that Moses handed down knowledge of the alphabet first to the Jews, from whom the Phoenicians received it, and from them in turn the Greeks.[62] The Jews here acquire priority. The text is frequently interpreted as a shot fired in the polemical campaign conducted by intellectuals over which nation invented the alphabet.[63] That interpretation somewhat misses the mark. Eupolemus, it should be noted, does not actually credit Moses with invention

---

61. The fragment is quoted by Clement *Strom.* 1.23.153.4, and, in somewhat fuller form, by Eusebius *PE* 9.25.4–9.26.1. Designation of Moses as τὸν Μωσῆν πρῶτον σοφὸν is not inconsistent with the assertion of "Pseudo-Eupolemus" that Abraham excelled all in εὐγενεία καὶ σοφία (Euseb. *PE* 9.17.3), and hence cannot prove that the two statements came from separate authors. On the setting of Moses among the Greek sages, see Gutman, *Beginnings*, II, 79–81 (Hebrew).

62. Euseb. *PE* 9.26.1: γράμματα παραδοῦναι τοῖς Ἰουδαίοις πρῶτον, παρὰ δὲ Ἰουδαίων Φοίνικας παραλαβεῖν, Ἕλληνας δὲ παρὰ Φοινίκων.

63. Wacholder, *Eupolemus*, 77–83; Attridge in Stone, *Jewish Writings*, 163–64; Hengel, *Judaism and Hellenism* I, 92, 129; Fallon in Charlesworth, *Old Testament Pseudepigrapha*, II, 865; Doran, *ANRW* II.20.1 (1987) 265; Droge, *Homer or Moses?* 15–17; Sterling, *Historiography and Self-*

of γράμματα. He simply "handed down" the knowledge.[64] The Egyptians, chief contenders for the claim of originating the alphabet, do not appear in the fragment. This indeed leaves open the possibility that Moses received it from them! Or, at the very least, it suggests that the debate over priority was not uppermost in Eupolemus' mind. The historian aimed to assure Moses a place as first among the sages and to give the Jews a principal role in the transmission of literacy and literature in the ancient Mediterranean. It may be best not to take this as serious intervention in a contentious debate. Gentile readers, if there were any, would hardly be persuaded. But Jewish intellectuals would take some satisfaction in imagining that Moses' delivery of the Tablets constituted a milestone in the history of letters.

Eupolemus adds a sentence with which few would have cause to quarrel: "Moses was first to write down laws for the Jews." Unfortunately, the sentence is frequently misunderstood to mean that Moses was the earliest lawgiver, thus to take priority over Lycurgus, Solon, and others, yet another salvo in the propaganda war over which culture can claim precedence in antiquity and initiative. Not so. Such was indeed the purpose of Josephus' unabashedly apologetic presentation of Moses as first of the lawgivers. But it is quite illegitimate to twist or mistranslate Eupolemus' text in order to have it conform to Josephus' ends.[65] Eupolemus' conviction did not require belligerence. He projected Moses, lawgiver of the Israelites, as earliest of the wise men and purveyor of letters to the Phoenicians from whom they descended to the world of Hellas. Greek traditions had long acknowledged Near Eastern priority with regard to the alphabet and other modes of learning.[66] Eupolemus, like Artapanus and "Pseudo-Eupolemus," simply injected ancient Israelite leaders into those traditions, not an irritant for the Greeks but a source of gratification for knowledgeable Hellenistic Jews.

Definition, 218–19. A comparable but more cautious view is expressed by Gutman, *Beginnings*, II, 81–82 (Hebrew).

64. Euseb. *PE* 9.26.1: παραδοῦναι. The point was observed by Freudenthal, *Alexander Polyhistor*, 116–17. For Wacholder, *Eupolemus*, 78, this means that Moses received it from God.

65. Euseb. *PE* 26.1: νόμους τε πρῶτον γράψαι Μωσῆν τοῖς Ἰουδαίοις. The translation of Holladay, *Fragments*, I, 113, "Also Moses was the first to write down laws, and he did so for the Jews," is unfounded. Wacholder, *Eupolemus*, 83, perhaps tries to introduce some ambiguity: "Also, laws were first written by Moses for the Jews." The interpretation of the text as apologetics is widespread; see works cited in n. 60. But Eupolemus' wording provides no basis for it. Josephus' apologia appears in *C. Apion.*, 2.154–56. Moses is not attested earlier as first of all lawgivers. Even Philo has him as "the best" but not "the first"; *V. Mos.* 2.12: νομοθετῶν ἄριστος τῶν πανταχοῦ πάντων.

66. See, e.g., Hecataeus of Miletus, *FGH*, I, fr. 20; Herodotus, 5.58; Diod. 3.67.1, 5.74.1. Other sources cited in Wacholder, *Eupolemus*, 78–83.

Moses took on still more imposing proportions in the hands of Artapanus. Although fully conversant with the Exodus narrative, Artapanus left it far behind in the construction of his imaginative tale. And the twists and turns of his narrative have a decidedly—though rarely recognized—jocular flavor. A summary of its contents can make that abundantly clear.

The story begins in familiar fashion. Moses, born to a Jewish family, was adopted by the daughter of a pharaoh.[67] From that point, Artapanus veers sharply away from the biblical account which resurfaces much later, and even then in a considerably altered form. Moses, we are told, acquired the name Mousaios from the Greeks, became the teacher of Orpheus, and conferred a host of benefits upon mankind, including the invention of ships, mechanisms for stone construction, Egyptian weaponry, hydraulic engines, implements of warfare—and even philosophy.[68] Further, he took the whole Egyptian political and religious structure in hand. Moses divided the nation into thirty-six nomes, assigned to each the god it was to worship, taught hieroglyphics to the priests, allotted special land for their use, and made divinities of cats, dogs, and ibises.[69] All of this won him the hearts of the people, earned him god-like stature in the eyes of the priests, and the name "Hermes" because of his ability to interpret sacred writings.[70] The pharaoh Chenephres, jealous of Moses' ἀρετή, sent him with a contingent of scratch troops to make war on the Ethiopians, in the expectation that he would not survive. But Moses conducted a ten years' war, winning battle after battle, and culminated his conquest by founding the city of Hermopolis, named after himself, to which the ibis was consecrated. The Ethiopians themselves then came to love Moses and acquired from his teachings the practice of circumcision.[71] For the Egyptians he added still another benefit, recommending a breed of oxen for plowing their fields, which prompted Chenephres to single out the bull named Apis and dedicate a temple to him.[72] Chenephres, however, persisted in his plots against Moses, even commissioning an assassin, but Moses managed to overcome his would-be slayer.[73]

Artapanus then manipulates the Exodus narrative of Moses' flight to Midian and marriage to a daughter of a Midian priest. In his version, Moses' new father-in-law urged an invasion of Egypt upon him—in vain—

67. Euseb. *PE* 9.27.1–3. Artapanus, to be sure, adds several novel details even here.
68. Euseb. *PE* 9.27.3–4.
69. Euseb. *PE* 9.27.4.
70. Euseb. *PE* 9.27.6.
71. Euseb. *PE* 9.27.7–10.
72. Euseb. *PE* 9.27.12.
73. Euseb. *PE* 9.27.13–18.

and settled instead for a plundering of the land.[74] There follows a variant on the burning bush narrative, significantly altered to have the divine voice direct Moses to wage war upon the Egyptians.[75] Artapanus now reverts to sheer invention: the pharaoh slaps Moses into prison, only to have the prison doors spontaneously open, and the hero escape. The scene reaches a climax when Moses pronounces the name of God, causing the king to collapse, and writes it on a tablet, bringing about the death of a contemptuous Egyptian priest.[76] The remainder of the text returns to Exodus, with the tale of the plagues, but even here Artapanus freely adapts, combines, abbreviates, adds, or omits material—including the insertion of a notice that Moses initiated the flooding of the Nile, and another that his use of the rod was taken up into Isis worship.[77] The fragment concludes with the Hebrews' departure from Egypt and their escape through the sea, with a few novel touches added by the Hellenistic author.[78]

This is a striking text, remarkable in conception and execution. It certainly offers no seamless narrative. At the very least, tension exists between the Moses figure at the outset who is benefactor of the Egyptians and beloved by them, and the later Moses who takes up arms against Egypt and becomes the agent of divine vengeance. But the fragments of Artapanus show little interest in consistency or tidiness. His work is learned and ingenious, rich in material drawn from Greek and Egyptian as well as Jewish sources, multiple in theme and content, and, not least, replete with wit and whimsy.[79]

Modern interpretations see a more pointed purpose. The general view reckons Artapanus' portrait of Moses as apologetic, patriotic, and national-istic, a piece of "competitive historiography" or "romantic national history," the glorification of Judaism, or even a point by point refutation of Manetho's slanders against the Jews.[80] But the author is not easily categorized, and the work merits a deeper probing.

74. Euseb. *PE* 9.27.19.
75. Euseb. *PE* 9.27.21–22. Cf. Exodus 3.1–10.
76. Euseb. *PE* 9.27.23–26.
77. Euseb. *PE* 9.27.27–33; see, especially, 9.27.28, 9.27.32.
78. Euseb. *PE* 9.27.34–37.
79. The assessment of Holladay, *Theios Aner*, 217, "far from being a creative piece of work, it merely assembles traditions and legends indiscriminately," undervalues Artapanus.
80. See, e.g., Freudenthal, *Alexander Polyhistor*, 160–62; Braun, *History and Romance*, 26–31; D. L. Tiede, *The Charismatic Figure as Miracle Worker* (Missoula, 1972) 148–50; Fraser, *Ptolemaic Alexandria*, I, 705–706; Walter, *Jüdische Schriften*, I.2, 125; Holladay, *Theios Aner*, 212–18, 231–32; idem, *Fragments*, I, 190–91; Collins, *Between Athens and Jerusalem*, 33–38; idem in Charlesworth, *Old Testament Pseudepigrapha*, II, 891–92; Goodman in Schürer, *History of the Jewish People*, III.1, 522–23; D. Georgi, *The Opponents of Paul in Second Corinthians* (Edinburgh, 1987) 124–26; van der

Artapanus had acquaintance with a range of sources, both pagan and Jewish, but shaped and molded them to his own taste. Although he fosters upon Moses a multiplicity of accomplishments, the extant text leaves out the one with which he was most commonly identified by Jew and Gentile alike: the delivery and promulgation of laws to the Jews.[81] Why this omission? The idea that Artapanus associated himself with those who disparaged Mosaic laws is highly implausible.[82] Moses receives only the most positive evaluations throughout. Perhaps Artapanus simply thumbed his nose at other interpretations: although some might see Moses as the great lawgiver of the Jews, he would develop a more colorful and arresting portrait of the man. This playful mocking and toppling of convention characterizes the text again and again.

Moses, to be sure, is cast as culture hero, somewhat in the mold of Eupolemus' presentation of him, and analogous to the image of Abraham delivered by Pseudo-Eupolemus and by Artapanus himself. But the benefactions of Moses to Egypt operate at a somewhat different level. He supplied the know-how for ships and weapons, for hydraulic and building devices—and, only as an afterthought, for philosophy.[83] The sequence suggests a bit of mischief on Artapanus' part. He proceeds to assign to Moses the responsibility for various Egyptian institutions: not only the division into nomes, the landed privileges of the priests, and the use of hieroglyphics, in all of which a Jewish readership could take pride, but even the apportioning of divinities to each nome and the inauguration of animal worship[84] This, of course, has distressed and disconcerted scholars who find it hard to reconcile the laudation of Moses and the Jews with a favorable judgment on pagan

---

Horst, *Essays*, 202–203; Droge, *Homer or Moses?* 30–32; Sterling, *Historiography and Self-Definition*, 182–84. A better analysis by Doran, *ANRW* II.20.1 (1987) 258–63, but he too embraces the notion that Artapanus' work constituted a response to Manetho's anti-Jewish tirade; so also J. M. G. Barclay, *Jews in the Mediterranean Diaspora* (Edinburgh.1996) 129–30. Gutman, *Beginnings*, II, 128, 133–34 (Hebrew) rightly dissents. On Manetho, see above, pp. 55–65.

81. On Hellenistic conceptions of Moses as lawgiver, see, e.g., Hecataeus of Abdera in Diod. 40.3.3; Eupolemus in Euseb. *PE* 9.26.1; Aristobulus in Euseb. *PE* 13.12.1–3; Pseudo-Longinus *On the Sublime* 9.9; Philo *Moses* 1.1, 1.162, 2.3, 2.12; Jos. *C. Apion.* 2.145, 2.154–56, 2.279–80.

82. For that idea, see Droge, *Homer or Moses?* 29.

83. Euseb. *PE* 9.27.4: καὶ γὰρ πλοῖα καὶ μηχανὰς πρὸς τὰς λιθοθεσίας καὶ τὰ Αἰγύπτια ὅπλα καὶ τὰ ὄργανα τὰ ὑδρευτικὰ καὶ πολεμικὰ καὶ τὴν φιλοσοφίαν ἐξευρεῖν.

84. Euseb. *PE* 9.27.4: καὶ ἑκάστῳ τῶν νομῶν ἀποτάξαι τὸν θεὸν σεφθήσεσθαι ... εἶναι δὲ καὶ αἰλούρους καὶ κύνας καὶ ἴβεις.

rites and animal gods.[85] But the discomfiture rests on too solemn a view of the text. Artapanus juggled a variety of traditions. He shrewdly exploited stories about Egyptian and other Near Eastern heroes and divinities, notably Sesostris, Semiramis, Isis, Osiris, and Hermes, most of them subsequently recorded in the first book of Diodorus Siculus. Exploits ascribed to one or more of these figures he simply transferred to Moses. Precedents in one form or another could be found for each of the achievements which Artapanus assigned to the Jewish forebear, including the division of Egypt into precisely thirty-six nomes by Sesostris and the consecration of animals by Isis.[86] The combination of these accomplishments centered in Moses of course signaled that the Israelite leader surpassed all his rivals. Artapanus engaged in some one-upmanship. But this was no somber contest for supremacy between Jewish and pagan intellectuals. Egyptians would hardly acknowledge Moses' initiation of animal worship—and Jews would certainly not take it seriously. Artapanus expropriated and transfigured pagan legends. And he thoroughly enjoyed himself.

The same can be said of the author's identification of Moses both with Hermes and with Mousaios. In each instance he records the fusion as attested by others: Egyptian priests amalgamated Moses with Hermes, and Greeks gave Moses the name Mousaios.[87] The ingenuity of the author here again comes to the fore. In the case of Hermes, he welded together various traits of Moses not so much with the Greek divinity as with the Egyptian version of him, namely Thot. Common characteristics included the skills of builders and craftsmen, a connection with the ibis, the exercise of magic, and, most particularly, the ability to interpret sacred writings.[88]

85. So, for instance, Freudenthal, *Alexander Polyhistor*, 143–53, was driven to conceive of Artapanus as a Jew writing in pagan guise in order to reach his audience. And Goodman in Schürer, *History of the Jewish People*, III.1, 523, tries to soften the blow by claiming that the "sacred animals were not so much worshipped as 'consecrated' to God." That distinction, if it exists, would be lost on Artapanus' readers. Various other efforts at explanation are usefully documented by Holladay, *Theios Aner*, 201–204. More recently, D. Flusser and S. Amorai-Stark, *JSQ* 1 (1993/1994) 225–31, argue that, for Artapanus, Moses' religious innovations only sought to provide stability to Egypt and animals were consecrated for their benefit to mankind, whereas Egyptian paganism was regarded as foolishness. This last idea finds no support in the fragments. See now the brief but sensible comments of Barclay, *Jews in the Mediterranean Diaspora*, 131–32, who, however, puts too much emphasis on Artapanus' "syncretism."

86. On all this, see the treatment by Braun, *History and Romance*, 26–31; and, especially, Tiede, *Charismatic Figure*, 151–77; cf. Holladay, *Theios Aner*, 209–12.

87. Euseb. *PE* 9.27.3: ὑπὸ δὲ τῶν Ἑλλήνων αὐτὸν ἀνδρωθέντα Μουσαῖον προςαγορευθῆναι; c.27.6: ὑπὸ τῶν ἱερέων ... προσαγορευθῆναι Ἑρμῆν.

88. For the utilization of Hermes/Thot traits by Artapanus, see Gutman, *Beginnings*, II, 120–122 (Hebrew), and Mussies in Voss et al., *Studies in Egyptian Religion*, 97–108.

This is no mere syncretism; it is appropriation. The fact emerges still more clearly with Moses-Mousaios. Artapanus not only claims that Greeks made the identification. He adds that Moses became the teacher of Orpheus—an exact reversal of the Hellenic legend which has Mousaios as son or disciple of Orpheus, the celebrated singer in ancient lore.[89] Moses, among his other skills, had now become the fount of song and poetry that enriched Hellenic life. Once again Artapanus surely did not anticipate conversion by Greeks or delusion by Jews. He relished the process of inverting and reshaping traditions. The Egypt of the pharaohs is only the ostensible canvas. Artapanus looked to contemporary Ptolemaic Egypt. His Moses, having absorbed Hermes and Mousaios, emerged as cultural progenitor of Hellas itself.

The culture hero also doubled as military hero. Moses not only turned back an Ethiopian invasion of Egypt but subdued the mighty Ethiopians with a patchwork army in an epic war of ten years' duration, thereby rivaling the storied exploits of Sesostris, Semiramis, and Osiris. And the founding of Hermopolis would leave a lasting memorial to Moses' glory. None of this has any basis in the Bible. Artapanus reworked Gentile traditions and perhaps Jewish folktales to elevate the ancestor of his own people.[90] And he took matters further than a war on Ethiopians. Moses, after declining his father-in-law's request to take up arms against Egypt, heeded the directives of the voice from the burning bush and mobilized against his native land itself.[91] What came of it is unknown, for a break in the text follows, perhaps an omission by Alexander Polyhistor. But Artapanus had no hesitation in ignoring the Scriptures and inventing martial heroics that would put Moses' military renown on a par with his cultural attainments.

The Hellenistic writer rarely missed an opportunity to reinterpret an event or an institution to the credit of Moses—and generally with tongue in cheek. The attitude undermines any notion of a stern competition for cultural supremacy. In addition to the wry humor already observed at various central points of the narrative, peripheral matters can illustrate it as well. Note for instance that the practice of circumcision, widely reckoned as originating

89. See references collected by Holladay, *Theios Aner*, 224.

90. Euseb. *PE* 9.27.7–9. A longer and very different version of Moses' campaign against the Ethiopians appears in Jos. *Ant.* 2.238–53. The degree to which Josephus drew on Artapanus or conveys elements that preceded Artapanus is much disputed and cannot here be explored. See, e.g., T. Rajak, *JJS* 29 (1978) 111–22; D. Runnalls, *JSJ* 14 (1983) 135–56, with further bibliography.

91. Euseb. *PE* 9.27.21–22: φωνὴν δ' αὐτῷ θείαν εἰπεῖν στρατεύειν ἐπ' Αἴγυπτον ... δύναμιν πολεμίαν ἐπάγειν διαγνῶναι τοῖς Αἰγυπτίοις. See above, p. 65.

with the Egyptians, became an invention of Moses who taught it to the Ethiopians—a reward for their compliance after defeat.[92] The consecration of Apis, a prime feature of Egyptian worship, resulted from a comment of Moses, and the burial of sacred animals was prompted by an effort to suppress Moses' initiative.[93] The city of Meroe, capital of Ethiopia, received its name from Moses who buried his adoptive mother Merris there.[94] By whispering the name of God in Chenephres' ear, Moses caused the pharaoh to keel over in a dead faint—no doubt quite a spectacle to the court.[95] And Moses' manipulation of the Nile to intimidate the king became the origin of the annual inundation of the river.[96]

The lengthy fragment of Artapanus on Moses sheds some valuable light on the disposition of Jewish-Hellenistic writers. They did not enlist in a deadly serious encounter to advance Jewish values against the claims of competing nations and cultures. Rather, they could exhibit a light touch, occasionally discerned in Pseudo-Eupolemus and Cleodemus Malchus, but readily obvious in Artapanus, a caprice and whimsy that tampered liberally with the Scriptures and inverted or transposed Gentile traditions to place the figures of Jewish legend in the center. The humor is mischievous rather than malicious. It sets the author in a superior posture of detachment, disengaged from ideological battle, and thereby augments the authority of his judgment.[97] What stands out is not so much polemics as inventive imagination.

•   •   •

Jewish twists on pagan tales could turn up in surprising places. The Greek Book of Ezra, which appears as I Esdras in the Septuagint and III Esdras in the Vulgate, offers an unusual case in point. The text reproduces the canonical Ezra with parts of II Chronicles and Nehemiah, although it reshuffles

---

92. Euseb. *PE* 9.27.10.
93. Euseb. *PE* 9.27.12.
94. Euseb. *PE* 9.27.16.
95. Euseb. *PE* 9.27.24–25.
96. Euseb. *PE* 9.27.28.
97. The Jews, of course, had no monopoly on playfulness and wit in literary production. Hellenistic writers indulged in it liberally. One need mention only (in different genres) Callimachus' droll touches in retelling the myth of Erysichthon who eats his family out of house and home (*Hymn*, 6.66–117), Apollonius' comic scene of the visit by Hera and Athena to Aphrodite's dwelling in which the latter moans about her inability to control her obstreperous son Eros (*Argonautica*, 3.1–110), and all the mocking mimes of Herodas. Jewish-Hellenistic writers, in this regard as in others, were part of a larger literary scene.

the material, omits some items and adds others. This is not the place to tackle the numerous chronological and interpretative problems raised by this notoriously troublesome work. Whether it represents a compilation and loose translation of the Masoretic texts or a Greek rendition of an earlier and lost Hebrew original can hardly now be ascertained. It is no easier to be secure about a date. Josephus did employ I Esdras rather than the canonical version, demonstrating that the work had circulation—and authority—in his time. Similarities of language or themes with works like Daniel and Esther might put it in the late second or early first century BCE, but one can go no further. The objectives of the work as a whole remain obscure: perhaps an effort to assemble material on the end of the First Temple, the Exile, and, particularly, the circumstances of the return and the reinstitution of worship, in order to affirm the ascendancy of the Temple cult; perhaps to pay special tribute to the achievements of Zerubbabel and Ezra, subordinating for some reason the role of Nehemiah; perhaps to underscore the collaborative relationship between Jews and the Persian regime, as reflection or harbinger of the situation that held between the Jewish state and the Hellenistic monarchies.[98] In any case, one story intrudes upon the narrative, with no counterpart in the Scriptures, sitting most awkwardly in its context, but an intriguing fable that illustrates once again the ingenuity and wit of Hellenistic Jews who wove pagan folktales into their own rewriting of the Bible.

First, the context. I Esdras opens with the Passover celebration of Josiah and the final years before the destruction of the Temple, a close correspondence to the account in II Chronicles.[99] The author proceeds to the first year of Cyrus' reign in Persia and the king's proclamation authorizing the restoration of the exiles and the rebuilding of the Temple, punctuated by recovery of the sacred treasures that had been carried off to Babylon. All of this is patterned on the opening chapters of the Book of Ezra.[100] The text then inexplicably leaps to the reign of Artaxerxes I, oblivious, so it seems, to the fact that almost a century had passed and three Persian rulers had inter-

---

98. Among the more valuable treatments of I Esdras, see C. C. Torrey, *Ezra Studies* (Chicago, 1910) 11–36; *idem, Louis Ginzberg Jubilee Volume* (New York, 1945) 395–410; R. H. Pfeiffer, *History of New Testament Times* (New York, 1949) 233–57; A. Lods, *Histoire de la littérature hébraique et juive* (Paris, 1950) 948–54; K. F. Pohlmann, *Studien zum dritten Ezra* (Göttingen, 1970) 14–73; J. M. Myers, *I and II Esdras* (Garden City, 1974) 1–19; R. J. Coggins and M. A. Knibb, *The First & Second Books of Esdras* (Cambridge, 1979) 1–7; H. Attridge in Stone, *Jewish Writings*, 159–60; Schürer, *History of the Jewish People*, III.2 (1987) 708–18, with bibliography.

99. I Esdras 1.1–58; cf. II Chron. 35–36.

100. I Esdras 2.1–15; cf. Ezra 1.

vened. The author records appeals by enemies of the Jews to Artaxerxes to put an end to the reconstruction of Jerusalem and its Temple, advice which Artaxerxes heeded, thus terminating the activity until the reign of Darius. This segment comes from a later portion of the canonical Ezra, but the chronological confusion is compounded by I Esdras.[101] We are suddenly thrust into the time of Darius, two generations before Artaxerxes, a reversal of which neither the author of Ezra nor that of I Esdras seems to have been aware. At this point I Esdras reports a tale altogether absent in the canonical book, but arresting in both content and implications.

The story involves a wager and contest among three young pages or bodyguards of Darius. A banquet of the king introduces the narrative. Darius lavishly hosted his family, household, officials of the realm, satraps, military commanders, and administrators from throughout the empire. After its conclusion the king intermittently slept and woke, while the three young guardsmen conceived a game among themselves. They determined that each would write down what one thing he considered to be "the strongest" and deposit it under Darius' pillow. When he should awake to find the notes, he and his top three advisers would select the wisest opinion and reward its holder with riches, glory, and the highest position in court.[102] The king duly awoke, read the three notes, and summoned all the chief officials of the realm to hear the arguments of the three young men.[103]

The first opted for wine as the strongest, pointing out its irresistible effect upon all, rich and poor, king and slave alike, addling their brains, inducing them to act in ways unimaginable when sober, and robbing them of all respect for convention and for their betters.[104] The second put his money on the strength of the king, emphasizing his mastery of land and sea, the unequivocal authority of his commands, and the absolute obedience paid by his subjects to any directive that he issues.[105] The third youth is the only one named, the Jew Zerubbabel. He first chose women as the most potent for they are responsible for bringing men into the world, nurturing and honoring them, and, more importantly, their allure and appeal can cause men to abandon all other loyalties and obligations, behave in irrational and heedless fashion, enslave themselves to the whims of their lovers, and throw away careers or lives for them, an affliction from which not even kings are

101. I Esdras 2.16–30; cf. Ezra 4.7–24.
102. I Esdras 3.1–9.
103. I Esdras 3.10–17.
104. I Esdras 3.18–24.
105. I Esdras 4.1–12.

immune.[106] This bodyguard, however, shifted his position in midstream. He turned to truth as the greatest and strongest of all elements. Whereas injustice can inhere in wine, kings, women, and men, causing all eventually to perish, truth abides forever, emblematic of objectivity and justice, the symbol of greatest authority through the ages. He concluded by hailing the God of truth.[107]

So ended the speeches. When everyone then heaped praise upon truth as the most powerful, Darius awarded the palm to the last speaker and offered to grant him any desire that he expressed. Zerubbabel then reminded the king of his vow to rebuild Jerusalem, restore the sacred vessels, and allow the erection of the Temple once again. Darius consented unhesitatingly, ordered the fulfillment of Zerubbabel's wish, directed his satraps in the area to offer every assistance, issued decrees to guarantee privileges for all the Jews, and furnished considerable financial support to assure both the implementation of his orders and the long-term maintenance of the Jews. He restored the holy vessels that Cyrus had confiscated from Babylon and, in general, brought all of Cyrus' commands regarding the Jews to fruition.[108] Zerubbabel then rendered thanks to the King of Heaven and Lord of his fathers and brought the news to his fellow countrymen who proceeded to celebrate for a week. The segment concludes with the departure of Jewish households for Jerusalem, accompanied by a cavalry escort and a band of musicians sent by Darius. The priests stood at their head, as did Zerubbabel whose wise words at the Persian court had brought it all about.[109] The text recounts the names of those who returned with Zerubbabel, here reverting once more to the canonical Ezra. The tale of the three bodyguards is not referred to again, an altogether separate and independent entity.

What to make of it? The story is incongruous and inconsistent, quite apart from being incredible. It possesses no historical value, of course. The author moves directly from the reign of Artaxerxes, presumably the first Persian monarch of that name, in the mid fifth century, to that of Darius two generations earlier, and Darius' directives for the rebuilding of the Temple and restoration of the sacred vessels simply duplicate what I Esdras had already ascribed to Cyrus two reigns earlier still. The chronological muddle in canonical Ezra is simply magnified here. Josephus who followed I Esdras tried to slip in a historical corrective, substituting Cambyses for Artaxerxes as

106. I Esdras 4.13–33.
107. I Esdras 4.34–40.
108. I Esdras 4.41–57.
109. I Esdras 4.58–5.6.

successor of Cyrus, but that did not help much.[110] The tale of the guardsmen, in any case, represents a jarring intrusion in the narrative. It has nothing to do with history and little with logic. For one thing, the narrator seems uncertain as to whether Darius was asleep or awake when the three youths developed their game.[111] The very idea that the pages would create this contest, offering Darius' favor, rewards, and elevation to the winner—without consulting the king—is quite preposterous.[112] And one need hardly comment on the notion that Zerubbabel, a Jew of royal lineage who would be instrumental in the reconstruction of the Temple in Jerusalem, began his career as a bodyguard in the Persian court. The story obviously has no place in its context and strains plausibility in almost every detail.

Its origins belong outside this setting. The contest of the guardsmen reads like a folktale, perhaps Greek, Persian, or even Egyptian in a previous incarnation. Certainly there is nothing peculiarly Jewish about it, apart from the appearance of Zerubbabel, a transparent insertion into the text.[113] Its prior form cannot be ascertained with any confidence. The present anomalies are so great as to demand the hypothesis of a better original.

---

110. Jos. *Ant.* 11.21–30.

111. I Esdras 3.3: καὶ ἐκοιμήθη καὶ ἔξυπνος ἐγένετο; cf. 3.8–9, 3.13. Torrey's suggestion, *Ezra Studies*, 34, that this mistranslates what had been a reference to the waking of the guardsmen, takes great liberties with the text.

112. I Esdras 3.4–9. Josephus, *Ant.* 11.33–37, recognizing the absurdity, tries to get around it by having Darius pose the alternatives and offer the rewards.

113. R. Laqueur, *Hermes* 46 (1911) 168–72, rightly sees it as a free-floating fable whose point resides in each contestant's meeting and overcoming the claims of his predecessor. W. Rudolph, *ZAW* 61 (1945–1948) 178, finds echoes of Greek stories concerning debates over the best, the strongest, or the wisest. For M. Heltzer, *Henoch* 2 (1980) 150–54, the accurate details of the Achaemenid court make it a story of Persian origin. That case is argued on broader grounds by Pfeiffer, *History of New Testament Times*, 251–53. The view of Torrey, *Ezra Studies*, 25–30, 37–39, that the tale belongs in the original version, is implausible. J. L. Crenshaw in B. O. Long, *Images of Man and God* (Sheffield, 1981) 77–79, sees various parallels in Jewish texts regarding the power of wine, kings, and women. But none of them is particularly close, nor do they provide any sound reason for believing in a Jewish composition at the outset. For precedents in Egyptian wisdom literature, see P. Humbert, *Orientalistische Literaturzeichnung* (1928) 148–49; Lods, *Histoire de la littérature*, 952–53. The original language, so it has been argued, was Aramaic; see, especially, Torrey, *Ezra Studies*, 20–25; F. Zimmerman, *JQR* 54 (1963/1964) 182–94. This, of course, would be consistent with a Persian tale. But even a Greek original cannot be ruled out; cf. Rudolph, *ZAW* 61 (1945–1948) 182–85. It matters little whether the fable was inserted independently by an interpolator or by the translator of the putative Aramaic version himself; see Pohlmann, *Studien zum dritten Ezra*, 35–52, for the first; W. T. In der Smitten, *VT* 22 (1972) 492–95, for the second. The present version, in any case, almost certainly represents Jewish adaptation of an earlier pagan folktale. The motif is a familiar one; see S. Thompson, *The Motif-Index of Folk-Literature*, 6 vols. (Bloomington, 1955–1958) III, H 631; cf. also H 501.

The sequence of propositions for the "strongest" as king, wine, and women would make more sense than the extant one of wine, king, and women—especially as the king is represented among those overcome by wine.[114] The three youths as initiators of the contest can hardly have been in the original. Nor does Josephus' revision improve matters much. Would the king have suggested royal power as only one of three alternatives, encouraging the other two pages to promote different options? More likely, the ruler cooked up the scheme without assigning answers to the contestants.[115] And the most glaring anomaly consists in the fact that four answers rather than three were forthcoming. The intrusive Zerubbabel not only makes a case for women but abruptly overtrumps himself by hauling in "truth" as ultimate victor. That will surely not have existed in the model, where, presumably, three (or four) respondents had one answer each. Nor must we see "truth" as a characteristically Jewish addition, stimulated by scriptural precedents. The theme of truth as supreme had strong and widespread pagan credentials. And Zerubbabel himself refers to it as an abstract entity, bringing in God only at the very end, a blatant insertion.[116] Why pervert what may have been a reasonably coherent fable into this twisted and illogical narrative which, on the face of it, does not even deliver a peculiarly Jewish message?

The most obvious answer, of course, lies in the character of Zerubbabel. He enters the story suddenly and surprisingly, a Jewish bodyguard of the Persian king, clumsily imposed upon the tale.[117] So, it has been argued, the spotlight falls on Zerubbabel, thereby to diminish the luster of Nehemiah. In fact, scholars have taken the conjecture further: the story represents a direct response to the festal letter of II Maccabees which celebrated and exaggerated the exploits of Nehemiah, a refutation of Hasmonaean propaganda by elevating Zerubbabel at Nehemiah's expense.[118] The explanation, even in moderate form, does not work. I Esdras as a whole may have downplayed the role of Nehemiah. But that end could readily be achieved without the

114. I Esdras 3.19. This has often been noticed; cf. Laqueur, *Hermes* 46 (1911) 171; Zimmerman, *JQR* 54 (1963/1964) 197. Crenshaw's doubts, in Long, *Images of Man and God*, 82, are unconvincing.

115. Cf. Zimmerman, *JQR* 54 (1963/1964) 195–96.

116. I Esdras 4.40: εὐλογητὸς ὁ θεὸς τῆς ἀληθείας. Cf. Rudolph, *ZAW* (1945–1948) 19–180; Pfeiffer, *History of New Testament Times*, 252–55; Myers, *I & II Esdras*, 55–56.

117. I Esdras 4.13: οὗτός ἐστιν Ζοροβαβελ.

118. Cf. Myers, *I & II Esdras*, 9–12. The more political interpretation by In der Smitten, *VT* 22 (1972) 494–95. The further hypothesis by Attridge in Stone, *Jewish Writings*, 160, that emphasis on the Temple was part of a polemic against the rival temples of Onias and the Tobiads, is highly speculative. The existence of such a polemic is itself questionable; see E. S. Gruen, *SCI* 16 (1997), 47–70.

invention or adaptation of the guardsmen's tale. It offers little help in understanding the motives for that creation. Zerubbabel serves a more plausible purpose. He represents the wise, knowledgeable, and articulate Jew at the court of the Gentile ruler who outstrips other counselors, finds the truth, and wins the favor of the monarch for himself or his people. That theme recurs in Jewish-Hellenistic literature, familiar from the Book of Daniel, from Esther, from the *Letter of Aristeas*, and rooted in the Genesis narrative of Joseph. Here it would have special resonance in calling attention to Jewish privileges earned by the shrewdness of a Jew, accorded and guaranteed by the Persian empire, thus providing a solid claim for the inviolability of the Temple and for the prerogatives of its worshippers.[119] Such a claim carried significance for Jews dwelling in the shadow of Hellenistic kingdoms.

That analysis, however plausible and meaningful, does not tell the whole story. The Jews did indeed owe restoration and protection to the generosity of Persian rulers, a fact that could be made more palatable by having a Jew outwit rivals and take credit for determining the policy of the suzerain. But there is more to it than that. The speech of Zerubbabel has a flavor very different from that of the loyal courtier expressing a cozy relationship with the king and sealing a collaboration between Jewish virtue and pagan authority. Instead the speech contains some sharp humor, more barbed than ingratiating, certainly far from a paean to Persian power.

A hint surfaces already in the speech of the first bodyguard, pointing out the potency of wine. He observes that it respects neither rich nor poor, slave nor free, and that its effects fall alike upon king and satrap.[120] That would hardly win the applause of any monarch. The second speaker, of course, endorses royal power as the most indomitable of entities. But his illustrations paint the ruler as autocratic despot, ruthless in his commands, intimidating subjects into servile obedience.[121] Few rulers could take pleasure in such a description of their authority. Zerubbabel subsequently took over and found jocular arguments that could only increase the king's discomfiture. In upholding the influence of women, his opening gambit noted that the king and all his people who rule land and sea were dependent upon the women who gave them birth.[122] He then became more personal and direct. He observed that the king's power is irresistible to every nation. Yet he is mere putty in the hands of his own concubine Apame. Zerubbabel gave

119. Cf. Laqueur, *Hermes* 46 (1911) 169–70; Rudolph, *ZAW* 61 (1945–1948) 185.
120. I Esdras 3.19–21.
121. I Esdras 4.3–12.
122. I Esdras 4.15.

an eyewitness account: he had seen Apame pull the diadem off Darius' head, put it on her own, and slap him with her left hand, while the king merely gaped at her. And that was just one occasion. Zerubbabel added that when she laughed, he laughed, and whenever she expressed irritation, he would resort to flattery in order to win back her affection.[123] It need hardly be said that no guardsman in his senses would utter such words in the presence of his sovereign. But, more significantly, the dialogue here tips off any reader that it is not to be taken as a serious piece of reporting. Even the final piece of wisdom delivered by Zerubbabel, the hymn to truth as all-powerful, normally taken as sober didacticism and the injection of morality and religion, has its own wry twist that ought not to be overlooked. The Jewish courtier, by hailing truth as the purveyor of justice, contrasts it with the injustice practiced by all elements of society—with explicit reference to the king among the perpetrators of injustice.[124] And what was Darius' response to these barbs and cavils? He praised Zerubbabel to the skies, named him as "kinsman," and offered to grant his every wish.[125]

The implications of this invented fable need to be brought out with clarity. Zerubbabel does not play the wise counselor, acting in the best interests of the king and thus advancing the ends of his own nation, a fruitful association in which Jews are the beneficiaries of the greater power. The speaker, in fact, twits the greater power, mocking and embarrassing him, but obtaining his blessing nonetheless. Irony and amusement run through the dialogue. It goes without saying that such a scenario was not composed for a Gentile readership. Hellenistic Jews, on the other hand, who read this version of the return from exile could take pleasure in a tale whereby their champion both outstripped his rival courtiers and made sport of a rather dense king who then ate out of his hand. The Jews, in short, regained their Temple and their homeland not through the condescension of the suzerain nation but through their own wit and ingenuity, making clear which was, in fact, the superior people.

•   •   •

Jewish levity in the rewriting of the Bible has been inadequately appreciated. The barbed shafts discernible in I Esdras' fable of the three bodyguards have comparable counterparts elsewhere, notably in the Greek additions to

---

123. I Esdras 4.28–33.
124. I Esdras 4.36–37.
125. I Esdras 4.42.

the Book of Daniel. Here the author or authors once again fiddled with a received text, inserting folktales of independent provenance, and applying some acid drollery to refashion the Jewish image.

The additions to Daniel consist of three separate items combined in two Greek recensions, the Septuagint and the version of Theodotion. The problems involved in understanding when, how, and by whom these accretions entered the tradition and subsequently dropped out are legion and cannot be explored here. Nor do we know with certainty whether the additions were originally composed in Greek or derived from Semitic prototypes. But one confident pronouncement can be made: the author or authors implanted these additions into the text of Daniel, where they sit quite awkwardly and incongruously, irrelevant to the overall narrative, and plain intrusions.[126] That, of course, only provokes a redoubled inquiry into the reasons for these inventions. The three additions are "The Prayer of Azariah and the Hymn of the Three Young Men," "Susanna," and "Bel and the Dragon." Of these, the first involves a prayer and a hymn that heighten the spiritual element, stress the religiosity of the characters, and convert the story from a narrative to a liturgical drama—features that stand outside our purview. The other two pieces of folklore have greater relevance and stronger appeal.

"Bel and the Dragon" actually contains two tales cobbled together and placed at the conclusion of what subsequently became the canonical text. They possess an unusually engaging character that attracts attention. A brief resumé will give some of the flavor. The first fable, concerning Bel, introduces Daniel as close adviser of king Cyrus, honored above all his friends. The king paid special homage to the god Bel whom the Babylonians served with tangible benefits: they lavished substantial portions of flour, sheep, and wine upon him every day. Cyrus wondered why Daniel did not share his enthusiasm for Bel, a manifest divinity who consumed so much food and drink daily. Daniel retorted that he worshipped only the God who

126. Valuable discussions of all these questions in Pfeiffer, *History of New Testament Times,* 433–56; Lods, *Histoire de la littérature,* 958–65; J. Schüpphaus, *ZAW* 83 (1971) 49–72; M. Delcor, *Le livre de Daniel* (Paris, 1971) 273–78, 289–92; C. A. Moore, *Daniel, Esther, and Jeremiah: The Additions* (Garden City, 1977) 23–34; Schürer, *History of the Jewish People,* III.2, 722–30, with bibliography. Date of composition is equally uncertain, but set by most authorities now in the later 2nd century BCE; see, especially, Moore, *op. cit.,* 28–29; M. J. Steussy, *Gardens in Babylon: Narrative and Faith in the Greek Legends of Daniel* (Atlanta, 1993) 28–32, with recent bibliography. The Hebrew/Aramaic text or, at least, *a* Hebrew/Aramaic text of Daniel was reckoned as authoritative by the time of I Maccabees; I Macc. 2.59–60. As the Qumran material shows, variant versions of Daniel circulated in this period; see J. J. Collins, *Daniel* (Minneapolis, 1993) 1–3, 72–79.

created heaven and earth, not some fabricated idol. And he had a laugh on the king, observing that Bel, constructed out of clay and bronze, was incapable of eating or drinking anything.[127] Cyrus, angry and determined to get at the truth, summoned the priests of Bel and ordered them, on pain of death, to prove that the god ate his stores; if they succeeded, Daniel would die in their stead. The priests then arranged a test whereby Cyrus would set out the food and drink in Bel's temple, close the door, and seal it with his own signet ring. They had full confidence in victory for they had a secret passageway beneath the table through which they regularly entered and confiscated the provisions.[128]

Daniel, however, saw through the ruse. And he had a trick up his sleeve. After the priests departed, he directed that ashes be scattered everywhere in the temple before it was sealed. Hence, when the priests, their wives, and their families, as usual, came up through the trap door and consumed the food and drink, they left tell-tale prints in the ashes. When morning dawned, the outer door was unsealed, and the stores were gone. Cyrus' first reaction was to hail the greatness of Bel. But Daniel had yet another laugh: he restrained the king from entering the temple and he pointed to the footprints of men, women, and children. The scales fell from Cyrus' eyes, he ordered the execution of the priests and their families, and he turned the statue of Bel over to Daniel who promptly destroyed it and its temple.[129]

The narrator proceeds directly to the next legend, that of the dragon or the snake. Here the king, still looking for a tangible deity to revere, points to the large snake which the Babylonians worship, and bids Daniel to pay it homage as well. The Jewish counselor, of course, sticks to his own God, and he offers to expose the snake's impotence by killing it without recourse to a weapon. Cyrus grants permission. Daniel then mixes a concoction of pitch, fat, and hair and feeds it to the snake which bursts open on the spot, allowing Daniel to crow, "Now look at your object of worship!"[130] The Babylonians struck back, hurled insults at the king for abandoning them, and vilified him as a converted Jew. Further, they applied blackmail: either turn over

127. Daniel 14.1–7: καὶ εἶπεν Δανιηλ γελάσας, μὴ πλανῶ, Βασιλεῦ· οὗτος γὰρ ἔσωθεν μέν ἐστι πηλὸς ἔξωθεν δὲ χαλκὸς καὶ οὐ βέβρωκεν οὐδὲ πέπωκεν πώποτε. The paraphrase presented here is based on Theodotion's version, preferable in this case to that of the Septuagint; see Moore, *Additions*, 139.

128. Daniel 14.8–13.

129. Daniel 14.14–22; note, especially, 14.19: ἐγέλασεν Δανιηλ καὶ ἐκράτησεν τὸν βασιλέα τοῦ μὴ εἰσελθεῖν αὐτὸν ἔσω.

130. Daniel 14.23–27: ἴδετε τὰ σεβάσματα ὑμῶν.

Daniel for punishment or the whole royal family will perish. The compliant Cyrus surrendered Daniel, and the Babylonians forthwith cast him into the lions' den.[131] But rescue was not long in coming. The prophet Habakkuk, preparing to distribute food to workers in the fields, was immediately whisked away by an angel, pulling him airborne by the hair, to deliver the sustenance to Daniel, still safe and sound.[132] When on the seventh day the king went to the pit to grieve for Daniel, he found him miraculously unharmed, heaped praise on Daniel's God, pulled out his counselor, and tossed his enemies to the lions.[133]

The tales are both amusing and revealing. Their origin remains obscure. A prevailing notion has it that the whole text constitutes an expansion on some verses of Jeremiah concerning Nebuchadnezzar's metaphorical swallowing of the prophet and the punishment of Bel. That idea hardly illuminates the quite distinct version of Daniel.[134] Nor does it help much to point to the battle between Marduk and Tiamat in the Babylonian *Enuma Elish* as a possible model, for the differences far exceed the similarities.[135] The stories themselves are something of a mishmash. The "dragon" tale alone consists of three largely unrelated episodes: the blowing up of the snake, Daniel in the lions' den, and the angelic flight of Habakkuk. And even the ostensible reminiscence of Daniel 6 by the lions' tale here is only superficial, for all the details are different. It is neither variant nor doublet.[136] Conjectures about Jewish or pagan prototypes do not get us far. The legends, whatever their archetypes, if any, constitute deliberate implantations onto the text, fanciful creations designed to capture the interests of readers.[137]

To what end? The most immediate and obvious objective would seem to be the contrast between Jewish monotheism and idol worship, a dominant

131. Daniel 14.28–32.

132. Daniel 14.33–39.

133. Daniel 14.40–42.

134. Jeremiah 51.34–35, 51.4. The idea is endorsed by Moore, *Additions*, 122–23; Schürer, *History of the Jewish People*, III.2, 723–24; cf. Steussy, *Gardens in Babylon*, 161–62. For Nickelsburg in Stone, *Jewish Writings*, 39, the stories represent midrashic interpretations of Isaiah 45–46. If so, however, the extant text has departed quite distantly from Isaiah and bears little relation to it.

135. Cf. Moore, *Additions*, 123–24. Pfeiffer, *History of New Testament Times*, 456, sees "Bel and the Dragon" as a parody of the Babylonian myth.

136. So, rightly, Moore, *Additions*, 147–48. See also J. J. Collins in J. A. Overman and R. S. MacLennan, *Diaspora Jews and Judaism* (Atlanta, 1992) 335–37. A different view in L. M. Wills, *The Jew in the Court of the Foreign King* (Minneapolis, 1990) 129–38.

137. The novelistic features of these tales are well brought out by L. M. Wills, *The Jewish Novel in the Ancient World* (Ithaca, 1995) 60–67, although his reconstructed evolution of the narratives is highly conjectural.

theme in biblical and post-biblical literature.[138] That undercurrent exists, to be sure. But theology hardly gets top billing in the narrative. Daniel makes only passing references to his God and says nothing about his beliefs. His sole prayer to God is one of gratitude for the food that Habakkuk delivered, a decidedly secondary and largely irrelevant aspect of the tale. The emphasis throughout rests not on divine intervention but on Daniel's own sagacity and resourcefulness.

A different approach will prove more profitable.[139] "Bel and the Dragon" possesses some striking resemblances, unnoticed by moderns, to the story of the three youths in I Esdras. The basic motif in each is that of the clever Jewish counselor at court who outstrips pagan adversaries, earning honor and reward at the hands of the king. But it is not the structure alone that arrests attention. Cyrus, of course, holds a high place in Jewish memory as the monarch responsible for the return of Jews from the Babylonian Exile, the very role played in the fictional account of I Esdras by Darius. In both of the narratives, however, the king, far from a magnanimous benefactor of the humble Jews, is represented as something of a dullard, manipulated and even mocked by those around him—including the shrewd Jew. On two occasions Daniel laughs at Cyrus' folly: when he took Bel for a living god on the assumption that he ate and drank the vast provisions supplied each day, and when he leaped to the conclusion that the god existed after unsealing the temple door and seeing the food and drink gone—forgetting about the ashes strewn just the night before. On the second occasion, in fact, Daniel has to restrain the oblivious king forcibly, lest he rush in and destroy the evidence![140] Cyrus fares no better in the "dragon" part of the story. He was as gullible about the snake as he had been about the idol. And even when Daniel exploded the unfortunate serpent, Cyrus was browbeaten and intimidated by his Babylonian subjects into yielding up his adviser for their

---

138. This is repeatedly characterized as a central point of the narrative; cf. Pfeiffer, *History of New Testament Times*, 455; Lods, *Histoire de la littérature*, 963–64; Moore, *Additions*, 127; Nickelsburg in Stone, *Jewish Writings*, 39; M. Delcor in W. D. Davies and L. Finkelstein, *The Cambridge History of Judaism* (Cambridge, 1989) II, 455–56. For M. W. M. Roth, *CBQ* 37 (1975) 42–43, the tales exemplify the genre of "idol parody." So also Wills, *Jew in the Court*, 131–33; idem, *Jewish Novel*, 62, 65. But see Steussy, *Gardens in Babylon*, 46–47.

139. For an instructive literary interpretation, quite different from the analysis here, see Steussy, *Gardens in Babylon*, 69–99. Her view that the story reflects ethnic rivalries between Jews and Greeks or Egyptians in Alexandria (*op. cit.*, 183–87) reads perhaps too much into the text. The tale need not, in any case, derive from Egypt; Collins in Overman and MacLennan, *Diaspora Jews*, 343–44.

140. Daniel 14.7, 14.19. See above nn. 127, 129.

vengeance.[141] The malleable monarch later gave way to regret and visited the lions' pit to grieve for Daniel's fate—only to find the would-be victim hale and hearty.[142] Hence he performed yet another about-face and extolled the power of Daniel's God. This is very far from a flattering portrait of the Persian king. The narrator misses no chance to expose his naiveté and deride his vacillation.[143] If this is the ruler under whom the Jews returned to their homeland, one must infer that a Jew pulled the strings on this hapless puppet.

The author of the fables plainly had great fun with them. Not only does he burlesque the king and humiliate the Babylonians, he also makes Daniel a master trickster. The text represents the Jewish hero less as champion of the ancestral faith against oppression and idolatry than as a clever chap with a repertoire of artifices. The sprinkling of ashes to detect the criminal makes Daniel a proto–Sherlock Holmes or Hercule Poirot. And the ludicrous blending of ingredients, not to poison the snake but to have it blow apart, can only have been designed to draw a laugh from the readership. Finally, one may note that, whatever scriptural model may have existed for it, the image of a baffled and reluctant Habakkuk being swept through the skies from Judaea to Babylon, by an angel tugging at his hair, just to bring some food to Daniel, surely reflects the mischievous frolic of the author.[144]

The episodes heretofore discussed have important elements in common. They all remold earlier stories to poke fun at Gentile rulers, exposing them as dim-witted, credulous, and readily deluded. The resourceful Jew in each instance outwits pagan rivals, manipulates the monarch, and demonstrates the superiority of Jewish belief and Jewish sagacity. The Jews may have to live under the rule of alien kings but the rewritten fables reassured them of how far they surpassed those kings in mental agility and insight. The irony reflects a shared perspective of author and reader, a joint laugh at the inadequacies of the political authority.

But the humor did not come only at the expense of the Gentile. Inventive Jewish writers could hold even their fellow Jews up to scorn, a striking sign of the self-confidence of their communities.

---

141. Daniel 14.28–30: ἀναγκασθεὶς παρέδωκεν αὐτοῖς τὸν Δανιηλ.

142. Daniel 14.40: ὁ δὲ βασιλεὺς ἦλθεν τῇ ἡμέρᾳ τῇ ἑβδόμῃ πενθῆσαι τὸν Δανιηλ.

143. The view of Collins in Overman and MacLennan, *Disapora Jews*, 336–43, that "the Gentile king is portrayed in very positive light" overlooks these features.

144. Moore, *Additions*, 145, suggests that the scene is patterned after the similar experience of Ezekiel; Ezek. 8.3. If so, however, the composer of the addition to Daniel transformed the episode from the sublime to the ridiculous.

That feature can be illustrated by another Greek addition to the Book of Daniel. The story of Susanna and the Elders has attracted much attention and interest over the centuries, and continues to do so. It serves to illuminate further some of the traits that Hellenistic Jews associated with their past and deployed to reflect on their present.

The tale can be briefly summarized. Susanna was the beautiful and devout daughter of pious parents and wife of Joakim, an eminent Jew in Babylon. Two of the elders of the people, appointed judges in that year, frequented the home of Joakim and were smitten by the sight of Susanna. Each independently lusted after her, then together they conspired to have her submit to their desires. They hid in the garden, spied upon her in the bath, and confronted her with an intimidating proposition: either have intercourse with them or be accused by them of committing adultery with a young man. Susanna, coerced into an unwelcome decision, chose the latter.[145] The lecherous elders then delivered their indictment before a gathering of the people, testifying that they had witnessed a sexual encounter between Susanna and her lover; they could not restrain the young man, but nabbed Susanna instead. Since they were elders, men of high standing in the community, and judges, their testimony persuaded the congregation which promptly condemned Susanna to death.[146] The unhappy woman then cried out to God to prevent this miscarriage of justice. And the plea took effect. God infused spirit into a youth named Daniel who roundly rebuked the people and denounced them for exercising peremptory judgment without even interrogating the elders on their testimony. He denied the validity of their statements and offered to grill them himself.[147] Daniel wisely took the precaution of separating the two men and questioning them independently. He excoriated both of them for a lifetime of wickedness, sinful lust, and injustice. And he put the same question to each: where did the act of intercourse take place? When each responded with a different location, Daniel triumphantly exposed their perjury, and the congregation cheered his success. The elders suffered execution, the virtuous Susanna was vindicated, her relatives praised the Lord, and Daniel gained great esteem among the people from that day on.[148]

Wherein lies the significance of this legend? Older theories proposed that it delivered a moral lesson, pitting the pious youth against the elderly

---

145. Daniel 13.1–27.
146. Daniel 13.28–41.
147. Daniel 13.42–51.
148. Daniel 13.52–64.

reprobates, or that its purpose focused on court procedures, advocating a more thorough and searching cross-examination, or that it represented a haggadic expansion of Jeremiah 29.21–23, or that it refashioned Greek myths that involved spying on virgin goddesses in their baths. None of these ideas carries full conviction. To draw out moral or didactic lessons may put too sober a construction on this fanciful tale. And the suggested Jewish and Greek models have very little in common with the Susanna story itself.[149] The motifs plainly have more to do with folklore than with instructional treatises, exegesis, or allegory. Analogous themes can be found in the Arabian Nights, Grimm's Fairy Tales, and a variety of eastern and near eastern literary texts.[150] But, whatever may have been the prototype, the version that appears among the Greek additions to Daniel has its own objectives and meaning. It clearly constitutes an alien element in the text, unconnected with and largely unsuitable to the rest of Daniel. Whether composed initially in Greek or in a Semitic language, it represents an independent insertion, readily separable, indeed rejected as part of the canon, but widely popular across the ages.[151] What purpose did it serve?

Standard interpretation emphasizes the religious elements. Although the folktale in an earlier incarnation may simply have mingled motifs like that of the wise youth and depraved elders and that of the chaste wife falsely accused, the extant rendition added frequent references or allusions to

149. On these various theories, see the trenchant comments of W. Baumgartner, *Archiv für Religionswissenschaft* 24 (1926) 261–68; cf. Pfeiffer, *History of New Testament Times*, 450–53; Moore, *Additions*, 84–88. A useful bibliography in Schürer, *History of the Jewish People*, III.2, 729–30. And see now the review of scholarship by Steussy, *Gardens in Babylon*, 49–54. Her effort to revive the idea that the Susanna story relates to Jeremiah 23.15 and 29 (*op. cit.*, 147–52), however, is unsuccessful. For a recent but rather strained attempt to recast the moral issues, see E. Stump in E. Spolsky, *The Judgment of Susanna: Authority and Witness* (Atlanta, 1996) 85–100. The voyeuristic aspect of the elders' behavior is not central in the text but becomes a major feature of later visual representations of the tale. See the acute remarks of M. Bal, *Biblical Interpretations* 1 (1993) 1–19. Note also E. Spolsky in Spolsky, *The Judgment of Susanna*, 101–17.

150. The patterns were discerned by G. Huet, *RHR* 65 (1912) 277–84; Baumgartner, *Archiv für Religionswissenschaft* 24 (1926) 268–80; *ibid.* 27 (1929) 187–88; B. Heller, *ZAW* 54 (1936) 281–87; and now widely adopted: e.g. Pfeiffer, *History of New Testament Times*, 453–54; Moore, *Additions*, 88–89; Wills, *Jew in the Court*, 76–79. For the motif, see Thompson, *Motif-Index*, IV, J 1153–54; K 2112.

151. On the original language, see the discussions of Zimmerman, *JQR* 48 (1957/1958) 236–41; Moore, *Additions*, 81–84, with bibliography. The incongruity of the tale in its context is widely recognized; cf. Moore, *op. cit.*, 90–91. For comparison of the two versions in the Septuagint and Theodotion, see Moore, *op. cit.*, 78–80; H. Engel, *Die Susanna-Erzählung* (Göttingen, 1985) 10–17, 55–77. On the Nachleben of the fable, see I. Lévi, *REJ* 95 (1933) 157–71; Engel, *op. cit.*, 29–54; and the various essays collected in Spolsky, *The Judgment of Susanna*, most of which deal with manipulation of the story in later eras.

the Lord, most significantly in Susanna's prayer to God, the divine spirit infused in Daniel, and the praise of the Lord after Susanna's acquittal and vindication.[152] Hence, it is claimed, religious considerations permeate the story, a Jewish reworking of pagan folklore in order to place God in the center and advance the theological concerns of Judaism.[153]

But there is more to it than that. Divine involvement is distant and oblique, alluded to rather than directly felt.[154] Certainly God plays no role through most of the text. And, although he may supply authority to Daniel, the young man performs his own task with personal energy and efficiency. Daniel's shrewdness, here as in the Bel and Dragon stories, carries the day. He foiled the libidinous but rather dull-witted scoundrels by interrogating them out of earshot of one another, thereby discovering and exhibiting the inconsistency of their stories. Daniel trounced the villains not as devout adherent of the faith but as a crafty prosecuting attorney. Nor do his lawyerly techniques embody exemplary justice. Daniel convicts the elders even before questioning them, and declares the first to be a lascivious perjurer although his story had yet to be contradicted.[155] Perhaps the scenario already appeared in a prior folktale. What matters, however, is that the Jewish interpolator had no qualms about casting Daniel in the part of the manipulative and aggressive accuser.[156]

Comic elements emerge in this story as well. One may note the spectacle of the two dirty old men parting company in Joakim's garden and then circling back surreptitiously—only to bump into one another.[157] And their doltish answers to Daniel's cross-examination displayed a gross ineptitude that made a travesty of their august public posts. Daniel also toyed with them

---

152. Daniel 13.42–45, 13.50, 13.60, 13.63.

153. Cf. Baumgartner, *Archiv für Religionswissenschaft* 24 (1926) 279–80; Pfeiffer, *History of New Testament Times*, 454; R. A. F. MacKenzie, *Canadian Journal of Theology* 3 (1957) 211–18; Moore, *Additions*, 89–90.

154. The one possible exception is God's rousing the holy spirit in Daniel; Daniel 13.45: ἐξήγειρεν ὁ θεὸς τὸ πνεῦμα τὸ ἅγιον παιδαρίου νεωτέρου (Theodotion's version). The Septuagint has an angel perform the task: καὶ ἔδωκεν ὁ ἄγγελος, καθὼς προσετάγη, πνεῦμα συνέσεως νεωτέρῳ. R. Dunn, *Christianity and Literature* 31 (1982) 22–24, exaggerates the difference here by interpreting the angel's role in the Septuagint as dictating Daniel's actions and reducing him to a mere instrument of divine will, whereas Theodotion's Daniel is a free agent merely inspired by God. The texts do not support so sharp a distinction.

155. Daniel 13.49: ψευδῆ γὰρ οὗτοι κατεμαρτύρησαν αὐτῆς ; 13.54–55: ὀρθῶς ἔψευσαι εἰς τὴν σεαυτοῦ κεφαλήν.

156. A different approach is taken by S. Sered and S. Cooper in Spolsky, *The Judgment of Susanna*, 43–55, for whom Daniel's role as trickster replaces the more common female trickster, thus to reinforce patriarchy.

157. Daniel 13.13–14.

in his questioning, twice employing puns to increase their discomfiture.[158] The outcome served less to point a moral than to entertain the reader.[159]

Perhaps more interesting still is the target of this ridicule. The author fires his shafts here at no foreign ruler or Gentile rivals, but at Jews themselves. Nor does he limit his attacks to the aging Don Juans, as if they were but two rotten apples in an otherwise healthy barrel. A noteworthy fact requires emphasis: the two elders held their high offices through appointment by the people, and their word alone sufficed to persuade the entire populace to pass a death sentence on Susanna without hesitation.[160] Hardly a favorable portrait of the Jewish nation. To be sure, public opinion turned around with enthusiasm once Daniel entered the scene.[161] But that only points up the fickle, malleable, and readily manipulated attitudes of leaders and citizenry alike.[162]

This addition to Daniel focuses exclusively on the internal. Only Jews appear on stage. They dwell in Babylon, to be sure, but their community is fully self-governing and ostensibly autonomous. Hence they also leave themselves vulnerable to the ironist's caricature. To read this yarn simply as a religious fable displaying God's protection of the innocent and punishment of the wicked misses much. The tale directs its mockery at a range of community failings: hypocrisy, false religiosity, inverted values, and unprincipled vacillation.

The humor, of course, had a serious purpose as well. The exposure of pomposity in the leadership and gullibility in the rank and file supplied a pointed reminder to the nation: Jews need to look to their own shortcomings. That such a message could be inserted into the text of Daniel is quite striking. It attests to a notable self-assurance on the part of Hellenistic Jews who exposed the foibles of fellow Jews to public scrutiny. It recalled to mind basic principles of justice and morality that needed to be observed,

---

158. See Daniel 13.54–55: σχῖνον ... σχίσει; 13.58–59: πρῖνον ... πρῖσαι.

159. The presence of comic elements was rightly discerned by Dunn, *Christianity and Literature* 31 (1982) 19–32. His probing article finds considerable differences in approach between the Septuagint version and that of Theodotion. But his analysis of the former virtually strips it of anything that can plausibly be called comic. And he goes perhaps too far in judging Theodotions' presentation as a social satire in which the reformist Daniel overturns the corrupt system of his elders.

160. Daniel 13.5: ἀπεδείχθησαν δύο πρεσβύτεροι ἐκ τοῦ λαοῦ κριταί; 13.41: ἡ συναγωγὴ [LXX: ἡ συναγωγὴ πᾶσα] ὡς πρεσβυτέροις τοῦ λαοῦ καὶ κριταῖς καὶ κατέκριναν αὐτὴν ἀποθανεῖν.

161. Daniel 13.50: καὶ ἀνέστρεψεν πᾶς ὁ λαὸς μετὰ σπουδῆς.

162. This aspect is not noted in the valuable study of the narrative by Steussy, *Gardens in Babylon*, 115–43.

especially in Jewish communities that governed their own activities. And it provided a subtle reminder that lapses in adherence to those principles could divide Jews internally, thus setting them up again for victimization by greater powers. The message, however, came not with prophetic thunder but with barbed levity. That dispassionate mode gave the reader a welcome sense of detachment rather than inflicting upon him the burden of anxiety.

·   ·   ·

Comparable conclusions can be advanced by examining another work. Greek additions to a Hebrew text occur also in the Book of Esther. Here again interpolators interjected material that fits ill with the received text, independent variants dramatically different from and even inconsistent with it that demand explanation and interpretation. The Scroll of Esther, in its Hebrew version, already told a lively and engrossing tale of Jewish success at the Persian court. It required no further spicing up.[163] Why then the additions? They possess a flavor and character ostensibly quite distinct from those to Daniel. Yet closer scrutiny exhibits some interesting parallels: features reminiscent of the sardonic character evident in other Jewish-Hellenistic writings, and a further indication of the growing self-confidence of Greek-speaking Jewish intellectuals.

As usual, textual questions abound but need no resolution here. The Greek text of Esther exists in two principal versions quite different from one another, and neither one is a close and faithful rendering of the MT.[164] This does not, however, affect analysis of the additions. Both of the extant Greek translations contain the supplements in nearly identical form. Just when they entered the corpus cannot be ascertained. Indeed, we know the dates of composition neither for the Hebrew Esther nor for the Greek

163. On the folktale themes in Esther, see S. Niditch, *Underdogs and Tricksters* (San Francisco, 1987) 126–45. She offers a better approach than the more rigid patterning found by A. Meinhold, *ZAW* 87 (1975) 306–24; *ZAW* 88 (1976) 72–93, who compares the Book of Esther to the Joseph story in Genesis.

164. This induced C. C. Torrey to argue that not only does each Greek text derive from a different Semitic original, but that neither employed the extant Hebrew version, and that the Greek translation derives from a lost text earlier than the MT; *JBL* 61 (1942) 131; *HTR* 37 (1944) 1–40. That may be extreme. See the useful summary of earlier works by Pfeiffer, *History of New Testament Times*, 307–309. Among more recent treatments, see J. Schildenberger, *Das Buch Esther* (Bonn, 1941) 1–23; R. Hanhart, *Esther* (Göttingen, 1966) 45–99; C. A. Moore, *ZAW* 79 (1967) 351–58; idem, *Esther: Introduction, Translation, and Notes* (Garden City, 1971) lxi–lxiii; D. J. Clines, *The Esther Scroll: The Story of the Story* (Sheffield, 1984) 69–114; L. M. Wills, *Jew in the Court*, 153–91; M. J. Fox, *The Redaction of the Books of Esther* (Atlanta, 1991) *passim*.

translation nor for the additions. Moreover, the additions themselves, quite distinct in form, style, and content, may date from different eras. This has invited a mass of speculation that we can happily ignore. One item of information, however, supplies an essential point of departure. The colophon that stands at the end of Greek Esther in the Septuagint reports that the Greek translation by a certain Lysimachus of Jerusalem was brought (presumably to the Alexandrian library) in the fourth year of the reign of Ptolemy and Cleopatra.[165] Such a subscription is unique among all the books of the Bible. That actually lends confidence in its authenticity. Comparable tags designed to assure the genuineness of disputed manuscripts were frequently applied to texts acquired by libraries. The Greek Esther had evidently been challenged, as indicated by the wording of the colophon which has the bearers of the manuscript declare its legitimacy.[166] We have no reason to doubt the accuracy of that attestation. Three dates are possible for a fourth year shared by Ptolemy and Cleopatra: 114/3, 78/7, or 49/8 BCE. The last, a turbulent time in the Mediterranean, would be an unlikely occasion for delivery of a manuscript. Either of the other two remains possible.[167] The Hebrew text which inspired the translation obviously has an earlier date, with modern conjectures ranging all the way from the Persian period to about 100 BCE. For our purposes a decision is unnecessary.[168]

The additions concern us here. Greek Esther contains six of them, readily grouped into three pairs and conventionally designated as A–F. The first and last convey, respectively, a dream of Mordecai and its interpretation. B and E purport to be documents issued by the Persian king, the first authorizing extermination of the Jews, the second rescinding the order. C presents the prayers of Mordecai and Esther prior to the latter's audience before the king, and D recounts the audience itself. When were the additions added? The colophon follows directly upon F, the interpretation of Mordecai's dream, which evidently belongs together with it, as, presumably, does A, the dream itself. In that case, both can be placed in the late Hellenistic period. The other

---

165. Esther, Add. F, 11: ἔτους τετάρτου βασιλεύοντος Πτολεμαίου καὶ Κλεοπάτρας.

166. Esther, Add. F, 11: Δωσίθεος ὃς ἔφη εἶναι ἱερεὺς καὶ Λευίτης καὶ Πτολεμαῖος ὁ υἱὸς αὐτοῦ τὴν προκειμένην ἐπιστολὴν τῶν φρουραι, ἣν ἔφασαν εἶναι. For the meaning of εἶναι here, see E. J. Bickerman, *JBL* 63 (1944) 351–55. Bickerman's erudite investigation demonstrated that such subscriptions attesting the genuineness of manuscripts were not uncommon in antiquity; *op. cit.*, 340–45.

167. Bickerman's case for 78/7 (*JBL* 63 [1944] 346–47), on the basis of the heading of the colophon, is instructive but not definitive. Cf. Goodman in Schürer, *History of the Jewish People*, III.1, 505–506.

168. See the discussion by Moore, *Esther*, lvii–lx.

two pairs, quite unconnected to the subscription or to one another, remain undatable. They were available by the time of Josephus who paraphrased them. Further precision would be illusory. Additions B and E, the king's proclamations, were almost certainly composed in Greek, the other four may or may not have had Semitic originals, thus leaving open the question of whether they (or some of them) preceded or followed the translation of Hebrew Esther into Greek.[169] In any case, they represent secondary impositions, created after the Book of Esther circulated in a prior version and, whether inserted singly or collectively into the text, they altered its character markedly and accord a very different flavor to the Greek Esther—another instance of free invention by Hellenistic Jews.

The overall change in tone provided by the additions is plain enough and long recognized. The original version conveyed a straightforward tale of intrigue at the Persian court in which the virtuous Jew and Jewess triumphed over their villainous antagonist. It lacked altogether any allusions to religious tenets, beliefs, or practices. And the God of the Hebrews played no part in the proceedings. The additions reinstate Yahweh, bring religion back to Mordecai and Esther, turn Haman into a raging anti-Semite, and convert what had been a personal conflict between Mordecai and Haman into a fundamental and implacable struggle between Jews and Gentiles on an international level. While the Masoretic text furnishes the setting for the festival of Purim, a lively and largely secular celebration, the supplements in Greek Esther leave Purim out of account and bring spiritual considerations into the forefront.[170] There can be no denying that the additions do serve to recast the Esther story along these lines, stressing the religiosity of the hero and heroine and having the Lord intervene to assure the triumph of Judaism over its enemies. Yet the supplements on scrutiny show more complex features, varied and discordant, allowing for a range of interpretations, and, at times, reminiscent of the sardonic character evident in other Jewish-Hellenistic writings.

Additions B and E present a serviceable starting point. They consist of the ostensibly verbatim reports of the ruler's edicts transmitted throughout the Persian empire, first to decree the annihilation of the Jews, and later to reverse

---

169. On all this, see the analyses of Moore, *JBL* 92 (1973) 382–93; *idem, Additions*, 155, 165–67; R. A. Martin, *JBL* 94 (1975) 65–72.

170. Cf. Bickerman, *JBL* 63 (1944) 360–62; Pfeiffer, *History of New Testament Times*, 311; Moore, *Additions*, 157–59, 181, 249. Clines, *Esther Scroll*, 168–74, argues that the additions were designed to bring the tale of Esther closer in form and content to scriptural norms exemplified in the books of Ezra, Nehemiah, and Daniel. The standard interpretation is reiterated by M. V. Fox, *Character and Ideology in the Book of Esther* (Columbia, S.C., 1991) 265–73.

the decree. The Hebrew narrative merely states that the vizier Haman who had the ear of King Ahasuerus persuaded him to order elimination of all Jews within his kingdom, for they resist assimilation and ignore the king's statutes, preferring to live by their own set of rules. Ahasuerus duly sent out dispatches to that effect to all the satrapies of his empire.[171] The Greek addition supplies the alleged decree with rhetorical flourish. King Artaxerxes opens by reminding his subjects that his primary concern is the peace and stability of his empire, an objective he strives for not out of any ambition for power but because he always acts with gentleness and in an agreeable manner.[172] He then notes that Haman, a man of conspicuous kindness and moderation, had informed him of a hostile people whose laws are antipathetic to those of all other nations and whose scorn of royal directives prevent the implementation of his benign rule.[173] Artaxerxes therefore determined that so perverse and anti-social a people had to be eradicated in order to keep his kingdom serene and secure—and he so decreed.[174]

As we know from the canonical text, however, the monarch did an about-face later. Convinced by the intercession of Esther, he hanged Haman on the gallows that had been erected for Mordecai, and sent out orders to revoke his previous instructions and authorize the Jews everywhere to revenge themselves upon their enemies.[175] The interpolator here inserted addition E, the letter that Artaxerxes supposedly issued throughout his empire. It goes well beyond the current situation. Artaxerxes indulges himself in sweeping ruminations about arrogant and wicked men who abuse power and deceive their sovereigns, conspiring to shed innocent blood, unaware that they cannot escape the all-seeing gaze of God.[176] He then names Haman explicitly as perpetrator of the wickedness, brands him as a "Macedonian" with not a drop of Persian blood, and condemns him for his plot against Mordecai, Esther, and all their nation—a scheme that would transfer hegemony from Persia to Macedon[177] The king proceeds to lavish praise upon the Jews, calling them children of the highest and greatest living God, ordering the

171. Esther 3.8–13.

172. Esther, Add. B, 2: μὴ τῷ θράσει τῆς ἐξουσίας ἐπαιρόμενος, ἐπιεικέστερον δὲ καὶ μετὰ ἡπιότητος ἀεὶ διεξάγων. The Septuagint, as is well known, regularly renders Ahasuerus as "Artaxerxes." But the relevant king is more likely to be Xerxes; see Moore, *Esther*, xxxv–xli.

173. Esther, Add. B, 3–4.

174. Esther, Add. B, 5–7.

175. Esther 5–8. The manipulation of the king by others is a common folktale motif. Cf. S. Talmon, *VT* 13 (1963) 441–43; Niditch, *Underdogs and Tricksters*, 133–34.

176. Esther, Add. E, 1–6.

177. Esther, Add. E, 7–14.

protection of all Jewish practices, and endorsing Jewish retaliation against their foes. He not only sanctions a Jewish festival to commemorate this reversal but directs that any city or territory in his realm which does not follow his instructions be destroyed root and branch.[178]

What is to be made of these royal letters? Standard interpretation has it that they lend authenticity to the narrative, boosting belief in its historicity by representing what appear to be official documents.[179] That idea does not deserve the long life it has enjoyed. Could any interpolator imagine that Jewish (let alone Gentile) readers would take these proclamations as legitimate decrees issuing from the palace? What they actually accomplish is to render the king ludicrous. The missives abound in high-flown rhetoric bordering on bombast. The excessive encomium that Artaxerxes applies to Haman in the first letter is rendered preposterous by the equally over-abundant condemnation of his minister in the second—thereby only calling attention to his own delusion and self-deception. The anachronistic allegation that Haman was a Macedonian and preparing the way for Macedonian hegemony may be a sly hint to readers that nothing in the royal edicts should be taken seriously. Artaxerxes simply succeeds in making himself absurd. The treatment presents some interesting analogies to that of the Bel and Dragon episode in Daniel and even to the three guardsmen's tale in I Esdras. One might note finally that the second letter contains the king's encourage-ment for the festival of Purim, claiming it to be the decision of God—the very festival that had virtually no religious overtones.[180] Artaxerxes' homage to the Jewish God hardly adds a note of spirituality to the text. It exhibits instead the somewhat malicious irony of the interpolator.

The Greek Esther begins with a dream of Mordecai and concludes with its interpretation, segments customarily designated as A and F. Neither has any prototype in the Hebrew text. The dream itself opens with turmoil and confusion, thunder and earthquake, heralding a battle between two mighty dragons. And when they sent up a great shout, all the nations readied themselves for war against the nation of the just. There followed dire signs of gloom, darkness, evil, and turbulence that terrified the righteous people and induced them to call out to God. That cry brought forth a great river from what had been a small spring. Light and sun appeared. The lowly arose

178. Esther, Add. E, 15–24.

179. E.g. Moore, *JBL* 92 (1973) 383–84; Nickelsburg in Stone, *Jewish Writings*, 136; Schürer, *History of the Jewish People*, III.2, 718. Wills' view, *Jewish Novel*, 117–20, that Addition B reflects Jewish uneasiness and embarrassment about their religious particularism seems difficult to sustain in light of Addition E.

180. Esther, Add. E, 21–22.

and consumed the renowned ones.[181] So the dream ended. Its interpretation was lodged after the last chapter of the Book of Esther. The triumph of the Jews reminded Mordecai of his dream, and now he understood its meaning. Esther was the river, Mordecai himself and Haman were the dragons. The nations that prepared themselves for war intended to eradicate the name of the Jews. And it was Israel that called out to God and was saved.[182] Mordecai proceeds to enlarge on the Lord's accomplishments, the rescue of his people from all evils, the great signs and wonders he delivered, and the distribution of two lots, one for the people of God and one for all other nations. The process came to fruition on the day of judgment when God remembered his people and justified his allotment. That event, says Mordecai, shall be celebrated through the ages.[183]

The dream and its interpretation present a picture dramatically different from anything that appears in the canonical Esther. The hand of God enters the scene with devastating effect. Preceded by natural and supernatural signs, the Lord transformed a personal battle between Mordecai and Haman into a titanic clash among the nations. He divided the peoples of the world into Jew and Gentile and set up a momentous contest in which his intervention determined the outcome. God not only rescued his people but exalted them over their enemies. Moderns have rightly called attention to these aspects of additions A and F. But to leave it at that may not catch all the notes struck by the texts. Troubling incongruities occur in the interpretation of the dream, awkward conjunctions and ambiguous meanings. For a start, the image of the dragons creates a problem. It would suit Haman well enough, but hardly Mordecai. Why cloak the Jewish champion in the garb of the monster? Moreover, the great river rising to a flood is not the most obvious symbol for Esther, whose behavior both in the canonical texts and in the additions is cautious and deliberate rather than aggressive. Further, the image of light and sun in the dream receives no exegesis in the interpretation, whereas the two lots that figure prominently in the latter do not even appear in the dream itself.[184] The discordances do not lend themselves to easy explanation. But

181. Esther, Add. A, 4–10.
182. Esther, Add. F, 1–6.
183. Esther, Add. F, 7–10.
184. The incongruities are compounded by discrepancies between the text of the LXX and the "Lucianic" version which, among other things, interprets the river not as Esther but as the enemy nations. These inconsistencies induced Moore to believe that the dream was an independent composition awkwardly grafted onto the Esther story, retaining some discordant details, and prompting divergent interpretations: *JBL* 92 (1973) 389–90; *idem, Additions,* 248–49. Fox, *Redaction,* 72–76, inferred that Additions A and F had two separate authors. Perhaps

a novel approach may be worth considering: perhaps the author indulged himself in a bit of parody. Mordecai as dragon and Esther as river are less than edifying symbols. The thunderings and earthquake, gloom, darkness, and turmoil of the dream do not resurface in its interpretation. But they, like the dragon and the river, the light and the sun, suggest apocalyptic visions. And the day of judgment in addition F, which has no direct counterpart in the dream, plainly introduces an eschatological motif, out of tune with the rest of the text.[185] One should not exclude the possibility that the creator of these supplements was playing about with the notorious ambiguity and malleability of apocalyptic pronouncements—and that he somewhat diminished both Mordecai and Esther in the process.

The personalities of Mordecai and Esther are central to additions C and D, perhaps the most remarkable supplements to the text. And one may detect further diminution of those characters. The royal edict against the Jews supplies the context. Mordecai's appeal to Esther to intercede with Ahasuerus precedes the insertions. Addition C invents prayers by both Mordecai and Esther, and D gives the actual encounter between Esther and the king.

Mordecai's prayer reads like a pious plea to the Lord, acknowledging his irresistible power and authority, and entreating him to save the people whom he had hitherto protected and to turn their sorrow into joy.[186] The supplication, to be sure, exhibits Mordecai's religiosity. But this is a far cry from the personage in the Hebrew text who developed his own plan and steeled Esther's resolve when she wavered.[187] In that text Mordecai's refusal to bow down before Haman is presented straightforwardly, a self-evident act of defiance that required no explanation.[188] In the prayer, however, Mordecai feels an obligation to justify and defend his decision. It was not done, so he claims, out of arrogance, overblown self-importance, or vanity. Indeed, he would gladly have kissed Haman's shoes, if that would save Israel.[189] No, Mordecai insists, he acted as he did solely to avoid putting the glory of man

---

so. But those are not the only possible explanations. On Mordecai's dream in later Jewish tradition, see E. L. Ehrlich, *Zeitschrift für Religions und Geistesgeschichte* 7 (1955) 73–74.

185. Esther, Add. F, 8: καὶ ἦλθον οἱ δύο κλῆροι οὗτοι εἰς ὥραν καὶ καιρὸν καὶ εἰς ἡμέραν κρίσεως ἐνώπιον τοῦ θεοῦ καὶ ἐν πᾶσι τοῖς ἔνθεσιν.

186. Esther, Add. C, 1–4, 8–10.

187. Esther 4.1–14.

188. Esther 3.2.

189. Esther, Add. C, 5–6: οὐκ ἐν ὕβρει οὐδὲ ἐν ὑπερηφανίᾳ οὐδὲ ἐν φιλοδοξίᾳ ἐποίησα τοῦτο, τὸ μὴ προσκυνεῖν τὸν ὑπερήφανον Αμαν, ὅτι ηὐδόκουν φιλεῖν πέλματα ποδῶν αὐτοῦ πρὸς σωτηρίαν Ισραηλ.

above that of God. He would bend his knee to no one except the Lord himself, and—so he reiterates still again—he was not motivated by self-importance.[190] Quite an intriguing speech. Why the need for this tortured apologia? It is hard to avoid the conclusion that Mordecai suffered from a bad conscience. His refusal to pay obeisance to Haman had thrust his entire nation into the gravest peril. His prayer to God, therefore, was at least as much for himself as for his people. And the double insistence that he did not act out of personal hauteur only underscores the plausibility of that charge. Whereas the Hebrew text took the propriety of Mordecai's deed for granted, the Greek addition has him labor mightily to vindicate it—which, of course, has the precise effect of questioning the virtue of his actions. The interpolator seems less concerned with Mordecai's piety than with his pretension.[191]

One might accord a similar analysis to Esther's prayer. The bad conscience emerges still more conspicuously here. Esther strips herself of the splendid garments supplied by the palace, covers herself with ashes and dung, and makes herself as unattractive now as she had been comely before.[192] She then utters an abject entreaty to God, begging him to forgive the sins of his people, including the past idolatry that has set them on the brink of destruction.[193] Esther here takes upon herself the burden not only of pleading for her nation's safety but for confessing all its prior transgressions. The queen proceeds, like Mordecai, to justify and explain away her own ostensible misdeeds. Yes, she concedes, she slept with the uncircumcised king—but she hated every minute of it.[194] Yes, she wears a crown, but only in public and only because she has to; in fact she despises the crown and never dons it when she is off duty.[195] She twice proclaims her loathing of the crown, and her comparison of it with a polluted, presumably menstrual,

---

190. Esther, Add. C, 7: ἀλλὰ ἐποίησα τοῦτο, ἵνα μὴ θῶ δόξαν ἀνθρώπου ὑπεράνω δόξης θεοῦ, καὶ οὐ προσκυνήσω οὐδένα πλὴν σοῦ τοῦ κυρίου μου καὶ οὐ ποιήσω αὐτὰ ἐν ὑπερηφανίᾳ .

191. Moore's characterization of this as "a beautiful and appropriate prayer" [*Additions*, 205] is hard to credit. Wills, *Jewish Novel*, 121, even more surprisingly, compares the prayer with contemporary martyr accounts in II Maccabees. Pohlmann, *History of New Testament Times*, 311–12, rightly perceived Mordecai to be speaking "unctuously—one would even say hypocritically," but he does not develop the insight.

192. Esther, Add. C, 12–13.

193. Esther, Add. C, 14–22.

194. Esther, Add. C, 26: οἶδας ὅτι ἐμίσησα δόξαν ἀνόμων καὶ βδελύσσομαι κοίτην ἀπεριτμήτων.

195. Esther, Add. C, 27: σὺ οἶδας τὴν ἀνάγκην μου, ὅτι βδελύσσομαι τὸ σημεῖον τῆς ὑπερηφανίας μου, ὅ ἐστιν ἐπὶ τῆς κεφαλῆς μου ἐν ἡμέραις ὀπτασίας μου. βδελύσσομαι αὐτὸ ὡς ῥάκος καταμηνίων καὶ οὐ φορῶ αὐτὸ ἐν ἡμέραις ἡσυχίας μου.

rag is strong language indeed. Like Mordecai, the queen protests too much. She insists even that she never took food at Haman's table, thus to declare her adherence to dietary laws—a statement at variance with the canonical account which betrays no concern on the matter.[196] The prayer goes well beyond an expression of faith and a plea for the salvation of the Jews. Esther exposes her own discomfort and self-consciousness about compromises with principle. The author of the addition makes the queen, through strained denials, direct attention to her weaknesses and bad faith.

A final scene buttresses this conclusion. Addition D describes the audience of Esther before the king. In the Hebrew text, she approaches this ordeal with grim determination: "If I perish, I perish."[197] Not so in the supplement. Esther is terrified. She had dressed herself once more in resplendent robes, she had summoned her God and savior, and she glowed at the peak of her beauty. But inside she was wracked with fear. As soon as she saw the king sitting magnificent and awesome on his throne, and flashing an angry glance at her, Esther passed out on the spot.[198] Indeed the queen fainted not once but twice. After Artaxerxes, induced by God into sweet reasonableness, revived and reassured Esther, the Jewess briefly took heart, then slipped from his grasp and sank again to the floor.[199] This is hardly the stuff of a heroine. Perhaps, as is often said, the scene provides her with genuinely human characteristics. But for the Hellenistic interpolator, this was surely not intended as a compliment. Between her two fainting spells Esther tried to explain away her nervousness: she was simply awestruck at the grandeur of the king who looked like an angel of God.[200] The excuse was forced and transparent, exhibiting the same lack of credibility as Esther's apologia for her conduct in the prayer to God. The narrative accentuates her disingenuousness when, despite the king's amiability, she keels over a second time. The interpolator evidently augmented the tale at Esther's expense.[201]

196. Esther 2.9; Add. C, 28: καὶ οὐκ ἔφαγεν ἡ δούλη σου τράπεζαν Αμαν.

197. Esther 4.16.

198. Esther, Add. D, 1–7: ἡ δὲ καρδία αὐτῆς ἀπεστενωμένη ἀπὸ τοῦ φόβου ... ἔπεσεν ἡ βασίλισσα καὶ μετέβαλεν τὸ χρῶμα αὐτῆς ἐν ἐκλύσει. Cf. the fainting spell of Agrippa I when he learned of Gaius' decision to erect a cult statue in the temple of Jerusalem; Philo *Leg. ad Gaium* 261–69.

199. Esther, Add. D, 8–15: ἔπεσεν ἀπὸ ἐκλύσεως αὐτῆς.

200. Esther, Add. D, 13: εἶδόν σε, κύριε, ὡς ἄγγελον θεοῦ, καὶ ἐταράχθη ἡ καρδία μου ἀπὸ φόβου τῆς δόξης σου. Cf. Genesis 33.10.

201. His sardonic irony can be discerned also in the overly generous assessment of Artaxerxes' magnanimity and his angelic quality—surely not to be taken seriously, as does W. H. Brownlee, *RevBibl* 73 (1966) 161–85. Wills, *Jewish Novel*, 121–26, points out the novelistic elements in these additions, but bypasses the irony.

Additions C and D drastically transform the characters of Mordecai and Esther—and certainly not to their advantage.[202]

The Greek supplements to the Scroll of Esther show a disposition unnoticed in modern treatments. Their author or authors do, of course, inoculate the narrative with a heavy dose of religion. The power of God is appealed to repeatedly in the prayers, given shape in the dream and its interpretation, and acknowledged even by the Persian king. They also accent a cosmic confrontation between the Jewish people, favorites of the Lord, and all other nations. Esther and Mordecai, who simply outwit Haman through their own resources in the canonical tale, become devotees of the divinity in the Greek additions and owe their success to his intervention. But there is more to be said. The additions possess further dimensions, greater complexity and subtlety. Their authors shared that sense of irony and dark humor that we have observed in several Jewish-Hellenistic writings. They exposed the vacuousness and vacillation of the Persian king, they hinted at hypocrisy in the prayers of Mordecai and Esther, and they parodied apocalyptic pronouncements in fashioning Mordecai's dream and its explanation. Their texts subverted Jewish as well as Gentile figures. Here, as so often, it is the ambiguity rather than the piety that sets off the character of these compositions.

•   •   •

Humor, of course, depends on the shared experience of writer and readership. A modern perspective risks the detection of jokes lost on or never intended by the ancients. Readily enough discerned in texts like Bel and the Dragon or the lampooning of Darius in I Esdras, they are more subtle and less obvious in the depiction of Mordecai and Esther. But not necessarily just the product of latter-day imposition on ancient mentality. Comedy occurs with too much frequency in Jewish-Hellenistic texts to be the product of modern imaginings. A diverse audience could appreciate or react to this material on more than one level. For many Jewish readers of the Greek text, the prayers of Mordecai and Esther, the reversal of Artaxerxes, and the punishment of Haman doubtless vindicated Judaism and confirmed their faith. In the hands of later writers like Josephus or the Church Fathers, who

---

202. That Jewish writers could take a detached and somewhat ironic view even of pious figures whom they admire can be illustrated in II Maccabees. The author delivers a glowing tribute to the saintly High Priest Onias III but does not refrain from a subtle dig at the motivation for some of his actions; cf. II Macc. 3.31–32.

preserved several of the texts discussed here and who had their own particular axes to grind, only the serious message counted. Other contemporaries, however, will have enjoyed the wit on a different plane, an "in-group" who could exchange knowing glances and discover a deeper meaning.

No single vision permeated the range and variety of writings touched on here. They span a spectrum from ostensibly historical reconstructions through whimsical recasting of the Scriptures to the invention of fanciful fables. For Jewish intellectuals of the Hellenistic age the Bible may have been a sacred text, but certainly not an inviolable one. It provoked novel creations that enriched, enlarged, and invigorated antique traditions.[203] Even the purportedly serious historian Eupolemus had no qualms about fabricating victories by David and making up a correspondence between Solomon and the king of Egypt. Other works went much further, envisioning Abraham as educator of Near Eastern peoples, ultimate source of Greek learning, and even progenitor of the companions of Heracles. Moses too rose to new heights in the works of imaginative Jewish writers. He passed on the alphabet to Jews, Phoenicians, and Greeks, trained Egyptians in building techniques and weaponry, conceived the whole political and religious structure of their nation, taught the father of Hellenic poetry and song—and conquered the Ethiopians to boot! All of this departed greatly from any basis in the Bible. Those authors at least presented their products as independent entities. Others, however, took the liberty even of introducing fresh material into the Greek editions of biblical texts. The legend of the three youths in I Esdras adapts a pagan folktale to highlight Jewish initiative in regaining the homeland after the Babylonian Exile. The tales attached to the Greek version of Daniel further exemplify Jewish ingenuity at the expense of Gentile rulers—and, in the case of the Susanna story, even at the expense of other Jews. That feature emerges still more strikingly in the additions to Esther which not only denigrate the Persian king but call into question the behavior of the Jewish figures. Hellenistic writers, as is clear, had astonishingly wide scope in manipulating biblical tales, whether by radical amplification of received texts or liberal infusion of new material.

The diversity of these writings precludes simplification but permits some inferences. That such legends circulated among Hellenistic Jews does not imply irreverence. Instead it reveals an open and pliable attitude toward sacred texts: they encouraged elaboration rather than shut off imagination.

203. This makes it difficult to concur with the conclusion of G. W. Bowersock, *Fiction as History: Nero to Julian* (Berkeley, 1994) 21–22, 119, that the real spurt of fictional writing in antiquity awaited the reign of Nero—and the compositions of Christians.

The tales might embellish the feats of ancient Israelite figures, thus to underscore a powerful legacy that stretched through the ages, or to claim a Hebraic contribution to the origins of a common Mediterranean culture. The self-esteem of Hellenistic Jews certainly provided stimulus for such creations. But it does not suffice to see this activity as a polemical engagement, a competitive battle to gain an edge on Gentiles or to counter the claims of rival nations on the genesis of culture. Nor is it adequate to explain the fictitious fables as arising from internal politics or current events within Palestine or the Diaspora. They have wider significance. They display a strong sense of identity and national self-consciousness rather than a scramble to fabricate it. For the tales could humble Jewish figures as well as Gentile ones. And a remarkable number of them exhibit humor, irony, and playfulness that give the lie to conventionally austere interpretations. To recall but a few instances: Solomon's gift of a golden column to grace the temple of Zeus in Tyre, Abraham's progeny participating in the conquests of Heracles, Moses introducing animal worship to Egypt and circumcision to Ethiopia, Zerubbabel twitting Darius for his infatuation with a concubine, Daniel mocking the fatuity of the Persian king as well as irresolute public opinion among the Jews, and Mordecai and Esther clumsily seeking to explain away their lapses with transparent sophistry. That Jews as well as Gentiles could be targets of these jibes demonstrates a notable level of self-confidence in the intellectual circles of Hellenistic Judaism. The stories were not intended to be taken with strict sobriety or reckoned as literal correspondence with history.

But their objectives were certainly serious ones. They admonished Jews for compromising principles and endangering the solidarity of the community. And they underscored Jewish intellectual and ethical superiority over the Gentiles in whose midst they lived. Pointed wit could bring out the distinctiveness of the Jews by deriding the deficiencies of the alien. But it could also make sport of Jewish shortcomings, a reminder to hold to their heritage in a society of potential adversaries. The stories gave scope for creativity and imagination, they provided entertainment value for the readership, and they buttressed the self-image of the Jews.

CHAPTER 6

Kings and Jews

Monarchs and monarchy prevailed in the Hellenistic world. The institution could be found almost everywhere in the Near East, not only the major kingdoms of the Seleucids, Ptolemies, and Attalids, but petty dynasts, princes, and pretenders who periodically dotted the landscape. Diaspora Jews, always a minority in the realms of the Greek powers, needed to accommodate themselves to those circumstances. The relatively gentle hand of the Persian empire had been removed. The distant seat in Persepolis gave way to Hellenic centers in Alexandria, Antioch, Babylon, and Pergamum where Jews felt more directly the authority of Hellenistic kings. And in Palestine itself, as we have seen, the ostensibly "autonomous" Judaean state, even when it took on monarchical trappings itself, remained very much in the orbit of Seleucids and Ptolemies. The process of adjustment required more than institutional change. Jewish intellectuals here again devised strategies and deployed fictitious inventions that emphasized both the integration of their people into the Hellenic world and also their special place within it. In this endeavor, creative energies directed themselves not to the rewriting or expansion of biblical traditions, but to the production of stories that gave Jewish matters a place in the high policy of Hellenistic kings.[1]

The fictions begin at the beginning. Jews wrote themselves into the campaign of Alexander the Great. The man around whom so many legends accumulated and whose conquest formed the basis for Hellenic rule in the east could hardly escape appropriation by Jews who sought to establish their position by linking it with the founder of the new world. Josephus

---

1. The claim of G. W. Bowersock, in his stimulating but controversial book, *Fiction as History: Nero to Julian* (Berkeley, 1994) 123, that narrative fiction in the form of history stemmed from the Gospels and the Acts of the Apostles ignores this whole realm of Jewish fiction.

records a celebrated and complex tale that captured the attention of its readers—and many scholars through the ages. Variants, additions, and altogether new creations appear subsequently in rabbinic texts and also in the Pseudo-Callisthenes *Alexander Romance*. They represent much later traditions, testimony to the spell that Alexander continued to cast, but not pertinent here.[2] Josephus preserves a Hellenistic invention, and on that we must train our focus. It sheds valuable light on Jewish recreation of the relationship between their nation and the empire of the Greeks.

Josephus' story is tangled, possibly multilayered. A fairly full summary will help. The narration opens with a brief reference to Alexander's coming to the throne, victory at the Granicus, and then subjugation of much of Asia Minor.[3] It then turns to internal matters, involving Jews and Samaritans. Manasses, brother of the Jewish High Priest Jaddous, had married the daughter of Sanaballetes, a man of Samaritan lineage and a Persian appointee as satrap of Samaria. The connection angered the elders of Jerusalem who held that intermarriage of this sort was prohibited and had been the root of past troubles for the Jews. They demanded that Manasses divorce his wife or give up his priestly status and functions, an opinion with which Jaddous concurred. Sanaballetes, unwilling to lose his son-in-law, offered him a better deal: he promised appointment to the governorship of Samaria and a high priestly office of his own, namely in Samaria where Sanaballetes promised to build a temple on Mt. Gerizim comparable to that in Jerusalem, counting upon the assent of the Persian monarch Darius III. Manasses happily accepted the deal, bringing with him to Samaria numerous Jews, including priests, whose marriages had put them in similar straits and who were welcomed by Sanaballetes with handsome rewards.[4] The scene then switches back to the contest between Alexander and Darius. The great Macedonian, although facing troops far superior in manpower, confounded the odds, defeated the Persian army at Issus, captured members of Darius'

2. For the rabbinic texts on Alexander's encounter with Jews in Judaea, see Megillat Ta'anit, 21 Kislev and BT Yoma, 69a. The story in the *Alexander Romance*, deriving from Josephus, can be found in Ps. Callisthenes, *Vita Alexandri*, in the ε recension, 20.2–5; on this and related texts, see the discussions of F. Pfister, *SitzHeid* (1914) Abt. 11; G. Delling, *JSJ* 12 (1981) 1–51; D. Pacella, *AnnPisa* 12 (1982) 1255–69. Useful translations and analysis in R. Marcus' Appendix C in the Loeb Library edition of *Josephus, Jewish Antiquities*, vol. VI (Cambridge, Mass., 1937) 512–32. Most recent treatments, with additional bibliography, by J. A. Goldstein, *Proceedings of the American Academy for Jewish Research* 59 (1993) 59–101; and R. Stoneman, *Studia Philonica Annual* 6 (1994) 37–53.

3. Jos. *Ant.* 11.304–305.

4. Jos. *Ant.* 11.302, 11.306–12.

family, and put the king to flight. He went on to occupy Damascus and Sidon, and then to undertake the siege of Tyre.[5]

Alexander now for the first time took notice of the Jews. He dispatched a message to the High Priest requesting military assistance, supplies for his army, and whatever gifts they had been accustomed to furnish Darius in the past. Jaddous' response, that he had to honor his vow to Darius never to take up arms against him, met with fury on the part of Alexander. The king promised that, once the conquest of Tyre was achieved, he would march on Jerusalem and deliver an object lesson on which vows were to be kept and for whom.[6]

Sanaballetes saw an opening and seized the occasion. Although doubtless crestfallen at the unexpected defeat of Darius, he found the right moment to switch sides. He brought a host of his subjects to Alexander at Tyre, announced his abandonment of the Persian cause, and offered his realm to the Macedonian. Alexander, in return, consented to the building of the Samaritan temple, impressed by Sanaballetes' argument that a divided constituency in Palestine would be to the king's advantage. Sanaballetes proceeded immediately to constructing the temple and appointing Manasses as high priest, tasks that he evidently accomplished before his own death a few months later.[7]

The moment of truth for the Jews approached. Alexander had taken Tyre and then Gaza, and now prepared for the march on Jerusalem. Jaddous was in a state of panic, not knowing how to halt the Macedonian juggernaut. He directed the Jews to make supplication to God and joined them in desperate sacrifice for deliverance. A dream came to the rescue. God spoke in oracular fashion to Jaddous in his sleep and reassured him that all would be well if the city were decorated with wreaths, the people dressed in white robes, and the priests themselves decked out in proper attire, to greet Alexander outside the gates of the city. Jaddous, much relieved, followed instructions and met Alexander on the heights of Mt. Scopus. The Phoenicians and "Chaldeans" in Alexander's train expected free rein for plunder and an agonizing death for the High Priest. But an astonishing event upset all expectations. Alexander was dazzled by the sight of the Jewish people clad in white garments, the priests in linen, and the High Priest himself in splendid regalia, sporting a golden plate on his headdress that carried the name of the Lord. Alexander immediately performed *proskynesis* before the High Priest.

5. Jos. *Ant.* 11.313–17.
6. Jos. *Ant.* 11.317–20.
7. Jos. *Ant.* 11.321–25.

His followers were stunned and took his actions as a sign of temporary insanity. The sage Parmenio, chief marshal of Alexander, could not believe his eyes and asked the king why, when all others prostrate themselves before him, he performed obeisance to a Jewish priest. Alexander responded that his *proskynesis* honored not the priest but the god whom he served, for that god, dressed in such attire, had appeared to him in a dream long ago in Macedon, promising him the conquest of the Persian empire. The omen now appeared to be confirmed, a divine sign that guaranteed the success of the expedition. Alexander proceeded to enter the city, grasping the hand of the High Priest, went up to the Temple, and there sacrificed to God, following the instructions of Jaddous. In the event that any lingering doubts might remain, the king was shown the book of Daniel which conveniently predicted the fall of Persia at the hands of a Greek. Alexander needed no further convincing. He offered any rewards the Jews might desire. Jaddous made three requests: that they might live in accord with their ancestral laws, that they enjoy exemption from taxes in the sabbatical year, and that their brethren who dwelled in Babylon and Media could also employ their own laws. Alexander cheerfully granted all requests, and even offered service in his army to all Jews who wished to join—an offer which many of them embraced with enthusiasm.[8]

But the tale was not quite finished. The Samaritans, seeing the splendid treatment accorded the Jews, hastened to approach Alexander and insisted that they too were actually Jews. Josephus adds the snide comment that when Jews are in trouble the Samaritans deny any connection with them, but when there is advantage to be had they suddenly remember a joint kinship. They now greeted Alexander once more with protestations of loyalty, invited him to visit their new temple, and asked for a tax exemption every seventh year like that awarded the Jews. The king pressed them on the question of their origins, and extracted an admission that they were not, after all, really Jews. He postponed any further action on the matter to a future date but did accept the Samaritan soldiers who were sent to join him, and would later supply them with land allotments in Egypt.[9] So ends the story, a surprisingly tepid closure to a tale whose dramatic climax had come rather earlier.

The limp and ineffective ending prompts speculation about the character of the narrative as a whole. Scholars have often argued, on other grounds, that the tale does not hang together as a unit. It appears to consist of

8. Jos. *Ant.* 11.326–39.
9. Jos. *Ant.* 11.340–45.

three or four separate strands, loosely and not very competently stitched together. The encounter of Alexander and Jaddous has an independent existence, unconnected with and irrelevant to the Samaritans' claims and requests of the Macedonian king. Indeed, the Samaritan part itself, so it has been maintained, divides into two portions, the first segment deriving from a favorable tradition that lends the authority of Alexander to the temple at Mt. Gerizim, the second from a hostile tradition stressing the duplicity of the Samaritans. And still a fourth strand can be discerned in the brief account, marginal to the rest, of Alexander's campaigns from the Granicus to the capture of Gaza. The muddled mélange can thus be ascribed either to Josephus' source or to Josephus himself.[10] Others, however, have taken a very different line: the narrative works as a single entity, with an anti-Samaritan *Tendenz* throughout. On this analysis, the noble Jaddous is contrasted with the devious Sanaballetes from the start, the campaigns of Alexander serve as a backdrop, and Macedonian authorization for the Samaritan temple actually means that it lacks divine sanction.[11]

Whichever stance they adopt, scholars strain to discover a date and occasion for the origins of the story or stories. Several solutions with dates that collectively range over two and a half centuries have won some support. To illustrate: the entire tale can be placed around 200 BCE, prompted by the Fifth Syrian War when Jews successfully shifted loyalties from Ptolemy to Antiochus while Samaria was supposedly crushed by the Seleucids; the fable stems from the mid second century BCE, generated by a dispute between Jews and Samaritans in Alexandria over the legitimacy of their respective temples; the Jaddous segment consists of one pre-Maccabaean piece composed when Jews lived contentedly under Hellenistic suzerains and a second post-Maccabaean piece designed to humble rulers, both deriving from Palestine; the story reflects the historical circumstances at the time of Julius Caesar who granted privileges to the Jews comparable to those ascribed to Alexander; the Jaddous legend derives from M. Agrippa's visit to Jerusalem, his sacrifice in the Temple and guarantee of Jewish civic prerogatives, and the

---

10. The case for separate pieces assembled later was made forcefully and capably long ago by A. Büchler, *REJ* 36 (1898) 1–26. The arguments, modified or qualified, have found widespread acceptance; e.g., F.-M. Abel, *RevBibl* 44 (1935) 48–56; Marcus, *Josephus*, VI, 530–32; A. Momigliano, *Athenaeum* 57 (1979) 443–44; S. J. D. Cohen, *AJS Review* 78 (1982/1983) 41–44; D. R. Schwartz *JSJ* 21 (1990) 187–92; Stoneman, *Studia Philonica Annual* 6 (1994) 39–41.

11. See A. Kasher, *Beth Miqra* 20 (1975) 187–208 (Hebrew); Goldstein, *Proceedings of the American Academy for Jewish Research* 59 (1993) 70–90. Kasher argues for the historicity of the tale, Goldstein gives it no credence but sees it as a coherent whole.

Samaritan portion alludes to a Jewish-Samaritan quarrel that belongs to 52 CE. An amusing array of answers.[12]

The diversity of suggestions and the absence of consensus characterize a common phenomenon: the scholarly drive to find particular historical events or circumstances that will disclose the motive for inventing a legend. That goal encourages ingenuity but may miss the point. Fictitious tales rarely spring full-blown from a specific occasion or delimited period. The legend of Alexander in Jerusalem can best be understood as one of several comparable fictions that gave voice to Hellenistic Jews seeking to define their place in a world governed by Greek monarchs.

That this intricate narrative presents a seamless whole is difficult to maintain. As already noted, the rather lackluster ending disappoints any reader who might have been stirred by the encounter of Alexander and the High Priest in Jerusalem. The story of that encounter surely has a life of its own, unconnected to the tangled tale of the Samaritans.[13] Whether the Samaritan episodes constitute a single entity or two separate strands, they reflect little credit upon that people. Sanaballetes, obsessed with the ambition of having his descendants carry High Priestly blood in their veins, offered lavish enticements to his son-in-law, even a great temple of his own, counted on Persian backing, and then, when Alexander's fortunes rose, immediately switched allegiance, winning the king's favor by a promise that the nation of the Jews would be divided and thus cause no trouble to Alexander. And all this in the allegedly "favorable" portion! The resumption of the narrative unequivocally exposes Samaritan duplicity, with editorial comments by Josephus, just in case anyone missed the point. Moreover, a Samaritan apologist would be unlikely to ascribe the origins of his temple to a foreign king lured by a political bribe, rather than to the blessings of

---

12. For 200 BCE, see Goldstein, *op. cit.*, 90–96. For pre- and post-Maccabaean segments from Palestine, see Cohen, *AJS Review* 78 (1982/1983) 65–68. For mid 2nd century Alexandria, see J. Freudenthal, *Alexander Polyhistor* (Breslau, 1874) 102–103; Momigliano, *Athenaeum* 57 (1979) 444–46; Stoneman, *Studia Philonica Annual* 6 (1994) 42–43. For the time of Julius Caesar, see Büchler, *REJ* 36 (1898) 15–22; Marcus, *Josephus*, VI, 529–32. For M. Agrippa and 52 CE, see H. Willrich, *Juden und Griechen vor der makkabäischen Erhebung* (Göttingen, 1895) 1–13. In addition to all this, there are scholars who defend the historicity of the narrative itself, and thus do not have to worry about discerning a date for invention; e.g., Kasher, *Bet Miqra* 20 (1975) 187–208 (Hebrew); D. Golan, *Berliner Theologische Zeitschrift* 8 (1991) 19–30.

13. The argument of Goldstein, *Proceedings of the American Academy for Jewish Research* 59 (1993) 81–90, that the stories belong together as a pointed contrast between Jaddous' fidelity and Sanaballetes' duplicity, founders on the fact that Jaddous also switched loyalty from Darius to Alexander—albeit with divine sanction.

heaven.[14] The Samaritan tale or tales plainly arose in Jewish circles hostile to that people, its leaders, and its rival temple. It is unnecessary to seek a specific time or place for its genesis, since the animosity stretched from at least the later Hellenistic period through the Roman era.[15] For our purposes here, the Samaritans can be set aside. The central yarn of Alexander and Jaddous is detachable—and quite instructive.

Alexander's visit to Jerusalem is outright fabrication. The king never approached Jerusalem. The historical narratives of his march breathe not a hint of any side trip to that city. Alexander went straight to Egypt after the siege of Gaza and, on his return, he went directly from Egypt to Tyre and from there to North Syria and Mesopotamia.[16] There was certainly no reason for our Greek sources to have suppressed a visit to the holy city. They regularly report Alexander's arrival at key shrines and sacred places, where he honored native gods and performed public acts of sacrifice.[17] Jerusalem would fit nicely into that repeated scenario, and the Alexander historians could hardly have missed or omitted it. The tale is a fiction. To what end?

14. Observe the absence of any reference to Alexander in the Samaritan speech at Jos. *Ant.* 12.258–61.

15. On Samaritan/Jewish relations generally, see M. Gaster, *The Samaritans* (London, 1925) 1–39; H. G. Kippenberg, *Garizim und Synagoge* (Berlin, 1971) 48–93; R. J. Coggins, *Samaritans and Jews* (Atlanta, 1975) 57–115; J. D. Purvis in W. D. Davies and L. Finkelstein, *The Cambridge History of Judaism* (Cambridge, 1989) II, 591–613; M. Mor in A. D. Crown, *The Samaritans* (Tübingen, 1989) 1–18. On this episode, see especially R. Egger, *Josephus Flavius und die Samaritaner* (Göttingen, 1986) 65–82, 252–60. Goldstein, *Proceedings of the American Academy for Jewish Research* 59 (1993) 81–84, argues persuasively that the Samaritan segments were probably not composed by a Samaritan, less persuasively that they hang together coherently with the Jaddous story—and even that they are based on historical fact (Samaritan aid to Alexander for which they gained authorization for their temple). That Sanaballetes may have been a historical personage was rendered more likely by discovery of the name among 4th century Samaritan papyri; see F. M. Cross, *Biblical Archaeologist* 26 (1963) 110–21; *idem, HTR* 59 (1966) 201–205; *JBL* 94 (1975) 4–18. But that is far from proof that the episode in Josephus has any historical validity; see the skepticism of L. L. Grabbe, *JBL* 106 (1987) 236–42, and Schwartz, *JSJ* 21 (1990) 175–99.

16. Arrian 3.1.1, 3.6.1, 3.6.4, 3.7.1–3; Diod. 17.49.1, 17.52.6; Curtius 4.7.1–2, 4.8.9–16; Plut. *Alex.* 29.1, 31.1. Kasher, *Bet Miqra* 20 (1975) 194–95 (Hebrew), points out that there was time for Alexander to make the visit after taking Gaza and before going on to Egypt. But he fails to account for the silence of the sources on any such visit. So also Golan, *Berliner Theologische Zeitschrift* 8 (1991) 19–30, who seems to rely heavily on Josephus' own claims about his historical accuracy. Golan supplies a useful bibliography on the subject, *op. cit.*, 20.

17. Cf. Arrian 3.1.4, 3.3–4, 3.16.4–5; Diod. 17.49.2–51.4; Curtius 4.7.5–28; Plut. *Alex.* 26.6–27.5. So, rightly, Goldstein, *Proceedings of the American Academy for Jewish Research* 59 (1993) 70.

The narrative of the Alexander/Jaddous confrontation, on the face of it, contains some awkwardness of its own. The Macedonian monarch begins to bear down on Jerusalem, full of fury, triggering dire alarm among the Jews and their High Priest who turn in despair to supplication of the Lord. From such an opening, one expects a divine intervention to thwart the villain's plans, humiliate him before Yahweh and his priests, and bring the Jews to glorious triumph. Nothing of the kind occurs. The greeting of Alexander by the populace of Jerusalem is warm and welcoming, the king returns the favor by honoring their deity and their observances, and offers to grant their every wish.[18] No humbling of the monarch takes place. If anything, the reverse. The awesome military might of Alexander goes unchallenged from start to finish. Just the prospect of his arrival terrifies the Jews and sends the High Priest into a state of panic.[19] The denouement delivers the main message. Alexander stays his hand not because of any divine epiphany. The figure he sees is the priest, not a deity, as he is well aware. Alexander did indeed see a vision, but it had come long before, only now confirmed and assured. The omen had appeared in his sleep far off at Dium in Macedon years earlier, before the expedition had begun. The apparition in his dream, clad in garb now duplicated by the High Priest, had promised him divine leadership of the army and rule over the empire of the Persians.[20] In short, the forecast and guarantee of Alexander's triumph in the east came not from Delphi, Dodona, or Didyma but from the God of the Jews. The High Priest's appearance evoked that dream once again and certified its authenticity. This was no surrender to the king but a reminder, however inadvertent, that he would be ruler of the east—but as surrogate of the Lord. Of course Alexander's power is undiminished at the end of the saga; indeed it is enhanced. Yahweh had predicted the fulfillment of his ambitions, and fulfilled they would be. Lest there be any lingering doubts, the priests showed Alexander a line in the Book of Daniel that predicted victory by a Greek king over the rulers of the Medes

18. Cohen, *AJS Review* 78 (1982/1983) 45–55, acutely observes that the story combines elements of two different conventions, the adventus narrative and the epiphany narrative. It does not follow, however, that these existed originally as independent tales that were later combined in a clumsy blend. The author may well have made use of both conventions in composing his construct.

19. Jos. *Ant.* 11.326: ὁ δὲ ἀρχιερεὺς Ἰαδδοῦς τοῦτ' ἀκούσας ἦν ἐν ἀγωνίᾳ καὶ δέει, πῶς ἀπαντήσει τοῖς Μακεδόσιν ἀμηχανῶν. Cf. the similar terror of the High Priest in II Macc. 3.16–17.

20. Jos. *Ant.* 11.334: αὐτὸς γὰρ ἡγήσεσθαί μου τῆς στρατιᾶς καὶ τὴν Περσῶν παραδώσειν ἀρχήν. On the vision of Alexander, see E. Bammel in W. Will, *Zu Alexander d. Gr.* (Amsterdam, 1987) 279–87.

and Persians.[21] Never mind that the campaigns of Alexander took place a century and a half before the composition of Daniel.[22] For the author of the legend, historical accuracy was a matter of indifference. A Jewish vision had foretold Alexander's victories; and a Jewish text confirmed it. Greek historians of Alexander's campaigns had recorded oracular predictions at Delphi and Siwah that spurred Alexander's campaigns and bolstered his spirits.[23] The inventor of our tall tale may well have been familiar with those accounts. Hence the substitution of Yahweh for Apollo or Ammon as the genuine guarantor of success and the introduction of Daniel as prophet of truth would supply a special twist. An informed readership could be expected to recognize the ironic allusion. One could hardly wish for a better example of Jewish expropriation and transformation of a Hellenistic theme.

A striking fact needs to be noticed. Although the narrative is plainly a Jewish invention, its central figure is not Jaddous the High Priest but Alexander the Great. The former is nearly paralyzed with fear and has no idea of how to meet the Macedonian menace. Only the nocturnal visitation provides him with instructions, duly and mechanically followed.[24] Jaddous, much relieved and overjoyed, has no hesitation in abandoning allegiance to Persia and embracing the cause of the invader. Not exactly the portrait of a commanding figure. Alexander, by contrast, takes charge. He marches his mighty forces on the city; he correctly identifies the High Priest's outfit, even at a great distance, as the divine emblem foreshadowed in his dream long ago (Jaddous himself had no idea why he was asked to dress up in this fashion); he responds articulately and persuasively to the baffled Parmenio (as he does so often in the Greek historical accounts); he sacrifices to God at the Temple itself; and he interprets the prediction in Daniel as applying to himself. Alexander further dismisses and then summons again the Jewish assemblage, he bestows favors upon the Jews, and he offers posts in his army to those who wished them. Far from a humbled foe, Alexander emerges

---

21. See Daniel 8.21; Jos. *Ant.* 11.337: δειχθείσης δ' αὐτῷ τῆς Δανιήλου Βίβλου, ἐν ᾗ τινα τῶν Ἑλλήνων καταλύσειν τὴν Περσῶν ἀρχὴν ἐδήλου.

22. There is no compelling reason to ascribe to Josephus himself the insertion of Daniel into the story, as do most scholars; see F. Pfister in R. Merkelbach et al., *Kleine Schriften zum Alexanderroman* (Meisenheim, 1976) 320; Kasher, *Bet Miqra* 20 (1975) 199; Momigliano, *Athenaeum* 57 (1979) 446–47; Cohen, *AJS Review* 78 (1982/1983) 64. It fits suitably with the rest of the tale, as endorsement of the earlier prognostication.

23. Delphi: Plut. *Alex.* 14.4; Diod. 17.93.4. Siwah: Curtius 4.7.26; Plut. *Alex.* 27.4; Diod. 17.51.2; Justin 11.11.10. Whether or not Alexander actually went to Delphi is irrelevant; cf. J. R. Hamilton, *Plutarch, Alexander: A Commentary* (Oxford, 1969) 34–35.

24. Josephus' depiction of Jaddous' dream and its literary context are explored by R. Gnuse, *JQR* 83 (1993) 349–68.

with greater strength than ever, the invincible warrior with conquest of Asia already foretold, the incisive interpreter of omens, the magnanimous benefactor, and even the effective recruiter of Jewish soldiers to beef up his own forces.[25]

The king indeed has taken on added dimensions. And they are of cardinal importance. The authoritative voice of prophecy issued from the god of the Jews and from a sacred book of the Jews. Alexander's spectacular successes could now be accounted for in the most satisfactory way: Yahweh was responsible for them. He sacrifices to the Lord in his very Temple under the guidance of the High Priest and he pays due honor to all of God's ministers.[26] This involves no diminution of Alexander's stature. Quite the contrary. He dispenses favors to priests and people alike, the benefactions of the overlord. He guarantees the rights and privileges of Jews not only in Palestine but in Babylon and Media as well. Never mind that Alexander had not yet even reached Babylon or Media. With the sanction of the Lord, his future successes are assured in advance. The invention here implies more than just a charter for Jewish prerogatives, a claim that the right to follow their ancestral laws was acknowledged by the conqueror of Persia and the first of the Hellenistic monarchs. It has still broader implications for the Jewish place in the new world. The story implied that Jews both of Palestine and of the Diaspora would become an integral part of the Macedonian empire—and that they would hold a distinct and privileged position within it. The suzerain's secular power is clear and unequivocal. But that power itself derives from the God of the Hebrew patriarchs whose authority Alexander openly and publicly recognizes. Time and place of the fable remain indeterminate. But its significance applies across the years and the nations. The historical narrative conveyed a sense of self-assurance about the Jews' own special role within the universe of the Hellenistic kingdoms. They are the beneficiaries of the king—but he is himself a beneficiary of their Lord.

Association with Alexander conferred dignity and pride. Jewish intellectuals who wrote their forefathers into the history of Alexander naturally did not omit an element of martial valor. The king's visit to Jerusalem, as we have seen, concluded with an offer for any Jews so inclined to join his forces, with no compromise of their ancestral practices. He got an enthusiastic response. Jews in large numbers leaped at the opportunity, enlisting in the ranks of

---

25. Jos. *Ant.* 11.326–39.

26. Jos. *Ant.* 11.336: καὶ ἀνελθὼν ἐπὶ τὸ ἱερὸν θύει μὲν τῷ θεῷ κατὰ τὴν τοῦ ἀρχιερέως ὑφήγησιν, αὐτὸν δὲ τὸν ἀρχιερέα καὶ τοὺς ἱερεῖς ἀξιοπρεπῶς ἐτίμησεν.

the Macedonian army.[27] Tales of Jewish exploits in the march of Alexander have not survived—a great pity, for we doubtless missed some entertaining anecdotes. The story of Mosollamos, to be discussed below, gives a hint of the possible whimsy they contained. That such concoctions circulated is clear from subsequent allusions to Jewish valor and loyalty to Alexander in the course of his campaigns. No details remain, but they might have been quite imaginative. We have reference, for instance, to zealous Jewish assistance to Alexander in his campaign against the Egyptians.[28] An interesting notice. Alexander never conducted a campaign against Egyptians; they yielded without a fight as soon as he showed up. The historical facts did not discourage Jewish creativity. The stories culminated in substantial and enduring rewards for the Jews. Josephus claims that Jewish civic privileges in Alexandria put them on a par with Greeks and Macedonians, a status accorded them by Alexander out of gratitude for their military service.[29] This too, if put to a historical test, could only generate mirth. The city of Alexandria was the king's own foundation, barely begun in his lifetime. There could have been no Jews in the city to request privileges.[30] But historical tests are plainly inappropriate and inapplicable. Readers welcomed edifying fictions in a quasi-historical context.

Another report belongs in the same category. Alexander, we are told, holding the Jews in high esteem for their reasonableness and fidelity, increased their territory by adding to it the land of Samaria free of tribute. That notice, according to Josephus, came from Hecataeus of Abdera.[31] No need to rehearse the much disputed question of whether the fragment is authentic Hecataeus or a Jewish Pseudo-Hecataeus. A Jew is far the more

27. Jos. *Ant.* 11.339: εἰπόντος δ' αὐτοῦ πρὸς τὸ πλῆθος, εἴ τινες αὐτῷ βούλονται συστρατεύειν τοῖς πατρίοις ἔθεσιν ἐμμένοντες καὶ κατὰ ταῦτα ζῶντες, ἑτοίμως ἔχειν ἐπάγεσθαι, πολλοὶ τὴν σὺν αὐτῷ στρατείαν ἠγάπησαν. Another notice, attributed to Hecataeus but doubtlessly penned by a Jewish author, remarks that Jews engaged in the campaigns of Alexander as well as in those of his successors; Jos. *C. Apion.* 1.200: Ἀλεξάνδρῳ τῷ βασιλεῖ συνεστρατεύσαντο.

28. Jos. *BJ* 2.487: χρησάμενος προθυμοτάτοις κατὰ τῶν Αἰγυπτίων Ἰουδαίοις Ἀλέξανδρος.

29. Jos. *BJ* 2.487: Ἀλέξανδρος γέρας τῆς συμμαχίας ἔδωκεν τὸ μετοικεῖν κατὰ τὴν πόλιν ἐξ ἰσομοιρίας πρὸς τοὺς Ἕλληνας; similarly, Jos. *C. Apion.* 2.72.

30. Josephus attempts to get around this elsewhere by having Alexander include the Jews among the original settlers of Alexandria; *C. Apion.* 2.35: εἰς κατοίκησιν δὲ αὐτοῖς ἔδωκεν τὸν τόπον Ἀλέξανδρος καὶ ἴσης παρὰ τοῖς Μακεδόσι τιμῆς ἐπέτυχον; 2.42: Ἀλέξανδρος τῶν ἡμετέρων τινὰς ἐκεῖ συνήθροισεν. Cf. *Ant.* 19.281.

31. Jos. *C. Apion.* 2.43: ἐτίμα γὰρ ἡμῶν τὸ ἔθνος, ὡς καί φησιν Ἑκαταῖος περὶ ἡμῶν, ὅτι διὰ τὴν ἐπιείκειαν καὶ πίστιν, ἣν αὐτῷ παρέσχον Ἰουδαῖοι, τὴν Σαμαρεῖτιν χώραν προσέθηκεν ἔχειν αὐτοῖς ἀφορολόγητον.

likely prospect as composer of this account, a fiction that fits well with the other claims of Alexander's favor toward that people.[32] To search for a historical basis to the tale is singularly pointless. Nothing in the Alexander histories gives the slightest ground for it. And even the invented narrative conveyed by Josephus that stitched together the anecdotes regarding Alexander, Jaddous, and the Samaritans has no hint of it.[33] Historians have consequently struggled to find the time and circumstances when the concoction of such a report would make political sense.

Two occasions seem appropriate: the era of Jonathan's High Priesthood, after 152 BCE, when the Seleucids authorized the annexation of three Samaritan districts by the Jews, and the end of the second century, when John Hyrcanus had forcibly subjected Samaria to Jewish control.[34] On each

32. The case for "Pseudo-Hecataeus" has now been made exhaustively and compellingly by B. Bar-Kochva, *Pseudo-Hecataeus, "On the Jews": Legitimizing the Jewish Diaspora* (Berkeley, 1996) 113–121. Prior proponents of this view were few, with highly speculative and tangled reconstructions; see, especially, B. Z. Wacholder, *Eupolemus: A Study of Judaeo-Greek Literature* (Cincinnati, 1974) 263–73; N. Walter, *Jüdische Schriften der hellenistisch-römischer Zeit* (Gütersloh, 1976) I.2, 146–48. The bibliography is vast, and need not be detailed here. For useful summaries of earlier opinions and references, see C. J. Holladay, *Fragments from Hellenistic Jewish Authors* (Chico, 1983) 277–90; J. D. Gauger, *JSJ* 13 (1982) 41–45; M. Goodman in E. Schürer, *The History of the Jewish People in the Age of Jesus Christ*, rev. ed. by G. Vermes, F. Millar, and M. Goodman (Edinburgh, 1986) III.1, 671–77; G. E. Sterling, *Historiography and Self-Definition: Josephos, Luke-Acts and Apologetic Historiography* (Leiden, 1992) 78–91; M. Pucci Ben Zeev, *JSJ* 24 (1993) 215–24.

33. Curtius Rufus, 4.8.9–11, reports that the Samaritans murdered Andromachus, Alexander's governor of Syria, thus prompting the king to hasten to Samaria, demand the guilty parties, and execute them. That information has tempted some to propose that Alexander further penalized the Samaritans by turning over some of their land to the Jews, thus a basis for Josephus' story. See, e.g., J. G. Gager, *ZNW* 60 (1969) 136; M. Stern, *Greek and Latin Authors on Jews and Judaism* (Jerusalem, 1976) I, 44; Gauger, *JSJ* 13 (1982) 38–39; J. J. Collins, *Between Athens and Jerusalem* (New York, 1983) 139; Sterling, *Historiography and Self-Definition*, 86–87, n. 120. Curtius' notice can be buttressed by papyrological finds at Wadi Daliyeh; Cross, *Biblical Archaeologist* 26 (1963) 110–19. But it provides no support for Josephus' account. Incorporation of Samaria into Judaea would have been of questionable value from a military or administrative point of view. And the two regions were quite distinct in the Ptolemaic and Seleucid eras; Polyb. 5.71.11, 16.39; II Macc. 14.12; Jos. *Ant.* 12.133, 12.154, 13.264. See the comments of Bar-Kochva, *Pseudo-Hecataeus*, 117.

34. On the authorization (or confirmation) of Jonathan's control over the three districts by Demetrius I and Demetrius II, see I Macc. 10.30, 10.38, 11.28, 11.34. For Hyrcanus' conquests, see Jos. *Ant.* 13.254–56, 13.275–81. Several scholars find annexation of the districts under Jonathan as impetus for the story of Alexander's award; see, e.g., B. Schaller, *ZNW* 54 (1963) 28–30; N. Walter, *Jüdische Schriften*, I.2, 147–48; Holladay, *Fragments*, I, 334, n. 55; Goodman in Schürer, *History of the Jewish People*, III.1, 675–76, n. 276; cf. Gauger, *JSJ* 13 (1982) 39. Others see the origin in Hyrcanus' occupation of Samaria; see, e.g., Willrich, *Juden und Griechen*, 21–22; Bar-Kochva, *Pseudo-Hecataeus*, 134–35.

hypothesis, the story reflects special conditions, its creation motivated by the political objectives of Jewish leaders, either to legitimize the absorption of Samaritan regions into Judaea or to justify the conquest of Samaria by appealing to a fictive grant by Alexander. But here too, as so often, the effort to pinpoint a distinct event or impulse that gave rise to a tall tale may overlook the broader significance. How many Jews—let alone Samaritans—would take comfort in the idea that the assimilation of Samaria by Judaea had been sanctioned two hundred years in advance? This Jewish invention, it can be suggested, has more to do with Alexander than with Samaria. It suits the pattern discernible in other reports of the Macedonian's benefactions to Jews, a proper return for their allegiance and their courage, thereby associating the nation with the achievements of the great conqueror. A swipe at Samaria in the process might, of course, be a welcome dividend to a Jewish readership. But this was no mere Hasmonaean vindication of expansionism. The story, like its counterparts, underscored the Jewish relationship with Macedonian power: valor and constancy earned them a share in the benefits of that power.

The special character of the Jews, however, remains a critical feature of these episodes. Pseudo-Hecataeus, as cited by Josephus, praises Jewish devotion to their laws, a steadfastness toward ancestral traditions that they maintain in the face of animosities, oppression, torture, and death. As illustration of this, he cites Alexander's directives to all his soldiers to rebuild the ancient and revered temple of Bel at Babylon, at that time lying in ruins. It was a measure of Alexander's own reverence toward ancient cults among the peoples who had come under his sway. The Jews alone, however, declined to participate. They could not engage in the resurrection of a pagan cult. And they refused the order even at the risk of heavy penalties and physical beatings. Alexander, previously unaware, so it seems, of Jewish zeal for the faith, relented and released them from this chore.[35] Here again the historicity of the anecdote is unverifiable and immaterial.[36] But its meaning admits of little doubt. Jewish soldiers were dutiful participants in Alexander's campaigns. They stood out from the rest, however, in commitment to their principles and traditions. The king and he alone had the authority to grant

35. Jos. *C. Apion.* 1.192: μόνους τοὺς Ἰουδαίους οὐ προσσχεῖν, ἀλλὰ καὶ πολλὰς ὑπομεῖναι πληγὰς καὶ ζημίας ἀποτῖσαι μεγάλας, ἕως αὐτοῖς συγγνόντα τὸν βασιλέα δοῦναι τὴν ἄδειαν.

36. That Alexander did rebuild the temple of Bel and respected the traditions of the Babylonians is well attested; Arrian 7.17.1; Strabo 16.1.5. But there is no other reference to Jewish involvement. For Gauger, *JSJ* 13 (1982) 32–33, their actions derive from a Jewish fiction taken up by Hecataeus.

an exemption, and grant it he did. The Jews were his subordinates, but they held a privileged place, acknowledged by the ruler himself. The episode, seen in this light, delivers a message akin to that of every other legend that joined Alexander and the Jews.

·   ·   ·

The inventions did not stop with Alexander. Tales circulated concerning the relationship between Jews and the shrewdest of Alexander's successors, Ptolemy I Soter, ruler of Egypt. Here the creators faced an uphill battle. Ptolemy's campaigns in Palestine and Coele-Syria were anything but gentle. And he counted Jerusalem and the Jews among his victims. The Hellenistic historian Agatharchides, who composed his works at least partially in Ptolemaic Alexandria of the mid second century, records the capture of Jerusalem by Ptolemy Soter a century and a half earlier. It occurred on a Sabbath when Jews could not or did not resist. The king and his army entered unopposed, occupied the city, and, according to Agatharchides, treated it cruelly.[37] A much later Greek source adds, with some exaggeration, that he destroyed the city.[38] More significantly, even a Jewish intellectual, the author of the *Letter of Aristeas*, records some nasty doings by Soter with regard to the Jews. His invasion of Coele-Syria resulted in the capture and deportation of 100,000 Jews, forcibly removed to Egypt, large numbers of them sold into slavery.[39] Not a happy beginning to the affiliation between Jews and the Ptolemaic dynasty. It would require some inventive rewriting to undo that damage. For Jews living under the later Ptolemies and eager to suggest a harmonious relationship from the start, such rewriting was a clear desideratum.

Jewish writers were up to the task. A full whitewash came from an author whom Josephus took to be Hecataeus of Abdera. He was, in fact, a Jew in pagan guise. His work, περὶ Ἰουδαίων , delivered an altogether different verdict on Ptolemy I Soter and his actions toward the Jews. In his account, Ptolemy's victory at Gaza in 312 made him master of Syria and its environs. And when word got round about his gentleness and humanitarianism, many of those who dwelled in the region expressed a desire to return with him to

---

37. Jos. *C. Apion.* 1.208–10: ἡ μὲν πατρὶς εἰλήφει δεσπότην πικρόν; *Ant.* 12.6: χαλεπὸν . . . δεσπότην. Whether this invasion took place in 312/311 or 302/301 cannot be definitively determined. For discussion, see V. Tcherikover, *Hellenistic Civilization and the Jews* (Philadelphia, 1959) 56–58; Bar-Kochva, *Pseudo-Hecataeus*, 74–78.

38. Appian, *Syr.* 50: ἦν δὴ καὶ Πτολεμαῖος . . . καθῃρήκει.

39. *LetArist* 12–14, 20–23, 35–36.

Egypt and to share in the affairs of that land.[40] Among them was Hezekiah, High Priest of the Jews, a man of sixty years, of distinguished reputation, known not only for his intellect and his oratory but even for his business sense. Hezekiah, so it appears, then migrated to Egypt with other Jews, having obtained distinction for himself and a charter for the Jewish settlement and political organization.[41] Of course, little or none of this concoction bears any relation to historical reality. No Hezekiah ever held the High Priesthood in Jerusalem. Numismatic evidence records only a Hezekiah who served as governor of Judaea for the Persians and perhaps continued in a comparable capacity under Macedonian rule.[42] The idea of a Jewish exodus to Egypt when Ptolemy, the kind and humane ruler, took over Coele-Syria is virtually senseless. Why not enjoy his kindliness and humanity at home? And few will give any credence to a supposed written document authorizing the Jewish settlement and political structure in Egypt. Ptolemy I would not readily welcome the colonization of his kingdom by peoples who had come under his sway abroad. Pseudo-Hecataeus offers an inverted picture that stands the whole story on its head. Ptolemy becomes a magnanimous monarch instead of a harsh master, Hezekiah is transformed from a Persian official into a Jewish High Priest, and a forced deportation is turned into a voluntary migration—with a foundation decree into the bargain. Creative Jews who felt free to rewrite the Bible would certainly not hesitate to rewrite history.[43]

---

40. Jos. *C. Apion.* 1.186: πολλοὶ τῶν ἀνθρώπων πυνθανόμενοι τὴν ἠπιότητα καὶ φιλανθρωπίαν τοῦ Πτολεμαίου συναπαίρειν εἰς Αἴγυπτον αὐτῷ καὶ κοινωνεῖν τῶν πραγμάτων ἠβουλήθησαν.

41. Jos. *C. Apion.* 1.187–89. The account is clearly reflected also in Jos. *Ant.* 12.9. The interpretation of *C. Apion.* 1.189, a confused and possibly corrupt passage, is highly problematical. Lewy's emendation of διαφορὰν to διφθέραν, *ZNW* 31 (1932) 122–24, has persuaded many; e.g., Stern, *Greek and Latin Authors*, I, 42; F. Millar, *JJS* 29 (1978) 7; Gauger, *JSJ* 13 (1982) 29–30; Holladay, *Fragments*, I, 327, n. 17. Even if accepted, however, it can hardly imply that the "settlement and the constitution" refer to biblical times. The reference is more likely to the purported settlement in Egypt by Hezekiah and his followers. See the discussion by Bar-Kochva, *Pseudo-Hecataeus*, 221–25.

42. Josephus' evidence on High Priests in this period leaves no room for Hezekiah; see Jos. *Ant.* 11.297, 11.302–303, 347; cf. D. R. Schwartz, *JQR* 72 (1981–1982) 252–54; Grabbe, *JBL* 106 (1987) 243–244. For discussion of the coins, see U. Rappaport, *JJS* 32 (1981) 1–17; Y. Meshorer, *Ancient Jewish Coinage* (New York, 1982) 13–34; D. P. Barag, *Israel Numismatic Journal* 9 (1986/1987) 4–21; B. Bar-Kochva and A. Kindler in Bar-Kochva, *Pseudo-Hecataeus*, 255–70. The notion that Hezekiah issued the coins as High Priest is untenable; see Bar-Kochva, *op. cit.*, 82–88, with extensive bibliographical references.

43. For Hellenistic Jews dwelling in Egypt the idea that their settlement in that land came voluntarily rather than as compulsory servitude was, of course, far more gratifying and acceptable. See now I. M. Gafni, *Land, Centre, and Diaspora* (Sheffield, 1997) 27–30.

In this matter Pseudo-Hecataeus had good company. The composer of the *Letter of Aristeas* had to swallow some unpalatable material about Ptolemy Soter. He evidently could not deny or suppress the data about his subjection of the Jews, removal of large numbers from their homeland, compulsory relocation to Egypt, and the sale of many into slavery. But he did not lack for ingenuity. "Aristeas" recast the information and softened its impact. Yes, Soter deported a great many Jews to Egypt. But they were good soldiers, he placed them in garrisons all around the country, enrolled them in the armed forces with handsome pay, and set up strongholds for those who had been in Egypt before and had thus established their loyalty.[44] Yes, many were sold into slavery. But that was not really Ptolemy's idea; his troops insisted on it, claiming that they deserved such rewards after years of service, and it was done against his better judgment.[45] Yes, the land was devastated and Jews were carried off. But that too was the doing of over-zealous soldiers.[46] And, according to the *Letter of Aristeas*, all this was reversed anyway by the generous actions of Ptolemy II. The author clearly made the best of some embarrassing material, having even the first of the Ptolemies acknowledge the quality of the Jews. The story thus came out right.

That version reappears in Josephus, not altogether dependent upon the *Letter of Aristeas*. The historian too has Ptolemy take Jewish captives to Egypt in order to settle them on the land and employ them as garrison troops because of their reputation for fidelity to oaths and pledges.[47] Indeed the king found them so reliable and valiant that he installed them to entrench his rule in Cyrene and various cities of Libya as well.[48] The information goes beyond what is contained in the *Letter of Aristeas*. Its author was evidently

---

44. *LetArist* 13–14: τρεῖς μυριάδας καθοπλίσας ἀνδρῶν ἐκλεκτῶν εἰς τὴν χώραν κατῴκισεν ἐν τοῖς φρουρίοις; 36: πλείονας εἰς τὸ στρατιωτικὸν σύνταγμα κατεχώρισεν ἐπὶ μείζοσι μισθοφορίαις, ὁμοίως δὲ καὶ τοὺς προόντας κρίνας πιστοὺς φρούρια κτίσας ἀπέδωκεν αὐτοῖς.

45. *LetArist* 14: οὐχ οὕτως τῇ προαιρέσει κατὰ ψυχὴν ἔχων, ὡς κατακρατούμενος ὑπὸ τῶν στρατιωτῶν; 23: νομίζομεν γὰρ καὶ παρὰ τὴν τοῦ πατρὸς ἡμῶν βούλησιν.

46. *LetArist* 23: διὰ δὲ τὴν στρατιωτικὴν προπέτειαν τήν τε χώραν αὐτῶν κατεφθάρθαι καὶ τὴν τῶν Ἰουδαίων μεταγωγὴν εἰς τὴν Αἴγυπτον γεγονέναι.

47. Jos. *Ant.* 12.7–8: ἐπεγνωκὼς δὲ τοὺς ἀπὸ τῶν Ἱεροσολύμων περί τε τὴν τῶν ὅρκων φυλακὴν καὶ τὰς πίστεις βεβαιοτάτους ὑπάρχοντας. The notice is not drawn exclusively from the *Letter of Aristeas*, for as testimony to Jewish steadfastness Josephus refers to the tale of Alexander and Jaddous.

48. Jos. *C. Apion.* 2. 44: πιστῶς ἅμα καὶ γενναίως φυλάξειν ὑπολαμβάνων. The addition of Cyrene and Libya also exceeds the information in the *Letter of Aristeas*.

not alone in reinterpreting the reign of Ptolemy Soter to the advantage of their forefathers—and of the king.[49]

The tradition that Jewish soldiers served in the ranks of Ptolemy I may or may not have historical validity. But it certainly spawned some stories. One fictive and engaging anecdote survives, a neat illustration of the sardonic humor in which Jewish-Hellenistic writers occasionally indulged. Josephus found it in the work "On the Jews," attributed to Hecataeus of Abdera. Ostensibly the author provided an eyewitness account, as participant in a march to the Red Sea with the Ptolemaic army. In fact, the episode came from the pen of a Jewish author—and one with a delightfully caustic wit.[50] The tale records a Ptolemaic advance on the Red Sea, with forces that included a troop of Jewish cavalry. One of its members was a certain Mosollamos, an expert archer and an impressive man both physically and intellectually.[51] Here was the ideal Jew, so it appears. Mosollamos became impatient when the army appeared stalled on its march, and inquired about the delay. The Greek seer who accompanied the forces explained that he needed to observe the movements of a particular bird, thereby to gain divine instructions for the army. If the bird moved forward, they should advance, if backward, retreat, and if it stayed in place, they should do the same. Mosollamos without hesitation pulled out his bow and arrow and shot the bird dead. The seer and others were beside themselves with fury, hurled curses at the Jewish archer, and demanded an explanation for the sacrilege. Mosollamos cooly retorted: if the bird were so smart and could forecast the future, why did he show up here to be shot by the arrow of Mosollamos the Jew?[52]

Only a Jew would have contrived such an anecdote. To be sure, somewhat comparable Greek yarns can be cited in which diviners and soothsayers are humiliated or exposed as charlatans.[53] But that is quite different from Mosollamos' act. The Jewish archer disposed of the very object which allegedly

49. That Jews served subsequently and regularly in the Ptolemaic army is, of course, true and well known. See the documents collected in *CPJ*, I, 18–32.

50. That the tale is not authentic Hecataeus was recognized by W. Burkert, *FondHardt* 18 (1971) 324, and fully argued by Bar-Kochva, *Pseudo-Hecataeus*, 57–71. A thorough bibliography on this issue is provided now by A. Kasher in H. Cancik, H. Lichtenberger, and P. Schäfer, *Geschichte—Tradition—Reflexion: Festschrift für Martin Hengel* (Tübingen, 1996) I, 148, 150. Kasher's belief in authenticity, however, fails to grapple with the problems of Greek divination.

51. Jos. *C. Apion.* 1.200–201: ἄνθρωπος ἱκανὸς κατὰ ψυχήν, εὔρωστος καὶ τοξότης δὴ πάντων ὁμολογουμένως καὶ τῶν Ἑλλήνων καὶ τῶν βαρβάρων ἄριστος.

52. Jos. *C. Apion.* 1.202–204.

53. Cf. Diog. Laert. 6.24; Cic. *De Div.* 2.9; Jos. *C. Apion.* 1.258; Lucian, *Deor. Dial.* 16.1. See Lewy, *ZNW* 31 (1932) 129–30.

carried divine signals. No Greek would have found that amusing. They did not regard birds themselves as prophets, with the capacity of predicting their own fates. Nor did they ever indulge in simplistic interpretation based on the creature's forward or backward movement.[54] This was a Jewish creation, punctuated by the final words "Mosollamos the Jew." Mosollamos' deed mocked the seer's incompetence, injecting an element of no-nonsense military efficiency into the scene. If there is to be a march on the Red Sea, let's get on with it! The able Jew thus shows himself more adept and more attuned to the needs of the Ptolemaic expedition than any other member of the king's contingent. The story underscores Jewish martial skills and pragmatic know-how. This is no critique of the Hellenistic ruler. Quite the contrary. It indirectly confirms his sound judgment, like that of Alexander before him, in recruiting Jewish fighters for his forces: they are loyal, accomplished, and smart.

Ptolemy I also got credit for one other act of generosity, with long-term benefits for the Jews. He allegedly accorded to them civic privileges in Alexandria equivalent to those enjoyed by the Macedonians. And he bound them in turn by a pledge that they would hold allegiance not only to him but to his descendants.[55] The import of that notice is plain enough: Jews formed a trusted and integral part of the Ptolemaic realm from the start— and throughout. Josephus in recording this claim got himself into a small dilemma. For, as we have seen, he elsewhere ascribes the origin of Jewish rights in Alexandria to the city's founder, not to Ptolemy Soter. But he wriggled out of it satisfactorily enough (at least to himself): he has Alexander bestow the privileges and his successors confirm them.[56] Jewish intellectuals plainly strained to save the reputation of Ptolemy I, thus to provide their ancestors with a reassuring pedigree in Egypt.

• • •

Soter's successor needed no rehabilitation. Ptolemy II Philadelphus enjoyed high repute in antiquity, an ideal figure around whom to construct a legend that linked Jewish fortunes with a Hellenistic kingdom. His reign provided the setting for the most celebrated of such legends: the story of

54. See Bar-Kochva, *Pseudo-Hecataeus*, 62–69, with additional arguments and references.

55. Jos. *Ant.* 12.8: τοῖς Μακεδόσιν ἐν Ἀλεξανδρείᾳ ποιήσας ἰσοπολίτας, ὅρκους ἔλαβε παρ' αὐτῶν ὅπως τοῖς ἐκγόνοις τοῦ παραθεμένου τὴν πίστιν διαφυλάξωσιν.

56. Jos. *BJ* 2.487–88: ἔδωκεν τὸ μετοικεῖν κατὰ τὴν πόλιν ἐξ ἰσομοιρίας πρὸς τοὺς Ἕλληνας· διέμεινεν δ' αὐτοῖς ἡ τιμὴ καὶ παρὰ τῶν διαδόχων. Cf. Jos. *C. Apion.* 2.35, 2.42, 2.72.

the composition of the Septuagint. That story framed the so-called *Letter of Aristeas*, a tale that reechoed in various versions through centuries of Jewish experience thereafter. And it supplies a key text for the theme pursued here.[57]

A summary will serve to highlight those aspects of special relevance. The work purports to be a communication from Aristeas, ostensibly a prominent figure at the court of Ptolemy II Philadelphus, to his brother Philocrates. Not, in fact, a letter but a διήγησις , a literary narrative.[58] According to "Aristeas," Demetrius of Phalerum, chief librarian in Alexandria, suggested to the king that the "laws of the Jews" (evidently the Pentateuch) were worthy of inclusion in the great library. But they required translation, for the script was peculiar and the available Hebrew texts were carelessly and improperly drawn up.[59] Ptolemy readily concurred. Moreover, he conceived the idea of contacting the High Priest in Jerusalem in order to facilitate the project. And he prepared the way by releasing from servitude all those Jews who had been victims of Ptolemy I's campaigns—while insisting, as we have seen, that his father had never wanted to enslave them in the first place.[60] The enterprise swiftly got underway. An exchange of letters between Philadelphus and Eleazer the Jewish High Priest, plus some lavish gifts sent by the king, brought about the dispatch of seventy-two elders, distinguished scholars, six from each of the twelve tribes, to Alexandria for the purpose of producing a Greek translation of the Scriptures.[61] "Aristeas" proceeds to describe at length the handsome gifts bestowed by Ptolemy and to provide a sketch of Jerusalem, Judaea, and the environs.[62] The narrator presents himself as one of the Ptolemaic envoys to the High Priest and recounts a disquisition by Eleazer, replying to the envoys' questions, on the religious beliefs and dietary prescriptions of the Jews, an extended

---

57. Among the more useful editions or commentaries, see R. Tramontano, *La Lettera di Aristea a Filocrate* (Naples, 1931); M. Hadas, *Aristeas to Philocrates* (New York, 1951); A. Pelletier, *Lettre d'Aristée à Philocrate* (Paris, 1962); N. Meisner, *Jüdische Schriften aus hellenistisch-römischer Zeit* (Gütersloh, 1973) II.1, 35–87. A general bibliography in Schürer, *History of the Jewish People*, III.1, 685–87.

58. *LetArist* 1, 8, 322. Cf. Hadas, *Aristeas to Philocrates*, 54–59.

59. *LetArist* 9–11, 29–30: τυγχάνει γὰρ Ἑβραικοῖς γράμμασι καὶ φωνῇ λεγόμενα, ἀμελέστερον δέ, καὶ οὐχ ὡς ὑπάρχει, σεσήμανται. The passage is a notorious crux. But it seems clear that the reference is to problematic Hebrew texts of the Bible, not to prior Greek versions; see D. W. Gooding, *VT* 13 (1963) 357–79; S. Jellicoe, *The Septuagint and Modern Study* (Oxford, 1968) 59–63, as against G. Zuntz, *JSemStud* 4 (1959) 109–26.

60. *LetArist* 11–27.

61. *LetArist* 31–51.

62. *LetArist* 51–120.

speech that extolled his people's principles and duly impressed the emissary of the king.[63]

The Jewish elders, selected for their profound learning in both Hebrew and Greek literature, arrived to a warm welcome in Alexandria. Ptolemy showed great respect for the impressive scrolls brought by the Jews, engraved in gold lettering in the Hebrew language. He paid signal honor to the sacred books, bowing seven times, deeply moved, and announced that the anniversary of the event would henceforth be celebrated as a festal day.[64] An extended symposium followed, seven full days of formal banquets—all served with kosher food—during which Philadelphus put a different question to each of his Jewish guests, most of them involving how best to govern a kingdom and to conduct one's life. Each of the sages responded promptly, included a reference to God as principal ingredient in the answer, and received warm compliments from the awe-struck king.[65] Having passed those prolonged tests with flying colors, the Jewish scholars were finally permitted to set about the task for which they had come. Demetrius of Phalerum gathered them in a splendid house situated in an attractive and quiet spot on the island of Pharos. There they systematically labored over their translations, comparing drafts with one another, and eventually agreed on a common version. The seventy-two sages completed their task in precisely seventy-two days, as if in accord with a divine plan. On the summons of Demetrius, the Jews of Alexandria assembled to hear the books of Moses read out to them in Greek by the translators; and they erupted in applause. The priests and leaders of the community gave their stamp of approval, pronounced the work satisfactory in every way, and even laid a curse on anyone who would alter a word of it. Ptolemy himself joined them in admiration. The king heaped praise upon Moses whose laws he could now understand and appreciate. He instructed that the newly composed books be treated with every care and respect, loaded gifts upon the Jewish scholars, and promised them similarly lavish hospitality whenever they should choose to return.[66] Thus ends the fable.

The tale, of course, should not be confused with history. How likely is it that Ptolemy II marshaled royal resources, commissioned a large number of Palestinian scholars, and financed an elaborate translation of the Books of

---

63. *LetArist* 128–71.
64. *LetArist* 121–22, 172–80.
65. *LetArist* 187–294.
66. *LetArist* 301–12, 317–21.

Moses just to add some volumes to the Alexandrian library?[67] The Jewish law code was hardly of burning interest to the Ptolemaic court. The number of Jews in Alexandria at the time of Philadelphus would not have been large enough to provoke a state-sponsored enterprise of this scale—and the Jews of Egypt, to judge from legal papyri, did not rigidly adhere to Mosaic law anyway.[68]

The historical setting is more than dubious. Demetrius of Phalerum, a noted scholar, writer, patron of the arts, and former ruler of Athens who sought refuge in Egypt, was a logical person around whom to concoct such a story. But no other evidence attests to his service as librarian of Alexandria. Indeed, Demetrius fell out of favor with Ptolemy II and was banished from the kingdom as soon as Ptolemy took the throne.[69] "Aristeas" simply seized upon a figure who represented high culture to advance his tale. In similar fashion he inserts the philosopher Menedemus of Eritrea to praise the wisdom of the Jewish sages and adds allusions to other Hellenic literary figures like the historians Hecataeus of Abdera and Theopompus and the tragic poet Theodectus.[70] To be sure, reference to a translation of the Hebrew law under Ptolemy II organized by Demetrius also appears in the fragments of the Jewish writer Aristobulus. But, despite much scholarly discussion, we do not know whether Aristobulus drew his remarks from the *Letter of Aristeas* or vice-versa, or whether both may have depended upon a third source—nor can we even be certain about Aristobulus' date. The fragment has no value as independent testimony for the validity of the tale.[71]

67. This idea has, in fact, been defended by E. Bickerman, *Studies in Jewish and Christian History* (Leiden, 1976) I, 167–75; *The Jews in the Greek Age* (Cambridge, Mass., 1988) 101–105; J. Mélèze-Modrzejewski, *The Jews of Egypt: From Rameses II to Emperor Hadrian* (Philadelphia, 1995) 99–106. Bickerman compares the compositions in Greek of Egyptian and Babylonian histories by Manetho and Berossus and the commissioned translations into Aramaic of an Egyptian law-code by Darius and of a Carthaginian agricultural treatise by the Roman senate. Mélèze-Modrzejewski adds the hypothesis that Darius' codification was rendered into Greek in the time of Ptolemy II. None of these, however, provides a close parallel. Philadelphus may indeed have had broad cultural interests, and he certainly welcomed additions to the library. But that is a far cry from commissioning a full-scale translation of a lengthy text just to add a Greek version to the shelves.

68. For arguments against Bickerman, without mentioning him by name, see S. Brock in S. Jellicoe, *Studies in the Septuagint* (New York, 1974) 541–50.

69. Hermippus of Smyrna in Diogenes Laertius, 5.78–79.

70. *LetArist* 31, 201, 314–16.

71. The fragment exists in two versions; Euseb. *PE* 13.12.1–2; Clement *Strom.* 1.22.148.1. The vast scholarly literature, going back to the 17th century, is usefully summarized now by C. R. Holladay, *Fragments from Hellenistic Jewish Authors: Aristobulus* (Atlanta, 1995) III, 49–65, 84–85, n. 79.

That Hellenistic Alexandria was the site for a translation of the Pentateuch we may well believe. As late as the time of Philo, Egyptian Jews still celebrated an annual festival on the island of Pharos to mark the completion of that task.[72] The needs of Greek-speaking Jews who had lost command of or even contact with Hebrew surely motivated the project to provide a Greek version for liturgical or instructional purposes or even for private worship.[73] That Palestinian scholars may have been called in to facilitate the job is perfectly possible—indeed a necessary postulate if most Alexandrian Jews had lost their mastery of biblical Hebrew.[74] But little else in the *Letter of Aristeas* commands confidence as history: the patronage of the Ptolemaic court, the involvement of eminent Greek literary figures, the diplomatic exchanges, the interrogation at the banquet—not to mention the still more fanciful details like Eleazer's lecture to Ptolemy's envoys on Jewish customs or the seventy-two days required for the translation by seventy-two elders. The yarn spun by the *Letter of Aristeas* is largely creative fiction.

Piles of papers and a multitude of suggestions have been applied to eliciting a date for this invention. That "Aristeas" was not, in fact, a contemporary of Ptolemy Philadelphus can be regarded as certain. His erroneous designation of Demetrius as librarian of Philadelphus suffices to show that he composed the tract at a substantial chronological distance from that reign. And other slips or inadvertent remarks give him away.[75] But a more precise dating may be illusory. Scholars have opted either for the period around 200 BCE or the mid second century BCE, the reign of Ptolemy VI or possibly Ptolemy VIII, the late second century BCE (the majority view), the first or second half of the first century BCE, and even as late as 33 CE. The issue cannot and need not be decided here.[76] Certain conclusions can, however, be stated

---

72. Philo *Moses* II.41.

73. The thesis is now widely accepted and needs no arguing here. A recent bibliography in Schürer, *History of the Jewish People*, III.1, 491–92.

74. Cf. Wacholder, *Eupolemus*, 274–76.

75. See, e.g., the comment that Ptolemaic "kings" regularly took measures through edicts and with great care for accuracy; *LetArist* 28. That would be an odd statement in the reign of Philadelphus, who had had only one predecessor. And the author elsewhere lets slip that some of the king's orders can "still be seen now"; *LetArist* 182: ἃ μὲν ἔτι καὶ νῦν ὁρᾷς.

76. The classic article by Bickerman, *ZNW* 29 (1930) 280–98, argued from the formulaic language in the *Letter's* documents that its composition came in the later 2nd century BCE. But terminology for institutions was used by E. Van't Dack, *Studia Hellenistica* 16 (1968) 263–78, to support a date in the early or mid 2nd century BCE. Hence even ostensibly "hard" data contain ambiguities and uncertainties. J. G. Février, *La date, la composition et les sources de la Lettre d'Aristée à Philocrate* (Paris, 1925) 22–31, argued against a unitary text, placing a core in the 1st century BCE and interpolations in the 1st century CE. Valuable reviews of the vast literature on this subject can be found in F. Parente, *AnnPisa* 2.1 (1972) 182–85, 189–90; P. M. Fraser,

with reasonable confidence. The author was a Hellenized Jew, residing in Egypt, presumably in Alexandria, some time in the later Ptolemaic era, and very probably a man close to the court. In any case, he professes a close acquaintance with the particulars of procedures at the highest levels. He makes reference to royal practice in the issuance of edicts.[77] He notes that when the Jewish elders were ushered immediately into Ptolemy's presence this was a break with court protocol which normally required a waiting period.[78] He knows the specific arrangements required for a formal banquet hosted by the king.[79] He points out the care and thoroughness with which every word and deed of Ptolemy is recorded from his first audience of the day to the moment he goes to bed, and then read out for corrections the next morning.[80] And one of the purported documents he reproduces, Ptolemy's decree releasing Jews from slavery and paying compensation to the slave owners, shows clear resemblance to an extant decree of Philadelphus on the matter of liberating slaves.[81] His vocabulary closely parallels that of the Septuagint, thus exhibiting familiarity with the Alexandrian Bible, and he shows equal command of the language of the Ptolemaic chancellery.[82] "Aristeas" was obviously a knowledgeable insider.

At the same time, the author of the *Letter* was no slavish reproducer of documents or mechanical duplicator of what he found in his sources.[83] The collection of diverse episodes, array of material, attention to detail, introduction of celebrated figures, and the striking content of documents, speeches, dialogue, and descriptions indicate a writer of unusual imagination. The reader enjoys a remarkable variety of presentations within this treatise: Ptolemy's letters, with their tortured efforts to get his father off the hook, a lengthy description of the furnishings supplied to the Jews, Eleazer's complex rationalizations of the most peculiar Jewish dietary restrictions, the rapid-fire

Ptolemaic Alexandria (Oxford, 1972) II, 970–72; Goodman in Schürer, *History of the Jewish People*, III.1, 679–84; L. Troiani in B. Virgilio, *Studi ellenistici*, II (Pisa, 1987) 50–58. More recently, J. A. Goldstein in M. Mor, *Eretz Israel, Israel, and the Jewish Diaspora: Mutual Relations* (Lanham, 1991) 1–23, sought to fix a time to the decade of the 130s. Bar-Kochva, *Pseudo-Hecataeus*, 271–88, places it in the years 125 to 112.

77. *LetArist* 28.
78. *LetArist* 174–75.
79. *LetArist* 183.
80. *LetArist* 298–300.
81. *LetArist* 22–25. For the extant decree on papyrus, see *SB*, 8008. The similarity was noted by W. L. Westerman, *AJP* 59 (1938) 19–30.
82. See the valuable discussion of Fraser, *Ptolemaic Alexandria*, I, 696–703. Cf. also Fevrier, *La date*, 49–55.
83. So, rightly, O. Murray, *Studia Patristica* 12 (1975) 123–28.

table talk of a Hellenistic banquet, and the professional manner in which scholars produced a consensus on the translation of the Pentateuch. It is no wonder that the *Letter of Aristeas* continues to exercise great fascination. The ingenuity of its author has helped to insure its endurance.

But what was the objective of the work? Proposals, of course, have proliferated. A large proportion view the *Letter* as literary polemic, part of a propaganda campaign by the Jews of Alexandria who felt beleaguered or who sought to expand the boundaries of their influence. The assumption of an internal debate among Jews dominates modern discussions. On one thesis, the work was a response to III Maccabees and its portrayal of an antagonistic relationship between Jews and the Ptolemies; the *Letter* endeavored to undo that damage by promoting a *modus vivendi* between Jews and Gentiles in Egypt.[84] On another, the reverse holds: the assimilationist message of the *Letter* was countered by the separatism of III Maccabees.[85] In a different formulation, "Aristeas" represented the Hellenized Jewish aristocracy of Alexandria, a reaction against their less cultivated brethren who clung to the traditionalism of Palestine but also against those who had gone too far in the other direction and abandoned too many Judaic practices.[86] The *Letter*, it has been argued, served as a manifesto for the Septuagint, recommending it to the Jews of Alexandria as against earlier renditions of the Bible and as an equivalent to the Hebrew Torah.[87] Others interpret the polemic as an attempt to undermine later Greek versions. The *Letter*, on this theory, not only supplied propaganda for the Septuagint but counter-propaganda against a rival translation, perhaps one produced at Leontopolis.[88] Or the thesis can be turned on its head: the Septuagint *was* the bible of Leontopolis, and "Aristeas," by according it the authority of Jerusalem, defended it against the hard-line traditionalists.[89] A variant on that analysis has the *Letter* as a response to charges leveled by Jerusalem that a rendition of the Bible in any

84. S. Tracy, *Yale Classical Studies* 1 (1928) 241–52.

85. M. Hadas, *HTR* 42 (1949) 175–84; *Aristeas to Philocrates*, 32–38.

86. V. Tcherikover, *HTR* 51 (1958) 80–85. For Parente, *AnnPisa* 2.1 (1972) 231–37, the *Letter* was an instrument of those Jews who held Alexandrian citizenship and had absorbed Greek culture against those for whom this was an unacceptable compromise of the faith.

87. P. Kahle, *The Cairo Geniza*, 2nd ed. (Oxford, 1959) 211–14; Hadas, *Aristeas to Philocrates*, 66–73; Goodman in Schürer, *History of the Jewish People*, III.1, 679.

88. A. Momigliano, *Aegyptus* 12 (1932) 161–72; P. Dalbert, *Die Theologie der hellenistisch-jüdischen Missions-Literatur unter Ausschluss von Philo und Josephus* (Hamburg, 1954) 93; A. F. J. Klijn, *NTS* 11 (1964/1965) 154–58; S. Jellicoe, *NTS* 12 (1966) 144–50. See the criticisms of Parente, *AnnPisa* 2.1 (1972) 193–202.

89. O. Murray, *JTS* 18 (1967) 361–69.

other language than Hebrew is an unacceptable departure from the Law.[90] One recent analysis offers a purely political interpretation: the *Letter*'s author wished to show that Jews had been better off under the gentle Ptolemy II than under the unpleasant contemporary Hasmonaeans and Seleucids.[91] Finally, some scholars see the work as an attempt to surmount the differences and tensions that divided Jewish communities and to make a case for the compatibility of Jewish values and Hellenic culture.[92]

As so often, discrepancies and inconsistencies among the proposed solutions suggest that presuppositions may be faulty. Must we believe that stresses among Jews called forth the *Letter of Aristeas*, either to take up the cudgels on one side or to advocate reconciliation? Testimony to support any of the reconstructions outlined above is inadequate or altogether absent. One will look long and hard to find any effort by either the *Letter* or III Maccabees to refute items in the other. In fact, as will be seen, their objectives are entirely in harmony. There is little to indicate that the Greek Bible of Alexandria faced competing translations against which it felt compelled to polemicize, an idea that rests on very fragile testimony and conjecture.[93] The notion of a manifesto by Alexandrian Jews as apologia for their Hellenism runs aground when one attempts to identify an appropriate readership. It is difficult to imagine isolationist Jews in Palestine reading, let alone being moved, by the tale. Nor is it likely to have circulated much among those outside the Alexandrian intelligentsia, the primary audience—and they did not have to be persuaded. A strictly political interpretation ignores the cultural meaning and implications that extended well beyond the specifics of any decade. Certainly the theme of harmony between Jewish principles and

90. G. Howard, *JTS* 22 (1971) 337–48. A modified view in Collins, *Between Athens and Jerusalem*, 84–86, who sees the text as an argument for Diaspora Judaism but not as polemic against Palestine.

91. Goldstein in M. Mor, *Eretz Israel*, 1–23, with characteristic ingenuity, finds particular parallels to events in the time of Simon and sees the author as apologist for the Ptolemies, critic of the Hasmonaeans, and opponent of Jewish traditionalists. Since generations of determined scholars failed to pick out these features, could the intended readership really be expected to penetrate them?

92. M. Hengel, *Judaism and Hellenism* (London, 1974) I, 264–65; G. W. E. Nickelsburg in M. Stone, *Jewish Writings of the Second Temple Period* (Philadelphia, 1984) 78–79; Murray in Virgilio, *Studi ellenistici*, II (Pisa, 1987) 17–18.

93. The remark of Aristobulus that earlier translations were available to Plato and Pythagoras is pure fantasy; Euseb. *PE* 13.12.1; Clement *Strom.* 1.22.150.1–3; cf. N. Walter, *Der Thoraausleger Aristobulos* (Berlin, 1964) 44–45. Equally dubious are the notices in *LetArist* 312–16 that certain Greek writers who preceded the Septuagint and sought to adapt biblical passages were afflicted with nervous disorders or cataracts. Earlier Hebrew versions, not Greek translations, are referred to in *LetArist* 30; see above, n. 59.

the Hellenic society of Egypt pervades the treatise. But to leave it at that would be simplistic. The *Letter of Aristeas* possesses richness and complexity that cannot be captured in a brief formula.

A principal aspect has relevance here: the Jewish attitude toward Hellenistic monarchy. Ptolemy II Philadelphus, as portrayed by "Aristeas" is, of course, kind, generous, and respectful. But another feature, equally pronounced, needs to be underscored. The king was in control throughout, his power and authority unquestioned by Jew and Gentile alike. Ptolemy issued the orders to write to the High Priest and get the project underway.[94] His magnanimity was responsible for the release of Jewish slaves and the payment of substantial expenses entailed by the process.[95] He was the employer of Jews, both in his army and, for those who were worthy, even at court and as ministers to the crown.[96] It was the king's decision to have the Hebrew Scriptures translated into Greek, that he might have them on the shelves of his library, along with the rest of the royal books.[97] The emphasis again and again is on Ptolemaic patronage, the king bestowing favors that elicit friendship and devotion.[98] He even orders the kosher meal for his guests and partakes of it as well, a gesture of his good nature, but also of his authority, the entire banquet orchestrated at his behest.[99] And he arranges the lavish parting gifts that send off the sages in high style.[100] In short, here, as in the fables noted earlier, the dependence of the Jews upon royal power is unequivocally acknowledged.[101] These are not subversive documents.

This monarch, however, stands out as a man of cultivation and learning. Philadelphus identifies high repute with completion of this intellectual endeavor.[102] He took a personal interest in the craftsmanship of the elaborate gifts sent to Jerusalem, a man dedicated to the arts.[103] His reputation for love of culture had reached as far as Jerusalem, for the High Priest knew that

94. *LetArist* 11.

95. *LetArist* 22–26: μεγαλομοιρίᾳ καὶ μεγαλοψυχίᾳ χρησάμενος.

96. *LetArist* 37: τοὺς δὲ δυναμένους καὶ περὶ ἡμᾶς εἶναι, τῆς περὶ τὴν αὐλὴν πίστεως ἀξίους, ἐπὶ χρειῶν καθεστάκαμεν.

97. *LetArist* 38: ἵν' ὑπάρχῃ καὶ ταῦτα παρ' ἡμῖν ἐν βιβλιοθήκῃ σὺν τοῖς ἄλλοις βασιλικοῖς βιβλίοις.

98. *LetArist* 44–45: τοῦτο γὰρ φιλίας καὶ ἀγαπήσεως σημεῖόν ἐστι.

99. *LetArist* 181.

100. *LetArist* 318–20.

101. Eleazer indeed promises compliance with all that is to the king's benefit, even if it be "contrary to nature"; *LetArist* 44: πάντα γὰρ ὅσα σοι συμφέρει, καὶ εἰ παρὰ φύσιν ἐστίν, ὑπακουσόμεθα.

102. *LetArist* 40: οἰόμεθα γὰρ ἐπιτελεσθέντος τούτου μεγάλην ἀποίσεσθαι δόξαν.

103. *LetArist* 80: φιλοδοξῶν εἰς τὰ καλῶς ἔχοντα.

Ptolemy had only the most distinguished men around him at court.[104] That characteristic is stressed again at the very end of the treatise, lest the reader miss the point: Ptolemy Philadelphus spent his money freely, not for empty pleasures but to have the company of educated men.[105] The treatise thereby associates Jewish interests with a king who not only possesses authority to confer benefits but who enjoys the refined sensibility to appreciate their distinctive qualities.

The *Letter of Aristeas* is thoroughly Hellenic in character, a fact of which the reader is repeatedly reminded. Greek men of learning and culture make an appearance or are referred to in the treatise: Demetrius of Phalerum, Hecataeus of Abdera, Menedemus of Eritrea, Theopompus, Theodectus. Eleazer the Jewish High Priest is described in terms that evoke a cultivated Hellenic aristocrat.[106] The scholars whom he sent to Alexandria not only command Greek as well as Jewish learning but express the noblest Hellenic ideal of striving for the "middle way."[107] The symposium in which the Jerusalemite sages were interrogated, of course, constitutes a fully Greek setting. And most of the sages respond with answers familiar from Greek philosophy or political theory: e.g., the need of the king to exercise restraint and honor justice, the definition of philosophy as reasoning well for every contingency, resisting impulses, and controlling the passions, and the designation of injustice as the greatest evil.[108] Eleazer himself, in accounting for the more peculiar dietary restrictions of the Jews, explains them either as having a rational basis with the objective of practicing justice or as having symbolic value demanding allegorical interpretation. They aim at truth and serve as a mark of right reason.[109] "Aristeas" has the High Priest speak like a Greek philosopher. The treatise plainly portrays cultivated Jews as comfortable in a Hellenic setting, attuned to Greek customs and modes of thought, and content under the protection of a Hellenistic monarch.

To leave it at that, however, misses the main message. The point of the *Letter* is not syncretism and assimilation. To be sure, "Aristeas," in a celebrated and much quoted passage, remarks to Ptolemy that the god revered by the Jews is

---

104. *LetArist* 43, 124–25.

105. *LetArist* 321: περὶ πολλοῦ ποιούμενος τοῖς πεπαιδευμένοις συνεῖναι, καὶ εἰς τοιούτους τὸν πλοῦτον κατατίθεσθαι δαψιλῶς, καὶ οὐκ εἰς μάταια.

106. *LetArist* 3: καλοκαγαθίᾳ καὶ δόξῃ προτετιμημένον.

107. *LetArist* 122: τὸ μέσον ἐζηλωκότες κατάστημα (τοῦτο γὰρ κάλλιστόν ἐστιν).

108. *LetArist* 209, 211, 222–23, 256, 292.

109. *LetArist* 128–170; see 161: πρὸς δ' ἀλήθειαν καὶ σημείωσιν ὀρθοῦ λόγου. Cf. the analysis of N. Janowitz, *SBL Seminar Papers* (1983) 355–56. It goes too far, however, to see Eleazer's exposition as "anti-Pharisaic"; so Parente, *AnnPisa* 2.1 (1972) 222–31.

the same divinity worshipped by all, only the names differ.[110] But that opinion
is put in the mouth of a pagan seeking to reassure his king. Eleazer sets
matters straight. For all his openness to Hellenism and eager collaboration
with the Alexandrian court, he insists on the distinctiveness of his people
and his religion. The High Priest in effect refutes the superficial judgment
of "Aristeas." He asserts that all other peoples believe in a multiplicity of
gods, themselves more powerful than the divinities they worship since they
fashion them out of stone and wood—an attitude of sheer folly.[111] Indeed,
he presses the point home with undisguised scorn: those who constructed
and created the myths are reckoned as the wisest of the Greeks; yet many,
even today, though more inventive and widely learned than the men of old,
would not outstrip them in performing obeisance.[112] Eleazer glories in the
Law transmitted by God which sets Jews apart, erecting barriers to keep
them pure in body and soul—and free of Gentile taint.[113] So much for the
Greeks. And the Egyptians, of course, who deify animals and pay homage to
snakes and monsters, both alive and dead, are simply unspeakable.[114] These
are strong words and powerful sentiments, not to be obscured or suppressed
in the warm glow of some alleged universalism.[115]

The superiority of Jewish insight and understanding comes across with
unmistakable clarity. "Aristeas" has Greek intellectuals acknowledge it themselves. Hecataeus of Abdera purportedly stated that Greek historians, poets,
and intellectuals held the Hebrew books in awe because of their rather sacred
and holy content.[116] Theopompus declared that when he once quoted carelessly from the Scriptures, he suffered from mental disorder for a month. And
the tragic poet Theodectus testified that his attempt to use a biblical passage

---

110. *LetArist* 16: τὸν γὰρ πάντων ἐπόπτην καὶ κτίστην θεὸν οὗτοι σέβονται, ὃν καὶ
πάντες, ἡμεῖς δέ, βασιλεῦ, προσονομάζοντες ἑτέρως Ζῆνα καὶ Δία.

111. *LetArist* 134–36: ὧν σέβονται ματαίως ... παντελῶς ἀνόητοι.

112. *LetArist* 137: καὶ γὰρ ἔτι καὶ νῦν εὑρεματικώτεροι καὶ πολυμαθέστεροι τῶν
ἀνθρώπων τῶν πρίν εἰσι πολλοί, καὶ οὐκ ἂν φθάνοιεν αὐτοὺς προσκυνοῦντες. καὶ
νομίζουσιν οἱ ταῦτα διαπλάσαντες καὶ μυθοποιήσαντες τῶν Ἑλλήνων οἱ σοφώτατοι
καθεστάναι. This refutes the idea of M. A. L. Beavis, *JSJ* 18 (1987) 147–48, that Eleazer
sought to associate Jewish monotheism with cultivated Greeks.

113. *LetArist* 139, 142.

114. *LetArist* 138.

115. A comparable point is made by J. M. G. Barclay, *Jews in the Mediterranean Diaspora*
(Edinburgh, 1996) 143–45. Cf. also C. R. Holladay in P. Bilde et al., *Ethnicity in Hellenistic Egypt*
(Aarhus, 1992) 147–49.

116. *LetArist* 31. Whether the statement came from Hecataeus or Pseudo-Hecataeus, or was
even invented by "Aristeas" makes no difference. See Bar-Kochva, *Pseudo-Hecataeus*, 140–42.
The author of the *Letter* used it for his own purposes.

in his play caused him to suffer from cataracts.[117] Those statements were duly endorsed by Demetrius of Phalerum.[118] The Egyptians too, according to the *Letter*, conceded Jewish uniqueness: their chief priests named the Jews "men of God," a designation accorded only to those who worship the true God.[119]

The table talk of the symposium further exemplified the superior wisdom of the Jews. Their representatives answered every question unhesitatingly, exhibiting their command of precepts familiar to the Greeks but incorporating in each response a reference to God as ultimate authority. The replies offer little that is distinctively Jewish—or even very specific. The sages never mention Moses, the Law, the Scriptures, or any practices peculiarly linked to Judaism. Indeed God often appears in mechanical, even irrelevant fashion. The intellectual context is strictly philosophical, not at all theological—and rather superficial philosophy at that.[120] What matters is that the Jewish elders impress the king, over and over again. He commends every statement made, never moving from one interlocutor to the next without complimenting the speaker. The upshot of the story, of course, is that biblical scholars display an insight eclipsing anything that could be mustered by Greek philosophers. Ptolemy acknowledges it explicitly: the Jewish elders stand out in virtue and discernment, for the foundation of their reasoning lies in God.[121] More tellingly, the Greek philosophers themselves admit that they cannot equal Jewish sagacity. Menedemus conceded it, and other philosophers led the applause in congratulating the Jews who, they proclaimed, far exceeded them in education and eloquence.[122]

The supreme compliment comes from the king himself. Ptolemy, as we have seen, exercised unchallenged rule. In the world of the Hellenistic

117. *LetArist* 314–16.

118. *LetArist* 312–13.

119. *LetArist* 140.

120. On the banquet and the dialogue, see Murray, *JTS* 18 (1967) 344–61, rightly disputing the notion of G. Zuntz, *JSS* 4 (1959) 21–31, that "Aristeas" largely reproduced a treatise on kingship here. Cf. Fraser, *Ptolemaic Alexandria*, 701–703. See also Parente, *AnnPisa* 2.2 (1972) 546–63, although his suggestion that some of the Jewish answers are directed against the Hasmonaean monarchy is implausible. J. J. Lewis, *NTS* 13 (1966/1967) 53–56, discerns parallels between the *Letter* and Pseudo-Phocylides—but this hardly warrants his conclusion that the work aimed to commend Judaism to the Gentiles. More interestingly, D. Mendels, *Aegyptus* 59 (1979) 127–36, points to similarities in issues raised at the banquet and those addressed in the Temple Scroll from Qumran, thus positing Jewish ideas as a common background for at least some of the material. G. Boccaccini, *Middle Judaism: Jewish Thought, 300 B.C.E. to 200 C.E.* (Minneapolis, 1991) 163–74, labors mightily to find theological precepts in this exchange, without much success.

121. *LetArist* 200: οἴομαι διαφέρειν τοὺς ἄνδρας ἀρετῇ, καὶ συνιέναι πλεῖον ... πάντες ἀπὸ θεοῦ τοῦ λόγου τὴν καταρχὴν ποιούμενοι.

122. *LetArist* 201, 235, 296.

kingdom, Jews were clients and dependents, recipients of the monarch's favor. But they occupy a special place, an acknowledged ascendancy in the spiritual sphere to which the ruler pays conspicuous homage. In this central regard, the *Letter of Aristeas* follows a pattern already discerned in the stories of Alexander the Great and Ptolemy I's relations with the Jews. Philadelphus does more than award them the palm for the acuity of their banquet rejoinders. He pays due reverence to their God, their principles, and their sacred books. His project for translation of the Pentateuch, according to the *Letter*, derived from piety toward the Jewish God.[123] When the Jewish delegates arrived in Alexandria, Ptolemy was overcome at the sight of the scrolls and even performed *proskynesis* seven times.[124] He declared that the day of their arrival would thereafter be celebrated as an annual festival.[125] And once the translation was complete, he bowed still again, this time to the Greek scrolls for which he ordered special care and permanent preservation.[126] The king may have been responsible for bringing the great enterprise to fruition. But it was the Lord of the Jews who shaped his desire and kept his kingdom secure so as to make the accomplishment possible.[127] Here, as elsewhere in the texts, royal power holds sway, but the Jews enjoy a unique relationship with it, their faith and their values its principal mainstay.

In the mountainous literature on the *Letter of Aristeas*, one element has attracted no attention. The composer of the work, while paying due deference to Hellenistic monarchy and exalting the special character of the Jewish place within it, did not lack a sense of humor. Beneath an ostensibly sober exterior, the treatise offers a droll commentary to delight the discerning reader.

Eleazer's denunciation of Greeks as idol-worshippers and myth-makers dismisses them as fools rather than knaves. He offers a clever twist to exhibit their naivete. Since the Greeks created the gods, made their images, and invented their stories, they are more powerful than the very divinities whose existence depends upon them. And he adds a sardonic conclusion: the supposedly wisest of the Greeks are the first to worship their own creations.[128] The Jewish readership will have enjoyed that parenthesis. No doubt they enjoyed still further the discomfiture of the philosophers who not only stood by while Jewish sages gave swift and commendable

---

123. *LetArist* 42: πρὸς τὸν θεὸν ἡμῶν εὐσέβειαν.
124. *LetArist* 177. This may, of course, have a double-edged connotation. See below, p. 219.
125. *LetArist* 180.
126. *LetArist* 317.
127. *LetArist* 18–20, 45.
128. *LetArist* 134–37. See above, nn. 111–12.

retorts to every query of the king, but had to suffer the embarrassment of Ptolemy's exposing their inferiority in public. At the end of the first day's banquet, when the assembled throng erupted in loud applause for the Jews, Ptolemy turned to the philosophers and opined that perhaps their answers indicated superior virtue and understanding. Menedemus, as spokesman for the philosophers, had no option but to agree.[129] "Aristeas" rubs it in later. After the third day's symposium, when the audience again raised a hearty applause, the philosophers conspicuously joined them, an implicit and doubtless disingenuous acknowledgment of Jewish intellectual ascendancy.[130] The narrator concludes his account of the seven banquets with a final dig at the Hellenic philosophers. In his own voice he observes that the scholars from Jerusalem were obviously worthy of the highest admiration from him, from those present—and especially from the philosophers.[131] That was no innocent remark.

The entire symposium scenario has something of the air of a spoof. The festivities went on for a week, with Ptolemy having to provide a different question for each of seventy-two Jewish elders and to commend each and every answer no matter how subtle or how banal. The dragging of God into every response, even when patently artificial or altogether immaterial, might well have coaxed a smile from the *Letter*'s readers.[132] "Aristeas" was not, of course, mocking the sages of Jerusalem, but exposing the gullibility of their audience.

Ptolemy II emerges as a wise, generous, and appreciative ruler. Yet even he does not escape the subtle jabs of the narrator. The king's nodding of agreement or even enthusiastic commendation of every single remark by his Jewish guests hardly suggests profound and discriminating judgment. And there is more. When the Jewish emissaries reached Egyptian shores with scrolls of the Torah, Ptolemy not only showed respect but performed *proskynesis* about seven times—and this before the sages had done anything! Nor

129. *LetArist* 200–201. See above, n. 121.

130. *LetArist* 235: συνεπιφωνούντων τῶν παρόντων, μάλιστα δὲ τῶν φιλοσόφων· καὶ γὰρ ταῖς ἀγωγαῖς καὶ τῷ λόγῳ πολὺ προέχοντες αὐτῶν ἦσαν.

131. *LetArist* 296: ἄξιοι θαυμασμοῦ κατεφαίνοντό μοι καὶ τοῖς παροῦσι, μάλιστα δὲ τοῖς φιλοσόφοις.

132. Cf., e.g., the answer to the king's question about how to find concord with a woman; *LetArist* 250–51. The sage refers to female enthusiasm, fickleness, lack of reasoning powers, and weak nature, thus recommending a healthy approach and avoidance of a quarrel. Whatever the value of that analysis, he proceeds to offer the analogy of a helmsman steering toward the proper goal of life. Not an obviously relevant remark. But it allows him to observe that life in all its aspects is steered by calling upon God. Ptolemy, as usual, expressed agreement. This is not an untypical instance.

does the narrator stop there. He has Ptolemy so overcome with emotion that he bursts into tears.[133] Not exactly proper royal behavior.[134] But "Aristeas" allows the king a little joke of his own. He declares that the date of the scholars' arrival would henceforth be celebrated each year as a national holiday throughout his lifetime. But why the anniversary of the arrival instead of the accomplishment of their task? Philadelphus observes that the envoys came at the right time: their advent happened to coincide with a Ptolemaic naval victory over the Macedonians. So they share by accident—and no credit of their own—in a patriotic commemoration.[135] The author of the *Letter* may have indulged in some whimsy.

The humorous undertones, here as elsewhere, go beyond mere amusement. They appear not in heavy-handed fashion but as subtle thrusts that afford a sense of distance to the reader. That strategy keeps the work outside the realm of polemic. The text represents the king in respectful terms but can also take him down a peg.[136] It bolsters Jewish feelings of superiority while permitting Ptolemy a joke at Jewish expense. The modest mockery invited winks and nods between author and audience—an edifying exchange for the *cognoscenti*.

The treatise of "Aristeas" is a complex, multilayered, and occasionally entertaining piece of work. In these regards, it exemplifies much of the Jewish literature in Greek that emerged in the Hellenistic period. No single

---

133. *LetArist* 176–78: προσκυνήσας σχεδὸν ἑπτάκις ... προήχθη δακρῦσαι τῇ χαρᾷ πεπληρωμένος.

134. To be sure, a Jewish source could describe royal tears in a sympathetic way, as Philo did with regard to Agrippa I; *Leg. ad Gaium*, 273–75. But the circumstances were altogether different. Agrippa was in despair over the prospective introduction of Caligula's statue into the Temple in Jerusalem. Ptolemy II, by contrast, shed tears of joy—a somewhat excessive reaction.

135. *LetArist* 180: μεγάλην δὲ τέθειμαι τὴν ἡμέραν ταύτην, ἐν ᾗ παραγεγόνατε ... συντέτυχε γὰρ καὶ τὰ κατὰ τὴν νίκην ἡμῖν προσπεπτωκέναι τῆς πρὸς Ἀντίγονον ναυμαχίας.

136. Ironic digs at the king in texts generally favorable to him can be paralleled in the Hellenistic poetry of Alexandria. Note, for example, Theocritus' praise of Ptolemy II's fine qualities which include a reference to him as ἐρωτικός, a sly allusion to his well-known amours. And while he lauds the king's generosity, he also adds an innuendo about its limits; Theocr. 14.61–65. In another poem, one of Theocritus' characters applauds the fact that Ptolemy has cracked down on ruffians and miscreants, but the words come as part of a lament that the streets of Alexandria are intolerably crowded and crushing—not least because of the menacing presence of the king's cavalry; Theocr. 15.46–53. One can cite also the mime of Herodas in which a speaker lists the pleasures and advantages of Alexandria, an array of motley items including riches, wine, and beautiful women without number. The "good king" receives mention in passing, in the midst of this catalogue of miscellanies; Herodas, 1.26–36.

purpose drove its composition. The idea, prevalent in modern scholarship, that it promoted a synthesis between Judaism and Hellenism is inadequate.[137] Eleazer affirms the uniqueness of Jewish practices and principles, Jewish sages surpass Greek philosophers, and the Torah receives obeisance from the king of Egypt. This narrative, like so many others, implies that Jews are fully at home in the world of Hellenic culture. The use of a fictive Greek as narrator and admirer of Judaism carries that implication clearly enough.[138] But the message is still more pointed: Jews have not only digested Hellenic culture, they have also surmounted it. The *Letter* plainly directs itself, first and foremost, at Jews. It would certainly serve no missionary purposes. Those Gentiles who happened to read the work would not have found it particularly edifying.[139] Insofar as one may detect a "synthesis," it is not between Judaism and Hellenism but between Diaspora Jews and the center in Jerusalem. The main theme of the treatise delivers this point unmistakably: the Septuagint, the Bible of the Greek Diaspora, was itself the creation of Jerusalem sages and had the blessing of the High Priest. Whatever the truth of that questionable proposition, the *Letter of Aristeas* proclaims that Jews of the homeland and those abroad share a stake in their common tradition.[140]

In the context of this discussion, a different but no less significant point can be stressed. Jews who dwell under the aegis of Hellenistic monarchy can prosper in the Gentile setting while preserving their own heritage. The fable of Ptolemy Philadelphus as director of a translation project that would not only benefit Alexandrian Jews but would expand his own cultural horizons surely speaks to that issue. The author of the *Letter* makes the king a benevolent master and the Jews compliant subjects who enjoy his protection and his favor. But he also has Ptolemy pay homage to the superior culture—

137. For this formulation, see, e.g., Tcherikover, *HTR* 51 (1958) 70, 82; Hengel, *Judaism and Hellenism*, I, 264–65; Nickelsburg in Stone, *Jewish Writings*, 80; L. H. Feldman, *Jew and Gentile in the Ancient World* (Princeton, 1993) 55–56.

138. Cf. Troiani in Virgilio, *Studi ellenistici*, II (Pisa, 1987) 35–47; R. Feldmeier in M. Hengel and A. M. Schwemer, *Die Septuaginta zwischen Judentum und Christentum* (Tübingen, 1994) 20–37; Barclay, *Jews in the Mediterranean Diaspora*, 145–48.

139. That case need not be argued here. It was made forcefully and persuasively by Tcherikover, *HTR* 51 (1958) 59–85, and now widely adopted. Cf., e.g., Murray in Virgilio, *Studi ellenistici*, II (Pisa, 1987) 17–18, reversing his earlier position in *JTS* 18 (1967) 345. Feldman's dissent, *Jew and Gentile*, 55–56, simply on the basis of the Greek pseudonym, does not shake the consensus. Nor does the argument of Barclay, *Jews in the Mediterranean Disapora*, 148–49, who can only point to Gentile reactions in the *Letter* itself.

140. H. M. Orlinsky, *HUCA* 46 (1975) 89–103; *idem* in Davies and Finkelstein, *Cambridge History of Judaism*, II, 540–48, notes allusions and parallels in the *Letter* to divine authorization of the Torah itself.

and he does not refrain even from a few sly pleasantries at the expense of the king and his ministers. Jewish readers would find it eminently gratifying.

•   •   •

No comparable legends settled upon the person of Ptolemy III Euergetes. At least none that survived. But Josephus does record one relevant story, with familiar resonance and an appropriate setting. Ptolemy Euergetes, fresh from a triumph over the Seleucid monarchy and now master of Syria, visited Jerusalem in order to offer thanks for his victory. There, instead of paying homage to Egyptian gods, he followed Jewish practice, making numerous sacrifices to the Lord. And he also dedicated offerings as a suitable return for his success.[141] That any truth resides in this account may be questioned. The episode is nowhere else on record, but our record on these matters is very sparse. For all we know, Ptolemy might have traversed Palestine after his victory, and the Temple in Jerusalem would be an appropriate site to visit if the king wished to cover all flanks and thank every god in the vicinity. But the event carries strong echoes of the Alexander/Jaddous story and the tale of Ptolemy IV discussed below. It represents yet another instance in which Hellenistic kings make public acknowledgment of the power and majesty of the Jewish god.[142] The persistence of the leitmotif raises legitimate doubts about the historicity of the incident. But it reinforces the importance of this theme in the perception of the Jews.

•   •   •

Far more dramatic was the confrontation of Jews with the subsequent ruler of Egypt: Ptolemy IV Philopator. So at least one memorable tradition would have us believe. The text of III Maccabees preserves the tale. On the face of it, that work presents a jarring contrast with the other accounts. No sweetness and light here, no concord and collaboration between king and Jews. Instead, the encounter was harsh and frightful, with dire threats and near calamity.

A resumé of the narrative will facilitate matters. It opens on the eve of Philopator's momentous clash with the forces of Antiochus III at the battle of Raphia in 217 BCE. The Egyptian king barely escaped assassination in his tent at the hands of a certain Theodotus. The quick-witted Dositheus, an

141. Jos. *C. Apion.* 2.48: πολλάς, ὡς ἡμῖν νόμιμόν ἐστιν, ἐπετέλεσε θυσίας τῷ θεῷ.
142. Cf. A. Paul, *ANRW* II.20.1 (1987) 305–306, who sees this as a stereotype.

apostate Jew, rescued him by substituting an unfortunate victim in his stead. Ptolemy had help also from his wife Arsinoe whose desperate exhortations—and offers of bribes—rallied the troops. As a consequence, Raphia proved to be a smashing triumph for the Ptolemaic cause.[143] That victory set the stage for Philopator's eventful meeting with the Jews. The initial dealings could hardly have been more cordial. A Jewish delegation came to meet and congratulate him, thus prompting a visit to Jerusalem where he offered sacrifices and thank offerings to God. So impressed was Ptolemy by the Temple, however, that he sought entrance into the Holy of Holies. The Jewish leaders pointed out politely that only the High Priest enjoyed that privilege—and then only once a year. But Ptolemy would not take no for an answer. He insisted upon admission, thereby prompting panic and desperate appeals by Jews of every station and rank, wails and pleas that raised a thunderous uproar but left the king unmoved. As last resort, the High Priest Simon lifted a piteous prayer to the Lord. Only then was Ptolemy's stubborn purpose thwarted and the sanctity of the inner shrine preserved. God heard the High Priest's prayer and felled Ptolemy with a stroke. The king suffered a violent fit and collapsed to the ground in a state of paralysis. The crisis was temporarily surmounted.[144]

But worse was to come. Ptolemy recovered and returned to Alexandria. Once there, he determined to make the Jews of Egypt pay for the humiliation he had suffered at their countrymen's hands. He posted a public notice that all Jews be subjected to registration and to servile status. Those who objected would suffer the death penalty. Further, the registered Jews would be branded with the ivy leaf of Dionysus and reduced to their former, limited station. He did, however, offer an alternative. Any Jews who chose to join those initiated in the mysteries could have privileges equal to the Alexandrians. The offer appealed to some, but most Jews held firm, clinging to their faith, paying a ransom to escape registration, and turning their wrath upon the apostates.[145]

The king's wrath was mightier still. He prepared to wreak vengeance not only on the Jews of Alexandria but on those of the *chora* as well. Venomous reports maligned the Jews and spurred him on. Ptolemy issued a public letter, recapitulating the insults he had endured from the Jews in Palestine, affirming the hostility and treachery of the entire race, and decreeing a mass genocide. Jews were now rounded up from everywhere, amidst bitter lamentation, to be herded into the hippodrome just outside Alexandria, and

143. III Macc. 1.1–5.
144. III Macc. 1.6–2.23.
145. III Macc. 2.24–33.

there to be slaughtered. Every member of the race was to be registered by name, tortured, and killed.[146]

Divine intervention, however, postponed, delayed, and ultimately frustrated the plan. The massive numbers proved an impossible burden upon those who attempted to register them. Forty days passed and countless Jews were still unregistered, while the scribes had run out of writing materials. Ptolemy thereupon ordered Hermon, his master of elephants, to drug five hundred of the beasts and prepare them to trample the captive Jews. Nothing remained but tears and prayers. But they proved effective. The king fell into a deep sleep and failed to give the order to loose the elephants. That, however, was but a brief respite. Everything was soon in readiness again, only this time the king suffered a bout of amnesia and forgot that he had ever had anything against the Jews. One last reversal remained. The befuddled Hermon once more readied the elephants, this time with extra doses of frankincense and unmixed wine. There seemed no recourse left for the doomed Jews, now reduced to helpless wailing and supplications. But at the eleventh hour, the Lord paid heed. Two angels descended, bedecked in glory and of terrifying aspect. Ptolemy's body shook, his soldiers were paralyzed, and the elephants turned about to trample the enemies of the Jews.[147]

All was now reversed in an instant. The king released the Jews and turned his wrath upon his advisers, blaming them for the malicious calumnies that had deceived him. The would-be victims suddenly emerged triumphant. Philopator honored them and their god, deflated their enemies, and declared a feast of seven days to celebrate their deliverance. A new proclamation was issued, overturning and inverting all that had been asserted in the previous one. Ptolemy heaped praise upon the Jews, scorn upon their foes, and honor upon the Lord. The liberated Jews had but one request to make of the sovereign: they sought permission to punish those of their own people who had left the flock. Permission once granted, the stalwarts executed more than three hundred of their fellows who had strayed from the faith, a slaughter which enlivened further the joyous festivities that marked their salvation.[148]

The treatise is clumsy and inelegant, a patchwork of inconsistencies and improbabilities. Researchers frequently castigate it for rhetorical bombast, incoherence, and literary ineptitude.[149] For our investigation these

---

146. III Macc. 3.1–4.14.
147. III Macc. 4.15–6.21.
148. III Macc. 6.22–7.23.
149. Cf. C. Emmet in R. H. Charles, *The Apocrypha and Pseudepigrapha of the Old Testament* (Oxford, 1913) I, 161–62; V. Tcherikover, *Scripta Hierosolymitana* 7 (1961) 1–11; Barclay, *Jews in the*

characteristics need not be liabilities, and may even be advantageous. What light does III Maccabees throw upon Hellenistic Jewry's perception of its place within the framework of a secular and alien monarchy?

First, date and circumstances. It is, of course, desirable to locate III Maccabees in time and place, thereby more confidently to elicit motives and aims. But the temptation too often leads to circularity. The evidence is ambiguous and inadequate. And, here as elsewhere, the drive to discover particular conditions that called forth a work of literary fiction (or largely literary fiction) may be misdirected. Suggestions for a date have focused primarily upon three possibilities: a period not long after 100 BCE, the early Augustan era, or the time of Caligula.[150] None has a decisive claim on confidence. The assaults on Alexandrian Jews in Caligula's reign might seem a logical occasion to prompt such a pamphlet, with Ptolemy IV a surrogate for the megalomaniacal Roman emperor. Yet the involvement of Caligula in the persecutions of Alexandria is itself questionable; the emperor is not held responsible in our fullest contemporary source, the *In Flaccum* of Philo. And the particulars of the story in III Maccabees have barely the slightest resemblance to the events of the early Empire.[151]

A date in the time of Augustus rests on the interpretation of the term λαογραφία. The author of III Maccabees has Ptolemy link the subjection of Jews to the λαογραφία with their reduction to servile status.[152] That

---

Mediterranean Diaspora, 192–95. For M. Hadas, *Chron.d'Égypte* 47 (1949) 97–104, the work most closely resembles the forms of popular Greek romances.

150. Complete bibliographical citations would be out of place here. For the period after 100 BCE, see especially Emmet in Charles, *Apocrypha and Pseudepigrapha*, I, 156–59; Bickerman, *RE* 19 (1928) 797–800; H. Anderson in J. H. Charlesworth, *Old Testament Pseudepigrapha* (New York, 1985) II, 510–12. For the early Augustan era, see M. Hadas, *The Third and Fourth Books of Maccabees* (New York, 1953) 18–21; Tcherikover, *Scripta Hierosolymitana* 7 (1961) 11–18; Paul, *ANRW* II.20.1 (1987) 331–33. For the age of Caligula, see the initial formulation of H. G. A. Ewald, *Geschichte des Volkes Israel*3 (Göttingen, 1864) IV, 611–14; cf. H. Willrich, *Hermes* 39 (1904) 244–58; Collins, *Between Athens and Jerusalem*, 105–11. A recent and valuable summary of the principal modern opinions may be found in F. Parente, *Henoch* 10 (1988) 150–68. Parente's own view is that the work went through two editions, one in the 1st century BCE, and a second in the early Empire; *op. cit.*, 168–81; cf. Nickelsburg in Stone, *Jewish Writings*, 83.

151. The point is adequately made by Emmet in Charles, *Apocrypha and Pseudepigrapha*, I, 158–59. See also R. B. Motzo, *Ricerche sulla letteratura e la storia giudaico-ellenistica* (Rome, 1977) 354–58. To be sure, Philo in his *Legatio ad Gaium* refers briefly to the Alexandrians as having been encouraged by Caligula's hatred of the Jews; *Leg. ad Gaium*, 120–21, 162–65. But even here there is no concrete action on his part. The circumstances in Alexandria are treated much more thoroughly in the *In Flaccum*, where Caligula, in fact, behaves in exemplary fashion.

152. III Macc. 2.28: πάντας δὲ τοὺς Ἰουδαίους εἰς λαογραφίαν καὶ οἰκετικὴν διάθεσιν ἀχθῆναι.

combination has led some to identify the "registration of the people" with the poll tax introduced by Augustus ca. 23 BCE which entailed a demotion of Jews to the same status as Egyptians. But the thesis is highly conjectural and vulnerable. The term λαογραφία occurs in Ptolemaic papyri, albeit of ostensibly local, rather than kingdom-wide, significance, with the meaning of "census."[153] There is no direct testimony that the Augustan census and imposition of a poll-tax reduced Jews to a station equivalent to that of Egyptians, and it is equally possible, for all we know, that Ptolemy levied a tax which encompassed Jews and which could have been regarded as a compromise of their privileges.[154]

A date in the early first century BCE depends more on philological and literary than on historical arguments. A line in III Maccabees appears to echo one of the verses in a Greek addition to Daniel, customarily dated to 100 BCE, thus supplying a *terminus post quem*.[155] The formulae employed by the king's letters reflect late Ptolemaic usage as attested in the papyri.[156] And the many parallels in themes, language, and episodes between III Maccabees on the one hand and II Maccabees, the *Letter of Aristeas*, and the Greek Esther on the other argue for a roughly contemporary composition for all of them, namely the early first century BCE.[157] That may be as near as we come to an answer. But it is hardly secure. The verbal echo of the Greek Daniel depends on a single word (and the date of the translation uncertain), the papyrological evidence is inconclusive (a later writer might have imitated earlier formulae), and the comparisons with other texts for chronological purposes is hazardous (and risks circularity since their dates are also controversial).[158]

153. P. Tebt. 103, 121, 189; P. Ryl. 667.

154. See the arguments of S. L. Wallace, *AJP* 59 (1938) 418–42. Cf. A. Kasher, *The Jews in Hellenistic and Roman Egypt* (Tübingen, 1985) 226–28. The hostile claim of Isidorus in the time of the emperor Claudius, that Jews were on a level with Egyptians in tax liability, is clearly propaganda; *CPJ*, 156c, lines 25–27. Cf. Kasher, *op. cit.*, 343–45. The text does not, in any case, specify *laographia*.

155. See III Macc. 6.6: διάπυρον δροσίσας; Dan. 3.50: πνεῦμα δρόσου.

156. Emmet in Charles, *Apocrypha and Pseudepigrapha*, 157–58; Bickerman, *RE* 19 (1928) 798.

157. Parallels with II Maccabees and the *Letter of Aristeas* are well brought out by Emmet in Charles, *Apocrypha and Pseudepigrapha*, 156–58; cf. also Anderson in Charlesworth, *Old Testament Pseudepigrapha*, II, 511, 515–16; M. Delcor in Davies and Finkelstein, *Cambridge History of Judaism*, II, 495. On III Maccabees and Esther, see Motzo, *Ricerche*, 285–93; cf. Bickerman, *RE* 19 (1928) 798–99. The association among these texts has now been studied anew and most effectively in the recent dissertation of S. Johnson, *Mirror, Mirror: Third Maccabees, Historical Fictions and Jewish Self-Fashioning in the Hellenistic Period* (Diss. Berkeley, 1996) 23–56.

158. As noted by J. Mélèze-Modrzejewski, *The Jews of Egypt* (Philadelphia, 1995) 141–42, even if one takes the extant version to have been composed in the 1st century BCE, the story itself may well be older.

One point, however, needs to be emphasized. There is nothing in III Maccabees that requires belief in a specific historical event or set of circumstances, whether a Ptolemaic persecution or a degrading Roman revenue system, that provoked the writer to compose this work. No Ptolemaic persecution stands on record, nor were Egyptian Jews the special victims of Roman taxation. The wider subject of the Jewish situation in a Hellenistic monarchy is at issue here.

This has not deterred moderns from seeking a historical basis for the tale. The author himself encourages it. III Maccabees opens with the battle of Raphia in 217, a historical event of some magnitude, and his account overlaps considerably with that of Polybius. This includes a number of particulars concerning the battle itself, the appearance of Arsinoe to exhort the troops, and even the thwarted plot of Theodotus to assassinate the king. But discrepancies also exist, only partially accounted for by condensation, and some notable additions in III Maccabees, most strikingly the apostate Jew Dositheus, son of Drimylus, who warned Ptolemy of the plot and saved his life.[159] The author clearly went to the trouble of consulting historical sources of some substance, whether Polybius himself or another authority or both. It should be observed that Dositheus, son of Drimylus, is a real figure, known independently from papyrological evidence as a priest of the royal cult.[160] Why bother? The narrative of Raphia does form a prelude to the visit of Ptolemy to Jerusalem. But the details are immaterial to it, and indeed the visit to Jerusalem, probably itself an invention, bears hardly any relevance to the bulk of the treatise that follows, which concerns itself with persecution in Alexandria. The author evidently opened his work with a major and well known historical event, thereby to lend an air of verisimilitude to his tale. The point surely was not to deceive readers into anticipating an authentic work of history. Embellishments and embroidery take place right at the outset. The weeping and wailing of Arsinoe and the transformation of Dositheus from a priest of the dynastic family to a renegade Jew exemplify them. The latter served nicely to foreshadow the issue of Jewish apostasy which would play a critical role in the story.[161] The narrator manipulated his material with some intelligence and imagination. Raphia supplied a convenient frame.

159. The parallel narrative in Polybius is 5.79–87.

160. On Dositheus, see *CPJ*, 127; cf. A. Fuks, *JJP* 8 (1954) 205–209. Ptolemy of Megalopolis has sometimes been postulated as a source for III Maccabees here; Emmet in Charles, *Apocrypha and Pseudepigrapha*, I, 159; Bickerman, *RE* 19 (1928) 799; Anderson in Charlesworth, *Old Testament Pseudepigrapha*, II, 513. But that is no more than a guess.

161. Cf. Paul, *ANRW* II.20.1 (1987) 299–303.

The author simply placed his work of fiction within a historical context. His readers would have understood perfectly well.[162]

That understanding does not presently prevail. A version of the elephant story can be found in Josephus' *Contra Apionem*. And this has been seized upon as proof that an authentic historical incident lies behind the fable in III Maccabees. Josephus' narrative is much briefer and quite different. He sets the event not in the reign of Ptolemy IV Philopator, the later third century, but at the time of Ptolemy VIII Euergetes II Physcon, in the middle of the second century. In Josephus' account, Physcon contended for the throne against Cleopatra II and her sons, whose army was captained by the Jewish generals Onias and Dositheus. Physcon did not have the courage to face the Jewish leaders' forces and instead rounded up all the Alexandrian Jews, including women and children, in order to have them trampled by inebriated elephants. But the pachyderms turned on cue, left the intended victims unharmed, and crushed Ptolemy's friends instead. The king's repentance then followed, prompted both by a menacing vision and by the importunings of his concubine. The Jews had their deliverance, and inaugurated a festival to mark the occasion thereafter.[163] The existence of this variant version has allowed scholars both to corroborate and to undermine the authority of III Maccabees. They find in the dual accounts indication that a real event did lie behind the fable of Ptolemy's persecution and repentance, but they prefer Josephus' report as the more reliable. The shorter and more straightforward presentation would seem to suggest that Physcon's quarrel with Cleopatra led to his retaliation against Alexandrian Jews, thus supplying a historical kernel for the legend.[164]

In fact, it does nothing of the kind. Josephus' inclusion of the intoxicated elephants' scene and the addition of a fearsome divine apparition hardly lend confidence in his trustworthiness. The diverse versions (Josephus even has two different possibilities as the name of Ptolemy's concubine) show only that a folktale circulated and that it could readily be adapted for different purposes. The author of III Maccabees found a suitable villain in Ptolemy Philopator, for that individual had the reputation of possessing numerous character flaws, including self-indulgence, debauchery, timidity,

162. See the fine analysis of this segment by Johnson, *Mirror, Mirror*, 82–93.

163. Jos. *C. Apion.* 2.51–55.

164. So Emmet in Charles, *Apocrypha and Pseudepigrapha*, I, 159–60; Tcherikover, *Scripta Hierosolymitana* 7 (1961) 7–9; Collins, *Between Athens and Jerusalem*, 105; Delcor in Davies and Finkelstein, *Cambridge History of Judaism*, II, 496–97. By contrast, Motzo, *Ricerche*, 380–86, Kasher, *Jews in Hellenistic and Roman Egypt*, 213–14, and Mélèze-Modrzejewski, *Jews of Egypt*, 146–53, find greater historical validity in III Maccabees' version.

and cruelty.[165] Josephus, for his part, had good reason to set the episode in Physcon's time or, at least, to choose the variant that set it there. Prominent Jews had fought for Physcon's rival. Hence this form of the tale would advance Josephus' argument against Apion that Jews were loyal to the legitimate claimant on the Ptolemaic throne, a claim sanctioned by divine intervention.[166] But none of this gives reason to believe in any actual Ptolemaic oppression of Jews.[167] The fable perhaps arose to account for a festival which celebrated the delivery of Jews from some danger but whose origins had fallen into obscurity.[168] And the author of III Maccabees enriched it with creative fantasy.

Documentary evidence too has been called as witness to defend a historical foundation for III Maccabees. Ptolemy IV Philopator was an ardent devotee of Dionysus, a fact attested not only by hostile sources which dwell on his revelries and drunkenness, but by authoritative and contemporary testimony. Ptolemy engaged in serious efforts to promote the cult and to monitor the legitimacy of its initiates. In particular, a royal decree, preserved on papyrus, directs all those initiated into the cult to gather in Alexandria, there to make formal declaration of their receipt of the rites for three generations and then to be registered by an official of the crown.[169] The papyrus has naturally fueled speculation about its relationship with Ptolemy's edict in III Maccabees for registration of Jews and reduction of their status, a registration associated with the brand of the ivy leaf, emblematic of Dionysus.[170] For some this establishes the basic historicity of the tale in III Maccabees: an enrollment of Jews into the rites of Dionysus or use of the

165. Cf. Polyb. 5.34; Plut. *Cleom.* 33; Justin 30.1–2. See the discusson of Johnson, *Mirror, Mirror*, 94–97.

166. So, rightly, Johnson, *Mirror, Mirror*, 73–76.

167. Willrich's effort, *Hermes* 39 (1904) 244–58, to find a persecution in the reign of Ptolemy X Alexander on the basis of a report in Jordanes—which does not even speak of Ptolemaic oppression—has fortunately found few takers. See the bibliography in Parente, *Henoch* 10 (1988) 154, n. 41. A refutation by I. Levy, *HUCA* 23 (1950/1951) 127–36; cf. Johnson, *Mirror, Mirror*, 76–78. Goodman in Schürer, *History of the Jewish People*, III.1, 539, holds it as possible.

168. Cf. Bickerman, *RE* 19 (1928) 800; J. Tromp, *Henoch* 17 (1995) 315–18.

169. *BGU*, VI, 1211. Philopator's concern with the Dionysiac mysteries is recorded also by the contemporary writer Satyros who has him put the Διονυσίας at the forefront of the Alexandrian tribes; *FGH*, III.C, 631, 180–82. Other evidence on Philopator and Dionysiac celebrations in Plut. *Cleom.* 33.1, 36.4; Justin 30.1; Steph. Byz., s.v. Γάλλος.

170. III Macc. 2.28–29: πάντας δὲ τοὺς Ἰουδαίους εἰς λαογραφίαν καὶ οἰκετικὴν διάθεσιν ἀχθῆναι ... τούς τε ἀπογραφομένους χαράσσεσθαι καὶ διὰ πυρὸς εἰς τὸ σῶμα παρασήμῳ Διονύσου κισσοφύλλῳ.

brand to distinguish their status.[171] But the language of the papyrus has little in common with that of Ptolemy's decree in III Maccabees. The recording of Dionysiac devotees who could trace their involvement in the mysteries for three generations seems hardly comparable to a measure designed to humble Jews or compel their subjection to a census. The scholarly notion, now widespread, that the author of III Maccabees had access to the royal document and adapted it in some fashion to compose his text is difficult to sustain.[172] If he did so, the adaptation is very loose and free, an imaginative transformation rather than a serious reproduction. And it has little bearing on historical reality.

The same conclusion holds with regard to the letters of the king as transmitted by III Maccabees. Two of them appear in the text, lengthy and elaborate, the first decreeing the extermination of the Jews, the second, after Ptolemy's *volte-face*, ordering their restoration, denouncing their enemies, and hailing their god.[173] The prescripts and some of the formulaic vocabulary indicate an acquaintance with the style of the officialdom. But no one will confuse these compositions with genuine documents. The rhetoric of the first letter, which includes a rehearsal of previous events and a justification for the king's wrath, serves to advance the narrative, not to reproduce a decree. And the second simply declares Ptolemy's own reversal of form and new-found dedication to the Jews—something no ruler would offer to public consumption. The chancery style lent an air of authenticity to the "documents" not to delude unwary readers but to maintain the illusion of the historical framework.[174] The true parallels to these letters are not items deposited in the royal archives but the closely corresponding fabrications of Artaxerxes' two decrees in the Greek additions to Esther. Here too the destruction of the Jews is justified with rhetorical embroidery in the first edict and reversed with equal flourish in the second.[175] These were literary compositions, an understood convention. No one was deceived.

171. So, in different formulations, P. Pedrizet, *REA* 12 (1910) 217–47; Motzo, *Ricerche*, 365–71; Kasher, *Jews in Hellenistic and Roman Egypt*, 211–32; Mélèze-Modrzejewski, *Jews of Egypt*, 149–53. See the criticisms of Parente, *Enoch* 10 (1988) 154–55, 161–66.

172. The view is held, among others, by J. Moreau, *Chron.d'Égypte* 31 (1941) 118–20; Tcherikover, *Scripta Hierosolymitana* 7 (1961) 3–5; Paul, *ANRW* II.20.1 (1987) 313–17; Johnson, *Mirror, Mirror*, 97–101.

173. III Macc. 3.11–29, 7.1–9.

174. See the discussion of the letters by Johnson, *Mirror, Mirror*, 101–108.

175. Additions to Esther B and E, discussed above, pp. 179–81. The parallels have not escaped notice. See, e.g., Motzo, *Ricerche*, 285–88; C. A. Moore, *Daniel, Esther, and Jeremiah: The Additions* (New York, 1977) 195–99; Paul, *ANRW* II.20.7 (1987) 322–23. Cf. also the purported repentance of Antiochus IV before his death; II Macc. 9.11–27.

What reaction could such a treatise be expected to evoke among an audience of Hellenized Jews? On the face of it, the author underscores tension and hostility between the ruler of a Greek kingdom and his Jewish subjects. The narrative depicts a brutal and reckless king, intent upon transgressing the sanctity of the Temple and then determined to commit genocide when thwarted. The Jews of Egypt narrowly escape destruction by a last-minute providential rescue, no thanks to the Hellenistic monarch or his people. It is hardly surprising that some scholars have seen III Maccabees and the *Letter of Aristeas* as representing two sharply different viewpoints, the one composed in an atmosphere of friction and menace, thereby portraying the king as an evil monster, the other reflecting a more harmonious time, and thus conveying the image of a benign Ptolemy entirely in accord with the Jews.[176] III Maccabees, on this understanding, delivers a dark and damaging verdict on the relationship of kings and Jews.

That may not be the correct reading. III Maccabees casts Ptolemy Philopator more as irrational or deranged than fundamentally wicked, his madcap activities an aberration, a temporary interruption of an otherwise harmonious association. One might observe that the initial expectations on both sides presupposed cordiality and concord. After Raphia a delegation from Jerusalem offered greeting and congratulations, inviting a visit to the city that the king eagerly welcomed. He proceeded to offer sacrifices to the Jewish god as a contributor to his triumph and was filled with admiration for the stately appearance of the Temple.[177] This was not a man predisposed to persecute Jews. A desire to enter the inner sanctum followed naturally, perhaps indeed as an act of homage. Even when told that entrance into the Holy of Holies was prohibited, Ptolemy's first reaction was incredulity.[178] It took a thoughtless remark by some unidentified individual to provoke the king to anger.[179] The hostile confrontation at the Temple then ensued, setting the stage for the still more hostile events in Alexandria. But it is worth bearing in mind that the king, in this scenario, had no anti-Jewish proclivities and that the whole sequence of episodes was triggered by contingencies.

Nor is the initial congeniality altogether suppressed thereafter. It resurfaces during Philopator's temporary amnesia—really his moment of lucidity—when he emerges briefly from his dementia to assert solidarity with

---

176. So, e.g., Tracy, *YCS* 1 (1928) 241–52; Hadas, *HTR* 42 (1949) 175–84; Nickelsburg in Stone, *Jewish Writings*, 82–83; Barclay, *Jews in the Mediterranean Diaspora*, 201–202.

177. III Macc. 1.6–9.

178. III Macc. 1.11: ὁ δὲ οὐδαμῶς ἐπείθετο.

179. III Macc. 1.14: καί τις ἀπρονοήτως ἔφη κακῶς αὐτὸ τοῦτο τερατεύεσθαι.

the Jews. He turns on his own courtiers and threatens them with destruction, while praising the Jews for long-standing fidelity to the house of the Ptolemies.[180] In the end, of course, all is restored to its natural order. Philopator's abrupt reversal should be understood as a return to his true nature, a reinstatement of the proper relationship between ruler and ruled. The point comes home through identification of the true villains. In his second letter Ptolemy levels stern charges against those friends and advisers whose malicious calumnies had turned him against the Jews, a blameless people who had shown nothing but loyalty to the Ptolemaic crown.[181] The rationalization parallels precisely Ptolemy II's apologia for his father in the *Letter of Aristeas*. There too he explains the enslavement of Jews as the result of pressure applied by others, against the real will and good nature of Ptolemy Soter. The son set matters right—as his father would have wished.[182] The harmony that prevails at the end of III Maccabees represents the true and enduring affiliation between the monarch and his Jewish flock, only briefly disturbed by Philopator's fleeting madness.[183]

And the Jews do their part as well. So long as the king does not transgress upon the cardinal principles of their faith, their allegiance to the crown is unequivocal. The treatise repeatedly reverts to this refrain. Even when some of the more intrepid Jerusalemites prepared to take up arms in order to prevent Ptolemy's invasion of the inner sanctum, their elder and wiser compatriots persuaded them to try prayer instead. Despite desperate straits, they refrained from breaking the ties that linked them to the Hellenic overlord.[184] When enemies sought to spread rumors of sedition, the narrator affirms that the Jews maintained good will and undeviating loyalty toward the kings.[185] Ptolemy echoes that claim himself when amnesia gives him insight: Jews have been preeminent in their total allegiance to me and my ancestors.[186] After the angels of the Lord turned the tide in Alexandria and caused the king to see the light, Ptolemy reasserted the statement in the most forceful terms: the Jews have exceeded all peoples in every manner of good

180. III Macc. 5.31.

181. III Macc. 7.3–7; cf. 6.25.

182. *LetArist* 14, 23.

183. Barclay's statement, *Jews in the Mediterranean Diaspora*, 196, that "the narrative ends with an enforced truce," is seriously misleading.

184. III Macc. 1.22–23.

185. III Macc. 3.3: οἱ δὲ Ἰουδαῖοι τὴν μὲν πρὸς τοὺς βασιλεῖς εὔνοιαν καὶ πίστιν ἀδιάστροφον ἦσαν φυλάσσοντες.

186. III Macc. 5.31: ἐμοὶ καὶ προγόνοις ἐμοῖς ἀποδεδειγμένων ὁλοσχερῆ βεβαίαν πίστιν ἐξόχως Ἰουδαίων. He had made reference to Jewish trustworthiness also in his first letter; III Macc. 3.21.

will toward us from the very beginning.[187] He reiterates the same in the formal letter to his generals: steadfast good will to us and our ancestors.[188] The Jews' acknowledgment of Ptolemy's authority persists to the end. When they undertook to inflict punishment upon their own compatriots for apostasy, they asked the king's permission first—and justified the request by claiming that such backsliders could never be trustworthy adherents of the crown.[189] The theme is consistent and unmistakable.[190]

III Maccabees, in short, places its stress on concord, not antagonism. The author makes that point also, and quite strikingly, with regard to Jews and Greeks. Although the Jews had their enemies at court and malevolent people who rejoiced at their suffering, the Alexandrian Greeks themselves offered sympathy, encouragement, and even clandestine assistance.[191] Further, the subtext that one finds in the *Letter of Aristeas*, that of solidarity between Palestinian and Diaspora Jewry, can be discerned in III Maccabees as well—albeit in unhappy rather than uplifting circumstances. The retaliation sought by Ptolemy against the Jews of Egypt for an incident that occurred in Jerusalem suffices to demonstrate it. The author need not spell out that implication: it is taken for granted in the very structure of the narrative.[192]

III Maccabees belongs in a category with the other traditions discussed here that linked Jewish fortunes with the power of the Hellenistic monarchy. Allegiance to the crown as a characteristic trait of the Jews reappears with consistency in all of them. And, of course, the obeisance paid by the king to the majesty and authority of God, thus recognizing the special place of Jewish worship within the kingdom, constitutes a central feature in the tale of Ptolemy IV, as it does in the comparable legends attached to each of his predecessors beginning with Alexander. The road to concord with Philopator was a bumpier one, but the protagonists did reach their destination. The lesson of III Maccabees taught that the most trying circumstances, including even the malevolent lunacy of a ruler, should be reckoned as merely transient

187. III Macc. 6.26: τοὺς ἐξ ἀρχῆς εὐνοίᾳ πρὸς ἡμᾶς κατὰ πάντα διαφέροντας πάντων ἐθνῶν.

188. III Macc. 7.7: βεβαίαν πρὸς ἡμᾶς καὶ τοὺς προγόνους ἡμῶν εὔνοιαν.

189. III Macc. 7.11: εὐνοήσειν μηδὲ τοῖς τοῦ βασιλέως πράγμασιν.

190. Cf. the observations of Johnson, *Mirror, Mirror*, 68–69.

191. III Macc. 3.8–10: οἱ δὲ κατὰ τὴν πόλιν Ἕλληνες ... παρεκάλουν δὲ καὶ δυσφόρως εἶχον ... καί τινες ... πίστεις ἐδίδουν συνασπιεῖν καὶ πᾶν ἐκτενὲς προσοίσεσθαι πρὸς ἀντίλημψιν. On rejoicing by unidentified ἔθνη, see III Macc. 4.1.

192. A recent suggestion by D. S. Williams, *JSP* 13 (1995) 17–29, sees the text as an apologia by Egyptian Jews directed at Palestinian Jews. The theme of solidarity between the two groups is clear enough. But there is no hard evidence for criticism of Diaspora Jewry by those in Palestine which would require a defensive response.

and ephemeral. The long-term relationship was unaffected. Prosperity for the Jews still depended on a critical combination: constancy in the ancestral faith and loyalty to the regime.

The author of III Maccabees, as we have seen, manipulated his material with the best of them. And one can detect yet another dimension missed by moderns, a quality unrecognized in many Jewish-Hellenistic writers: an instinct for the comic and the absurd.[193]

His portrait of the schizophrenic king is memorable. It borders on farce and could even be adapted for the stage. Artaxerxes in Greek Esther, the ruler whose about-face rendered him ridiculous, might have supplied a model. In the Additions to Esther, Artaxerxes defended both of his contradictory positions with rhetorical bombast. Ptolemy Philopator in III Maccabees cuts a still more ludicrous figure. He reverses himself three or four times, and always with utmost conviction. His first letter already announces his own inconsistencies. In almost the same breath, Ptolemy affirms the long-standing services of Jews to the crown and declares them as harboring hostilities in every possible way.[194] He dwells on his own kindness and benevolence, while authorizing atrocities and executions of men, women, and children.[195] The author has already set Ptolemy up as someone completely oblivious to his own inconsistencies. The initial plan to crush the Jews under the weight of crazed elephants could not be carried out, however, because Philopator dropped off into a stupor from which he had to be rudely awakened. And then, forgetting that he had failed to give the order, denounced his minister Hermon for failing to carry it out[196] They tried again the following day. This time the king was awake but afflicted with total amnesia. He expressed astonishment at the preparations and once again fiercely reprimanded Hermon—only this time for planning an assault on innocent Jews who, he claimed, had shown unequivocal loyalty to the regime.[197] The complete reversal held only briefly. Another *volte-face* occurred, prompting Philopator to berate the hapless Hermon once more: "how often do I have to tell you to do the same thing, you wretch?"[198] The words, of course, are self-condemnatory, as the reader knows. The king's final flip-flop upended all that came before,

---

193. It is noted in passing by L. M. Wills, *The Jewish Novel in the Ancient World* (Ithaca, 1995) 204, but only to disparage the author. In the most recent analysis, Barclay delivers an unrelievedly dark and somber characterization of the work, *Jews in the Mediterranean Diaspora*, 192–203.

194. III Macc. 3.21, 3.24.

195. III Macc. 3.15, 3.18, 3.25.

196. III Macc. 5.10–20.

197. III Macc. 5.26–32.

198. III Macc. 5.37: ποσάκις δὲ δεῖ σοι περὶ τούτων αὐτῶν προστάττειν, ἀθλιώτατε.

exonerated the Jews, and, as usual, blamed everything on scapegoats.[199] And, despite the protests about his benevolence and fair-mindedness, Ptolemy in the end once again condemns himself out of his own mouth. At the conclusion of his letter to his generals, he acknowledges that it was not his good nature or altruism that prompted release of the Jews, but sheer terror. To act against the Jews would bring the vengeance of the Lord—inescapable, in every way, and for all time.[200] The story thus has a happy ending. But Philopator emerges less as tyrant or benefactor than as buffoon.

Comic touches recur periodically. The initial frustration of Ptolemy's plan can only be described as a burlesque. For reasons quite unfathomable, he had determined to have every Jew enrolled by scribes on a register prior to their execution. But the dutiful clerks, try as they might, could not keep up with the vast numbers who arrived for certification. Forty days went by and the lists were still far from complete. Ptolemy finally had to scrap the whole idea when his scribes reported that their sources of supply could no longer produce enough paper or pens for the purpose! It is quite remarkable that commentators have missed the humor here.[201] A sardonic element may lurk also in the report of Ptolemy's branding of Jews with the ivy leaf of Dionysus. Since the king was himself an ardent disciple of the cult and evidently sported a tattoo on his own body, the author may well have had a good joke with this episode: Ptolemy already carried the very mark of degradation that he ordered for the Jews.[202] Further, III Maccabees has some fun with the forlorn figure of Hermon, the elephant driver, repeatedly buffeted about by the king's tergiversations. Hermon's jaw must have dropped every time Ptolemy reversed himself and blamed each blunder on him. The turnabouts drove even the king's kinsmen to exasperation—without having the slightest effect upon him.[203] The author of III Maccabees may not have invented the

---

199. III Macc. 6.22–27.

200. III Macc. 7.9: γινώσκετε γὰρ ὅτι κατὰ τούτων ἐάν τι κακοτεχνήσωμεν πονηρὸν ἢ ἐπιλυπήσωμεν αὐτοὺς τὸ σύνολον, οὐκ ἄνθρωπον, ἀλλὰ τὸν πάσης δεσπόζοντα δυνάμεως θεὸν ὕψιστον ἀντικείμενον ἡμῖν ἐπ' ἐκδικήσει τῶν πραγμάτων κατὰ πᾶν ἀφεύκτως διὰ παντὸς ἕξομεν. Cf. 6.23–24.

201. III Macc. 4.20: λεγόντων μετὰ ἀποδείξεως καὶ τὴν χαρτηρίαν ἤδη καὶ τοὺς γραφικοὺς καλάμους, ἐν οἷς ἐχρῶντο, ἐκλελοιπέναι. Tcherikover, *Scripta Hierosolymitana* 7 (1961) 7, suggests that the author has mindlessly combined two traditions, one on registration of all Jews and one on elimination of a certain group in the hippodrome. This gives far too little credit to the ingenuity of the author—and overlooks the humor.

202. III Macc. 2.29. See above, n. 170. On Ptolemy's own brand, see Steph. Byz. s.v. Γάλλος; cf. Perdrizet, *REA* 12 (1910) 230–38; Emmet in Charles, *Apocrypha and Pseudepigrapha*, I, 165; Parente, *Henoch* 10 (1988) 164.

203. III Macc. 5.39–42.

idea of inebriated elephants as executioners. It appears also in Josephus'
text and perhaps represents a tale independent of both of them. But he
certainly made the most of it. By contrast with Josephus' spare account, III
Maccabees has the beasts drugged three times and brought to fever pitch
by huge quantities of unmixed wine, spiced by frankincense.[204] The vivid
image of frenzied pachyderms surely entertained the audience.

The appeal to amusement here advanced the objectives of the treatise.
Comic relief subverted the aura of foreboding and fear. By deriding the
mental powers of Ptolemy, III Maccabees rendered him less malevolent
and less menacing. The result undermined any notion of irremediable
conflict between ruler and ruled. Concord was only briefly interrupted
by the madcap activities of a befuddled monarch.

III Maccabees hardly qualifies as a sterling example of Greek literature.
But its composer merits more respect than he has generally enjoyed. The
observations above do not pretend to cover all aspects of the work.[205] One
can, however, state with confidence that it is no aberration or anomaly. The
treatise falls comfortably in the category of concocted legends designed to
express the interrelationships between Jews and Hellenistic kings and the
centrality of Jews within Hellenistic kingdoms. Its author, in fact, exercised
more imagination than most. Not only did he intimate that harmonious
relations can survive hostile confrontations and erratic rulers. He eschewed
the simple tale of wicked and cruel tyrant transformed into wise and gentle
shepherd of his flock. His king is a comic character bouncing between the
poles, a fictive caricature whose antics could draw a laugh as well as teach a
lesson. III Maccabees communicated a fundamental continuity that survived
the schemes of the wicked and restored the balance upset by the irrational.

•   •   •

Collaboration between the crown and its loyal Jewish subjects yields mutual
benefits. That recurrent theme holds central place in yet another fiction
concocted by Hellenistic Jews. The so-called "tales of the Tobiads" ostensibly
transpired in the reign of the next king of Egypt, Ptolemy V Epiphanes.
Here no issue of religious belief, holy books, conviction, faith, or divine
intervention arises at all. The story is strictly secular. But the main message
provides close parallels to the legends associated with each of the previous
monarchs.

204. III Macc. 5.2, 5.45.
205. That is no longer necessary in view of Johnson's incisive study, *Mirror, Mirror, passim.*

No need to rehearse the narrative. A summary appears above in connection with the image of the biblical Joseph which the Tobiad stories exploited and manipulated.[206] In brief, the version as transmitted by Josephus centers upon two Jewish figures, father and son, Joseph and Hyrcanus, each of whom won the favor of Ptolemy, the first becoming chief collector of revenues for the king in Coele-Syria, Phoenicia, and Judaea, the second obtaining Ptolemaic endorsement, ruling his own Transjordanian barony, and extorting income from the Arab peoples under his domain.[207] The stories, of course, encompass far more than this and raise a host of questions not relevant here. As so often, scholarly treatments devote most of their attention to the historicity or lack thereof contained in these yarns. That the Tobiads existed, a family of prominence and power in Judaea over several generations, is well known and undisputed. And various points of the tale in Josephus can be interpreted (or squeezed) to match a putative history of the Tobiads in the third and second centuries.[208] But his narrative possesses the predominant flavor of a folktale, with a host of inventions stretched over a historical framework. Many of them, as we have seen, deliberately recall the Genesis account of Joseph, his traits distributed between father and son in the Tobiad house. Here we focus upon a different aspect.

As in the legends recounted above, this Ptolemy too carries absolute and unquestioned authority over the lands and peoples within his realm— including the Jews who dwell therein. When the stingy High Priest Onias declined to provide the tribute payments due to the crown, Ptolemy's wrath was mighty indeed. A royal envoy charged Onias with insubordination and threatened wholesale expropriation of Jewish land which would then be allotted to and settled by the soldiers of the king.[209] The ascendancy of Joseph and the power wielded later by Hyrcanus derived exclusively from authorization through Ptolemy—who gave them both free rein.[210] Joseph later had to conceal his own break with Hyrcanus out of fear of the king.[211] Hyrcanus' suicide came right after the death of his patron and the accession of a rival Hellenistic monarch.[212] There is never any question that real sovereignty lay in the court. The successful Jews were the loyal ones. Joseph outmaneuvered the High Priest because the latter looked more to his own

---

206. See above, pp. 100–102.
207. Jos. *Ant.* 12.154–236.
208. See above, pp. 102–104.
209. Jos. *Ant.* 12.158–59.
210. Jos. *Ant.* 12.182: ἐφίησιν αὐτῷ ποιεῖν ὅ τι βούλεται; 12.219.
211. Jos. *Ant.* 12.221: φοβούμενος τὸν βασιλέα.
212. Jos. *Ant.* 12.236: ὁρῶν μεγάλην δύναμιν ἔχοντα τὸν Ἀντίοχον.

advantage than to the interests of the crown.[213] Joseph played the role of courtier to perfection, as did his son after him.[214]

But this was no toadyism or passive receptivity. Joseph reached high position through wit and resourcefulness, qualities which Hyrcanus too possessed in abundance. The elder Tobiad won Ptolemy's approval by wheedling and wooing his envoy and then treating Onias with patronizing disdain.[215] Hyrcanus showed comparable ingenuity, outdistancing his rivals with deceit and gaining hearty laughter from Ptolemy with barbed wit at their expense.[216] His shrewd employment of cash even allowed him to buy off would-be assassins.[217] The tales of the Tobiads deliver no lessons about Jewish religious superiority. Their orientation is relentlessly secular. Nor do they celebrate moral character. Josephus or his source pays lip service to the seriousness, intelligence, and righteousness of Joseph, the courage and understanding of Hyrcanus.[218] In fact, however, their actions are ruthless and their objectives shamelessly self-aggrandizing. The elder Tobiad extorted revenues from the king's subjects with unrestrained brutality, aiming simply at the entrenchment of his own power through the profits he raked in.[219] Hyrcanus roughed up his father's own steward to extract the cash he needed, then went on to bigger and better things by imposing heavy exactions upon Arabs and butchering or taking prisoner those who resisted.[220] The stories honored no spiritual or moral values, just practical success through superior Jewish shrewdness. Ptolemaic fortunes rested on the capabilities of Jewish stewards—who feathered their own nests while advancing the interests of the suzerain.

Ptolemy may have ultimate sovereignty. But not only does he rely on Jews. Like some of his counterparts in these legends, he is subtly mocked and derided by them. The author or authors of the Tobiad saga also shared with other Jewish-Hellenistic writers an appreciation for irony and satire.

Joseph's reputation had preceded him when he reached Alexandria. He had already charmed the king's envoy in Jerusalem. Ptolemy was totally

213. Jos. *Ant.* 12.158–66, 175–76.
214. Jos. *Ant.* 12.185, 12.200, 12.219.
215. Jos. *Ant.* 12.165–66, 12.172–73.
216. Jos. *Ant.* 12.207–12.
217. Jos. *Ant.* 12.218.
218. Jos. *Ant.* 12.160: ἐπὶ σεμνότητι δὲ καὶ προνοίᾳ δικαιοσύνης δόξαν ἔχων; 12.190: τὴν φυσικὴν ἀνδρείαν καὶ σύνεσιν; 12.224: ἀνὴρ ἀγαθὸς γενόμενος καὶ μεγαλόφρων.
219. Jos. *Ant.* 12.180–84: εἰς τὸ διαμεῖναι τὴν ὑπάρχουσαν αὐτῷ δύναμιν.
220. Jos. *Ant.* 12.204, 12.222, 12.229, 12.236.

taken in. Joseph had only to supply a witticism that both excused and disparaged Onias: he was an old man, and old men have about the same level of intelligence as infants. The king needed to hear no more; he immediately honored Joseph with signal favor at his court.[221] One might wonder in consequence about Ptolemy's own level of intelligence. The sequel reinforces that impression. In the competition for obtaining tax farming rights in Palestine, Ptolemy asked Joseph about sureties for his bid. Joseph promptly replied that he would offer the most reliable of guarantors, namely the king and queen themselves, each of whom would provide assurance of the other's share.[222] An extraordinarily arrogant statement, quite inconceivable in fact, of course. Ptolemy, however, greeted it with laughter and approval, and awarded the tax contract to Joseph on the spot, without requiring any security.[223] The author plainly portrayed Ptolemy as a pliable simpleton, ready to applaud anything Joseph said or did—rather like Ptolemy Philadelphus in the *Letter of Aristeas* who was mightily impressed by every comment made by a Jew at his banquet.

The king had become no smarter by the time Hyrcanus reached his court. When the young Tobiad was questioned about the severe treatment he had meted out to his steward, he too had a quick retort: masters have to punish recalcitrant slaves lest they be held in contempt by them—a principle that the king too would do well to heed.[224] Unsolicited and uppity advice of that sort would hardly be welcomed by rulers. But the docile and amiable Ptolemy, as usual, simply laughed admiringly.[225] Hyrcanus' joke at the expense of his rivals at the king's banquet, not an especially witty or clever one, nevertheless induced Ptolemy both to applaud his acumen and to order all others to applaud it![226] The whole fable of the contest for Ptolemy's favor through competing gifts presupposes that he would be most impressed by the most lavish presents. And indeed Hyrcanus wins the competition by the rather vulgar presentation of two hundred young boys and virgins each carrying

---

221. Jos. *Ant.* 12.171–74.

222. Jos. *Ant.* 12.177–78: ὦ βασιλεῦ, σέ τε καὶ τὴν γυναῖκα τὴν σὴν ὑπὲρ ἑκατέρου μέρους ἐγγυησομένους δίδωμί σοι.

223. Jos. *Ant.* 12.178.

224. Jos. *Ant.* 12.207: ἂν οὖν μὴ κολάζωμεν τοὺς τοιούτους, καὶ σὺ προσδόκα ὑπὸ τῶν ἀρχομένων καταφρονηθήσεσθαι.

225. Jos. *Ant.* 12.207. There is sly irony also in the steward's rebuke of Hyrcanus that prompted his punishment. He contrasted Hyrcanus' reckless extravagance with Joseph's great self-restraint; 12.203. But the latter quality had hardly been evident in Joseph's career as presented by the narrator himself.

226. Jos. *Ant.* 12.213–14.

a talent for the rulers. Ptolemy was completely won over by this crass display and promised Hyrcanus anything his heart desired.[227]

No monarch of Egypt could ever have heard the tales of the Tobiads with pleasure. But they were not intended for his ears. Canny Jews composed this narrative, employing a historical frame but freely recasting it for circulation among themselves. The setting and objectives strongly suggest a creation in the Jewish community of Alexandria in the late Ptolemaic era.[228] The cynical cast and strictly secular character of the narrative give it a somewhat different flavor from those centered upon the previous Ptolemies and Alexander before them. But kindred ideas recur. The authors affirm Jewish allegiance to the throne and recognize the advantages of collaborating with royal authority. And there is an additional, perhaps more central, message. The undertones of these texts leave the implication that the (often mediocre) occupants of the throne depend on Jewish wit for their achievements or the Jewish faith for their success.

· · ·

A final episode warrants brief notice. It occurred, if Josephus be believed, in the reign of Ptolemy VI Philometor, i.e., between 181 and 145 BCE. The text recounts a quarrel between Jews and Samaritans dwelling in Alexandria. The parties claimed legitimacy for their own temples, the Jews for Jerusalem, the Samaritans for Mt. Gerizim, each tracing authority from the laws of Moses. The dispute was submitted for resolution to the tribunal of Ptolemy himself, sitting in state with his φίλοι. His decision would not only award victory to the spokesmen of one party but render a death verdict to those of the other. Once the king's counselors had assembled in impressive numbers, the Alexandrian Jews began to panic lest their temple be subject to destruction. But the Samaritans allowed Andronicus, the Jewish representative, to deliver the opening speech. He swiftly marshaled evidence from Mosaic law, the unbroken sequence of High Priests in Jerusalem, and

227. Jos. *Ant.* 12.217–19.

228. The notion of a "Tobiad chronicle" as responsible for the tales does not account for the folktale elements and the fictive inventions in the narrative. Too much of the modern discussion focuses on Josephus' putative source and its hypothetical propaganda purposes. See, especially, Tcherikover, *Hellenistic Civilization and the Jews*, 140–42; M. Stern, *Tarbiz* 32 (1962) 36–40 (Hebrew); Hengel, *Judaism and Hellenism*, I, 269–70; Goldstein in J. Neusner, *Christianity, Judaism, and Other Greco-Roman Cults* (Leiden, 1975) III, 104–16 (to be read with great caution). The best analysis is that of D. Gera in A. Kasher, U. Rappaport, and G. Fuks, *Greece and Rome in Eretz Israel* (Jersualem, 1990) 35–38.

the lavish gifts bestowed upon the Jewish temple by Asian kings over the ages—by contrast with Mt. Gerizim which could boast nothing of the sort. Andronicus' arguments were compelling. The Samaritans never even got a say. Philometor found for the Jews, declared their temple to be in accord with Moses' laws, and passed a death sentence upon the Samaritans.[229] Josephus, it appears, alludes to this episode on an earlier occasion as well. When speaking of Jewish migration to Egypt in the time of Ptolemy Philadelphus, he notes that their descendants would engage in disputes with Samaritans over which temple was the sacred one and thus the proper recipient of sacrifices.[230]

The event receives little attention in the literature. And, when noted, its historicity is normally taken for granted.[231] Yet the story contains peculiarities, implausibilities, and transparent fictions. The very notion of a contest between Jews and Samaritans, in which the latter are worsted, immediately arouses suspicion. The tale fits into an ongoing polemic against Samaritans that surfaces more than once in Josephus' text.[232] And the particulars of the narrative increase misgivings. Why would squabbling Jews and Samaritans turn to Ptolemy to determine the sanctity of their respective temples in Palestine? Why should he waste his time, let alone summon a huge gathering of counselors, to hear arguments on the relative merits of shrines in Palestine? What information would he have or criteria could he apply to render a verdict? Indeed, why should he wish to offend one ethnic group or the other within Alexandria, thereby causing himself unnecessary trouble? And, assuming that he did agree to pass judgment, what implementation would there be? Would the losing party abandon its temple and honor the other? Would Ptolemy enforce his decision and raze the temple of the defeated claimant—in a land that he did not control? The absurdities mount. That Ptolemy could determine (or care) which of the temples more closely

229. Jos. *Ant.* 13.74–79.

230. Jos. *Ant.* 12.9–10. There is no reason to see this as reference to a different quarrel in the time of Philadelphus. Josephus refers explicitly to τοῖς ἐκγόνοις αὐτῶν. So, rightly, Kippenberg, *Garizim und Synagoge*, 66–67; Fraser, *Ptolemaic Alexandria*, II, 446; Egger, *Josephus*, 234–36.

231. So, e.g., Gaster, *Samaritans*, 118–19; Momigliano, *Athenaeum* 57 (1979) 445; Egger, *Josephus*, 95–101; Purvis in Davies and Finkelstein, *Cambridge History of Judaism*, II, 602; A. Kasher in M. Mor, *Eretz Israel, Israel, and the Jewish Diaspora: Mutual Relations* (Lanham, 1991) 25, 31; Goldstein, *Proceedings of the American Academy for Jewish Research* 59 (1993) 83.

232. Motzo, *Ricerche*, 645–71, finds a priestly anti-Samaritan source behind several stories in Josephus. On Josephus' attitude toward Samaritans, see Egger, *Josephus, passim*, with bibliography. A brief treatment by R. J. Coggins in L. H. Feldman and G. Hata, *Josephus, Judaism, and Christianity* (Detroit, 1987) 257–73.

conformed to Mosaic law strains credulity. And the more closely one looks at specifics, the odder they become. The two parties jointly take the initiative to seek Ptolemaic arbitration. But when he accepts the job, the Alexandrian Jews suddenly fear for the destruction of their temple—an outcome that had not even been hinted at before.[233] Spokesmen are chosen for both sides, but only the Jew speaks. The Samaritans generously let their opponent make the first address. And then they found themselves forthwith executed without the opportunity for a rebuttal.[234] Indeed, the very idea of a contest agreed upon by contestants in which the loser forfeits his life has far more to do with folktale motifs than with historical reality.[235]

The episode is best understood as creative fiction. That it plays a part in presumed polemics against Samaritans seems clear enough on the face of it. But to concentrate on that aspect may misplace the emphasis. The implications of the narrative have affinities with other tales told of Jews and kings. Josephus' presentation seems cramped and abbreviated. He took what he wished for the purposes of his history, in this context a resumé of the Jewish experience in Egypt under Ptolemy Philometor. The arbitration is juxtaposed with an account of the self-exiled Onias IV gaining Ptolemy's permission for the temple in Leontopolis.[236] But the original story available to Josephus or his source may have been considerably more elaborate—and more interesting. One can readily imagine the preliminaries which set up this *Wettstreit*, the rivalry between Jewish and Samaritan representatives in Alexandria, the willingness of both sides to lay their lives on the line, the ceremonial features of the royal tribunal with its numerous advisers and attendants of the king, the rhetoric employed by the Jewish spokesman, the outmaneuvering of the Samaritan contestants, and the solemn pronouncements of Ptolemy VI.

233. Jos. *Ant.* 13.77: οἱ δ᾽ ἐν τῇ Ἀλεξανδρείᾳ τυγχάνοντες Ἰουδαῖοί σφόδρα ἠγωνίων ... χαλεπῶς γὰρ ἔφερον εἰ τοῦτό τινες καταλύσουσιν.

234. Jos. *Ant.* 13.78-79.

235. Cf. the Bel and Dragon episode in the Greek additions to Daniel. Scholars have done their best to rewrite the story so as to make it approximate reality. So, for instance, A. Büchler, *Die Tobiaden und die Oniaden* (Vienna, 1899) 248-63, supposes that the quarrel concerned Jewish and Samaritan temples in Egypt rather than in Palestine—in direct contradiction to Josephus' own text. Egger, *Josephus*, 99-100, connects the arbitration with Ptolemy's putative desire to establish that Jews and Samaritans in Alexandria owed allegiance to Palestinian temples rather than to the shrine in Leontopolis—as if Ptolemy took the intiative in this affair. For Gaster, *Samaritans*, 34-35, 118-19, the argument concerned competing translations of the Scriptures, not the temples at all—a purely imaginary construct.

236. Jos. *Ant.* 13.62-79. Note, in particular, 13.79: καὶ τὰ μὲν γενόμενα τοῖς ἐν Ἀλεξανδρείᾳ Ἰουδαίοις κατὰ Πτολεμαῖον τὸν Φιλομήτορα ταῦτα ἦν.

The sober source of Josephus stripped the story of its real vigor, leaving a rather dull residue. But the kernel remains. Ptolemy is the final arbiter, his verdict decisive. And that verdict not only sanctions Jewish ascendancy over rivals in Alexandria but acknowledges the authority of their temple in Jerusalem. One might note the argument of Andronicus on which the narrative lays greatest stress. He claimed that all the kings of Asia regularly honored the Jerusalem temple with dedications and lavish gifts while paying not the slightest attention to Mt. Gerizim.[237] That apparently was enough to convince Philometor that the Jewish shrine conformed to the laws of Moses![238] Mutual deference underlies this story—like all the rest. The Jews rely on Hellenistic rulers for certification. And the rulers in turn recognize the august quality of the faith. That concept of reciprocity—not synthesis, syncretism, or assimilation—holds central place in tale after tale.

•   •   •

Jewish literary imagination found a fertile field in discussing the deeds—and the foibles—of Hellenistic sovereigns. A lengthy tradition lay behind it. The "Jew at court" motif had a solid pedigree, exemplified in Daniel, the Book of Esther, and stretching back, of course, to Joseph in Genesis. But the later Hellenistic tales go well beyond this hackneyed theme. They exhibit the concerns and reflections of Jewish communities within the dominions of absolute rulers and in the setting of a Greek cultural environment. Adjustment to those circumstances stimulated a rash of fictive tales. But more than adjustment was at stake. Jewish writers helped to build the confidence of their fellow Jews with a series of stories that gave their religion, their holy books, and their special shrewdness privileged positions within the councils of the realm. And they did so very often with a brand of humor that promoted the longevity of the legends.

Alexander the Great offered an irresistible subject. The invention of his visit to Jerusalem allowed Jews to capitalize on his charisma. The fountainhead of Hellenistic monarchy himself discovered the source of his power in Jewish prophecy and the favor of Jehovah. The very conquest of the Persian empire was sanctioned in Jerusalem, and the mighty conqueror paid due homage to the Temple, its priests, and its divinity. Alexander further

---

237. Jos. *Ant.* 13.78: πάντες οἱ τῆς Ἀσίας βασιλεῖς τὸ ἱερὸν ἐτίμησαν ἀναθήμασιν καὶ λαμπροτάταις δωρεαῖς. Cf. II Macc. 3.2.

238. Jos. *Ant.* 13.79: πείθει τὸν βασιλέα κρῖναι μὲν κατὰ τοὺς Μωυσέος νόμους οἰκοδομηθῆναι τὸ ἐν Ἱεροσολύμοις ἱερόν.

accorded privileges and enlisted Jews in his armies—thereby giving them a role at the outset in the creation of Hellenistic imperialism itself. The concocters of these tales had more than just amusement in mind.

The surviving evidence is limited and one-sided. Most of the extant tales seem to have stemmed from Alexandrian Jews, thus fastening upon the personalities of the Ptolemies. Stories sprang up about each of the first six Greek rulers of Egypt and their encounters with Jews under their aegis. The imbalance may not be fortuitous. To celebrate the sovereignty of Seleucids would be awkward for Jews in the Hasmonaean era. And Jewish communities were perhaps not sufficiently sizable or developed to produce a comparable output in the dominions of the Antigonids or the dynasts of Asia Minor.[239] The voices from Alexandria alone, however, have resonant force. They elevate the exploits of Jewish soldiers in the time of Ptolemy I, they have Jewish scholars awe Ptolemy II, they place Ptolemy III in Jerusalem emulating the homage paid by Alexander the Great, they record divine intervention that transforms the bizarre Ptolemy IV into a proponent of Jewish values, they tie the financial fortunes of Ptolemy V to the guidance of Jewish counselors, and they credit Ptolemy VI with a decision that authenticates the sanctity of the Temple in Jerusalem.

Key themes run through the testimony. Jewish loyalty to the regime receives repeated emphasis. None of the texts is subversive; far from it. They orient the reader toward the acknowledgment of monarchic power and the benefits it can bestow. Loyal Jews became part of Ptolemy Soter's military establishment, enjoyed respect and honor from Philadelphus, gained public endorsement for long-standing allegiance by the reformed Philopator, and actively pursued Ptolemaic interests, as well as their own, under Epiphanes. The actions in no way denote docile compliance. Jews hold firmly to their own convictions, without compromise or assimilation. The point is made unequivocally by Jews who resisted Alexander's demand that they rebuild the temple of Bel, by the High Priest Eleazer who underscored Jewish distinctiveness in the time of Ptolemy II, and by the triumphant Jews who gained Ptolemy IV's permission to execute their own renegades. Superior Jewish character, intelligence, and beliefs constitute recurrent refrains, from the canny pragmatism of the archer Mosollamos or the Tobiad financiers to the noble presence of Eleazer, the unshaken faith of Jews in the hippodrome,

---

239. Evidence for Jews in Asia Minor during the Hellenistic period is frustratingly slim, although there certainly were important Jewish communities in some of the cities. See the testimony and discussion by P. Trebilco, *Jewish Communities in Asia Minor* (Cambridge, 1991) 5–36.

and the rhetorical skill of the advocate Andronicus. Such legends would boost the self-esteem of Jewish readers in a precarious diaspora.

The sense of superiority emerged also in another feature of the fables. The authors eschewed somberness or solemnity. Comic touches enlivened the narratives and confirmed the advantages of being Jewish. They come in every variety and every context. One need mention only Mosollamos' decisive exposure of Greek seers, the outstripping of Hellenic philosophers by Jewish elders or of rival tax gatherers and courtiers by the Tobiads, and the succession of naive, gullible, or absurd rulers of Egypt from the pliable Philadelphus and Epiphanes to the doltish Philopator. The monarchs were no mere playthings of God, either agents or victims of divine power. They held authority and exercised it. The subordinate and dependent status of the Jews is unequivocal. Absence of power, however, did not drive them to consolation, let alone lamentation. The pen provided an active and positive mode of expression. Anecdotes that poked fun at the kings' foibles and mocked their mental acuity called attention to the craft, wit, and ascendant cultural values that distinguished the Jews from their political masters.

Consistent themes and reiterated lessons predominate. They transcend attempts to tie these tales to particular episodes, special circumstances, or narrow political motivation. They represent efforts by Jewish intellectuals to shore up the self-assurance of their people in a cultural world not of their own making. The legends give prominence to Jewish values and character. But, for the most part, they avoid sermons and preaching. Their authors spiced the narratives with levity and irony. The imaginative and occasionally light-hearted recreations of Hellenistic history accorded readers pride in Jewish heritage—and also some amusement in the reinvention of that heritage.

CHAPTER 7

Pride and Precedence

The pride of Jews in the precedence of their character, creed, and accomplishments sustained them through this era. Adjustment to the Hellenistic world expressed itself not as accommodation but as reaffirmation of their own lustrous legacy. A multiplicity of modes and an abundance of ingenuity marked the process. Jews, as we have seen, recast biblical tales and rewrote history in order both to embellish antique traditions and to elevate their place within the recent past. But that represents just a part of what they did. Their inventiveness found a still greater variety of means whereby to broadcast associations with Hellenic culture and society while underscoring Jewish superiority. A select and diverse sample can illustrate the range of creative activity on this score.

A favored fiction involved the derivation of Greek ideas from Jewish roots. Among purveyors of this notion a certain Aristobulus occupies a principal place. A mere handful of fragments survive, and the identification of Aristobulus himself is disputed. But his emphasis on Jewish priority in concepts later conveyed by Greeks is plain enough. Clement of Alexandria picked up the notion and cited Aristobulus for confirmation.[1] Clement and Eusebius preserve the extant fragments which, whatever their origins, leave little doubt about their meaning.[2]

The name Aristobulus appears as addressee of a purported letter sent by Judas Maccabaeus ca. 164 BCE and attached to the text of II Maccabees. There he is identified as belonging to a family of anointed Jewish priests and

---

1. Clement *Strom.* 1.15.72.4, 5.14.97.7.

2. A new edition of the fragments, with translation, thorough notes, and comprehensive bibliography, has now been produced by C. R. Holladay, *Fragments from Hellenistic Jewish Authors: Volume III: Aristobulus* (Atlanta, 1995) thus obviating the need for any extensive treatment.

serving as teacher to king Ptolemy of Egypt. Clement never questioned the authenticity of the letter and reckoned Aristobulus as tutor to Ptolemy VI Philometor in the mid second century.[3] The accuracy of that conclusion can be and has been questioned. But whether or not Aristobulus actually worked at the court in Alexandria, no good reason exists to deny him a Hellenistic date. He was clearly a Hellenized Jew conversant with Greek philosophical and literary traditions and eager to establish Jewish precedents for many of those traditions.[4] The form of his work itself cannot be determined with certainty. It seems to have consisted of a commentary, or extended exegetical remarks, on the Torah, perhaps structured as a dialogue between author and king. Whatever the form, Aristobulus wrote at great length, a fact no longer reflected in the meager remains.[5] And he devoted at least a portion of his study to establishing the claims of the Bible as a source for the Greek intellectual achievement.

In Aristobulus' construct, Moses provides stimulus for Hellenic philosophers and poets.[6] But this is not the Moses of Eupolemus or Artapanus, the active conveyor of culture to other peoples, the inventor or transmitter of letters, poetry, and technology. The contribution of Aristobulus' Moses is the Torah, the law code of the Israelites, from which others would find

3. II Macc. 1.10; Clement *Strom.* 1.22.150.1, 5.14.97.7; Euseb. *PE* 8.9.38. For Eusebius, *Chron.* Ol. 151, Aristobulus wrote commentaries on Moses addressed to Ptolemy Philometor. A full list of testimonia on Aristobulus is compiled by Holladay, *Fragments*, III, 114–26.

4. The case was argued most fully and persuasively by N. Walter, *Der Thoraausleger Aristobulos* (Berlin, 1964) 35–123, followed in the main by subsequent scholars. The lengthy and tedious scholarly debate is summarized by Holladay, *Fragments*, III, 49–75, with moderate and sane conclusions. See also the remarks of D. Winston, *Studia Philonica Annual* 8 (1996) 155–60. Among the more valuable recent contributions, see Y. Gutman, *The Beginnings of Jewish-Hellenistic Literature*, 2 vols. (Jerusalem, 1958, 1963), I, 186–220 (Hebrew); A.-M. Denis, *Introduction aux Pseudépigraphes grecs d'ancien testament* (Leiden, 1970) 277–83; P. M. Fraser, *Ptolemaic Alexandria* (Oxford, 1972) I, 694–96; II, 963–70; M. Hengel, *Judaism and Hellenism* (London, 1974) I, 163–69; II, 105–10; N. Walter, *Jüdische Schriften aus hellenistisch-römischer Zeit* (Gütersloh, 1980) III.2, 261–79; J. J. Collins, *Between Athens and Jerusalem* (New York, 1983) 175–78; A. Y. Collins in J. H. Charlesworth, *Old Testament Pseudepigrapha* (Garden City, 1985) II, 831–42; M. Goodman in E. Schürer, *The History of the Jewish People in the Age of Jesus Christ*, rev. ed. by G. Vermes, F. Millar, and M. Goodman (Edinburgh, 1986) III.1, 579–87; J. M. G. Barclay, *Jews in the Mediterranean Diaspora* (Edinburgh, 1996) 150–58. That Aristobulus was a Jew is obvious from several of the fragments; e.g. Euseb. *PE* 8.10.3, 13.12.11, 13.12.13. That he was an Alexandrian is not quite so obvious as most scholars would have it.

5. For the work as commentary, see Euseb. *PE* 7.13.7; *Chron.* Ol. 151; *PE* 7.32.16. On its size, Clement *Strom.* 5.14.97.7. The dialogue form may be indicated by Euseb. *PE* 8.10.7, 13.12.2. Cf. Holladay, *Fragments*, III, 74, 92–94.

6. Euseb. *PE* 8.10.4: φιλόσοφοι καὶ ... ποιηταὶ παρ' αὐτοῦ μεγάλας ἀφορμὰς εἰληφότες.

inspiration. Aristobulus asserted that Plato's ideas followed the path laid out by the legislation of Moses, indeed that he was assiduous in working through every particular contained in it.[7] And he cited an earlier case still, an equally distinguished name, the sixth century philosopher Pythagoras, who also found much in the Hebrew teachings which he could adapt for his own doctrines.[8] The chronology created a problem. How would these Greek sages have had access to the Hebrew Scriptures generations or centuries before the Septuagint? Aristobulus had no qualms about fabricating one fiction to save another. He reassures potential skeptics by maintaining that translations of the Israelite escape from Egypt, conquest and settlement of the new land, and all the details of the law code were available long before the composition of the Septuagint.[9] This, of course, was transparent invention, a necessary adjunct to preserve his thesis—and perhaps taken more seriously by some moderns than by his ancient readership.

Another fragment of Aristobulus expands upon this construct. He includes Socrates with Pythagoras and Plato among those whose reference to a divine voice in contemplating the creation of the cosmos derives from the words of Moses.[10] Nor does he rest content here. Aristobulus offers a broadly embracing doctrine that sweeps all of Greek philosophy within the Jewish orbit. He affirms universal agreement among philosophers that only pious opinions must be held about God. And that view, of course, appears preeminently in the Jewish way of thinking, embedded in Mosaic law framed to promote piety, righteousness, self-control, and all the other virtues consonant with truth.[11] It would follow, therefore, that Jewish conceptualizing supplied the wellspring for Hellenic philosophizing.

Aristobulus extended the reach of the Jews from philosophy to poetry. And he ranged unhesitatingly between the mythological and the near contemporary. He conjures up Orpheus, the legendary singer and source of Greek poetics. By interpreting his supposed verses on God as all-encompassing power, origin of life, and supreme being in light of Jewish precepts, Aristobulus could claim the father of Hellenic song as well for the camp of Moses'

---

7. Euseb. *PE* 13.12.1: κατηκολούθησεν ὁ Πλάτων τῇ καθ' ἡμᾶς νομοθεσίᾳ καὶ φανερός ἐστι περιειργασμένος ἕκαστα τῶν ἐν αὐτῇ; Clement *Strom.* 1.22.150.1.

8. Euseb. *PE* 13.12.1: Πυθαγόρας πολλὰ τῶν παρ' ἡμῖν μετενέγκας εἰς τὴν ἑαυτοῦ δογματοποιίαν κατεχώρισεν; Clement *Strom.* 1.22.150.3. Cf. Jos. *C. Apion.* 1.165.

9. Euseb. *PE* 13.12.1; Clement *Strom.* 1.22.150.2. Gutman, *Beginnings*, I, 189–92 (Hebrew), argues, unconvincingly, for the validity of Aristobulus' claim.

10. Euseb. *PE* 13.12.3–4; Clement *Strom.* 5.14.99.3.

11. Euseb. *PE* 13.12.8. Cf. Gutman, *Beginnings*, I, 192–99 (Hebrew).

followers.[12] With equal dexterity, he brings matters up to date by quoting the Hellenistic poet Aratus of Soli, finding suitable material in the opening lines of his great astronomical poem, the *Phaenomena*. Through the simple substitution of "God" for "Zeus" in those lines, Aristobulus transformed Aratus' paean to Zeus into a pantheistic hymn for the Jewish deity.[13]

The inventive writer took a still further step. He either fabricated or (more likely) adapted and reproduced a full-scale monotheistic poem which he credited to Orpheus himself. The extant text survives in multiple recensions, a nightmare for moderns seeking to reconstruct its stemma and odyssey. The version followed here appears in Eusebius, who claims to have found it in the work of Aristobulus. It takes the form of advice rendered by the mythical Orpheus to his son and star pupil Musaeus. In effect, the ancient bard counseled his son to abandon previous (presumably polytheistic) beliefs, to look to the divine word, and to contemplate the immortal creator of the universe. He characterizes the divinity as complete in himself but completer of all things, in which he roams everywhere, though visible only to the mind not to the eye, the sole god, none other beside him, entrenched on a golden throne in high heaven with earth at his feet, his power extending to the ends of the ocean, causing the mountains and the depths of the sea to tremble.[14] Whether the rendition preserved by Eusebius actually represents that of Aristobulus has been disputed. A shorter version of the Orphic poem, perhaps an earlier one, exists in two works attributed to Justin Martyr, and still other variants are cited in scattered fashion by Clement and contained in later authorities. The text transmitted by Aristobulus cannot be determined with certainty.[15] But no matter. The monotheistic vision of the awesome deity, delivered by the ancestor of pagan poets, certainly originated in the mental world of Hellenistic Judaism. Whether Aristobulus or some compatriot conceived them, certain striking verses in the Orphic hymn illuminate the core of this mental world. The poet asserts that God appears in a cloud that obscures him from mortal vision; even Orpheus'

12. Euseb. *PE* 13.12.4.

13. Euseb. *PE* 13.12.6–7; cf. Clement *Strom.* 5.14.101.4b.

14. Euseb. *PE* 13.12.5. Text, apparatus, and translation in Holladay, *Fragments*, III, 165–71.

15. Walter, *Der Thoraausleger*, 103–15, 202–61, argued at length that Aristobulus quoted an Orphic poem altogether different from that in the Eusebian recension, an extreme position that has not carried the day. On the tangled question of the different versions and their possible interrelations, see, e.g., Collins, *Between Athens and Jerusalem*, 204–207; M. Lafargue in Charlesworth, *Old Testament Pseudepigrapha*, II, 795–97; Goodman in Schürer, *History of the Jewish People*, III.2, 661–67. The whole subject is reassessed now by Holladay, whose exhaustive study of the fragments, sources, and scholarship will be the starting point for all future work; *Fragments from Hellenistic Jewish Authors, Vol. IV: Orphica* (Atlanta, 1996).

perception is blurred, that of other men ten times dimmer still. Just a single individual had the privilege of perceiving God, namely the man of the Chaldean race, whose insights pierced the mysteries of the stars and the movements of the heavenly sphere. The reference is almost certainly to Abraham.[16] In short, even the progenitor of Hellenic song, who sets himself apart from the rest of mankind, must ultimately give the palm to the Hebrew patriarch. Not only does Orpheus hymn the majesty of the sole god, he also acknowledges the precedence of the Chosen People.[17]

Numerology could be manipulated for similar ends. Aristobulus shrewdly fastened upon the mystical number seven to link Jewish precepts to the greatest of Greek poets. He associates the institution of the Sabbath as enjoined by Genesis with a universal principle emblematized by the number seven.[18] And he summons up the verses of Homer and Hesiod to affirm that Greek epic poetry endorsed the biblical sanctification of the holy day. Here Aristobulus or his Jewish source exercised special liberties in twisting the texts to his will. Hesiod's reference to a seventh day of the month became the seventh day of the week and a Homeric allusion to the "fourth day" was transformed through emendation to the "seventh day." Other lines quoted by Aristobulus but not attested in the extant texts of Homer and Hesiod may also have been tampered with or simply invented.[19] The subtle—or not so subtle—reworking had Homer and Hesiod acknowledge the consecration of the Sabbath. From the vantage point of Aristobulus it was all in a good cause: to demonstrate the dependence of Greece's most ancient bards upon the teachings of the Torah. And if their antiquity did not suffice as authority, Aristobulus could call up a legendary figure, the shadowy Linus, variously

16. Euseb. *PE* 13.12.5: αὐτὸν δ' οὐχ ὁρόω· περὶ γὰρ νέφος ἐστήρικται λοιπὸν ἐμοί· 'στᾶσιν δὲ δεκάπτυχον ἀνθρώποισιν. οὐ γάρ κέν τις ἴδοι θνητῶν μερόπων κραίνοντα, εἰ μὴ μουνογενής τις ἀπορρὼξ φύλου ἄνωθεν Χαλδαίων· ἴδρις γὰρ ἔην ἄστροιο πορείης καὶ σφαίρης κίνημ' ἀμφὶ χθόνα ὡς περιτέλλει κυκλοτερές τ' ἐν ἴσῳ, κατὰ δὲ σφέτερον κνώδακα. That the man "of Chaldean race" might be Moses, on the basis of Philo *Moses* 1.5, is much less likely. The identification with Abraham is made explicitly by Clement *Strom.* 5.14.123.

17. Subsequent lines in the Eusebian recension make clear reference to Moses as well, the man "born in the water" and recipient of the law in double tablets; Euseb. *PE* 13.12.5. These lines, however, do not appear in Clement and may not have been in Aristobulus' version; cf. Walter, *Der Thoraausleger*, 108–15, 221–22, 237–39. But this need not preclude a Hellenistic date; see Goodman in Schürer, *History of the Jewish People*, III.1, 665–66.

18. Euseb. *PE* 13.12.12. On the philosophical underpinnings of this notion, see Gutman, *Beginnings*, I, 203–10 (Hebrew); Walter, *Der Thoraausleger*, 68–81; Holladay, *Fragments*, III, 230–32.

19. Euseb. *PE* 13.12.13–15; Clement *Strom.* 5.14.107.1–3. See the careful discussion of Walter, *Der Thoraausleger*, 150–58, with reference to the relevant Homeric and Hesiodic lines; cf. Gutman, *Beginnings*, I, 210–12 (Hebrew); Holladay, *Fragments*, III, 234–37.

identified as son of Apollo or music master of Heracles. The verses attributed to him here bear all the marks of Jewish creation or adaptation. Linus is made to proclaim that all things were completed on the seventh day, a day most auspicious of all and a number most perfect of all.[20] Observance of the Sabbath, in short, was no mere idiosyncrasy of an alien and self-segregated sect, but a principle cherished in Hellenic poetry. Aristobulus thereby harnessed some of the most celebrated Greek thinkers and artists, real or legendary, to the antique traditions of the Jews.

Aristobulus himself remains an obscure personage, more discussed and debated by moderns than noticed by the ancients. Clement designated him as a "Peripatetic," but the surviving fragments show little influence of the Aristotelian school. Researchers have strained to detect other philosophical traces in the work, notably Stoicism and Pythagoreanism, even a touch of Cynicism.[21] That issue can here be left aside. Familiarity with certain philosophical concepts, often arguably superficial, does not make Aristobulus a philosopher. It has been argued indeed that he aimed not to establish the priority of Jewish wisdom but to employ the allegorical method in explaining the Scriptures to Hellenic or hellenized intellectuals.[22] Speculation on Aristobulus' main motive, however, is unprofitable and unnecessary. The scantiness of the extant fragments precludes any confidence. What matters is the fact that his writings took part in a broader Jewish enterprise that declared the dependence of distinctive Greek thought on the Torah. Manipulation of texts and even forgery of verses could serve that end. If Homer gained inspiration from the Bible and Plato plagiarized Moses, the Jews had good reason for pride in their heritage.

In this venture Aristobulus was by no means alone. Jewish intellectuals ransacked the texts of Greek drama, chasing after verses that might suggest Hellenic borrowing from Hebraic ideas. And when they did not find appropriate lines, they simply manufactured them. Concepts with Jewish resonance were ascribed to the great tragedians Aeschylus, Sophocles, and Euripides, and to the comic poets Menander, Philemon, and Diphilus. The sources of these selective, doctored, or fabricated lines can no longer be traced. They are preserved now in the Church Fathers, in Clement, Eusebius,

---

20. Euseb. *PE* 13.12.16: Λίνος δέ φησιν οὕτως· ἑβδομάτη δ᾽ ἠοῖ τετελεσμένα πάντα τέτυκται. See Walter, *Der Thoraausleger*, 158–66; Hengel, *Judaism and Hellenism*, I, 166–67; Holladay, *Fragments*, III, 237–40. Clement *Strom.* 5.14.107.4, less plausibly, attributes the fragment to Callimachus.

21. Clement *Strom.* 1.15.72.4; cf. Denis *Introduction*, 281; Walter *Jüdische Schriften*, III.2, 262–63; Holladay, *Fragments*, III, 72–73; a more skeptical line by Fraser, *Ptolemaic Alexandria*, I, 694–95.

22. Walter, *Der Thoraausleger*, 26–31, 43–45; *Jüdische Schriften*, III.2, 263–64.

and two treatises erroneously assigned to Justin Martyr. But they plainly derive from a collection or collections of passages from Greek dramatists put together by Jewish compilers.[23]

Thunderous verses allegedly composed by Aeschylus exalt the authority of God. The great tragedian warns mortals to acknowledge his splendor and to recognize his presence in every manifestation of nature, an omnipotence that can shake the earth, the mountains, and the depths of the sea: "The glory of the highest god is all-powerful."[24] Such sentiments, whether authentic Aeschylus or not, would certainly play into Jewish hands. Sophocles too was exploited for similar purposes. Three separate fragments with suitable theological pronouncements survive through patristic sources. Sophocles trumpeted the unity and uniqueness of the Lord, rebuking mortals who installed graven images of bronze, stone, gold, or ivory.[25] He even supplied an eschatological text that forecast the destruction of the universe in an all-consuming flame to issue in the salvation of the righteous.[26] The third fragment, purely pagan and possibly genuine, speaks of Zeus' philandering in mortal guise, probably cited as contrast with the loftier morality of the Jewish divinity.[27] Euripides too served to advance the cause. A passage assigned to him by Clement asserts that no dwelling fashioned by mortal hands can contain the spirit of God, and another characterizes God as one who sees all but who is himself invisible.[28] These concocted lines—and doubtless many others no longer extant—conscripted the Attic tragedians in the service of Hellenistic Judaism.

A similar process enlisted Greek comic poets. Here the tradition becomes more complex and confused. The Christian sources disagree as to which verses belong to which dramatist, whether to Philemon, Diphilus,

23. The fragments can be found in A.-M. Denis, *Fragmenta pseudepigraphorum quae supersunt graeca* (Leiden, 1970) 161–74. A translation by H. Attridge in Charlesworth, *Old Testament Pseudepigrapha*, II, 824–30. And see the valuable treatment by Goodman in Schürer, *History of the Jewish People*, III.1, 656–61, 667–71, with bibliographies.

24. πάντα δυνατὴ γὰρ δόξα ὑψίστου θεοῦ. The lines appear in Ps. Justin *De Monarch*. 2; Clement *Strom*. 5.14.131.2–3; Euseb. *PE* 13.13.60.

25. Ps. Justin *De Monarch*. 2; Clement *Strom*. 5.14.113.2; Euseb. *PE* 13.13.40. Clement found the passage in a work, "On Abraham and the Egyptians," attributed to Hecataeus of Abdera. The author, of course, was a Jewish Pseudo-Hecataeus, as all scholars recognize. How many of the other fabricated fragments of the dramatists may have been drawn from Pseudo-Hecataeus' composition cannot be determined.

26. Ps. Justin *De Monarch*. 3; Clement *Strom*. 5.14.121.4–122.1; Euseb. *PE* 13.13.48.

27. Clement *Strom*. 5.14.111.4–6; Euseb. *PE* 13.13.38.

28. The first passage in Clement *Strom*. 5.11.75.1; the second in Clement *Protr*. 6.68.3. The latter is attributed by Ps. Justin *De Monarch*. 2, not to Euripides but to the comic poet Philemon.

or Menander—or indeed even to Euripides. Specific attributions, however, matter little, especially if the lines themselves were forged. The concepts, in any case, disclose the objectives of the forgers. They include admonitions to the wicked, assertions that God punishes the unjust, insistence that upright conduct is more important than sacrificial offerings, and exhortation to honor the one god who is father for all time, the inventor and creator of every good.[29] Hellenistic Jews were evidently tireless in rummaging through the Greek classics to find opinions and sentiments that evoked scriptural teachings. They had no hesitation in rewriting lines, interpolating verses, or manufacturing passages. They recruited philosophers from Pythagoras to Plato, poets from Homer to Menander, and even the legendary writers Orpheus and Linus to show that the precepts of the Bible and the Jewish conception of the deity inspired the most sublime of Hellenic writings. The assiduous efforts gave forceful reminders to their countrymen of Jewish priority in the thinking of great thoughts.

• • •

The pattern of purported association between Jew and Greek in which the former takes precedence warrants illustration in another sphere. A long-standing practice in the Hellenic world promoted fictitious kinship connections between states. The bonds that linked friendly cities and nations might often be expressed as deriving from blood ties, even as stemming from a common, usually legendary, ancestor, a staple item in Hellenic folklore.[30] The Jews seized readily upon that convention. Their hand may be detected in the striking fiction of an affiliation with the people of Sparta.[31]

29. The last sentiment is ascribed to Diphilus by Clement *Strom.* 5.14.133.3: πατέρα τοῦτον διὰ τέλους τίμα μόνον, ἀγαθῶν τοσούτων εὑρετὴν καὶ κτίστορα. So also Euseb. *PE* 13.13.62. Ps. Justin *De Monarch.* 5, no doubt erroneously, assigns it to a supposed play "Diphilus" of Menander. For the other fragments attributed to various comic poets, see Ps. Justin *De Monarch.* 2–4; Clement *Strom.* 5.14.119.2, 5.14.121.1–3; Euseb. *PE* 13.13.45–47.

30. See, for instance, the supposed appeal of Xerxes to Argos in 480 BCE, claiming that Perses, son of Perseus, was the ancestor of Persians and thus supplied a link with the men of Argos; Herod. 7.150. Such fictitious kinship alignments were even recorded on stone. A recently published Hellenistic inscription discloses the web of interlocking divine and heroic ancestors that linked Xanthos in Lycia with Doris on the mainland; J. Bousquet, *REG* 101 (1988) 12–53, lines 14–33. A full collection of epigraphic testimony on legendary kinship connections between Greek states, with texts, translations, and commentary, is now available in O. Curty, *Les parentés legéndaires entre cités grecques* (Geneva, 1995) 3–212.

31. What follows is an adaptation of the essay by E. S. Gruen in R. W. Wallace and E. M. Harris, *Transitions to Empire: Essays in Greco-Roman History, 300–146 BC, in Honor of E. Badian* (Norman, 1996) 254–69.

Spartans and Jews might seem, on the face of it, to be the most unlikely partners. Yet a remarkable tale affirms not only political and diplomatic association but even consanguinity: both nations claimed Abraham as an ancestor. This story piques the imagination in a special way. For it does not occur in epic, drama, or a work of romantic fiction. Instead, it appeals to ostensible documents and diplomatic correspondence. Scholarly literature accumulates on the subject. Clever conjectures have proposed occasions that called forth this connection and circumstances that rendered it advantageous. The quest, however, has almost invariably concentrated upon presumed political motivation, specific conditions and objectives that prompted Spartans or Jews to initiate the association—or forgers to invent it.

A different approach may be more productive. The reputed kinship may have broader cultural ramifications. As with the other cases considered here, Jewish efforts to redefine and enhance their own identity in the circumstances of the Hellenistic world provide the appropriate setting.

The supposed Jewish-Spartan kinship will repay close inspection. Three letters constitute the principal testimony, recorded in I Maccabees and reproduced in a variant form by Josephus. The exchange began with a missive from king Areus of Sparta to the Judaean High Priest Onias. The individuals are historical and the ostensible time of the communication can be approximated: the early third century BCE.[32] Areus offered friendly greeting, announcing that he had discovered the kinship of the two peoples in a written text: Jews and Spartans are brothers, both from the stock of Abraham. He hopes for a reply with news of the Jews' current circumstances and affirms that their goods and property are joint possessions.[33]

32. Only two Spartan kings carried the name Areus, the second of whom died as a small boy. Hence the presumed author of the letter must be Areus I whose regnal years fell between 309 and 265 BCE and whose active role occupied the last decade and a half of that period. The alleged recipient is either Onias I who became High Priest in the late 4th century or Onias II who held the office in the reign of Ptolemy III Euergetes (246–221). On Areus, see G. Marasco, *Sparta agli inizi dell'età ellenistica: il regno di Areo I* (Florence, 1980). For Onias I, see Jos. *Ant.* 11.347; for Onias II, Jos. *Ant.* 12.157–67. Given the dates, most commentators opt for Onias I as the probable correspondent. But Areus' chief exploits came in the later years of his reign. And Onias II was evidently of advanced age in the reign of Ptolemy III; Jos. *Ant.* 12.158–63. Hence the story may well allude to the later Onias. See the discussions of V. Tcherikover, *Heilenistic Civilization and the Jews* (New York, 1959) 128–29; J. A. Goldstein in J. Neusner, *Christianity, Judaism, and Other Greco-Roman Cults* (Leiden, 1975) 94–95; *idem, I Maccabees* (New York, 1976) 455–56. Josephus, *Ant.* 12.225–27, wrongly considers the recipient to be Onias III. The latter, who was High Priest in the early 2nd century, could hardly have received a letter from Areus.

33. I Macc. 12.20–23; Jos. *Ant.* 12.225–27. Josephus' close paraphrase makes it nearly certain that he used I Maccabees as usual. But he evidently had additional information as well; cf. 12.227.

The affiliation was reaffirmed more than a century later when Jonathan, successor to Judas Maccabaeus as leader of the Jews, sent an embassy to Sparta ca. 144, with the consent of the Jewish Council of Elders. His message addressed the Lacedaemonians as "brothers," acknowledged Areus' letter of long ago, and enclosed a copy. Jonathan added a reference to friendship and alliance between the nations, now overdue for renewal since so many years had passed without direct communication. But he observed that his countrymen over the years regularly mentioned Spartans in their prayers and sacrifices and rejoiced at their fame. Further, the letter reported Jewish successes against all the enemies in their vicinity, successes attained without the assistance of allies. They supplied the occasion for envoys sent with this announcement to Rome and to Sparta, in the latter place to renew the bonds of brotherhood. The letter concluded with a polite request for a reply.[34]

The Lacedaemonian response arrived only after the death of Jonathan, addressed in our text to his successor Simon, perhaps in the year 142. Spartan envoys conveyed their government's desire to renew the friendship and alliance. The letter which they brought greeted the Jews as brothers, reporting the warm welcome with which Jewish delegates had been received in Sparta and the decision to inscribe their speeches for preservation in the Spartan archives.[35]

One other piece of evidence alludes to the kinship association. In 168 BCE, according to II Maccabees, Jason, the former Jewish High Priest, failed in his violent efforts to reclaim the office and was driven out of Judaea. Hunted down by his enemies, the fugitive sought refuge among the Nabataean Arabs, then in Egypt, and finally headed for Sparta, where he hoped to find safety in view of their συγγένεια but perished instead.[36]

So much for the testimony. To what extent does it warrant confidence? The extraordinary diplomatic exchange has engendered a lengthy and still lengthening list of scholarly publications. The authenticity of the letters has often been impugned in whole or in part, questions raised about one, two, or

---

34. I Macc. 12.6–18. On use of the term ἀδελφοί rather than συγγενεῖς, perhaps an inaccurate rendering of the Hebrew original, see O. Curty, *Historia* 41 (1992) 246–48. The letter of Areus in this narrative is supplied by Jonathan's envoys to remind Sparta that the kinship had been initially acknowledged by one of their monarchs. Josephus, *Ant.* 12.225–27, records the letter independently of Jonathan's mission, but adverts to it again in the latter context; *Ant.* 13.164–70.

35. I Macc. 14.16–23; cf. Jos. *Ant.* 13.170.

36. II Macc. 5.6–10.

all three of the missives. But a growing number of commentators now incline to accept the correspondence as genuine.[37]

Ingenuity of a high order has been expended in defense of Areus' letter. Scholars have proposed a variety of explanations for it. Perhaps the Spartan king took note of a Jewish community in his midst and sought to establish relations with Judaea, now a Ptolemaic dependency, in order to strengthen ties with the rulers of Egypt.[38] A link with the Jews, reinforcing the Ptolemaic connection, might bolster Spartan resistance to encroachment of the Peloponnese by the Antigonids of Macedon.[39] Recruitment of Jewish mercenaries could even help fill up the depleted ranks of the Spartiatai![40] Other motives too have been hypothesized. The Spartan overture, so one interpreter proposes, represented an offer to establish commercial relations in joint business activities.[41] The Spartans may actually have read the Scriptures (before composition of the Septuagint), learned of Abraham, and embraced the idea of kinship.[42] And, it has been suggested, they employed scribes literate in Aramaic to communicate their zeal for the Jewish connection.[43] So much for the sampling of diverse opinions.

The ingenuity is misplaced. That Areus in the early third century would have sought either military or moral support from a tiny, distant, and impotent dependency of the Ptolemaic empire surely strains imagination. The Spartans did indeed enjoy an alliance with Ptolemy II Philadelphus, concluded at some time prior to the Chremonidean War in the 260s.[44] That, if anything, makes it even less likely that they would engage in independent relations with a principality under Ptolemaic authority. As for Macedonian aggression, Sparta could hardly hope to buttress resistance by courting

37. Bibliographical summaries can be found in B. Cardauns, *Hermes* 95 (1967) 317–18, n. 1; R. Katzoff, *AJP* 106 (1985) 485, n. 1; Cl. Orrieux in R. Lonis, *L'étranger dans le monde grec* (Nancy, 1987) 187, n. 7.

38. M. S. Ginsburg, *CP* 29 (1934) 117–22; V. Ehrenberg, *RE* IIIA.2 (1929) 1425, 1445; H. Michell, *Sparta* (Cambridge, 1952) 92; P. Oliva, *Sparta and her Social Problems* (Amsterdam, 1971) 207. That the Egyptian connection might account for Areus' interest in the Jews is allowed as a possibility by P. Cartledge and A. Spawforth, *Hellenistic and Roman Sparta* (London, 1989) 36–37.

39. S. Schuller, *JSemStud* 1 (1956) 259.

40. Goldstein, *I Maccabees*, 457; Orrieux in Lonis, *L'étranger*, 174.

41. W. Wirgin, *PEQ* 101 (1969) 15–17.

42. Wirgin, *op. cit.*, 15.

43. Goldstein, *I Maccabees*, 456–57. Josephus' enigmatic remark, *Ant.* 12.227, about the Spartan missive conveyed in "square writings" hardly proves that it was composed in Aramaic. What reason would Josephus or an archivist have for expressing the fact in such circuitous language?

44. The alliance is attested by the Chremonidean decree; *Syll.*3 434/5.

a Jewish connection. The Peloponnese was no more than a sidelight for Antigonid ambitions anyway.[45] The notion that Areus contracted with Jews to supply soldiers for the Lacedaemonian forces or to enter into cooperative business ventures is most improbable. Even if the king had such unattested objectives, he did not need to invent a mythology to attain them. Where indeed would the Spartans have ever encountered legends of the patriarchal age in Israel? That Areus' contemporaries had access to a Greek translation of the Scriptures (or a part thereof) prior to the commissioning of the Septuagint is a fanciful idea altogether devoid of testimony or plausibility.[46] Perhaps then Spartan intellectuals, including king Areus himself, had learned of Abraham through reading the work of Hecataeus of Abdera?[47] If so, it must have been in some portion of Hecataeus that subsequently vanished. The extant fragments make no mention of Abraham.[48] Belief in genuineness requires great credulity.

Jonathan's letter has better credentials, but by no means a secure claim on historicity. One might note, to begin, that it appears as part of the same record in I Maccabees that contains the spurious letter of Areus. And a more fundamental question can be posed. What reason would Jews have to enter into diplomatic negotiations with Sparta in the mid second century BCE? Scholars have manufactured motives. A connection with Sparta, it is claimed, would put the Jews in touch with the one Peloponnesian state that retained some independence.[49] Or Sparta might serve as an avenue to a greater power. An approach to the Lacedaemonians in the late 140s can be seen as a means to curry favor with Rome. The western power had smashed Achaea in 146, leaving political devastation in its wake. But Sparta had been spared, indeed protected by Rome, its position strengthened by Rome's forceful intervention in the Peloponnese.

45. See Cartledge and Spawforth, *Hellenistic and Roman Sparta*, 29–31.

46. As we have seen, the reference by Aristobulus to translations earlier than the Septuagint is plainly invented in order to account for his assertion that Greek philosophers imitated the legal code of the Hebrews; Euseb. *PE* 13.12.1. The *Letter of Aristeas*, 30, notes the existence of early Hebrew scrolls in the Alexandrian library—by no means a clear allusion to Greek translations; see above, p. 207. No one can take seriously the tale of divine intervention to prevent Theopompus and Theodectus from quoting Greek passages in the Scriptures; *LetArist* 312–15.

47. So Goldstein, *I Maccabees*, 450, 458–59.

48. The alleged work of Hecataeus on Abraham (Jos. *Ant.* 1.159; Clement *Strom.* 5.113; Euseb. *PE* 13.13.40) is spurious; cf. M. Stern, *Greek and Latin Authors on Jews and Judaism* (Jerusalem, 1974) I, 22.

49. Schüller, *JSemStud* 1 (1956) 266; A. Momigliano, *Prime linee di storia della tradizione maccabaica*[2] (Amsterdam, 1968) 143–44.

Hence assertion of an ancestral bond with Sparta offered the Jews an indirect route to Rome.[50]

The speculation carries little conviction. That Jews courted the patronage of Rome by linking themselves to a Roman ally simply will not do. The Romans had their own reasons for assaulting the Achaean League in 146, reasons that did not stem from closeness to Sparta. Nor did the Lacedaemonians receive any conspicuous favors in the aftermath of the Achaean War.[51] If Jonathan sought out Sparta as an intermediary with Rome, it is most peculiar that the Jewish embassy, according to I Maccabees, went to Rome first and only stopped in at Sparta on the way home.[52] In fact, the Jews already had a treaty of alliance with Rome, one which had been in force since 161 and which Jonathan's envoys now took the occasion to renew. They plainly had no need of Spartans as intermediaries.[53] Little practical advantage would accrue from connection with a relatively weak Hellenic state which might embroil the Jews in distant affairs. Certainly they could expect no Spartan assistance in the Near East! Efforts to find political motives underlying the putative συγγένεια seem doomed to failure.[54]

No need to dwell on the ostensible third letter, the purported response of Sparta to Jonathan's overtures. Its historicity is bound up with the embassy that called it forth. And the text of I Maccabees appears to muddle the missions. The Spartan message refers to Jonathan's delegates but

50. Goldstein, *I Maccabees*, 448; L. Feldman, *Jew and Gentile in the Ancient World* (Princeton, 1993) 143.

51. E. S. Gruen, *The Hellenistic World and the Coming of Rome* (Berkeley, 1984) II, 520–27.

52. The sequence is clear in I Macc. 12.1–5, and Jos. *Ant.* 13.163–64.

53. On the treaty of 161, see I Macc. 8; Jos. *Ant.* 12.414–419; cf. *BJ* 1.38. To be sure, not all scholars accept the treaty as genuine, but no good reasons exist for falsification or invention. Bibliography on the subject is enormous. See summaries of the literature in E. Schürer, *The History of the Jewish People in the Age of Jesus Christ*, rev. ed. by G. Vermes and F. Millar (Edinburgh, 1973) I, 171–72, n. 33; J.-D. Gauger, *Beiträge zur jüdischen Apologetik* (Cologne-Bonn, 1977) 156–61. Recent cases for authenticity in Gruen, *Hellenistic World*, II, 42–46, with additional bibliography, and, in fuller detail, M. Stern, *Zion* 51 (1985–1986) 3–28 (Hebrew) = *idem* in M. Amit, I. Gafni, and M. D. Herr, *Studies in Jewish History: The Second Temple Period* (Jerusalem, 1991) 51–76 (Hebrew). On the renewal, see I Macc. 12.1–4, 12.16; Jos. *Ant.* 13.163–65, 13.169.

54. At a different level of interpretation, Katzoff suggests that Jonathan saw in Sparta a kindred spirit, a society honored by other Greeks but one whose institutions stood outside the Hellenic mainstream; *AJP* 106 (1985) 488–89. The texts, however, point in a somewhat different direction. Sparta serves to exemplify the best that Greeks had to offer, not a deviant from Hellenism. See below, pp. 261–62.

makes response to Simon.[55] No subsequent sign of the partnership surfaces in the testimony. In fact, after Simon sent his own embassy to Rome to confirm his alliance with that state, the Romans despatched messages to a wide variety of cities and kings requesting them to refrain from any hostilities toward the Jews—among them the Spartans. The passage obviously evinces no knowledge of any special relationship between Lacedaemonians and Jews.[56]

Jason's supposed flight or attempted flight to Sparta adds little weight to the case. The ex-High Priest allegedly expected sanctuary because of συγγένεια between the peoples.[57] But the report of Jason's movements, even if true, has him flee from city to city before finally hoping for haven in Sparta—and then in vain.[58] The ascription of motive can hardly count as independent testimony. It means only that the tale of the συγγένεια was known to the author of II Maccabees or to Jason of Cyrene whose work he abridged.

The quest for authenticity runs into a blind alley. It has, in any case, commanded excessive scholarly energies. Whatever conclusion is drawn about Jonathan's diplomacy, the correspondence of Areus is certainly an invention. And inventions often have more to reveal than genuine documents. They can speak to deeper cultural objectives.

The invention in this case is clearly a Jewish one. The idea of joint descent from Abraham can have no other meaning. The language of Areus' letter should suffice to make the point. As conveyed in I Maccabees, it includes the striking phrase, with biblical overtones, "your cattle and goods are ours, and ours are yours."[59] No Spartan would have expressed himself in that manner. More telling still is the tone of Jonathan's missive, which has not received adequate emphasis in modern scholarship. Even if there were an exchange between the two nations, it would hardly have taken this form. Far from petitioning for Spartan aid, the letter underscores Jewish primacy. Jonathan asserts that the Jews have at every opportunity remembered Sparta in their

---

55. I Macc. 14.16–23. Goldstein's suggestion, *I Maccabees*, 492, that a private Jewish traveller reported the news of Jonathan's death while the latter's envoys were still in Sparta, is inventive but unlikely.

56. I Macc. 14.24, 15.15–24. The point is noted by Cardauns, *Hermes* 95 (1967) 321.

57. II Macc. 5.9.

58. II Macc. 5.7–9.

59. I Macc. 12.23: τὰ κτήνη ὑμῶν καὶ ἡ ὕπαρξις ὑμῶν ἡμῖν ἐστι, καὶ τὰ ἡμῶν ὑμῖν ἐστιν. Cf. I Kings 22.4; II Kings 3.7. Josephus modifies the text to supply a more Hellenic flavor; *Ant.* 12.227: τά τε ὑμέτερα ἴδια νομιοῦμεν καὶ τὰ αὐτῶν κοινὰ πρὸς ὑμᾶς ἕξομεν.

sacrifices and their prayers during festivals and other suitable occasions.[60] The Jews, in short, are the benefactors, not the beneficiaries.

This prompts a further query. If Jews conceived the Hellenic connection, why fasten upon the Spartans in particular? Spartans would hardly seem the most logical Greeks with whom to claim a kinship that had religious and cultural reverberations. The problem has inspired considerable conjecture. Some discern in Hecataeus of Abdera's narrative of migrations from Egypt to Judaea and Greece the roots of the affiliation. Hecataeus records the banishment of aliens from Egypt, some of whom, led by Danaus and Cadmus, reached Hellenic shores; the majority, however, settled in Judaea, taken there by Moses.[61] The tale brings to mind the legend of the Danaids, settlers in the Peloponnese and progenitors of the Spartan royal dynasties.[62] But this is still quite some distance from suggesting a link between Spartans and Jews. Readers of Hecataeus would not readily extract that association from his text. The hypothesis has had further extension. In the formulation of the obscure early Imperial writer Claudius Iolaus, one of the "Spartoi" sown by Cadmus as ancestors of the Thebans was a certain "Oudaios" from whose name derives the appellation Judaea.[63] To reckon this tradition as lurking behind the Spartan-Jewish affiliation, however, is, on the most generous assessment, far-fetched. The tale of Cadmus and the "Spartoi" concerns the origins of Thebes, not Sparta. And the conjecture of Claudius Iolaus, based on nothing more than a similarity of sound and preserved only in Stephanus of Byzantium, carries little weight.[64] It would be reaching indeed to consider such remote associations as prompting the fabricated correspondence in I Maccabees.[65]

---

60. I Macc. 12.11: ἡμεῖς οὖν ἐν παντὶ καιρῷ ἀδιαλείπτως ἔν τε ταῖς ἑορταῖς καὶ ταῖς λοιπαῖς καθηκούσαις ἡμέραις μιμνησκόμεθα ὑμῶν, ἐφ᾽ ὧν προσφέρομεν θυσιῶν, καὶ ἐν ταῖς προσευχαῖς; Jos. *Ant.* 13.168.

61. Diod. 40.3.2. Cf. Ginsburg, *CP* 29 (1934) 120–21; Schüller, *JSemStud* 1 (1956) 262–63; Hengel, *Judaism and Hellenism*, II, 50–51, n. 124; L. J. Piper, *Spartan Twilight* (New Rochelle, 1986) 148–49.

62. The Egyptian-Spartan connection is known to Herodotus; 2.91, 6.53.2; cf. 2.80, 6.55.

63. *FGH*, IIIC, 788 Fr. 4 = Stern, *Greek and Latin Authors*, I, 249.

64. The hypothesis has marginal support from the fact that a cult of Cadmus existed at Sparta; Paus. 3.15.8. But it requires quite a leap from that to a kinship connection between Spartans and Jews.

65. Still more indirect is the association inferred from Cleodemus Malchus' story of marriage alliance between Heracles and the house of Abraham; Jos., *Ant.* 1.239–41; Euseb. *PE* 9.20.2–4. The legend has been cited in this connection on the grounds that Heracles was a putative ancestor of Sparta; so, e.g., Momigliano, *Prime linee*, 144–45; Goldstein, *I Maccabees*, 458; Hengel, *Judaism and Hellenism*, II, 50–51, n. 124; Feldman, *Jew and Gentile*, 143. But the tale

Strained surmises can be left aside. Certain features of the Spartan character—or at least the Spartan image—would have appealed to Hellenistic Jews. For those knowledgeable about Spartan traditions and public posture, parallels might well have suggested themselves. Hecataeus of Abdera had already left an account of Moses that set him in the mold of a recognizable Hellenic lawgiver. Moses, in Hecataeus' conception, not only ordered religious and civic institutions for his people, but provided for physical training and martial prowess. His legislation aimed at inculcating the military arts through a compulsory program for Jewish youth that prepared them for manly virtue, endurance, and tolerance of every form of suffering.[66] The model of the Spartan ἀγωγή appears to lie in the background here. And Hecataeus' further description puts the matter beyond doubt. He has Moses follow up his military victories and territorial acquisitions with an apportioning of land in equal lots and a requirement that those lots be inalienable. Such legislation would prevent the greedy from acquiring the land, squeezing the poor, and causing a decline in manpower.[67] The parallel to Spartan traditions associated with the legendary lawgiver Lycurgus, both in measures and in motives, seems quite incontestable. In the Spartans' conception of their system's origin, Lycurgus too allocated land to fellow citizens in equal κλῆροι to break down the vast discrepancies in wealth and power that plagued Spartan society. And he firmly discouraged the alienation of land in order to preserve that equality.[68]

The analogy becomes more explicit in Josephus. He names Lycurgus himself as exemplary in Greek eyes, and the Spartan system as a source of admiration among Hellenes, for its citizens adhered for the longest time to the precepts of their lawgiver. The πολιτεία of Lycurgus thus became the benchmark whereby to judge the virtues and successes of all commonwealths. The Jews, however, in Josephus' formulation, had exceeded Spartan achievements. Their faithfulness to ancestral laws remained unshaken long after the Lacedaemonian system collapsed. And the hardships en-

---

itself has nothing to do with Sparta and could hardly justify the συγγένεια of Lacedaemonians and Jews.

66. Diod. 40.3.6: ἐποιήσατο δ' ὁ νομοθέτης τῶν τε πολεμικῶν ἔργων πολλὴν πρόνοιαν καὶ τοὺς νέους ἠνάγκαζεν ἀσκεῖν ἀνδρειάν τε καὶ καρτερίαν καὶ τὸ σύνολον ὑπομονὴν πάσης κακοπαθείας.

67. Diod. 40.3.7: καὶ πολλὴν κατακτησάμενος χώραν κατεκληρούχησε, τοῖς μὲν ἰδιώταις ἴσους ποιήσας κλήρους ... οὐκ ἐξῆν δὲ τοῖς ἰδιώταις τοὺς ἰδίους κλήρους πωλεῖν, ὅπως μή τινες διὰ πλεονεξίαν ἀγοράζοντες τοὺς κλήρους ἐκθλίβωσι τοὺς ἀπορωτέρους καὶ κατασκευάζωσιν ὀλιγανδρίαν.

68. Plut. *Lyc.* 8; *Agis* 5.1; Polyb. 6.45.3, 6.48.2–3; Aristotle *Pol.* 2.6.10; Heracleides Lembos 373.12, Dilts.

dured by the Jews, the tests put to their courage, far outstrip the Hellenic model, obedience to the law the clearest demonstration of Jewish nobility of spirit.[69]

The appeal of a Spartan affiliation is intelligible. The Jews could associate themselves with a society reckoned as a yardstick for Hellenic excellence and achievement. But why select Areus as the Spartan who first authenticated the kinship? He was far from the most celebrated of Lacedaemonian leaders, hardly an obvious choice to affirm a fictitious bond between the peoples. That troublesome fact has served to strengthen the hand of those who argue for the genuineness of an exchange between Spartans and Jews in the third century: no forger would have dug up Areus for the purpose.[70]

The conclusion is hasty and unwarranted. Areus' repute stood much higher in the Hellenistic era than it does today. The absence of a biography by Plutarch constitutes an unjust liability. Few contemporary observers on the international scene would, for instance, have ranked the "reformer" king Agis IV (the subject of a Plutarch biography) on a level with Areus. The latter had a dramatic career, pushing himself and his city into major events of Hellenistic politics and diplomacy. A coalition of Greek states, we are told, chose Areus as leader in an assault upon the Aetolian League, an indirect thrust against the power of Macedon in Hellas in 280. Although the venture ended in failure, it attests to the stature and reputation of Areus.[71] He expanded his connections in subsequent years on the island of Crete, which served as a source of mercenaries, and its cities were soon linked in alliance with Sparta.[72] Greater notoriety came from the incursions of Pyrrhus into the Peloponnese in the late 270s. The Epirote invasion of Laconia occurred during Areus' absence in Crete. A valiant Spartan resistance thwarted Pyrrhus, Macedonian mercenaries entered the fray, and then Areus returned with a force from Crete. Pyrrhus withdrew and turned his attention to Argos.[73] Areus now took a prominent part in the contest, first harassing Pyrrhus on his route, then commanding Spartan and Cretan troops against him in battle, which led to the death of the redoubtable Epirote prince.[74] Areus' renown rapidly spread. Indeed he promoted it actively through the minting of Sparta's first silver coinage, tetradrachms inscribed with his name and displaying

69. Jos. *C. Apion.* 2.225–35.
70. Cf. Goldstein, *I Maccabees*, 456.
71. Justin 24.1.1–7; cf. Polyb. 2.41.11–12; Marasco, *Il regno di Areo I*, 63–73.
72. Cf. *Syll.*3 434/5, lines 25–26, 39–41; see Marasco, *Il regno di Areo I*, 84–90.
73. Plut. *Pyrrh.* 26.7–30.1.
74. Plut. *Pyrrh.* 30.2–34.2; Marasco, *Il regno di Areo I*, 100–14.

an image modeled on the types of Alexander the Great. Areus plainly projected himself as in the line of the Diadochoi, a major figure on the international stage.[75]

The resurgence of Spartan power can be read without ambiguity in the famed Chremonidean Decree from Athens in 268. The measure sets forth a string of Spartan allies, the fruit of Areus' policy: Elis, Achaea, Tegea, Mantinea, Orchomenus, Phigalea, and Caphyae. Sparta had reaffirmed ascendancy in the Peloponnese. Its network, in fact, went beyond Greece proper. The decree records Sparta's formal links with the Cretans, and, as a capstone, the alliance with Ptolemy I of Egypt.[76] Areus' prominence gains explicit acknowledgment in the document: the king is singled out for mention among the Lacedaemonians as a whole five different times.[77] There seems little doubt that Areus was the pivotal figure in assembling the grand anti-Macedonian coalition reflected in the decree of Chremonides.[78] Statues of him were dedicated by Orchomenus, by the Eleans and others at Olympia, by Polyrrhenia in Crete, and, most strikingly, by Ptolemy Philadelphus himself, also at Olympia.[79] Areus had a high profile in the world of Hellenistic politics. It should not therefore cause surprise that attestation of the genealogical tie between Spartans and Jews was ascribed to Areus, a figure who would lend stature to the connection.[80] But that certainly does not vouch for its authenticity.

Jewish initiative and Jewish inventiveness created this fictive συγγένεια. Scrutiny of the text in I Maccabees puts the matter beyond question. Jonathan's purported letter asks nothing of the Spartans, asserting instead the special position of the Jews, the senior partner in the association. After alluding to Areus' missive that attested the kinship and to the warm

75. On the coins, see A. R. Bellinger, *Essays on the Coinage of Alexander the Great* (New York, 1963) 89–90; S. Grunauer-von Hoerschelmann, *Die Münzprägung der Lakedaimonier* (Berlin, 1978) 1–4, 112–13, Tafel 1. Cf. Marasco, *Il regno di Areo I*, 124–27; Cartledge and Spawforth, *Hellenistic and Roman Sparta*, 34–35.

76. *Syll.*3 434/5, lines 21–26, 35–41.

77. *Syll.*3 434/5, lines 26, 29, 40, 50, 55. See, e.g., lines 25–26: ὅσοι εἰσὶν ἐν τεῖ συμμ[αχίαι τ]εῖ Λακεδαιμονίων καὶ Ἀρέως καὶ τῶν ἄλλων συμμάχω[ν].

78. Cf. H. Heinen, *Untersuchungen zur hellenistischen Geschichte des 3. Jahrhunderts v. Chr. Zur Geschichte der Zeit des Ptolemaios Keraunos und zum chremonideischen Krieg* (Wiesbaden, 1972) 126–32; Marasco, *Il regno di Areo I*, 131–35.

79. Orchomenus: L. Moretti, *Iscrizioni storiche ellenistiche* (Florence, 1967) I, 54 (also noting Areus' connection with Ptolemy); statuary at Olympia: Paus. 6.12.5, 6.15.9; Polyrrhenia: *IC*, II, xxiii, 12; Ptolemy: *Syll.*3 433.

80. The reputation of Areus is recognized by Momigliano, *Prime linee*, 146, and Marasco, *Il regno di Areo I*, 161–65.

reception of Sparta's envoy by Onias who hailed the message of friendship and alliance, Jonathan sets it all in perspective. The Jews, so his letter asserts, have no need of these bonds for they have in their hands the holy books as encouragement.[81] They seek to renew the fraternity and friendship only in order not to have the long absence of contact weaken the relationship.[82] The tone borders on patronizing. Jonathan insists that Jewish success owes nothing to alliance or partnership with other states. His people fended off attacks from neighboring kings and hostile powers without requesting the aid of Sparta or other allies. The assistance of heaven suffices to rescue the Jews from their enemies and to lay those enemies low.[83] Jonathan delivers a clear message of Jewish ascendancy in this relationship. The Spartans, in their reply which reached Jerusalem after the death of Jonathan, acknowledged the ambassadorial speeches that declared Jewish fame and prestige and noted that copies of them had been deposited in their own public records.[84]

The Judeo-centric quality of all this is unmistakable. The fact that Abraham, the Hebrew patriarch, appears as ultimate ancestor of both Spartans and Jews makes the point without ambiguity. In this regard it parallels the legend recounted by Cleodemus Malchus that the sons of Abraham joined with Heracles in his war on the Libyan giant Antaeus and that the Greek hero married the daughter of one of those sons who became the eponymous forebear of Africa.[85]

81. I Macc. 12.8–9: καὶ ἡμεῖς οὖν ἀπροσδεεῖς τούτων ὄντες παράκλησιν ἔχοντες τὰ βιβλία τὰ ἅγια τὰ ἐν ταῖς χερσὶν ἡμῶν. Josephus' paraphrase alters the meaning quite substantially. In his version Jonathan declares that the Jews did not need Spartan proof of the kinship for which they could trust in their own sacred writings; *Ant.* 13.167: περὶ τῆς ὑπαρχούσης ἡμῖν πρὸς ὑμᾶς συγγενείας ... οὐ δεόμενοι τῆς τοιαύτης ἀποδείξεως διὰ τὸ ἐκ τῶν ἱερῶν ἡμῶν πεπιστεῦσθαι γραμμάτων. This makes for a more polite reply, perhaps a deliberate effort on Josephus' part to supply suitable diplomatic language. But it undercuts the real thrust of the remarks in I Maccabees.

82. I Macc. 12.10; cf. Jos. *Ant.* 13.168.

83. I Macc. 12.13–15: οὐκ ἠβουλόμεθα οὖν παρενοχλεῖν ὑμῖν καὶ τοῖς λοιποῖς συμμάχοις καὶ φίλοις ἡμῶν ἐν τοῖς πολέμοις τούτοις· ἔχομεν γὰρ τὴν ἐξ οὐρανοῦ βοήθειαν βοηθοῦσαν ἡμῖν καὶ ἐρρύσθημεν ἀπὸ τῶν ἐχθρῶν ἡμῶν, καὶ ἐταπεινώθησαν οἱ ἐχθροὶ ἡμῶν; Jos. *Ant.* 13.169.

84. I Macc. 14.20–23: οἱ πρεσβευταὶ οἱ ἀποσταλέντες πρὸς τὸν δῆμον ἡμῶν ἀπήγγειλαν ἡμῖν περὶ τῆς δόξης ὑμῶν καὶ τιμῆς. The preceding lines, I Macc. 14.16–19, appear to refer to a Roman rather than a Spartan response to the Jews; cf. F.-M. Abel, *Les livres des Maccabées* (Paris, 1949) 252–53. The efforts of Goldstein, *I Maccabees*, 494, to excise references to Rome and to a treaty with Judas as interpolations, are tempting but beyond proof.

85. Jos. *Ant.* 1.239–41; Euseb. *PE* 9.20.2–4.

The fiction of Spartan-Jewish affiliation, like all the inventions recounted above, puts the prestige of the Jews on display. When will such a tale have gained currency? Any attempt to pinpoint its emergence with precision brings frustration. Indeed, efforts along these lines have plagued scholarship by prompting a fruitless search for specific historical occasions that provoked the invention. The most that can be said with confidence is that the kinship story surfaced prior to the composition of I Maccabees, probably at the end of the second century BCE.[86] It was known also to Jason of Cyrene or his epitomator, the author of II Maccabees, who included the notice that Jason the Oniad fled to Sparta because of the affiliation. The complexities and uncertainties in attempting to date this work, however, are so formidable that no hypothesis is likely to win much assent. The relationship between I and II Maccabees remains highly controversial, not to mention disputes over possible common sources, different levels of composition, and the problems involved in detecting what material derives from Jason of Cyrene and what from his abridger.[87] A conservative guess would place Jason some time in the later second century BCE and the abridgment of his history no later than the early first century BCE.[88] The tale of a Spartan-Jewish

---

86. The date of composition has attained at least a broad consensus. The laudatory remarks on Rome make unlikely a time of writing after Pompey's conquest of Jerusalem in 63 BCE: I Macc. 8.1–16; cf. 14.40, 15.15–24. At I Macc. 13.30, the author refers to a mausoleum constructed at the time of Simon ca. 142 as still standing in his own day—thus implying the perspective of at least a generation later. And, more telling, the work closes with a citation of the "book of days" of John Hyrcanus' High Priesthood, a biblical phrase that indicates a date after Hyrcanus' death in 104; I Macc. 16.23–24; cf. I Kings 14.29, 16.27; II Kings 20.20. It is, of course, possible to argue that the two passages were later additions or interpolations, but that constitutes special pleading. For discussion, see Abel, *Les livres de Maccabées*, xxviii–xxix; J. C. Dancy, *I Maccabees: A Commentary* (Oxford, 1954) 87–89; Goldstein, *I Maccabees*, 62–63; H. W. Attridge in M. Stone, *Jewish Writings of the Second Temple Period* (Assen-Philadelphia, 1984) 171; Schürer, *History of the Jewish People*, III.1, 181; J. Sievers, *The Hasmoneans and their Supporters* (Atlanta, 1990) 3. The recent attempt by B. Bar-Kochva, *Judas Maccabaeus* (Cambridge, 1989) 151–70, to put the book early in Hyrcanus' reign on grounds of the vividness of the battle narratives is unconvincing. Even if such vividness did imply eyewitness testimony, Bar-Kochva too hastily discounts the possibility that the author of I Maccabees made use of a prior account. S. Schwartz, *JJS* 42 (1991) 36–38, also argues for an early date on other grounds—but only by ascribing the final lines of the work to a later reviser.

87. It is certainly unwarranted to take the notice of Jason the Oniad's flight as giving a *terminus ante quem* of 168 for the kinship tale, as do, e.g., Hengel, *Judaism and Hellenism*, I, 72, and Momigliano, *Alien Wisdom* (Cambridge, 1975) 113–14.

88. The assertion at II Macc. 15.37 that Jerusalem was still in the hands of the Hebrews suggests a date before 63 BCE, as do the friendly references to Rome; II Macc. 4.11, 11.34–38. One of the letters attached at the beginning of the text is dated to 124 BCE; II Macc. 1.10. Whether this offers a clue to the date of Jason or of the summarizer or of yet a third editor

kinship, therefore, circulated among Jewish intellectuals around the end of the second century.

What objectives did those who created or disseminated the legend have in view? As we have seen, proposed answers tend to concentrate upon political advantage and special circumstances—like an indirect Spartan overture to the Ptolemies or an indirect Jewish overture to Rome. A recent study offers a mishmash of motives, each of similarly circumscribed scope. Perhaps the story represents Hasmonaean propaganda to justify control of the high-priesthood by having a neutral state like Sparta acknowledge their legitimacy? Or anti-Oniad polemic by the supporters of Jonathan and Simon? Or a ruse by the renegade Jason to pave the way for his exile in Sparta? Or a product of the "Hellenizing party" in Jerusalem prior to the Maccabaean revolt?[89] One will not make much headway in this fashion.

The course of the second century BCE brought the Jews into increasing contact with Hellenic literature, legends, and traditions, both in Palestine and the Diaspora. Cultivated Jews who learned Greek and absorbed Greek culture faced squarely the burden of articulating their own people's place within the broader cultural community. The creation of the Spartan linkage belongs in that context, together with the fictitious dependence of Greek poets and philosophers on the Bible and the adaptation of Sibylline pronouncements to augur Jewish glories. The process is too often considered as apologia or assimilation. So, a great scholar characterized the Jews' embrace of the Spartan συγγένεια as "a ticket of admission to the Hellenic club."[90] For that purpose, however, the purported ancestor of both peoples should be a Greek hero or legendary figure, hardly a Hebrew patriarch. Identification of Abraham as the common forefather delivers the appropriate message. The Jews attempted to assimilate Greeks into their own traditions, rather than subordinating themselves to Hellenism. The distinction is a critical one.

Jews are no mere passive recipients of a tradition here. Nor did they promote a connection for political, military, or economic advantage. The cultural character of this association holds pride of place. Sparta served as an eminently suitable vehicle. In the fragmented and turbulent scene

---

remains altogether uncertain. Among many treatments, see Abel, *Les livres des Maccabées*, xlii–xliii; J. G. Bunge, *Untersuchungen zum zweiten Makkabäerbuch* (Bonn, 1971) 573–617; C. Habicht, *2 Makkabäerbuch* (Gütersloh, 1976) 169–77; Goldstein, *I Maccabees*, 62–89; *idem, II Maccabees* (Garden City, 1983) 28–83; Attridge in Stone, *Jewish Writings*, 176–78. A valuable bibliography of recent works in Schürer, *History of the Jewish People*, III.1, 536–37. See now the sensible and sober remarks of Bar-Kochva, *Judas Maccabaeus*, 182–85, and Sievers, *The Hasmoneans*, 4–7.

89. These and other possiblities are canvassed by Orrieux in Lonis, *L'étranger*, 176–86.

90. E. Bickerman, *The Jews in the Greek Age* (Cambridge, Mass., 1988) 184.

of the post-Alexander era, the image of Sparta still glowed brightly, at least in the impression of intellectuals. Perception, as so often, counted for more than reality. Sparta continued to stand for martial virtue, voluntary sacrifice, order, stability, and the rule of law.[91] The Spartan model, evoking respect and admiration, would be an ideal one—especially when shaped to Jewish advantage. The invention of the συγγένεια did more than to assert bonds between the Jewish and Hellenic worlds. It constituted a Jewish expropriation and transformation of the Spartan mystique to declare the primacy of the Jews.

The Spartan affiliation surely did not exhaust Jewish inventiveness on this score. To what degree Jews claimed comparable connections with other states or peoples lie beyond our grasp. But hints survive to suggest that they found fictitious bonds to be a serviceable form of projecting their identity.

One instance surfaces in a purported Pergamene decree. The decree occurs amidst a series of texts assembled by Josephus to demonstrate favors bestowed and privileges guaranteed to the Jews over the years by Roman officials, emperors, and the senate. The decree of Pergamum registers a Jewish mission to Rome in the time of the High Priest Hyrcanus, presumably John Hyrcanus I in the later second century BCE. The embassy received a senatorial declaration admonishing the Seleucid king against any acts that might cause damage to the Jews. Hyrcanus' envoys evidently circulated the notice around the Mediterranean, stopping, among other places, in Pergamum. The Pergamenes duly honored the envoys, proclaimed their compliance with Roman wishes, and affirmed their friendship with the Jews. The decree which described these events then concluded the diplomatic niceties with a notable statement. The Pergamenes acknowledged that friendly relations with the Jews extended as far back as the era of Abraham, "the father of all Hebrews"—a fact recorded in the public archives of Pergamum itself.[92]

The authenticity of the document need not be argued here. That question is bound up with the larger issue of Josephus' reliability in the transmission

---

91. Note, for example, the claim by the people of Selge in Pisidia to a συγγένεια with the Lacedaemonians; Polyb. 5.76.11. For the persistence of the Spartan image, see F. Ollier, *Le mirage spartiate*, 2 vols. (Paris, 1933–1943); E. N. Tigerstedt, *The Legend of Sparta in Classical Antiquity*, 3 vols. (Stockholm, 1965, 1974, 1978); E. Rawson, *The Spartan Tradition in European Thought* (Oxford, 1969). On the molding of that image in antiquity, see now N. M. Kennell, *The Gymnasium of Virtue* (Chapel Hill, 1995).

92. Jos. *Ant.* 14.247–55; see, especially, 14.255: μεμνημένον τε ὡς καὶ ἐν τοῖς κατὰ Ἄβραμον καιροῖς, ὃς ἦν πάντων Ἑβραίων πατήρ, οἱ πρόγονοι ἡμῶν ἦσαν αὐτοῖς φίλοι, καθὼς ἐν τοῖς δημοσίοις εὑρίσκομεν γράμμασιν.

of pagan edicts and decrees involving the Jews.[93] Even the most credulous, however, might query the idea that Pergamum held in its public registry a notice dating relations with the Jews back to Abraham! Plainly that item at least stems from Jewish interpolators.[94] The link here does not involve kinship ties but an ancient association assigned to a period centuries before Pergamum even came into existence. The supposed reference to Abraham as ancestor of all Hebrews in the Pergamene archives clearly represents a Jewish imposition upon the story of this diplomatic exchange. It discloses the existence of a tradition, surely not invented for this occasion alone, in which Jews defined their relations to Hellenistic powers through reference to biblical antiquity.

One other tradition may belong in this company. Among diverse pagan speculations about the origins of the Jews, one tale identified them with the Solymi, a Lycian people celebrated in the poems of Homer. The name triggered an association with Hierosolyma, a typical etymological inference leading to a dubious ethnic conclusion.[95] The hypothesis doubtless derived from a pagan source. But one can readily imagine that Jewish writers snapped up and propagated a story that gave them an illustrious place in the Homeric epics.

●   ●   ●

Jews were assiduous in exhibiting the superiority of their faith and nation through usurpation of pagan conventions. The practice took a multitude of

93. Among treatments of this issue, see E. Bickerman, *Studies in Jewish and Christian History* (Leiden, 1980) II, 24–43; H. Moehring in Neusner, *Christianity, Judaism*, III, 124–58; C. Saulnier, *RevBibl* 88 (1981) 161–98; M. Pucci Ben Zeev, *SCI* 13 (1994) 46–59.

94. The date and circumstances of the decree, if genuine, are uncertain. For discussion, see T. Fischer, *Untersuchungen zum Partherkrieg Antiochos' VII* (Tübingen, 1970) 73–82; A. Giovannini and H. Muller, *MH* 28 (1971) 156–58; Schürer, *History of the Jewish People*, I, 204–206; J. D. Gauger, *Beiträge*, 321–24; Gruen, *Hellenistic World*, II, 750–51; P. Trebilco, *Jewish Communities in Asia Minor* (Cambridge, 1991) 7–8; M. Pucci Ben Zeev in R. Katzoff, *Classical Studies in Honor of D. Sohlberg* (Ramat Gan, 1996) 214–16—none of whom questions its authenticity. H. Moehring, *ANRW* II.21.2 (1984) 894–97, expresses doubts on different grounds.

95. The tale is preserved, along with several other conjectures on Jewish origins, by Tacitus, *Hist.* 5.2.3: *clara illi Iudaeorum initia: Solymos, carminibus Homeri celebratam gentem, conditae urbi Hierosolyma nomen e suo fecisse.* Reference to the Solymi in Homer, *Iliad*, 6.184 and *Odyssey*, 5.283. Cf. Jos. *C. Apion.* 1.172–74; *Ant.* 7.67. The idea of I. Lévy, *Latomus* 5 (1946) 334–39, that this version derived from a Jewish exegete, is improbable. See Feldman, *Jew and Gentile*, 520, n. 55. On the Solymi and the association with Jews, see Stern, *Greek and Latin Authors*, II, 34–35; III, 5–6; and now Feldman, *REJ* 150 (1991) 351–54; *idem, Jew and Gentile*, 192, 520–22, with important bibliography.

forms. None, however, was more dramatic than commandeering the voice of the Sibyl. Her potent pronouncements, excoriating the foibles of humanity and forecasting the dreadful doom of the wicked, rang through the classical landscape. The prophecies of the divinely inspired Sibyl or Sibyls held a prominent place in pagan tradition. Collections of the Sibylline Oracles, duly edited, expanded, or invented, had wide circulation in the Greco-Roman world—long before Jewish writers exploited them for their own purposes. But circumstances of transmission, as so often, produce peculiar ironies. The Gentile originals that served as models have largely been lost, surviving only in fragments or reconstructions. The extant corpus of Sibylline Books, drawing upon but refashioning those models, derive from Jewish and Christian compilers who had their own agenda to promote. The role of Hellenized Jews in this development is pivotal. Rehabilitation of the originals may no longer be possible, but assessment of the means and motives for the transformation raises even more significant issues of Jewish self-image.

In this quest, the Third Sibylline Oracle possesses special importance. It contains the earliest material in the collection and its composition is predominantly Jewish. That much can confidently be stated. Beyond lies controversy, dispute, and division. A large and burgeoning scholarly literature daunts the researcher, with innumerable disagreements in detail. And irony enters here as well. A few issues do command a broad consensus, issues of centrality and importance, thus affording an ostensible reassurance. Yet the very ground on which that consensus rests is shaky, and may well have clouded rather than clarified understanding. The areas of agreement touch on fundamental matters that have not been subjected to adequate scrutiny. The time is overdue for a closer look.

First, the matter of unity or diversity of composition. Opinions vary widely on specifics. But a heavy majority of scholars have always discerned a main corpus or a principal core produced or redacted at a particular historical time. Earlier material might have been incorporated and accretions subsequently added, but the body of the work, so most have claimed, can be tied to identifiable historical circumstances that called it forth. The favored times, each boasting notable champions, are the mid second century BCE, the early first century BCE, and the later first century BCE.[96] Second, and in close

---

96. In the first edition of real importance and influence, C. Alexandre, *Oracula Sibyllina*, 2 vols. (Paris, 1841–1856), assigned well over half of the text to a Jewish redactor of ca. 168 BCE. The notion of a principal author dating to the mid 2nd century prevailed until the sustained assault by J. Geffcken, *Komposition und Entstehungszeit der Oracula Sibyllina* (Leipzig, 1902) 1–17, which has had wide impact in the scholarship. Geffcken, as a committed pluralist, dissected the Third Book with scrupulous care but excessive confidence, labelling various segments as

conjunction with the first, various pointers in the text to what appear to be historical episodes have regularly been taken as disclosing the *Sitz-im-Leben* of the text—a sign of the author's attitude to contemporary leaders, nations, or events. The most common referents identified by interpreters are Antiochus Epiphanes, the Maccabees, Ptolemy VI or VIII, Mithridates, the Roman triumvirs, and Cleopatra.[97] And third, a firm unanimity among scholars holds that the bulk of Book III derives from the Jewish community in Egypt, whether in Alexandria or Leontopolis. The Egyptian provenance, so it is asserted or assumed, accounts for the attitudes expressed and the general thrust of, at least, the main corpus of the work.[98]

---

products of the Babylonian Sibyl, the Persian Sibyl, the Erythraean Sibyl, or the Jewish Sibyl. Even his atomistic structure, however, includes a Jewish composer from the Maccabaean period for nearly one quarter of the lines and a Jewish revision of the Erythraean Sibyl, constituting more than a third of the whole, in the early 1st century BCE. W. Bousset, *RE für protestantische Theologie und Kirche* 18 (1906) 270–71, detected divisions in places other than those noted by Geffcken, but ascribed more than half of the text to an author living in the early 1st century. E. Schürer, *Geschichte des jüdischen Volkes im Zeitalter Jesu Christi* (Leipzig, 1886) II, 794–99, believed that almost all came from the pen of a Jewish writer in the mid 2nd century. Similar judgments were expressed by H. Lanchester in R. H. Charles, *The Apocrypha and Pseudepigrapha of the Old Testament*, II (Oxford, 1913) 371–72, and A. Rzach, *RE* II.A.2 (1923) 2127–28. A. Peretti, *La Sibilla babilonese nella propaganda ellenistica* (Florence, 1943) 96–99, 143–47, 317–40, 350–51, 397–99, 459–68, holds that the core of the text was composed in the early 1st century, and certainly prior to 63 BCE, the taking of Jerusalem by Pompey, and then subject to subsequent accretions. The strongest argument for unity came from V. Nikiprowetzky, *La Troisième Sibylle* (Paris, 1970) 195–225, who set almost the entire work in the time of the later 1st century BCE, the period of Cleopatra VII and the triumvirate. That verdict has not found favor among more recent commentators. The current consensus inclines to the composite interpretation of Geffcken, but discerns a main corpus, encompassing more than two thirds of the whole, as a product of the mid 2nd century BCE. That is the conclusion of J. J. Collins, who has written extensively on the subject; *The Sibylline Oracles of Egyptian Judaism* (Missoula, 1974) 21–33; in J. H. Charlesworth, *The Old Testament Pseudepigrapha*, I (Garden City, 1983) 354–55; in M. E. Stone, *Jewish Writings of the Second Temple Period* (Philadelphia, 1984) 365–71; *ANRW* II.20.1 (1987) 430–36. Similarly, Fraser, *Ptolemaic Alexandria*, I, 709, 711. The position has been endorsed in recent works; e.g. J. D. Newsome, *Greeks, Romans, Jews* (Philadelphia, 1992) 93–97; Feldman, *Jew and Gentile*, 294; cf. M. Delcor in W. D. Davies and L. Finkelstein, *The Cambridge History of Judaism*, II (Cambridge, 1989) 487–89. A more pluralistic interpretation by Goodman in Schürer, *History of the Jewish People*, III.1, 632–38. Most recently, Barclay, *Jews in the Mediterranean Diaspora*, 216–25, offers a fresh and welcome intepretation, but follows the consensus in assigning the bulk of the material to the 2nd century while allowing for subsequent changes and modifications. Arguments about the Sibylline Oracles generally began already among Renaissance humanists; see A. Grafton, *Defenders of the Text* (Cambridge, Mass., 1991) 172–77.

97. No need to rehearse the bibliography here. Specifics will emerge in subsequent discussions.

98. See, e.g., Collins, *The Sibylline Oracles*, 35–55.

The modern literature, in short, has sought to locate the Third Sibyl in time and place. The aim is logical and laudable enough. Yet the search for historical specificity may miss the essence of the Sibyl's message, its apocalyptic character, and its significance for the interaction of Judaism and Hellenism. A reconsideration of the three propositions outlined above is in order.

Is there, in fact, a "main corpus" in Book III, in which earlier oracles were incorporated and later material tacked on? The idea runs into trouble from the start. Chronological indicators are few, scattered, and usually ambiguous. The problem can be readily illustrated. Verse 46 speaks of a time when Rome ruled Egypt, a passage that can hardly be earlier than the battle of Actium.[99] A mention of Beliar who comes from the Sebastenoi occurs in verse 63. The Sebastenoi very likely signify the line of Roman emperors or Augusti, and the arrogant Beliar who comes to a bad end probably denotes Nero. Hence, this passage evidently postdates 68 CE.[100] The sequence of kingdoms given in lines 156–61 places Rome after Egypt, again implying a date after 30 BCE, the fall of Egypt into Roman hands.[101] By contrast, the following oracle, offering yet another series of kingdoms that will rise and fall, sets the Romans after the Macedonians, gives Macedon as their prime victim, and, in describing them as "white, many-headed, from the western sea," obviously alludes to the Republic and presumably to the defeat of Macedon in 168 or 148.[102] The fierce hostility and rage directed against Rome and the vengeance promised from Asia in verses 350–80 belong more suitably to the late Republic when Roman expansionism and imperial exactions had left deep scars in the east.[103] Yet the oracle that appears next in the text reverts to an earlier time, lamenting the mighty power of Macedon and the sorrows it

99. Sib. Or. 3.46: αὐτὰρ ἐπεὶ Ῥώμη καὶ Αἰγύπτου βασιλεύσει . The suggestion of Lanchester in Charles, *Apocrypha and Pseudepigrapha*, II, 371, that this may allude to Popillius Laenas' mission to Egypt in 168 BCE, is out of the question. Rome exercised no sovereignty over Egypt at that time. Nor after the bequests of either Ptolemy Apion or Ptolemy Auletes, the other possibilities canvassed by Lanchester.

100. So Collins, *The Sibylline Oracles*, 80–87, citing as parallel Ascension of Isaiah 4.1. Beliar, however, can have other connotations; see Nikiprowetzky, *La Troisième Sibylle*, 138–43.

101. Collins, *The Sibylline Oracles*, 26, implausibly prefers the 2nd century BCE on the grounds that Rome was already a world empire by that time. That skirts the significance of the sequence of empires, each kingdom replacing or subduing the previous.

102. Sib. Or. 3.162–90, esp. 176: λευκὴ καὶ πολύκρανος ἀφ' ἑσπερίοιο θαλάσσης.

103. That conclusion is generally accepted, although commentators differ as to whether the lines allude to the Mithridatic war or to Cleopatra's resistance to Rome; cf. Bousset, *RE für protestantische Theologie und Kirche* 18 (1906) 271; Peretti, *La Sibilla babilonese*, 329–57; Collins, *The Sibylline Oracles*, 57–64. On this, see below, pp. 280–82.

brings and looking ahead to its demise.[104] Later, the Sibyl proclaims the dire fate of Italy as consequence not of foreign war but of civil bloodshed, and refers also to a murderous man from Italy, the destroyer of Laodicea. Those verses must recall the Roman Social and civil wars of the early first century BCE and the ravages by Sulla in the east that fell in that very period.[105] Yet the succeeding lines raise the specter of a previous time, two generations earlier, that witnessed the eradication of Carthage and Corinth.[106] And the Sibyl could also recall a much earlier era, when savage Gauls devastated Thrace in the early third century BCE.[107] One could proceed to passages of more speculative date. But no need. It seems clear that the third Book of the Sibylline Oracles constitutes a conglomerate, a gathering of various prophecies that stem from different periods ranging from the second century BCE through the early Roman Empire. To postulate a main corpus or a primary redaction reflecting special circumstances does not get us far.[108] The significance of the composition transcends any specific era.

The ostensible historical pointers in the text require reassessment. The cornerstone for the idea of a principal edition in the second century rests upon three references to a seventh king of Egypt: verses 193, 318, 608. Since he is explicitly described in two of the three passages as "from the race of the Greeks," the allusion is apparently to a Ptolemaic monarch. Scholars have wrangled over how to calculate the sequence of kings. Does Alexander the Great count as the first or not? Does one include the short and overlapping reign of Ptolemy VII Philopator? The uncertainties have caused some argument over whether "the seventh king" is Ptolemy VI Philometor (180–145), Ptolemy VII Philopator (145–144), or Ptolemy VIII Euergetes (145–116). The first stands as favorite, but near unanimity, in any case, prevails in identifying the period in question as the mid second century.[109] That has engendered the further conclusion that this work represents the propaganda

104. Sib. Or. 3.381–400.

105. Sib. Or. 3.464–73.

106. Sib. Or. 3.484–88.

107. Sib. Or. 3.508–10.

108. The conglomerate mixture is reflected also in the confused and overlapping manuscript transmission. The tangled strands permit no neat stemma, suggesting a number of layers built over time by diverse interests and sources. See J. Geffcken, *Die Oracula Sibyllina* (Leipzig, 1902) xxi–liii; Rzach, *RE* II.A.2 (1923) 2119–22; Goodman in Schürer, *History of the Jewish People*, III.1, 628–31.

109. The conclusion is taken for granted by Lanchester in Charles, *Apocrypha and Pseudepigrapha*, II, 382. A fuller discussion by Collins, *The Sibylline Oracles*, 28–32; *Bull. Inst. Jewish Studies* 2 (1974) 1–5. See also Rzach, *RE* II.A.2 (1923) 2127–28; Fraser, *Ptolemaic Alexandria*, II, 992; Goodman in Schürer, *History of the Jewish People*, III.1, 635–36; Barclay, *Jews in the*

of Egyptian Jews to ingratiate themselves with the Ptolemaic dynasty and to express a common basis for relations between Jews and Gentiles in Egypt.[110] How legitimate is that analysis?

The first mention of the "seventh king" causes misgivings right away. It follows upon the Sibyl's recounting of the rise and fall of kingdoms. Among them the Greeks are singled out as arrogant and impious and the Macedonians as bringing a fearsome cloud of war upon mortals. The God of Heaven, however, will eradicate them, paving the way for Roman rule, the ascendancy of the many hoary-headed men from the western sea, whose dominion too will prove oppressive, thus prompting a mighty fall, whose morals will degenerate, who will provoke hatred, and who will engage in every form of deceit until the time of the seventh kingdom when an Egyptian monarch of Greek lineage will be sovereign.[111] Do these really suit the era of Ptolemy VI or Ptolemy VIII? No *ex eventu* forecast could have set the fall of Roman power to that period, a time when its might was increasing and its reach extending. Nor can one imagine the Sibyl (or her recorder) making such a pronouncement in the reigns of Philometor or Euergetes themselves when its falsity was patent. The idea collides abruptly with reality.[112] The Sibyl must be looking forward to a demise of Rome that had not yet occurred. Hence the "seventh king" can hardly refer to a present or past scion of the Ptolemaic dynasty.

Mediterranean Diaspora, 218, 222–23 (more cautiously). The sole dissenter is Nikiprowetzky, *La Troisième Sibylle*, 208–17, whose proposal that the seventh king is Cleopatra has rightly found no takers.

110. So Collins in Charlesworth, *Old Testament Pseudepigrapha*, I, 356; *ANRW* II.20.1 (1987) 432.

111. Sib. Or. 3.165–95; see esp. 191–93: μῖσος δ' ἐξεγερεῖ καὶ πᾶς δόλος ἔσσεται αὐτοῖς, ἄχρι πρὸς ἑβδομάτην βασιληΐδα, ἧς βασιλεύσει Αἰγύπτου βασιλεύς, ὃς ἀφ' Ἑλλήνων γένος ἔσται.

112. Geffcken, *Oracula Sibyllina*, 58, recognized the problem and simply bracketed lines 192–93, thus removing the seventh kingdom from the passage. Peretti, *La Sibilla babilonese*, 178–96, took a different route, separating out the verses on Roman conquest (lines 175–78) and seeing the rest of the segment as a denunciation of Macedonian imperialism. Such dissection, however, is unwarranted and implausible. Geffcken's solution is arbitrary, and Peretti's reconstruction ignores the problem of the Macedonian realm coming to an end at the time when Egypt was ruled by a king of Macedonian lineage. The unity of the whole passage is ably defended by Nikiprowetzky, *La Troisième Sibylle*, 209–13. Collins, *The Sibylline Oracles*, 31–32, argues that an anti-Roman attitude by Egyptian Jews might well have been prompted by Ptolemy Philometor who had reason to feel aggrieved at the Romans. The suggestion carries little conviction. No evidence exists for any animosity on Philometor's part toward Rome, let alone for any prodding of Jews by him for this purpose. Even if the conjecture were right, however, it fails to address the question of how the collapse of Roman power could be set in Philometor's reign.

The Sibyl's next reference to a seventh king comes in the midst of numerous woeful prophecies. She dwells on the grievous fate that has either overtaken or will eventually overtake a number of nations. Egypt indeed is among them, with a heavy blow to come, unanticipated and dreadful, in the seventh generation of kings—and then she will rest.[113] The oracle proceeds to detail the evils that will befall numerous other places, reiterating once more that the baleful race of Egypt is approaching its own destruction.[114] In the context of so dire a set of predictions, with the afflictions of Egypt doubly noted, it strains the point to place emphasis upon a single line alluding to a pause in the seventh generation. Nothing in the passage gives any reason to evoke the era of Philometor and Euergetes.[115] Indeed, what is predicted for the seventh generation is dispersal, death, and famine, and only subsequently will it cease.[116] The apocalyptic visions predominate in the long string of verses. A search for historical specificity obscures that fact.

The third passage is still more problematic. It too lies embedded in an eschatological prophecy. The oracle foresees calamity, war, and pestilence inflicted by the Immortal upon those who fail to acknowledge his existence and persist instead in the worship of idols. Destruction will fall upon Egypt in the time of the young (or new) seventh king reckoned from the rule of the Greeks. And the divine instrument is named: a great king from Asia whose infantry and cavalry will despoil the land, spread every evil, overthrow the Egyptian kingdom, and cart off its possessions over the sea. Then they will bend their knees to God, the great king, the immortal one, while all works made by the hand of man collapse in a flame of fire.[117] A standard line has it that the Asian invader is Antiochus IV Epiphanes and the young Egyptian king is Ptolemy Philometor, victim of the Seleucid's assault.[118]

---

113. Sib. Or. 3.295–318. See esp. 314–18: ἥξει σοι πληγὴ μεγάλη, Αἴγυπτε, πρὸς οἴκους, δεινή, ἣν οὔπω ποτ' ἐξήλπισας ἐρχομένην σοι ... θάνατος καὶ λιμὸς ἐφέξει ἑβδομάτῃ γενεῇ βασιλήων, καὶ τότε παύσῃ.

114. Sib. Or. 3.319–49. See 348: ἴσθι τότ' Αἰγύπτου ὀλοὸν γένος ἐγγὺς ὀλέθρου.

115. That the allusion in line 316 to a sword passing through their midst refers to civil conflict between Philometor and Euergetes is pure conjecture, made even less substantial by the fact that the line itself is corrupt. The conjecture was offered by Lanchester in Charles, *Apocrypha and Pseudepigrapha*, II, 384; endorsed by Fraser, *Ptolemaic Alexandria*, I, 710; II, 994; Collins, *The Sibylline Oracles*, 31; rightly dismissed by Nikiprowetzky, *La Troisième Sibylle*, 198. The Sibyl could indeed appeal to biblical authority for civil strife in Egypt; Isaiah 19.2.

116. Sib. Or. 3.316, quoted above, n. 113.

117. Sib. Or. 3.601–18.

118. See Lanchester in Charles, *Apocrypha and Pseudepigrapha*, II, 389; Fraser, *Ptolemaic Alexandria*, II, 998–99; A. Momigliano, *Sesto contributo alla storia degli studi classici*, 2 (Rome, 1980) 557. Collins, *The Sibylline Oracles*, 29–30, shrinks from too narrow or definite a judgment on the Asian king, but adheres to the view that Egypt's monarch must be Philometor or Euergetes:

Again, however, the effort to find direct historical allusions encounters serious stumbling-blocks. If the Sibyl intended Antiochus IV as the Asian king, her timing would have had to be very precise indeed. Seleucid success and deposition of the Ptolemies came as consequence of Epiphanes' first invasion in 170; the second, in 168, was thwarted by Rome and followed by reinstatement of Ptolemaic authority. An *ex eventu* prophecy would make no sense except in that narrow corridor of time—far too tight a squeeze. The idea of a direct allusion to Antiochus Epiphanes can be discarded. Threats to Egypt from Asia were endemic in Egyptian history and lore. The Sibyl simply fastened upon the traditional foe as anticipated ravager of the land, not a particular monarch, nor an identifiable invasion.[119] The passage also provides little comfort to those who argue that a cordial relationship between Ptolemy Philometor and the Jews and the elevation of Jewish leaders under his aegis justify a dating of the oracle to his reign. On the contrary, the relevant verses hold no brief, indeed hold no hope, for the seventh king. The invasion will come in his time, bringing with it not only devastation and pestilence but the fall of the Egyptian kingdom that had been founded by Macedonians.[120] Far better then to divorce these verses from the particular events that marked the reign of Ptolemy VI—or anyone else for that matter. The Sibyl predicts catastrophe for Egyptian idolaters, laid low

---

if the term νέος in line 608 means "young," it could suit the youthful Philometor at the time of Antiochus' invasion; if the meaning is "new," this might be the product of an oracle issued late in either king's reign. Collins leaves the options open. One might even consider the possibility of an allusion to the title of Ptolemy Neos Philopator. Goodman in Schürer, *History of the Jewish People*, III.1, 636, declines to take a stand.

119. This is correctly noted by Collins, *The Sibylline Oracles*, 29–30, 39–40, who points to invasions by Hyksos and Persians and to oracular pronouncements in the Potter's Oracle and elsewhere. But he still considers Epiphanes' invasion as a prod for the Sibyl's forecast. On Antiochus' two military expeditions into Egypt, see Gruen, *Hellenistic World*, II, 651–60, with bibliography. Antiochus did, allegedly, acknowledge the power of the Jewish god at the end, as recounted by II Macc. 9.11–17; cf. I Macc. 6.12–13. But this is certainly not alluded to by Sib. Or. 3.616–17, where those who will bend a knee to God are clearly repentant Egyptians. Peretti's notion, *La Sibilla babilonese*, 389–93, that the Asian king represents the coming Messiah, drastically misconceives his role in the text—which is that of destroyer, not reclaimer.

120. Sib. Or. 3.608–15: ὁπόταν Αἰγύπτου βασιλεὺς νέος ἕβδομος ἄρχῃ τῆς ἰδίης γαίης ἀριθμούμενος ἐξ Ἑλλήνων ἀρχῆς, ἧς ἄρξουσι Μακηδόνες ἄσπετοι ἄνδρες. ἔλθῃ δ' ἐξ Ἀσίης βασιλεὺς μέγας ... ῥίψει δ' Αἰγύπτου βασιλήιον. The opposition here between an Asian ruler and a kingdom founded by Macedonians makes it even less likely that the former could be a Seleucid. Collins, *ANRW* II.20.1 (1987) 431–32, remarks upon "the enthusiasm for the Egyptian king in Sib. Or. III." There is certainly no sign of it here. If anything, the reverse. Barclay, *Jews in the Mediterranean Diaspora*, 222–23, independently reached similar conclusions.

by the hand of God through the agency of an Asian conqueror, and then redeemed when they prostrate themselves before the true Immortal. The model should more properly be sought in something like the thunderings of Isaiah than in the special circumstances of a Ptolemaic reign.[121] Once again, the eschatology holds central place and drives the entire passage. In this context it looks ahead to the smashing of idolatry, to transformation, conversion, and redemption. A narrow political interpretation would be simplistic and distorting.[122]

A noteworthy point demands attention, one missed by all those who have written on the subject. Designations like Ptolemy VI or Ptolemy VII may be a convenience for modern scholars, but they lack ancient authority. The Greek rulers of Egypt nowhere identified themselves by numbers. One will look in vain for such a title in official documents, whether on stone, papyri, or coinage. Petitions to the crown do not address the kings in this fashion, nor are they so referred to indirectly in transactions between private persons. The Ptolemies, of course, regularly appear with cult titles (Soter, Euergetes, Philometor and the like), other epithets of dignity and honor, and patronymics, but they did not place themselves in a numerical sequence.[123] Perhaps more striking, our fullest and most reliable Hellenistic literary source, the historian Polybius, refers to the Ptolemies regularly and frequently, but never attaches numbers to them.[124] One can go further still. Jewish sources, contemporary or nearly contemporary with the Ptolemaic monarchy, namely I, II, and III Maccabees, and the *Letter of Aristeas*, speak of the Egyptian kings—but not by number.[125] The same indeed holds for Josephus' *Antiquitates* which employs cult titles, no numerals.[126] In a word, apart from very rare exceptions, neither the technical language in documents nor the less formal designations by literary sources, whether pagan or Jewish,

---

121. Nikiprowetzky, *La Troisième Sibylle*, 208, rightly points to parallels between Isaiah 2.18–21, 30.22–24, and Sib. Or. 3.604–607, 616–23.

122. Cf. the reference to a coalition of kings organized for a concerted assault on the Temple; Sib. Or. 3.657–68. No historical circumstance has been suggested or can be found for that purported episode. Cf. Psalms 2.1–2.

123. To take only the most celebrated examples, see the titulature exhibited in the Canopus decree, the Rosetta Stone, and Ptolemy Euergetes' will that bequeathed his kingdom to Rome; *OGIS* 56; *OGIS* 90; *SEG* IX.7.

124. See, e.g., Polyb. 5.34.1: Πτολεμαῖος ὁ κληθεὶς Φιλοπάτωρ; 14.3–4, 31.10.

125. See I Macc. 10.51, 10.55, 11.8; II Macc. 1.10, 4.21; III Macc. 1.1, 3.12, 7.1; *LetArist* 13, 35, 41.

126. E.g. Jos. *Ant.* 12.2–3, 12.11, 12.118, 12.235, 12.243, 13.62, 13.79–80, 13.103, 13.285, 13.328, 13.370. The numbers do appear, though very rarely, in other Josephan texts; *BJ* 1.31: Πτολεμαῖον τὸν ἕκτον; *C. Apion.* II.48: τρίτος Πτολεμαῖος.

employ a numbering system to distinguish the Ptolemies. When the Sibyl makes mention of a seventh king, she could hardly expect her readers to take it as a specific Ptolemy.

The number seven possessed high symbolic import for the Jews. The centrality of the Sabbath as a defining feature of Judaism suffices to demonstrate the fact.[127] One could assemble biblical instances aplenty.[128] The number recurs also in apocalyptic literature.[129] More striking still, it appears twice more in the Third Sibyl, without reference to any kings, let alone Ptolemies. The prophetess forecasts a dismal desolation for Jews, to endure for "seven decades of time" before God elevates them to glory.[130] And elsewhere she visualizes the time of peace when Jews will gather the weapons of enemies for "seven lengths of annually revolving times."[131] The number must be understood as carrying mystical import, an abstract and spiritual sense, not the denotation of a royal tenure.

One additional passage needs treatment in this connection. The Sibyl describes a grisly period of civil strife, cataclysmic warfare among kings and peoples, seizure of territory and riches, foreign rule over the Greek world, the destructive power of greed for wealth that terminates in utter ruin, death, and devastation. But rescue will come when God sends a king from the sun to put an end to war, slaying some and binding others with oaths of loyalty—an end achieved not by private counsel but by obeying the worthy precepts of the great God.[132] This image too has been associated with the Ptolemies, and "the king from the sun" reckoned as identical with the "seventh king."[133] Precedents and parallels in the Egyptian material ostensibly lend credence to the association. The nearest analogy, however, appears in the Potter's Oracle which looks to a king from the sun appointed by the goddess Isis. And that is an expression of Egyptian nationalist sentiment, certainly not advocacy of

---

127. Gen. 2.2–3.

128. Note, e.g., the famed tale of Joseph with its seven years of abundance and seven of famine; Gen. 41.

129. Cf. I Enoch 91.12–17, 93.3–10.

130. Sib. Or. 3.273–83; see 280: ἑπτὰ χρόνων δεκάδας. The text draws on Jeremiah 25.11.

131. Sib. Or. 3.728: ἑπτὰ χρόνων μήκη περιτελλομένων ἐνιαυτῶν. See Ezekiel 39.9.

132. Sib. Or. 3.635–56.

133. A strong argument for this identification is made by Collins, *Bull. Inst. Jewish Studies* 2 (1974) 5–8; *The Sibylline Oracles*, 40–44; *Between Athens and Jerusalem*, 68–70. Accepted by O. Camponovo, *Königtum, Königsherrschaft und Reich Gottes in den frühjüdischen Schriften* (Freiburg, 1984) 344–45. But Collins' claim that "the identification is inevitable" greatly overstates the case. Momigliano, *Sesto contributo*, 556, and Barclay, *Jews in the Mediterranean Diaspora*, 223, rightly question the connection. See also the comments of Nikiprowetzky, *La Troisième Sibylle*, 133–37.

Ptolemaic rule.[134] To be sure, connection of the king with the sun might well be appropriated by the Ptolemies too. But the relationship has its roots in Pharaonic imagery and ancient Egyptian religion. These lines in the Third Sibylline Book represent Jewish adaptation of Egyptian lore to forecast a Messiah who will stamp out strife and restore tranquillity. The "king from the sun" is an emissary of God, not a Ptolemaic monarch.[135] Indeed the author of these lines had a solidly Jewish text to employ as inspiration: the verse of Isaiah in which the Lord proclaims the coming of one from the rising sun to trample down rulers everywhere.[136] In short, the standard theory of a central core for the Third Sibyl in the mid second century is a ramshackle structure on the most fragile foundations.

Similar historical markers have been discerned (or imagined) for the later first century BCE—most notably in alleged allusions to the "second triumvirate" and to Cleopatra VII, last of the Ptolemies. They do not easily survive scrutiny.

A verse in the early part of the text furnishes the sole basis for finding the "second triumvirate" amidst the Sibylline pronouncements. The oracle speaks of a time when Rome will rule over Egypt, when the greatest kingdom of the immortal king will materialize among men, when the holy sovereign will take universal dominion. At that time, inexorable anger will fall upon the men of Latium, and three with woeful destiny will rain destruction upon Rome. And all will perish in their own abodes when a cataract of fire rushes from Heaven.[137] Scholars regularly repeat identification of the cryptic "three" with the triumvirate of Antony, Octavian, and Lepidus.[138] But the text itself provides grave difficulties for that hypothesis. The opening line of the passage has Rome exercising dominion over Egypt, an explicit statement that makes sense only after annexation of the land as a Roman province in 30 BCE. But the triumvirate no longer existed at that time: Lepidus had been dropped, Antony was dead, and Octavian unopposed. Furthermore,

---

134. See the text in L. Koenen, *ZPE* 2 (1968) 206, lines 38–41. Collins' efforts to get around this, most recently in L. Bormann et al., *Religious Propaganda and Missionary Competition in the New Testament World* (Leiden, 1994) 57–69, are unsuccessful. He appeals to the myth of Horus and Seth but has to acknowledge that the Third Sibyl has no one to correspond to Seth.

135. Cf. the discussion of D. Frankfurter, *Elijah in Upper Egypt* (Minneapolis, 1993) 176–82, 186, with references.

136. Isaiah 41.25.

137. Sib. Or. 3.46–54: αὐτὰρ ἐπεὶ Ῥώμη καὶ Αἰγύπτου βασιλεύσει ... τρεῖς Ῥώμην οἰκτρῇ μοίρῃ καταδηλήσονται.

138. So, e.g., Geffcken, *Komposition*, 13–14; A. Kurfess, *Sibyllinische Weissagungen* (Berlin, 1951) 288; Peretti, *La Sibilla babilonese*, 342–45. Doubts expressed by M. Simon in D. Hellholm, *Apocalypticism in the Mediterranean World and the Near East* (Tübingen, 1983) 224.

the forecast that the trio will destroy Rome hardly applies to the triumvirate. Rome stood intact, and the empire had expanded. No *ex eventu* oracle could have uttered such patently false phrases. And a genuine prediction would not likely have conceived Rome's destruction at the hands of the triumvirate after the conquest of Egypt.[139] Nor is it likely that the Sibyl projects three future rulers of Rome who will do in the empire.[140] She foresees the destruction of Rome as the deed of the deathless monarch, the holy prince as sovereign over all the earth, doubtless a reference to the divinity. The three who administer the mournful fate to Rome should therefore be agents of God, not identifiable personages from Roman history.[141]

Does Cleopatra appear in the Third Sibylline Book? Many have found her in lines that describe the world as being in the hands of a woman, a world governed and obedient in every regard. The Sibyl goes on to characterize the woman as a widow, reigning over all the universe, hurling gold and silver into the deep, as well as the brass and iron of ephemeral men. Then all parts of the cosmos will be bereft when God rolls up the sky like a scroll and the heavens themselves fall upon the earth, followed by a cataract of fire to burn earth and sea, eradicating daylight and nightfall, as well as all the seasons, a terrible divine judgment.[142] Only guesswork can offer an identity for the "woman" and the "widow." And there has been plenty of that. Many scholars, both early and recent, favor Cleopatra.[143] The reasons fall well short of compelling. Cleopatra, to be sure, was a widow after the death of her brother-husband Ptolemy XIII. But her widowhood was hardly conspicuous at a time when she ruled much of the east together with and largely as consequence of her consort M. Antony. Nor is it likely that the widow allusion refers to Cleopatra's association with Isis, on the grounds that Isis lost her husband Osiris every year (only to regain him again) and

139. The remark of W. W. Tarn, *JRS* 22 (1932) 142, that once Roman rule was established over Egypt, it could itself be used as a date, is unfathomable. Collins, *The Sibylline Oracles*, 65, rightly sees that the oracle must have been composed after Actium but fails to recognize the implications for any reference to the triumvirate.

140. So Nikiprowetzky, *La Troisième Sibylle*, 150–54, who usefully points to the motif of three Roman kings in Jewish apocalyptic.

141. Note Sib. Or. 3.533–36, which refers to "five" who will arouse a mighty wrath and who will shamelessly engage one another in frightful and tumultuous war, bringing joy to their enemies but woe to the Greeks. The author evidently blended an echo of Isaiah 30.17 with an allusion to Roman civil wars. The number "five," it is clear, lacks any specific denotation here. And there is no more reason to assign specificity to the number "three" in Sib. Or. 3.52.

142. Sib. Or. 3.75–92.

143. E.g. Tarn, *JRS* 22 (1932) 142: "That the widow is Cleopatra ... seems certain"; Collins, *The Sibylline Oracles*, 66–70; Goodman in Schürer, *History of the Jewish People*, III.1, 641.

that Cleopatra was twice widowed. That is far-fetched, and out of tune with the context of the passage. The widow in question rules the world— not simply the lands of the east on the sufferance of a Roman dynast.[144] Only one power fits that description: Rome itself. Characterization of the great city as a widow has parallels in biblical prophecies about Babylon.[145] The metaphorical bereavement of the superpower may signify the loss of divine support, presaging an imminent demise, which indeed follows shortly thereafter in the passage. That sense is reinforced by repetition of the widow metaphor in connection with the divine judgment: all elements of the universe will be bereft when God rolls up the heavens.[146] The oracle, like so much else in the Third Book, directs itself against Rome, not Cleopatra.[147]

Another oracle involves an explicit attack on Rome. This too has been identified with Cleopatra, only here she takes the positive role as the avenger of Roman misdeeds. Such at least is the theory.[148] The passage itself makes that conclusion less than obvious. In the Sibylline pronouncement, vengeance will fall upon Rome, a three-fold exaction taken by Asia, previously its victim, now its conqueror, and a twenty-fold return in Italian slaves for the Asians once enslaved by Rome, a down payment on a debt of myriads. Rome, the virgin, often intoxicated with numerous suitors, will be wed unceremoniously as a slave. The mistress will frequently snip her locks and, passing judgment, will cast her from heaven to earth and then again from earth to heaven. After destruction, however, will come

144. Sib. Or. 3.75–77: καὶ τότε δὴ κόσμος ὑπὸ ταῖς παλάμῃσι γυναικός ... ἔνθ' ὁπόταν κόσμου παντὸς χήρη βασιλεύσῃ. Indeed κόσμος appears yet a third time in line 81.

145. Isaiah 47.8–9; Apocalypse of John, 17–18. This was acutely noted by Nikiprowetzky, *La Troisième Sibylle*, 147–48. The equation of Babylon and Rome in later Jewish and Christian authors is well known; e.g. Sib. Or. 5.137–44, 5.155–61; 4 Ezra 15.43–16.1; Rev. 14.8, 16.19, 18.2, 18.21.

146. Sib. Or. 3.80–82: τότε δὴ στοιχεῖα πρόπαντα χηρεύσει κόσμου, ὁπόταν θεὸς αἰθέρι ναίων οὐρανὸν εἱλίξῃ.

147. The idea of Rome as the referent here was suggested long ago but has found little favor in the last century. See C. Alexandre, *Excursus ad Sibyllina* (Paris, 1856) 517; Lanchester in Charles, *Apocrypha and Pseudepigrapha*, II, 371. A. Rzach, *RE* II.A.2 (1923) 2131, rules out Cleopatra and reckons the widow as an apocalyptic figure. The argument of Nikiprowetzky, *La Troisième Sibylle*, 146–49, that the widow represents the Messiah or the coming of New Jerusalem, confusingly amalgamates both the world ruler and the dominion which follows the divine destruction.

148. So Tarn, *JRS* 22 (1932) 135–41; H. Jeanmaire, *La Sibylle et le retour de l'age d'Or* (Paris, 1939) 55–61. Collins, *The Sibylline Oracles*, 57–64, questions many of Tarn's arguments, but adopts his conclusion.

reconciliation, peace, and prosperity, a time of concord and the flight of all evils.[149]

Is Cleopatra the *despoina*, the mistress? Does this represent a Jewish reflection of the Ptolemaic queen's propaganda against Rome? Not a likely inference. The oracle pits Asia against Rome, unambiguously favoring the former and projecting an eventual era of harmony. Depiction of the struggle between Cleopatra and Octavian as one between east and west was, of course, the product of propaganda from Rome, a blackening of the shameless and power-mad woman who leads barbaric hordes against the valiant Italians.[150] It is quite unthinkable that Cleopatra herself would embrace that distorted portrait. Egypt had suffered no depredation from Rome, Cleopatra had no reason to seek reparations or exact revenge for past iniquities. The notion that she looked toward conquest of Rome itself rests on a hostile and thoroughly unreliable tradition. The queen's ambitions in fact directed themselves toward revival of the Ptolemaic empire—with the assistance of Rome.

Once again, the Sibyl's meaning transcends a specific historical circumstance. The mistress who shears the head of Roma, the newly enslaved servant, may well be Asia itself, a broad and vague allusion to the sufferings of the east at Roman hands, now to be reversed and compensated for many times over.[151] The forecast, plainly a wishful hope for a future that never came to pass, expresses fierce eastern resentment against Roman exploitation and looks ahead to a happier time when the empire will be crushed, its reparations plenteous, and the outcome one of concord. Cleopatra has no place here.

Similar doubts need to be applied to other inferences about historical events or personages lurking behind the Sibyl's dark pronouncements. The

---

149. Sib. Or. 3.350–80. See esp. 356–60: ὦ χλιδανὴ ζάχρυσε Λατινίδος ἔκγονε Ῥώμη, παρθένε, πολλάκι σοῖσι πολυμνήστοισι γάμοισιν οἰνωθεῖσα, λάτρις νυμφεύσεαι οὐκ ἐνὶ κόσμῳ, πολλάκι δ᾽ ἁβρὴν σεῖο κόμην δέσποινά τε κείρει ἠδὲ δίκην διέπουσα ἀπ᾽ οὐρανόθεν ποτὶ γαῖαν ῥίψει, ἐκ δὲ γαίης πάλιν οὐρανὸν εἷς ἀνεγείρει.

150. Cf. Horace, *Epode*, 9; *Carm.* 1.37; Vergil, *Aen.* 8.675–728; Propertius, 3.11, 4.6. To be sure, the war of Actium is portrayed as a clash of Europe against Asia also by Philo *Leg.* 144, a point stressed by Collins, *The Sibylline Oracles*, 60. But Philo, whose objective in this section of his work was to contrast the virtues of Caligula's predecessors with his own megalomania, clearly took up the Augustan line and represents no independent Jewish viewpoint—let alone a reflection of Cleopatra's attitude. His account, in fact, omits any allusion to the Ptolemaic queen, depicting the contest as one headed by rival Romans: ἡγεμόνας ἔχουσαι καὶ προαγωνιστὰς Ῥωμαίων τοὺς ἐν τέλει δοκιμωτάτους. Moreover, Augustus appears not as leader of Rome against a Greek ruler but as champion of Hellenism and civilizer of the barbarians; Philo *Leg.* 147.

151. So Peretti, *La Sibilla babilonese*, 351–54.

very passage just discussed has been ascribed to the time of the Mithridatic wars, an anticipated vengeful retaliation by Mithridates against Romans who had despoiled the east.[152] But Mithridates would hardly qualify as a "mistress." And his fearsome war against Romans and Italians would certainly not suit a prediction of subsequent peace and harmony.

Elsewhere, a cryptic oracle regarding Macedonian terrors unleashed upon Asia has stimulated a wealth of scholarly speculation. The Sibyl bewails afflictions imposed upon Asia, and even upon Europe, by the horrific Macedon becoming mistress of all lands under the sun, climaxed by the conquest of Babylon. The evils wrought upon Asia are ascribed to an untrustworthy man, clad in purple cloak, characterized as barbaric and fiery, who came to place Asia under a wicked yoke. Ultimately, however, so the Sibyl forecast, the very race he sought to destroy will bring about the destruction of his own race. A still more cryptic pronouncement follows: the destroyer provides a single root which he will cut off from ten horns and will leave another side-shoot; then, after slaying the warrior progenitor of a purple race, he will perish at the hands of his sons, and the side-horn will rule.[153] Opinions divide on the identity of the malignant Macedonian conqueror whose race will perish by the hand of those whom he oppressed. Some opt for Alexander the Great, some for Antiochus IV Epiphanes.[154] Or, as almost all commentators now seem to concur, the original oracle had Alexander as its villain but was then reworked by a Jewish Sibyllist who directed its fire against Antiochus Epiphanes, arch-enemy of the Jews, and saw the collapse of Macedonian power in the internecine warfare of the Seleucid house.[155]

---

152. So Bousset, *RE für protestantische Theologie und Kirche* 18 (1906) 271; Lanchester in Charles, *Apocrypha and Pseudepigrapha*, II, 372; Peretti, *La Sibilla babilonese*, 329–40; Geffcken, *Komposition*, 8–9; B. C. McGing, *The Foreign Policy of Mithridates VI Eupator* (Leiden, 1986) 104–105. Goodman in Schürer, *History of the Jewish People*, III.1, 636, declines to choose between Mithridates and Cleopatra.

153. Sib. Or. 3.381–400. The oracle is often divided into two, with a break after line 387. But even if the division is justified, the forecasts are closely related and belong together.

154. For Antiochus, see, e.g., Lanchester in Charles, *Apocrypha and Pseudepigrapha*, II, 385; H. H. Rowley, *ZAW* 44 (1926) 324–27; Fraser, *Ptolemaic Alexandria*, II, 995–96. The argument for Alexander, at least as the initial figure in lines 388–91, was forcefully made by Bousset, *ZNW* 3 (1902) 34–41, followed by many in subsequent years.

155. Peretti, *La Sibilla babilonese*, 372–74; S. K. Eddy, *The King is Dead* (Lincoln, 1961) 11–14; Collins, *The Sibylline Oracles*, 27; Goodman in Schürer, *History of the Jewish People*, III.1, 634. The dispute over whether the first part of the forecast, in lines 381–87, derives from a "Persian Sibyl," a "Babylonian Sibyl," or neither one need not be explored here. See the valuable discussion, with bibliography, by Nikiprowetzky, *ANRW* II.20.1 (1987) 474–75, 524–28.

But how much is gained from this speculation? Focus upon historical personages and their actions veers away from the central significance. The purple-clad invader of Asia may well be Alexander the Great, but he is cited as emblematic of Macedonian power and ruthlessness, not with regard to specific deeds of the individual. The one explicit reference to conquest of Babylon should have made that clear to commentators: Alexander did gain control of Babylon, but postured as its liberator, respected its religion and traditions, and treated it with generosity.[156] The Sibyl is concerned with the broader consequences of Macedonian dominance, not with historical particulars. By the same token, the narrow interpretation of the oracle's conclusion which seeks to identify individuals in the house of Antiochus Epiphanes has little point. To be sure, the Sibyl here has adopted the image of the ten horns and their offshoot that can be found in Daniel 7.7–8, but it does not follow that the image carries the same significance—even if we knew for certain to what Daniel does refer. What matters here is the sharp hostility to Hellenic overlordship in the east, at least as exercised by savage rulers, and the prediction of its violent demise. The thrust of the oracle is out of tune with much else in the Third Book. Knowledge of Daniel implies a Jewish hand at work. But the message contains no hint of divine retribution or intervention. And this is the one segment in the Third Book in which Macedonians, rather than the more usual Romans, are the targets of oracular venom. Insofar as Jewish authorship is involved, whether in origin or as redaction, it is best seen as expressing resentment against foreign oppression, wherever it manifests itself in the east.

Of course, the Book's verses belong to time and circumstances. But accretions and admixtures obscure their origins and set them largely beyond our grasp. Occasional references, however dark, to particular periods or personalities do survive, as already noted. Unfortunately, they have received undue attention. The very character of apocalyptic texts fosters ambiguity, their allusions deliberately designed for adaptability to diverse settings. Oracular voices resonate beyond the particular and give greater meaning to the whole text.[157]

The quest for geographical specificity has also been overemphasized. Egypt is the favored provenance, with the Hellenized Jews of Alexandria or Leontopolis as principal sites for authors.[158] The theory connects closely

156. Arrian 3.16.3–5, 7.17.1–2. See also Ps. Hecataeus in Jos. *C. Apion.*, 1.192, for a favorable Jewish view of Alexander at Babylon; cf. 2.43.

157. See the sensible general remarks of Simon in Hellholm, *Apocalypticism*, 224–25.

158. The case is made most fully by Collins, *Bull. Inst. Jewish Studies* 2 (1974) 1–18; *The Sibylline Oracles*, 35–55. Collins' argument for Leontopolis as the principal site of composition, however, has little force. The absence of any allusion to Leontopolis in the text fatally weakens

with the idea that a cozy relationship between Jews and the Ptolemies of mid second century Egypt finds voice in the utterances of the Third Sibyl. The weakness of that reconstruction has already been indicated above. And the corollary correspondingly falls. Since no unequivocal reference to the relevant Ptolemies exists in the text, further speculation about the significance of an alleged Jewish-Egyptian provenance lacks warrant.

In fact, many of the Sibyl's pronouncements would dishearten the devotees of Ptolemaic Egypt. Almost the very opening lines of the Third Book denounce Egyptians for their idolatry that includes not only the erection of stone statues to people, but the worship of snakes and the rendering of sacrifice to cats.[159] The early verses, to be sure, may actually belong to Book II, and hence have no bearing on the attitude of the authors of the Third Sibyl.[160] But it is perhaps not irrelevant that those who ordered the extant edition found ostensible congruence. In any event, later passages are comparably uncomplimentary to Egyptians. When God's wrath falls upon the nations, Egypt will suffer together with others, indeed doubly so.[161] The Egyptians are characterized as a destructive race.[162] The Sibyl brackets them, together with Phoenicians, Romans, and others, as moral transgressors, indulging in homosexual vice.[163] And it is noteworthy that the projected time of peace and prosperity will come *after* the collapse of Egypt, done in by an Asian king.[164]

That some verses in the collection stem from Hellenized Jews in Egypt can be readily acknowledged. The denunciations of Egypt noted above belong in that category. So do the lines that give Egypt prominence in the sequence of empires, singling out its royal rule twice.[165] And one may plausibly infer Egyptian provenance for the passage on the "king from the sun," a Jewish reworking of material rooted in their adopted land.[166] All of this, however,

---

the idea, forcing Collins to postulate a very narrow corridor of time for the composition: after Onias' arrival in Egypt but before he built the temple at Leontopolis. However, the recent immigration of Onias and his followers from Judaea and their relatively conservative ideology, which Collins himself acknowledges, make them the least likely persons to embrace the quintessentially Hellenic form of Sibylline prophecy to convey their message.

159. Sib. Or. 3.29–45.

160. See Geffcken, *Komposition*, 47–53; Bousset, *RE für protestantische Theologie und Kirche* 18 (1906) 273–74; Rzach, *RE* II.A.2 (1923) 2123, 2130.

161. Sib. Or. 3.314–18, 348–49.

162. Sib. Or. 3.348–49: Αἰγύπτου ὀλοὸν γένος.

163. Sib. Or. 3.596–600. Cf. the harsh attacks on Egyptians in Wisdom 11.5–16. 12.23–27, 15.14–19, 17.7–21, 10.13–17.

164. Sib. Or. 3.611–23.

165. Sib. Or. 3.156–61.

166. Sib. Or. 3.619–56.

amounts to no more than a fraction of the 829 verses in Book III. Much of the remainder could just as readily derive from Palestinian Jews.[167] And parts indeed need not even be Jewish in origin.[168] In short, it is hazardous to see the centrality of Egypt in the work, let alone Jewish favor toward Ptolemy VI or Ptolemy VIII as stimulus for its composition.[169] The Sibyl has a wider canvas.

Eschatology is the central ingredient throughout. Reference both to past disasters and to ills still to come issue in forecasts of terrifying divine judgments and usually the glorious elevation of the Jewish faithful. That is surely the significance of the "king from the sun," not a historical personage but a Messianic figure.[170] And eschatological overtones may be caught also in lines that allude to construction of the second Temple but also carry deeper meaning embodied in a king sent by the Lord to deliver judgment in blood and fire.[171]

The Sibyl's realm of concern stretches to the world at large—at least the world as she knew it, the lands of the Mediterranean. And there the dominant power was Rome, ruthless, tyrannical, and appalling. Rome is the prime villain of the verses, overwhelmingly so. Only misguided scholarly ingenuity has obscured that otherwise conspicuous fact.

The evils of Rome, Romans, and the Roman empire recur repeatedly. A forecast near the outset of Book III issues a severe condemnation. When the imperial power stretches over Egypt, its days become numbered. Despite all the splendid cities with their temples, stadia, fora, and statuary, the empire stands doomed, to be destroyed by the fiery cataract of the Supreme Being

167. E.g., Sib. Or. 3.63–74, 97–155, 196–294, 381–400, 489–600, 657–808.

168. Sib. Or. 3.350–80, 401–88.

169. A similar criticism with regard to reductive interpretations of the Oracula Sibyllina Book 7 was delivered by J. G. Gager, *HTR* 65 (1972) 91–97. See also Frankfurter, *Elijah in Upper Egypt*, 211–38, on the Apocalypse of Elijah.

170. Sib. Or. 3.652–56; see above, pp. 277–78.

171. Sib. Or. 3.282–94, esp. 286–87: καὶ τότε δὴ θεὸς οὐράνιος πέμψει βασιλῆα, κρινεῖ δ' ἄνδρα ἕκαστον ἐν αἵματι καὶ πυρὸς αὐγῇ. Cf. Peretti, *La Sibilla babilonese*, 393–95, whose speculations about the influence of Iranian eschatology, however, need to be taken with caution. The Messianic interpretation of these lines is not in fashion; cf. Nikiprowetzky, *La Troisième Sibylle*, 133–37; Collins, *The Sibylline Oracles*, 38–39. J. Nolland, *JTS* 30 (1979) 158–66, with valuable bibliography, rightly endeavored to revive it. But his effort to pinpoint it to the early Maccabaean period, despite the absence of any Maccabaean allusion, is unpersuasive. Cf. Collins, *Between Athens and Jerusalem*, 66–68. Nothing in the Third Book gives any hint of Jewish resistance to the Seleucid persecutions. That resounding silence also undermines the thesis of Momigliano, *Sesto contributo*, 553–56, that lines 194–95, predicting the future strength of the Jews, refer to the success of the Maccabaean uprising—a thesis endorsed now by Barclay, *Jews in the Mediterranean Diaspora*, 223–24.

who will reign over the earth.[172] The very next oracle directs itself against Beliar from the Sebastenoi, the latter probably signifying the line of Roman emperors and the former perhaps Nero, who will lead men away from God but will perish by divine fire, as will those who put trust in him.[173] There follows the passage in which "the widow," quite probably Rome, who rules the entire world, will herself be swept away by the mighty wrath of a divine judgment.[174] Not long thereafter in the text, a list of kingdoms culminating in Rome provokes a prophecy whereby the imperial forces of the Roman Republic will wreak widespread destruction only to fall afoul of their own arrogance, impiety, and moral corruption.[175] A harsher fate for Rome is proclaimed later in the text: retribution three-fold for exactions made from Asia, twenty-fold for the numbers enslaved, and ten thousand-fold for debts imposed; vengeance will reduce Rome to a mere street.[176] Yet another oracle bewails the devastation and destruction to be wrought by Romans upon the east but also foretells civil war that will tear Italy apart, the land described not as mother of good men but as nurse of wild beasts.[177] Finally, the large barbarian horde, which will devastate the Greeks, rampage, lay waste the earth, enslave and rape the conquered, and place a heavy yoke upon the Hellenes until God unleashes his deadly fire, unquestionably refers to the Romans.[178]

The Sibyl's rage needs explanation. She directs her fury against Rome, against the terror, destructiveness, and corruption of the Roman empire. Her verses, of course, are no political clarion call. Efforts to locate the message in precise time and place, with concrete intent and expectation, lead to blind alleys. The fall of Rome will come only through a cataclysmic divine intervention. But why this vitriol against Rome? Jews did not suffer at Roman hands in the Hellenistic period prior to the advent of Pompey, and rarely thereafter before the time of Caligula. Indeed, they generally enjoyed tolerance, alliance, and signal favor. What would prompt a Jewish Sibyl of this era to assault the Romans? The question, a difficult and troubling

---

172. Sib. Or. 3.46–62.

173. Sib. Or. 3.63–74. On Beliar as Nero, see Collins, *The Sibylline Oracles*, 80–87. *Contra*: Nikiprowetzky, *La Troisième Sibylle*, 138–43; cf. Goodman in Schürer, *The History of the Jewish People*, III.1, 640–41.

174. Sib. Or. 3.75–92. See above, pp. 279–280.

175. Sib. Or. 3.156–95.

176. Sib. Or. 3.350–64.

177. Sib. Or. 3.464–88; see 469: ἔσσῃ δ᾽ οὐκ ἀγαθῶν μήτηρ, θηρῶν δὲ τιθήνη.

178. Sib. Or. 3.520–44. The suggestion that this may allude to the Gallic invasion of Greece is ruled out by line 530 which states that the Greeks will have no one to give them a little aid in war and to preserve their lives.

one, seldom even arises in the scholarship. A tentative suggestion may be put forward.

The divine judgment that will eventually blast the Romans to perdition is, of course, a triumphant vindication of Jewish faith. Ultimate glory for the Jews is a repeated refrain of the Third Sibyl.[179] A noteworthy feature, however, needs emphasis here. Whereas the oracle mounts a heavy assault upon Roman wickedness, no comparable attacks are leveled at the Greeks. To the contrary. The Sibyl reaches out to the Hellenic world, exhorting its people to repentance, urging acknowledgment of the true God, and offering hope of salvation. Oracular verses expose the folly of trust in mortal leaders and resort to idolatry, proclaiming instead the need to recognize the great God, thereby to escape the woes that will fall upon Hellas.[180] A further call to repentance comes several lines later, prescribing sacrifices, prayers, and righteous behavior to earn divine favor.[181] The disasters to befall Greece will eventually be lifted by God through the agency of a king from the sun.[182] And the Sibyl subsequently repeats her appeal to unhappy Hellas to abandon haughtiness and embrace the true God—which will bring a share in the blissful peace to come.[183] Insofar as the Third Book contains negative aspersions upon Greeks, it includes them among wayward peoples whose failure to see the truth has led them into arrogance, impiety, and immorality, thus provoking divine vengeance.[184] But Greeks alone are singled out for encouragement to enter the fold of the true believers.[185]

179. Cf. Sib. Or. 3.211–17, 282–94, 573–600, 669–731, 767–808.

180. Sib. Or. 3.545–72.

181. Sib. Or. 3.624–34. Since these lines follow directly upon a passage that speaks of Greco-Macedonians bending a knee to God who then brings about peace and prosperity, 601–23, the exhortation must be directed to Greeks.

182. Sib. Or. 3.635–56.

183. Sib. Or. 3.732–61.

184. Sib. Or. 3.196–210, 295–365, 594–600. Only the anti-Macedonian prophecy of lines 381–400, with its parallel to the forecast of Daniel, gives no ostensible hope for reconciliation. But the reference is to the aggressions of royal imperialists, not to the Hellenic people as such. The thesis of E. Kocsis, *NT* 5 (1962) 105–10, that the oracles drew a sharp contrast between the favored east and the savage west, is unconvincing. One needs only to cite the destructive king from Asia in Sib. Or. 3.611–18. Barclay, *Jews in the Mediterranean Diaspora*, 223–25, underplays the attitude toward Greeks and overemphasizes an aggressive nationalism in the Third Sibyl.

185. The Sibyl's hostile comments about Egyptian practices might be thought to reflect ill upon the Hellenic masters of that land. Not so. The opening verses unambiguously condemn the idolatry of native Egyptians, worship of snakes and reverence for cats; Sib. Or. 3.29–45. Later, the baleful race of Egypt whose doom is nigh is evidently contrasted with the Alexandrians who seem to be put in a different category; Sib. Or. 3.348–49: ἴσθι τότ' Αἰγύπτου ὀλοὸν γένος ἐγγὺς ὀλέθρου, καὶ τότ' Ἀλεξανδρεῦσιν ἔτος τὸ παρελθὸν

The verbal assault on Rome suitably fits the context. The Greeks had indeed been victimized by the western power, especially in the later Hellenistic era. Greek resentment bursts out with pointed force in lines preserved by the Third Sibyl herself and plainly deriving from Hellenic circles.[186] Adoption of the anti-Roman line by Hellenized Jews who helped to shape this compilation signaled a community of interest between the two cultures.

The gesture of the Sibyl is noble and magnanimous. Is it an invitation to conversion? Did inventive Jews employ the Sibyl as a front for proselytism? Not likely. Few Greeks could be expected to read the work. How many of them would welcome a text that maligned Homer, denounced Hellenic beliefs as idolatry, and branded the Greek conquest of Persia as destructive savagery? The authors of the Third Sibylline Oracle surely wrote for a readership that would consist, for the most part, of Hellenized Jews—with perhaps a sprinkling of Gentiles.[187] This was no conscious campaign for conversion. To interpret it in that vein is to fall into the same historicist fallacy already undermined above. The text is of symbolic import, not a manifesto for missionary activity. The Third Sibyl transcended the realms of time and space. She asserted common cultural bonds that could encompass the traditions of both Hellas and Judaism.

The roots of the Sibyl's utterances reside in biblical prophecy, the powerful voices who denounced contemporaries and heralded destruction from the skies: an Amos, a Hosea, or an Isaiah. No less potent in inspiration for the Sibyl was the apocalyptic literature of Hellenistic Judaism: Daniel, I Enoch, Jubilees, IV Ezra, and a variety of other texts, now further illuminated by the Qumran documents. The Sibylline pronouncements fit snugly within that setting, a complex of thoroughly Jewish traditions.[188]

ἄμεινον. That the Sibyl did not subsume Greeks under Egypt is plain from lines 594–600. The cryptic allusions to the seventh king of Egypt remain elusive, but clearly imply no reproach of the Hellenic dwellers in that land; Sib. Or. 3.191–95, 314–18, 608. See above, pp. 272–77. C. R. Holladay in P. Bilde et al., *Ethnicity in Hellenistic Egypt* (Aarhus, 1992) 155, surprisingly sees the Sibyl as more hostile to Greeks than to Egyptians. The text does not bear out that conclusion.

186. The bitterness is unmistakable in Sib. Or. 3.350–80, 464–88, which are surely of Greek origin.

187. Cf. N. Walter in J. C. Reeves and J. Kampen, *Pursuing the Text: Studies in Honor of Ben Zion Wacholder* (Sheffield, 1994) 153–54.

188. This emerges forcefully in Nikiprowetzky's discussion; *La Troisième Sibylle*, 95–99, 127–37, 160–76, 248–267. The lengthy and repetitious treatment by Peretti, *La Sibilla babilonese*, 363–444, tracing the apocalyptic statements to Iranian eschatology, as exemplified by the Oracle of Hystaspes, is altogether speculative.

But, of course, that is not the whole story. The authors or compilers of this collection, whether from Palestine or the Diaspora, purposefully and pointedly donned the cloak of the pagan Sibyl. Declarations issuing forth from oracular shrines, subsequently assimilated, expanded, or fabricated in written form, had long been a feature of Hellenic religious culture. They could even take shape as a full-scale piece of literature, as in the case of Lycophron's *Alexandra*. Sibylline prophecies constituted an important part of this development, widely circulated in private hands, available for consultation by public authorities, and the basis for literary invention. The authority of the Sibyls spread through much of the Greek world, most especially the prophetess at Erythrae, but also a number of others located at various Mediterranean sites.[189] Jewish intellectuals tapped into the tradition and embraced the Hellenic oracular form. A Hebrew Sibyl eventually took her place among the venerable female seers acknowledged by pagan writers. Verses in the extant Third Book that concern the tower of Babel, the reign of the Titans, and the myth of Kronos and his sons are attributed to the Sibyl by Alexander Polyhistor already in the first century BCE.[190] By the second century CE Pausanias could make specific reference to a Sibyl of the Hebrews in Palestine alongside the Erythraean, Libyan, and Cumaean Sibyls.[191]

The Jews successfully usurped the Hellenic medium. The Jewish Sibyl speaks in proper Homeric hexameters. She pronounces her prophecies under divine prodding, a mouthpiece, even a somewhat reluctant one, of the greater power who speaks through her.[192] She has a grasp of Greek mythology and the epic tradition.[193] Indeed she forecasts both the fall of Troy and the Exodus from Egypt.[194] Employment of Hellenic forms, language, and themes in the service of advancing Judaic ideas enlivened the intellectual circles of Hellenistic Judaism. The composers of the Third Sibylline Oracle stand shoulder to shoulder with Ezekiel the tragedian, the historians Demetrius and Eupolemus, and the imaginative reinventors of a Hebraic-Hellenic past like Artapanus, Aristobulus, and Pseudo-Eupolemus. And they inhabited the same mental world that produced the fabricated verses and refashioned

189. On the Sibyls and Sibylline oracles, see Alexandre, *Oracula Sibyllina*, II, 1–101; Rzach, *RE* IIA.2 (1923) 2073–183; H. W. Parke, *Sibyls and Sibylline Prophecy in Classical Antiquity* (London, 1988) 1–50; D. Potter, *Prophets and Emperors* (Cambridge, Mass., 1994) 71–93.

190. See Eusebius, *Chron.* I, 23 (Schoene).

191. Paus. 10.12; cf. Schol. Plato, *Phaedrus*, 315. See Nikiprowetzky, *La Troisième Sibylle*, 37–53; Peretti, *La Sibilla babilonese*, 53–69.

192. See Sib. Or. 3.1–7, 162–64, 196–98, 295–99, 489–91, 698–99.

193. Sib. Or. 3.110–55, 401–32.

194. Sib. Or. 3.248–56, 414–18.

sentiments of Greek thinkers, thus bringing them into line with the teachings of the Torah.

Preparation for the Eschaton can unite Hebrew and Hellene. The Sibylline declarations extend a hand to Greeks and a promise of divine deliverance—an expression of common ground between the two heritages. But a central ingredient demands emphasis. This cultural solidarity is one in which Jewish traditions take clear precedence. To put it plainly, Greeks who show themselves worthy are invited to partake of the values of the Jews. The provenance of the Third Sibyl makes the point unambiguously. She presents herself as daughter-in-law of Noah, thus with a claim on the most distant antiquity and the hoariest biblical and Near Eastern legacies. The Hellenic connection is a decidedly secondary one. The Sibyl moved from Babylon to Greece, there to be associated with Erythrae. But her memory stretches back to the Flood, a divine prescience, infallible as the gift of God.[195] Here is appropriation indeed. The Sibyl's origins precede even Babel. She thus asserts the most ancient lineage, embodying Hebrew traditions and later subsuming the authority of the Erythraean Sibyl, most venerated of the Hellenic prophetesses. Jewish identity stands in the forefront here. The keepers of the faith who had also absorbed pagan learning, literature, and legends claimed a place in both worlds but held firm to their core. The oracular voice promises a happy fate for the Jewish faithful, and shows a willingness to extend that fate to the Greeks—provided that they embrace the values and ideals of the Chosen People.

•   •   •

Hellenistic Jews conceived a plethora of means whereby to sharpen their self-image and brace their self-esteem. The relationship with Greek culture and society was an abiding obsession. Writers and intellectuals devoted considerable creativity to the presentation of that relationship. They developed strategies both to articulate the intertwining bonds between Judaism and Hellenism and to display the primacy of the former. The discussion here has endeavored to illustrate certain facets of that strategic design.

The leading lights of Hellas' literary and philosophical history turned out to be readers of the Torah. Pythagoras and Plato took ideas from the Mosaic code, Homer and Hesiod honored the Sabbath, Orpheus sang the praises of monotheism, and Greek dramatists celebrated the glories of God. Various lines of Hellenic prose and poetry were interpreted or fabricated so

195. Sib. Or. 3.809–29.

as to place the literary creations and intellectual achievements of the classical world in Jewish debt. The Jews could consequently reckon themselves as an integral part of that world—as well as its cultural forerunners.

Fictitious kinship connections served similar purposes. Jews adopted a standard Hellenic convention to express solidarity with those states whose image best encapsulated Jewish self-perception. But they made sure to insist that the admirable traits linking the peoples owed their origins to Jewish progenitors and principles.

Gentile institutions could also be turned to Jewish ends. The Sibylline Oracle spouted prophecies of doom, delivering awesome apocalyptic visions that ensured the destruction of wicked idolaters and the ultimate triumph of the Jewish faithful. The commissioning of this pagan vehicle allowed Jews to speak in Greek guise, to claim that Hellenic medium as their own, and to offer a share in future glory to those Greeks who saw the light, while simultaneously and dramatically reaffirming the ascendancy of their own creed.

CHAPTER 8

Conclusion

The fashioning and refashioning of identity constitutes a staple item in Jewish history. The matter took on particular urgency in an age when Hellenic power and Greek culture held sway in the Near East. Jews remained true to ancestral traditions, the faith of their fathers, and the sanctity of the Scriptures. But they found themselves cheek by jowl with Hellenistic communities in Palestine, and they were part and parcel of Hellenistic societies in the Diaspora. The Jews were not so much permeated by the culture of the Greeks as they were an example of it. This made it all the more important to exhibit the features of their own legacy in the terms and language of their adopted one.

The process had no uniform pattern. And what patterns there were can scarcely be traced in the meager evidence. Adjustment to the Hellenic world presented a challenge in Palestine as well as in the Diaspora. Even those dwelling in Judaea could not be oblivious to the temptations and allure of Hellenism. The material examined here by no means belongs exclusively to the Diaspora. For several authors, texts, or segments, a Palestinian provenance is perfectly possible, and for more still the origin is pure guesswork. The range and diversity of Jewish reactions to Greek culture cannot be catalogued by location and only rarely by chronology. But the surviving texts, whether full or fragmentary, testify to the cleverness, imagination, and enterprise with which Hellenized Jews captured the media of the Mediterranean to express the superiority of their own heritage.

The development transcends a Diaspora mentality. The surviving products do not present a struggle for identity in an alien world, an apologia for strange customs and beliefs, or propaganda meant to persuade the Gentile. The texts instead display a positive quality, bold and inventive, sometimes startling, often light-hearted and engaging, and throughout directed internally to Jews conversant with or altogether inseparable from the culture of the Greeks. The relationships portrayed rarely have an antagonistic or adversarial quality—at least not without reconciliation and a happy ending. The imaginative fictions made political subordination palatable by pointing to the Jewish roots of pagan accomplishments and Jewish involvement in the course of Hellenistic history.

This proud self-perception held for Palestine as well as the Diaspora. The Hasmonaeans indeed never fully escaped the suzerainty of larger powers, but they exploited the patronage of Hellenic kings and embraced the trappings of Hellenic authority, thus advancing the interests of their nation as well as themselves within the circumstances of the new world.

Hasmonaean strategy serves to symbolize the designs of Hellenistic Jews on a broader front. They redefined themselves in the terms of a culture that they had now made their own but left intact the core of their ancestral legacy. They displayed a talent not so much for adaptation as for expropriation.

The land of Egypt stimulated the process. Jews showed an aptitude for manipulating Egyptian as well as Hellenic traditions. The Exodus legend provides a prime exhibit. It long served and still serves as founding myth of the Israelite claim on the promised land. But for Hellenistic Jews who returned to Egypt and endeavored to reassure themselves of a rightful place in that realm, a revamped tale could be advantageous. Diverse versions developed, and some very probably owe their origins to Jewish artifice. Those that made the Hebrews conquerors of Egypt, topplers of idol worship, and ancient rulers of the country best suited the psyche of Egyptian Jews in the Hellenistic age. The ancient Hebrews were thus transformed from victims and expatriates into the masters of Egypt in its remote past—an uplifting myth for their descendants in that land.

The self-confidence of Jews writing in Greek manifests itself quite intriguingly in the freedom with which they reassessed and refashioned their own biblical heroes. The figure of Joseph supplies an instructive example. His demeanor and actions in Genesis show an ambiguous personality that lent itself to multiple interpretations. And Jews of the Hellenistic era provided them. Joseph received treatment in a diversity of media, both Hebrew and Greek, that surfaced in this era: biblical exegesis, wisdom literature, the imaginary testaments, philosophy, romance, and political sagas. Different dimensions of the persona received emphasis or suppression, depending upon the inclinations of the author and the nature of the text. Joseph could be either a saintly or a sanctimonious character, a champion of rectitude or a conveyor of pious platitudes, a noble and generous soul or a prickly and insufferable prude, a sensitive dispenser of justice or an autocratic wielder of power. In general, the texts in Hebrew presented a one-dimensional Joseph, normally stripped of shortcomings, whereas Hellenized Jews brought out the complexities, took some pride in the authority he exercised over Egypt, but also depicted craft, deviousness, and arrogance. The result was not a debunking of the biblical patriarch. Jews played with the image of Joseph, felt entirely comfortable with an ancestor who, like most Hellenistic leaders, combined admirable prestige with defects of character, and had no hesitation in rewriting, manipulating, and even abandoning the account in Genesis.

Reverence for Scripture could go hand in hand with a liberal remodeling of it. Jews thoroughly imbued with Greek culture but committed to the authority of the Book felt full confidence in reproducing its material in forms familiar to their Hellenized compatriots. The historian Demetrius treated problems and ostensible inconsistencies that emerged from the biblical text, straining to show that rational interpretations can explain away the difficulties and reassure the doubters. Aristeas sharply reduced the tale of Job to repress the conflicts and provide a more edifying version. The story of Dinah's rape and the sack of Shechem found expression in a Greek epic by Theodotus whose verses rendered it more readily palatable to troubled readers. The poetry of Philo and the drama of Ezekiel bestowed added distinction upon the grand figures of the Bible whom they celebrated in elegant phrases and Hellenic forms. These works of history, epic, and tragedy, while placing scriptural stories in Greek molds, aimed to confirm and enhance, not to question, their authority.

Other writers handled the Scriptures with much greater freedom, elaborating the tales out of all proportion and exaggerating the exploits of heroes at will. Jewish artistry, imagination, and even whimsicality showed itself to excellent effect. In the conception of writers like "Pseudo-Eupolemus" and Artapanus, the biblical Abraham became the inventor of astrology and the conveyer of culture to Egyptians and Phoenicians as well as Jews. Moses' accomplishments acquired still larger dimensions. Eupolemus portrays him as provider of the alphabet to the lands of the Near East, while Artapanus has him as bringer of technological, institutional, and religious innovations to Egypt, as military hero who vanquishes the Ethiopians, and as the source even of Greek poetic genius. Eupolemus' work further extended David's conquests into lands he could not have heard of and turned Solomon into an international figure who engaged in diplomatic exchanges like a Hellenistic king. Little or none of this has roots in the Bible. The Jews of the Greek age had considerable room for invention. Some of them indeed supplemented (and even sharply altered the impression of) canonical texts by inserting new segments in Greek based on pagan models. The story of the three bodyguards in I Esdras made a Jew responsible for the return from the Babylonian Exile. The additions to Daniel gave a secular flavor to a religious work, while the additions to Esther injected religious elements into a secular text. These Greek insertions served a variety of ends, encompassing an emphasis on Jewish acumen and dexterity, a ridicule of Gentile rulers, and even a subtle reminder of hypocrisy and inconstancy among Jews themselves. The buoyant self-confidence exhibited itself not only in the license with which biblical texts were tampered with but the jocular quality of tales that mocked Jew and Gentile alike. Having Abraham's family take some credit for the feats of Heracles, making Moses responsible for animal worship in Egypt, depicting Persian kings as manipulated by Zerubbabel and Daniel, and turning Jewish elders into lecherous buffoons manifested the mischievous levity with which Hellenistic Jews expanded, exploited, and supplemented the Bible. Their irreverence could entertain readers but never demeaned the faith.

Entertainment value was higher still in the stories concocted by Jews regarding their encounters with Hellenistic kings. Improvised episodes had Alexander the Great perform obeisance to the Jewish god, Ptolemy Philadelphus praise the acumen and learning of Jewish sages, and Ptolemy Philometor pronounce the sanctity of the Temple in Jerusalem. The inventions extended to stories that made Ptolemy Epiphanes a dunce and Ptolemy Philopator a laughing-stock. But they involved more than mere comedy. Jews lacked political power in Hellenistic realms, their position and security dependent upon the favor of the monarchs, a fact undisguised in these fables. Jewish loyalty to the crown constitutes a recurrent theme. But the twist in the tales places Jews in a situation of moral, spiritual, and intellectual ascendancy. The shrewdness of a Jewish archer exceeds the power of Greek mantics, Jewish sages outshine Greek philosophers, Jews administer financial affairs at the Ptolemaic court, Jewish faith impresses Alexander and overawes kings and elephants alike. The legends both record the political authority of the monarchy and celebrate the significance of Jewish values.

The modes of promoting Jewish pride in Hellenic fashion proliferated. Writers like Aristobulus acclaimed the Torah as model for the noblest ideas of Pythagoras, Socrates, and Plato, as the fountainhead of Greek music and poetry, and as a stimulus for purported Homeric and Hesiodic verses on the Sabbath. Aristobulus and others not only interpreted Greek pronouncements to Jewish taste but even invented monotheistic allusions to be put into the mouths of luminaries like Aeschylus, Euripides, and Menander. Here was literary enterprise indeed. And they were not the only Hellenic media enlisted by Jewish ingenuity. The long-standing pagan institution of creating imaginary kinship relations between peoples was exploited by Jews to express their own priority over Hellenic partners. And the Sibylline Oracle herself issued prophecies that heralded the salvation and triumph of the Jews.

The character, level, and extent of Jewish readership for these works remain elusive. Data are almost nonexistent and guesswork does not get us far. Degrees of literacy play a role, but they too evade any confident estimate. Even if calculation were possible, the result would tell only part of the story. Many of the texts now extant may have circulated orally in a earlier form, and, even when committed to writing, could still be recited or presented viva voce to those who lacked literacy. Different segments of society, whether in Palestine or abroad, in the cities or the countryside, would find different examples of this rich productivity diverting, meaningful, or edifying.

Familiarity with the Scriptures, certainly with the Pentateuch, in Hebrew or Greek, can be assumed in both the homeland and the Diaspora. Variants on biblical stories will have found knowledgeable recipients at all social levels. For the Jews of Egypt, claiming an honored place in that ancient land, manipulations of the Exodus tale to display Jewish military as well as moral superiority were doubtless welcome on a wide front. Ezekiel's *Exagoge* may have been performed on stage to a still wider audience. Recitals of epic poetry were perhaps limited to smaller groups; only few could fathom the elevated, often opaque, verses of the poet Philo. But circulation of fanciful tales about the patriarchs like those by Artapanus, Cleodemus Malchus, and "Pseudo-Eupolemus" certainly reached beyond narrow confines. Just a small circle was likely to show interest in Demetrius' chronological researches, but many more would take pleasure in Eupolemus' retelling of exploits by David and Solomon. And, of course, the entertaining tales that attached themselves to later biblical texts like Ezra, Esther, and Daniel appealed to a broad constituency.

No particular profile of a postulated audience can suffice. It required some learning to appreciate Aristobulus' references to Plato and Pythagoras, still more to grasp the significance of monotheistic statements discovered or implanted in classical tragedians and comic poets. But Homer could claim wider recognition, as could some Hellenic myths like that of Orpheus. Narratives such as *Joseph and Aseneth*, the tales of the Tobiads, and the many stories that described Jewish encounters with Hellenic kings demanded no special qualifications from their audiences. The creations catered to different levels of comprehension. One could enjoy the romance of Joseph and Aseneth without decoding the allegory, delight in the triumphs of Esther and Daniel while missing some of the nuance and irony, and take comfort in the apocalyptic vision of the Sibyl without awareness of classical antecedents or contemporary allusions.

The world of Greek culture was not an alien one to Hellenistic Jews. They thrived within it and they made its conventions their own. They engaged in Hellenic discourse but addressed their message to fellow Jews. Their free adaptation of the Scriptures, imaginative fictions, and light-hearted recreations of Hellenistic history gave readers pride in Jewish heritage and amusement in its novel reformulation.

ABBREVIATIONS

AJP	*American Journal of Philology*
AJSReview	*Association for Jewish Studies Review*
AnnPisa	*Annali della Scuola Normale Superiore di Pisa, Classe di Lettere e Filosofia*
ANRW	*Aufstieg und Niedergang der römischen Welt: Geschichte und Kultur Roms im Spiegel der neueren Forschung*
AttiTorino	*Atti della Accademia della Scienze di Torino, Classe di Scienze morali, storiche e filologiche*
BullLittEccl	*Bulletin de Littérature Ecclésiastique*
CBQ	*Catholic Biblical Quarterly*
Chron.d'Egypte	*Chronique d'Égypte*
CP	*Classical Philology*
CQ	*Classical Quarterly*
EOS	*Eos: commentarii Societatis Philologae Polonorum*
EphTheoLov	*Ephemerides Theologicae Lovaniensis*
FGH	Felix Jacoby, *Die Fragmente der griechischen Historiker*
FondHardt	*Entretiens Fondation Hardt*
HSCP	*Harvard Studies in Classical Philology*
HTR	*Harvard Theological Review*
HUCA	*Hebrew Union College Annual*
HZ	*Historische Zeitschrift*
IEJ	*Israel Exploration Journal*
JBL	*Journal of Biblical Literature*
JBR	*Journal of Bible and Religion*
JEA	*Journal of Egyptian Archaeology*
Jhrb.Heid.Akad.	*Jahrbuch der Heidelberger Akademie der Wissenschaften*

JJP	*Journal of Juristic Papyrology*
JJS	*Journal of Jewish Studies*
JQR	*Jewish Quarterly Review*
JR	*Journal of Religion*
JSemStud	*Journal of Semitic Studies*
JSJ	*Journal for the Study of Judaism*
JSP	*Journal for the Study of the Pseudepigrapha*
JTS	*Journal of Theological Studies*
MH	*Museum Helveticum*
NTS	*New Testament Studies*
RE	Pauly-Wissowa, *Realencyclopädie der klassischen Altertums-wissenschaft*
REA	*Revue des Études Anciennes*
REG	*Revue des Études Grecques*
REJ	*Revue des Études Juives*
RevBibl	*Revue Biblique*
RHR	*Revue de l'Histoire des Religions*
RivFilol	*Rivista di filologia*
RivStorItal	*Rivista Storica Italiana*
SBL Seminar Papers	*Society of Biblical Literature Seminar Papers*
SCI	*Scripta Classica Israelica*
SCO	*Studi classici e orientali*
SitzHeid	*Sitzungsberichte der Heidelberger Akademie der Wissenschaften*
VT	*Vetus Testamentum*
ZAW	*Zeitschrift für die Alttestamentliche Wissenschaft*
ZNW	*Zeitschrift für die Neutestamentliche Wissenschaft und die Kunde der älteren Kirche*
ZPE	*Zeitschrift für Papyrologie und Epigraphik*

BIBLIOGRAPHY

Abel, F.-M. "Alexandre le Grand en Syrie et en Palestine." *RevBibl* 44 (1935) 42–61.
———. *Les livres des Maccabées.* Paris, 1949.
Alexandre, C. *Oracula Sibyllina.* 2 vols. Paris, 1841–1856.
———. *Excursus ad Sibyllina.* Paris, 1856.
Amit, D., and H. Eshel. *The Hasmonean Period.* Jerusalem, 1995. (Hebrew)
Anderson, H. "3 Maccabees." In J. H. Charlesworth, II, 509–29.
———. "2 Maccabees." In J. H. Charlesworth, II, 531–64.
Applebaum, S. "Hellenistic Cities of Judaea and its Vicinity—Some New Aspects."
In B. Levick, ed., *The Ancient Historian and his Materials*, 59–73. Westmead, 1975.
———. "Jewish Urban Communities and Greek Influences." *SCI* 5 (1979/1980)
158–77.
Aptowitzer, V. "Aseneth, the Wife of Joseph: A Haggadic Literary-Historical Study."
HUCA 1 (1924) 239–306.
Arenhoevel, D. *Die Theokratie nach dem 1. und 2. Makkabäerbuch.* Mainz, 1967.
Attridge, H. W. "Historiography." In M. E. Stone, *Jewish Writings of the Second Temple
Period*, 157–84. Assen and Philadelphia, 1984.
———. "Philo the Epic Poet." In J. H. Charlesworth, II, 781–84.
Aziza, C. "L'utilisation polémique du récit de l'Exode chez les écrivains alexan-
drins." *ANRW* II.20.1 (1987) 41–65.
Bal, M. "The Elders and Susanna." *Biblical Interpretation* 1 (1993) 1–19.
Bammel, E. "Der Zeuge des Judentums." In W. Will, *Zu Alexander d. Gr.* 279–87.
Amsterdam, 1987.
Barag, D., and S. Qedar. "The Beginning of Hasmonean Coinage." *Israel Numismatic
Journal* 4 (1980) 8–21.
———. "A Silver Coin of Yohanan the High Priest and the Coinage of Judea in
the Fourth Century, B.C." *Israel Numismatic Journal* 9 (1986/1987) 4–21.
———. "New Evidence on the Foreign Policy of John Hyrcanus I." *Israel Numismatic
Journal* 12 (1992/1993) 1–12.
Barclay, J. M. G. *Jews in the Mediterranean Diaspora.* Edinburgh, 1996.

Bar-Kochkva, B. *The Seleucid Army*. Cambridge, 1976.

———. "Manpower, Economics, and Internal Strife in the Hasmonean State." In A. Chastagnol et al., *Armées et fiscalité dans le monde antique*, 167–94. Paris, 1977.

———. *Judas Maccabaeus*. Cambridge, 1989.

———. "On Josephus and the Maccabees: Philology and Historiography." *Tarbiz* 62 (1992) 115–32. (Hebrew)

———. "Judaism and Hellenism: Between Scholarship and Journalism." *Tarbiz* 63 (1994) 451–80. (Hebrew)

———. *Pseudo-Hecataeus, "On the Jews": Legitimizing the Diaspora*. Berkeley, 1996.

———. *Anti-Semitism and Idealization of Judaism*. (forthcoming)

Barraclough, R. "Philo's Politics, Roman Rule and Hellenistic Judaism." *ANRW* II.21.1 (1984) 417–553.

Baumgartner, W. "Susanna: Die Geschichte einer Legende." *Archiv für Religionswissenschaft* 24 (1926) 259–80.

———. "Der weise Knabe und die des Ehebruchs beschuldigte Frau." *Archiv für Religionswissenschaft* 27 (1929) 187–88.

Beavis, M. A. L. "Anti-Egyptian Polemic in the Letter of Aristeas 130–165 (The High Priest's Discourse)." *JSJ* 18 (1987) 145–51.

Becker, J. *Untersuchungen zur Entstehungsgeschichte der Testamente der zwölf Patriarchen*. Leiden, 1970.

Bellinger, A. R. *Essays on the Coinage of Alexander the Great*. New York, 1963.

Bickerman, E. "Makkabäerbücher (III)" *RE* 19 (1928) 797–800.

———. "Zur Datierung des Pseudo-Aristeas." *ZNW* 29 (1930) 280–96.

———. *Der Gott der Makkabäer*. Berlin, 1937.

———. *Institutions des Séleucides*. Paris, 1938.

———. "The Colophon of the Greek Book of Esther." *JBL* 63 (1944) 339–62.

———. "Origines Gentium." *CP* 47 (1952) 65–81.

———. "The Jewish Historian Demetrius." In J. Neusner, *Christianity, Judaism, and Other Greco-Roman Cults* III, 72–84. Leiden, 1975.

———. *Studies in Jewish and Christian History*. Leiden, 1976.

———. *The Jews in the Greek Age*. Cambridge, Mass., 1988.

Blenkinsopp, J. *Prophecy and Canon*. Notre Dame, 1977.

Boccaccini, G. *Middle Judaism: Jewish Thought, 300 B.C.E. to 200 C.E.* Minneapolis, 1991.

Bohak, G. "CPJ III, 520: The Egyptian Reaction to Onias' Temple." *JSJ* 26 (1995) 32–41.

———. *Joseph and Aseneth and the Jewish Temple in Heliopolis*. Atlanta, 1996.

Borgen, P. *Early Christianity and Hellenistic Judaism*. Edinburgh, 1996.

Bormann, L., et al. *Religious Propaganda and Missionary Competition in the New Testament World*. Leiden, 1994.

Bousquet, J. "La Stèle des Kyténiens au Létôon de Xanthos." *REG* 101 (1988) 12–53.

Bousset, W. "Die Beziehungen der ältesten jüdischen Sibylle zur chaldäischen Sibylle und einige weitere Beobachtungen über den synkretistischen Charakter der spätjüdischen Litteratur." *ZNW* 3 (1902) 23–49.

————. "Sibyllen und Sibyllinische Bücher." *RE für protestantische Theologie und Kirche* 18 (1906) 265–80.

Bowersock, G. W. *Fiction as History: Nero to Julian.* Berkeley, 1994.

Braun, M. *Griechischer Roman und hellenistische Geschichtsschreibung.* Frankfurt, 1934.

————. *History and Romance in Graeco-Oriental Literature.* Oxford, 1938.

Bresciani, E. "The Persian Occupation of Egypt." In I. Gershevitch, *The Cambridge History of Iran* II, 502–28. Cambridge, 1985.

Brock, S. P. *Pseudepigrapha Veteris Testamenti Graece.* 2. Leiden, 1967.

————. "The Phenomenon of Biblical Tradition in Antiquity." In S. Jellicoe, *Studies in the Septuagint,* 541–71. New York, 1974.

Brownlee, W. H. "Le livre grec d'Esther et la royauté divine." *RevBibl* 73 (1966) 161–85.

Büchler, A. "La Relation de Josèphe concernant Alexandre le Grand." *REJ* 36 (1898) 1–26.

————. *Die Tobiaden und die Oniaden.* Vienna, 1899.

Bull, R. J. "A Note on Theodotus' Description of Shechem." *HTR* 60 (1967) 221–27.

Bunge, J. G. *Untersuchungen zum zweiten Makkabäerbuch.* Bonn, 1971.

————. "Zur Geschichte und Chronologie des Untergangs der Oniaden und des Aufstiegs der Hasmonäer." *JSJ* 6 (1975) 1–46.

Burchard, C. *Untersuchungen zur Joseph und Aseneth.* Tübingen, 1965.

————. "Joseph et Aséneth: Questions actuelles." In W. C. van Unnik, *La littérature juive entre Tenach et Mischna,* 77–100. Leiden, 1974.

————. "Joseph and Aseneth." In J. H. Charlesworth, II, 177–247.

Burgmann, H. "Das umstrittene Intersacerdotium in Jerusalem, 159–152 v. Chr." *JSJ* 11 (1980) 135–76.

Burkert, W. In discussion of M. Hengel, "Anonymität, Pseudepigraphie und 'Literarische Fälschung.' " *FondHardt* 18 (1971) 231–329.

Camponovo, O. *Königtum, Königsherrschaft und Reich Gottes in den frühjüdischen Schriften.* Freiburg, 1984.

Cardauns, B. "Juden und Spartaner." *Hermes* 95 (1967) 317–24.

Cartledge, P., and A. Spawforth, *Hellenistic and Roman Sparta: A Tale of Two Cities.* London and New York, 1989.

Catastini, A. "Le testimonianze di Manetone e la 'storia di Giuseppe' (Genesis 37–50)." *Henoch* 17 (1995) 279–300.

Cazeaux, J. "Nul n'est prophète en son pays: Contribution a l'étude de Joseph et après Philon." In J. F. Kenney, *The School of Moses: Studies in Philo and Hellenistic Religion,* 41–81. Atlanta, 1995.

Charles, R. H. *The Testaments of the Twelve Patriarchs.* London, 1908.

Charlesworth, J. H. *Old Testament Pseudepigrapha.* 2 vols. Garden City, 1983 and 1985.

Chesnutt, R. D. "The Social Setting and Purpose of Joseph and Aseneth." *JSP* 2 (1988) 21–48.

————. *From Death to Life: Conversion in Joseph and Aseneth.* Sheffield, 1995.

Clines, D. J. *The Esther Scroll: The Story of the Story.* Sheffield, 1984.

Coggins, R. J. *Samaritans and Jews.* Atlanta, 1975.

————. "The Samaritans in Josephus." In L. H. Feldman and G. Hata, *Josephus, Judaism, and Christianity*, 257–73. Detroit, 1987.

Coggins, R. J., and M. A. Knibb. *The First and Second Book of Esdras*. Cambridge, 1979.

Cohen, N. G. "The Names of the Translators in the Letter of Aristeas: A Study in the Dynamics of Cultural Transition." *JSJ* 15 (1984) 32–64.

Cohen, S. J. D. "Sosates the Jewish Homer." *HTR* 74 (1981) 391–96.

————. "Alexander the Great and Jaddus the High Priest according to Josephus." *ASJ Review* 78 (1982/1983) 41–68.

————. *From the Maccabees to the Mishna*. Philadelphia, 1987.

————. "Religion, Ethnicity and 'Hellenism' in the Emergence of Jewish Identity in Maccabean Palestine." In P. Bilde, T. Engberg-Pedersen, L. Hannestad, and J. Zahle, *Religion and Religious Practice in the Seleucid Kingdom*, 204–23. Aarhus, 1990.

Collins, A. Y. "Aristobulus." In J. H. Charlesworth, II, 831–42.

Collins, J. J. *The Sibylline Oracles of Egyptian Judaism*. Missoula, 1974.

————. "The Provenance of the Third Sibylline Oracle." *Bulletin of the Institute of Jewish Studies* 2 (1974) 1–18.

————. "The Epic of Theodotus and the Hellenism of the Hasmoneans." *HTR* 73 (1980) 91–104.

————. *Between Athens and Jerusalem*. New York, 1983.

————. "Testaments." In M. E. Stone, *Jewish Writings of the Second Temple Period*, 325–56. Philadelphia, 1984.

————. "The Testamentary Literature in Recent Scholarship." In R. A. Kraft and G. W. E. Nickelsburg, *Early Judaism and its Modern Interpreters*, 268–78. Atlanta, 1986.

————. "Sibylline Oracles." In J. H. Charlesworth, I, 317–472.

————. "Artapanus." In J. H. Charlesworth, II, 889–903.

————. "The Development of the Sibylline Tradition." *ANRW* II.20.1 (1987) 421–59.

————. " 'The King has Become a Jew?' The Perspective on the Gentile World in Bel and the Snake." In J. A. Overman and R. S. MacLennan, *Diaspora Jews and Judaism*, 335–45. Atlanta, 1992.

————. *Daniel*. Minneapolis, 1993.

Collins, N. L. "Ezekiel, the Author of the *Exagoge*: His Calendar and Home." *JSJ* 22 (1991) 201–11.

Crenshaw, J. L. "The Contest of Darius' Guards." In B. O. Long, *Images of Man and God*, 74–88. Sheffield, 1981.

Crowley, A. *Aramaic Papyri of the Fifth Century* BC. Oxford, 1923.

Crown, A. D. "Redating the Schism Between the Judaeans and the Samaritans." *JQR* 82 (1991) 17–50.

Cross, F. M. "The Discovery of the Samaria Papyri." *Biblical Archaeologist* 26 (1963) 110–21.

————. "Aspects of Samaritan and Jewish History in Late Persian and Hellenistic Times." *HTR* 59 (1966) 201–11.

————. "A Reconstruction of the Judean Restoration." *JBL* 94 (1975) 4–18.

Curty, O. "À propos de la parenté entre Juifs et Spartiates." *Historia* 41 (1992) 246–48.

———. *Les parentés legéndaires entre cités grecques.* Geneva, 1995.

Dalbert, P. *Die Theologie der hellenistisch-j"udischen Missions-Literatur unter Ausschluss von Philo und Josephus.* Hamburg, 1954.

Dancy, J. *A Commentary on I Maccabees.* Oxford, 1954.

Daniel, J. L. "Anti-Semitism in the Hellenistic-Roman World." *JBL* 98 (1979) 45–65.

Davies, W. D., and L. Finkelstein, *Cambridge History of Judaism.* 2 vols. Cambridge, 1989.

de Jonge, M. *The Testaments of the Twelve Patriarchs.* Leiden, 1953.

Delcor, M. "Un roman d'amour d'origine thérapeute: Le livre de Joseph et Asénath." *BullLittEccl* 63 (1962) 3–27.

———. *Le livre de Daniel.* Paris, 1971.

———. "The Apocrypha and Pseudepigrapha of the Hellenistic Period." In Davies and Finkelstein, II, 409–503.

———. "Jewish Literature in Hebrew and Aramaic in the Greek Era." In Davies and Finkelstein, II, 352–84.

Delling, G. "Einwirkungen der Sprache der Septuaginta in 'Joseph und Aseneth.'" *JSJ* 9 (1978) 29–56.

———. "Alexander der Grosse als Bekenner des jüdischen Gottesglaubens." *JSJ* 12 (1981) 1–51.

Denis, A.-M. *Fragmenta Pseudepigraphorum Quae Supersunt Graeca.* Leiden, 1970.

———. *Introduction aux pseudépigraphes grecs d'ancien testament.* Leiden, 1970.

———. "L'historien anonyme d'Eusèbe (Praef. Ev., 9.17–18) et la crise des Macchabées." *JSJ* 8 (1977) 42–49.

Develin, R., and J. C. Yardley. *Justin: Epitome of the Philippic History of Pompeius Trogus.* Atlanta, 1994.

Diamond, F. H. "Hecataeus of Abdera and the Mosaic Constitution." In S. M. Burstein and L. A. Okin, *Panhellenica: Essays in Ancient History and Historiography in Honor of Truesdell S. Brown,* 77–95. Lawrence, Kansas, 1980.

Doran, R. *Temple Propaganda: The Purpose and Character of 2 Maccabees.* Washington, 1981.

———. "Aristeas the Exegete." In J. H. Charlesworth, II, 855–59.

———. "Pseudo-Eupolemus." In J. H. Charlesworth, II, 873–82.

———. "Cleodemus Malchus." In J. H. Charlesworth, II, 883–87.

———. "The Jewish Hellenistic Historians before Josephus." *ANRW* II.20.1 (1987) 246–97.

———. "The Non-Dating of Jubilees: Jub 34–38; 23:14–32 in Narrative Context." *JSJ* 20 (1989) 1–11.

———. "Jason's Gymnasion." In H. Attridge, J. Collins, and T. Toblin, eds., *Of Scribes and Scrolls,* 99–109. Lanham, 1990.

Droge, A. J. "Josephus Between Greeks and Barbarians." In L. H. Feldman and J. R. Levison, *Josephus' Contra Apionem: Studies in its Character and Context with a Latin Concordance to the Portion Missing in Greek,* 115–42. Leiden, 1996.

———. *Homer or Moses?* Tübingen, 1989.

Dunn, R. "Discriminations in the Comic Spirit in the Story of Susanna." *Christianity and Literature* 31 (1982) 19–31.

Eddy, S. K. *The King is Dead*. Lincoln, 1961.

Efron, J. *Studies in the Hasmonean Period*. Leiden, 1987.

Egger, R. *Josephus Flavius und die Samaritaner*. Göttingen, 1986.

Ehrenberg, V. "Sparta (Geschichte)" *RE* IIIA.2 (1929) 1373–453.

Ehrlich, E. L. "Der Traum des Mardochai." *Zeitschrift für Religions und Geistesgeschichte* 7 (1955) 69–74.

Ellis, E. E. *The Old Testament in Early Christianity*. Tübingen, 1991.

Emmet, C. "The Third Book of Maccabees." In R. H. Charles, *The Apocrypha and Pseudepigrapha of the Old Testament* I, 155–73. Oxford, 1913.

Engel, H. *Die Susanna-Erzählung*. Göttingen, 1985.

Eschel, H. *The Samaritans in the Persian and Hellenistic Periods: The Origins of Samaritanism*. Diss. Hebrew University, 1994. (Hebrew with English summary)

Ewald, H. G. A. *Geschichte des Volkes Israel*[3]. 8 vols. Göttingen, 1864–1868.

Fallon, F. "Theodotus." In J. H. Charlesworth, II, 785–93.

Feldman, L. "Anti-Semitism in the Ancient World." In D. Berger, ed., *History and Hate: The Dimensions of Anti-Semitism*, 15–42. Philadelphia, 1986.

———. "Pro-Jewish Intimations in Anti-Jewish Remarks Cited in Josephus' *Against Apion*." *JQR* 78 (1988) 187–251.

———. "Pro-Jewish Intimations in Tacitus' Account of Jewish Origins." *REJ* 150 (1991) 331–60.

———. "Josephus' Portrait of Joseph." *RevBibl* 99 (1992) 379–417; 504–28.

———. *Jew and Gentile in the Ancient World*. Princeton, 1993.

———. "Reading Between the Lines: Appreciation of Judaism in Anti-Jewish Writers." In L. H. Feldman and J. R. Levison, *Josephus' Contra Apionem: Studies in its Character and Context with a Latin Concordance to the Portion Missing in Greek*, 115–42. Leiden, 1996.

Feldmeier, R. "Weise hinter 'eisernen Mauern.'" In M. Hengel and A. M. Schwemer, *Die Septuaginta zwischen Judentum und Christentum*, 20–37. Tübingen, 1994.

Février, J. G. *La date, la composition et les sources de la Lettre d'Aristée à Philocrate*. Paris, 1925.

Fischer, T. *Untersuchungen zum Partherkrieg Antiochos VII*. Tübingen, 1970.

———. *Seleukiden und Makkabäer*. Bochum, 1980.

———. "Hasmoneans and Seleucids: Aspects of War and Policy in the 2nd and 1st Centuries B.C.E." In A. Kasher et al., *Greece and Rome in Eretz Israel*, 3–19. Jerusalem, 1990.

Flusser, D., and S. Amorai-Stark. "The Goddess Thermuthis, Moses, and Artapanus." *JSQ* 1 (1993/1994) 217–33.

Fox. M. V. *The Redaction of the Books of Esther*. Atlanta, 1991.

———. *Character and Ideology in the Book of Esther*. Columbia, S.C., 1991.

Frankfurter, D. "Lest Egypt's City be Deserted: Religion and Ideology in the Egyptian Response to the Jewish Revolt, 116–117 CE." *JJS* 43 (1992) 203–20.

———. *Elijah in Upper Egypt*. Minneapolis, 1993.

Fraser, P. M. *Ptolemaic Alexandria*. 3 vols. Oxford, 1972.

Freedman, D. N. *Anchor Bible Dictionary*. 6 vols. New York, 1992.

Freudenthal, J. *Alexander Polyhistor*. Breslau, 1874/1875.

Freyne, S. *Galilee from Alexander the Great to Hadrian, 323 B.C.E.–135 C.E.* Wilmington, 1980.

Frick, C. *Chronica Minora*. Leipzig, 1892.

Fuks, A. "Dositheos son of Drimylos: A Prosopographical Note." *JJP* 8 (1954) 205–209.

Funkenstein, A. "Anti-Jewish Propaganda: Pagan, Christian, and Modern." *The Jerusalem Quarterly* 19 (1981) 56–72.

———. *Perceptions of Jewish History*. Berkeley, 1993.

Gabba, E. "The Growth of Anti-Judaism or the Greek Attitude towards Jews." In Davies and Finkelstein, II, 614–56.

Gafni, I. M. *Land, Centre and Diaspora*. Sheffield, 1997.

Gager, J. G. "Pseudo-Hecataeus again." *ZNW* 60 (1969) 130–39.

———. *Moses in Greco-Roman Paganism*. Nashville, 1972.

———. "Some Attempts to Label the Oracula Sibyllina, Book I." *HTR* 65 (1972) 91–97.

Gaster, M. *The Samaritans*. London, 1925.

Gauger, J.-D. *Beiträge zur jüdischen Apologetik*. Cologne and Bonn, 1977.

———. "Eine missverstandene Strabonstelle." *Historia*. 28 (1979) 211–24.

———. "Zitate in der jüdischen Apologetik und die Authentizität der Hekataios-Passagen bei Flavius Josephus und im Ps. Aristeas-Brief." *JSJ* 13 (1982) 6–46.

Geffcken, J. *Die Oracula Sibyllina*. Leipzig, 1902.

———. *Komposition und Entstehungszeit der Oracula Sibyllina*. Leipzig, 1902.

Geiger, J. "The History of Judas Maccabaeus: One Aspect of Hellenistic Historiography." *Zion* 49 (1984/1985) 1–8. (Hebrew)

———. "Form and Content in Jewish-Hellenistic Historiography." *SCI* 8–9 (1985/1988) 120–29.

Georgi, D. *The Opponents of Paul in Second Corinthians*. Edinburgh, 1987.

Gera, D. "On the Credibility of the History of the Tobiads." In A. Kasher, U. Rappaport, and G. Fuks, *Greece and Rome in Eretz Israel*, 21–38. Jerusalem, 1990.

Giblet, J. "Eupolème et l'historographie du Judaisme hellénistique." *EphTheoLov* (1963) 539–54.

Ginsburg, M. S. "Sparta and Judaea." *CP* 29 (1934) 117–22.

Giovannini, A., and H. Müller. "Die Beziehungen zwischen Rom und den Juden im 2. Jh. v. Chr." *MH* 28 (1971) 156–71.

Gnuse, R. "The Temple Experience of Jaddus in the *Antiquities* of Josephus: A Report of Jewish Dream Incubation." *JQR* 83 (1993) 349–68.

Golan, D. "Der Besuch Alexanders in Jerusalem." *Berliner Theologische Zeitschrift* 8 (1991) 19–30.

Goldberg, A. M. "Joseph in der Sicht des Judentums der Antike." *Bibel und Kirche* 21 (1966) 11–15.

Goldstein, J. "The Tales of the Tobiads." In J. Neusner, *Christianity, Judaism, and Other Greco-Roman Cults: Studies for Morton Smith at Sixty* III, 85–123. Leiden, 1975.

———. *I Maccabees*. Garden City, 1976.

——— . "Jewish Acceptance and Rejection of Hellenism." In E. P. Sanders, *Jewish and Christian Self-Definition* II, 64–87, 318–26. Philadelphia, 1981.

——— . *II Maccabees*. Garden City, 1983.

——— . "The Message of *Aristeas to Philokrates* in the Second Century B.C.E.: Obey the Torah, Venerate the Temple of Jerusalem, But Speak Greek and Put Your Hopes in the Ptolemaic Dynasty." In M. Mor, *Eretz Israel, Israel and the Jewish Diaspora: Mutual Relation*, 1–23. Lanham, 1991.

——— . "Alexander and the Jews." *Proceedings of the American Academy for Jewish Research*. 59 (1993) 59–101.

——— . "The Hasmonean Revolt and the Hasmonean Dynasty." In Davies and Finkelstein, II, 292–351.

Goodenough, E. R. *By Light, Light: The Mystic Gospel of Hellenistic Judaism*. New Haven, 1935.

——— . *The Politics of Philo Judaeus: Practice and Theory*. New Haven, 1938.

Gooding, D. W. "Aristeas and Septuagint Origins." *VT* 13 (1963) 357–79.

Goodman, M. *Mission and Conversion: Proselytizing in the Religious History of the Roman Empire*. Oxford, 1994.

Grabbe, L. L. "Josephus and the Reconstruction of the Judaean Restoration." *JBL* 106 (1987) 231–46.

——— . "On Some Papyri and Josephus' Sources and Chronology for the Persian Period." *JSJ* 21 (1990) 175–99.

Grafton, A. *Defenders of the Text*. Cambridge, Mass., 1991.

Griffiths, J. G. "Apocalyptic in the Hellenistic Era." In D. Hellholm, *Apocalypticism in the Mediterranean World and the Near East*, 273–293. Tübingen, 1983.

Gruen, E. S. *The Hellenistic World and the Coming of Rome*. 2 vols. Berkeley, 1984.

——— . "Hellenism and Persecution: Antiochus IV and the Jews." In P. Green, ed., *Hellenistic History and Culture*, 238–64. Berkeley, 1993.

——— . "The Purported Jewish-Spartan Affiliation." In R. W. Wallace and E. M. Harris, *Transitions to Empire: Essays in Greco-Roman History, 300–146 B.C., in Honor of E. Badian*, 254–69. Norman, Oklahoma, 1996.

——— . "The Origins and Objectives of Onias' Temple." *SCI* 16 (1997) 47–70.

Grunauer–von Hoerschelmann, S. *Die Münzprägung der Lakedaimonier*. Berlin, 1978.

Gudeman, A. "Lysimachos. Griechischer Grammatiker." *RE* 14 (1928) 32–39.

Gutman, Y. "Philo the Epic Poet." *Scripta Hierosolymitana* 1 (1954) 36–63.

——— . *The Beginnings of Jewish-Hellenistic Literature*. 2 vols. Jerusalem, 1958, 1963. (Hebrew)

Habicht, C. "Die herrschende Gesellschaft in den hellenistischen Monarchien." *Vierteljahrschrift für Sozial und Wirtschaftsgeschichte* 45 (1958) 1–16.

——— . "Hellenismus und Judentum in der Zeit des Judas Makkabäus." *Jhrb.Heid.-Akad.* (1974) 97–110.

——— . "Royal Documents in Maccabees II." *HSCP* 80 (1976) 1–18.

——— . *2 Makkabäerbuch*. Gütersloh, 1976.

Hadas, M. "III Maccabees and the Tradition of Patriotic Romance." *Chron.d'Égypte* 47 (1949) 97–104.

————. "Aristeas and III Maccabees." *HTR* 42 (1949) 175–84.

————. *Aristeas to Philocrates*. New York, 1951.

————. *The Third and Fourth Book of Maccabees*. New York, 1953.

Hamerton-Kelly, R. "Sources and Traditions in Philo Judaeus: Prolegomena to an Analysis of His Writings." *Studia Philonica* 1 (1972) 3–26.

Hamilton, J. R. *Plutarch, Alexander: A Commentary*. Oxford, 1969.

Hanhart, R. *Esther*. Göttingen, 1966.

Hanson, J. "Demetrius the Chronographer." In J. H. Charlesworth, II, 843–54.

Harrelson, W. "Patient Love in the Testament of Joseph." In G. W. E. Nickelsburg, 29–35.

Harrington, D. J. "The Original Language of Pseudo-Philo's *Liber Antiquitatem Biblicarum*." *HTR* 63 (1970) 503–14.

————. "Pseudo-Philo." In J. H. Charlesworth, II, 297–377.

Harris, H. A. *Greek Athletics and the Jews*. Cardiff, 1976.

Hata, G. "The Story of Moses Interpreted Within the Context of Anti-Semitism." In L. H. Feldman, and G. Hata, *Josephus, Judaism, and Christianity*, 180–97. Detroit, 1987.

Heckel, W., and J. C. Yardley. *Justin, Epitome of the Philippic History of Pompeius Trogus*. Vol. 1. Oxford, 1997.

Heinen, H. *Untersuchungen zur hellenistischen Geschichte des 3. Jahrhunderts v. Chr. Zur Geschichte der Zeit des Ptolemaios Keraunos und zum chremonideischen Krieg*. Wiesbaden, 1972.

————. "Ägyptische Grundlagen des antiken Judaismus." *Trierer Theologische Zeitschrift* 101 (1992) 124–49.

Heller, B. "Die Susannaerzählung: ein Märchen." *ZAW* 54 (1936) 281–87.

Heltzer, M. "The Greek Text of I Esdras, III, 1–2: Its Date and Subordination at the Achaemenian Court." *Henoch* 2 (1980) 150–55.

Hengel, M. "Anonymität, Pseudepigraphie und 'Literarische Fälschung' in der jüdisch-hellenistische Literatur." *FondHardt* 18 (1971) 229–329.

————. *Judaism and Hellenism*. London, 2 vols., 1974.

Herman, G. "The 'Friends' of the Early Hellenistic Rules: Servants or Officials?" *Talanta* 12–13 (1980/1981) 103–49.

Hilgert, E. "The Dual Image of Joseph in Hebrew and Early Jewish Literature." *Biblical Research* 30 (1985) 5–21.

Holladay, C. "The Portrait of Moses in Ezekiel the Tragedian." *SBL Seminar Papers* (1976) 447–52.

————. *Theios Aner in Hellenistic Judaism*. Missoula, 1977.

————. *Fragments from Hellenistic Jewish Authors*. Vol. I: *The Historians*. Chico, California, 1983.

————. *Fragments from Hellenistic Jewish Authors*. Vol. II: *The Poets*. Atlanta, 1989.

————. "Jewish Responses to Hellenistic Culture in Early Ptolemaic Egypt." In P. Bilde et al., *Ethnicity in Hellenistic Egypt*, 139–63. Aarhus, 1992.

————. *Fragments from Hellenistic Jewish Authors*. Vol III: *Aristobulus*. Atlanta, 1995.

————. *Fragments from Hellenistic Jewish Authors*. Vol IV: *Orphica*. Atlanta, 1996.

Hollander, H. W. *Joseph as an Ethical Model in the Testaments of the Twelve Patriarchs.* Leiden, 1981.

Holtz, T. "Christliche Interpolationen in 'Joseph und Aseneth.'" *NTS* 14 (1967/1968) 482–97.

Horsley, R. A. *Galilee: History, Politics, People.* Valley Forge, 1995.

Howard, G. E. "The Letter of Aristeas and Diaspora Judaism." *JTS* 22 (1971) 337–48.

Huet, G. "Daniel et Susanne." *RHR* 65 (1912) 277–84.

Humbert, P. "'Magna est veritas et praevalet' (3 Esra 4, 35)." *Orientalistische Literaturzeichnung* (1928) 148–50.

Ilan, T. "The Greek Names of the Hasmoneans." *JQR* 78 (1987) 1–20.

In der Smitten, W. T. "Zur Pagenerzählung in 3 Esra (3 Esr. III.1–V.6)." *VT* 22 (1972) 492–95.

Isaac, J. *Genèse de l'antisémitisme.* Vanves, 1956.

Jacobson, H. "The Identity and Role of Chum in Ezekiel's *Exagoge.*" *Hebrew University Studies in Literature* 9 (1981) 139–46.

———. "Mysticism and Apocalyptic in Ezekiel's *Exagoge.*" *Illinois Classical Studies* 6 (1981) 272–93.

———. *The Exagoge of Ezekiel.* Cambridge, 1983.

———. *A Commentary on Pseudo-Philo's Liber Antiquitatum Biblicarum.* Leiden, 1996.

Jacoby, F. "Hekataios." *RE* 7 (1912) 2750–69.

———. *Die Fragmente der griechischen Historiker.* 3 parts in 15 vols. Berlin and Leiden, 1923–1958.

Jaeger, W. *Diokles von Karystos.* Berlin, 1938.

———. "Greeks and Jews." *JR* 18 (1938) 127–43.

Janowitz, N. "Translating Cult: The Letter of Aristeas and Hellenistic Judaism." *SBL Seminar Papers* (1983) 347–57.

Jeanmaire, H. *La Sibylle et la retour de l'age d'Or.* Paris, 1939.

Jellicoe, S. "The Occasion and Purpose of the Letter of Aristeas: A Re-Examination." *NTS* 12 (1966) 144–50.

———. *The Septuagint and Modern Study.* Oxford, 1968.

Johnson, S. *Mirror, Mirror: Third Maccabees, Historical Fictions and Jewish Self-Fashioning in the Hellenistic Period.* Diss. Berkeley, 1996.

Kahle, P. *The Cairo Geniza*[2]. Oxford, 1959.

Kampen, J. *The Hasideans and the Origins of Pharisaism: A Study in 1 and 2 Maccabees.* Atlanta, 1988.

Kasher, A. "The Propaganda Goals of Manetho's Accusations in the Matter of the Low Origins of the Jews." In B. Oded et al., *Studies in the History of the Jewish People and the Land of Israel* III, 69–84. Haifa, 1974. (Hebrew)

———. "Alexander of Macedon's Campaign in Palestine." *Bet Miqra* 20 (1975) 187–208. (Hebrew)

———. *The Jews in Hellenistic and Roman Egypt.* Tübingen, 1985.

———. *Jews, Idumaeans, and Ancient Arabs.* Tübingen, 1988.

———. *Jews and Hellenistic Cities in Eretz-Israel.* Tübingen, 1990.

————. "Changes in Manpower and Ethnic Composition of the Hasmonean Army (167–63 BCE)." *JQR* 81 (1991) 325–52.

————. "Political and National Connections Between the Jews of Ptolemaic Egypt and their Brethren in Eretz Israel." In M. Mor, *Eretz Israel, Israel, and the Jewish Diaspora: Mutual Relations*, 24–41. Lanham, 1991.

————. "Hecataeus of Abdera on Mosollamus the Jewish Mounted Archer (*Contra Apionem*, I, 200–204)." In H. Cancik, H. Lichtenberger, and P. Schäfer, *Geschichte— Tradition—Reflexion: Festschrift für Martin Hengel*, I, 147–58. Tübingen, 1996.

————. "Polemic and Apologetic." In L. H. Feldman and J. R. Levison, *Josephus' Contra Apionem: Studies in its Character and Context with a Latin Concordance to the Portion Missing in Greek*, 250–70. Leiden, 1996.

Katzoff, R. "Jonathan and Late Sparta." *AJP* 106 (1985) 485–89.

Kee, H. C. "The Socio-Cultural Setting of Joseph and Aseneth." *NTS* 29 (1983) 394–413.

————. "Testaments of the Twelve Patriarchs." In J. H. Charlesworth, I, 775–81.

Kennell, N. M. *The Gymnasium of Virtue*. Chapel Hill, 1995.

Kippenberg, H. G. *Garizim und Synagoge*. Berlin, 1971.

Klijn, A. F. J. "The Letter of Aristeas and the Greek Translation of the Pentateuch in Egypt." *NTS* 11 (1964/1965) 154–58.

Koenen, L. "Die Prophezeiungen des 'Töpfers.'" *ZPE* 2 (1968) 178–209.

Kraeling, E. G. *The Brooklyn Museum Aramaic Papyri*. New Haven, 1953.

Kraemer, R. *Her Share of the Blessings*. New York, 1992.

Kraft, R. "Philo and the Sabbath Crisis: Alexandrian Jewish Polities and the Dating of Philo's Works." In B. Pearson, *The Future of Early Christianity*, 131–41. Minneapolis, 1991.

Kugel, J. L. *In Potiphar's House*. New York, 1990.

————. "The Story of Dinah in the Testament of Levi." *HTR* 85 (1992) 1–34.

Kuiper, K. "Le poète juif Ezéchiel." *REJ* 46 (1903) 48–73.

Kurfess, A. *Sibyllinische Weissagungen*. Berlin, 1951.

Lafargue, M. "Orphica." In J. H. Charlesworth, II, 795–801.

Lanchester, H. "The Sibylline Oracles." In R. H. Charles, *The Apocrypha and Pseudepigrapha of the Old Testament* II, 368–406. Oxford, 1913.

Laporte, J. *De Josepho (Les Oeuvres de Philon d'Alexandrie*, 21). Paris, 1962.

Laqueur, R. "Ephoros." *Hermes* 46 (1911) 161–206.

————. "Griechische Urkunden in der jüdisch-hellenistischen Literatur." *HZ* 136 (1927) 229–52.

————. "Manethon." *RE* 14 (1928) 1060–101.

Lévi, I. "La dispute entre les Égyptiens et les Juifs." *REJ* 63 (1912) 211–15.

————. "L'histoire 'De Suzanne et les deux vieillards' dans la littérature juive." *REJ* 95 (1933) 157–71.

Levy, I. "Tacite et l'origine du people juif." *Latomus* 5 (1946) 331–40.

————. "Ptolémée Lathyre et les Juifs," Part II. *HUCA* 23 (1950/1951) 127–36.

Lewis, J. J. "The Table-Talk Section in the Letter of Aristeas." *NTS* 12 (1966/1967) 53–56.

Lewis, J. P. "What Do We Mean by Jabneh?" *JBR* 32 (1964) 125–32.

Lewy, H. "Hekataios von Abdera περὶ Ἰουδαίων." *ZNW* 31 (1932) 117–32.

Lloyd-Jones, H., and P. Parsons. *Supplementum Hellenisticum*. Berlin, 1983.

Lods, A. *Histoire de la littérature hébraique et juive*. Paris, 1950.

Ludwich, A. *De Theodoti carmine graeco-iudaico*. Königsberg, 1899.

McCown, C. C. "Hebrew and Egyptian Apocalyptic Literature." *HTR* 18 (1925) 357–411.

McGing, B. C. *The Foreign Policy of Mithridates VI Eupator*. Leiden, 1986.

MacKenzie, R. A. F. "The Meaning of the Susanna Story." *Canadian Journal of Theology* 3 (1957) 211–18.

McKnight, S. *A Light among the Gentiles*. Minneapolis, 1991.

Mack, B. "Exegetical Traditions in Alexandrian Judaism: A Program for the Analysis of the Philonic Corpus." *Studia Philonica* 3 (1974/1975) 71–112.

Maier, J. *The Temple Scroll*. Sheffield, 1985.

Marasco, G. *Sparta agli inizi dell'età ellenistica: Il regno di Areo I*. Florence, 1980.

Marcus, R. "Appendix C." In *Josephus, Jewish Antiquities* VI, 512–32. Cambridge, Mass., 1937.

Martin, R. A. "Syntax Criticism of the LXX Additions to the Book of Esther." *JBL* 94 (1975) 65–72.

Mazar, B. "The Tobiads." *IEJ* 7 (1957) 137–45; 229–38.

Meeks, W. A. *The Prophet King*. Leiden, 1967.

———. "Moses as God and King." In J. Neusner, *Religions in Antiquity: Essays in Memory of E. R. Goodenough*, 354–71. Leiden, 1968.

Meinhold, A. "Die Gattung der Josephsgeschichte und des Estherbuches: Diasporanovelle I." *ZAW* 87 (1975) 306–24.

———. "Die Gattung der Josephsgeschichte und des Estherbuches: Diasporanovelle II." *ZAW* 88 (1976) 72–93.

Meisner, N. "Aristeasbrief." *Jüdische Schriften aus hellenistisch-römischer Zeit* 2.1 (1973) 35–85.

Mélèze-Modrzejewski, J. "L'image du Juif dans la pensée grecque vers 300 avant notre ère." In A. Kasher et al., *Greece and Rome in Eretz Israel*, 105–18. Jerusalem, 1990.

———. *The Jews of Egypt: From Rameses II to Emperor Hadrian*. Philadelphia, 1995.

Mendels, D. "'On Kingship' in the 'Temple Scroll' and the Ideological Vorlage of the Seven Banquets in the 'Letter of Aristeas to Philocrates.'" *Aegyptus* 59 (1979) 127–36.

———. "Hecataeus of Abdera and a Jewish *patrios politeia* of the Persian Period (Diodorus Siculus XL, 3)." *ZAW* 95 (1983) 95–110.

———. *The Land of Israel as a Political Concept in Hasmonean Literature*. Tübingen, 1987.

———. "Creative History in the Hellenistic Near East in the Third and Second Centuries BCE: The Jewish Case." *JSP* 2 (1988) 13–20.

———. "The Polemical Character of Manetho's *Aegyptiaca*." *Studia Hellenistica* 30 (1990) 91–123.

———. *The Rise and Fall of Jewish Nationalism*. New York, 1992.

Meshorer, Y. *Ancient Jewish Coinage*. Dix Hills, New York, 1982.

————. "Ancient Jewish Coinage: Addendum I." *Israel Numismatic Journal* 11 (1990/1991) 104–32.

Meyer, E. *Aegyptische Chronologie*. Berlin, 1904.

Michell, H. *Sparta*. Cambridge, 1952.

Millar, F. "The Background of the Maccabean Revolution: Reflections on Martin Hengel's 'Judaism and Hellenism.'" *JJS* 29 (1978) 1–21.

Moehring, H. "The *Acta Pro Judaeis* in the *Antiquitates* of Flavius Josephus." In J. Neusner, *Christianity, Judaism, and Other Greco-Roman Cults* III, 124–58. Leiden, 1975.

————. "Joseph ben Matthia and Flavius Josephus: The Jewish Prophet and Roman Historian." *ANRW* II.21.2 (1984) 864–944.

Mölleken, W. "Geschichtsklitterung im I. Makkabäerbuch (Wann wurde Alkimus Hoherpriester?)." *ZAW* 65 (1953) 205–28.

Momigliano, A. "Intorno al *Contro Apione*." *RivFilol* 9 (1931) 485–503.

————. "I Tobiadi nella preistoria del moto maccabaico." *Atti Torino* 67 (1931/1932) 165–200.

————. "Per la data e la caratteristica della lettera di Aristea." *Aegyptus* 12 (1932) 161–72.

————. *Prime linee di storia della tradizione maccabaica*2. Amsterdam, 1968.

————. *Alien Wisdom: The Limits of Hellenization*. Cambridge, 1975.

————. "Ebrei e Greci." *RivStorItal* 88 (1976) 425–43.

————. "Flavius Josephus and Alexander's Visit to Jerusalem." *Athenaeum* 57 (1979) 442–48.

————. "La portata storica dei vaticani sul settino re nel terzo libro degli oracoli sibillini." *Sesto contributo alla storia degli studi classici*. 2 (1980) 551–59.

Moore, C. A. "A Greek Witness to a Different Hebrew Text of Esther." *ZAW* 79 (1967) 351–58.

————. *Esther: Introduction, Translation, and Notes*. Garden City, 1971.

————. "On the Origins of the LXX Additions to the Book of Esther." *JBL* 92 (1973) 382–93.

————. *Daniel, Esther, and Jeremiah: The Additions*. Garden City, 1977.

Mor, M. "Samaritan History: The Persian, Hellenistic and Hasmonean Period." In A. D. Crown, *The Samaritans*, 1–18. Tübingen, 1989.

————. "Theodotos, the Epos of Schechem and the Samaritans: A New Interpretation." In I. M. Gafni, A. Oppenheimer, and D. R. Schwartz, *The Jews in the Hellenistic-Roman World: Studies in Memory of Menahem Stern*, 345–59. Jerusalem, 1996. (Hebrew)

Moreau, J. "Le troisième livre des Maccabées." *Chron.d'Égypte* 31 (1941) 111–22.

Moretti, L. *Iscrizioni storiche ellenistiche*. Florence, 1967.

Motzo, R. B. *Ricerche sulla letteratura e la storia giudaico-ellenistica*. Rome, 1977.

Murphy, F. J. *Pseudo-Philo: Rewriting the Bible*. New York, 1993.

Murray, O. "Aristeas and Ptolemaic Kingship." *JTS* 18 (1967) 337–71.

————. "Hecataeus of Abdera and Pharaonic Kingship." *JEA* 56 (1970) 141–71.

————. "Aristeas and his Sources." *Studia Patristica* 12 (1975) 123–28.

————. "The Letter of Aristeas." In B. Virgilio, *Studi ellenistici* II, 15–27. Pisa, 1987.

Mussies, G. "The Interpretatio Judaica of Thot-Hermes." In M. Voss et al., *Studies in Egyptian Religion*, 87–120. Leiden, 1982.

Myers, J. M. *I and II Esdras*. Garden City, 1974.

Naveh, J. "The Development of the Aramaic Script." *Proceedings of the Israel Academy of Sciences and Humanities* 5 (1971–1976) 62–64.

Newsome, J. D. *Greek, Romans, Jews*. Philadelphia, 1992.

Nickelsburg, G. W. E. *Studies on the Testament of Joseph*. Missoula, 1975.

——— . "Stories of Biblical and Early Post-Biblical Times." In M. E. Stone, *Jewish Writings*, 33–85.

Niditch, S. "Father-Son Folktale Patterns and Tyrant Typologies in Josephus' Ant. 12.160–222." *JJS* 32 (1981) 47–55.

——— . *Underdogs and Tricksters*. San Francisco, 1987.

Niehoff, M. *The Figure of Joseph in Post-Biblical Literature*. Leiden, 1992.

Nikiprowetzky, V. "ΚΥΡΙΟΥ ΠΡΟΣΘΕΣΙΣ: Note critique sur Philon d'Alexandrie, *De Josepho*, 28." *REJ* 127 (1968) 387–92.

——— . *La Troisième Sibylle*. Paris, 1970.

——— . "La Sibylle juive et le 'Troisième Livre' des Pseudo-Oracles Sibyllins depuis Charles Alexandre." *ANRW* II.20.1 (1987) 460–542.

Nock, A. D. *Conversion: The Old and the New in Religion from Alexander the Great to Augustine of Hippo*. Oxford, 1933.

Nolland, J. "Sib. Or. III.265–294, An Early Maccabaean Messianic Oracle." *JTS* 30 (1979) 158–66.

Oliva, P. *Sparta and her Social Problems*. Amsterdam, 1971.

Ollier, F. *Le mirage spartiate*. 2 vols. Paris, 1933–1943.

Orlinsky, H. M. "The Septuagint as Holy Writ and the Philosophy of the Translators." *HUCA* 46 (1975) 89–114.

——— . "The Septuagint and its Hebrew Text." In Davies and Finkelstein, II, 534–62.

Orrieux, C. "Flavius-Joséphe est il crédible?" *Kentron* 2 (1986) 8–11.

——— . "La 'parenté' entre Juifs et Spartiates." In R. Lonis, *L'étranger dans le monde grec*, 169–91. Nancy, 1987.

——— . "Flavius-Joséphe est il crédible? (II)" *Kentron* 4–5 (1988) 133–41.

Pacella, D. "Alessandra e i Ebrei." *AnnPisa* 12 (1982) 1255–69.

Parente, F. "La lettera di Aristea come fonte per la storia del Giudaismo Alessandrino durante la prima metà del I secolo a.C." *AnnPisa* 2.1 (1972) 177–237.

——— . "La lettera di Aristea come fonte per la storia del Giudaismo Alessandrino durante la prima metà del I secolo a.C." *AnnPisa* 2.2 (1972) 517–67.

——— . "The Third Book of Maccabees as Ideological Document and Historical Source." *Henoch* 10 (1988) 148–82.

Parente, F., and J. Sievers. *Josephus and the History of the Greco-Roman Period*. Leiden, 1994.

Parke, H. W. *Sibyls and Sibylline Prophecy in Classical Antiquity*. London, 1988.

Paul, A. "Le troisième livre des Macchabées." *ANRW* II.20.1 (1987) 298–336.

Pedrizet, P. "Le fragment de Satyros sur les dèmes d'Alexandrie." *REA* 12 (1910) 217–47.

Pelletier, A. *Lettre d'Aristée à Philocrate*. Paris, 1962.

Peretti, A. *La Sibilla babilonese nella propaganda ellenistica*. Florence, 1943.

Perrot, C., and P.-M. Bogaert. *Pseudo-Philon: Les antiquités bibliques*. Paris, 1976.

Pervo, R. I. "Joseph and Aseneth and the Greek Novel." In *SBL Seminar Papers*, 171–81. Missoula, 1976.

Pfeiffer, R. H. *History of New Testament Times with an Introduction to the Apocrypha*. Westport, Conn., 1949.

Pfister, F. "Eine jüdische Gründungsgeschichte Alexandrias." *SitzHeid* (1914) Abt. 11.

——— . "Eine jüdische Gründungsgeschichte Alexandrias." In R. Merkelbach et al., *Kleine Schriften Zum Alexanderroman*, 80–103. Meisenheim, 1976.

Philonenko, M. *Joseph et Aséneth*. Leiden, 1968.

Piper, L. J. *Spartan Twilight*. New Rochelle, 1986.

Pohlmann, K. F. *Studien zum dritten Ezra*. Göttingen, 1970.

Porten, B. *Archives from Elephantine: The Life of a Military Colony*. Berkeley, 1968.

——— . "The Jews in Egypt." In Davies and Finkelstein, I, 372–400.

Potter, D. *Prophets and Emperors*. Cambridge, Mass., 1994.

Priessnig, A. "Die literarische Form der Patriarchenbiographien des Philon von Alexandrien." *Monatsschrift für Geschichte und Wissenschaft des Judentums* 73 (1929) 143–55.

Pucci ben Zeev, M. "The Reliability of Josephus Flavius: The Case of Hecataeus' and Manetho's Accounts of Jews and Judaism." *JSJ* 24 (1993) 215–34.

——— . "Greek and Roman Documents from Republican Times in the *Antiquities*." *SCI* 13 (1994) 46–59.

——— . "*Ant.* 14.186–267: A Problem of Authenticity." In R. Katzoff, *Classical Studies in Honor of D. Sohlberg*, 193–221. Ramat Gan, 1996.

Pummer, R. "The Book of Jubilees and the Samaritans." *Église et Théologie* 10 (1979) 147–78.

——— . "Antisamaritanische Polemik in jüdischen Schriften aus der intertestamentarischen Zeit." *Biblische Zeitschrift* 26 (1982) 224–42.

——— . "Genesis 34 in Jewish Writings of the Hellenistic and Roman Periods." *HTR* 75 (1982) 177–88.

Pummer, R., and M. Roussel. "A Note on Theodotus and Homer." *JSJ* 13 (1982) 177–82.

Purvis, J. D. "The Samaritans." In Davies and Finkelstein, II, 591–613.

Rainbow, P. A. "The Last Oniad and the Teacher of Righteousness." *JJS* 48 (1997) 30–52.

Rajak, T. "Moses in Ethiopia: Legend and Literature." *JJS* 29 (1978) 111–22.

——— . "Roman Intervention in a Seleucid Siege of Jerusalem?" *GRBS* 22 (1981) 65–81.

——— . "The Hasmoneans and the Uses of Hellenism." In P. R. Davies and R. T. White, eds., *A Tribute to Geza Vermes*, 261–80. Sheffield, 1990.

——— . "The Jews under Hasmonean Rule." In J. A. Crook, A. Lintott, and E. Rawson, eds., *Cambridge Ancient History*[2], IX, 274–309. Cambridge, 1994.

————. "Hasmonean Kingship and the Invention of Tradition." In P. Bilde et al., *Aspects of Hellenistic Kingship*, 99–105. Aarhus, 1996.

Rappaport, U. "The Emergence of Hasmonean Coinage." *AJS Review* 1 (1976) 171–186.

————. "The First Judaean Coinage." *JJS* 32 (1981) 1–17.

————. "The Hellenization of the Hasmoneans." In M. Mor, *Jewish Assimilation, Acculturation, and Accommodation*, 1–13. London, 1992.

Rawson, E. *The Spartan Tradition in European Thought*. Oxford, 1969.

Redford, D. B. *Pharaonic King-Lists, Annals, and Day Books*. Mississauga, Ontario, 1986.

Reinhold, M. *History of Purple as a Status Symbol in Antiquity*. Brussels, 1970.

Robertson, R. G. "Ezekiel the Tragedian." In J. H. Charlesworth, II, 803–19.

Roth, M. W. M. "For Life, He Appeals to Death (Wis 13:18): A Study of Old Testament Idol Parodies." *CBQ* 37 (1975) 21–47.

Rowley, H. H. "The Interpretation and Date of Sibylline Oracles, III.388–400." *ZAW* 44 (1926) 324–27.

Rudolph, W. "Der Wettstreit der Leibwächter des Darius. 3 Esr. 3.1–5.6." *ZAW* 61 (1945–1948) 176–90.

Ruether, R. *Faith and Fratricide: The Theological Roots of Antisemitism*. Minneapolis, 1974.

Runnalls, D. "Moses' Ethiopian Campaign." *JSJ* 14 (1983) 135–56.

Rzach, A. "Sibyllen." *RE* II A.2 (1923) 2073–183.

Sanders, J. A. *From Sacred Story to Sacred Text*. Philadelphia, 1987.

Sandmel, S. *Philo of Alexandria: An Introduction*. New York, 1979.

Sänger, D. "Bekehrung und Exodus: zum jüdischen Traditionshintergrund von 'Joseph und Aseneth.'" *JSJ* 10 (1979) 11–36.

————. "Erwägung zur historischen Einordung und zur Datierung von 'Joseph und Aseneth.'" *ZNW* 76 (1985) 86–106.

————. *Antikes Judentum und die Mysterien*. Tübingen, 1980.

Saulnier, C. "Lois romaines sur les juifs selon Flavius Josèphe." *RevBibl* 88 (1981) 161–95.

Schäfer, P. "The Exodus Tradition in Pagan Greco-Roman Literature." In I. M. Gafni, A Oppenheimer, and D. R. Schwartz, *The Jews in the Hellenistic-Roman World: Studies in Memory of Menahem Stern*, 9–38. Jerusalem, 1996.

————. *Judeophobia: Attitudes toward the Jews in the Ancient World*. Cambridge, Mass., 1997.

Schaller, B. "Hekataios von Abdera über die Juden, zur Frage der Echtheit und Datierung." *ZNW* 54 (1963) 15–31.

————. *Jüdische Schriften aus hellenistisch-römischer Zeit*. Gütersloh, 1979.

————. "Das Testament Hiobs und die Septuaginta—Übersetzung des Buches Hiobs." *Biblica* 61 (1980) 377–406.

Schildenberger, J. *Das Buch Esther*. Bonn, 1941.

Schüller, S. "Some Problems Connected with the Supposed Common Ancestry of Jews and Spartans and their Relations during the Last Three Centuries B.C." *JSemStud* 1 (1956) 257–68.

Schüpphaus, J. "Der Verhältnis von LXX- und Theodotion-Text in den apokryphen Zusätzen zum Danielbuch." *ZAW* 83 (1971) 49–72.

Schürer, E. *Geschichte des jüdischen Volkes im Zeitalter Jesu Christi* II. Leipzig, 1886.

——— . *The History of the Jewish People in the Age of Jesus Christ* I. Rev. ed. by G. Vermes and F. Millar. Edinburgh, 1973.

——— . *The History of the Jewish People in the Age of Jesus Christ* II. Rev. ed. by G. Vermes, F. Millar, and M. Black. Edinburgh, 1979.

——— . *The History of the Jewish People in the Age of Jesus Christ* III. Rev. ed by G. Vermes, F. Millar, and M. Goodman. Edinburgh, 1986.

Schwartz, D. R. "KATA TOYTON TON KAIPON: Josephus' Source on Agrippa II." *JQR* 72 (1981/1982) 241–68.

——— . "Philonic Anonyms of the Roman and Nazi Periods: Two Suggestions." *The Studia Philonica Annual* 1 (1989) 63–73.

——— . *Agrippa I: The Last King of Judaea*. Tübingen, 1990.

——— . *Studies in the Jewish Background to Christianity*. Tübingen, 1992.

——— . "Hasidim in First Maccabees 2:42?" *SCI* 13 (1994) 7–18.

Schwartz, S. "Israel and the Nations Roundabout: 1 Maccabees and the Hasmonean Expansion." *JJS* 42 (1991) 16–38.

——— . "On the Autonomy of Judaea in the 4th and 3rd Centuries B.C." *JJS* 45 (1994) 157–68.

——— . "John Hyrcanus I's Destruction of the Gerizim Temple and Judaean-Samaritan Relations." *Jewish History* 7 (1993) 9–25.

Schwyzer, H. R. *Chairemon*. Leipzig, 1932.

Sered, S., and S. Cooper. "Sexuality and Social Control: Anthropological Reflections on the Book of Susanna." In E. Spolsky, *The Judgment of Susanna: Authority and Witness*, 43–55. Atlanta, 1996.

Sevenster, J. N. *The Roots of Pagan Anti-Semitism in the Ancient World*. Leiden, 1975.

Shatzman, I. "The Hasmonaeans in Greco-Roman Historiography." *Zion* 57 (1992) 5–62. (Hebrew)

——— . *The Armies of the Hasmonaeans and Herod*. Tübingen, 1991.

Sievers, J. *The Hasmoneans and their Supporters from Mattathias to the Death of John Hyrcanus I*. Atlanta, 1990.

——— . "Jerusalem, the Akra, and Josephus." In Parente and Sievers, 195–209.

Siker, J. S. "Abraham in Graeco-Roman Paganism." *JSJ* 18 (1987) 188–208.

Simon, M. "Sur quelques aspects des Oracles Sibyllins juifs." In D. Hellholm, *Apocalypticism in the Mediterranean World and the Near East*, 219–33. Tübingen, 1983.

——— . *Versus Israel*. Oxford, 1986.

Slingerland, H. D. *The Testaments of the Twelve Patriarchs: A Critical History of Research*. Missoula, 1977.

Smith, E. W. "Joseph Material in Joseph and Asenath and Josephus Relating to the Testament of Joseph." In G. Nickelsberg, *Studies*, 133–37.

Smith, M. *Studies in the Cult of Yahweh*. Leiden, 1996.

Spolsky, E. "Law or the Garden: The Betrayal of Susanna in Pastoral Painting." In E. Spolsky, *The Judgment of Susanna: Authority and Witness*, 101–117. Atlanta, 1996.

Spródowsky, H. *Die Hellenisierung der Geschichte von Joseph in Ägypten bei Flavius Josephus.* Greifswald, 1937.

Standhartinger, A. "'Um zu sehen die Töchter des Landes.' Die Perspektive Dinas in der jüdisch-hellenistischen Diskussion um Gen 34." In L. Bormann et al., *Religious Propaganda and Missionary Competition in the New Testament World*, 89–116. Leiden, 1994.

———. *Das Frauenbild im Judentum der hellenistischen Zeit: Ein Beitrag anhand von "Joseph und Aseneth".* Leiden, 1995.

Starobinski-Safran, E. "Un poète judéo-hellénistique: Ezéchiel le tragique." *MH* 31 (1974) 216–24.

Stegemann, H. *Die Entstehung der Qumrangemeinde.* Bonn, 1971.

Sterling, G. E. *Historiography and Self-Definition: Josephos, Luke-Acts, and Apologetic Historiography.* Leiden, 1992.

Stern, M. "Notes on the Story of Joseph, son of Tobias." *Tarbiz* 32 (1962) 35–47. (Hebrew)

———. "A Fragment of Greco-Egyptian Prophecy and the Tradition of the Jews' Expulsion from Egypt in Chaeremon's History." *Zion* 28 (1963) 223–27. (Hebrew)

———. *Greek and Latin Authors on Jews and Judaism.* 3 vols. Jerusalem, 1976.

———. "Relations Between the Hasmoneans and Ptolemaic Egypt in Light of the International Relations of the Second and First Centuries." *Zion* 50 (1985) 81–106. (Hebrew)

———. "The Treaty between Judaea and Rome in 161 B.C.E." *Zion* 51 (1986) 3–28. (Hebrew)

Steussy, M. J. *Gardens in Babylon: Narrative and Faith in the Greek Legends of Daniel.* Atlanta, 1993.

Stoneman, R. "Jewish Traditions on Alexander the Great." *Studia Philonica Annual* 6 (1994) 37–53.

Stump, E. "Susanna and the Elders: Wisdom and Folly." In E. Spolsky, *The Judgment of Susanna: Authority and Witness*, 85–100. Atlanta, 1996.

Sundberg, A. C. *The Old Testament of the Early Church.* Cambridge, Mass., 1964.

Tarn, W. W. "Alexander Helios and the Golden Age." *JRS* 22 (1932) 135–60.

Tcherikover, V. "Jewish Apologetic Literature Reconsidered." *EOS* 48.3 (1956) 169–93.

———. "The Ideology of the Letter of Aristeas." *HTR* 51 (1958) 59–85.

———. *Hellenistic Civilization and the Jews.* Philadelphia, 1959.

———. "The Third Book of Maccabees as a Historical Source of Augustus' Time." *Scripta Hierosolymitana* 7 (1961) 1–26.

Tcherikover, V., and A. Fuks, *Corpus Papyrorum Judaicarum.* 3 vols. Cambridge, Mass., 1957–1964.

Thompson, S. *The Motif-Index of Folk-Literature.* 6 vols. Bloomington, 1955–1958.

Tiede, D. L. *The Charismatic Figure as Miracle Worker.* Missoula, 1972.

Tigerstedt, E. N. *The Legend of Sparta in Classical Antiquity.* 3 vols. Stockholm, 1965, 1974, 1978.

Torrey, C. C. *Ezra Studies.* Chicago, 1910.

———. "The Aramaic of the Gospels." *JBL* 61 (1942) 71–85.

————. "A Revised View of First Esdras." In *Louis Ginzberg Jubilee Volume*, 395–410. New York, 1945.

————. "The Older Book of Esther." *HTR* 37 (1944) 1–40.

Tov, E. "The Text of the OT." In A. van der Woude, *The World of the Bible*, 156–90. Grand Rapids, 1986.

Tracy, S. "III Maccabees and Ps. Aristeas: A Study." *Yale Classical Studies* 1 (1928) 241–52.

Tramontano, R. *La Lettera di Aristea a Filocrate*. Naples, 1931.

Trebilco, P. *Jewish Communities in Asia Minor*. Cambridge, 1991.

Troiani, L. "Sui frammenti di Manetone." *SCO* 24 (1975) 97–126.

————. "Il libro di Aristea ed il giudaismo ellenistico." In B. Virgilio, *Studi ellenistici* II, 31–61. Pisa, 1987.

Tromp, J. "The Formation of the Third Book of Maccabees." *Henoch* 17 (1995) 311–28.

Ulrich, G. "The Bible in the Making: The Scriptures at Qumran." In G. Ulrich and J. VanderKam, *The Community of the Renewed Covenant*, 77–93. Notre Dame, 1994.

van den Broek, R. *The Myth of the Phoenix According to Classical and Early Christian Traditions*. Leiden, 1971.

van der Horst, P. W. "Moses' Throne Vision in Ezekiel the Dramatist." *JJS* 34 (1983) 21–29.

————. *Chaeremon: Egyptian Priest and Stoic Philosopher*. Leiden, 1984.

————. "Some Notes on the *Exagoge* of Ezekiel." *Mnemosyne* 37 (1984) 354–75.

————. *Essays on the Jewish World of Early Christianity*. Göttingen, 1990.

————. "'Thou Shalt Not Revile the Gods': The LXX Translation of Ex.22:28." *Studia Philonica Annual* 5 (1993) 1–8.

VanderKam, J. *Textual and Historical Studies in the Book of Jubilees*. Missoula, 1977.

————. "Hannukah: Its Timing and Significance." *JSP* 1 (1987) 23–40.

van der Woude, A. S. "Wicked Priest or Wicked Priests? Reflections on the Identification of the Wicked Priest in the Habbakuk Commentary." *JJS* 33 (1982) 349–59.

van Henten, J.-W., and R. Abusch. "The Jews as Typhonians and Josephus' Strategy of Refutation in *Contra Apionem*." In L. H. Feldman and J. R. Levison, *Josephus' Contra Apionem: Studies in its Character and Context with a Latin Concordance to the Portion Missing in Greek*, 271–309. Leiden, 1996.

Van't Dack, E. "La date de la lettre d'Aristée." *Studia Hellenistica* 16 (1968) 263–78.

Velde, H. te. *Seth, God of Confusion*. Leiden, 1967.

Vermes, G. *Scripture and Tradition in Judaism*. Leiden, 1961.

Wacholder, B. Z. "Pseudo-Eupolemus' Two Greek Fragments on the Life of Abraham." *HUCA* 34 (1963) 83–113.

————. *Eupolemus: A Study of Judaeo-Greek Literature*. Cincinnati, 1974.

Waddell, W. G. *Manetho*. Cambridge, Mass., 1940.

Wallace, S. L. "Census and Poll Tax in Ptolemaic Egypt." *AJP* 59 (1938) 418–42.

Walter, N. *Der Thoraausleger Aristobulos*. Berlin, 1964.

————. "Zu Pseudo-Eupolemos." *Klio* 43–5 (1965) 282–90.

————. *Jüdische Schriften aus hellenistisch-römischer Zeit*. Gütersloh, 1976.

————. "Jewish-Greek Literature of the Greek Period." In Davies and Finkelstein, 385–408.

————. "Jüdisch-hellenistische Literatur vor Philon von Alexandrien." *ANRW* II.20.1 (1987) 67–120.

————. "Kann man als Jude auch Grieche sein? Erwägung zur jüdisch-hellenistischen Pseudepigraphie." In J. C. Reeves and J. Kampen, *Pursuing the Text: Studies in Honor of Ben Zion Wacholder*, 148–63. Sheffield, 1994.

Weinfeld, M. *The Promise of the Land*. Berkeley, 1993.

Welles, C. B. *Royal Correspondence in the Hellenistic Period: A Study in Greek Epigraphy*. New Haven, 1934.

Wellhausen, J. *Israelitische und jüdische Geschichte*. Berlin, 1921.

Werman, C. "Jubilees 30: Building a Paradigm for the Ban on Intermarriage." *HTR* 90 (1997) 1–22.

West, S. "*Joseph and Aseneth*: A Neglected Greek Romance." *CQ* 68 (1974) 70–81.

Westerman, W. L. "Enslaved Persons Who Are Free." *AJP* 59 (1938) 1–30.

Wiencke, J. *Ezekielis Iudaei poetae Alexandrini fabulae quae inscribitur Ἐξαγωγή fragmenta*. Münster, 1931.

Will, E., and C. Orrieux. *Ioudaismos-Hellènismos: Essai sur le judaisme judéen à l'époque hellénistique*. Nancy, 1986.

————. "*Prosélytisme Juif"*? Histoire d'une erreur*. Paris, 1992.

Williams, D. S. "3 Maccabees: A Defense of Diaspora Judaism?" *JSP* 13 (1995) 17–29.

Willrich, H. *Juden und Griechen vor der makkabäischen Erhebung*. Göttingen, 1895.

————. "Der historische Kern des III. Makkabäerbuches." *Hermes* 39 (1904) 244–58.

————. *Urkundenfälschung in der hellenistisch-jüdischen Literatur*. Göttingen, 1924.

Wills, L. M. *The Jew in the Court of the Foreign King: Ancient Jewish Court Legends*. Minneapolis, 1990.

————. *The Jewish Novel in the Ancient World*. Ithaca, 1995.

Winston, D. *The Wisdom of Solomon*. Garden City, 1979.

————. "Aristobulus from Walter to Holladay." *Studia Philonica Annual* 8 (1996) 155–66.

Wintermute, O. S. "Jubilees." In J. H. Charlesworth, II, 35–142.

Wirgin, W. "Judah Maccabee's Embassy to Rome and the Jewish-Roman Treaty." *PEQ* 101 (1969) 15–20.

Yavetz, Z. "Judeophobia in Classical Antiquity: A Different Approach." *JJS* 44 (1993) 1–22.

Yoyotte, J. "L'Égypte ancienne et les origines de l'antijudaisme." *RHR* 163 (1963) 133–43.

Zambelli, M. *Miscellanea greca e romana*. Rome, 1965.

Zimmerman, F. "The Story of Susanna and its Original Language." *JQR* 48 (1957/1958) 236–41.

————. "The Story of the Three Guardsmen." *JQR* 54 (1963/1964) 179–200.

Zuntz, G. "Aristeas Studies II: Aristeas on the Translation of the Torah." *JSemStud* 4 (1959) 109–26.

INDEX

Compositor:	Humanist Typesetting & Graphics, Inc.
	(Theodora Stillwell MacKay 1938–1998)
Printer:	Data Reproductions
Binder:	Data Reproductions
Text:	10/12 Baskerville
Display:	Baskerville
Greek:	Ibycus by Silvio Levy
	modified by Pierre A. MacKay